CENSUS OF INDIA 1931

Census of India 1871-1951, 9 Sets In 384 Bindings (9788121258876) Rs. 700000

Census of India 1931, 28 Vols. In 52 Bindings (9788121271233) Rs. 100000

1. India - Report (9788121276153) Rs. 2820 (Vol. I, Part 1)
2. India - Imeriral Tables (9788121276139) Rs. 770 (Vol. I, Part 2)
3. India - Ethnographical and Administration Report (9788121276115) Rs. 2900 (Vol. I, Part 3 & 5)
4. The Andaman And Nicobar Island - Report, Tables (9788121276078) Rs. 720 (Vol. II,Pt. 1, pt. 2)
5. Assam - Report (9788121276054) Rs. 1340 (Vol. III, Pt. 1)
6. Assam - Tables and Administrative Report (9788121276030) Rs. 1830 (Vol. III, Pt. 2 & 3)
7. Baluchistan - Report, Imeprial and Provincial Tables and Administrative Report (9788121276016) Rs. 2320 (Vol. IV, Pt. 1 & 2 & 3)
8. Bengal & Sikkim - Report (9788121275972) Rs. 2860 (Vol. V, Pt. 1)
9. Bengal & Sikkim - Tables (9788121275958) Rs. 1660 (Vol. V, Pt. 2)
10. Calcutta (9788121275910) Rs. 960 (Vol. VI, Pt. 1 & 2)
11. Bengal, Sikkim And Calcutta - Administrative Report (9788121275934) Rs. 580 (Vol. V & VI, Pt. 3)
12. Bihar And Orissa - Report (9788121275897) Rs. 1780 (Vol. VII, Pt. 1)
13. Bihar And Orissa - Tables and Administrative Report (9788121275873) Rs. 1190 (Vol. VII, Pt. 2 & 3)
14. Bombay Presidency - General Report (9788121275835) Rs. 3620 (Vol. VIII, Pt. 1)
15. Bombay - Statistical tables (9788121275811) Rs. 3060 (Vol. VIII, Pt. 2)
16. Bombay Presidency Aden - report and tables and Administrative report (9788121275798) Rs. 520 (Vol. VIII, Pt. 3 & 4)
17. Cities of the Bombay Presidency Report & Statistical tables (9788121275750) Rs. 2020 (Vol. IX, Pt. 1 & 2)
18. The Western India States Agency, In Two Parts - The Report & The Statistical Tables (9788121275736) Rs. 2560 (Vol. X, Pt. 1 & 2)
19. Burma - Report (9788121275712) Rs. 1860 (Vol. XI, Pt. 1)
20. Burma - Tables and Administrative Report (9788121275699) Rs. 1690 (Vol. XI, Pt. 2 & 3)
21. Central Provinces & Berar - Report (9788121275651) Rs. 2340 (Vol. XII, Pt. 1)
22. Central Provinces & Berar - Tables and Administrative Report (9788121275637) Rs. 3120 (Vol. XII, Pt. 2 & 3)
23. Coorg - Report And Tables and Madras - Report (9788121275613) Rs. 2680 (Vol. Vol. XIV, Pt. 1)
24. Madras - Imperial And Provincial Tables and The Administration Report (9788121275576) Rs. 1950 (Vol. XIV, Pt. 2 & 4)
25. North - West Frontier Province - Report & Tables (9788121275538) Rs. 2300 (Vol. XV, Pt. 1 & 2)
26. Delhi - Report & Tables (9788121275514) Rs. 1180 (Vol. XVI, Pt. 1 & 2)
27. Punjab - Report (9788121275491) Rs. 2070 (Vol. XVII, Pt. 1)
28. Punjab - Tables (9788121275477) Rs. 1690 (Vol. XVII, Pt. 2)
29. United Provinces of Agra And Oudh - Report (9788121275453) Rs. 3380 (Vol. XVIII, Pt. 1)
30. United Provinces of Agra And Oudh - Imperial And Provincial Tables and Administrative (9788121275439) Rs. 3600 (Vol. XVIII, Pt. 2 & 3)
31. Baroda - Report (9788121275415) Rs. 2800 (Vol. XIX, Pt. 1)
32. Baroda - Tables (9788121275392) Rs. 730 (Vol. XIX, Pt. 2)
33. Baroda - Administrative (9788121275378) Rs. 780 (Vol. XIX, Pt. 3)
34. Central India Agency - Report (9788121275354) Rs. 1690 (Vol. XX, Pt. 1)
35. Central India Agency - Tables and Administrative (9788121275330) Rs. 2260 (Vol. XX, Pt. 2 & 3)
36. Cochin - Report & Tables (9788121275293) Rs. 2460 (Vol. XXI, Pt. 1 & 2 - A & B.)
37. Gwalior - Report (9788121275279) Rs. 1470 (Vol. XXII, Pt. 1)
38. Gwalior - Tables (9788121275255) Rs. 980 (Vol. XXII, Pt. 2)
39. H. E. H. The Nizam's Dominions (Hyderabad State) - Report (9788121275231) Rs. 1540 (Vol. XXIII, Pt. 1)
40. H. E. H. The Nizam's Dominions (Hyderabad State) - Tables (9788121275217) Rs. 1510 (Vol. XXIII, Pt. 2)
41. Jammu & Kashmir State - Report (9788121275194) Rs. 2060 (Vol. XXIV, Pt. 1)
42. Jammu & Kashmir State - Imperial & State Tables (9788121275170) Rs. 1940 (Vol. XXIV, Pt. 2 & 3)
43. Mysore - Report (9788121275156) Rs. 1950 (Vol. XXV, Pt. 1)
44. Mysore - Tables (9788121275132) Rs. 1380 (Vol. XXV, Pt. 2)
45. Ajmer-Merwara - Report And Tables (9788121275118) Rs. 780 (Vol. XXVI)
46. Rajputana Agency And Ajmer-Merwara - Report and Tables and Administrative (9788121275095) Rs. 2380 (Vol. XXVII, Pt. 1 & 2)
47. Travancore - Report (9788121276092) Rs. 2960 (Vol. XXVIII, Pt. 1)
48. Travancore - Tables & Administrative (9788121275996) Rs. 1360 (Vol. XXVIII, Pt. 2 & 4)
49. Jaipur State- Report (9788121275859) Rs. 1280 (Pt. 1)
50. Jaipur State- Tables (9788121275774) Rs. 2030 (Pt. 2)
51. Mayurbhanj state- Report (9788121275675) Rs. 3180 (Pt. 1)
52. Mayurbhanj state- Tables (9788121275552) Rs. 3070 (Pt. 2)

Owing to the antiquity and rarity of this book, certain pages are regrettably absent, and readability is compromised due to the blurring of the original text. If you possess any insights regarding the availability of these missing sections, kindly inform us. Your assistance is crucial in ensuring the completion of this significant work for the benefit of future generations.

CENSUS OF INDIA, 1931

BOOK - 44: VOLUME - XXV

MYSORE

PART II - TABLES

M. VENKATES IYENGAR

GYAN

Published by

Gyan Publishing House
5, Ansari Road
Daryaganj, New Delhi-110002
Phone: 011-47034999, 9811692060
E-mail: books@gyanbooks.com

Distribution Network
gyanbooks.com
India, USA, Canada, UK, Australia

ISBN: 978-81-212-7123-3 (Set) 28 Vols. In 52 Bindings

ISBN: 978-81-212-7513-2 (PB) Book-44, Vol. XXV, Pt. II

First Published, 1933

2nd Impression 2024

Printed at: Gyan Press, Delhi.

CENSUS OF INDIA 1931

Census of India, 1931

VOLUME XXV

MYSORE

PART II—TABLES

BY

M. VENKATESA IYENGAR, M.A.,
Superintendent of Census Operations, Mysore State.

BANGALORE:
PRINTED AT THE GOVERNMENT PRESS
1932

TABLE OF CONTENTS

Table XII Unemployment of educated persons is omitted from the list of Imperial Tables and given as a Subsidiary Table in Chapter VIII of the report proper (Vol. I). Table XVIII Plus and Minus figures for Primitive Tribes has not been compiled for the State.

ADDENDA AND CORRIGENDA.

Page	*Table*	*Column*	*Line*	*For*	*Read*
11	IV	14	9	...540	+540
27	VI	38	19	25.274	25,275
30	,,	28	72	insert	1
30	,,	28	73	insert	1
73	VIII	12	19	8	58
87	X	29	9	5,154	51,574
101	,,	268	7	1	13
101	,,	282	8	15	155
102	,,	294	1	1,436	1,456
132	,,	839	14	insert	2
133	,,	860	14	insert	1
161	,,	1,359	5	103	108
172	XI (a)	91	16	1	...
172	,,	92	18	...	1
177	XIII	7	5	62,184	62,814
201	XIV	10	11	107	106
201	,,	10	13	17,359	17,859
217	XV (ii)	16	7	insert	4
227	XVI	34	2	11,598	11,958
231	XVII	19	24	260	2,607
239	Provincial Table I	Note 2	13	After 'cases' read 'except Seringapatam.'	
241	,,	1	16	Saklespur	Manjarabad
248 & 249	Provincial Table II	1	6	Do	Do
249		Title	...	Literary	Literacy

MYSORE CENSUS, 1931.

TABLE I—Area, Houses and Population.

NOTE 1.—Areas of Districts and Cities have been taken to the nearest square mile. Details of fractions omitted or rounded off are given below :—

Omitted		Rounded off	
Bangalore District ...	0·41	Bangalore City	0·82
Kolar District ...	0·16	Mysore District	0·79
Tumkur District ..	0·14	Hassan District	0·52
Chitaldrug District ...	0·12	Kadur District	0·96
Shimoga District ...	0·06	Civil and Military Station, Bangalore	0·50

NOTE 2.—There is a net decrease of about 149 square miles as compared with the figure of the last Census in the area of the State including Civil and Military Station, Bangalore. The decrease is due to accurate measurement and area computation of tracts not subjected to such processes before.

NOTE 3.—Statistics of population by taluks will be found in Provincial Tables I and II at the end of this volume.

TABLE I.

Area, Houses and Population.

District or State	Area in square miles	Towns	Inhabited villages	Occupied houses			Population								
				Total	In towns	In villages	Persons			Males			Females		
							Total	Urban	Rural	Total	Urban	Rural	Total	Urban	Rural
1	2	3	4	5	6	7	8	9	10	11	12	13	14	15	16
MYSORE STATE, INCLUDING CIVIL AND MILITARY STATION, BANGALORE.	**29,326**	**108**	**16,483**	**1.311,445**	**205.567**	**1,105,878**	**6,557.302**	**1.045.042**	**5,512,260**	**3.353,963**	**546,822**	**2,807,141**	**3,203,339**	**498,220**	**2,705,119**
MYSORE STATE, EXCLUDING CIVIL AND MILITARY STATION, BANGALORE.	**29,312**	**107**	**16,483**	**1.289,833**	**183,955**	**1.105,878**	**6,423,189**	**910,929**	**5,512.260**	**3,284,554**	**477,413**	**2.807,141**	**3,138,635**	**433,516**	**2,705,119**
Bangalore City	12	1	...	34,657	34,657	...	172.357	172,357	...	91,680	91,680	...	80,677	80,677	...
Bangalore District	2,922	13	2,478	176,955	15,631	161,324	908,056	77,990	830,066	461,905	39,827	422,078	446,151	38,163	407,988
Kolar Gold Fields (City)	30	1	...	19,448	19,448	...	85,103	85,103	...	45,051	45,051	...	40,052	40,052	...
Kolar District	3,161	11	2,751	150,993	13,710	137,283	763,934	70,040	693,894	389,262	35,766	353,496	374,672	34,274	340,398
Tumkur District	4,082	10	2,381	171,184	12,083	159,101	861,405	61,586	799,819	439,144	32,182	406,962	422,261	29,404	392,857
Mysore City	10	1	...	21,715	21,715	...	107,142	107,142	...	56,772	56,772	...	50,370	50,370	...
Mysore District	5,492	26	2,709	291,050	23,526	267,524	1,403,984	115,056	1,288,928	703,838	58,862	644,976	700,146	56,194	643,952
Chitaldrug District	4,149	11	1,239	124,798	13,369	111,429	656,569	66,451	590,118	336,786	34,586	302,200	319,783	31,865	287,918
Hassan District	2,635	12	2,252	122,435	10,560	111,875	596,937	52,567	544,370	300,746	27,525	273,221	296,191	25,042	271,149
Kadur District	2,771	9	959	73,649	7,985	65,664	347,715	39,911	307,804	184,389	21,328	163,061	163,326	18,583	144,743
Shimoga District	4,048	12	1,714	102,949	11,271	91,678	519,987	62,726	457,261	274,981	33,834	241,147	245,006	28,892	216,114
Civil and Military Station, Bangalore.	**14**	**1**	...	**21,612**	**21,612**	...	**134,113**	**134,113**	...	**69,409**	**69,409**	...	**64,704**	**64,704**	...

MYSORE CENSUS, 1931.

TABLE II.—Variation in Population since 1881.

TABLE II.

Variation in Population since 1881.

District or State	Persons						Variation, Increase (+), Decrease (−)					Net variation in period 1881-1931 Increase (+) Decrease (−)
	1931	1921	1911	1901	1891	1881	1921 to 1931	1911 to 1921	1901 to 1911	1891 to 1901	1881 to 1891	
1	2	3	4	5	6	7	8	9	10	11	12	13
MYSORE STATE, INCLUDING CIVIL AND MILITARY STATION, BANGALORE.	**6,557,302**	**5,978,892**	**5,806,193**	**5,539,399**	**4,943,604**	**4,186,188**	**+578,410**	**+172,699**	**+266,794**	**+595,795**	**+757,416**	**+2,371,114**
MYSORE STATE, EXCLUDING CIVIL AND MILITARY STATION, BANGALORE.	**6,423,189**	**5,859,952**	**5,705,359**	**5,449,800**	**4,843,523**	**4,092,648**	**+563,237**	**+154,593**	**+255,559**	**+606,277**	**+750,875**	**+2,330,541**
Bangalore City	172,357	118,556	88,651	69,447	80,285	62,317	+53,801	+29,905	+19,204	−10,838	+17,968	+110,040
Bangalore District	908,056	788,379	759,522	720,217	622,545	523,750	+119,677	+28,857	+39,305	+97,672	+98,795	+384,306
Kolar Gold Fields (City) ...	85,103	87,682	83,743	70,874	24,111	*...	−2,579	+3,939	+12,869	+46,763	+24,111	+85,103
Kolar District...	763,934	704,657	696,410	652,726	567,002	481,191	+59,277	+8,247	+43,684	+85,724	+85,811	+282,743
Tumkur District	861,405	773,122	735,346	670,377	572,978	447,053	+88,283	+37,776	+64,969	+97,399	+125,925	+414,352
Mysore City	107,142	83,951	71,306	68,111	74,048	60,292	+23,191	+12,645	+3,195	−5,937	+13,756	+46,850
Mysore District	1,403,984	1,319,368	1,270,765	1,227,061	1,107,766	972,366	+84,616	+48,603	+43,704	+119,295	+135,400	+431,618
Chitaldrug District	656,569	574,179	564,243	511,062	424,899	318,534	+82,390	+9,936	+53,181	+86,163	+106,365	+338,035
Hassan District	596,937	583,960	580,200	568,919	511,975	428,344	+12,977	+3,760	+11,281	+56,944	+83,631	+168,593
Kadur District	347 715	333,538	338,457	359,270	328,918	291,377	+14,177	−4,919	−20,813	+30,352	+37,541	+56,338
Shimoga District	519,987	492,560	516,716	531,736	528,996	507,424	+27,427	−24,156	−15,020	+2,740	+21,572	+12,563
Civil and Military Station, Bangalore.	**134,113**	**118,940**	**100,834**	**89,599**	**100,081**	**93,540**	**+15,173**	**+18,106**	**+11,235**	**−10,482**	**+6,541**	**+40,573**

* K. G. F. (City) was not in existence in this year.

TABLE II.

Variation in Population since 1881—*concld.*

District or State	Males						Females					
	1931	1921	1911	1901	1891	1881	1931	1921	1911	1901	1891	1881
	14	15	16	17	18	19	20	21	22	23	24	25
MYSORE STATE, INCLUDING CIVIL AND MILITARY STATION, BANGALORE.	**3,353,963**	**3,047,117**	**2,934,621**	**2,797,024**	**2,483,451**	**2,085,842**	**3,203,339**	**2,931,775**	**2,871,572**	**2,742,375**	**2,460,153**	**2,100,346**
MYSORE STATE, EXCLUDING CIVIL AND MILITARY STATION, BANGALORE.	**3,284,554**	**2,985,541**	**2,882,869**	**2,751,902**	**2,433,262**	**2,038,865**	**3,138,635**	**2,874,411**	**2,822,490**	**2,697,898**	**2,410,261**	**2,053,783**
Bangalore City	91,680	63,911	45,997	35,964	40,873	30,950	80,677	54,645	42,654	33,483	39,412	31,367
Bangalore District	461,905	399,872	382,726	360,826	308,382	258,054	446,151	388,507	376,796	359,391	314,163	265,696
Kolar Gold Fields (City)	45,051	47,487	46,521	39,810	13,323	...	40,052	40,195	37,222	31,064	10,788	...
Kolar District	389,262	357,474	349,825	327,873	284,374	238,164	374,672	347,183	346,585	324,853	282,628	243,027
Tumkur District	439,144	394,897	372,030	337,626	287,062	220,987	422,261	378,225	363,316	332,751	285,916	226,066
Mysore City	56,772	48,783	36,112	34,328	36,691	28,979	50,370	40,168	35,194	33,783	37,357	31,313
Mysore District	703,838	659,148	629,516	606,822	544,046	476,227	700,146	660,220	641,249	620,239	563,720	496,139
Chitaldrug District	336,786	294,955	287,030	259,979	215,230	160,426	319,763	279,224	277,213	251,083	209,669	158,108
Hassan District	300,746	292,249	287,360	283,043	258,554	210,568	296,191	291,711	292,840	285,876	258,421	217,756
Kadur District	184,389	174,615	177,074	188,373	173,340	151,284	163,326	158,923	161,383	170,897	155,578	140,093
Shimoga District	274,981	257,150	268,678	277,258	276,387	263,206	245,006	235,410	248,038	254,478	252,609	244,218
Civil and Military Station, Bangalore.	**69,409**	**61,576**	**51,752**	**45,122**	**50,189**	**46,977**	**64,704**	**57,364**	**49,082**	**44,477**	**49,892**	**46,563**

MYSORE CENSUS, 1931.

TABLE III.—Towns and Villages classified by Population.

TABLE III

Towns and Villages classified by Population.

District or State	Total number of inhabited towns and villages	Population	Under 500		500—1,000		1.000—2 000		2,000—5,000		5,000—10,000		10 000—20,000		20,000—50,000		50,000—100,000		100,000 & over		Encampments, Railway travellers and special Blocks
			Number	Population	Number	Population	Number	Population	Number	Population	Number	Population	Number	Population	Number	Population	Number	Population	Number	Population	
1	2	3	4	5	6	7	8	9	10	11	12	13	14	15	16	17	18	19	20	21	22
MYSORE STATE, INCLUDING CIVIL AND MILITARY STATION, BANGALORE.	16,591	6,557,302	13,282	2,721,707	2,406	1,611,984	702	931,888	157	440,571	31	205,686	7	92,596	2	43,632	1	85,058	3	412,871	11,309
MYSORE STATE, EXCLUDING CIVIL AND MILITARY STATION, BANGALORE.	16,590	6,423,189	13,282	2,721,707	2,406	1,611,984	702	931,888	157	440,571	31	205,686	7	92,596	2	43,632	1	85,058	2	278,758	11,309
Bangalore City	1	172,357	...	...	...	...	...	...	...	...	...	...	...	...	...	...	...	...	1	172,357	...
Bangalore District ...	2,491	908,056	2,009	424,983	366	249,743	92	125,676	17	51,558	6	41,136	1	13,815	...	...	...	...	...	...	1,145
Kolar Gold Fields* (City) ...	1	85,103	...	...	...	...	...	...	...	...	...	...	...	...	...	...	1	85,058	...	...	45
Kolar District	2,762	763,934	2,468	464,905	224	144,424	54	72,199	11	34,925	3	19,050	2	27,244	...	...	...	...	...	...	1,187
Tumkur District	2,391	861,405	1,913	403,547	357	240,652	101	131,562	13	31,511	6	35,500	1	18,034	...	...	...	...	...	...	599
Mysore City	1	107,142	...	...	...	...	...	...	...	...	...	...	...	...	...	...	...	...	1	106,401	741
Mysore District	2,735	1,403,984	1,795	407,342	627	436,493	233	311,636	73	196,434	7	50,170	...	...	...	...	...	...	...	...	1,904
Chitaldrug District ...	1,250	656,569	823	228,854	296	180,901	109	145,808	17	46,875	3	18,570	1	10,732	1	23,101	...	...	...	...	1,728
Hassan District	2,264	596,937	2,013	369,789	210	135,560	29	38,126	9	27,131	2	13,859	1	10,546	...	...	...	...	...	...	1,926
Kadur District	968	347,715	771	154,813	157	108,553	30	38,241	7	20,441	2	13,052	1	12,225	...	...	...	...	...	...	390
Shimoga District	1,726	519,987	1,490	267,474	169	115,653	54	68,640	10	31,696	2	14,349	...	...	1	20,531	...	...	...	...	1,644
Civil and Military Station, Bangalore.	1	134,113	...	...	...	...	...	...	...	...	...	...	...	...	...	...	...	...	1	134,113	...

*The Population of the Kolar Gold Fields includes the population of the Mining Area and that of 81 villages under the jurisdiction of the K. G. F. Sanitary Board.

MYSORE CENSUS, 1931.

TABLE IV.--Towns classified by Population with variation since 1881.

NOTE 1.—Six new towns (*Vide* names within marked with an asterisk) have come into existence since the last Census and their populations at the previous Censuses which should be taken into account to make the figures for the several years comparable, are shown below:—

Names		1921	1911	1901	1891	1881
1. Belakavadi	.. ...	5,817	4,060	5.183	2,795	2,537
2. Yelandur	... ...	3,693	3,686	3,803	3,566	3,273
3. Agara-Mamballi	... ...	4,261	4,826	5,838	5,218	4,529
4- Banavara	... ...	2,663	2,382	2,422	2,172	2,141
5. Mirle	... ...	2,895	2,593	2,682	2,511	2,110
6. Konanur	... ...	2,383	2,536	2,328	2,433	2,034
Total	...	21,712	20,083	22,256	18,695	16,624

NOTE 2.—The totals of the urban population for the 1921 and previous Censuses include the population of the following three places which have now ceased to be towns and are consequently not shown in the table. Their population in 1931 and in previous Census years, which should be taken into account to make the total figures for this and the previous Censuses comparable, are also noted below:—

Names		1931	1921	1911	1901	1891	1881
1. Male-Bennur	...	2,332	2,177	2,138	2,056	1,909	1,637
2. Sivani	...	2,328	2,019	2,106	2,130	2,411	1,549
3. Sulabele	...	1,691	1,734	2,041	2,186	1,927	1,701
Total	...	6,351	5,930	6,285	6,372	6,247	4,887

TABLE IV.

Towns classified by Population with variation since 1881.

Town	District or State	Municipality, Suburb, Cantonment, etc.	Population 1931	Population 1921	Population 1911	Population 1901	Population 1891	Population 1881	Variation: Increase (+), Decrease (−) 1921 to 1931	1911 to 1921	1901 to 1911	1891 to 1901	1881 to 1891	Variation in period 1881-1931 Increase (+) Decrease (−)	Males 1931	Males 1921	Males 1911	Females 1931	Females 1921	Females 1911
1	2	3	4	5	6	7	8	9	10	11	12	13	14	15	16	17	18	19	20	21
TOTAL, TOWNS INCLUDING CIVIL AND MILITARY STATION, BANGALORE.			**1,045,042**	**862,628**	**729,118**	**712,569**	**675,617**	**561,899**	**+182,414**	**+133,509**	**+16,550**	**+36,952**	**+113,718**	**+483,143**	**546,822**	**450,659**	**375,617**	**498,220**	**411,969**	**353,502**
TOTAL, TOWNS EXCLUDING CIVIL AND MILITARY STATION, BANGALORE.			**910,929**	**743,688**	**628,285**	**622,970**	**575,536**	**468,359**	**+167,241**	**+115,403**	**+ 5,315**	**+47,434**	**+107,177**	**+442,570**	**477,413**	**389,083**	**323,865**	**433,516**	**354,605**	**304,420**
Bangalore City ...	Bangalore...	Municipalities	**172,357**	118,556	88,651	69,447	80,285	62,317	+53,801	+29,905	+19,204	−10,838	+17,968	+110,040	**91,680**	63,911	45,997	**80,677**	54,645	42,654
Mysore City ...	Mysore ...		**107,142**	83,951	71,306	68,111	74,048	60,292	+23,191	+12,645	+ 3,195	− 5,987	+13,756	+46,850	**56,772**	43,783	36,112	**50,370**	40,168	35,194
Kolar Gold Fields (City)	Kolar ...		**85,103**	87,682	83,743	70,874	24,111	...	− 2,579	+ 3,939	+12,869	+46,763	+24,111	+85,103	**45,051**	47,487	46,521	**40,052**	40,195	37,222
Davangere ...	Chitaldrug.		**23,155**	16,971	10,074	10,402	8,061	6,362	+ 6,184	+ 6,897	− 328	+ 2,341	+ 1,699	+16,793	**12,069**	8,978	5,257	**11,086**	7,993	4,817
Shimoga ...	Shimoga ...		**20,661**	15,090	13,118	6,240	11,340	12,040	+ 5,571	+ 1,972	+ 6,878	− 5,100	− 700	+ 8,621	**11,056**	7,995	6,617	**9,605**	7,095	6,501
Tumkur ...	Tumkur ...		**18,196**	14,246	6,039	11,888	11,086	9,909	+ 3,950	+ 8,207	− 5,849	+ 802	+ 1,177	+ 8,287	**9,880**	7,599	3,267	**8,316**	6,647	2,772
Kolar ...	Kolar ...		**16,161**	13,368	8,193	12,210	12,148	11,172	+ 2,793	+ 5,175	− 4,017	+ 62	+ 976	+ 4,989	**8,196**	6,818	4,097	**7,965**	6,550	4,096
Channapatna ...	Bangalore...		**13,858**	11,846	7,624	10,425	9,160	8,885	+ 2,012	+ 4,222	− 2,801	+ 1,265	+ 275	+ 4,973	**7,151**	6,054	3,796	**6,707**	5,792	3,828
Chikmagalur ...	Kadur ...		**12,225**	10,207	8,537	9,515	8,000	7,569	+ 2,018	+ 1,670	− 978	+ 1,515	+ 431	+ 4,656	**6,741**	5,488	4,496	**5,484**	4,719	4,041
Chikballapur ...	Kolar ...		**11,508**	10,431	7,661	5,521	10,623	9,133	+ 1,077	+ 2,770	+ 2,140	− 5,102	+ 1,490	+ 2,375	**5,833**	5,235	3,923	**5,675**	5,196	3,738
Chitaldrug ...	Chitaldrug.		**10,732**	8,520	6,986	5,792	4,946	4,271	+ 2,212	+ 1,534	+ 1,194	+ 846	+ 675	+ 6,461	**5,640**	4,415	3,573	**5,092**	4,105	3,413
Hassan ...	Hassan ...		**10,544**	8,096	7,461	8,241	6,654	5,950	+ 2,448	+ 635	− 780	+ 1,587	+ 704	+ 4,594	**5,468**	4,268	3,717	**5,076**	3,828	3,744
Chamrajnagar ...	Mysore ...		**9,538**	6,934	6,556	5,973	5,507	4,123	+ 2,604	+ 378	+ 583	+ 466	+ 1,384	+ 5,415	**4,931**	3,501	3,305	**4,607**	3,433	3,251
Bhadravati ...	Shimoga ...		**9,137†**	3,789	1,810	2,676	2,270	2,334	+ 5,348	+ 1,979	− 866	+ 406	− 64	+ 6,803	**5,313**	2,066	938	**3,824**	1,723	872
Dodballapur ...	Bangalore...		**8,853**	7,588	7,272	7,094	7,141	7,082	+ 1,265	+ 316	+ 178	− 47	+ 109	+ 1,821	**4,509**	3,855	3,594	**4,344**	3,733	3,678
Malvalli ...	Mysore ...		**8,348**	7,400	5,461	7,270	6,308	5,078	+ 948	+ 1,939	− 1,809	+ 962	+ 1,230	+ 3,270	**4,302**	3,776	2,775	**4,046**	3,624	2,686
Holenarsipur ...	Hassan ...		**8,238**	6,679	6,862	6,256	5,758	4,647	+ 1,559	− 183	+ 606	+ 498	+ 1,111	+ 3,591	**4,166**	3,447	3,349	**4,072**	3,232	3,513
Nanjangud ...	Mysore ...		**8,215**	7,453	7,246	5,991	7,292	5,701	+ 762	+ 207	+ 1,255	− 1,301	+ 1,591	+ 2,514	**4,277**	3,756	3,628	**3,938**	3,697	3,618
Tarikere ...	Kadur ...		**8,211**	7,858	6,618	10,164	7,056	5,266	+ 353	+ 1,240	− 3,546	+ 3,108	+ 1,790	+ 2,945	**4,293**	4,282	3,521	**3,918**	3,576	3,097
Kankanhalli ...	Bangalore...		**7,203**	5,759	4,870	5,588	4,986	4,360	+ 1,444	+ 889	− 718	+ 602	+ 626	+ 2,848	**3,732**	2,937	2,501	**3,471**	2,822	2,369
Sira ...	Tumkur ...		**6,894**	5,596	5,573	4,059	3,595	3,154	+ 1,298	+ 23	+ 1,514	+ 464	+ 441	+ 3,740	**3,506**	2,824	2,767	**3,388**	2,772	2,806
Harihar ...	Chitaldrug.		**6,884**	5,904	5,408	5,783	6,385	4,679	+ 980	+ 496	− 375	− 602	+ 1,706	+ 2,205	**3,527**	2,996	2,697	**3,357**	2,908	2,711
Hunsur ...	Mysore ...		**6,777**	4,463	4,772	6,673	6,427	6,653	+ 2,314	− 309	− 1,901	+ 246	− 226	+ 124	**3,464**	2,312	2,458	**3,313**	2,151	2,314
Bowringpet ...	Kolar ...		**6,668**	5,893	2,908	2,893	2,613	1,302	+ 775	+ 2,985	+ 15	+ 280	+ 1,311	+ 5,366	**3,411**	3,147	1,545	**3,257**	2,746	1,363
Chiknaikanhalli ...	Tumkur ...		**6,612**	6,432	5,188	6,113	4,863	3,553	+ 180	+ 1,244	− 925	+ 1,250	+ 1,310	+ 3,059	**3,316**	3,275	2,551	**3,296**	3,157	2,637
Arsikere ...	Hassan ...		**6,611**	4,723	3,685	3,565	2,472	928	+ 1,888	+ 1,038	+ 120	+ 1,093	+ 1,544	+ 5,683	**3,717**	2,832	1,974	**2,894**	1,891	1,711
Closepet ...	Bangalore...		**6,571**	5,552	3,506	6,099	6,236	4,832	+ 1,019	+ 2,046	− 2,593	− 137	+ 1,404	+ 1,739	**3,445**	2,857	1,812	**3,126**	2,695	1,694
Sidlaghatta ...	Kolar ...		**6,368**	3,697	6,512	7,636	6,572	5,804	+ 2,671	− 2,815	− 1,124	+ 1,064	+ 768	+ 564	**3,220**	1,888	3,206	**3,148**	1,809	3,306
Magadi ...	Bangalore...		**6,335**	5,182	3,024	3,608	3,452	3,080	+ 1,203	+ 2,108	− 584	+ 156	+ 372	+ 3,255	**3,127**	2,526	1,493	**3,208**	2,606	1,531
Anekal ...	Bangalore...		**6,307**	6,326	4,587	5,174	7,719	5,995	− 19	+ 1,739	− 587	− 2,545	+ 1,724	+ 312	**3,102**	3,183	2,213	**3,205**	3,143	2,374
Seringapatam ...	Mysore ...		**6,300**	7,217	7,457	8,584	12,553	11,734	− 917	− 240	− 1,127	− 3,969	+ 819	− 5,434	**3,155**	3,614	3,614	**3,145**	3,603	3,843
Devanhalli ...	Bangalore...		**6,152**	5,387	6,313	6,649	6,698	5,774	+ 765	− 926	− 336	− 44	+ 919	+ 378	**3,132**	2,712	3,112	**3,020**	2,675	3,201
Mulbagal ...	Kolar ...		**6,131**	5,671	2,677	6,562	5,163	4,441	+ 460	+ 2,994	− 3,885	+ 1,399	+ 722	+ 1,690	**3,055**	2,860	1,346	**3,076**	2,811	1,331
Mandya ...	Mysore ...		**5,958**	4,887	4,255	4,496	4,100	3,770	+ 1,071	+ 632	− 241	+ 396	+ 330	+ 2,188	**3,160**	2,496	2,089	**2,798**	2,391	2,166
Madhugiri ...	Tumkur ...		**5,865**	5,143	4,545	4,060	3,536	2,846	+ 722	+ 598	+ 485	+ 524	+ 690	+ 3,019	**3,060**	2,600	2,284	**2,805**	2,543	2,261

† Bhadravati Town 4,695 + Bhadravati Iron Works 4,442.

TABLE IV.

Towns classified by Population with variation since 1881—*contd.*

Town	District or State	Munici-pality, Suburb, Canton-ment, etc.	Population						Variation: Increase (+) Decrease (−)					Variation in period 1881—1931 Increase (+) Decrease (−)	Males			Females		
			1931	1921	1911	1901	1891	1881	1921 to 1931	1911 to 1921	1901 to 1911	1891 to 1901	1881 to 1891		1931	1921	1911	1931	1921	1911
1	2	3	4	5	6	7	8	9	10	11	12	13	14	15	16	17	18	19	20	21
TOWNS—*contd.*																				
Gundlupet ...	Mysore ...	Municipalities	**5,759**	4,594	4.187	4,065	4,022	2.951	+ 1,165	+ 407	+ 122	+ 43	+ 1,071	+ 2,808	**3,145**	2,351	2,089	**2,614**	2,243	2,098
Sagar ...	Shimoga ...		**5,696**	4,987	3,684	3.103	2,869	2,284	+ 709	+ 1,303	+ 581	+ 234	+ 585	+ 3.412	**3,316**	2,698	1,942	**2,380**	2,289	1.742
Gubbi ...	Tumkur ...		**5,663**	5.263	3,464	5.593	4,187	3,793	+ 400	+ 1,799	− 2,129	+ 1,406	+ 394	+ 1,870	**2,884**	2,703	1,767	**2,779**	2,560	1,697
Kunigal ...	Tumkur ...		**5,341**	3,044	1,405	1,802	4,406	3,654	+ 2,297	+ 1,639	− 397	− 2,604	+ 752	+ 1,687	**2,757**	1,561	712	**2,584**	1,483	693
Tiptur ...	Tumkur ...		**5,160**	4,311	2,581	3,560	2,260	2,169	+ 849	+ 1,780	− 1,029	+ 1,300	+ 91	+ 2,991	**2,798**	2,244	1,423	**2,362**	2,067	1,106
Birur ...	Kadur ...		**5,109**	4,207	4,853	5,701	4,828	3.786	+ 902	− 646	− 848	+ 873	+ 1,042	+ 1,323	**2,628**	2,063	2,477	**2,481**	2,144	2,376
Ramasamudra ...	Mysore ...		**4,990**	4,748	4,396	4,200	3,820	3,802	+ 242	+ 352	+ 196	+ 380	+ 18	+ 1.188	**2,466**	2,405	2,192	**2,524**	2,343	2,204
Chintamani ...	Kolar ...		**4.985**	6,161	2,570	2,430	2,788	5,119	− 1,176	+ 3,591	+ 140	− 358	− 2,331	− 134	**2,546**	3.114	1,262	**2,439**	3,047	1,308
Hoskote ...	Bangalore...		**4,960**	4,532	4,552	3,184	4,917	4,377	+ 428	− 20	+ 1,368	− 1,793	... 540	+ 583	**2,578**	2.825	2,298	**2,382**	2,207	2,254
Arkalgud ...	Hassan ...		**4,908**	4,458	5,060	4,903	4,374	3,575	+ 450	− 602	+ 157	+ 529	+ 799	+ 1.333	**2,481**	2,321	2,538	**2,427**	2,137	2,522
Bannur ...	Mysore ...		**4,906**	4,458	4,505	5,119	4,925	4,446	+ 448	− 47	− 614	+ 194	+ 479	+ 460	**2,525**	2.256	2,232	**2,381**	2,202	2,273
Shikarpur ...	Shimoga ...		**4,872**	4,366	4,970	5,007	5,011	4.428	+ 506	− 604	− 37	− 4	+ 583	+ 444	**2.480**	2,205	2,582	**2,392**	2,161	2,388
Malur ...	Kolar ...		**4.770**	3,779	4,212	3,632	3.185	2,875	+ 991	− 433	+ 580	+ 447	+ 310	+ 1.895	**2,551**	1,908	2,124	**2,719**	1,871	2.088
Goribidnur ...	Kolar ...		**4,606**	1,842	2,617	2,441	1,765	1.392	+ 2,764	− 775	+ 176	+ 676	+ 373	+ 3,214	**2,382**	972	1,327	**2,224**	870	1,290
Talakad ...	Mysore ...		**4,521**	4,115	4,184	3,857	3,273	3,379	+ 406	− 69	+ 327	+ 584	− 106	+ 1.142	**2,243**	2,038	2,039	**2,278**	2,077	2,145
Saligrama ...	Mysore ...		**4,163**	3,909	3.148	2,744	3,788	3,291	+ 254	+ 761	+ 404	− 1,044	+ 497	+ 872	**2,090**	1,988	1,576	**2,073**	1,921	1,572
Belakavadi* ...	Mysore ...		**4,001**	...	...	...	...	...	...	...	...	...	...	...	**1,985**	...	...	**2,016**	...	...
Honnali ...	Shimoga ...		**3.968**	3,860	1,049	3,891	3.467	2.351	+ 108	+ 2,811	− 2,842	+ 424	+ 1,116	+ 1,617	**2,021**	2,026	561	**1,947**	1.834	488
Mugur ...	Mysore ...		**3,941**	3,540	4,112	4,231	3,735	2,881	+ 401	− 572	− 119	+ 496	+ 854	+ 1,060	**1.946**	1,801	2,000	**1.995**	1,739	2,112
Challakere ...	Chitaldrug.		**3,846**	2,529	2,505	2,000	1,710	1,513	+ 1,317	+ 24	+ 505	+ 290	+ 197	+ 2.333	**2,065**	1,328	1,302	**1,791**	1,201	1,203
Tyamagondlu ...	Bangalore...		**3,823**	3,391	3.022	4.099	3,748	3,299	+ 432	+ 369	− 1,077	+ 351	+ 449	+ 524	**1.945**	1,765	1,539	**1,878**	1,626	1,483
Kadur ...	Kadur ...		**3,822**	3,155	2,900	3,881	2,716	2,216	+ 667	+ 255	− 981	+ 1,165	+ 500	+ 1,606	**1,935**	1,642	1,505	**1,887**	1,513	1,895
Nelamangala ...	Bangalore...		**3,820**	3,354	1.666	4,025	4.171	3.742	+ 466	+ 1,688	− 2,359	− 146	+ 429	+ 78	**1,977**	1,736	862	**1,843**	1,618	804
Vadigenahalli ...	Bangalore...		**3.820**	3,730	4,376	4,008	3,970	3,422	+ 90	− 646	+ 368	+ 38	+ 548	+ 898	**1.910**	1,893	2,175	**1,910**	1,837	2,201
Srinivaspur ...	Kolar ...		**3,812**	3,119	3,430	3,158	2,741	2,403	+ 693	− 311	+ 272	+ 417	+ 338	+ 1,409	**1,927**	1,574	1,676	**1,885**	1,545	1,754
Nagamangala ...	Mysore ...		**3.780**	3,474	3,633	3.516	2,928	2,897	+ 306	− 159	+ 117	+ 588	+ 531	+ 1,383	**1,892**	1,735	1,829	**1,888**	1,739	1,604
Channagiri ...	Shimoga ...		**3,739**	3,996	4,168	4,775	3,787	3,141	− 257	− 172	− 607	+ 988	+ 646	+ 598	**1,912**	2,011	2,050	**1,827**	1,985	2,118
Jagalur ...	Chitaldrug.		**3.707**	2,668	3,632	3.307	3,249	2,510	+ 1,039	− 964	+ 325	+ 58	+ 739	+ 1,197	**1.879**	1,370	1,896	**1,828**	1,298	1,736
Tirthahalli ...	Shimoga ...		**3.538**	3.336	2,718	2,623	2,359	2,092	+ 202	+ 618	+ 95	+ 264	+ 267	+ 1,446	**1.991**	1,852	1,550	**1,547**	1,484	1,168
Hosdurga ...	Chitaldrug.		**3,512**	2.594	2.176	2,263	2,061	1,648	+ 918	+ 418	− 87	+ 202	+ 413	+ 1,864	**1,804**	1,374	1,108	**1,708**	1,220	1,068
Channarayapatna ...	Hassan ...		**3,473**	3,106	2,989	3,222	3,081	2,608	+ 367	+ 117	− 233	+ 141	+ 473	+ 865	**1,733**	1,564	1,498	**1,740**	1,542	1,491
Yelandur* ...	Mysore ...		**3,453**	...	...	...	...	...	...	...	...	...	...	...	**1,688**	...	...	**1,765**	...	...
Agara-Mamballi* ...	Mysore ...		**3,450**	...	...	...	...	...	...	...	...	...	...	...	**1,760**	...	...	**1,690**	...	...
Nyamti ...	Shimoga ...		**3.362**	3,209	3,062	3,461	3,102	2,753	+ 153	+ 147	− 399	+ 359	+ 349	+ 609	**1,704**	1,647	1,523	**1,658**	1,562	1,539
Yedatore ...	Mysore ...		**3,349**	2.105	1,655	2,706	2,413	2,015	+ 1,244	+ 450	− 1,051	+ 293	+ 398	+ 1,334	**1,758**	1,119	855	**1,591**	986	800
Molakalmuru ...	Chitaldrug.		**3.331**	3,359	3,054	2,915	2,421	1,711	− 28	+ 305	+ 139	+ 494	+ 710	+ 1,620	**1,751**	1,716	1,563	**1,580**	1,643	1,491
Yelahanka ...	Bangalore...		**3.315**	2,558	2,336	2,437	2,668	2,808	+ 757	+ 222	− 101	− 231	+ 360	+ 1,007	**1,678**	1,297	1,152	**1,637**	1,261	1,184
Belur ...	Hassan ...		**3.278**	2.859	2,631	3,862	3,084	2,917	+ 419	+ 228	− 1,231	+ 778	+ 167	+ 361	**1.664**	1,422	1,308	**1,614**	1,437	1,323
Ajjampur ...	Kadur ...		**3,255**	2,352	2,546	2,164	2,890	2,306	+ 903	− 194	+ 392	− 726	+ 584	+ 949	**1,700**	1,223	1,319	**1,555**	1,129	1,227
Holalkere ...	Chitaldrug.		**3,243**	3,184	3,746	3,418	2,783	1,855	+ 59	− 562	+ 328	+ 635	+ 928	+ 1,388	**1,652**	1,648	1,927	**1,591**	1,536	1,819

* *Vide* note 1 on title page.

TABLE IV.

Towns Classified by Population with Variation since 1881.—*concld.*

Town	District or State	Municipality, Suburb, Cantonment, etc.	Population 1931	Population 1921	Population 1911	Population 1901	Population 1891	Population 1881	Variation Increase (+) Decrease (−) 1921 to 1931	1911 to 1921	1901 to 1911	1891 to 1901	1881 to 1891	Variation in period 1881-1931 Increase (+) Decrease (−)	Males 1931	Males 1921	Males 1911	Females 1931	Females 1921	Females 1911
1	2	3	4	5	6	7	8	9	10	11	12	13	14	15	16	17	18	19	20	21
TOWNS—*concld.*																				
Periyapatna ...	Mysore ...	Municipalities.	**3,216**	3,108	3,404	3,872	3,712	3,811	+ 108	− 296	− 468	+ 160	− 99	− 595	**1,635**	1,534	1,690	**1,581**	1,574	1,714
Banavar* ...	Hassan ...		**3,127**	...	...	...	...	...	...	...	...	...	...	...	**1,627**	...	...	**1.500**	...	...
Maddur ...	Mysore ...		**3,093**	2,816	2,279	2,597	2,392	2,117	+ 277	+ 537	− 318	+ 205	+ 275	+ 976	**1,608**	1,488	1,194	**1,485**	1,333	1,085
French-Rocks ...	Mysore ...		**3,016**	2,407	1,922	1,983	2,470	3,327	+ 609	+ 485	− 61	− 487	− 857	− 311	**1,631**	1,287	1,029	**1.385**	1,120	893
Sarjapura ...	Bangalore ...		**2,973**	2,639	2,681	3,056	3,017	2,629	+ 334	− 42	− 375	+ 39	+ 388	+ 344	**1,541**	1,370	1,332	**1,432**	1,269	1,349
Kortagere ...	Tumkur ...		**2,969**	3,028	2,965	2,811	2,541	2,016	− 59	+ 63	+ 154	+ 270	+ 525	+ 953	**1,484**	1,580	1,500	**1,485**	1,448	1,465
Saklespur ...	Hassan ...		**2,925**	2,270	804	2,140	1,591	1,432	+ 655	+ 1,466	− 1,336	+ 549	+ 159	+ 1,493	**1,725**	1,247	460	**1,200**	1,023	344
Nayakanahatti ...	Chitaldrug.		**2,902**	2,704	2,610	2,858	2,468	1,716	+ 198	+ 94	− 248	+ 390	+ 752	+ 1,186	**1,505**	1,401	1,338	**1,397**	1,303	1,272
Sirala-Koppa ...	Shimoga ...		**2,855**	2,230	2,482	2,270	2,125	1,954	+ 625	− 252	+ 212	+ 145	+ 171	+ 901	**1,498**	1,155	1,280	**1,357**	1,075	1,202
T.-Narsipur ...	Mysore ...		**2,806**	4,768	4,033	2,406	1,650	1,419	− 1,962	+ 735	+ 1,627	+ 756	+ 231	+ 1,387	**1,466**	2,405	2,006	**1,340**	2,363	2,027
Gudibanda ...	Kolar ...		**2,803**	2,450	2,392	2,384	1,957	1,788	+ 353	+ 58	+ 8	+ 427	+ 169	+ 1,015	**1,460**	1,207	1,230	**1,343**	1,243	1,162
Krishnarajpete ...	Mysore ...		**2,750**	3,226	2,337	2,181	1,662	1,401	− 476	+ 889	+ 206	+ 469	+ 261	+ 1,349	**1,349**	1,593	1,165	**1,401**	1,633	1,172
Pavagada ...	Tumkur ...		**2,750**	2,529	2,594	2,840	1,930	1,591	+ 221	− 65	− 246	+ 910	+ 339	+ 1,159	**1,419**	1,276	1,297	**1,331**	1,253	1,297
Hiriyur ...	Chitaldrug.		**2,748**	2,616	2,533	2,313	2,863	2,270	+ 132	+ 83	+ 220	− 550	+ 593	+ 478	**1,436**	1,304	1,339	**1,312**	1,312	1,194
Melkote ...	Mysore ...		**2,733**	6,307	2,535	3,129	2,789	2,302	− 3,574	+ 3,772	− 594	+ 340	+ 487	+ 431	**1,338**	3,145	1,266	**1,395**	3,162	1,269
Mirle* ...	Mysore ...		**2,674**	...	...	...	...	...	...	...	...	...	...	...	**1,364**	...	...	**1,310**	...	...
Konanur* ...	Hassan ...		**2,637**	...	...	...	...	...	...	...	...	...	...	...	**1,458**	...	...	**1,179**	...	...
Sringeri ...	Kadur ...		**2,579**	1,889	2,971	2,430	1,987	1,994	+ 690	− 1,082	+ 541	+ 443	− 7	+ 585	**1,372**	968	1,639	**1,207**	921	1,332
Harnahalli ...	Hassan ...		**2,459**	2,171	2,025	2,117	2,338	1,727	+ 288	+ 146	− 92	− 221	+ 611	+ 732	**1,248**	1,154	1,055	**1,211**	1,017	970
Mayakonda ...	Chitaldrug.		**2,391**	2,081	2,426	1,894	1,646	1,308	+ 310	− 345	+ 532	+ 248	+ 338	+ 1,083	**1,268**	1,038	1,247	**1,123**	1,043	1,179
Sravanabelgola ...	Hassan ...		**2,371**	1,923	2,163	1,926	1,763	1,315	+ 448	− 260	+ 257	+ 163	+ 448	+ 1,056	**1,197**	952	1,081	**1,174**	971	1,102
Narasimharajapura ...	Kadur ...		**2,232**	1,997	1,855	2,266	1,837	1,702	+ 235	+ 142	− 411	+ 429	+ 135	+ 530	**1,212**	1,071	965	**1,020**	926	890
Bagepalli ...	Kolar ...		**2,228**	1,716	1,962	1,769	1,389	1,242	+ 512	− 246	+ 173	+ 400	+ 147	+ 986	**1,185**	863	998	**1,043**	853	964
Kumsi ...	Shimoga ...		**2,160**	2,128	1,895	2,001	1,656	1,676	+ 32	+ 233	− 106	+ 345	− 20	+ 484	**1,128**	1,039	982	**1,032**	1,069	963
Turuvekere ...	Tumkur ...		**2,136**	1,936	2,685	2,333	1,610	1,688	+ 200	− 749	+ 352	+ 723	− 78	+ 448	**1,078**	993	1,302	**1,058**	943	1,388
Saragur ...	Mysore ...		**2,069**	2,265	2,471	2,284	1,902	1,832	− 196	− 206	+ 187	+ 382	+ 70	+ 237	**1,027**	1,168	1,243	**1,042**	1,097	1,228
Alur ...	Hassan ...		**1,996**	1,984	988	1,299	1,822	1,683	+ 12	+ 996	− 311	− 523	+ 139	+ 313	**1,041**	1,009	522	**955**	975	466
Sorab ...	Shimoga ...		**1,661**	1,482	1,792	1,622	1,661	1,585	+ 179	− 310	+ 170	− 39	+ 76	+ 76	**825**	755	884	**836**	727	908
Mudgere ...	Kadur ...		**1,607**	1,278	1,390	1,675	1,149	950	+ 329	− 112	− 285	+ 526	+ 199	+ 657	**911**	702	781	**696**	576	609
Heggaddevankote ...	Mysore ...		**1,250**	1,242	1,346	1,298	1,295	1,204	+ 8	− 104	+ 48	+ 3	+ 91	+ 46	**657**	632	661	**593**	610	685
Hosanagar† ...	Shimoga ...		**1,077**	1,011	1,000	918	624	571	+ 66	+ 11	+ 82	+ 294	+ 53	+ 506	**590**	554	553	**487**	457	447
Koppa ...	Kadur ...		**871**	858	1,198	1,018	782	827	+ 13	− 340	+ 180	+ 236	− 45	+ 44	**536**	519	738	**335**	339	460
Civil and Military Station, Bangalore.			**134,113**	**118,940**	**100,834**	**89,599**	**100,081**	**98,540**	**+15,178**	**+18,106**	**+11,235**	**−10,482**	**+ 6,541**	**+40,573**	**69,409**	**61,576**	**51,752**	**64,704**	**57,364**	**49,082**

See note I on title page. †Formerly Kallurkatte.

MYSORE CENSUS, 1931.

TABLE V.—Towns arranged Territorially with Population by Religion.

NOTE 1.—The Civil and Military Population of the Civil and Military Station, Bangalore, is as shown below.—

Military	...	...	...	9,163
Civil	...	...	.	124,950

The figures for the Military population are those obtained from the Census of the strictly Military area.

NOTE 2.—Population shown under "animist" in previous Censuses has been shown as "Tribal" in this Census.

TABLE V.

Towns arranged Territorially with Population by Religion.

District or State	Town, Municipality, Suburb or Cantonment	Population			Hindu			Jain			Sikh			Buddhist		
		Persons	Males	Females	Persons	Males	Females	Persons	Males	Females	Persons	Males	Females	Persons	Males	Females
1	2	3	4	5	6	7	8	9	10	11	12	13	14	15	16	17
MYSORE STATE, INCLUDING CIVIL AND MILITARY STATION, BANGALORE.		**1,045,042**	**546,822**	**498,220**	**800.606**	**417,321**	**383,285**	**7,461**	**4,443**	**3,018**	**49**	**40**	**9**	**1,237**	**639**	**598**
MYSORE STATE, EXCLUDING CIVIL AND MILITARY STATION, BANGALORE.		**910,929**	**477,413**	**433,516**	**726.602**	**378.784**	**347,818**	**6,647**	**3,959**	**2,688**	**17**	**11**	**6**	**977**	**496**	**481**
BANGALORE CITY ...		**172,357**	**91,680**	**80,677**	**144,529**	**76,645**	**67,884**	**1,153**	**724**	**429**	...	...	...	**35**	**18**	**17**
BANGALORE DISTRICT		**77,990**	**39,827**	**38,163**	**61,751**	**31,392**	**30,359**	**11**	**8**	**3**	...	...	...	...	...	...
	Channapatna	13,858	7,151	6,707	8,215	4,206	4,009	9	6	3	...	...	...	...	...	...
	Dodballapur	8,853	4,509	4,344	7,282	3,707	3,575	1	1	...	...	...	...	...	...	...
	Anekal	6,307	3,102	3,205	5,379	2,628	2,751	...	...	...	...	...	...	...	...	...
	Kankanhalli	7,203	3,732	3,471	6,358	3,279	3,079	...	...	...	...	...	...	...	...	...
	Closepet	6,571	3,445	3,126	4,186	2,189	1,997	...	...	...	...	...	...	...	...	...
	Devanhalli	6,152	3,132	3,020	5,635	2,867	2,768	...	...	...	...	...	...	...	...	...
	Magadi	6,335	3,127	3,208	5,479	2,689	2,790	...	...	...	...	...	...	...	...	...
	Hoskote	4,960	2,578	2,382	4,193	2,152	2,041	...	...	...	...	...	...	...	...	...
	Vadigenahalli	3,820	1,910	1,910	3,461	1,727	1,734	...	...	...	...	...	...	...	...	...
	Tyamagondlu	3,823	1,945	1,878	2,997	1,519	1,478	...	...	...	...	...	...	...	...	...
	Nelamangala	3,820	1,977	1,843	3,302	1,715	1,587	1	1	...	...	...	...	...	...	...
	Sarjapura	2,973	1,541	1,432	2,391	1,261	1,130	...	...	...	...	...	...	...	...	...
	Yelahanka	3,315	1,678	1,637	2,873	1,453	1,420	...	...	...	...	...	...	...	...	...
KOLAR GOLD FIELDS.		**85,103**	**45,051**	**40,052**	**62,313**	**32,695**	**29,618**	**447**	**262**	**185**	...	...	...	**920**	**469**	**451**
KOLAR DISTRICT ...		**70,040**	**35,766**	**34,274**	**51,112**	**25,918**	**25,194**	**352**	**225**	**127**	...	...	...	**2**	**1**	**1**
	Kolar	16,161	8,196	7,965	10,559	5,333	5,226	59	44	15	...	...	...	...	...	...
	Chikballapur	11,508	5,833	5,675	9,358	4,712	4,646	19	16	3	...	...	...	...	...	...
	Chintamani	4,985	2,546	2,439	3,793	1,908	1,885	2	2	...	...	...	...	...	...	...
	Bowringpet	6,668	3,411	3,257	4,544	2,275	2,269	57	46	11	...	...	...	2	1	1
	Mulbagal	6,131	3,055	3,076	4,176	2,050	2,126	3	1	2	...	...	...	...	...	...
	Malur	4,770	2,551	2,219	4,055	2,151	1,904	...	...	...	...	...	...	...	...	...
	Sidlaghatta	6,368	3,220	3,148	4,668	2,368	2,300	...	...	...	...	...	...	...	...	...
	Srinivaspur	3,812	1,927	1,885	2,421	1,223	1,198	...	...	...	...	...	...	...	...	...
	Gudibanda	2,809	1,460	1,349	2,089	1,059	1,030	27	15	12	...	...	...	...	...	...
	Goribidnur	4,606	2,382	2,224	3,710	1,910	1,800	180	97	83	...	...	...	...	...	...
	Bagepalli	2,228	1,185	1,043	1,789	929	810	5	4	1	...	...	...	...	...	...

TABLE V.

Towns arranged Territorially with Population by Religion.—*contd.*

District or State	Town, Municipality, Suburb or Cantonment	Musalman			Christian			Parsi			Tribal			Jew			Others		
		Persons	Males	Females	Persons	Males	Females	Persons	Males	Females	Persons	Males	Females	Persons	Males	Females	Persons	Males	Females
		18	19	20	21	22	23	24	25	26	27	28	29	30	31	32	33	34	35
MYSORE STATE, INCLUDING CIVIL AND MILITARY STATION, BANGALORE.		170,349	91,744	78,605	64,219	32,064	32,155	323	163	160	653	344	309	39	13	26	106	51	55
MYSORE STATE, EXCLUDING CIVIL AND MILITARY STATION, BANGALORE.		141,724	76,346	65,378	34,197	17,412	16,785	79	43	36	653	344	309	18	7	11	15	11	4
BANGALORE CITY ...		19,831	10,975	8,856	6,754	3,291	3,463	28	11	17	...	...	...	12	5	7	15	11	4
BANGALORE DISTRICT		15,688	8,165	7,523	540	262	278	...	...	...	...	...	...	...	...	...	...	...	...
	Channapatna	5,538	2,904	2,634	96	35	61	...	...	...	...	...	...	...	...	...	...	...	...
	Dodballapur	1,522	776	746	48	25	23	...	...	...	...	...	...	...	...	...	...	...	...
	Anekal	807	407	400	121	67	54	...	...	...	...	...	...	...	...	...	...	...	...
	Kankanhalli	807	433	374	38	20	18	...	...	...	...	...	...	...	...	...	...	...	...
	Closepet	2,276	1,197	1,079	109	59	50	...	...	...	...	...	...	...	...	...	...	...	...
	Devanhalli	500	258	242	17	7	10	...	...	...	...	...	...	...	...	...	...	...	...
	Magadi	848	434	414	8	4	4	...	...	...	...	...	...	...	...	...	...	...	...
	Hoskote	764	423	341	3	3	...	...	...	...	...	...	...	...	...	...	...	...	...
	Vadigenahalli	354	181	173	5	2	3	...	...	...	...	...	...	...	...	...	...	...	...
	Tyamagondlu	815	422	393	11	4	7	...	...	...	...	...	...	...	...	...	...	...	...
	Nelamangala	513	258	255	1	3	1	...	...	...	...	...	...	...	...	...	...	...	...
	Sarjapura	578	280	298	4	...	4	...	...	...	...	...	...	...	...	...	...	...	...
	Yelahanka	366	192	174	76	33	43	...	...	...	...	...	...	...	...	...	...	...	...
KOLAR GOLD FIELDS.		6,771	4,045	2,726	14,651	7,579	7,072	...	...	...	1	1	...	...	...	...	...	...	...
KOLAR DISTRICT ...		16,963	8,844	8,119	1,611	778	833	...	...	...	...	...	...	...	...	...	...	...	...
	Kolar	4,628	2,413	2,215	915	406	509	...	...	...	...	...	...	...	...	...	...	...	...
	Chikballapur	1,852	963	889	279	142	137	...	...	...	...	...	...	...	...	...	...	...	...
	Chintamani	1,184	634	550	6	2	4	...	...	...	...	...	...	...	...	...	...	...	...
	Bowringpet	1,807	943	864	258	146	112	...	...	...	...	...	...	...	...	...	...	...	...
	Mulbagal	1,930	990	940	22	11	8	...	...	...	...	...	...	...	...	...	...	...	...
	Malur	671	378	293	44	22	22	...	...	...	...	...	...	...	...	...	...	...	...
	Sidlaghatta	1,656	827	829	44	25	19	...	...	...	...	...	...	...	...	...	...	...	...
	Srinivaspur	1,386	701	685	5	3	2	...	...	...	...	...	...	...	...	...	...	...	...
	Gudibanda	685	386	299	2	...	2	...	...	...	...	...	...	...	...	...	...	...	...
	Goribidnur	680	357	323	36	18	18	...	...	...	...	...	...	...	...	...	...	...	...
	Bagepalli	484	252	232	...	...	...	...	...	...	...	...	...	...	...	...	...	...	...

TABLE V.

Towns arranged Territorially with Population by Religion—*contd.*

District or State	Town, Municipality, Suburb or Cantonment	Population			Hindu			Jain			Sikh			Buddhist		
		Persons	Males	Females	Persons	Males	Females	Persons	Males	Females	Persons	Males	Females	Persons	Males	Females
1	2	3	4	5	6	7	8	9	10	11	12	13	14	15	16	17
TUMKUR DISTRICT ...		**61,586**	**32,182**	**29,404**	**48,414**	**25,185**	**23,229**	**611**	**315**	**296**	...	...	...	...	...	...
	Tumkur	18,196	9,880	8,316	14,223	7,675	6,548	306	166	140	...	...	...	...	...	...
	Chiknaikanhalli ...	6,612	3,316	3,296	5,869	2,943	2,926	5	2	3	...	...	...	...	...	...
	Sira	6,894	3,506	3,388	4,325	2,194	2,131	3	3	...	...	...	...	...	...	...
	Gubbi	5,663	2,884	2,779	4,844	2,440	2,404	122	66	56	...	...	...	...	...	...
	Madhugiri	5,865	3,060	2,805	4,534	2,375	2,159	99	41	58	...	...	...	...	...	...
	Tiptur	5,160	2,798	2,362	3,956	2,153	1,803	16	12	4	...	...	...	...	...	...
	Kunigal	5,341	2,757	2,584	3,744	1,902	1,842	11	2	9	...	...	...	...	...	...
	Kortagere	2,969	1,484	1,485	2,559	1,270	1,289	13	4	9	...	...	...	...	...	...
	Pavegada	2,750	1,419	1,331	2,477	1,277	1,200	36	19	17	...	...	...	...	...	...
	Turuvekere	2,136	1,078	1,058	1,883	956	927	...	...	...	...	...	...	...	...	...
MYSORE CITY ...		**107,142**	**56,772**	**50,370**	**84,789**	**44,734**	**40,055**	**549**	**372**	**177**	**17**	**11**	**6**	**19**	**7**	**12**
MYSORE DISTRICT ...		**115,056**	**58,862**	**56,194**	**100,430**	**51,075**	**49,355**	**893**	**425**	**468**	...	...	...	...	...	...
	Nanjangud	8,215	4,277	3,938	7,468	3,855	3,613	8	5	3	...	...	...	...	...	...
	Malvalli	8,348	4,302	4,046	7,533	3,869	3,664	10	5	5	...	...	...	...	...	...
	Seringapatam	6,300	3,155	3,145	5,366	2,665	2,701	2	1	1	...	...	...	...	...	...
	Chamrajnagar ...	9,538	4,931	4,607	7,869	4,030	3,839	172	81	91	...	...	...	...	...	...
	Melkote	2,733	1,338	1,395	2,686	1,308	1,378	...	...	...	...	...	...	...	...	...
	Mandya	5,958	3,160	2,798	5,278	2,809	2,469	149	67	82	...	...	...	...	...	...
	T.-Narsipur	2,806	1,466	1,340	2,598	1,347	1,251	...	...	...	...	...	...	...	...	...
	[illegible]amasamudra ...	4,990	2,466	2,524	4,833	2,381	2,452	18	8	10	...	...	...	...	...	...
	Gundlupet	5,759	3,145	2,614	4,901	2,677	2,224	2	1	1	...	...	...	...	...	...
	Hunsur	6,777	3,464	3,313	5,590	2,832	2,758	4	2	2	...	...	...	...	...	...
	Pannur	4,906	2,525	2,381	3,997	2,036	1,961	...	...	...	...	...	...	...	...	...
	Talakad	4,521	2,243	2,278	4,328	2,144	2,184	6	2	4	...	...	...	...	...	...
	Saligrama	4,163	2,090	2,073	3,472	1,739	1,733	424	205	219	...	...	...	...	...	...
	Mugur	3,941	1,946	1,995	3,880	1,914	1,966	...	...	...	...	...	...	...	...	...
	Nagamangala	3,780	1,892	1,888	2,588	1,264	1,324	...	...	...	...	...	...	...	...	...
	Krishnarajpete ...	2,750	1,349	1,401	2,374	1,162	1,212	...	...	...	...	...	...	...	...	...
	Periyapatna	3,216	1,635	1,581	2,758	1,395	1,363	...	...	...	...	...	...	...	...	...
	Maddur	3,093	1,608	1,485	2,294	1,179	1,115	1	1	...	...	...	...	...	...	...
	French-Rocks... ...	3,016	1,631	1,385	2,274	1,225	1,049	2	2	...	...	...	...	...	...	...
	Saragur	2,069	1,027	1,042	1,869	920	949	93	43	50	...	...	...	...	...	...
	Yedatore	3,349	1,758	1,591	2,672	1,404	1,268	...	...	...	...	...	...	...	...	...

TABLE V.

Towns arranged Territorially with Population by Religion—*contd.*

District or State	Town, Municipality, Suburb or Cantonment	Musalman			Christian			Parsi			Tribal			Jew			Others		
		Persons	Males	Females	Persons	Males	Females	Persons	Males	Females	Persons	Males	Females	Persons	Males	Females	Persons	Males	Females
		18	19	20	21	22	23	24	25	26	27	28	29	30	31	32	33	34	35
TUMKUR DISTRICT ...		**11,488**	**6,080**	**5,408**	**1,038**	**588**	**450**	**1**	**1**	...	**34**	**13**	**21**	...	...	...	...	...	...
	Tumkur	2,872	1,578	1,294	795	461	334	...	...	...	...	...	...	...	...	...	...	...	...
	Chiknaikanhalli ...	736	370	366	2	1	1	...	...	...	...	...	...	...	...	...	...	...	...
	Sira	2,559	1,308	1,251	7	1	6	...	...	...	...	...	...	...	...	...	...	...	...
	Gubbi	600	321	279	97	57	40	...	...	...	...	...	...	...	...	...	...	...	...
	Madhugiri	1,219	638	581	13	6	7	...	...	...	...	...	...	...	...	...	...	...	...
	Tiptur	1,139	608	531	49	25	24	...	...	...	...	...	...	...	...	...	...	...	...
	Kunigal	1,540	831	709	45	21	24	1	1	...	...	...	...	...	...	...	...	...	...
	Koratagere	379	202	177	7	3	4	...	...	...	11	5	6	...	...	...	...	...	...
	Pavagada	225	116	109	12	7	5	...	...	...	...	...	...	...	...	...	...	...	...
	Turuvekere	219	108	111	11	6	5	...	...	...	23	8	15	...	...	...	...	...	...
MYSORE CITY ...		**17,772**	**9,661**	**8,111**	**3,947**	**1,956**	**1,991**	**36**	**23**	**13**	**7**	**6**	**1**	**6**	**2**	**4**	...	...	...
MYSORE DISTRICT ...		**12,943**	**6,917**	**6,026**	**783**	**440**	**343**	...	...	...	**7**	**5**	**2**	...	...	...	...	...	...
	Nanjangud	720	402	318	19	15	4	...	...	...	...	...	...	...	...	...	...	...	...
	Malvalli	764	403	361	41	25	16	...	...	...	...	...	...	...	...	...	...	...	...
	Seringapatam	830	437	393	102	52	50	...	...	...	...	...	...	...	...	...	...	...	...
	Chamrajnagar ...	1,468	801	667	29	19	10	...	...	...	...	...	...	...	...	...	...	...	...
	Melkote	46	29	17	1	1	...	...	...	...	...	...	...	...	...	...	...	...	...
	Mandya	393	214	179	138	70	68	...	...	...	...	...	...	...	...	...	...	...	...
	T.-Narsipur	206	117	89	2	2	...	...	...	...	...	...	...	...	...	...	...	...	...
	hamasamudra... ...	137	75	62	2	2	...	...	...	...	...	...	...	...	...	...	...	...	...
	Gundlupet	832	451	381	24	16	8	...	...	...	...	...	...	...	...	...	...	...	...
	Hunsur	1,098	581	517	82	46	36	...	...	...	3	3	...	...	...	...	...	...	...
	Bannur	907	487	420	2	2	...	...	...	...	...	...	...	...	...	...	...	...	...
	Talakad	154	81	73	33	16	17	...	...	...	...	...	...	...	...	...	...	...	...
	Saligrama	260	142	118	7	4	3	...	...	...	...	...	...	...	...	...	...	...	...
	Mugur	48	24	24	13	8	5	...	...	...	...	...	...	...	...	...	...	...	...
	Nagamangala	1,175	619	556	17	9	8	...	...	...	...	...	...	...	...	...	...	...	...
	Krishnarajpete ...	368	182	186	8	5	3	...	...	...	...	...	...	...	...	...	...	...	...
	Periyapatna	448	235	213	6	3	3	...	...	...	4	2	2	...	...	...	...	...	...
	Maddur	780	415	365	18	13	5	...	...	...	...	...	...	...	...	...	...	...	...
	French-Rocks	567	309	258	173	95	78	...	...	...	...	...	...	...	...	...	...	...	...
	Saragur	103	62	41	4	2	2	...	...	...	...	...	...	...	...	...	...	...	...
	Yedatore	645	337	308	32	17	15	...	...	...	...	...	...	...	...	...	...	...	...

TABLE V

Towns arranged Territorially with Population by Religion—*contd.*

District or State	Town, Municipality, Suburb, or Cantonment	Population			Hindu			Jain			Sikh			Buddhist		
		Persons	Males	Females	Persons	Males	Females	Persons	Males	Females	Persons	Males	Females	Persons	Males	Females
1	2	3	4	5	6	7	8	9	10	11	12	13	14	15	16	17
MYSORE DISTRICT—*concld.*	Heggaddevanakote ...	1,250	657	593	1,109	575	534	2	2	...	...	...	...	...	...	...
	Mirle ...	2,674	1,364	1,310	2,627	1,338	1,289	...	...	...	...	...	...	...	...	...
	Belakavadi ...	4,001	1,985	2,016	3,693	1,832	1,861	...	...	...	...	...	...	...	...	...
	Yelandur ...	3,453	1,688	1,765	3,184	1,544	1,640	...	...	...	...	...	...	...	...	...
	Agara-Mamballi ...	3,450	1,760	1,690	3,189	1,631	1,558	...	...	...	...	...	...	...	...	...
CHITALDRUG DISTRICT.		**66,451**	**34,586**	**31,865**	**52,155**	**27,118**	**25,037**	**677**	**417**	**260**	...	...	...	...	...	...
	Davangere ...	23,155	12,069	11,086	18,119	9,397	8,722	271	174	97	...	...	...	...	...	...
	Chitaldrug ...	10,732	5,640	5,092	7,934	4,179	3,755	104	78	26	...	...	...	...	...	...
	Harihar ...	6,884	3,527	3,357	5,040	2,572	2,468	27	21	6	...	...	...	...	...	...
	Molakalmuru ...	3,331	1,751	1,580	2,364	1,262	1,102	...	...	...	...	...	...	...	...	...
	Holalkere ...	3,243	1,652	1,591	2,494	1,284	1,210	63	30	33	...	...	...	...	...	...
	Nayakanahatti ...	2,902	1,505	1,397	2,618	1,360	1,258	...	...	...	...	...	...	...	...	...
	Jagalur ...	3,707	1,879	1,828	3,108	1,572	1,536	5	4	1	...	...	...	...	...	...
	Hiriyur ...	2,748	1,436	1,312	1,929	1,024	905	11	7	4	...	...	...	...	...	...
	Hosdurga ...	3,512	1,804	1,708	3,027	1,541	1,486	142	70	72	...	...	...	...	...	...
	Challakere ...	3,846	2,055	1,791	3,290	1,756	1,534	38	22	16	...	...	...	...	...	...
	Mayakonda ...	2,391	1,268	1,123	2,232	1,171	1,061	16	11	5	...	...	...	...	...	...
HASSAN DISTRICT ...		**52,567**	**27,525**	**25,042**	**41,756**	**21,728**	**20,028**	**1,298**	**717**	**581**	...	...	...	1	1	...
	Hassan ...	10,544	5,468	5,076	8,042	4,232	3,810	413	197	216	...	...	...	...	...	...
	Holenarsipur ...	8,238	4,166	4,072	7,165	3,592	3,573	20	9	11	...	...	...	...	...	...
	Arsikere ...	6,611	3,717	2,894	4,741	2,659	2,082	104	74	30	...	...	...	1	1	...
	Arkalgud ...	4,908	2,481	2,427	4,315	2,171	2,144	...	...	...	...	...	...	...	...	...
	Chennarayapatna ...	3,473	1,733	1,740	2,794	1,394	1,400	15	11	4	...	...	...	...	...	...
	Belur ...	3,278	1,664	1,614	2,618	1,299	1,319	41	32	9	...	...	...	...	...	...
	Banavar ...	3,127	1,627	1,500	2,537	1,292	1,245	38	26	12	...	...	...	...	...	...
	Sakalespur ...	2,925	1,725	1,200	2,170	1,250	920	40	32	8	...	...	...	...	...	...
	Konanur ...	2,637	1,458	1,179	2,345	1,291	1,054	11	10	1	...	...	...	...	...	...
	Harnahalli ...	2,459	1,248	1,211	2,066	1,043	1,023	...	...	...	...	...	...	...	...	...
	Sravanabelgola ...	2,371	1,197	1,174	1,560	778	782	606	316	290	...	...	...	...	...	...
	Alur ...	1,996	1,041	955	1,403	727	676	10	10	...	...	...	...	...	...	...
KADUR DISTRICT ...		**39,911**	**21,328**	**18,583**	**31,928**	**16,780**	**15,148**	**326**	**255**	**71**	...	...	...	...	...	...
	Chikmagalur ...	12,225	6,741	5,484	8,909	4,814	4,095	154	124	30	...	...	...	...	...	...
	Tarikere ...	8,211	4,293	3,918	6,711	3,462	3,249	51	38	13	...	...	...	...	...	...

TABLE V.

Towns arranged Territorially with Population by Religion—*contd.*

District or State	Town, Municipality, Suburb or Cantonment	Musalman			Christian			Parsi			Tribal			Jew			Others		
		Persons	Males	Females	Persons	Males	Females	Persons	Males	Females	Persons	Males	Females	Persons	Males	Females	Persons	Males	Females
		18	19	20	21	22	23	24	25	26	27	28	29	30	31	32	33	34	35
MYSORE DISTRICT.— *contd.*	Heggaddevankote ...	135	77	58	4	3	1	...	...	...	...	...	...	...	...	...	...	...	...
	Mirle ...	37	19	18	10	7	3	...	...	...	...	...	...	...	...	...	...	...	...
	Belakavadi ...	304	151	153	4	2	2	...	...	...	...	...	...	...	...	...	...	...	...
	Yelandur ...	266	144	122	3	...	3	...	...	...	...	...	...	...	...	...	...	...	...
	Agara-Mamballi ...	252	123	129	9	6	3	...	...	...	...	...	...	...	...	...	...	...	...
CHITALDRUG DISTRICT.		**12,679**	**6,565**	**6,114**	**376**	**192**	**184**	**8**	**5**	**3**	**556**	**289**	**267**	...	...	...	...	...	...
	Davangere ...	4,182	2,190	1,992	131	67	64	8	5	3	444	236	208	...	...	...	...	...	...
	Chitaldrug ...	2,456	1,262	1,194	165	87	78	...	...	...	73	34	39	...	...	...	...	...	...
	Harihar ...	1,791	920	871	15	7	8	...	...	...	11	7	4	...	...	...	...	...	...
	Molakalmuru ...	951	480	471	16	9	7	...	...	...	...	...	...	...	...	...	...	...	...
	Holalkere ...	684	338	346	2	...	2	...	...	...	...	...	...	...	...	...	...	...	...
	Nayakanahatti ...	282	145	137	2	...	2	...	...	...	...	...	...	...	...	...	...	...	...
	Jagalur ...	562	289	273	4	2	2	...	...	...	28	12	16	...	...	...	...	...	...
	Hiriyur ...	802	400	402	6	5	1	...	...	...	...	...	...	...	...	...	...	...	...
	Hosdurga ...	330	189	141	13	4	9	...	...	...	...	...	...	...	...	...	...	...	...
	Challakere ...	496	266	230	22	11	11	...	...	...	...	...	...	...	...	...	...	...	...
	Mayakonda ...	143	86	57	...	...	...	...	...	...	...	...	...	...	...	...	...	...	...
HASSAN DISTRICT ...		**8,349**	**4,545**	**3,804**	**1,159**	**532**	**627**	...	...	...	**4**	**2**	**2**	...	...	...	...	...	...
	Hassan ...	1,547	830	717	542	209	333	...	...	...	...	...	...	...	...	...	...	...	...
	Hole-Narsipur...	1,008	540	468	45	25	20	...	...	...	...	...	...	...	...	...	...	...	...
	Arsikere ...	1,295	742	553	470	241	229	...	...	...	...	...	...	...	...	...	...	...	...
	Arkalgud ...	593	310	283	...	...	...	...	...	...	...	...	...	...	...	...	...	...	...
	Chennarayapatna	652	323	329	12	5	7	...	...	...	...	...	...	...	...	...	...	...	...
	Belur ...	597	322	275	22	11	11	...	...	...	...	...	...	...	...	...	...	...	...
	Banavar ...	548	307	241	...	...	...	...	...	...	4	2	2	...	...	...	...	...	...
	Sakalespur ...	661	413	248	54	30	24	...	...	...	...	...	...	...	...	...	...	...	...
	Konanur ...	281	157	124	...	...	...	...	...	...	...	...	...	...	...	...	...	...	...
	Harnahalli ...	387	199	188	6	6	...	...	...	...	...	...	...	...	...	...	...	...	...
	Sravanabelgola	205	103	102	...	...	...	...	...	...	...	...	...	...	...	...	...	...	...
	Alur ...	575	299	276	8	5	3	...	...	...	...	...	...	...	...	...	...	...	...
KADUR DISTRICT ...		**6,719**	**3,791**	**2,928**	**932**	**499**	**433**	**6**	**3**	**3**	...	...	...	...	...	...	...	...	...
	Chikmagalur ...	2,541	1,476	1,065	615	324	291	6	3	3	...	...	...	...	...	...	...	...	...
	Tarikere ...	1,371	752	619	78	41	37	...	...	...	...	...	...	...	...	...	...	...	...

TABLE V.
Towns by Religion.

TABLE V.

Towns arranged Territorially with Population by Religion—*concld.*

District or State	Town, Municipality, Suburb or Cantonment	Population			Hindu			Jain			Sikh			Buddhist		
		Persons	Males	Females	Persons	Males	Females	Persons	Males	Females	Persons	Males	Females	Persons	Males	Females
1	2	3	4	5	6	7	8	9	10	11	12	13	14	15	16	17
KADUR DISTRICT.—*concld.*	Birur	5,109	2,628	2,481	4,416	2,256	2,160	12	10	2	...	...	...	...	...	...
	Kadur	3,822	1,935	1,887	3,390	1,689	1,701	10	10	...	...	...	...	...	...	...
	Ajjampur	3,255	1,700	1,555	3,177	1,657	1,520	5	5	...	...	...	...	...	...	...
	Sringeri	2,579	1,372	1,207	2,282	1,200	1,082	42	27	15	...	...	...	...	...	...
	Narasimharajapura ..	2,232	1,212	1,020	1,633	899	734	24	16	8	...	...	...	...	...	...
	Mudgere	1,607	911	696	763	429	334	18	16	2	...	...	...	...	...	...
	Koppa	871	536	335	647	374	273	10	9	1	...	...	...	...	...	...
SHIMOGA DISTRICT ...		**62.726**	**33,834**	**28.892**	**47.425**	**25,514**	**21,911**	**330**	**239**	**91**	...	...	...	...	...	...
	Shimoga	20,661	11,056	9,605	14,884	7,951	6,933	133	92	41	...	...	...	...	...	...
	Sagar	5,696	3,316	2,380	4,396	2,568	1,828	26	22	4	...	...	...	...	...	...
	Shikarpur	4,872	2,480	2,392	3,855	1,954	1.901	65	46	19	...	...	...	...	...	...
	Bhadravati	9,137	5,313	3,824	7,161	4,136	3,025	32	25	7	...	...	...	...	...	...
	Honnali	3,968	2.021	1.947	2.978	1,508	1.470	14	8	6	...	...	...	...	...	...
	Chennagiri	3.739	1.912	1,827	2,539	1,307	1,232	7	7	...	...	...	...	...	...	...
	Tirthahalli	3,538	1,991	1,547	2,810	1,531	1,279	13	12	1	...	...	...	...	...	...
	Nyamati	3,362	1,704	1,658	3.059	1,554	1,505	...	...	...	...	...	...	...	...	...
	Shiralkoppa	2.855	1,498	1,357	1,827	969	858	18	18	...	...	...	...	...	...	...
	Kumsi	2,160	1,128	1,032	1,774	921	853	1	1	...	...	...	...	...	...	...
	Sorab	1,661	825	836	1,301	656	645	16	8	8	...	...	...	...	...	...
	Hosanagar ...	1.077	590	487	841	459	382	5	...	5	...	...	...	...	...	...
CIVIL AND MILITARY STATION, BANGALORE.		**134,113**	**69.409**	**64.704**	**74,004**	**38,537**	**35.467**	**814**	**484**	**330**	**32**	**29**	**3**	**260**	**143**	**117**

TABLE V.

Towns by Religion.

TABLE V.

Towns arranged Territorially with Population by Religion—*concld.*

District or State	Town, Municipality, Suburb or Cantonment	Musalman			Christian			Parsi			Tribal			Jew			Others		
		Persons	Males	Females	Persons	Males	Females	Persons	Males	Females	Persons	Males	Females	Persons	Males	Females	Persons	Males	Females
		18	19	20	21	22	23	24	25	26	27	28	29	30	31	32	33	34	35
KADUR DISTRICT.— *concld.*	Birur	654	347	307	27	15	12	...	...	...	...	...	...	...	...	...	...	...	...
	Kadur	390	220	170	32	16	16	...	...	...	...	...	...	...	...	...	...	...	...
	Ajjampur	69	36	33	4	2	2	...	...	...	...	...	...	...	...	...	...	...	...
	Sringeri	231	133	98	24	12	12	...	...	...	...	...	...	...	...	...	...	...	...
	Narasimharajapura ...	553	287	266	22	10	12	...	...	...	...	...	...	...	...	...	...	...	...
	Mudgere	734	412	322	92	54	38	...	...	...	...	...	...	...	...	...	...	...	...
	Koppa	176	128	48	38	25	13	...	...	...	...	...	...	...	...	...	...	...	...
SHIMOGA DISTRICT.—		**12,521**	**6,758**	**5,763**	**2,406**	**1,295**	**1,111**	...	...	...	**44**	**28**	**16**	...	...	...	...	...	...
	Shimoga	4,595	2,459	2,136	1,027	544	483	...	...	...	22	10	12	...	...	...	...	...	...
	Sagar	995	567	428	279	159	120	...	...	...	...	...	...	...	...	...	...	...	...
	Shikarpur	932	468	464	15	7	8	...	...	...	5	5	...	...	...	...	...	...	...
	Bhadravati	1,229	749	480	702	393	309	...	...	...	13	10	3	...	...	...	...	...	...
	Honnali	950	493	457	26	12	14	...	...	...	...	...	...	...	...	...	...	...	...
	Chennagiri	1,181	593	588	12	5	7	...	...	...	...	...	...	...	...	...	...	...	...
	Tirthahalli	488	337	151	223	108	115	...	...	...	4	3	1	...	...	...	...	...	...
	Nyamti	293	143	150	10	7	3	...	...	...	...	...	...	...	...	...	...	...	...
	Shiralkoppa	999	506	493	11	5	6	...	...	...	...	...	...	...	...	...	...	...	...
	Kumsi	372	198	174	13	8	5	...	...	...	...	...	...	...	...	...	...	...	...
	Sorab	333	156	177	11	5	6	...	...	...	...	...	...	...	...	...	...	...	...
	Hosanagar	154	89	65	77	42	35	...	...	...	...	...	...	...	...	...	...	...	...
CIVIL AND MILITARY STATION, BANGALORE.		**28,625**	**15,398**	**13,227**	**30,022**	**14,652**	**15,370**	**244**	**120**	**124**	...	...	...	**21**	**6**	**15**	**91**	**40**	**51**

MYSORE CENSUS, 1931.

TABLE VI—Birthplace.

NOTE 1.—Figures are given for the individual Districts and States of Bombay and Madras Presidencies only where the number of immigrants is considerable.

NOTE 2.—Of the birth districts in the State 'Bangalore District' includes Bangalore City and the Civil and Military Station, Bangalore: 'Kolar District' includes Kolar Gold Fields (City); and 'Mysore District' includes Mysore City.

NOTE 3.—The phrase "Within British Dominions" in column 1 of this Table should be taken to mean "Within the British Empire and Mandated Territories."

Number	District, State, Province or Country where born	City, District or State								
		Mysore State including Civil and Military Station, Bangalore			Mysore State excluding Civil and Military Station, Bangalore			Bangalore City		
		Persons	Males	Females	Persons	Males	Females	Persons	Males	Females
	1	2	3	4	2 (a)	3 (a)	4 (a)	5	6	7
1	**TOTAL POPULATION** ...	**6,557,302**	**3,353,963**	**3,203,339**	**6,423,189**	**3,284,554**	**3,138,635**	**172,357**	**91,680**	**80,677**
2	*A. BORN IN INDIA*	**6,553,410**	**3,351,314**	**3,202,096**	**6,422,020**	**3,283,829**	**3,138,191**	**172,071**	**91,535**	**80,536**
3	(i) **Mysore**	**6,212,710**	**3,163,517**	**3,049,193**	**6,113,261**	**3,113,461**	**2,999,800**	**135,120**	**71,278**	**63,842**
4	Bangalore District	1,101,138	561,342	539,796	1,008,512	514,491	494,021	108,682	56,335	52,297
5	Kolar do	786,442	403,751	382,691	784,207	402,725	381,482	6,787	3,714	3,073
6	Tumkur do	856,898	439,855	417,043	856,543	439,680	416,863	5,233	3,034	2,199
7	Mysore do	1,512,864	759,684	753,180	1,508,984	757,837	751,147	10,863	5,991	4,872
8	Chitaldrug do	625,935	322,[illegible]	303,576	625,912	322,345	303,567	707	473	234
9	Hassan do	571,55[illegible]	286,572	284,986	571,445	286,519	284,926	1,286	746	540
10	Kadur do	292,5[illegible]	148,729	143,834	292,499	148,707	143,792	672	410	262
11	Shimoga do	465,312	241,225	224,087	465,159	241,157	224,002	940	575	365
12	(ii) **Provinces and States in India beyond Mysore**	**340,700**	**187,797**	**152,903**	**308,759**	**170,368**	**138,391**	**36,951**	**20,257**	**16,694**
13	(a) Provinces adjacent to Mysore* ...	**327,333**	**179,330**	**148,003**	**300,360**	**164,638**	**135,722**	**35,300**	**19,164**	**16,136**
	(i) British Territory—									
14	Bombay ...	30,606	16,395	14,211	29,138	15,617	13,521	1,629	1,003	626
15	*Dharwar*	*16,296*	*8,027*	*8,269*	*16,242*	*7,995*	*8,247*	*366*	*217*	*149*
16	*North Canara*	*5,869*	*3,525*	*2,344*	*5,837*	*3,498*	*2,339*	*106*	*79*	*27*
17	*Elsewhere*	*8,441*	*4,843*	*3,598*	*7,059*	*4,124*	*2,935*	*1,157*	*707*	*450*
18	Coorg	2,703	1,320	1,383	2,473	1,187	1,286	175	96	79
19	Madras including Laccadives ...	294,024	161,615	132,409	268,749	147,834	120,915	33,496	18,065	15,431
20	*Anantapur*	*33,617*	*14,961*	*18,656*	*33,280*	*14,785*	*18,495*	*1,651*	*896*	*755*
21	*Bellary*	*18,730*	*8,917*	*9,813*	*18,000*	*8,549*	*9,451*	*693*	*343*	*350*
22	*Chittoor*	*29,694*	*14,257*	*15,437*	*28,789*	*13,759*	*15,030*	*6,248*	*3,190*	*3,058*
23	*Coimbatore*	*12,464*	*6,376*	*6,088*	*11,910*	*6,068*	*5,842*	*1,146*	*584*	*562*
24	*Cuddapah*	*3,315*	*1,846*	*1,469*	*3,186*	*1,777*	*1,409*	*355*	*198*	*157*
25	*Malabar*	*6,139*	*4,578*	*1,561*	*4,889*	*3,772*	*1,117*	*890*	*592*	*298*
26	*Nilgiris*	*1,157*	*555*	*602*	*548*	*275*	*273*	*69*	*35*	*34*
27	*North Arcot*	*41,983*	*22,709*	*19,274*	*34,494*	*18,513*	*15,981*	*6,757*	*3,633*	*3,124*
28	*Salem*	*24,862*	*11,983*	*12,879*	*22,987*	*10,943*	*12,044*	*3,944*	*2,072*	*1,872*
29	*South Canara*	*72,267*	*47,937*	*24,330*	*71,998*	*47,790*	*24,208*	*1,009*	*744*	*265*
30	*Elsewhere*	*49,796*	*27,496*	*22,300*	*38,668*	*21,603*	*17,065*	*10,734*	*5,778*	*4,956*
31	(b) Other Provinces and States in India—	**12,592**	**8,029**	**4,563**	**7,901**	**5,436**	**2,465**	**1,531**	**1,021**	**510**
32	(i) British Territory—	4,027	2,566	1,461	1,769	1,304	465	426	277	149
33	Ajmer—Merwara	183	140	43	167	129	38	19	12	7
34	Andamans and Nicobars ...	10	6	4	5	3	2	...	...	...
35	Assam	11	5	6	2	1	1	...	...	...
36	Baluchistan	95	68	27	65	48	17	23	18	5
37	Bengal	617	311	306	181	112	69	65	38	27
38	Bihar and Orissa	58	43	15	28	20	8	4	3	1
39	Burma	382	163	219	107	52	55	31	12	19
40	Central Provinces and Berar ...	693	371	322	235	154	81	87	56	31
41	Delhi	132	86	46	77	49	28	26	17	9
42	North-West Frontier Province ...	93	60	33	31	20	11	6	5	1
43	Punjab	1,193	922	271	657	562	95	92	69	23
44	United Provinces of Agra and Oudh	560	391	169	214	154	60	73	47	26
45	(ii) States and Agencies—	**8,565**	**5,463**	**3,102**	**6,132**	**4,132**	**2,000**	**1,105**	**744**	**361**
46	Assam States	1	1	...	1	1	...	...	...	...
47	Baroda	51	30	21	36	18	18	13	9	4
48	Bombay States	461	240	221	423	225	198	39	15	24
49	Central India Agency ...	110	79	31	87	67	20	...	...	...
50	Gwalior	26	12	14	18	11	7	...	...	...
51	Hyderabad	4,224	2,384	1,840	2,796	1,652	1,144	389	227	162
52	Kashmir	73	47	26	25	19	6	19	14	5
53	Madras States (including Cochin and Travancore)	1,058	732	326	840	607	233	219	139	80
54	*Cochin*	*543*	*400*	*143*	*476*	*356*	*120*	*71*	*41*	*30*
55	*Travancore*	*422*	*283*	*139*	*278*	*207*	*71*	*88*	*67*	*21*
56	Punjab States	3	2	1	3	2	1	...	...	...
57	Rajaputana Agency	2,348	1,793	555	1,739	1,417	322	365	309	56
58	Western India Agency ...	210	143	67	164	113	51	61	31	30
59	(c) French and Portuguese Settlements	585	304	281	345	197	148	90	52	38
60	(d) India Unspecified	190	134	56	153	97	56	30	20	10

*There are no States adjacent to Mysore.

where enumerated

Bangalore District			Kolar Gold Fields (City)			Kolar District			Tumkur District			
Persons	Males	Females	Persons	Males	Females	Persons	Males	Females	Persons	Males	Females	Number
8	9	10	11	12	13	14	15	16	17	18	19	
908,056	461,905	446,151	85,103	45,051	40,052	763,934	389,262	374,672	861,405	439,144	422,261	1
907,958	461,855	446,103	84,657	44,718	39,939	763,902	389,250	374,652	861,391	439,136	422,255	2
888,842	452,284	436,558	47,309	24,141	23,168	729,266	374,000	355,266	843,611	431,588	412,023	3
852,627	437,079	415,548	3,364	1,646	1,718	11,603	4,481	7,122	12,136	4,884	7,252	4
14,185	5,751	8,434	43,424	22,250	21,174	712,363	367,278	345,085	3,287	1,386	1,901	5
10,353	4,122	6,236	48	29	19	3,631	1,419	2,212	813,615	419,594	394,021	6
10,693	4,826	5,867	373	173	200	1,092	517	575	6,619	2,531	4,088	7
183	92	91	12	3	9	214	127	87	3,307	1,297	2,010	8
380	186	194	12	6	6	176	84	92	3,798	1,493	2,305	9
143	82	61	7	4	3	53	29	24	378	167	211	10
273	146	127	69	30	39	134	65	69	471	236	235	11
19,116	9,571	9,545	37,343	20,577	16,771	34,636	15,250	19,386	17,780	7,548	10,232	12
18,834	9,395	9,438	36,297	19,861	16,436	34,309	15,029	19,280	17,591	7,412	10,179	13
166	96	70	111	55	56	90	50	40	249	163	86	14
35	24	11	3	2	1	30	21	9	107	62	45	15
20	4	16	...	...	...	7	4	3	4	4	...	16
111	68	43	108	53	55	53	25	28	138	97	41	17
40	19	21	10	6	4	4	1	3	29	15	14	18
18,628	9,281	9,347	36,176	19,800	16,376	34,215	14,978	19,237	17,313	7,234	10,079	19
1,242	689	553	33	16	17	9,006	3,814	5,192	14,185	5,531	8,654	20
244	125	119	117	57	60	188	89	99	530	274	256	21
2,354	1,277	1,077	3,394	1,786	1,608	14,808	6,339	8,469	258	108	150	22
847	422	425	355	207	148	320	188	132	164	98	66	23
784	451	333	70	42	28	739	370	369	132	90	42	24
99	65	34	1,763	1,454	309	65	50	15	101	33	68	25
26	16	10	138	78	60	8	5	3	34	20	14	26
1,740	1,033	707	20,697	11,052	9,645	1,768	825	943	170	105	65	27
8,434	3,785	4,649	2,972	1,553	1,419	5,142	2,133	3,009	204	102	102	28
142	116	26	31	15	16	97	67	30	134	103	31	29
2,716	1,302	1,414	6,606	3,540	3,066	2,074	1,098	976	1,401	770	631	30
261	165	96	941	656	285	319	219	100	174	129	45	31
137	89	48	366	314	52	37	25	12	35	24	11	32
...	...	...	3	2	1	...	...	...	...	...	...	33
...	...	...	1	...	1	...	...	...	4	3	1	34
...	...	...	...	...	...	...	...	...	...	...	...	35
2	2	...	3	1	2	1	1	...	...	...	...	36
34	15	19	31	18	13	3	1	2	4	3	1	37
3	2	1	6	4	2	1	1	...	...	...	...	38
12	8	4	19	9	10	4	2	2	1	...	1	39
18	14	4	23	12	11	6	3	3	14	9	5	40
10	5	5	7	6	1	2	1	1	1	...	1	41
7	7	...	7	4	3	...	...	...	...	...	...	42
38	26	12	256	252	4	10	8	2	1	1	...	43
13	10	3	10	6	4	10	8	2	10	8	2	44
124	76	48	575	342	233	282	194	88	139	105	34	45
...	...	...	...	...	...	1	1	...	...	...	...	46
3	2	1	...	...	...	1	...	1	3	1	2	47
...	...	...	14	7	7	1	1	...	9	7	2	48
...	...	...	5	4	1	1	1	...	...	...	...	49
...	...	...	...	...	...	...	...	...	...	...	...	50
71	42	29	158	90	68	139	85	54	53	38	15	51
...	...	...	1	1	...	2	1	1	...	...	...	52
44	28	16	99	60	39	32	19	13	11	9	2	53
28	15	13	59	31	28	19	9	10	5	5	...	54
15	12	3	36	26	10	13	10	3	...	...	...	55
...	...	...	...	...	...	...	...	...	...	...	...	56
6	4	2	298	180	118	105	86	19	50	42	8	57
...	...	...	...	...	...	...	...	...	13	8	5	58
21	10	11	110	60	50	8	2	6	2	1	1	59
...	...	...	...	...	...	...	...	...	13	6	7	60

Number	District, State, Province or Country where born	City, District or State								
		Mysore City			Mysore District			Chitaldrug District		
		Persons	Males	Females	Persons	Males	Females	Persons	Males	Females
		20	21	22	23	24	25	26	27	28
1	**TOTAL POPULATION ...**	**107,142**	**56,772**	**50,370**	**1,403,984**	**708,838**	**700,146**	**656,569**	**336,786**	**319,783**
2	*A. BORN IN INDIA ... ...*	**107,052**	**56,736**	**50,316**	**1,403,932**	**703,797**	**700,135**	**656,561**	**336,780**	**319.781**
3	(1) **Mysore ... ...**	**99,626**	**52,548**	**47,078**	**1,389,810**	**696,056**	**693,754**	**625,001**	**321,199**	**303,802**
4	Bangalore District	5,630	2,865	2,765	6,247	2,787	3,460	1,281	657	624
5	Kolar do	1,084	630	454	922	494	428	358	181	177
6	Tumkur do	1,453	856	597	3,117	1,140	1,977	6,356	2,891	3,465
7	Mysore do	88,988	46,784	42,204	1,373,663	689,313	684,350	940	521	419
8	Chitaldrug do	282	176	106	167	99	68	607,856	313,526	294,330
9	Hassan do	1,381	773	608	5,272	1,991	3,281	739	319	420
10	Kadur do	327	179	148	170	90	80	2,101	838	1,263
11	Shimoga do	481	285	196	252	142	110	5,370	2,266	3,104
12	(ii) **Provinces and States in India beyond Mysore ... ...**	**7,426**	**4,188**	**3,238**	**14,122**	**7,741**	**6,381**	**31,560**	**15,581**	**15,979**
13	(a) Provinces adjacent to Mysore* ...	**6,758**	**3,713**	**3,045**	**13,786**	**7,522**	**6,264**	**30,263**	**14,766**	**15,497**
	(i) British Territory—									
14	Bombay	477	304	173	487	282	205	7,885	3,863	4,022
15	*Dharwar ... ...*	*136*	*91*	*45*	*119*	*64*	*48*	*5,493*	*2,545*	*2,948*
16	*North Canara ... ...*	*10*	*7*	*3*	*8*	*4*	*4*	*158*	*106*	*52*
17	*Elsewhere ... ...*	*331*	*206*	*125*	*367*	*214*	*153*	*2,234*	*1,212*	*1,022*
18	Coorg	296	141	155	401	218	186	15	8	7
19	Madras including Laccadives ...	5,985	3,268	2,717	12,895	7,022	5,873	22,363	10,895	11,468
20	*Anantapur ... ...*	*284*	*145*	*139*	*177*	*97*	*80*	*5,349*	*2,658*	*2,691*
21	*Bellary ... ...*	*270*	*139*	*131*	*234*	*134*	*100*	*14,028*	*6,435*	*7,593*
22	*Chittoor ... ...*	*174*	*90*	*84*	*159*	*109*	*50*	*104*	*54*	*50*
23	*Coimbatore ... ...*	*1,066*	*548*	*518*	*6,749*	*3,277*	*3,472*	*399*	*227*	*172*
24	*Cuddapah ... ...*	*28*	*17*	*11*	*774*	*431*	*343*	*175*	*108*	*67*
25	*Malabar ... ...*	*235*	*163*	*72*	*419*	*337*	*82*	*63*	*49*	*14*
26	*Nilgiris ... ...*	*77*	*37*	*40*	*102*	*53*	*49*	*3*	*1*	*2*
27	*North Arcot ... ...*	*353*	*180*	*173*	*361*	*152*	*209*	*127*	*79*	*48*
28	*Salem ... ...*	*456*	*243*	*213*	*393*	*211*	*182*	*128*	*78*	*50*
29	*South Canara ... ...*	*387*	*285*	*102*	*428*	*340*	*88*	*311*	*237*	*74*
30	*Elsewhere ... ...*	*2,655*	*1,421*	*1,234*	*3,099*	*1,881*	*1,218*	*1,676*	*969*	*707*
31	(b) Other Provinces and States in India—	**635**	**454**	**181**	**328**	**212**	**116**	**1,263**	**792**	**471**
32	(i) British Territory—	202	144	58	153	114	39	101	83	18
33	Ajmer—Merwara	1	1	...	...	...	...	70	58	12
34	Andamans and Nicobars ...	...	...	...	...	...	...	...	...	...
35	Assam	...	...	...	...	...	...	...	...	...
36	Baluchistan	2	2	...	31	21	10	2	2	...
37	Bengal	11	9	2	3	3	...	7	5	2
38	Bihar and Orissa	3	3	...	...	...	...	3	3	...
39	Burma	23	7	16	7	7	...	2	1	1
40	Central Provinces and Berar ...	24	17	7	7	6	1	6	6	...
41	Delhi	14	7	7	3	2	1	3	2	1
42	North-West Frontier Province ...	2	...	2	7	4	3	...	...	...
43	Punjab	83	65	18	79	58	21	5	4	1
44	United Provinces of Agra and Oudh	39	33	6	16	13	3	3	2	1
45	(ii) States and Agencies	**433**	**310**	**123**	**175**	**98**	**77**	**1,162**	**709**	**453**
46	Assam States	...	...	...	...	...	...	...	...	...
47	Baroda	2	1	1	1	...	1	1	1	...
48	Bombay States	14	8	6	16	10	6	92	53	39
49	Central India Agency ...	56	49	7	13	7	6	...	...	...
50	Gwalior	1	1	...	...	...	...	...	...	...
51	Hyderabad	155	91	64	100	49	51	846	475	371
52	Kashmir	...	...	...	3	3	...	...	...	...
53	Madras States (including Cochin and Travancore) ...	111	74	37	35	24	11	18	11	7
54	*Cochin ... ...*	*57*	*42*	*15*	*19*	*13*	*6*	*5*	*1*	*4*
55	*Travancore ... ...*	*48*	*30*	*18*	*16*	*11*	*5*	*13*	*10*	*3*
56	Punjab States	...	...	...	3	2	1	...	...	...
57	Rajputana Agency	93	86	7	4	3	1	191	159	32
58	Western India Agency ...	1	...	1	...	...	...	14	10	4
59	(c) French and Portuguese Settlements...	33	21	12	8	7	1	4	2	2
60	(d) India Unspecified	...	...	...	...	...	...	30	21	9

* There are no States adjacent to Mysore.

where enumerated

Hassan District			Kadur District			Shimoga District			Civil and Military Station Bangalore			Number
Persons	Males	Females	Persons	Males	Females	Persons	Males	Females	Persons	Males	Females	
29	30	31	32	33	34	35	36	37	38	39	40	
596,937	**300,746**	**296,191**	**347,715**	**184,389**	**163,326**	**519,987**	**274,981**	**245,006**	**134,113**	**69,409**	**64,704**	1
596,901	**300,720**	**296,181**	**347,628**	**184,333**	**163,295**	**519,967**	**274,969**	**244,998**	**131,390**	**67,485**	**63,905**	2
577,736	**288,663**	**289,073**	**301,291**	**154,861**	**146,930**	**475,649**	**247,343**	**228,306**	**99,449**	**50,056**	**49,393**	3
2,319	1,164	1,155	2,055	1,146	909	2,618	1,447	1,171	92,626	46,851	45,775	4
486	287	199	535	327	208	776	427	349	2,235	1,026	1,209	5
7,246	3,259	3,987	2,930	1,770	1,160	2,556	1,566	990	355	175	180	6
10,856	4,156	6,700	1,920	1,207	713	2,977	1,818	1,159	3,880	1,847	2,033	7
1,076	569	507	3,379	1,734	1,645	8,729	4,249	4,480	23	14	9	8
550,743	277,118	273,625	6,562	3,193	3,369	1,096	610	486	113	53	60	9
4,558	1,888	2,670	280,611	143,413	137,198	3,479	1,607	1,872	64	22	42	10
452	222	230	3,299	1,571	1,728	453,418	235,619	217,799	153	68	85	11
19,165	**12,057**	**7,108**	**46,337**	**29,972**	**16,365**	**44,318**	**27,626**	**16,692**	**31,941**	**17,429**	**14,512**	12
18,605	**11,597**	**7,008**	**45,711**	**29,472**	**16,239**	**42,906**	**26,706**	**16,200**	**26,973**	**14,692**	**12,281**	13
719	369	350	621	384	237	16,704	9,048	7,656	1,468	778	690	14
161	93	68	284	157	127	9,515	4,719	4,796	54	32	22	15
297	105	192	151	99	52	5,076	3,086	1,990	32	27	5	16
261	171	90	186	128	58	2,113	1,243	870	1,382	719	663	17
1,276	527	749	162	114	48	62	42	20	230	133	97	18
16,610	10,701	5,909	44,928	28,974	15,954	26,140	17,616	8,524	25,274	13,781	11,494	19
175	103	72	567	419	148	611	417	194	337	176	161	20
266	155	111	322	185	137	1,108	613	495	730	368	362	21
273	169	104	843	516	327	174	121	53	905	498	407	22
409	239	170	176	111	65	279	167	112	554	308	246	23
60	31	29	16	11	5	53	28	25	129	69	60	24
419	354	65	395	305	90	440	370	70	1,250	806	444	25
57	13	44	17	7	10	17	10	7	609	280	329	26
580	365	215	1,018	557	461	923	532	391	7,489	4,196	3,293	27
182	112	70	702	400	302	430	254	176	1,875	1,040	835	28
11,676	7,666	4,010	38,483	24,941	13,542	19,300	13,276	6,024	269	147	122	29
2,513	1,494	1,019	2,389	1,522	867	2,805	1,828	977	11,128	5,893	5,235	30
542	**444**	**98**	**586**	**478**	**108**	**1,321**	**866**	**455**	**4.691**	**2,593**	**2,098**	31
107	76	31	76	54	22	129	104	25	2,258	1,262	996	32
22	11	11	4	4	...	48	41	7	16	11	5	33
...	...	...	...	...	...	...	...	...	5	3	2	34
...	...	...	2	1	1	...	...	...	9	4	5	35
...	...	...	...	...	...	1	1	...	30	20	10	36
2	2	...	6	4	2	15	14	1	436	199	237	37
1	1	...	...	...	...	7	3	4	30	23	7	38
4	3	1	1	1	...	3	2	1	275	111	164	39
7	5	2	37	20	17	6	6	...	158	217	241	40
2	1	1	6	6	...	3	2	1	55	37	18	41
...	...	...	...	...	...	2	...	2	62	40	22	42
51	42	9	13	12	1	29	25	4	536	360	176	43
18	11	7	7	6	1	15	10	5	346	237	109	44
435	**368**	**67**	**510**	**424**	**86**	**1,192**	**762**	**430**	**2,433**	**1,331**	**1,102**	45
...	...	...	...	...	...	...	...	...	...	...	...	46
2	...	2	3	3	...	7	1	6	15	12	3	47
4	3	1	34	18	16	200	103	97	38	15	23	48
...	...	...	...	...	...	12	6	6	28	12	11	49
2	2	...	13	8	5	2	...	2	8	1	7	50
60	39	21	69	42	27	756	474	282	1,428	732	696	51
...	...	...	...	...	...	...	...	...	48	28	20	52
130	124	6	112	102	10	29	17	12	218	125	93	53
120	117	3	76	70	6	17	12	5	67	44	23	54
10	7	3	31	29	2	8	5	3	144	76	68	55
...	...	...	...	...	...	...	...	...	...	...	...	56
195	166	29	246	221	25	186	161	25	609	376	233	57
42	34	8	33	30	3	...	...	...	46	30	16	58
8	7	1	30	17	13	31	18	13	240	107	133	59
10	9	1	10	5	5	60	36	24	37	37	...	60

Number	District, State, Province or Country where born	Mysore State including Civil and Military Station, Bangalore			Mysore State excluding Civil and Military Station, Bangalore			City, District or State: Bangalore City		
		Persons	Males	Females	Persons	Males	Females	Persons	Males	Females
	1	2	3	4	2 (a)	3 (a)	4 (a)	5	6	7
61	***B. OTHER ASIATIC COUNTRIES***	**468**	**278**	**190**	**254**	**168**	**86**	**76**	**55**	**21**
62	(i) Within British Dominions ...	235	118	117	98	60	38	17	8	9
63	Ceylon	200	102	98	83	52	31	14	5	9
64	Straits Settlements and Malaya	34	15	19	14	7	7	3	3	...
65	Elsewhere	1	1	...	1	1	...	...	...	...
66	(ii) Outside British Dominions ...	215	146	69	153	106	47	59	47	12
67	Afghanistan	78	70	8	78	70	8	37	34	3
68	China	25	21	4	8	5	3	6	4	2
69	Nepal	25	18	7	12	8	4	4	4	...
70	Elsewhere	87	37	50	55	23	32	12	5	7
71	(iii) Asia unspecified	18	14	4	3	2	1	...	...	...
72	***C. EUROPE***	**3,162**	**2,241**	**921**	**832**	**517**	**315**	**184**	**77**	**107**
73	(i) United Kingdom and Ireland ...	2,903	2,110	793	712	453	259	153	71	82
74	(ii) British possessions in Europe ...	2	...	2	2	...	2	2	...	2
75	(iii) Continental Europe ...	253	128	125	114	61	53	29	6	23
76	(iv) Europe unspecified	4	3	1	4	3	1	...	...	...
77	***D. AFRICA.***	**167**	**86**	**81**	**35**	**20**	**15**	**13**	**8**	**5**
78	(i) Within British Dominions ...	31	14	17	14	7	7	2	1	1
79	Kenya (British East Africa) ...	2	2	...	1	1	...	...	...	...
80	Natal	14	7	7	13	6	7	2	1	1
81	Zanzibar	15	5	10	...	...	...	...	...	...
82	Elsewhere	...	...	...	...	...	...	...	...	...
83	(ii) Outside British Dominions ...	1	1	...	...	...	...	...	...	...
84	Elsewhere	1	1	...	...	...	...	...	...	...
85	(iii) Africa unspecified	135	71	64	21	13	8	11	7	4
86	***E. AMERICA***	**63**	**26**	**37**	**32**	**11**	**21**	**10**	**4**	**6**
87	(i) Within British Dominions ...	5	1	4	2	...	2	...	...	...
88	Canada	4	1	3	2	...	2	...	...	...
89	Elsewhere	1	...	1	...	...	...	...	...	...
90	(ii) Outside British Dominions ...	32	16	16	4	2	2	...	...	...
91	United States	31	16	15	3	2	1	...	...	...
92	Elsewhere	1	...	1	1	...	1	...	...	...
93	(iii) America unspecified	26	9	17	26	9	17	10	4	6
94	***F. AUSTRALASIA***	**30**	**17**	**13**	**15**	**9**	**6**	**3**	**1**	**2**
95	(i) Within British Dominions ...	14	8	6	12	8	4	...	...	...
96	Australia	9	6	3	9	6	3	...	...	...
97	Fiji Islands	1	1	...	1	1	...	...	...	...
98	New Zealand	4	1	3	2	1	1	...	...	...
99	Elsewhere	...	...	...	...	...	...	...	...	...
100	(ii) Outside British Dominions ...	...	...	...	...	...	...	...	...	...
101	(iii) Australasia unspecified	16	9	7	3	1	2	3	1	2
102	***G. BORN AT SEA***	**2**	**1**	**1**	**1**	...	**1**	...	...	...
103	***H. BIRTHPLACE UNSPECIFIED***	...	...	...	...	...	...	...	...	...

where enumerated

Bangalore District			Kolar Gold Fields (City)			Kolar District			Tumkur District			Number
Persons	Males	Females	Persons	Males	Females	Persons	Males	Females	Persons	Males	Females	
8	9	10	11	12	13	14	15	16	17	18	19	
25	21	4	33	17	16	9	5	4	6	5	1	61
18	14	4	28	15	13	8	1	2	1	1	...	62
16	13	3	21	13	8	3	1	2	1	1	...	63
2	1	1	7	2	5	...	...	...	...	...	...	64
...	...	...	...	...	...	...	...	...	...	...	...	65
7	7	...	5	2	3	6	4	2	5	4	1	66
5	5	...	1	1	...	4	3	1	...	...	...	67
...	...	...	...	...	...	...	...	...	1	1	...	68
1	1	...	...	...	...	2	1	1	3	2	1	69
1	1	...	4	1	3	...	...	...	1	1	...	70
...	...	...	...	...	...	...	...	...	...	...	...	71
66	27	39	389	301	88	9	3	6	8	3	5	72
45	21	24	341	259	82	8	3	5	8	8	5	73
...	...	...	...	...	...	...	...	...	...	...	...	74
21	6	15	48	42	6	1	...	1	...	...	...	75
...	...	...	...	...	...	...	...	...	...	...	...	76
1	...	1	10	5	5	3	2	1	...	...	...	77
1	...	1	7	3	4	1	...	1	...	...	...	78
...	...	...	...	...	...	...	...	...	...	...	...	79
1	...	1	7	3	4	1	...	1	...	...	...	80
...	...	...	...	...	...	...	...	...	...	...	...	81
...	...	...	...	...	...	...	...	...	...	...	...	82
...	...	...	...	...	...	...	...	...	...	...	...	83
...	...	...	...	...	...	...	...	...	...	...	...	84
...	...	...	3	2	1	2	2	...	...	...	...	85
5	2	3	4	3	1	11	2	9	...	...	...	86
1	...	1	1	...	1	...	...	...	...	...	...	87
1	...	1	1	...	1	...	...	...	...	...	...	88
...	...	...	...	...	...	...	...	...	...	...	...	89
4	2	2	...	...	...	...	...	...	...	...	...	90
3	2	1	...	...	...	...	...	...	...	...	...	91
1	...	1	...	...	...	...	...	...	...	...	...	92
...	...	...	8	8	...	11	2	9	...	...	...	93
1	...	1	9	7	2	...	...	...	...	...	...	94
1	...	1	9	7	2	...	...	...	...	...	...	95
...	...	...	8	6	2	...	...	...	...	...	...	96
...	...	...	1	1	...	...	...	...	...	...	...	97
1	...	1	...	...	...	...	...	...	...	...	...	98
...	...	...	...	...	...	...	...	...	...	...	...	99
...	...	...	...	...	...	...	...	...	...	...	...	100
...	...	...	...	...	...	...	...	...	...	...	...	101
...	...	...	1	...	1	...	...	...	...	...	...	102
...	...	...	...	...	...	...	...	...	...	...	...	103

Number	District, State, Province or Country where born	City, District or State								
		Mysore City			Mysore District			Chitaldrug District		
		Persons	Males	Females	Persons	Males	Females	Persons	Males	Females
		20	21	22	23	24	25	26	27	28
61	*B. OTHER ASIATIC COUNTRIES.*	**33**	**11**	**22**	**29**	**25**	**4**	**6**	**5**	**1**
62	(i) Within British Dominions ...	10	4	6	7	6	1	5	4	1
63	Ceylon	9	4	5	7	6	1	4	3	1
64	Straits Settlements and Malaya	1	...	1	...	...	...	...	...	
65	Elsewhere	...	...	...	...	...	...	1	1	...
66	(ii) Outside British Dominions ...	23	7	16	22	19	3	1	1	...
67	Afganistan	2	2	...	22	19	3	...	...	...
68	China	1	...	1	...	...	...	...	...	...
69	Nepal	2	...	2	...	...	...	...	...	...
70	Elsewhere	18	5	13	...	...	...	1	1	...
71	(iii) Asia unspecified	...	...	...	...	...	...	...	...	...
72	*C. EUROPE*	**55**	**25**	**30**	**19**	**13**	**6**	**2**	**1**	
73	(i) United Kingdom and Ireland ...	45	21	24	19	13	6	2	1	
74	(ii) British Possessions in Europe ...	...	...	...	...	...	...	...	...	...
75	(iii) Continental Europe	10	4	6	...	...	...	...	...	...
76	(iv) Europe unspecified	...	...	...	...	...	...	...	...	...
77	*D. AFRICA*	...	...	...	**2**	**2**	...	...	...	...
78	(i) Within British Dominions ...	...	...	...	2	2	...	...	...	...
79	Kenya (British East Africa) ...	...	...	...	...	...	...	...	...	...
80	Natal	...	...	...	2	2	...	...	...	...
81	Zanzibar	...	...	...	...	...	...	...	...	...
82	Elsewhere	...	...	...	...	...	...	...	...	...
83	(ii) Outside British Dominions ...	...	...	...	...	...	...	...	...	...
84	Elsewhere	...	...	...	...	...	...	...	...	...
85	(iii) Africa unspecified	...	...	...	...	...	...	...	...	...
86	*E. AMERICA*	**2**	...	**2**	...	...	...	...	...	...
87	(i) Within British Dominions ...	...	...	...	...	...	...	...	...	...
88	Canada	...	...	...	...	...	...	...	...	...
89	Elsewhere	...	...	...	...	...	...	...	...	...
90	(ii) Outside British Dominions ...	...	...	...	...	...	...	...	...	...
91	United States	...	...	...	...	...	...	...	...	...
92	Elsewhere	...	...	...	...	...	...	...	...	...
93	(iii) America unspecified	2	...	2	...	...	...	...	...	...
94	*F. AUSTRALASIA*	...	...	...	**2**	**1**	**1**	...	...	...
95	(i) Within British Dominions ...	...	...	...	2	1	1	...	...	...
96	Australia	...	...	...	1	...	1	...	...	...
97	Fiji Islands	...	...	...	...	...	...	...	...	...
98	New Zealand	...	...	...	1	1	...	...	...	...
99	Elsewhere	...	...	...	...	...	...	...	...	...
100	(ii) Outside British Dominions ...	...	...	...	...	...	...	...	...	...
101	(iii) Australasia unspecified	...	...	...	...	...	...	...	...	...
102	*G. BORN AT SEA*	...	...	...	...	...	...	...	...	...
103	*H. BIRTHPLACE UNSPECIFIED.*	...	...	...	...	...	...	...	...	...

where enumerated

Hassan District			Kadur District			Shimoga District			Civil and Military Station, Bangalore			
Persons	Males	Females	Persons	Males	Females	Persons	Males	Females	Persons	Males	Females	Number
29	30	31	32	33	34	35	36	37	38	39	40	
...	...	...	25	15	10	12	9	3	214	110	104	61
...	...	...	6	5	1	3	2	1	137	58	79	62
...	...	...	6	5	1	2	1	1	117	50	67	63
...	...	...	...	...	...	1	1	...	20	8	12	64
...	...	...	...	...	...	...	...	...	...	...	...	65
...	...	...	18	9	9	7	6	1	62	40	22	66
...	...	...	...	...	...	7	6	1	...	...	...	67
...	...	...	...	...	...	...	...	...	17	16	1	68
...	...	...	...	...	...	...	...	...	13	10	3	69
...	...	...	18	9	9	...	...	...	32	14	18	70
...	...	...	1	1	...	2	1	1	15	12	3	71
34	25	9	59	39	20	7	3	4	2,330	1,724	606	72
33	24	9	51	34	17	7	3	4	2,191	1,657	534	73
...	...	...	...	...	...	...	...	...	...	...	...	74
...	...	...	5	3	2	...	...	...	139	67	72	75
1	1	...	3	2	1	...	...	...	...	...	...	76
2	1	1	3	2	1	1	...	1	132	66	66	77
...	...	...	1	1	...	...	...	...	17	7	10	78
...	...	...	1	1	...	...	...	...	1	1	...	79
...	...	...	...	...	...	...	...	...	1	1	...	80
...	...	...	...	...	...	...	...	...	15	5	10	81
...	...	...	...	...	...	...	...	...	...	...	...	82
...	...	...	...	...	...	...	...	...	1	1	...	83
...	...	...	...	...	...	...	...	...	1	1	...	84
2	1	1	2	1	1	1	...	1	114	58	56	85
...	...	...	...	...	...	...	...	...	31	15	16	86
...	...	...	...	...	...	...	...	...	3	1	2	87
...	...	...	...	...	...	...	...	...	2	1	1	88
...	...	...	...	...	...	...	...	...	1	...	1	89
...	...	...	...	...	...	...	...	...	28	14	14	90
...	...	...	...	...	...	...	...	...	28	14	14	91
...	...	...	...	...	...	...	...	...	...	...	...	92
...	...	...	...	...	...	...	...	...	...	...	...	93
...	...	...	...	...	...	...	...	...	15	8	7	94
...	...	...	...	...	...	...	...	...	2	...	2	95
...	...	...	...	...	...	...	...	...	...	...	...	96
...	...	...	...	...	...	...	...	...	...	...	...	97
...	...	...	...	...	...	...	...	...	2	...	2	98
...	...	...	...	...	...	...	...	...	...	...	...	99
...	...	...	...	...	...	...	...	...	...	...	...	100
...	...	...	...	...	...	...	...	...	13	8	5	101
...	...	...	...	...	...	...	...	...	1	1	...	102
...	...	...	...	...	...	...	...	...	...	...	...	103

MYSORE CENSUS, 1931.

TABLE VII.—Age, Sex and Civil Condition.

NOTE 1.—Details for the total population and each religion are given for Mysore State including the Civil and Military Station, Bangalore, and Mysore State excluding the Civil and Military Station, Bangalore. For Districts and Cities details are given for the total population and the following religions only—Hindu, Musalman, Christian, Jain and Tribal under the following age-groups 0-1, 1-2, 2-3, 3-4, 4-5, 5-10, 10-15, 15-20, 20-30, 30-40, 40-50, 50-60 and 60 and over.

NOTE 2.—Details for "Others" are shown below.—

Religion	Place	Population		
		Persons	Males	Females
Confucian	Bangalore City	11	9	2
Religion unspecified ...	Do	4	2	2
Do ...	Civil and Military Station, Bangalore.	91	40	51

TABLE VII—Age, Sex & Civil Condition.

Mysore State, Including Civil and Military Station, Bangalore.

AGE	POPULATION			UNMARRIED			MARRIED			WIDOWED		
	Persons	Males	Females	Persons	Males	Females	Persons	Males	Females	Persons	Males	Females
1	2	3	4	5	6	7	8	9	10	11	12	13
All Religions.												
All ages ...	**6,557,302**	**3,353,963**	**3,208,339**	**3,161,713**	**1,866,180**	**1,295,533**	**2,657,614**	**1,318,017**	**1,339,597**	**737,975**	**169,766**	**568,209**
0-1	**176,771**	86,822	89,949	**176,771**	86,822	89,949	...	...	...	...	...	...
1-2	**181,494**	88,935	92,559	**181,494**	88,935	92,559	...	...	...	...	...	...
2-3	**191,638**	93,117	98,521	**191,638**	93,117	98,521	...	...	...	...	...	...
3-4	**190,352**	93,004	97,348	**190,332**	92,999	97,333	**19**	5	14	**1**	...	1
4-5	**189,705**	93,976	95,729	**189,674**	93,970	95,704	**31**	6	25	...	...	....
Total 0—5 ...	**929,960**	455,854	474,106	**929,909**	455,848	474,066	**50**	11	39	**1**	...	1
5-10	**882,466**	440,978	441,488	**860,544**	440,602	419,942	**21,583**	359	21,224	**339**	17	322
10-15	**814,673**	420,275	394,398	**735,179**	417,989	317,240	**77,969**	2,270	75,699	**1,525**	66	1,459
15-20	**602,622**	305,621	297,001	**314,133**	260,784	53,349	**277,113**	43,851	233,262	**11,376**	986	10,390
20-25	**612,368**	295,141	317,227	**195,529**	180,474	15,055	**392,858**	111,695	281,163	**23,981**	2,972	21,009
25-30	**549,596**	272,035	277,561	**63,838**	59,277	4,561	**436,548**	204,546	232,002	**49,210**	8,212	40,998
30-35	**501,043**	262,459	238,584	**30,322**	26,985	3,337	**407,510**	223,715	183,795	**63,211**	11,759	51,452
35-40	**409,297**	228,090	181,207	**12,066**	9,823	2,243	**315,760**	201,770	113,990	**81,471**	16,497	64,974
40-45	**341,640**	192,177	149,463	**7,452**	5,740	1,712	**250,077**	168,307	81,770	**84,111**	18,130	65,981
45-50	**255,608**	139,621	115,987	**4,154**	3,012	1,142	**164,476**	116,840	47,636	**86,978**	19,769	67,209
50-55	**199,137**	104,432	94,705	**2,923**	2,043	880	**117,065**	84,009	33,056	**79,149**	18,380	60,769
55-60	**153,599**	78,970	74,629	**2,000**	1,325	675	**74,871**	58,157	16,714	**76,728**	19,488	57,240
60-65	**130,456**	66,415	64,041	**1,591**	1,019	572	**58,082**	46,825	11,257	**70,783**	18,571	52,212
65-70	**69,937**	36,518	33,419	**830**	525	305	**27,669**	23,645	4,024	**41,438**	12,848	29,090
70 and over ...	**104,900**	55,377	49,523	**1,243**	789	454	**35,983**	32,017	3,966	**67,674**	22,571	45,103
Hindu—Brahmanic.												
All ages ...	**6,015,759**	**3,066,255**	**2,949,504**	**2,877,288**	**1,698,271**	**1,179,017**	**2,443,495**	**1,207,944**	**1,235,551**	**694,976**	**160,040**	**534,936**
0-1	**161,712**	79,266	82,446	**161,712**	79,266	82,446	...	...	...	...	...	...
1-2	**165,349**	80,858	84,491	**165,349**	80,858	84,491	...	...	...	...	...	...
2-3	**174,570**	84,717	89,853	**174,570**	84,717	89,853	...	...	...	...	...	...
3-4	**173,429**	84,722	88,707	**173,410**	84,718	88,692	**18**	4	14	**1**	...	1
4-5	**172,469**	85,536	86,933	**172,438**	85,530	86,908	**31**	6	25	...	...	...
Total 0—5 ...	**847,529**	415,099	432,430	**847,479**	415,089	432,390	**49**	10	39	**1**	...	1
5-10	**806,987**	402,395	404,592	**785,839**	402,058	383,781	**20,826**	320	20,506	**322**	17	305
10-15	**746,551**	384,510	362,041	**671,744**	382,327	289,417	**73,364**	2,119	71,245	**1,443**	64	1,379
15-20	**550,111**	278,179	271,932	**283,481**	236,597	46,884	**255,899**	40,693	215,206	**10,731**	889	9,842
20-25	**559,155**	267,779	291,376	**174,817**	162,023	12,794	**361,613**	103,001	258,612	**22,725**	2,755	19,970
25-30	**504,700**	248,377	256,323	**57,360**	53,417	3,943	**400,574**	187,246	213,328	**46,766**	7,714	39,052
30-35	**461,432**	240,374	221,058	**27,402**	24,489	2,913	**374,017**	204,836	169,181	**60,013**	11,049	48,964
35-40	**378,010**	209,836	168,174	**10,976**	9,026	1,950	**290,070**	185,217	104,853	**76,964**	15,593	61,371
40-45	**315,638**	176,915	138,723	**6,805**	5,308	1,497	**229,542**	154,408	75,134	**79,291**	17,199	62,092
45-50	**235,928**	128,156	107,772	**3,740**	2,745	995	**150,570**	106,720	43,850	**81,618**	18,691	62,927
50-55	**183,964**	95,842	88,122	**2,637**	1,880	757	**107,044**	76,556	30,488	**74,283**	17,406	56,877
55-60	**142,338**	72,673	69,665	**1,773**	1,195	578	**68,461**	53,061	15,400	**72,104**	18,417	53,687
60-65	**121,209**	61,290	59,919	**1,438**	937	501	**53,186**	42,812	10,374	**66,585**	17,541	49,044
65-70	**64,975**	33,686	31,289	**717**	466	251	**25,343**	21,633	3,710	**38,915**	11,587	27,328
70 and over ...	**97,232**	51,144	46,088	**1,080**	714	366	**32,937**	29,312	3,625	**63,215**	21,118	42,097
Brahmo.												
All ages ...	**76**	**41**	**35**	**44**	**28**	**16**	**28**	**12**	**16**	**4**	**1**	**3**
0-1	**3**	1	2	**3**	1	2	...	...	...	...	...	...
1-2	**3**	1	2	**3**	1	2	...	...	...	...	...	...
2-3	**3**	1	2	**3**	1	2	...	...	...	...	...	...
3-4	**5**	3	2	**5**	3	2	...	...	...	...	...	...
4-5	**2**	2	...	**2**	2	...	...	...	...	...	...	...
Total 0—5 ...	**16**	8	8	**16**	8	8	...	...	...	...	...	...
5-10	**8**	5	3	**8**	5	3	...	...	...	...	...	...
10-15	**11**	8	3	**11**	8	3	...	...	...	...	...	...
15-20	**8**	4	4	**5**	4	1	3	...	3	...	...	...
20-25	**11**	4	7	**4**	3	1	6	1	5	**1**	...	**1**
25-30	**5**	2	3	...	...	...	5	2	3	...	...	...
30-35	**3**	2	1	...	...	...	3	2	1	...	...	...
35-40	**5**	4	1	...	...	...	5	4	1	...	...	...
40-45	**3**	1	2	...	...	...	2	1	1	**1**	...	**1**
45-50	...	...	...	...	...	...	...	...	...	...	...	...
50-55	**1**	...	1	...	...	...	1	...	1	...	...	...
55-60	**3**	1	2	...	...	...	1	...	1	**2**	**1**	**1**
60-65	**1**	1	...	...	...	...	1	1	...	...	...	...
65-70	**1**	1	...	...	...	...	1	1	...	...	...	...
70 and over ...	...	...	...	...	...	...	...	...	...	...	...	...

TABLE VII—Age, Sex & Civil Condition.

Mysore State, Including Civil and Military Station, Bangalore.

AGE	POPULATION			UNMARRIED			MARRIED			WIDOWED		
	Persons	Males	Females	Persons	Males	Females	Persons	Males	Females	Persons	Males	Females
1	2	3	4	5	6	7	8	9	10	11	12	13
Arya.												
All ages ...	**45**	**36**	**9**	**35**	**31**	**4**	**9**	**5**	**4**	**1**	...	**1**
0–1	1	1	...	1	1	...	...	...	...	...	...	...
1–2	2	1	1	2	1	1	...	...	...	...	...	...
2–3	...	...	...	...	...	...	...	...	...	...	...	...
3–4	...	...	...	...	...	...	...	...	...	...	...	...
4–5	...	...	...	...	...	...	...	...	...	...	...	...
Total 0—5 ...	3	2	1	3	2	1	...	...	...	...	...	...
5–10	8	6	2	8	6	2	...	...	...	...	...	...
10–15	8	7	1	7	7	...	1	...	1	...	...	...
15–20	9	8	1	9	8	1	...	...	...	...	...	...
20–25	6	4	2	4	4	...	2	...	2	...	...	...
25–30	3	3	...	1	1	...	2	2	...	...	...	...
30–35	2	1	1	...	...	...	2	1	1	...	...	...
35–40	2	2	...	1	1	...	1	1	...	...	...	...
40–45	1	...	1	...	...	...	...	...	...	1	...	1
45–50	2	2	...	1	1	...	1	1	...	...	...	...
50–55	...	...	...	...	...	...	...	...	...	...	...	...
55–60	...	...	...	...	...	...	...	...	...	...	...	...
60–65	1	1	...	1	1	...	...	...	...	...	...	...
65–70	...	...	...	...	...	...	...	...	...	...	...	...
70 and over ...	...	...	...	...	...	...	...	...	...	...	...	...
Total Hindu.												
All ages ...	**6,015,880**	**3,066,332**	**2,949,548**	**2,877,367**	**1,698,330**	**1,179,037**	**2,443,532**	**1,207,961**	**1,235,571**	**694,981**	**160,041**	**534,940**
0–1	161,716	79,268	82,448	161,716	79,268	82,448	...	...	...	...	...	...
1–2	165,354	80,860	84,494	165,354	80,860	84,494	...	...	...	...	...	...
2–3	174,573	84,718	89,855	174,573	84,718	89,855	...	...	...	...	...	...
3–4	173,434	84,725	88,709	173,415	84,721	88,694	18	4	14	1	...	1
4–5	172,471	85,538	86,933	172,440	85,532	86,908	31	6	25	...	...	...
Total 0—5 ...	847,548	415,109	432,439	847,498	415,099	432,399	49	10	39	1	...	1
5–10	807,003	402,406	404,597	785,855	402,069	383,786	20,826	320	20,506	322	17	305
10–15	746,570	384,525	362,045	671,762	382,342	289,420	73,365	2,119	71,246	1,443	64	1,379
15–20	550,128	278,191	271,937	283,495	236,609	46,886	255,902	40,693	215,209	10,731	889	9,842
20–25	559,172	267,787	291,385	174,825	162,030	12,795	361,621	103,002	258,619	22,726	2,755	19,971
25–30	504,708	248,382	256,326	57,361	53,418	3,943	400,581	187,250	213,331	46,766	7,714	39,052
30–35	461,437	240,377	221,060	27,402	24,489	2,913	374,022	204,839	169,183	60,013	11,049	48,964
35–40	378,017	209,842	168,175	10,977	9,027	1,950	290,076	185,222	104,854	76,964	15,593	61,371
40–45	315,642	176,916	138,726	6,805	5,308	1,497	229,544	154,409	75,135	79,293	17,199	62,094
45–50	235,930	128,158	107,772	3,741	2,746	995	150,571	106,721	43,850	81,618	18,691	62,927
50–55	183,965	95,842	88,123	2,637	1,880	757	107,045	76,556	30,489	74,283	17,406	56,877
55–60	142,341	72,674	69,667	1,773	1,195	578	68,462	53,061	15,401	72,106	18,418	53,688
60–65	121,211	61,292	59,919	1,439	938	501	53,187	42,813	10,374	66,585	17,541	49,044
65–70	64,976	33,687	31,289	717	466	251	25,344	21,634	3,710	38,915	11,587	27,328
70 and over ...	97,232	51,144	46,088	1,080	714	366	32,937	29,312	3,625	63,215	21,118	42,097
Musalman.												
All ages ...	**398,628**	**213,381**	**185,247**	**208,990**	**124,513**	**84,477**	**159,357**	**82,067**	**77,290**	**30,281**	**6,801**	**23,480**
0–1	10,996	5,539	5,457	10,996	5,539	5,457	...	...	...	...	...	...
1–2	12,047	5,981	6,066	12,047	5,981	6,066	...	...	...	...	...	...
2–3	12,772	6,225	6,547	12,772	6,225	6,547	...	...	...	...	...	...
3–4	12,805	6,213	6,592	12,805	6,213	6,592	...	...	...	...	...	...
4–5	13,301	6,478	6,823	13,301	6,478	6,823	...	...	...	...	...	...
Total 0—5 ...	61,921	30,436	31,485	61,921	30,436	31,485	...	...	...	...	...	...
5–10	57,145	29,284	27,861	56,593	29,256	27,337	538	28	510	14	...	14
10–15	50,954	26,955	23,999	47,287	26,848	20,439	3,605	105	3,500	62	2	60
15–20	38,074	20,184	17,890	21,632	17,840	3,792	16,013	2,278	13,735	429	66	363
20–25	38,610	20,020	18,590	14,263	13,349	914	23,493	6,516	16,977	854	155	699
25–30	32,593	17,228	15,365	4,185	4,014	171	26,719	12,850	13,869	1,689	364	1,325
30–35	28,846	16,207	12,639	1,758	1,649	109	24,836	14,041	10,795	2,252	517	1,735
35–40	22,829	13,505	9,324	573	504	69	19,109	12,372	6,737	3,147	629	2,518
40–45	18,826	11,270	7,556	298	257	41	15,160	10,370	4,790	3,368	643	2,725
45–50	14,195	8,445	5,750	180	149	31	10,239	7,576	2,663	3,776	720	3,056
50–55	10,913	6,309	4,604	106	84	22	7,346	5,556	1,790	3,461	669	2,792
55–60	8,022	4,560	3,462	75	48	27	4,660	3,789	871	3,287	723	2,564
60–65	6,570	3,688	2,882	36	24	12	3,552	2,959	593	2,982	705	2,277
65–70	3,473	2,034	1,439	36	23	13	1,695	1,478	217	1,742	533	1,209
70 and over ...	5,657	3,256	2,401	47	32	15	2,392	2,149	243	3,218	1,075	2,143

TABLE VII—Age, Sex & Civil Condition.

Mysore State, Including Civil and Military Station, Bangalore.

AGE	POPULATION			UNMARRIED			MARRIED			WIDOWED		
	Persons	Males	Females	Persons	Males	Females	Persons	Males	Females	Persons	Males	Females
1	2	3	4	5	6	7	8	9	10	11	12	13
Christian.												
All ages ...	**87,538**	**45,164**	**42,374**	**48,321**	**27,048**	**21,273**	**32,363**	**16,671**	**15,692**	**6,854**	**1,445**	**5,409**
0–1	**2,499**	1,256	1,243	**2,499**	1,256	1,243	...	...	...	...	...	...
1–2	**2,557**	1,322	1,235	**2,557**	1,322	1,235	...	...	...	...	...	...
2–3	**2,634**	1,353	1,281	**2,634**	1,353	1,281	...	...	...	...	...	...
3–4	**2,442**	1,247	1,195	**2,442**	1,247	1,195	...	...	...	...	...	...
4–5	**2,317**	1,161	1,156	**2,317**	1,161	1,156	...	...	...	...	...	...
Total 0–5 ...	**12,449**	6,339	6,110	**12,449**	6,339	6,110	...	...	...	...	...	...
5–10	**10,904**	5,520	5,384	**10,870**	5,516	5,354	**34**	4	30	...	...	...
10–15	**10,345**	5,180	5,165	**9,959**	5,161	4,798	**381**	19	362	**5**	...	5
15–20	**9,134**	4,490	4,644	**6,294**	4,070	2,224	**2,744**	410	2,334	**96**	10	86
20–25	**9,269**	4,666	4,603	**4,745**	3,504	1,241	**4,322**	1,137	3,185	**202**	25	177
25–30	**7,573**	3,994	3,579	**1,722**	1,314	408	**5,479**	2,616	2,863	**372**	64	308
30–35	**6,578**	3,562	3,016	**888**	587	301	**5,213**	2,885	2,328	**477**	90	387
35–40	**5,140**	2,812	2,328	**396**	176	220	**4,039**	2,520	1,519	**705**	116	589
40–45	**4,412**	2,379	2,033	**275**	104	171	**3,349**	2,151	1,198	**788**	124	664
45–50	**3,348**	1,799	1,549	**180**	68	112	**2,290**	1,566	724	**878**	165	713
50–55	**2,668**	1,425	1,243	**149**	51	98	**1,726**	1,221	505	**793**	153	640
55–60	**1,975**	1,062	913	**123**	56	67	**1,125**	827	298	**727**	179	548
60–65	**1,625**	866	759	**103**	44	59	**854**	650	204	**668**	172	496
65–70	**899**	475	424	**67**	28	39	**392**	321	71	**440**	126	314
70 and over ...	**1,219**	595	624	**101**	30	71	**415**	344	71	**703**	221	482
Jain.												
All ages ...	**29,613**	**15,920**	**13,693**	**13,899**	**8,833**	**5,066**	**11,800**	**6,094**	**5,706**	**3,914**	**993**	**2,921**
0–1	**763**	378	385	**763**	378	385	...	...	...	...	...	...
1–2	**688**	359	329	**688**	359	329	...	...	...	...	...	...
2–3	**764**	392	372	**764**	392	372	...	...	...	...	...	...
3–4	**767**	377	390	**767**	377	390	...	...	...	...	...	...
4–5	**747**	363	384	**747**	363	384	...	...	...	...	...	...
Total 0–5 ...	**3,729**	1,869	1,860	**3,729**	1,869	1,860	...	...	...	...	...	...
5–10	**3,685**	1,857	1,828	**3,556**	1,852	1,704	**126**	5	121	**3**	...	3
10–15	**3,555**	1,899	1,656	**3,155**	1,884	1,271	**387**	15	372	**13**	...	13
15–20	**3,015**	1,669	1,346	**1,541**	1,368	173	**1,394**	289	1,105	**80**	12	68
20–25	**3,004**	1,626	1,378	**1,039**	1,009	30	**1,828**	597	1,231	**137**	20	117
25–30	**2,541**	1,377	1,164	**379**	364	15	**1,895**	971	924	**267**	42	225
30–35	**2,253**	1,292	961	**208**	202	6	**1,723**	1,023	700	**322**	67	255
35–40	**1,795**	1,054	741	**101**	100	1	**1,266**	847	419	**428**	107	321
40–45	**1,551**	892	659	**63**	62	1	**1,044**	719	325	**444**	111	333
45–50	**1,235**	694	541	**45**	43	2	**729**	517	212	**461**	134	327
50–55	**929**	495	434	**27**	26	1	**501**	359	142	**401**	110	291
55–60	**779**	415	364	**23**	22	1	**359**	281	78	**397**	112	285
60–65	**661**	354	307	**13**	13	...	**284**	232	52	**364**	109	255
65–70	**387**	207	180	**9**	8	1	**137**	126	11	**241**	73	168
70 and over ...	**494**	220	274	**11**	11	...	127	113	14	**356**	96	260
Tribal.*												
All ages ...	**23,828**	**12,230**	**11,598**	**12,177**	**6,922**	**5,255**	**9,827**	**4,845**	**4,982**	**1,824**	**463**	**1,361**
0–1	**735**	351	384	**735**	351	384	...	...	...	...	...	...
1–2	**796**	383	413	**796**	383	413	...	...	...	...	...	...
2–3	**824**	393	431	**824**	393	431	...	...	...	...	...	...
3–4	**834**	406	428	**834**	406	428	...	...	...	...	...	...
4–5	**819**	409	410	**819**	409	410	...	...	...	...	...	...
Total 0–5 ...	**4,008**	1,942	2,066	**4,008**	1,942	2,066	...	...	...	...	...	...
5–10	**3,512**	1,798	1,714	**3,457**	1,797	1,660	**55**	1	54	...	...	...
10–15	**3,048**	1,618	1,430	**2,828**	1,607	1,221	**219**	11	208	**1**	...	1
15–20	**2,073**	999	1,074	**1,052**	826	226	**984**	164	820	**37**	9	28
20–25	**2,124**	951	1,173	**578**	524	54	**1,487**	410	1,077	**59**	17	42
25–30	**2,015**	964	1,051	**159**	145	14	**1,746**	791	955	**110**	28	82
30–35	**1,796**	946	850	**53**	49	4	**1,603**	862	741	**140**	35	105
35–40	**1,411**	819	592	**15**	13	2	**1,185**	757	428	**211**	49	162
40–45	**1,125**	670	455	**8**	7	1	**910**	613	297	**207**	50	157
45–50	**826**	486	340	**6**	5	1	**592**	426	166	**228**	55	173
50–55	**609**	336	273	**3**	1	2	**410**	295	115	**196**	40	156
55–60	**445**	238	207	**5**	4	1	**243**	183	60	**197**	51	146
60–65	**363**	200	163	...	...	...	**192**	158	34	**171**	42	129
65–70	**185**	106	79	**1**	...	1	**93**	78	15	**91**	28	63
70 and over ...	**288**	157	131	**4**	2	2	**108**	96	12	**176**	59	117

* See Note 2 to Table V.

TABLE VII.--Age, Sex & Civil Condition.

Mysore State, Including Civil and Military Station, Bangalore.

AGE	POPULATION			UNMARRIED			MARRIED			WIDOWED		
	Persons	Males	Females	Persons	Males	Females	Persons	Males	Females	Persons	Males	Females
1	2	3	4	5	6	7	8	9	10	11	12	13
Buddhist.												
All ages ...	**1,239**	**640**	**599**	**633**	**363**	**270**	**521**	**266**	**255**	**85**	**11**	**74**
0-1	**40**	19	21	**40**	19	21	...	...	...	...	...	...
1-2	**42**	24	18	**42**	24	18	...	...	...	...	...	...
2-3	**52**	28	24	**52**	28	24	...	...	...	...	...	...
3-4	**52**	26	26	**52**	26	26	...	...	...	...	...	...
4-5	**40**	20	20	**40**	20	20	...	...	...	...	...	...
Total 0-5 ...	**226**	117	109	**226**	117	109	...	...	...	...	...	...
5-10	**153**	82	71	**150**	81	69	**3**	1	2	...	...	...
10-15	**132**	64	68	**120**	63	57	**11**	1	10	**1**	...	1
15-20	**128**	53	75	**67**	44	23	**58**	9	49	**3**	...	3
20-25	**132**	59	78	**47**	39	8	**82**	20	62	**3**	...	3
25-30	**116**	64	52	**16**	13	3	**95**	51	44	**5**	...	5
30-35	**98**	59	39	**5**	4	1	**87**	54	33	**6**	1	5
35-40	**72**	44	28	**2**	2	...	**59**	40	19	**11**	2	9
40-45	**56**	36	20	...	...	...	**49**	34	15	**7**	2	5
45-50	**44**	25	19	...	...	...	**33**	23	10	**11**	2	9
50-55	**33**	16	17	...	...	...	**23**	15	8	**10**	1	9
55-60	**18**	7	11	...	...	...	**9**	6	3	**9**	1	8
60-65	**18**	9	9	...	...	...	**8**	8	...	**10**	1	9
65-70	**7**	3	4	...	...	...	**3**	3	...	**4**	...	4
70 and over ...	**6**	2	4	...	...	...	**1**	1	...	**5**	1	4
Parsi.												
All ages ...	**331**	**169**	**162**	**205**	**112**	**93**	**104**	**49**	**55**	**22**	**8**	**14**
0-1	**12**	6	6	**12**	6	6	...	...	...	...	...	...
1-2	**8**	5	3	**8**	5	3	...	...	...	...	...	...
2-3	**8**	4	4	**8**	4	4	...	...	...	...	...	...
3-4	**11**	6	5	**10**	5	5	**1**	1	...	...	...	...
4-5	**6**	4	2	**6**	4	2	...	...	...	...	...	...
Total 0-5 ...	**45**	25	20	**44**	24	20	**1**	1	...	...	...	...
5-10	**41**	21	20	**40**	21	19	**1**	...	1	...	...	...
10-15	**42**	22	20	**42**	22	20	...	...	...	...	...	...
15-20	**36**	17	19	**32**	17	15	**4**	...	4	...	...	...
20-25	**27**	14	13	**20**	12	8	**7**	2	5	...	...	...
25-30	**30**	16	14	**12**	8	4	**18**	8	10	...	...	...
30-35	**23**	10	13	**8**	5	3	**15**	5	10	...	...	...
35-40	**15**	7	8	**2**	1	1	**11**	5	6	**2**	1	1
40-45	**15**	6	9	**1**	...	1	**12**	6	6	**2**	...	2
45-50	**19**	7	12	**2**	1	1	**13**	5	8	**4**	1	3
50-55	**14**	7	7	**1**	1	...	**9**	5	4	**4**	1	3
55-60	**11**	8	3	**1**	...	1	**6**	5	1	**4**	3	1
60-65	**6**	4	2	...	...	...	**3**	3	...	**3**	1	2
65-70	**6**	4	2	...	...	...	**3**	3	...	**3**	1	2
70 and over ...	**1**	1	...	...	...	...	**1**	1	...	...	...	...
Sikh.												
All ages ...	**100**	**63**	**37**	**37**	**22**	**15**	**56**	**38**	**18**	**7**	**3**	**4**
0-1	**5**	3	2	**5**	3	2	...	...	...	...	...	...
1-2	...	...	...	...	...	...	...	...	...	...	...	...
2-3	**4**	1	3	**4**	1	3	...	...	...	...	...	...
3-4	**2**	...	2	**2**	...	2	...	...	...	...	...	...
4-5	**3**	2	1	**3**	2	1	...	...	...	...	...	...
Total 0-5 ...	**14**	6	8	**14**	6	8	...	...	...	...	...	...
5-10	**7**	4	3	**7**	4	3	...	...	...	...	...	...
10-15	**9**	5	4	**8**	5	3	**1**	...	1	...	...	...
15-20	**16**	12	4	**6**	5	1	**10**	7	3	...	...	...
20-25	**17**	13	4	**2**	2	...	**15**	11	4	...	...	...
25-30	**8**	5	3	...	...	...	**7**	5	2	**1**	...	1
30-35	**4**	2	2	...	...	...	**4**	2	2	...	...	...
35-40	**7**	4	3	...	...	...	**6**	4	2	**1**		1
40-45	**6**	4	2	...	...	...	**4**	3	1	**2**	1	1
45-50	**3**	2	1	...	...	...	**2**	1	1	**1**	1	...
50-55	**2**	1	1	...	...	...	**2**	1	1	...	...	...
55-60	**3**	2	1	...	...	...	**3**	2	1	...	...	...
60-65	**1**	1	...	...	...	...	**1**	1	...	...	...	...
65-70	**2**	1	1	...	...	...	**1**	1	...	**1**	...	1
70 and over ...	**1**	1	...	...	...	...	...	...	...	**1**	1	...

TABLE VII—Age, Sex & Civil Condition.

Mysore State, Including Civil and Military Station, Bangalore.

AGE	POPULATION			UNMARRIED			MARRIED			WIDOWED		
	Persons	Males	Females	Persons	Males	Females	Persons	Males	Females	Persons	Males	Females
1	2	3	4	5	6	7	8	9	10	11	12	13
Jew.												
All ages ...	39	13	26	24	6	18	15	7	8	...	...	...
0–1	1	...	1	1	...	1	...	...	...	...	...	...
1–2	...	...	...	...	...	...	...	...	...	...	...	...
2–3	3	1	2	3	1	2	...	...	...	...	...	...
3–4	1	...	1	1	...	1	...	...	...	...	...	...
4–5	...	...	...	...	...	...	...	...	...	...	...	...
Total 0–5 ...	5	1	4	5	1	4	...	...	...	...	...	...
5–10	7	2	5	7	2	5	...	...	...	...	...	...
10–15	7	2	5	7	2	5	...	...	...	...	...	...
15–20	5	1	4	4	1	3	1	...	1	...	...	...
20–25	2	...	2	1	...	1	1	...	1	...	...	...
25–30	2	1	1	...	...	...	2	1	1	...	...	...
30–35	1	1	...	...	...	...	1	1	...	...	...	...
35–40	3	1	2	...	...	...	3	1	2	...	...	...
40–45	1	...	1	...	...	...	1	...	1	...	...	...
45–50	3	2	1	...	...	...	3	2	1	...	...	...
50–55	1	...	1	...	...	...	1	...	1	...	...	...
55–60	2	2	...	...	...	...	2	2	...	...	...	...
60–65	...	...	...	...	...	...	...	...	...	...	...	...
65–70	...	...	...	...	...	...	...	...	...	...	...	...
70 and over ...	...	...	...	...	...	...	...	...	...	...	...	...
Others.*												
All ages ...	106	51	55	60	31	29	39	19	20	7	1	6
0–1	4	2	2	4	2	2	...	...	...	...	...	...
1–2	2	1	1	2	1	1	...	...	...	...	...	...
2–3	4	2	2	4	2	2	...	...	...	...	...	...
3–4	4	4	...	4	4	...	...	...	...	...	...	...
4–5	1	1	...	1	1	...	...	...	...	...	...	...
Total 0—5 ...	15	10	5	15	10	5	...	...	...	...	...	...
5–10	9	4	5	9	4	5	...	...	...	...	...	...
10–15	11	5	6	11	5	6	...	...	...	...	...	...
15–20	13	5	8	10	4	6	3	1	2	...	...	...
20–25	11	5	6	9	5	4	2	...	2	...	...	...
25–30	10	4	6	4	1	3	6	3	3	...	...	...
30–35	7	3	4	...	...	...	6	3	3	1	...	1
35–40	8	2	6	...	...	...	6	2	4	2	...	2
40–45	6	4	2	2	2	...	4	2	2	...	...	...
45–50	5	3	2	...	...	...	4	3	1	1	...	1
50–55	3	1	2	...	...	...	2	1	1	1	...	1
55–60	3	2	1	...	...	...	2	1	1	1	1	...
60–65	1	1	...	...	...	...	1	1	...	...	...	...
65–70	2	1	1	...	...	...	1	1	...	1	...	1
70 and over ...	2	1	1	...	...	...	2	1	1	...	...	...

*See Note 2 on the Fly leaf

TABLE VII—Age, Sex & Civil Condition.

Mysore State, Excluding Civil and Military Station, Bangalore.

AGE	POPULATION			UNMARRIED			MARRIED			WIDOWED		
	Persons	Males	Females	Persons	Males	Females	Persons	Males	Females	Persons	Males	Females
1	2	3	4	5	6	7	8	9	10	11	12	13
All Religions.												
All ages ...	**6,423,189**	**3,284,554**	**3,138,635**	**3,092,648**	**1,826,177**	**1,266,471**	**2,604,412**	**1,291,162**	**1,313,250**	**726,129**	**167,215**	**558,914**
0-1	**173,223**	85,057	88,166	**173,223**	85,057	88,166	...	...	...	...	...	...
1-2	**177,586**	86,990	90,596	**177,586**	86,990	90,596	...	...	...	...	...	...
2-3	**187,590**	91,104	96,486	**187,590**	91,104	96,486	...	...	...	...	...	...
3-4	**186,482**	91,085	95,397	**186,462**	91,080	95,382	**19**	5	14	**1**	...	1
4-5	**186,064**	92,145	93,919	**186,033**	92,139	93,894	**31**	6	25	...	...	...
Total 0-5 ...	**910,945**	446,381	464,564	**910,894**	446,370	464,524	**50**	11	39	**1**	...	1
5-10	**865,528**	432,320	433,208	**843,788**	431,954	411,834	**21,406**	349	21,057	**334**	17	317
10-15	**799,078**	412,400	386,678	**720,699**	410,109	310,590	**76,871**	2,226	74,645	**1,508**	65	1,443
15-20	**588,880**	298,782	290,098	**306,021**	254,907	51,114	**271,645**	42,909	228,736	**11,214**	966	10,248
20-25	**598,081**	287,867	310,214	**189,378**	175,479	13,899	**385,051**	109,456	275,595	**23,652**	2,932	20,720
25-30	**538,188**	266,038	272,150	**61,789**	57,609	4,180	**427,853**	200,335	227,518	**48,546**	8,094	40,452
30-35	**491,068**	257,084	234,084	**29,281**	26,217	3,064	**399,405**	219,227	180,178	**62,382**	11,590	50,792
35-40	**401,471**	223,767	177,704	**11,635**	9,572	2,063	**309,530**	197,905	111,625	**80,306**	16,290	64,016
40-45	**334,962**	188,527	146,435	**7,161**	5,584	1,577	**244,999**	165,032	79,967	**82,802**	17,911	64,891
45-50	**250,481**	136,929	113,552	**3,969**	2,922	1,047	**161,037**	114,503	46,534	**85,475**	19,504	65,971
50-55	**195,029**	102,303	92,726	**2,776**	1,975	801	**114,502**	82,212	32,290	**77,751**	18,116	59,635
55-60	**150,513**	77,295	73,218	**1,879**	1,266	613	**73,150**	56,831	16,319	**75,484**	19,198	56,286
60-65	**127,834**	64,989	62,845	**1,489**	971	518	**56,716**	45,735	10,981	**69,629**	18,283	51,346
65-70	**68,475**	35,731	32,744	**762**	495	267	**27,034**	23,113	3,921	**40,679**	12,123	28,556
70 and over ...	**102,656**	54,191	48,465	**1,127**	747	380	**35,163**	31,318	3,845	**66,366**	22,126	44,240
Hindu—Brahmanic.												
All ages ...	**5,941,783**	**3,027,732**	**2,914,051**	**2,841,190**	**1,676,948**	**1,164,242**	**2,412,389**	**1,192,171**	**1,220,218**	**688,204**	**158,613**	**529,591**
0-1	**159,572**	78,219	81,353	**159,572**	78,219	81,353	...	...	...	...	...	...
1-2	**163,070**	79,751	83,319	**163,070**	79,751	83,319	...	...	...	...	...	...
2-3	**172,162**	83,524	88,638	**172,162**	83,524	88,638	...	...	...	...	...	...
3-4	**171,180**	83,607	87,573	**171,161**	83,603	87,558	**18**	4	14	**1**	...	1
4-5	**170,421**	84,512	85,909	**170,390**	84,506	85,884	**31**	6	25	...	...	...
Total 0-5 ...	**836,405**	409,613	426,792	**836,355**	409,603	426,752	**49**	10	39	**1**	...	1
5-10	**797,683**	397,651	400,032	**776,677**	397,319	379,358	**20,687**	315	20,372	**319**	17	302
10-15	**738,238**	380,293	357,945	**664,192**	378,136	286,056	**72,614**	2,093	70,521	**1,432**	64	1,368
15-20	**542,700**	274,447	268,253	**279,636**	233,511	46,125	**252,436**	40,060	212,376	**10,628**	876	9,752
20-25	**551,274**	263,770	287,504	**171,953**	159,496	12,457	**356,796**	101,545	255,251	**22,525**	2,729	19,796
25-30	**498,365**	245,035	253,330	**56,581**	52,729	3,852	**395,432**	184,664	210,768	**46,352**	7,642	38,710
30-35	**455,769**	237,246	218,523	**27,033**	24,177	2,856	**369,233**	202,119	167,114	**59,503**	10,950	48,553
35-40	**373,539**	207,291	166,248	**10,840**	8,922	1,918	**286,416**	182,896	103,520	**76,283**	15,473	60,810
40-45	**311,880**	174,798	137,082	**6,714**	5,237	1,477	**226,636**	152,487	74,149	**78,530**	17,074	61,456
45-50	**233,120**	126,660	106,460	**3,682**	2,704	978	**148,686**	105,414	43,272	**80,752**	18,542	62,210
50-55	**181,754**	94,684	87,070	**2,599**	1,854	745	**105,678**	75,575	30,103	**73,477**	17,255	56,222
55-60	**140,724**	71,790	68,934	**1,747**	1,176	571	**67,589**	52,367	15,222	**71,388**	18,247	53,141
60-65	**119,857**	60,548	59,309	**1,417**	924	493	**52,510**	42,252	10,258	**65,930**	17,372	48,558
65-70	**64,280**	33,317	30,963	**704**	459	245	**25,054**	21,383	3,671	**38,522**	11,475	27,047
70 and over ...	**96,195**	50,589	45,606	**1,060**	701	359	**32,573**	28,991	3,582	**62,562**	20,897	41,665
Brahmo.												
All ages ...	**59**	**33**	**26**	**35**	**22**	**13**	**22**	**10**	**12**	**2**	**1**	**1**
0-1	**3**	1	2	**3**	1	2	...	...	...	...	...	...
1-2	**2**	1	1	**2**	1	1	...	...	...	...	...	...
2-3	**3**	1	2	**3**	1	2	...	...	...	...	...	...
3-4	**4**	2	2	**4**	2	2	...	...	...	...	...	...
4-5	**1**	1	...	**1**	1	...	...	...	...	...	...	...
Total 0-5 ...	**13**	6	7	**13**	6	7	...	...	...	...	...	...
5-10	**7**	5	2	**7**	5	2	...	...	...	...	...	...
10-15	**8**	6	2	**8**	6	2	...	...	...	...	...	...
15-20	**6**	3	3	**4**	3	1	**2**	...	2	...	...	...
20-25	**9**	3	6	**3**	2	1	**5**	1	4	**1**	...	1
25-30	**3**	1	2	...	...	...	**3**	1	2	...	...	...
30-35	**2**	2	...	...	...	...	**2**	2	...	...	...	...
35-40	**4**	3	1	...	...	...	**4**	3	1	...	...	...
40-45	**2**	1	1	...	...	...	**2**	1	1	...	...	...
45-50	...	...	...	...	...	...	...	...	...	...	...	...
50-55	**1**	...	1	...	...	...	**1**	...	1	...	...	...
55-60	**2**	1	1	...	...	...	**1**	...	1	**1**	1	...
60-65	**1**	1	...	...	...	...	**1**	1	...	...	...	...
65-70	**1**	1	...	...	...	...	**1**	1	...	...	...	...
70 and over ..	...	...	...	...	...	...	...	...	...	...	...	...

TABLE VII—Age, Sex & Civil Condition.

Mysore State, Excluding Civil and Military Station, Bangalore.

AGE	POPULATION			UNMARRIED			MARRIED			WIDOWED		
	Persons	Males	Females	Persons	Males	Females	Persons	Males	Females	Persons	Males	Females
1	2	3	4	5	6	7	8	9	10	11	12	13
Arya.												
All ages ...	**34**	**30**	**4**	**30**	**28**	**2**	**3**	**2**	**1**	**1**	...	**1**
0-1	1	1	...	1	1	...	...	...	...	...	...	...
1-2	...	...	...	...	...	...	...	...	...	...	...	...
2-3	...	...	...	...	...	...	...	...	...	...	...	...
3-4	...	...	...	...	...	...	...	...	...	...	...	...
4-5	...	...	...	...	...	...	...	...	...	...	...	...
Total 0-5 ...	1	1	...	1	1	...	...	...	...	...	...	...
5-10	6	5	1	6	5	1	...	...	...	...	...	...
10-15	7	7	...	7	7	...	...	...	...	...	...	...
15-20	8	7	1	8	7	1	...	...	...	...	...	...
20-25	5	4	1	4	4	...	1	...	1	...	...	...
25-30	2	2	...	1	1	...	1	1	...	...	...	...
30-35	...	...	...	...	...	...	...	...	...	...	...	...
35-40	1	1	...	1	1	...	...	...	...	...	...	...
40-45	1	...	1	...	...	...	...	...	...	1	...	1
45-50	2	2	...	1	1	...	1	1	...	...	...	...
50-55	...	...	...	...	...	...	...	...	...	...	...	...
55-60	...	...	...	...	...	...	...	...	...	...	...	...
60-65	1	1	...	1	1	...	...	...	...	...	...	...
65-70	...	...	...	...	...	...	...	...	...	...	...	...
70 and over ...	...	...	...	...	...	...	...	...	...	...	...	...
Total Hindu.												
All ages ...	**5,941,876**	**3,027,795**	**2,914,081**	**2,841,255**	**1,676,998**	**1,164,257**	**2,412,414**	**1,192,183**	**1,220,231**	**688,207**	**158,614**	**529,593**
0-1	159,576	78,221	81,355	159,576	78,221	81,355	...	...	...	...	...	...
1-2	163,072	79,752	83,320	163,072	79,752	83,320	...	...	...	...	...	...
2-3	172,165	83,525	88,640	172,165	83,525	88,640	...	...	...	...	...	...
3-4	171,184	83,609	87,575	171,165	83,605	87,560	18	4	14	1	...	1
4-5	170,422	84,518	85,909	170,391	84,507	85,884	31	6	25	...	...	...
Total 0-5 ...	836,419	409,620	426,799	836,369	409,610	426,759	49	10	39	1	...	1
5-10	797,696	397,661	400,035	776,690	397,329	379,361	20,687	315	20,372	319	17	302
10-15	738,253	380,306	357,947	664,207	378,149	286,058	72,614	2,093	70,521	1,432	64	1,368
15-20	542,714	274,457	268,257	279,648	233,521	46,127	252,438	40,060	212,378	10,628	876	9,752
20-25	551,288	263,777	287,511	171,960	159,502	12,458	356,802	101,546	255,256	22,526	2,729	19,797
25-30	498,370	245,038	253,332	56,582	52,730	3,852	395,436	184,666	210,770	46,352	7,642	38,710
30-35	455,771	237,248	218,523	27,033	24,177	2,856	369,235	202,121	167,114	59,503	10,950	48,553
35-40	373,544	207,295	166,249	10,841	8,923	1,918	286,420	182,899	103,521	76,283	15,473	60,810
40-45	311,883	174,799	137,084	6,714	5,237	1,477	226,638	152,488	74,150	78,531	17,074	61,457
45-50	233,122	126,662	106,460	3,683	2,705	978	148,687	105,415	43,272	80,752	18,542	62,210
50-55	181,755	94,684	87,071	2,599	1,854	745	105,679	75,575	30,104	73,477	17,255	56,222
55-60	140,726	71,791	68,935	1,747	1,176	571	67,590	52,367	15,223	71,389	18,248	53,141
60-65	119,859	60,550	59,309	1,418	925	493	52,511	42,253	10,258	65,930	17,372	48,558
65-70	64,281	33,318	30,963	704	459	245	25,055	21,384	3,671	38,522	11,475	27,047
70 and over ...	96,195	50,589	45,606	1,060	701	359	32,573	28,991	3,582	62,562	20,897	41,665
Musalman.												
All ages ...	**370,003**	**197,983**	**172,020**	**194,024**	**115,551**	**78,473**	**147,957**	**76,167**	**71,790**	**28,022**	**6,265**	**21,757**
0-1	10,355	5,215	5,140	10,355	5,215	5,140	...	...	...	...	...	...
1-2	11,238	5,579	5,659	11,238	5,579	5,659	...	...	...	...	...	...
2-3	11,957	5,830	6,127	11,957	5,830	6,127	...	...	...	...	...	...
3-4	11,985	5,823	6,162	11,985	5,823	6,162	...	...	...	...	...	...
4-5	12,477	6,075	6,402	12,477	6,075	6,402	...	...	...	...	...	...
Total 0-5 ...	58,012	28,522	29,490	58,012	28,522	29,490	...	...	...	...	...	...
5-10	53,318	27,348	25,970	52,793	27,323	25,470	513	25	488	12	...	12
10-15	47,427	25,160	22,267	43,994	25,063	18,931	3,375	96	3,279	58	1	57
15-20	35,128	18,632	16,496	19,847	16,456	3,391	14,882	2,113	12,769	399	63	336
20-25	35,574	18,399	17,175	12,943	12,172	771	21,841	6,078	15,763	790	149	641
25-30	30,144	15,930	14,214	3,752	3,612	140	24,832	11,981	12,851	1,560	337	1,223
30-35	26,723	15,013	11,710	1,539	1,450	89	23,091	13,086	10,005	2,093	477	1,616
35-40	21,170	12,519	8,651	488	431	57	17,752	11,502	6,250	2,930	586	2,344
40-45	17,416	10,429	6,987	250	218	32	14,056	9,618	4,438	3,110	593	2,517
45-50	13,117	7,797	5,320	157	131	26	9,485	7,008	2,477	3,475	658	2,817
50-55	10,083	5,809	4,274	94	74	20	6,797	5,125	1,672	3,192	610	2,582
55-60	7,445	4,210	3,235	64	39	25	4,318	3,497	821	3,063	674	2,389
60-65	6,089	3,401	2,688	25	15	10	3,282	2,727	555	2,782	659	2,123
65-70	3,186	1,855	1,331	29	19	10	1,557	1,354	203	1,600	482	1,118
70 and over ...	5,171	2,959	2,212	37	26	11	2,176	1,957	219	2,958	976	1,982

TABLE VII—Age, Sex & Civil Condition.

Mysore State, Excluding Civil and Military Station, Bangalore.

AGE	POPULATION			UNMARRIED			MARRIED			WIDOWED		
	Persons	Males	Females	Persons	Males	Females	Persons	Males	Females	Persons	Males	Females
1	2	3	4	5	6	7	8	9	10	11	12	13
Christian.												
All ages ...	**57,516**	**30,512**	**27,004**	**31,068**	**17,785**	**13,283**	**22,300**	**11,840**	**10,460**	**4,148**	**887**	**3,261**
0–1	**1,771**	882	889	**1,771**	882	889	...	...	...	...	...	...
1–2	**1,782**	908	874	**1,732**	908	874	...	...	...	...	...	...
2–3	**1,854**	950	904	**1,854**	950	904	...	...	...	...	...	...
3–4	**1,683**	855	828	**1,683**	855	828	...	...	...	...	...	...
4–5	**1,581**	777	804	**1,581**	777	804	...	...	...	...	...	...
Total 0–5 ...	**8,671**	4,372	4,299	**8,671**	4,372	4,299	...	...	...	...	...	...
5–10	**7,263**	3,631	3,632	**7,241**	3,629	3,612	**22**	2	20	...	...	...
10–15	**6,758**	3,412	3,346	**6,479**	3,401	3,078	**275**	11	264	**4**	...	4
15–20	**5,932**	3,038	2,894	**3,911**	2,735	1,176	**1,953**	297	1,656	**68**	6	62
20–25	**6,085**	3,127	2,958	**2,850**	2,269	581	**3,096**	840	2,256	**139**	18	121
25–30	**5,088**	2,717	2,371	**912**	756	156	**3,922**	1,915	2,007	**254**	46	208
30–35	**4,502**	2,529	1,973	**448**	339	109	**3,730**	2,127	1,603	**324**	63	261
35–40	**3,580**	2,073	1,457	**188**	104	84	**2,891**	1,892	999	**451**	77	374
40–45	**2,980**	1,735	1,245	**126**	60	66	**2,342**	1,591	751	**512**	84	428
45–50	**2,167**	1,284	883	**81**	40	41	**1,524**	1,127	397	**562**	117	445
50–55	**1,641**	975	666	**53**	20	33	**1,101**	852	249	**487**	103	384
55–60	**1,107**	634	473	**41**	26	15	**632**	497	135	**434**	111	323
60–65	**854**	479	375	**33**	18	15	**446**	362	84	**375**	99	276
65–70	**430**	242	188	**19**	9	10	**188**	167	21	**223**	66	157
70 and over ...	**508**	264	244	**15**	7	8	**178**	160	18	**315**	97	218
Jain.												
All ages ...	**28,799**	**15,436**	**13,363**	**13,540**	**8,583**	**4,957**	11,416	**5,881**	**5,535**	**3,843**	**972**	**2,871**
0–1	**744**	368	376	**744**	368	376	...	...	...	...	...	...
1–2	**664**	348	316	**664**	348	316	...	...	...	...	...	...
2–3	**743**	381	362	**743**	381	362	...	...	...	...	...	...
3–4	**751**	368	383	**751**	368	383	...	...	...	...	...	...
4–5	**729**	353	376	**729**	353	376	...	...	...	...	...	...
Total 0–5 ...	**3,631**	1,818	1,813	**3,631**	1,818	1,813	...	...	...	...	...	...
5–10	**3,606**	1,811	1,795	**3,477**	1,806	1,671	**126**	5	121	**3**	...	3
10–15	**3,470**	1,848	1,622	**3,082**	1,834	1,248	**376**	14	362	**12**	...	12
15–20	**2,900**	1,596	1,304	**1,488**	1,318	170	**1,333**	266	1,067	**79**	12	67
20–25	**2,882**	1,553	1,329	**1,000**	971	29	**1,747**	563	1,184	**135**	19	116
25–30	**2,468**	1,334	1,134	**371**	357	14	**1,832**	936	896	**265**	41	224
30–35	**2,198**	1,253	945	**205**	199	6	**1,675**	989	686	**318**	65	253
35–40	**1,742**	1,020	722	**101**	100	1	**1,222**	817	405	**419**	103	316
40–45	**1,502**	861	641	**61**	60	1	**1,007**	693	314	**434**	108	326
45–50	**1,203**	676	527	**42**	41	1	**712**	504	208	**449**	131	318
50–55	**909**	485	424	**27**	26	1	**492**	352	140	**390**	107	283
55–60	**766**	408	358	**22**	21	1	**354**	277	77	**390**	110	280
60–65	**652**	350	302	**13**	13	...	**278**	228	50	**361**	109	252
65–70	**383**	205	178	**9**	8	1	**136**	125	11	**238**	72	166
70 and over ...	**487**	218	269	**11**	11	...	**126**	112	14	**350**	95	255
Tribal.												
All ages ...	**23,828**	**12,230**	**11,598**	**12,177**	**6,922**	**5,255**	**9,827**	**4,845**	**4,982**	**1,824**	**463**	**1,361**
0–1	**735**	351	384	**735**	351	384	...	...	...	...	...	...
1–2	**796**	383	413	**796**	383	413	...	...	...	...	...	...
2–3	**824**	393	431	**824**	393	431	...	...	...	...	...	...
3–4	**834**	406	428	**834**	406	428	...	...	...	...	...	...
4–5	**819**	409	410	**819**	409	410	...	...	...	...	...	...
Total 0–5 ...	**4,008**	1,942	2,066	**4,008**	1,942	2,066	...	...	...	...	...	...
5–10	**3,512**	1,798	1,714	**3,457**	1,797	1,660	**55**	1	54	...	...	...
10–15	**3,048**	1,618	1,430	**2,828**	1,607	1,221	**219**	11	208	**1**	...	1
15–20	**2,073**	999	1,074	**1,052**	826	226	**984**	164	820	**37**	9	28
20–25	**2,124**	951	1,173	**578**	524	54	**1,487**	410	1,077	**59**	17	42
25–30	**2,015**	964	1,051	**159**	145	14	**1,746**	791	955	**110**	28	82
30–35	**1,796**	946	850	**53**	49	4	**1,603**	862	741	**140**	35	105
35–40	**1,411**	819	592	**15**	13	2	**1,185**	757	428	**211**	49	162
40–45	**1,125**	670	455	**8**	7	1	**910**	613	297	**207**	50	157
45–50	**826**	486	340	**6**	5	1	**592**	426	166	**228**	55	173
50–55	**609**	336	273	**3**	1	2	**410**	295	115	**196**	40	156
55–60	**445**	238	207	**5**	4	1	**243**	183	60	**197**	51	146
60–65	**363**	200	163	...	...	...	**192**	158	34	**171**	42	129
65–70	**185**	106	79	**1**	...	1	**93**	78	15	**91**	28	63
70 and over ...	**288**	157	131	**4**	2	2	**108**	96	12	**176**	59	117

TABLE VII.

Age, Sex & Civil Condition.

TABLE VII—Age, Sex & Civil Condition.

Mysore State, Excluding Civil and Military Station, Bangalore.

AGE	POPULATION			UNMARRIED			MARRIED			WIDOWED		
	Persons	Males	Females	Persons	Males	Females	Persons	Males	Females	Persons	Males	Females
1	2	3	4	5	6	7	8	9	10	11	12	13
Buddhist												
All ages ...	**979**	**497**	**482**	**485**	**280**	**205**	**422**	**209**	**213**	**72**	**8**	**64**
0–1	**34**	16	18	**34**	16	18	...	...	...	...	...	...
1–2	**32**	19	13	**32**	19	13	...	...	...	...	...	...
2–3	**40**	22	18	**40**	22	18	...	...	...	...	...	...
3–4	**41**	22	19	**41**	22	19	...	...	...	...	...	...
4–5	**33**	16	17	**33**	16	17	...	...	...	...	...	...
Total 0–5 ...	**180**	95	85	**180**	95	85	...	...	...	...	...	...
5–10	**117**	62	55	**114**	61	53	**3**	1	2	...	...	...
10–15	**100**	45	55	**88**	44	44	**11**	1	10	**1**	...	1
15–20	**105**	45	60	**54**	38	16	**48**	7	41	**3**	...	3
20–25	**108**	48	60	**37**	32	5	**68**	16	52	**3**	...	3
25–30	**88**	47	41	**9**	7	2	**75**	40	35	**4**	...	4
30–35	**72**	43	29	**2**	2	...	**66**	41	25	**4**	...	4
35–40	**59**	35	24	**1**	1	...	**49**	33	16	**9**	1	8
40–45	**47**	29	18	...	...	...	**41**	27	14	**6**	2	4
45–50	**34**	19	15	...	...	...	**26**	18	8	**8**	1	7
50–55	**27**	12	15	...	...	...	**18**	11	7	**9**	1	8
55–60	**16**	6	10	...	...	...	**8**	5	3	**8**	1	7
60–65	**15**	7	8	...	...	...	**6**	6	...	**9**	1	8
65–70	**6**	2	4	...	...	...	**2**	2	...	**4**	...	4
70 and over ...	**5**	2	3	...	...	...	**1**	1	...	**4**	1	3
Parsi.												
All ages ...	**87**	**49**	**38**	**47**	**27**	**20**	**33**	**17**	**16**	**7**	**5**	**2**
0–1	**3**	1	2	**3**	1	2	...	...	...	...	...	...
1–2	**2**	1	1	**2**	1	1	...	...	...	...	...	...
2–3	**2**	1	1	**2**	1	1	...	...	...	...	...	...
3–4	**2**	2	...	**1**	1	...	**1**	1	...	...	...	...
4–5	...	...	...	...	...	...	...	...	...	...	...	...
Total 0–5 ...	**9**	5	4	**8**	4	4	**1**	1	...	...	...	...
5–10	**5**	3	2	**5**	3	2	...	...	...	...	...	...
10–15	**8**	4	4	**8**	4	4	...	...	...	...	...	...
15–20	**15**	7	8	**13**	7	6	**2**	...	2	...	...	...
20–25	**10**	6	4	**7**	6	1	**3**	...	3	...	...	...
25–30	**10**	7	3	**4**	2	2	**6**	5	1	...	...	...
30–35	**3**	2	1	**1**	1	...	**2**	1	1	...	...	...
35–40	**5**	2	3	**1**	...	1	**3**	1	2	**1**	1	...
40–45	**4**	1	3	...	...	...	**3**	1	2	**1**	...	1
45–50	**7**	2	5	...	...	...	**6**	2	4	**1**	...	1
50–55	**2**	1	1	...	...	...	**2**	1	1	...	...	...
55–60	**5**	5	...	...	...	...	**2**	2	...	**3**	3	...
60–65	**1**	1	...	...	...	...	...	...	...	**1**	1	...
65–70	**2**	2	...	...	...	...	**2**	2	...	...	...	...
70 and over ...	**1**	1	...	...	...	...	**1**	1	...	...	...	...
Sikh.												
All ages ...	**68**	**34**	**34**	**34**	**20**	**14**	**29**	**13**	**16**	**5**	**1**	**4**
0–1	**5**	3	2	**5**	3	2	...	...	...	...	...	...
1–2	...	...	...	...	...	...	...	...	...	...	...	...
2–3	**3**	1	2	**3**	1	2	...	...	...	...	...	...
3–4	**2**	...	2	**2**	...	2	...	...	...	...	...	...
4–5	**3**	2	1	**3**	2	1	...	...	...	...	...	...
Total 0–5 ...	**13**	6	7	**13**	6	7	...	...	...	...	...	...
5–10	**7**	4	3	**7**	4	3	...	...	...	...	...	...
10–15	**8**	4	4	**7**	4	3	**1**	...	1	...	...	...
15–20	**9**	6	3	**5**	4	1	**4**	2	2	...	...	...
20–25	**9**	5	4	**2**	2	...	**7**	3	4	...	...	...
25–30	**3**	...	3	...	...	...	**2**	...	2	**1**	...	1
30–35	**2**	...	2	...	...	...	**2**	...	2	...	...	...
35–40	**5**	2	3	...	...	...	**4**	2	2	**1**	...	1
40–45	**3**	1	2	...	...	...	**2**	1	1	**1**	...	1
45–50	**1**	...	1	...	...	...	**1**	...	1	...	...	...
50–55	**2**	1	1	...	...	...	**2**	1	1	...	...	...
55–60	**2**	2	...	...	...	...	**2**	2	...	...	...	...
60–65	**1**	1	...	...	...	...	**1**	1	...	...	...	...
65–70	**2**	1	1	...	...	...	**1**	1	...	**1**	...	1
70 and over ...	**1**	1	...	...	...	...	...	...	...	**1**	1	...

TABLE VII—Age, Sex & Civil Condition.

Mysore State, Excluding Civil and Military Station, Bangalore.

AGE	POPULATION			UNMARRIED			MARRIED			WIDOWED		
	Persons	Males	Females	Persons	Males	Females	Persons	Males	Females	Persons	Males	Females
1	2	3	4	5	6	7	8	9	10	11	12	13
Jew.												
All ages ...	18	7	11	10	3	7	8	4	4	...	...	...
0–1	...	...	...	...	...	...	...	...	...	...	...	...
1–2	...	...	...	...	...	...	...	...	...	...	...	...
2–3	1	...	1	1	...	1	...	...	...	...	...	...
3–4	...	...	...	...	...	...	...	...	...	...	...	...
4–5	...	...	...	...	...	...	...	...	...	...	...	...
Total 0–5 ...	1	...	1	1	...	1	...	...	...	...	...	...
5–10	3	1	2	3	1	2	...	...	...	...	...	...
10–15	4	1	3	4	1	3	...	...	...	...	...	...
15–20	3	1	2	2	1	1	1	...	1	...	...	...
20–25	...	...	...	...	...	...	...	...	...	...	...	...
25–30	...	...	...	...	...	...	...	...	...	...	...	...
30–35	...	...	...	...	...	...	...	...	...	...	...	...
35–40	2	1	1	...	...	...	2	1	1	...	...	...
40–45	...	...	...	...	...	...	...	...	...	...	...	...
45–50	3	2	1	...	...	...	3	2	1	...	...	...
50–55	1	...	1	...	...	...	1	...	1	...	...	...
55–60	1	1	...	...	...	...	1	1	...	...	...	...
60–65	...	...	...	...	...	...	...	...	...	...	...	...
65–70	...	...	...	...	...	...	...	...	...	...	...	...
70 and over ...	...	...	...	...	...	...	...	...	...	...	...	...
Others.												
All ages ...	15	11	4	8	8	...	6	3	3	1	...	1
0–1	...	...	...	...	...	...	...	...	...	...	...	...
1–2	...	...	...	...	...	...	...	...	...	...	...	...
2–3	1	1	...	1	1	...	...	...	...	...	...	...
3–4	...	...	...	...	...	...	...	...	...	...	...	...
4–5	...	...	...	...	...	...	...	...	...	...	...	...
Total 0–5 ...	1	1	...	1	1	...	...	...	...	...	...	...
5–10	1	1	...	1	1	...	...	...	...	...	...	...
10–15	2	2	...	2	2	...	...	...	...	...	...	...
15–20	1	1	...	1	1	...	...	...	...	...	...	...
20–25	1	1	...	1	1	...	...	...	...	...	...	...
25–30	2	1	1	...	...	...	2	1	1	...	...	...
30–35	1	...	1	...	...	...	1	...	1	...	...	...
35–40	3	1	2	...	...	...	2	1	1	1	...	1
40–45	2	2	...	2	2	...	...	...	...	...	...	...
45–50	1	1	...	...	...	...	1	1	...	...	...	...
50–55	...	...	...	...	...	...	...	...	...	...	...	...
55–60	...	...	...	...	...	...	...	...	...	...	...	...
60–65	...	...	...	...	...	...	...	...	...	...	...	...
65–70	...	...	...	...	...	...	...	...	...	...	...	...
70 and over ...	...	...	...	...	...	...	...	...	...	...	...	...

TABLE VII.

Age, Sex & Civil Condition.

Bangalore City.

AGE	POPULATION			UNMARRIED			MARRIED			WIDOWED		
	Persons	Males	Females	Persons	Males	Females	Persons	Males	Females	Persons	Males	Females
1	2	3	4	5	6	7	8	9	10	11	12	13
All Religions.												
All ages ...	**172,357**	**91,680**	**80,677**	**81,019**	**49,698**	**31,321**	**75,777**	**38,573**	**37,204**	**15,561**	**3,409**	**12,152**
0–1	**4,662**	2,312	2,350	**4,662**	2,312	2,350	...	...	...	...	...	...
1–2	**4,830**	2,388	2,442	**4,830**	2,388	2,442	...	...	...	...	...	...
2–3	**5,155**	2,539	2,616	**5,155**	2,539	2,616	...	...	...	...	...	...
3–4	**5,004**	2,456	2,548	**5,004**	2,456	2,548	...	...	...	...	...	...
4–5	**4,619**	2,287	2,332	**4,618**	2,287	2,331	**1**	...	1	...	...	...
Total 0–5 ...	**24,270**	11,982	12,288	**24,269**	11,982	12,287	**1**	...	1	...	...	...
5–10	**20,870**	10,564	10,306	**20,344**	10,546	9,798	**521**	18	503	**5**	...	5
10–15	**19,553**	10,185	9,368	**17,223**	10,122	7,101	**2,299**	62	2,237	**31**	1	30
15–20	**18,870**	10,165	8,705	**9,533**	8,327	1,206	**9,074**	1,810	7,264	**263**	28	235
20–30	**34,442**	18,390	16,052	**8,166**	7,577	589	**24,792**	10,539	14,253	**1,484**	274	1,210
30–40	**23,648**	13,483	10,165	**985**	822	163	**19,800**	12,096	7,704	**2,863**	565	2,298
40–50	**15,215**	8,619	6,596	**273**	180	93	**11,168**	7,721	3,447	**3,774**	718	3,056
50–60	**8,621**	4,673	3,948	**126**	79	47	**5,176**	3,878	1,298	**3,319**	716	2,603
60 and over ...	**6,868**	3,619	3,249	**100**	63	37	**2,916**	2,449	497	**3,822**	1,107	2,715
Hindu.												
All ages ...	**144,529**	**76,645**	**67,884**	**66,467**	**41,034**	**25,433**	**64,406**	**32,619**	**31,787**	**13,656**	**2,992**	**10,664**
0–1	**3,940**	1,924	2,016	**3,940**	1,924	2,016	...	...	...	...	...	...
1–2	**4,065**	1,987	2,078	**4,065**	1,987	2,078	...	...	...	...	...	...
2–3	**4,307**	2,108	2,199	**4,307**	2,108	2,199	...	...	...	...	...	...
3–4	**4,169**	2,041	2,128	**4,169**	2,041	2,128	...	...	...	...	...	...
4–5	**3,838**	1,911	1,927	**3,837**	1,911	1,926	**1**	...	1	...	...	...
Total 0–5 ...	**20,319**	9,971	10,348	**20,318**	9,971	10,347	**1**	...	1	...	...	...
5–10	**17,409**	8,813	8,596	**16,913**	8,799	8,114	**491**	14	477	**5**	...	5
10–15	**16,367**	8,547	7,820	**14,246**	8,491	5,755	**2,090**	55	2,035	**31**	1	30
15–20	**15,858**	8,589	7,269	**7,663**	6,929	734	**7,957**	1,635	6,322	**238**	25	213
20–30	**28,807**	15,347	13,460	**6.298**	6,008	290	**21,185**	9,098	12,087	**1,324**	241	1,083
30–40	**19,829**	11,264	8,565	**679**	592	87	**16,610**	10,175	6,435	**2,540**	497	2,043
40–50	**12,744**	7,157	5,587	**192**	141	51	**9,273**	6,389	2,884	**3,279**	627	2,652
50–60	**7,305**	3,894	3,411	**90**	59	31	**4,314**	3,203	1,111	**2,901**	632	2,269
60 and over ...	**5,891**	3,063	2,828	**68**	44	24	**2,485**	2,050	435	**3,338**	969	2,369
Musalman.												
All ages ...	**19,831**	**10,975**	**8,856**	**10,058**	**6,209**	**3,849**	**8,415**	**4,459**	**3,956**	**1,358**	**307**	**1,051**
0–1	**491**	264	227	**491**	264	227	...	...	...	...	...	...
1–2	**538**	281	257	**538**	281	257	...	...	...	...	...	...
2–3	**593**	301	292	**593**	301	292	...	...	...	...	...	...
3–4	**601**	297	304	**601**	297	304	...	...	...	...	...	...
4–5	**579**	275	304	**579**	275	304	...	...	...	...	...	...
Total 0–5 ...	**2,802**	1,418	1,384	**2,802**	1,418	1,384	...	...	...	...	...	...
5–10	**2,510**	1,268	1,242	**2,489**	1,267	1,222	**21**	1	20	...	...	...
10–15	**2,275**	1,191	1,084	**2,105**	1,186	919	**170**	5	165	...	...	...
15–20	**2,121**	1,153	968	**1,235**	1,019	216	**866**	131	735	**20**	3	17
20–30	**3,984**	2,231	1,753	**1,211**	1,130	81	**2,664**	1,076	1,588	**109**	25	84
30–40	**2,721**	1,631	1,090	**164**	152	12	**2,328**	1,428	900	**229**	51	178
40–50	**1,764**	1,089	675	**31**	23	8	**1,382**	1,000	382	**351**	66	285
50–60	**939**	576	363	**13**	9	4	**628**	507	121	**298**	60	238
60 and over ...	**715**	418	297	**8**	5	3	**356**	311	45	**351**	102	249
Christian.												
All ages ...	**6,754**	**3,291**	**3,463**	**3,890**	**2,023**	**1,867**	**2,401**	**1,180**	**1,221**	**463**	**88**	**375**
0–1	**205**	109	96	**205**	109	96	...	...	...	...	...	...
1–2	**200**	105	95	**200**	105	95	...	...	...	...	...	...
2–3	**223**	115	108	**223**	115	108	...	...	...	...	...	...
3–4	**204**	104	100	**204**	104	100	...	...	...	...	...	...
4–5	**176**	89	87	**176**	89	87	...	...	...	...	...	...
Total 0–5 ...	**1,008**	522	486	**1,008**	522	486	...	...	...	...	...	...
5–10	**815**	402	413	**811**	401	410	**4**	1	3	...	...	...
10–15	**767**	354	413	**742**	353	389	**25**	1	24	...	...	...
15–20	**720**	308	412	**535**	287	248	**181**	21	160	**4**	...	4
20–30	**1,344**	612	732	**574**	360	214	**729**	248	481	**41**	4	37
30–40	**934**	481	453	**130**	66	64	**727**	403	324	**77**	12	65
40–50	**605**	312	293	**45**	11	34	**443**	284	159	**117**	17	100
50–60	**326**	177	149	**22**	10	12	**200**	146	54	**104**	21	83
60 and over ...	**235**	123	112	**23**	13	10	**92**	76	16	**120**	34	86

Bangalore City—*concld.*

AGE	POPULATION			UNMARRIED			MARRIED			WIDOWED		
	Persons	Males	Females	Persons	Males	Females	Persons	Males	Females	Persons	Males	Females
1	2	3	4	5	6	7	8	9	10	11	12	13
Jain.												
All ages ...	**1,153**	**724**	**429**	**560**	**409**	**151**	**513**	**294**	**219**	**80**	**21**	**59**
0–1	**26**	15	11	**26**	15	11	...	...	...	...	...	...
1–2	**25**	14	11	**25**	14	11	...	...	...	...	...	...
2–3	**30**	14	16	**30**	14	16	...	...	...	...	...	...
3–4	**30**	14	16	**30**	14	16	...	...	...	...	...	...
4–5	**24**	12	12	**24**	12	12	...	...	...	...	...	...
Total 0–5 ...	**135**	69	66	**135**	69	66	...	...	...	...	...	...
5–10	**124**	75	49	**120**	74	46	**4**	1	3	...	...	...
10–15	**132**	88	44	**119**	87	32	**13**	1	12	...	...	...
15–20	**156**	107	49	**89**	84	5	**66**	23	43	**1**	...	1
20–30	**293**	192	101	**79**	77	2	**204**	111	93	**10**	4	6
30–40	**154**	104	50	**12**	12	...	**127**	87	40	**15**	5	10
40–50	**92**	56	36	**4**	4	...	**62**	44	18	**26**	8	18
50–60	**43**	21	22	**1**	1	...	**27**	18	9	**15**	2	13
60 and over ...	**24**	12	12	**1**	1	...	**10**	9	1	**13**	2	11

TABLE VII.

Age, Sex and Civil Condition.

Bangalore District.

AGE	POPULATION			UNMARRIED			MARRIED			WIDOWED		
	Persons	Males	Females	Persons	Males	Females	Persons	Males	Females	Persons	Males	Females
1	2	3	4	5	6	7	8	9	10	11	12	13
All Religions.												
All ages ...	**908,056**	**461,905**	**446,151**	**433,052**	**252,002**	**181,050**	**381,262**	**188,259**	**193,003**	**93,742**	**21,644**	**72,098**
0–1	**25,908**	12,685	13,223	**25,908**	12,685	13,223	...	...	...	...	...	...
1–2	**27,086**	13,230	13,856	**27,086**	13,230	13,856	...	...	...	...	...	...
2–3	**28,529**	13,883	14,646	**28,529**	13,883	14,646	...	...	...	...	...	...
3–4	**28,389**	13,914	14,475	**28,389**	13,914	14,475	...	...	...	...	...	...
4–5	**28,379**	14,153	14,226	**28,379**	14,153	14,226	...	...	...	...	...	...
Total 0–5 ...	**138,291**	67,865	70,426	**138,291**	67,865	70,426	...	...	...	...	...	...
5–10	**126,495**	63,267	63,228	**123,339**	63,200	60,139	**3,125**	67	3,058	**31**	...	31
10–15	**111,923**	57,640	54,283	**100,318**	57,352	42,966	**11,441**	279	11,162	**164**	9	155
15–20	**79,621**	39,593	40,028	**38,253**	33,043	5,210	**40,050**	6,424	33,626	**1,318**	126	1,192
20–30	**152,790**	72,156	80,634	**28,047**	26,506	1,541	**116,760**	44,494	72,266	**7,983**	1,156	6,827
30–40	**120,844**	64,370	56,474	**3,219**	2,834	385	**101,456**	58,699	42,757	**16,169**	2,837	13,332
40–50	**81,975**	46,103	35,872	**865**	674	191	**60,548**	41,196	19,352	**20,562**	4,233	16,329
50–60	**49,174**	26,089	23,085	**394**	304	90	**28,518**	20,804	7,714	**20,262**	4,981	15,281
60 and over ...	**46,943**	24,822	22,121	**326**	224	102	**19,364**	16,296	3,068	**27,253**	8,302	18,951
Hindu.												
All ages ...	**833,552**	**422,950**	**410,602**	**392,859**	**228,756**	**164,108**	**352,189**	**173,654**	**178,535**	**88,504**	**20,540**	**67,964**
0–1	**23,633**	11,558	12,075	**23,633**	11,558	12,075	...	...	...	...	...	...
1–2	**24,577**	11,992	12,585	**24,577**	11,992	12,585	...	...	...	...	...	...
2–3	**25,867**	12,594	13,273	**25,867**	12,594	13,273	...	...	...	...	...	...
3–4	**25,785**	12,654	13,131	**25,785**	12,654	13,131	...	...	...	...	...	...
4–5	**25,722**	12,847	12,875	**25,722**	12,847	12,875	...	...	...	...	...	...
Total 0–5 ...	**125,584**	61,645	63,939	**125,584**	61,645	63,939	...	...	...	...	...	...
5–10	**115,228**	57,534	57,694	**112,167**	57,467	54,700	**3,033**	67	2,966	**28**	...	28
10–15	**102,194**	52,516	49,678	**91,231**	52,245	38,986	**10,808**	262	10,546	**155**	9	146
15–20	**72,790**	36,052	36,738	**34,413**	29,903	4,510	**37,148**	6,044	31,104	**1,229**	105	1,124
20–30	**140,502**	66,075	74,427	**25,122**	23,798	1,324	**107,797**	41,183	66,614	**7,583**	1,094	6,489
30–40	**111,691**	59,309	52,382	**2,913**	2,595	318	**93,475**	54,021	39,454	**15,303**	2,693	12,610
40–50	**76,007**	42,646	33,361	**782**	623	159	**55,852**	37,981	17,871	**19,373**	4,042	15,331
50–60	**45,747**	24,154	21,593	**354**	275	79	**26,271**	19,132	7,139	**19,122**	4,747	14,375
60 and over ...	**43,809**	23,019	20,790	**293**	205	88	**17,805**	14,964	2,841	**25,711**	7,850	17,861
Musalman.												
All ages ...	**60,276**	**31,744**	**28,532**	**32,947**	**19,193**	**13,754**	**23,356**	**11,749**	**11,607**	**3,973**	**802**	**3,171**
0–1	**1,823**	908	915	**1,823**	908	915	...	...	...	...	...	...
1–2	**2,038**	1,005	1,033	**2,038**	1,005	1,033	...	...	...	...	...	...
2–3	**2,169**	1,048	1,121	**2,169**	1,048	1,121	...	...	...	...	...	...
3–4	**2,142**	1,037	1,105	**2,142**	1,037	1,105	...	...	...	...	...	...
4–5	**2,189**	1,077	1,112	**2,189**	1,077	1,112	...	...	...	...	...	...
Total 0–5 ...	**10,361**	5,075	5,286	**10,361**	5,075	5,286	...	...	...	...	...	...
5–10	**9,293**	4,741	4,552	**9,219**	4,741	4,478	**71**	...	71	**3**	...	3
10–15	**7,992**	4,226	3,766	**7,469**	4,209	3,260	**516**	17	499	**7**	...	7
15–20	**5,574**	2,916	2,658	**3,170**	2,620	550	**2,345**	286	2,059	**59**	10	49
20–30	**9,944**	4,985	4,959	**2,430**	2,292	138	**7,210**	2,645	4,565	**304**	48	256
30–40	**7,307**	4,106	3,201	**224**	195	29	**6,424**	3,807	2,617	**659**	104	555
40–50	**4,700**	2,732	1,968	**42**	34	8	**3,726**	2,562	1,164	**932**	136	796
50–60	**2,679**	1,530	1,149	**18**	17	1	**1,790**	1,345	445	**871**	168	703
60 and over ...	**2,426**	1,433	993	**14**	10	4	**1,274**	1,087	187	**1,138**	336	802
Christian.												
All ages ...	**8,036**	**4,067**	**3,969**	**4,277**	**2,322**	**1,955**	**3,168**	**1,596**	**1,572**	**591**	**149**	**442**
0–1	**256**	113	143	**256**	113	143	...	...	...	...	...	...
1–2	**274**	135	139	**274**	135	139	...	...	...	...	...	...
2–3	**279**	135	144	**279**	135	144	...	...	...	...	...	...
3–4	**264**	125	139	**264**	125	139	...	...	...	...	...	...
4–5	**269**	130	139	**269**	130	139	...	...	...	...	...	...
Total 0–5 ...	**1,342**	638	704	**1,342**	638	704	...	...	...	...	...	...
5–10	**1,138**	582	556	**1,138**	582	556	...	...	...	...	...	...
10–15	**1,009**	525	484	**958**	525	433	**51**	...	51	...	...	...
15–20	**717**	354	363	**412**	298	114	**294**	54	240	**11**	2	9
20–30	**1,309**	605	704	**305**	237	68	**962**	359	603	**42**	9	33
30–40	**1,042**	530	512	**56**	19	37	**895**	493	402	**91**	18	73
40–50	**699**	403	296	**34**	10	24	**561**	375	186	**104**	18	86
50–60	**419**	233	186	**18**	8	10	**260**	189	71	**141**	36	105
60 and over ...	**361**	197	164	**14**	5	9	**145**	126	19	**202**	66	136

Bangalore District—*concld.*

AGE	POPULATION			UNMARRIED			MARRIED			WIDOWED		
	Persons	Males	Females	Persons	Males	Females	Persons	Males	Females	Persons	Males	Females
1	2	3	4	5	6	7	8	9	10	11	12	13
Jain.												
All ages ...	**3,532**	**1,777**	**1,755**	**1,691**	**994**	**697**	**1,360**	**672**	**688**	**481**	111	**370**
0-1	**100**	53	47	**100**	53	47	...	...	...	...	...	...
1-2	**102**	53	49	**102**	53	49	...	...	...	...	...	...
2-3	**111**	56	55	**111**	56	55	...	...	...	...	...	...
3-4	**105**	50	55	**105**	50	55	...	...	...	...	...	...
4-5	**108**	51	57	**108**	51	57	...	...	...	...	...	...
Total 0-5 ...	**526**	263	263	**526**	263	263	...	...	...	...	...	...
5-10	**473**	221	252	**460**	221	239	**13**	...	13	...	...	...
10-15	**425**	211	214	**379**	211	168	**44**	...	44	**2**	...	2
15-20	**327**	170	157	**163**	144	19	**148**	19	129	**16**	7	9
20-30	**586**	292	294	**129**	122	7	**414**	168	246	**43**	2	41
30-40	**442**	239	203	**21**	20	1	**336**	200	136	**85**	19	66
40-50	**325**	166	159	**6**	6	...	**209**	134	75	**110**	26	84
50-60	**204**	104	100	**3**	3	...	**114**	80	34	**87**	21	66
60 and over ...	**224**	111	113	**4**	4	...	**82**	71	11	**138**	36	102
Tribal.												
All ages ...	**2,645**	**1,357**	**1,288**	**1,272**	**732**	**540**	**1,182**	**584**	**598**	**191**	**41**	**150**
0-1	**94**	52	42	**94**	52	42	...	...	...	...	...	...
1-2	**95**	45	50	**95**	45	50	...	...	...	...	...	...
2-3	**103**	50	53	**103**	50	53	...	...	...	...	...	...
3-4	**93**	48	45	**93**	48	45	...	...	...	...	...	...
4-5	**91**	48	43	**91**	48	43	...	...	...	...	...	...
Total 0-5 ...	**476**	243	233	**476**	243	233	...	...	...	...	...	...
5-10	**362**	188	174	**354**	188	166	**8**	...	8	...	...	...
10-15	**301**	161	140	**280**	161	119	**21**	...	21	...	...	...
15-20	**212**	100	112	**95**	78	17	**114**	20	94	**3**	2	1
20-30	**445**	196	249	**59**	55	4	**375**	138	237	**11**	3	8
30-40	**360**	186	174	**5**	5	...	**325**	178	147	**30**	3	27
40-50	**244**	156	88	**1**	1	...	**200**	144	56	**43**	11	32
50-60	**123**	66	57	**1**	1	...	**82**	57	25	**40**	8	32
60 and over ...	**122**	61	61	**1**	...	1	**57**	47	10	**64**	14	50

TABLE VII.

Age, Sex & Civil Condition.

Kolar Gold Fields (City)

AGE	POPULATION			UNMARRIED			MARRIED			WIDOWED		
	Persons	Males	Females	Persons	Males	Females	Persons	Males	Females	Persons	Males	Females
1	2	3	4	5	6	7	8	9	10	11	12	13
All Religions.												
All ages ...	**85,103**	**45,051**	**40,052**	**40,299**	**23,962**	**16,337**	**37,746**	**19,726**	**18,020**	**7,058**	**1,363**	**5,695**
0-1	**2,452**	1,202	1,250	**2,452**	1,202	1,250	...	...	...	...	...	...
1-2	**2,489**	1,221	1,268	**2,489**	1,221	1,268	...	...	...	...	...	...
2-3	**2,761**	1,385	1,376	**2,761**	1,385	1,376	...	...	...	...	...	...
3-4	**2,623**	1,313	1,310	**2,623**	1,313	1,310	...	...	...	...	...	...
4-5	**2,368**	1,165	1,203	**2,368**	1,165	1,203	...	...	...	...	...	...
Total 0-5 ...	**12,693**	6,286	6,407	**12,693**	6,286	6,407	...	...	...	...	...	...
5-10	**10,443**	5,205	5,238	**10,241**	5,204	5,037	**200**	1	199	**2**	...	**2**
10-15	**9,176**	4,659	4,517	**8,345**	4,633	3,712	**817**	26	791	**14**	...	**14**
15-20	**7,980**	4,091	3,889	**4,188**	3,459	729	**3,669**	621	3,048	**123**	11	**112**
20-30	**16,286**	8,419	7,867	**4,022**	3,683	339	**11,654**	4,636	7,018	**610**	100	**510**
30-40	**12,764**	7,284	5,480	**578**	522	56	**10,902**	6,520	4,382	**1,284**	242	**1,042**
40-50	**8,578**	5,143	3,435	**155**	122	33	**6,552**	4,696	1,856	**1,871**	325	**1,546**
50-60	**4,426**	2,485	1,941	**52**	36	16	**2,687**	2,119	568	**1,687**	330	**1,357**
60 and over ...	**2,757**	1,479	1,278	**25**	17	8	**1,265**	1,107	158	**1,467**	355	**1,112**
Hindu.												
All ages ...	**62,313**	**32,695**	**29,618**	**28,658**	**17,133**	**11,525**	**28,094**	**14,454**	**13,640**	**5,561**	**1,108**	**4,453**
0-1	**1,744**	836	908	**1,744**	836	908	...	...	...	...	...	...
1-2	**1,773**	872	901	**1,773**	872	901	...	...	...	...	...	...
2-3	**1,925**	950	975	**1,925**	950	975	...	...	...	...	...	...
3-4	**1,843**	903	940	**1,843**	903	940	...	...	...	...	...	...
4-5	**1,687**	834	853	**1,687**	834	853	...	...	...	...	...	...
Total 0-5 ...	**8,972**	4,395	4,577	**8,972**	4,395	4,577	...	...	...	...	...	...
5-10	**7,560**	3,759	3,801	**7,381**	3,758	3,623	**177**	1	176	**2**	...	**2**
10-1	**6,679**	3,386	3,293	**6,007**	3,364	2,643	**662**	22	640	**10**	...	**10**
15-20	**5,770**	2,950	2,820	**2,906**	2,474	432	**2,767**	467	2,300	**97**	9	**88**
20-30	**11,889**	6,071	5,818	**2,814**	2,636	178	**8,595**	3,352	5,243	**480**	83	**397**
30-40	**9,540**	5,340	4,200	**420**	383	37	**8,106**	4,763	3,343	**1,014**	194	**820**
40-50	**6,410**	3,798	2,612	**106**	83	23	**4,847**	3,455	1,392	**1,457**	260	**1,197**
50-60	**3,337**	1,829	1,508	**33**	25	8	**1,960**	1,535	425	**1,344**	269	**1,075**
60 and over ...	**2,156**	1,167	989	**19**	15	4	**980**	859	121	**1,157**	293	**864**
Musalman.												
All ages ...	6,771	**4,045**	**2,726**	**3,187**	**1,966**	**1,221**	**3,224**	**1,997**	**1,227**	**360**	**82**	**278**
0-1	**177**	92	85	**177**	92	85	...	...	...	...	...	...
1-2	**179**	86	93	**179**	86	93	...	...	...	...	...	...
2-3	**209**	103	106	**209**	103	106	...	...	...	...	...	...
3-4	**207**	103	104	**207**	103	104	...	...	...	...	...	...
4-5	**197**	96	101	**197**	96	101	...	...	...	...	...	...
Total 0-5 ...	969	480	489	**969**	480	489	...	...	...	...	...	...
5-10	**842**	436	406	**833**	436	397	**9**	...	9	...	...	...
10-15	**730**	392	338	**669**	391	278	**60**	1	59	**1**	...	1
15-20	**607**	346	261	**331**	287	44	**271**	58	213	**5**	1	4
20-30	**1,270**	743	527	**326**	314	12	**917**	423	494	**27**	6	21
30-40	**1,062**	727	335	**43**	43	...	**958**	664	294	**61**	20	41
40-50	**728**	552	176	**10**	10	...	**633**	522	111	**85**	20	65
50-60	**364**	257	107	**6**	5	1	**267**	230	37	**91**	22	69
60 and over ...	**199**	112	87	...	...	...	**109**	99	10	**90**	13	77
Christian.												
All ages ...	14,651	**7,579**	**7,072**	**7,780**	**4,457**	**3,323**	**5,833**	**2,969**	**2,864**	**1,038**	**153**	**885**
0-1	**477**	248	229	**477**	248	229	...	...	...	...	...	...
1-2	**492**	240	252	**492**	240	252	...	...	...	...	...	...
2-3	**572**	302	270	**572**	302	270	...	...	...	...	...	...
3-4	**518**	277	241	**518**	277	241	...	...	...	...	...	...
4-5	**439**	211	228	**439**	211	228	...	...	...	...	...	...
Total 0-5 ...	**2,498**	1,278	1,220	**2,498**	1,278	1,220	...	...	...	...	...	...
5-10	**1,883**	926	957	**1,874**	926	948	**9**	...	9	...	...	...
10-15	**1,626**	813	813	**1,549**	812	737	**75**	1	74	**2**	...	**2**
15-20	**1,452**	720	732	**879**	642	237	**555**	77	478	**18**	1	**17**
20-30	**2,850**	1,459	1,391	**819**	678	141	**1,936**	770	1,166	**95**	11	**84**
30-40	**1,972**	1,099	873	**107**	88	19	**1,675**	988	687	**190**	23	**167**
40-50	**1,322**	717	605	**36**	26	10	**983**	656	327	**303**	35	**268**
50-60	**675**	376	299	**12**	5	7	**431**	335	96	**232**	36	**196**
60 and over ...	**373**	191	182	**6**	2	4	**169**	142	27	**198**	47	**151**

Kolar Gold Fields (City)—*concld.*

AGE	POPULATION			UNMARRIED			MARRIED			WIDOWED		
	Persons	Males	Females	Persons	Males	Females	Persons	Males	Females	Persons	Males	Females
1	2	3	4	5	6	7	8	9	10	11	12	13
Jain.												
All ages ...	**447**	**262**	**185**	**221**	**143**	**78**	**193**	**107**	**86**	**33**	**12**	**21**
0–1	21	10	11	21	10	11	...	...	...	...	...	...
1–2	15	6	9	15	6	9	...	...	...	...	...	...
2–3	16	8	8	16	8	8	...	...	...	...	...	...
3–4	16	9	7	16	9	7	...	...	...	...	...	...
4–5	15	8	7	15	8	7	...	...	...	...	...	...
Total 0–5 ...	83	41	42	83	41	42	...	...	...	...	...	...
5–10	52	27	25	49	27	22	3	...	3	...	...	...
10–15	48	26	22	38	25	13	10	1	9	...	...	...
15–20	53	34	19	22	22	...	30	12	18	1	...	1
20–30	90	56	34	20	19	1	67	37	30	3	...	3
30–40	64	41	23	5	5	...	51	32	19	8	4	4
40–50	41	30	11	3	3	...	26	20	6	12	7	5
50–60	10	7	3	1	1	...	6	5	1	3	1	2
60 and over ...	6	...	6	...	...	...	...	...	...	6	...	6
Tribal.												
All ages ...	**1**	**1**	...	...	...	...	**1**	**1**	...	...	...	...
0–1	...	...	...	...	...	...	...	...	...	...	...	...
1–2	...	...	...	...	...	...	...	...	...	...	...	...
2–3	...	...	...	...	...	...	...	...	...	...	...	...
3–4	...	...	...	...	...	...	...	...	...	...	...	...
4–5	...	...	...	...	...	...	...	...	...	...	...	...
Total 0–5 ...	...	...	...	...	...	...	...	...	...	...	...	...
5–10	...	...	...	...	...	...	...	...	...	...	...	...
10–15	...	...	...	...	...	...	...	...	...	...	...	...
15–20	...	...	...	...	...	...	...	...	...	...	...	...
20–30	...	...	...	...	...	...	...	...	...	...	...	...
30–40	1	1	...	...	...	...	1	1	...	...	...	...
40–50	...	...	...	...	...	...	...	...	...	...	...	...
50–60	...	...	...	...	...	...	...	...	...	...	...	...
60 and over ...	...	...	...	...	...	...	...	...	...	...	...	...

TABLE VII.

Age, Sex & Civil Condition

Kolar District.

AGE	POPULATION			UNMARRIED			MARRIED			WIDOWED		
	Persons	Males	Females	Persons	Males	Females	Persons	Males	Females	Persons	Males	Females
1	2	3	4	5	6	7	8	9	10	11	12	13
All Religions.												
All ages ...	763,934	389,262	374,672	346,286	205,004	141,282	328,610	161,081	167,529	89,038	23,177	65,861
0–1	18,027	8,626	9,401	18,027	8,626	9,401	...	...	...	...	...	...
1–2	18,896	9,165	9,731	18,896	9,165	9,731	...	...	...	...	...	...
2–3	21,781	10,566	11,215	21,781	10,566	11,215	...	...	...	...	...	...
3–4	22,709	11,100	11,609	22,709	11,100	11,609	...	...	...	...	...	...
4–5	22,380	11,134	11,246	22,380	11,134	11,246	...	...	...	...	...	...
Total 0–5 ...	103,793	50,591	53,202	103,793	50,591	53,202	...	...	...	...	...	...
5–10	99,568	49,869	49,699	96,998	49,826	47,172	2,540	43	2,497	30	...	30
10–15	88,360	45,408	42,952	79,246	45,107	34,139	8,949	296	8,653	165	5	160
15–20	64,861	32,182	32,679	31,542	26,827	4,715	32,096	5,226	26,870	1,223	129	1,094
20–30	133,322	63,620	69,702	27,454	26,142	1,312	98,189	36,178	62,011	7,679	1,300	6,379
30–40	107,364	56,692	50,672	4,694	4,386	308	87,586	49,086	38,500	15,084	3,220	11,864
40–50	74,475	41,392	33,083	1,376	1,182	194	53,978	35,488	18,490	19,121	4,722	14,399
50–60	46,969	25,080	21,889	653	519	134	26,717	19,246	7,471	19,599	5,315	14,284
60 and over ...	45,222	24,428	20,794	530	424	106	18,555	15,518	3,037	26,137	8,486	17,651
Hindu.												
All ages ...	696,319	353,912	342,407	311,375	184,681	126,694	300,831	147,211	153,620	84,113	22,020	62,093
0–1	16,139	7,725	8,414	16,139	7,725	8,414	...	...	...	...	...	...
1–2	16,854	8,171	8,683	16,854	8,171	8,683	...	...	...	...	...	...
2–3	19,509	9,468	10,041	19,509	9,468	10,041	...	...	...	...	...	...
3–4	20,437	9,979	10,458	20,437	9,979	10,458	...	...	...	...	...	...
4–5	20,003	9,927	10,076	20,003	9,927	10,076	...	...	...	...	...	...
Total 0–5 ...	92,942	45,270	47,672	92,942	45,270	47,672	...	...	...	...	...	...
5–10	89,517	44,704	44,813	87,062	44,666	42,396	2,426	38	2,388	29	...	29
10–15	79,707	40,879	38,828	71,265	40,605	30,660	8,289	270	8,019	153	4	149
15–20	58,750	29,068	29,682	28,319	24,166	4,153	29,272	4,789	24,483	1,159	113	1,046
20–30	121,777	57,858	63,919	24,952	23,808	1,144	89,521	32,833	56,688	7,304	1,217	6,087
30–40	98,912	52,041	46,871	4,406	4,136	270	80,190	44,842	35,348	14,316	3,063	11,253
40–50	68,860	38,161	30,699	1,300	1,124	176	49,521	32,525	16,996	18,039	4,512	13,527
50–60	43,564	23,191	20,373	620	497	123	24,509	17,630	6,879	18,435	5,064	13,371
60 and over ...	42,290	22,740	19,550	509	409	100	17,103	14,284	2,819	24,678	8,047	16,631
Musalman.												
All ages ...	58,760	30,790	27,970	30,450	17,738	12,712	24,363	12,164	12,199	3,947	888	3,059
0–1	1,662	788	874	1,662	788	874	...	...	...	...	...	...
1–2	1,840	890	950	1,840	890	950	...	...	...	...	...	...
2–3	2,029	975	1,054	2,029	975	1,054	...	...	...	...	...	...
3–4	2,028	1,000	1,028	2,028	1,000	1,028	...	...	...	...	...	...
4–5	2,105	1,069	1,036	2,105	1,069	1,036	...	...	...	...	...	...
Total 0–5 ...	9,664	4,722	4,942	9,664	4,722	4,942	...	...	...	...	...	...
5–10	8,839	4,564	4,275	8,744	4,559	4,185	95	5	90	...	...	...
10–15	7,533	3,956	3,577	6,932	3,935	2,997	589	20	569	12	1	11
15–20	5,249	2,681	2,568	2,731	2,295	436	2,470	373	2,097	48	13	35
20–30	10,017	5,018	4,999	2,099	1,991	108	7,634	2,959	4,675	284	68	216
30–40	7,304	4,043	3,261	207	184	23	6,492	3,733	2,759	605	126	479
40–50	4,824	2,792	2,032	45	36	9	3,901	2,597	1,304	878	159	719
50–60	2,877	1,602	1,275	18	11	7	1,922	1,412	510	937	179	758
60 and over ...	2,453	1,412	1,041	10	5	5	1,260	1,065	195	1,183	342	841
Christian.												
All ages ...	2,679	1,319	1,360	1,594	820	774	933	461	472	152	38	114
0–1	82	36	46	82	36	46	...	...	...	...	...	...
1–2	76	41	35	76	41	35	...	...	...	...	...	...
2–3	89	49	40	89	49	40	...	...	...	...	...	...
3–4	83	44	39	83	44	39	...	...	...	...	...	...
4–5	97	53	44	97	53	44	...	...	...	...	...	...
Total 0–5 ...	427	223	204	427	223	204	...	...	...	...	...	...
5–10	408	199	209	408	199	209	...	...	...	...	...	...
10–15	378	180	198	378	180	198	...	...	...	...	...	...
15–20	308	134	174	204	115	89	101	18	83	3	1	2
20–30	433	193	240	141	92	49	276	99	177	16	2	14
30–40	310	157	153	21	8	13	262	148	114	27	1	26
40–50	197	104	93	11	2	9	155	96	59	31	6	25
50–60	121	61	60	4	1	3	80	49	31	37	11	26
60 and over ...	97	68	29	...	...	...	59	51	8	38	17	21

Kolar District—*concld.*

AGE	POPULATION			UNMARRIED			MARRIED			WIDOWED		
	Persons	Males	Females	Persons	Males	Females	Persons	Males	Females	Persons	Males	Females
1	2	3	4	5	6	7	8	9	10	11	12	13
Jain.												
All ages ...	**6,052**	**3,173**	**2,879**	**2,803**	**1,724**	**1,079**	**2,426**	**1,218**	**1,208**	**823**	**231**	**592**
0-1	**138**	75	63	**138**	75	63	...	...	...	...	...	...
1-2	**125**	63	62	**125**	63	62	...	...	...	...	...	...
2-3	**149**	71	78	**149**	71	78	...	...	...	...	...	...
3-4	**159**	76	83	**159**	76	83	...	...	...	...	...	...
4-5	**170**	82	88	**170**	82	88	...	...	...	...	...	...
Total 0-5 ...	**741**	367	**374**	**741**	367	**374**	...	...	...	...	...	...
5-10	**783**	388	395	**763**	388	375	**19**	...	19	**1**	...	**1**
10-15	**724**	382	342	**654**	376	278	**70**	6	64	...	...	...
15-20	**546**	295	251	**285**	248	37	**248**	45	203	**13**	2	**11**
20-30	**1,075**	540	535	**258**	247	11	**743**	280	463	**74**	13	**61**
30-40	**820**	443	**377**	**60**	58	2	**624**	355	269	**136**	30	**106**
40-50	**583**	329	**254**	**20**	20	...	**390**	264	126	**173**	45	**128**
50-60	**401**	223	178	**11**	10	**1**	**201**	152	49	**189**	61	**128**
60 and over ...	**379**	206	173	**11**	10	**1**	**131**	116	15	**237**	80	**157**
Tribal.												
All ages ...	**122**	**67**	**55**	**63**	**40**	**23**	**57**	**27**	**30**	**2**	...	**2**
0-1	**6**	**2**	**4**	**6**	2	**4**	...	...	...	...	...	...
1-2	**1**	...	**1**	**1**	...	**1**	...	...	...	...	...	...
2-3	**5**	3	**2**	**5**	3	**2**	...	...	...	...	...	...
3-4	**1**	...	**1**	**1**	...	**1**	...	...	...	...	...	...
4-5	**5**	3	**2**	**5**	3	**2**	...	...	...	...	...	...
Total 0-5 ...	**18**	8	10	**18**	8	10	...	...	...	...	...	...
5-10	**21**	14	**7**	**21**	14	**7**	...	...	...	...	...	...
10-15	**18**	11	**7**	**17**	11	6	**1**	...	**1**	...	...	...
15-20	**8**	4	**4**	**3**	3	...	**5**	**1**	**4**	...	...	...
20-30	**19**	11	**8**	**4**	4	...	**15**	**7**	**8**	...	...	...
30-40	**18**	8	10	...	...	...	**18**	8	10	...	...	...
40-50	**11**	6	**5**	...	...	...	**11**	6	**5**	...	...	...
50-60	**6**	3	**3**	...	...	...	**5**	3	**2**	**1**	...	**1**
60 and over ...	**3**	2	1	...	...	...	**2**	2	...	**1**	...	**1**

TABLE VII.

Age, Sex & Civil Condition.

Tumkur District.

AGE	POPULATION			UNMARRIED			MARRIED			WIDOWED		
	Persons	Males	Females	Persons	Males	Females	Persons	Males	Females	Persons	Males	Females
1	2	3	4	5	6	7	8	9	10	11	12	13
All Religions.												
All ages ...	**861,405**	**439,144**	**422,261**	**422,411**	**248,400**	**174,011**	**343,522**	**167,813**	**175,709**	**95,472**	**22,931**	**72,541**
0–1	**24,378**	12,216	12,162	**24,378**	12,216	12,162	...	...	...	...	...	...
1–2	**24,437**	12,023	12,414	**24,437**	12,023	12,414	...	...	...	...	...	...
2–3	**25,931**	12,500	13,431	**25,931**	12,500	13,431	...	...	...	...	...	...
3–4	**26,381**	12,928	13,453	**26,372**	12,927	13,445	**9**	1	8	...	...	...
4–5	**26.251**	13,086	13,165	**26,233**	13,083	13,150	**18**	3	15	...	...	...
Total 0–5 ...	**127,378**	62,753	64,625	**127,351**	62,749	64,602	**27**	4	23	...	...	...
5–10	**119,478**	59,568	59,910	**116,709**	59,489	57,220	**2,709**	73	2,636	**60**	6	54
10–15	**107,861**	55,421	52,440	**97,543**	55,125	42,418	**10,130**	287	9,843	**188**	9	179
15–20	**76,238**	38,272	37,966	**38,995**	32,766	6,229	**35,873**	5,399	30,474	**1,370**	107	1,263
20–30	**146,836**	70,688	76,148	**32,615**	30,553	2,062	**105,302**	38,931	66,371	**8,919**	1,204	7,715
30–40	**115,977**	62,029	53,948	**6,038**	5,334	704	**92,459**	53,419	39,040	**17,480**	3,276	14,204
40–50	**76,574**	42,491	34,083	**1,677**	1,310	367	**53,811**	36,246	17,565	**21,086**	4,935	16,151
50–60	**46,784**	24,435	22,349	**810**	594	216	**25,641**	18,675	6,966	**20,333**	5,166	15,167
60 and over ...	**44,279**	23,487	20,792	**673**	480	193	**17,570**	14,779	2,791	**26,036**	8,228	17,808
Hindu.												
All ages ...	**806,673**	**410,649**	**396,024**	**393,396**	**231,385**	**162,011**	**322,221**	**157,334**	**164,887**	**91,056**	**21,930**	**69,126**
0–1	**22,788**	11,394	11,394	**22,788**	11,394	11,394	...	...	...	...	...	...
1–2	**22,753**	11,178	11,575	**22,753**	11,178	11,575	...	...	...	...	...	...
2–3	**24,121**	11,621	12,500	**24,121**	11,621	12,500	...	...	...	...	...	...
3–4	**24,529**	12,025	12,504	**24,520**	12,024	12,496	**9**	1	8	...	...	...
4–5	**24,394**	12,164	12,230	**24,376**	12,161	12,215	**18**	3	15	...	...	...
Total 0–5 ...	**118,585**	58,382	60,203	**118,558**	58,378	60,180	**27**	4	23	...	...	...
5–10	**111,199**	55,373	55,826	**108,544**	55,299	53,245	**2,597**	68	2,529	**58**	6	52
10–15	**100,554**	51,591	48,963	**90,789**	51,308	39,481	**9,589**	274	9,315	**176**	9	167
15–20	**71,232**	35,707	35,525	**36,236**	30,500	5,736	**33,686**	5,110	28 576	**1,310**	97	1,213
20–30	**137,733**	66,164	71,569	**30,470**	28,540	1,930	**98,680**	36,480	62,200	**8,583**	1,144	7,439
30–40	**109,252**	58,375	50,877	**5,759**	5,080	679	**86,745**	50,155	36,590	**16,748**	3,140	13,608
40–50	**72,078**	39,878	32,200	**1,604**	1,243	361	**50,366**	33,893	16,473	**20,108**	4,742	15,366
50–60	**44,184**	23,031	21,153	**780**	571	209	**24,052**	17,500	6,552	**19,352**	4,960	14,392
60 and over ...	**41,856**	22,148	19,708	**656**	466	190	**16,479**	13,850	2,629	**24,721**	7,882	16,889
Musalman.												
All ages ...	**44,390**	**23,116**	**21,274**	**23,952**	**13,967**	**9,985**	**17,127**	**8,432**	**8,695**	**3,311**	**717**	**2,594**
0–1	**1,314**	689	625	**1,314**	689	625	...	...	...	...	...	...
1–2	**1,413**	698	715	**1,413**	698	715	...	...	...	...	...	...
2–3	**1,510**	723	787	**1,510**	723	787	...	...	...	...	...	...
3–4	**1,541**	750	791	**1,541**	750	791	...	...	...	...	...	...
4–5	**1,566**	782	784	**1,566**	782	784	...	...	...	...	...	...
Total 0–5 ...	**7,344**	3,642	3,702	**7,344**	3,642	3,702	...	...	...	...	...	...
5–10	**6,872**	3,504	3,368	**6,800**	3,501	3,299	**70**	3	67	**2**	...	2
10–15	**6,034**	3,167	2,867	**5,597**	3,157	2,440	**429**	10	419	**8**	...	8
15–20	**4,069**	2,100	1,969	**2,272**	1,865	407	**1,754**	227	1,527	**43**	8	35
20–30	**7,315**	3,622	3,693	**1,689**	1,585	104	**5,377**	1,991	3,386	**249**	46	203
30–40	**5,363**	2,896	2,467	**184**	165	19	**4,634**	2,635	1,999	**545**	96	449
40–50	**3,553**	2,082	1,471	**45**	40	5	**2,789**	1,915	874	**719**	127	592
50–60	**2,007**	1,092	915	**13**	7	6	**1,236**	929	307	**758**	156	602
60 and over ...	**1,833**	1,011	822	**8**	5	3	**838**	722	116	**987**	284	703
Christian.												
All ages ...	**1,620**	**892**	**728**	**947**	**571**	**376**	**582**	**298**	**284**	**91**	**23**	**68**
0–1	**52**	28	24	**52**	28	24	...	...	...	...	...	...
1–2	**58**	33	25	**58**	33	25	...	...	...	...	...	...
2–3	**53**	27	26	**53**	27	26	...	...	...	...	...	...
3–4	**56**	28	28	**56**	28	28	...	...	...	...	...	...
4–5	**54**	24	30	**54**	24	30	...	...	...	...	...	...
Total 0–5 ...	**273**	140	133	**273**	140	133	...	...	...	...	...	...
5–10	**240**	126	114	**238**	125	113	**2**	1	1	...	...	...
10–15	**205**	124	81	**201**	124	77	**4**	...	4	...	...	...
15–20	**150**	87	63	**111**	82	29	**38**	5	33	**1**	...	1
20–30	**299**	154	145	**108**	89	19	**185**	63	122	**6**	2	4
30–40	**199**	108	91	**11**	7	4	**171**	99	72	**17**	2	15
40–50	**123**	74	49	**1**	1	...	**95**	67	28	**27**	6	21
50–60	**68**	43	25	**3**	2	1	**49**	37	12	**16**	4	12
60 and over ...	**63**	36	27	**1**	1	...	**38**	26	12	**24**	9	15

TABLE VII.

Age, Sex & Civil Condition.

Tumkur District—*concld.*

AGE	POPULATION			UNMARRIED			MARRIED			WIDOWED		
	Persons	Males	Females	Persons	Males	Females	Persons	Males	Females	Persons	Males	Females
1	2	3	4	5	6	7	8	9	10	11	12	13
Jain.												
All ages ...	**7,340**	**3,814**	**3,526**	**3,406**	**2,097**	**1,311**	**3,004**	**1,483**	**1,521**	**928**	**234**	**694**
0–1	**167**	80	87	**167**	80	87	...	...	...	...	...	...
1–2	**162**	84	78	**162**	84	78	...	...	...	...	...	...
2–3	**196**	103	93	**196**	103	93	...	...	...	...	...	...
3–4	**201**	99	102	**201**	99	102	...	...	...	...	...	...
4–5	**191**	94	97	**191**	94	97	...	...	...	...	...	...
Total 0–5 ...	**917**	460	457	917	460	457	...	...	...	...	...	...
5–10	**958**	473	485	**925**	472	453	**33**	1	32	...	...	...
10–15	**898**	461	437	**803**	459	344	**91**	2	89	**4**	...	4
15–20	**684**	332	352	**332**	282	50	**337**	48	289	**15**	2	13
20–30	**1,263**	647	616	**308**	303	5	**880**	336	544	**75**	8	67
30–40	**1,003**	566	437	**76**	75	1	**764**	454	310	**163**	37	126
40–50	**695**	389	306	**26**	25	1	**462**	312	150	**207**	52	155
50–60	**460**	236	224	**13**	13	...	**258**	179	79	**189**	44	145
60 and over ...	**462**	250	212	**8**	8	...	**179**	151	28	**275**	91	184
Tribal.												
All ages ...	**1,381**	**672**	**709**	**707**	**379**	**328**	**588**	**266**	**322**	**86**	**27**	**59**
0–1	**57**	25	32	**57**	25	32	...	...	...	...	...	...
1–2	**51**	30	21	**51**	30	21	...	...	...	...	...	...
2–3	**51**	26	25	**51**	26	25	...	...	...	...	...	...
3–4	**54**	26	28	**54**	26	28	...	...	...	...	...	...
4–5	**46**	22	24	**46**	22	24	...	...	...	...	...	...
Total 0–5 ...	**259**	129	130	**259**	129	130	...	...	...	...	...	...
5–10	**209**	92	117	**202**	92	110	**7**	...	7	...	...	...
10–15	**170**	78	92	**153**	77	76	**17**	1	16	...	...	...
15–20	**103**	46	57	**44**	37	7	**58**	9	49	**1**	...	1
20–30	**226**	101	125	**40**	36	4	**180**	61	119	**6**	4	2
30–40	**160**	84	76	**8**	7	1	**145**	76	69	**7**	1	6
40–50	**124**	67	57	...	...	...	**99**	59	40	**25**	8	17
50–60	**65**	33	32	**1**	1	...	**46**	30	16	**18**	2	16
60 and over ...	**65**	42	23	...	...	...	**36**	30	6	**29**	12	17

TABLE VII.

Age, Sex & Civil Condition.

Mysore City.

AGE	POPULATION			UNMARRIED			MARRIED			WIDOWED		
	Persons	Males	Females	Persons	Males	Females	Persons	Males	Females	Persons	Males	Females
1	2	3	4	5	6	7	8	9	10	11	12	13
All Religions.												
All ages ...	**107,142**	**56,772**	**50,370**	**50,340**	**31,014**	**19,326**	**46,007**	**23,346**	**22,661**	**10,795**	**2,412**	**8,383**
0-1	**2,470**	1,248	1,222	**2,470**	1,248	1,222	...	...	...	...	...	...
1-2	**2,576**	1,290	1,286	**2,576**	1,290	1,286	...	...	...	...	...	...
2-3	**2,957**	1,444	1,513	**2,957**	1,444	1,513	...	...	...	...	...	...
3-4	**2,938**	1,443	1,495	**2,938**	1,443	1,495	...	...	...	...	...	...
4-5	**2,818**	1,396	1,422	**2,818**	1,396	1,422	...	...	...	...	...	...
Total 0-5 ...	**13,759**	6,821	6,938	**13,759**	6,821	6,938	...	...	...	...	...	...
5-10	**13,695**	7,091	6,604	**13,357**	7,083	6,274	**332**	8	324	**6**	...	6
10-15	**13,024**	6,947	6,077	**11,613**	6,910	4,703	**1,389**	37	1,352	**22**	...	22
15-20	**11,036**	5,975	5,061	**5,830**	1,996	834	**5,010**	959	4,051	**196**	20	176
20-30	**20,153**	10,539	9,614	**4,933**	4,541	392	**14,233**	5,812	8,421	**987**	186	801
30-40	**14,865**	8,089	6,776	**544**	458	86	**12,338**	7,246	5,092	**1,983**	385	1,598
40-50	**10,042**	5,619	4,423	**169**	120	49	**7,269**	4,979	2,290	**2,604**	520	2,084
50-60	**5,898**	3,209	2,689	**78**	49	29	**3,436**	2,613	823	**2,384**	547	1,837
60 and over ...	**4,670**	2,482	2,188	**57**	36	21	**2,000**	1,692	308	**2,613**	754	1,859
Hindu.												
All ages ...	**84,789**	**44,734**	**40,055**	**38,914**	**24,123**	**14,791**	**36,842**	**18,618**	**18,224**	**9,033**	**1,993**	**7,040**
0-1	**1,961**	979	982	**1,961**	979	982	...	...	...	...	...	...
1-2	**2,047**	1,003	1,044	**2,047**	1,003	1,044	...	...	...	...	...	...
2-3	**2,344**	1,135	1,209	**2,344**	1,135	1,209	...	...	...	...	...	...
3-4	**2,306**	1,136	1,170	**2,306**	1,136	1,170	...	...	...	...	...	...
4-5	**2,202**	1,095	1,107	**2,202**	1,095	1,107	...	...	...	...	...	...
Total 0-5 ...	**10,860**	5,348	5,512	**10,860**	5,348	5,512	...	...	...	...	...	...
5-10	**10,817**	5,603	5,214	**10,498**	5,596	4,902	**314**	7	307	**5**	...	5
10-15	**10,317**	5,539	4,778	**9,088**	5,508	3,580	**1,208**	31	1,177	**21**	...	21
15-20	**8,701**	4,780	3,921	**4,394**	3,913	481	**4,139**	850	3,289	**168**	17	151
20-30	**15,846**	8,250	7,596	**3,520**	3,311	209	**11,468**	4,786	6,682	**858**	153	706
30-40	**11,856**	6,368	5,488	**363**	309	54	**9,791**	5,748	4,043	**1,702**	311	1,391
40-50	**8,043**	4,433	3,610	**111**	81	30	**5,741**	3,916	1,825	**2,191**	436	1,755
50-60	**4,705**	2,498	2,207	**49**	34	15	**2,674**	2,010	664	**1,982**	454	1,528
60 and over ...	**3,644**	1,915	1,729	**31**	23	8	**1,507**	1,270	237	**2,106**	622	1,484
Músalman.												
All ages ...	17,772	9,661	**8,111**	8,846	**5,422**	**3,424**	**7,539**	**3,898**	**3,641**	**1,387**	**341**	**1,046**
0-1	**386**	196	190	**386**	196	190	...	...	...	...	...	...
1-2	**415**	221	194	**415**	221	194	...	...	...	...	...	...
2-3	**494**	251	243	**494**	251	243	...	...	...	...	...	...
3-4	**513**	251	262	**513**	251	262	...	...	...	...	...	...
4-5	**502**	248	254	**502**	248	254	...	...	...	...	...	...
Total 0-5 ...	**2,310**	1,167	1,143	**2,310**	1,167	1,143	...	...	...	...	...	...
5-10	**2,307**	1,199	1,108	**2,289**	1,198	1,091	**18**	1	**17**	...	...	...
10-15	**2,130**	1,114	1,016	**1,979**	1,110	869	**151**	4	147	...	...	...
15-20	**1,784**	915	869	**1,043**	824	219	**722**	88	634	**19**	3	16
20-30	**3,415**	1,835	1,580	**1,041**	963	78	**2,280**	845	1,435	**94**	27	67
30-40	**2,418**	1,396	1,022	**126**	114	12	**2,079**	1,221	858	**213**	61	152
40-50	**1,601**	964	637	**28**	26	2	**1,245**	872	373	**328**	66	262
50-60	**968**	592	376	**15**	10	5	**634**	511	123	**319**	71	248
60 and over ...	**839**	479	360	**15**	10	5	**410**	356	54	**414**	113	301
Christian.												
All ages ...	3,947	**1,956**	**1,991**	**2,236**	**1,215**	**1,021**	**1,390**	**683**	**707**	**321**	**58**	**263**
0-1	**105**	63	42	**105**	63	42	...	...	...	...	...	...
1-2	**100**	58	42	**100**	58	42	...	...	...	...	...	...
2-3	**105**	51	54	**105**	51	54	...	...	...	...	...	...
3-4	**104**	49	55	**104**	49	55	...	...	...	...	...	...
4-5	**98**	46	52	**98**	46	52	...	...	...	...	...	...
Total 0-5 ...	**512**	267	245	**512**	267	245	...	...	...	...	...	...
5-10	**497**	243	254	**497**	243	254	...	...	...	...	...	...
10-15	**501**	239	262	**473**	237	236	**27**	2	25	**1**	...	1
15-20	**468**	218	250	**336**	205	131	**124**	13	111	**8**	...	8
20-30	**755**	362	393	**323**	221	102	**403**	138	265	**29**	3	26
30-40	**503**	263	240	**44**	25	19	**403**	229	174	**56**	9	47
40-50	**344**	186	158	**26**	9	17	**245**	164	81	**73**	13	60
50-60	**202**	102	100	**14**	5	9	**113**	79	34	**75**	18	57
60 and over ...	**165**	76	89	**11**	3	8	**75**	58	17	**79**	15	64

TABLE VII.

Age, Sex & Civil Condition.

Mysore City—*concld.*

AGE	POPULATION			UNMARRIED			MARRIED			WIDOWED		
	Persons	Males	Females	Persons	Males	Females	Persons	Males	Females	Persons	Males	Females
1	2	3	4	5	6	7	8	9	10	11	12	13
Jain.												
All ages ...	**549**	**372**	177	**296**	**226**	70	**205**	**128**	**77**	**48**	**18**	**30**
0–1	**14**	8	6	**14**	8	6	...	...	...	...	...	...
1–2	**13**	7	6	**13**	7	6	...	...	...	...	...	...
2–3	**12**	6	6	**12**	6	6	...	...	...	...	...	...
3–4	**13**	6	7	**13**	6	7	...	...	...	...	...	...
4–5	**13**	6	7	**13**	6	7	...	...	...	...	...	...
Total 0–5 ...	**65**	33	32	**65**	33	32	...	...	...	...	...	...
5–10	**66**	42	24	**65**	42	23	...	...	...	**1**	...	1
10–15	**64**	48	16	**61**	48	13	**3**	...	3	...	...	...
15–20	**72**	56	16	**48**	48	...	**24**	8	16	...	...	...
20–30	**124**	85	39	**44**	42	2	**75**	40	35	**5**	3	2
30–40	**74**	53	21	**9**	9	...	**54**	41	13	**11**	3	8
40–50	**45**	31	14	**4**	4	...	**30**	22	8	**11**	5	6
50–60	**21**	15	6	...	...	...	**13**	11	2	**8**	4	4
60 and over ...	**18**	9	9	...	...	...	**6**	6	...	**12**	3	9
Tribal.												
All ages ...	**7**	6	1	...	...	...	**7**	6	1	...	...	...
0–1	...	...	...	...	...	...	...	...	...	...	...	...
1–2	...	...	...	...	...	...	...	...	...	...	...	...
2–3	...	...	...	...	...	...	...	...	...	...	...	...
3–4	...	...	...	...	...	...	...	...	...	...	...	...
4–5	...	...	...	...	...	...	...	...	...	...	...	...
Total 0–5 ...	...	...	...	...	...	...	...	...	...	...	...	...
5–10	...	...	...	...	...	...	...	...	...	...	...	...
10–15	...	...	...	...	...	...	...	...	...	...	...	...
15–20	...	...	...	...	...	...	...	...	...	...	...	...
20–30	**1**	1	...	...	...	...	**1**	1	...	...	...	...
30–40	**4**	3	1	...	...	...	**4**	3	1	...	...	...
40–50	**2**	2	...	...	...	...	**2**	2	...	...	...	...
50–60	...	...	...	...	...	...	...	...	...	...	...	...
60 and over ...	...	...	...	...	...	...	...	...	...	...	...	...

TABLE VII.

Age, Sex & Civil Condition.

Mysore District.

AGE	POPULATION			UNMARRIED			MARRIED			WIDOWED		
	Persons	Males	Females	Persons	Males	Females	Persons	Males	Females	Persons	Males	Females
1	2	3	4	5	6	7	8	9	10	11	12	13
All Religions.												
All ages ...	**1,403,984**	**703,838**	**700,146**	**667,778**	**388,276**	**269,502**	**589,897**	**288,600**	**301,297**	**156,309**	**26,962**	**129,347**
0-1	**37,475**	18,381	19,094	**37,475**	18,381	19,094	...	...	...	...	...	...
1-2	**39,343**	19,410	19,933	**39,343**	19,410	19,933	...	...	...	...	...	...
2-3	**41,201**	20,149	21,052	**41,201**	20,149	21,052	...	...	...	...	...	...
3-4	**40,185**	19,691	20,494	**40,185**	19,691	20,494	...	...	...	...	...	...
4-5	**40,352**	20,107	20,245	**40,352**	20,107	20,245	...	...	...	...	...	...
Total 0-5 ...	**198,556**	97,738	100,818	**198,556**	97,738	100,818	...	...	...	...	...	...
5-10	**193,075**	96,699	96,376	**185,546**	96,690	88,847	**7,460**	...	7,460	**69**	...	69
10-15	**179,097**	92,838	86,259	**157,592**	92,229	65,363	**21,160**	594	20,566	**345**	15	330
15-20	**125,816**	63,025	62,791	**62,271**	53,128	9,143	**61,218**	9,731	51,487	**2,327**	166	2,161
20-30	**236,802**	110,844	125,958	**45,667**	42,113	3,554	**177,090**	67,087	110,003	**14,045**	1,644	12,401
30-40	**193,334**	100,494	92,840	**5,605**	4,651	954	**158,093**	91,767	66,326	**29,636**	4,076	25,560
40-50	**130,350**	69,623	60,727	**1,504**	1,071	433	**92,461**	62,796	29,665	**36,385**	5,756	30,629
50-60	**78,824**	39,260	39,564	**593**	386	207	**44,113**	32,692	11,421	**34,118**	6,182	27,936
60 and over ...	**68,130**	33,317	34,813	**444**	261	183	**28,302**	23,933	4,369	**39,384**	9,123	30,261
Hindu.												
All ages ...	**1,348,180**	**674,201**	**673,979**	**629,297**	**371,176**	**258,121**	**567,342**	**277,097**	**290,245**	**151,541**	**25,928**	**125,613**
0-1	**35,995**	17,644	18,351	**35,995**	17,644	18,351	...	...	...	...	...	...
1-2	**37,755**	18,596	19,159	**37,755**	18,596	19,159	...	...	...	...	...	...
2-3	**39,547**	19,309	20,238	**39,547**	19,309	20,238	...	...	...	...	...	...
3-4	**38,567**	18,883	19,684	**38,567**	18,883	19,684	...	...	...	...	...	...
4-5	**38,594**	19,224	19,370	**38,594**	19,224	19,370	...	...	...	...	...	...
Total 0-5 ...	**190,458**	93,656	96,802	**190,458**	93,656	96,802	...	...	...	...	...	...
5-10	**185,177**	92,625	92,552	**177,733**	92,625	85,108	**7,375**	...	7,375	**69**	...	69
10-15	**171,909**	89,036	82,873	**150,924**	88,430	62,494	**20,648**	591	20,057	**337**	15	322
15-20	**120,571**	60,269	60,302	**59,298**	50,703	8,595	**59,027**	9,409	49,618	**2,246**	157	2,089
20-30	**226,981**	105,910	121,071	**43,154**	39,766	3,388	**170,202**	64,588	105,614	**13,625**	1,556	12,069
30-40	**185,895**	96,294	89,601	**5,287**	4,354	933	**151,837**	88,045	63,792	**28,771**	3,895	24,876
40-50	**125,474**	66,743	58,731	**1,441**	1,016	425	**88,752**	60,196	28,556	**35,281**	5,531	29,750
50-60	**75,962**	37,635	38,327	**569**	371	198	**42,330**	31,300	11,030	**33,063**	5,964	27,099
60 and over ...	**65,753**	32,033	33,720	**433**	255	178	**27,171**	22,968	4,203	**38,149**	8,810	29,339
Musalman.												
All ages ...	**43,485**	**23,231**	**20,254**	**22,591**	**13,639**	**8,952**	**17,224**	**8,801**	**8,423**	**3,670**	**791**	**2,879**
0-1	**1,109**	568	541	**1,109**	568	541	...	...	...	...	...	...
1-2	**1,243**	638	605	**1,243**	638	605	...	...	...	...	...	...
2-3	**1,294**	651	643	**1,294**	651	643	...	...	...	...	...	...
3-4	**1,283**	638	645	**1,283**	638	645	...	...	...	...	...	...
4-5	**1,364**	680	684	**1,364**	680	684	...	...	...	...	...	...
Total 0-5 ...	**6,293**	3,175	3,118	**6,293**	3,175	3,118	...	...	...	...	...	...
5-10	**6,271**	3,228	3,043	**6,212**	3,228	2,984	**59**	...	59	...	...	...
10-15	**5,721**	3,041	2,680	**5,335**	3,041	2,294	**378**	...	378	**8**	...	8
15-20	**4,069**	2,192	1,877	**2,374**	1,961	413	**1,640**	225	1,415	**55**	6	49
20-30	**7,551**	3,856	3,693	**2,033**	1,926	108	**5,214**	1,870	3,344	**304**	63	241
30-40	**5,673**	3,205	2,468	**264**	249	15	**4,753**	2,818	1,935	**656**	138	518
40-50	**3,750**	2,202	1,548	**52**	45	7	**2,850**	1,994	856	**848**	163	685
50-60	**2,263**	1,292	971	**20**	12	8	**1,418**	1,110	308	**825**	170	655
60 and over ...	**1,894**	1,038	856	**8**	3	5	**912**	784	128	**974**	251	723
Christian.												
All ages ...	**3,375**	**1,828**	**1,547**	**1,763**	**1,068**	**695**	**1,348**	**709**	**639**	**264**	**51**	**213**
0-1	**112**	53	59	**112**	53	59	...	...	...	...	...	...
1-2	**95**	48	47	**95**	48	47	...	...	...	...	...	...
2-3	**97**	52	45	**97**	52	45	...	...	...	...	...	...
3-4	**80**	44	36	**80**	44	36	...	...	...	...	...	...
4-5	**114**	61	53	**114**	61	53	...	...	...	...	...	...
Total 0-5 ...	**498**	258	240	**498**	258	240	...	...	...	...	...	...
5-10	**462**	239	223	**462**	239	223	...	...	...	...	...	...
10-15	**414**	212	202	**387**	212	175	**27**	...	27	...	...	...
15-20	**341**	184	157	**204**	165	39	**133**	19	114	**4**	...	4
20-30	**632**	336	296	**184**	168	16	**421**	164	257	**27**	4	23
30-40	**461**	265	196	**23**	21	2	**380**	232	148	**58**	12	46
40-50	**301**	189	112	**4**	4	...	**232**	167	65	**65**	18	47
50-60	**160**	93	67	**1**	1	...	**106**	85	21	**53**	7	46
60 and over ...	**106**	52	54	...	...	...	**49**	42	7	**57**	10	47

Mysore District—*concld.*

AGE	POPULATION			UNMARRIED			MARRIED			WIDOWED		
	Persons	Males	Females	Persons	Males	Females	Persons	Males	Females	Persons	Males	Females
1	2	3	4	5	6	7	8	9	10	11	12	13
Jain.												
All ages ...	**2,514**	**1,250**	**1,264**	**1,121**	**684**	**437**	**1,006**	**500**	**506**	**387**	**66**	**321**
0-1	81	40	41	81	40	41	...	...	...	...	...	...
1-2	66	34	32	66	34	32	...	...	...	...	...	...
2-3	67	36	31	67	36	31	...	...	...	...	...	...
3-4	58	30	28	58	30	28	...	...	...	...	...	...
4-5	75	38	37	75	38	37	...	...	...	...	...	...
Total 0-5 ...	347	178	169	347	178	169	...	...	...	...	...	...
5-10	317	162	155	305	162	143	12	...	12	...	...	...
10-15	292	150	142	255	150	105	37	...	37	...	...	...
15-20	239	122	117	106	92	14	127	30	97	6	...	6
20-30	439	206	233	87	82	5	307	118	189	45	6	39
30-40	326	173	153	12	11	1	244	155	89	70	7	63
40-50	238	122	116	4	4	...	153	102	51	81	16	65
50-60	156	70	86	2	2	...	68	49	19	86	19	67
60 and over ...	160	67	93	3	3	...	58	46	12	99	18	81
Tribal.												
All ages ...	**6,390**	**3,312**	**3,078**	**2,987**	**1,700**	**1,287**	**2,961**	**1,487**	**1,474**	**442**	**125**	**317**
0-1	176	75	101	176	75	101	...	...	...	...	...	...
1-2	184	94	90	184	94	90	...	...	...	...	...	...
2-3	193	100	93	193	100	93	...	...	...	...	...	...
3-4	195	96	99	195	96	99	...	...	...	...	...	...
4-5	204	103	101	204	103	101	...	...	...	...	...	...
Total 0-5 ...	952	468	484	952	468	484	...	...	...	...	...	...
5-10	845	444	401	831	444	387	14	...	14	...	...	...
10-15	758	398	360	688	395	293	70	3	67	...	...	...
15-20	591	255	336	286	205	81	289	47	242	16	3	13
20-30	1,191	531	660	207	170	37	941	346	595	43	15	28
30-40	975	556	419	19	16	3	876	516	360	80	24	56
40-50	583	366	217	3	2	1	471	336	135	109	28	81
50-60	281	169	112	1	...	1	189	147	42	91	22	69
60 and over ...	214	125	89	...	...	...	111	92	19	103	33	70

TABLE VII.

Age, Sex & Civil Condition.

Chitaldrug District.

AGE	POPULATION			UNMARRIED			MARRIED			WIDOWED		
	Persons	Males	Females	Persons	Males	Females	Persons	Males	Females	Persons	Males	Females
1	2	3	4	5	6	7	8	9	10	11	12	13
All Religions.												
All ages ...	**656,569**	**336,786**	**319,783**	**328,182**	**192,182**	**136,000**	**254,337**	**124,632**	**129,705**	**74,050**	**19,972**	**54,078**
0–1	**18,381**	9,064	9,317	**18,381**	9,064	9,317	...	...	...	...	...	...
1–2	**18,772**	9,089	9,683	**18,772**	9,089	9,688	...	...	...	...	...	...
2–3	**20,262**	9,723	10,539	**20,262**	9,723	10,539	...	...	...	...	...	...
3–4	**20,564**	9,939	10,625	**20,553**	9,935	10,618	**10**	4	6	**1**	...	1
4–5	**20,593**	9,980	10,613	**20,581**	9,977	10,604	12	3	9	...	...	...
Total 0–5 ...	**98,572**	47,795	50,777	**98,549**	47,788	50,761	**22**	7	15	**1**	...	**1**
5–10	**89,502**	44,499	45,003	**87,780**	44,439	43,341	**1,683**	56	1,627	**39**	4	35
10–15	**81,562**	42,109	39,453	**74,110**	41,889	32,221	**7,292**	210	7,082	**160**	10	150
15–20	**61,093**	30,779	30,314	**32,286**	26,516	5,770	**27,600**	4,149	23,451	**1,207**	114	1,093
20–30	**116,782**	57,060	59,722	**27,358**	25,210	2,148	**81,342**	30,643	50,699	**8,082**	1,207	6,875
30–40	**88,907**	48,235	40,672	**5,500**	4,619	881	**68,222**	40,257	27,965	**15,185**	3,359	11,826
40–50	**56,323**	31,994	24,329	**1,493**	1,073	420	**38,153**	26,370	11,783	**16,677**	4,551	12,126
50–60	**33,296**	17,564	15,732	**605**	376	229	**17,785**	12,825	4,960	**14,906**	4,363	10,543
60 and over ...	**30,532**	16,751	13,781	**501**	272	229	**12,238**	10,115	2,123	**17,793**	6,364	11,429
Hindu.												
All ages ...	**614,755**	**314,839**	**299,916**	**306,277**	**179,460**	**126,817**	**237,676**	**116,241**	**121,435**	**70,802**	**19,138**	**51,664**
0–1	**17,039**	8,388	8,651	**17,039**	8,388	8,651	...	...	...	...	...	...
1–2	**17,403**	8,430	8,973	**17,403**	8,430	8,973	...	...	...	...	...	...
2–3	**18,803**	9,043	9,760	**18,803**	9,043	9,760	...	...	...	...	...	...
3–4	**19,023**	9,234	9,789	**19,013**	9,231	9,782	**9**	3	6	**1**	...	1
4–5	**18,932**	9,276	9,656	**18,920**	9,273	9,647	**12**	3	9	...	...	...
Total 0–5 ...	**91,200**	44,371	46,829	**91,178**	44,365	46,813	**21**	6	15	**1**	...	**1**
5–10	**83,448**	41,399	42,049	**81,826**	41,349	40,477	**1,587**	46	1,541	**35**	4	81
10–15	**76,356**	39,288	37,068	**69,382**	39,089	30,293	**6,822**	189	6,633	**152**	10	142
15–20	**57,144**	28,740	28,404	**30,262**	24,817	5,445	**25,719**	3,814	21,905	**1,163**	109	1,054
20–30	**109,463**	53,346	56,117	**25,809**	23,753	2,056	**75,871**	28,447	47,424	**7,783**	1,146	6,637
30–40	**83,671**	45,296	38,375	**5,302**	4,438	864	**63,825**	37,646	26,179	**14,544**	3,212	11,332
40–50	**53,205**	30,138	23,067	**1,444**	1,029	415	**35,777**	24,709	11,068	**15,984**	4,400	11,584
50–60	**31,411**	16,493	14,918	**585**	358	227	**16,612**	11,948	4,664	**14,214**	4,187	10,027
60 and over ...	**28,857**	15,768	13,089	**489**	262	227	**11,442**	9,436	2,006	**16,926**	6,070	10,856
Musalman.												
All ages ...	**36,841**	**19,271**	**17,570**	**19,315**	**11,183**	**8,132**	**14,650**	**7,356**	**7,294**	**2,876**	**732**	**2,144**
0–1	**1,184**	605	579	**1,184**	605	579	...	...	...	...	...	...
1–2	**1,208**	578	630	**1,208**	578	630	...	...	...	...	...	...
2–3	**1,289**	598	691	**1,289**	598	691	...	...	...	...	...	...
3–4	**1,346**	614	732	**1,346**	614	732	...	...	...	...	...	...
4–5	**1,497**	631	866	**1,497**	631	866	...	...	...	...	...	...
Total 0–5 ...	**6,524**	3,026	3,498	**6,524**	3,026	3,498	...	...	...	...	...	...
5–10	**5,343**	2,734	2,609	**5,257**	2,727	2,530	**82**	7	75	**4**	...	4
10–15	**4,597**	2,473	2,124	**4,164**	2,455	1,709	**426**	18	408	**7**	...	7
15–20	**3,488**	1,793	1,695	**1,783**	1,495	288	**1,667**	294	1,373	**38**	4	34
20–30	**6,449**	3,258	3,191	**1,355**	1,271	84	**4,828**	1,933	2,895	**266**	54	212
30–40	**4,581**	2,566	2,015	**171**	155	16	**3,848**	2,289	1,559	**562**	122	440
40–50	**2,726**	1,616	1,110	**40**	36	4	**2,071**	1,446	625	**615**	134	481
50–60	**1,645**	927	718	**13**	11	2	**1,021**	767	254	**611**	149	462
60 and over ...	**1,488**	878	610	**8**	7	1	**707**	602	105	**773**	269	504
Christian.												
All ages ...	**515**	**275**	**240**	**271**	**153**	**118**	**222**	**118**	**104**	**22**	**4**	**18**
0–1	**19**	7	12	**19**	7	12	...	...	...	...	...	...
1–2	**22**	10	12	**22**	10	12	...	...	...	...	...	...
2–3	**24**	12	12	**24**	12	12	...	...	...	...	...	...
3–4	**23**	11	12	**23**	11	12	...	...	...	...	...	...
4–5	**10**	4	6	**10**	4	6	...	...	...	...	...	...
Total 0–5 ...	**98**	44	54	**98**	44	54	...	...	...	...	...	...
5–10	**62**	31	31	**62**	31	31	...	...	...	...	...	...
10–15	**52**	29	23	**51**	29	22	**1**	...	1	...	...	...
15–20	**52**	25	27	**26**	20	6	**26**	5	21	...	...	...
20–30	**109**	58	51	**27**	25	2	**77**	32	45	**5**	1	4
30–40	**68**	43	25	**3**	2	1	**61**	40	21	**4**	1	3
40–50	**39**	22	17	**1**	...	1	**31**	21	10	**7**	1	6
50–60	**26**	17	9	**1**	1	...	**21**	15	6	**4**	1	3
60 and over ...	**9**	6	3	**2**	1	1	**5**	5	...	**2**	...	2

Chitaldrug District—*concld.*

AGE	POPULATION			UNMARRIED			MARRIED			WIDOWED		
	Persons	Males	Females	Persons	Males	Females	Persons	Males	Females	Persons	Males	Females
1	2	3	4	5	6	7	8	9	10	11	12	13
Jain.												
All ages ...	**1,180**	**696**	**484**	**571**	**392**	**179**	**463**	**263**	**200**	**146**	**41**	**105**
0-1	**35**	16	19	**35**	16	19	...	...	...	...	...	...
1-2	**24**	13	11	**24**	13	11	...	...	...	...	...	...
2-3	**28**	17	11	**28**	17	11	...	...	...	...	...	...
3-4	**34**	17	17	**34**	17	17	...	...	...	...	...	...
4-5	**25**	11	14	**25**	11	14	...	...	...	...	...	...
Total 0-5 ...	**146**	74	72	**146**	74	72	...	...	...	...	...	...
5-10	**140**	79	61	**132**	76	56	**8**	3	5	...	...	...
10-15	**144**	85	59	**125**	85	40	**18**	...	18	**1**	...	1
15-20	**136**	83	53	**74**	66	8	**58**	17	41	**4**	...	4
20-30	**240**	151	89	**70**	67	3	**157**	82	75	**13**	2	11
30-40	**168**	107	61	**14**	14	...	**121**	79	42	**33**	14	19
40-50	**100**	62	38	**4**	4	...	**66**	51	15	**30**	7	23
50-60	**60**	36	24	**4**	4	...	**25**	22	3	**31**	10	21
60 and over ...	**46**	19	27	**2**	2	...	**10**	9	1	**34**	8	26
Tribal.												
All ages ...	**3,269**	**1,699**	**1,570**	**1,744**	**991**	**753**	**1,322**	**652**	**670**	**203**	**56**	**147**
0-1	**103**	48	55	**103**	48	55	...	...	...	...	...	...
1-2	**115**	58	57	**115**	58	57	...	...	...	...	...	...
2-3	**118**	53	65	**118**	53	65	...	...	...	...	...	...
3-4	**137**	62	75	**137**	62	75	...	...	...	...	...	...
4-5	**129**	58	71	**129**	58	71	...	...	...	...	...	...
Total 0-5 ...	**602**	279	323	**602**	279	323	...	...	...	...	...	...
5-10	**508**	255	253	**502**	255	247	**6**	...	6	...	...	...
10-15	**413**	234	179	**388**	231	157	**25**	3	22	...	...	...
15-20	**273**	138	135	**141**	118	23	**130**	19	111	**2**	1	1
20-30	**519**	245	274	**95**	92	3	**409**	149	260	**15**	4	11
30-40	**418**	223	195	**10**	10	...	**366**	203	163	**42**	10	32
40-50	**251**	155	96	**4**	4	...	**206**	142	64	**41**	9	32
50-60	**153**	90	63	**2**	2	...	**106**	73	33	**45**	15	30
60 and over ...	**132**	80	52	...	...	...	**74**	63	11	**58**	17	41

TABLE VII.

Age, Sex & Civil Condition.

Hassan District.

AGE	POPULATION			UNMARRIED			MARRIED			WIDOWED		
	Persons	Males	Females	Persons	Males	Females	Persons	Males	Females	Persons	Males	Females
1	2	3	4	5	6	7	8	9	10	11	12	13
All Religions.												
All ages ...	**596,937**	**300,746**	**296,191**	**300,766**	**174,155**	**126,611**	**224,662**	**111.314**	**113.348**	**71.509**	**15,277**	**56,232**
0–1	**16,162**	7,915	8,247	**16,162**	7,915	8,247	...	...	...	...	...	...
1–2	**16,209**	7,984	8,225	**16,209**	7,984	8,225	...	...	...	...	...	...
2–3	**16,380**	7,963	8,417	**16,380**	7,963	8,417	...	...	...	...	...	...
3–4	**15,711**	7,580	8,131	**15,711**	7,580	8,131	...	...	...	...	...	...
4–5	**16,066**	7,850	8,216	**16,066**	7,850	8,216	...	...	...	...	...	...
Total 0–5 ...	**80,528**	39,292	41,236	**80,528**	39,292	41,236	...	...	...	...	...	...
5–10	**80,219**	39,531	40,688	**79,413**	39,497	39,916	**782**	33	749	**24**	1	**23**
10–15	**78,177**	40,141	38,036	**73,819**	39,964	33,855	**4,256**	174	4,082	**102**	3	**99**
15–20	**56,405**	29,030	27,375	**34,144**	25,902	8,242	**21,343**	3,064	18,279	**918**	64	854
20–30	**108,894**	52,553	56,341	**27,248**	24,604	2,644	**74,112**	26,785	47,327	**7,534**	1,164	6,370
30–40	**86,391**	45,555	40,836	**4,232**	3,837	395	**66,189**	38,658	27,531	**15,970**	3,060	12,910
40–50	**54,225**	29,391	24,834	**897**	721	176	**35,411**	24,901	10,510	**17,917**	3,769	14,148
50–60	**29,694**	14,565	15,129	**299**	211	88	**14,665**	11,044	3,621	**14,730**	3,310	11,420
60 and over ...	**22.404**	10,688	11,716	**186**	127	59	**7,904**	6,655	1,249	**14,314**	3,906	10,408
Hindu.												
All ages ...	567,139	**284,490**	**282,649**	**285,018**	**164,638**	**120,380**	**213,064**	**105,109**	**107,955**	**69,057**	**14,743**	**54,314**
0–1	**15,263**	7,463	7,800	**15,263**	7,463	7,800	...	...	...	...	...	...
1–2	**15,297**	7,524	7,773	**15,297**	7,524	7,773	...	...	...	...	...	...
2–3	**15,502**	7,531	7,971	**15,502**	7,531	7,971	...	...	...	...	...	...
3–4	**14,838**	7,170	7,668	**14,838**	7,170	7,668	...	...	...	...	...	...
4–5	**15,062**	7,358	7,704	**15,062**	7,358	7,704	...	...	...	...	...	...
Total 0–5 ...	**75,962**	37,046	38,916	**75,962**	37,046	38,916	...	...	...	...	...	...
5–10	**76,267**	37,506	38,761	**75,494**	37,473	38,021	**751**	32	719	**22**	1	**21**
10–15	**74,512**	38,164	36,348	**70,342**	37,996	32,346	**4,072**	165	3,907	**98**	3	**95**
15–20	**53,495**	27,416	26,079	**32,318**	24,436	7,882	**20,294**	2,920	17,374	**883**	60	**823**
20–30	**103,255**	49,488	53,767	**25,600**	23,074	2,526	**70,351**	25,298	45,053	**7,304**	1,116	6,188
30–40	**82,227**	43,064	39,163	**3,994**	3,614	380	**62,740**	36,494	26,246	**15,493**	2,956	**12,537**
40–50	**51,692**	27,851	23,841	**851**	683	168	**33,536**	23,524	10,012	**17,305**	3,644	13,661
50–60	**28,338**	13,802	14,536	**278**	196	82	**13,869**	10,406	3,463	**14,191**	3,200	10,991
60 and over ...	**21,391**	10,153	11,238	**179**	120	59	**7,451**	6,270	1,181	**13,761**	3,763	9,998
Musalman.												
All ages ...	**21.487**	**11.835**	**9,652**	**11.347**	**6,948**	**4,399**	**8,462**	**4,547**	**3,915**	**1,678**	**340**	**1,338**
0–1	**643**	333	310	**643**	333	310	...	...	...	...	...	...
1–2	**664**	343	321	**664**	343	321	...	...	...	...	...	...
2–3	**646**	320	326	**646**	320	326	...	...	...	...	...	...
3–4	**656**	301	355	**656**	301	355	...	...	...	...	...	...
4–5	**805**	396	409	**805**	396	409	...	...	...	...	...	...
Total 0–5 ...	**3,414**	1,693	1,721	**3,414**	1,693	1,721	...	...	...	...	...	...
5–10	**2,868**	1,488	1,380	**2,845**	1,487	1,358	**21**	1	20	**2**	...	**2**
10–15	**2,616**	1,438	1,178	**2,466**	1,431	1,035	**147**	7	140	**3**	...	**3**
15–20	**2,066**	1,160	906	**1,282**	1,064	218	**760**	94	666	**24**	2	**22**
20–30	**4,037**	2,230	1,807	**1,152**	1,096	56	**2,736**	1,102	1,634	**149**	32	**117**
30–40	**2,938**	1,764	1,174	**152**	147	5	**2,465**	1,547	918	**321**	70	**251**
40–50	**1,830**	1,119	711	**24**	21	3	**1.385**	1,021	364	**421**	77	344
50–60	**980**	550	430	**9**	6	3	**603**	483	120	**368**	61	307
60 and over ...	**738**	393	345	**3**	3	...	**345**	292	53	**390**	98	292
Christian.												
All ages ...	**5,280**	**2.840**	**2,440**	**2,884**	**1,657**	**1,227**	**1,972**	**1,074**	**898**	**424**	**109**	**315**
0–1	**160**	76	84	**160**	76	84	...	...	...	...	...	...
1–2	**161**	79	82	**161**	79	82	...	...	...	...	...	...
2–3	**147**	74	73	**147**	74	73	...	...	...	...	...	...
3–4	**130**	64	66	**130**	64	66	...	...	...	...	...	...
4–5	**122**	58	64	**122**	58	64	...	...	...	...	...	...
Total 0–5 ...	**720**	351	369	**720**	351	369	...	...	...	...	...	...
5–10	**680**	336	344	**678**	336	342	**2**	...	2	...	...	...
10–15	**668**	336	332	**656**	335	321	**12**	1	11	...	...	...
15–20	**541**	286	255	**380**	260	120	**157**	26	131	**4**	...	**4**
20–30	**1,041**	556	485	**359**	301	58	**644**	248	396	**38**	7	31
30–40	**816**	492	324	**65**	56	9	**659**	414	245	**92**	22	**70**
40–50	**442**	267	175	**14**	9	5	**311**	228	83	**117**	30	87
50–60	**222**	136	86	**9**	6	3	**124**	102	22	**89**	28	61
60 and over ...	**150**	80	70	**3**	3	...	**63**	55	8	**84**	22	62

Hassan District—*concld.*

AGE	POPULATION			UNMARRIED			MARRIED			WIDOWED		
	Persons	Males	Females	Persons	Males	Females	Persons	Males	Females	Persons	Males	Females
1	2	3	4	5	6	7	8	9	10	11	12	13
Jain.												
All ages ...	**1,941**	**1,044**	**897**	**935**	**598**	**337**	**754**	**388**	**366**	**252**	**58**	**194**
0–1	**62**	30	32	**62**	30	32	...	...	...	...	...	...
1–2	**52**	28	24	**52**	28	24	...	...	...	...	...	...
2–3	**47**	21	26	**47**	21	26	...	...	...	...	...	...
3–4	**48**	23	25	**48**	23	25	...	...	...	...	...	...
4–5	**41**	19	22	**41**	19	22	...	...	...	...	...	...
Total 0–5 ...	**250**	121	129	**250**	121	129	...	...	...	...	...	...
5–10	**235**	120	115	**228**	120	108	**7**	...	7	...	...	...
10–15	**238**	132	106	**215**	131	84	**22**	1	21	**1**	...	1
15–20	**220**	124	96	**116**	104	12	**98**	19	79	**6**	1	5
20–30	**371**	194	177	**97**	94	3	**239**	94	145	**35**	6	29
30–40	**260**	157	103	**19**	18	1	**195**	130	65	**46**	9	37
40–50	**172**	102	70	**6**	6	...	**117**	85	32	**49**	11	38
50–60	**104**	52	52	**3**	3	...	**43**	33	10	**58**	16	42
60 and over ...	**91**	42	49	**1**	1	...	**33**	26	7	**57**	15	42
Tribal.												
All ages ...	**1,089**	**536**	**553**	**581**	**313**	**268**	**410**	**196**	**214**	**98**	**27**	**71**
0–1	**34**	13	21	**34**	13	21	...	...	...	...	...	...
1–2	**35**	10	25	**35**	10	25	...	...	...	...	...	...
2–3	**38**	17	21	**38**	17	21	...	...	...	...	...	...
3–4	**39**	22	17	**39**	22	17	...	...	...	...	...	...
4–5	**36**	19	17	**36**	19	17	...	...	...	...	...	...
Total 0–5 ...	**182**	81	101	**182**	81	101	...	...	...	...	...	...
5–10	**169**	81	88	**168**	81	87	**1**	...	1	...	...	...
10–15	**143**	71	72	**140**	71	69	**3**	...	3	...	...	...
15–20	**83**	44	39	**48**	38	10	**34**	5	29	**1**	1	...
20–30	**189**	84	105	**39**	38	1	**142**	43	99	**8**	3	5
30–40	**150**	78	72	**2**	2	...	**130**	73	57	**18**	3	15
40–50	**89**	52	37	**2**	2	...	**62**	43	19	**25**	7	18
50–60	**50**	25	25	...	...	...	**26**	20	6	**24**	5	19
60 and over ...	**34**	20	14	...	...	...	**12**	12	...	**22**	8	14

TABLE VII.

Age, Sex & Civil Condition.

Kadur District.

AGE	POPULATION			UNMARRIED			MARRIED			WIDOWED		
	Persons	Males	Females	Persons	Males	Females	Persons	Males	Females	Persons	Males	Females
1	2	3	4	5	6	7	8	9	10	11	12	13
All Religions.												
All ages ...	347,715	184,389	163,326	175,049	105,076	69,973	130,102	68,272	61,830	42,564	11,041	31,523
0–1	9,174	4,428	4,746	9,174	4,428	4,746	...	...	...	...	...	...
1–2	8,999	4,355	4,644	8,999	4,355	4,644	...	...	...	...	...	...
2–3	8,913	4,307	4,606	8,913	4,307	4,606	...	...	...	...	...	...
3–4	8,546	4,146	4,400	8,546	4,146	4,400	...	...	...	...	...	...
4–5	8,633	4,193	4,440	8,633	4,193	4,440	...	...	...	...	...	...
Total 0–5 ...	44,265	21,429	22,836	44,265	21,429	22,836	...	...	...	...	...	...
5–10	44,713	22,292	22,421	44,192	22,274	21,918	505	15	490	16	3	13
10–15	44,590	23,133	21,457	41,726	23,041	18,685	2,777	87	2,690	87	5	82
15–20	34,976	18,445	16,531	20,848	16,314	4,534	13,365	2,066	11,299	763	65	698
20–30	68,999	36,422	32,577	19,141	17,646	1,495	44,275	17,724	26,551	5,583	1,052	4,531
30–40	52,796	30,673	22,123	3,735	3,451	284	38,569	24,602	13,967	10,492	2,620	7,872
40–50	31,336	18,444	12,892	784	667	117	19,679	14,829	4,850	10,873	2,948	7,925
50–60	15,783	8,387	7,396	238	176	62	7,456	5,976	1,480	8,089	2,235	5,854
60 and over ...	10,257	5,164	5,093	120	78	42	3,476	2,973	503	6,661	2,113	4,548
Hindu.												
All ages ...	319,277	167,771	151,506	160,380	95,728	64,652	118,654	61,583	57,071	40,243	10,460	29,783
0–1	8,430	4,067	4,363	8,430	4,067	4,363	...	...	...	...	...	...
1–2	8,268	3,983	4,285	8,268	3,983	4,285	...	...	...	...	...	...
2–3	8,211	3,956	4,255	8,211	3,956	4,255	...	...	...	...	...	...
3–4	7,894	3,828	4,066	7,894	3,828	4,066	...	...	...	...	...	...
4–5	7,998	3,890	4,108	7,998	3,890	4,108	...	...	...	...	...	...
Total 0–5 ...	40,801	19,724	21,077	40,801	19,724	21,077	...	...	...	...	...	...
5–10	41,326	20,562	20,764	40,828	20,545	20,283	482	14	468	16	3	13
10–15	41,140	21,272	19,868	38,456	21,185	17,271	2,603	82	2,521	81	5	76
15–20	31,964	16,654	15,310	18,843	14,678	4,165	12,391	1,915	10,476	730	61	669
20–30	63,022	32,827	30,195	17,046	15,668	1,378	40,642	16,165	24,477	5,334	994	4,340
30–40	48,424	27,833	20,591	3,361	3,095	266	35,076	22,249	12,827	9,987	2,489	7,498
40–50	28,684	16,655	12,029	712	602	110	17,721	13,262	4,459	10,251	2,791	7,460
50–60	14,418	7,520	6,898	221	161	60	6,618	5,244	1,374	7,579	2,115	5,464
60 and over ...	9,498	4,724	4,774	112	70	42	3,121	2,652	469	6,265	2,002	4,263
Musalman.												
All ages ...	19,430	11,141	8,289	10,075	6,347	3,728	7,785	4,431	3,354	1,570	363	1,207
0–1	502	244	258	502	244	258	...	...	...	...	...	...
1–2	502	251	251	502	251	251	...	...	...	...	...	...
2–3	486	238	248	486	238	248	...	...	...	...	...	...
3–4	474	226	248	474	226	248	...	...	...	...	...	...
4–5	481	226	255	481	226	255	...	...	...	...	...	...
Total 0–5 ...	2,445	1,185	1,260	2,445	1,185	1,260	...	...	...	...	...	...
5–10	2,481	1,276	1,205	2,467	1,275	1,192	14	1	13	...	...	...
10–15	2,453	1,342	1,111	2,324	1,342	982	125	...	125	4	...	4
15–20	1,997	1,164	833	1,288	1,063	225	687	98	589	22	3	19
20–30	3,948	2,311	1,637	1,286	1,224	62	2,513	1,052	1,461	149	35	114
30–40	2,927	1,875	1,052	215	213	2	2,376	1,577	799	336	85	251
40–50	1,712	1,128	584	36	33	3	1,267	1,006	261	409	89	320
50–60	914	545	369	10	8	2	542	462	80	362	75	287
60 and over ...	553	315	238	4	4	...	261	235	26	288	76	212
Christian.												
All ages ...	6,575	4,110	2,465	3,388	2,231	1,157	2,735	1,741	994	452	138	314
0–1	180	89	91	180	89	91	...	...	...	...	...	...
1–2	173	94	79	173	94	79	...	...	...	...	...	...
2–3	157	83	74	157	83	74	...	...	...	...	...	...
3–4	121	61	60	121	61	60	...	...	...	...	...	...
4–5	109	53	56	109	53	56	...	...	...	...	...	...
Total 0–5 ...	740	380	360	740	380	360	...	...	...	...	...	...
5–10	610	303	307	608	303	305	2	...	2	...	...	...
10–15	690	361	329	665	357	308	25	4	21	...	...	...
15–20	762	483	279	564	448	116	191	34	157	7	1	6
20–30	1,511	980	531	648	600	48	808	368	440	55	12	43
30–40	1,072	732	340	128	112	16	851	595	256	93	25	68
40–50	702	515	187	26	22	4	540	449	91	136	44	92
50–60	346	261	85	5	5	...	243	224	19	98	32	66
60 and over ...	142	95	47	4	4	...	75	67	8	63	24	39

Kadur District—*concld.*

AGE	POPULATION			UNMARRIED			MARRIED			WIDOWED		
	Persons	Males	Females	Persons	Males	Females	Persons	Males	Females	Persons	Males	Females
1	2	3	4	5	6	7	8	9	10	11	12	13
Jain.												
All ages ...	**1,360**	**798**	**562**	**645**	**439**	**206**	**527**	**316**	**211**	**188**	**43**	**145**
0–1	**35**	15	20	**35**	15	20	...	...	...	...	...	...
1–2	**27**	15	12	**27**	15	12	...	...	...	...	...	...
2–3	**28**	15	13	**28**	15	13	...	...	...	...	...	...
3–4	**26**	13	13	**26**	13	13	...	...	...	...	...	...
4–5	**18**	9	9	**18**	9	9	...	...	...	...	...	...
Total 0–5 ..	**134**	67	67	**134**	67	67	...	...	...	...	...	...
5–10	**143**	69	74	**136**	69	67	**7**	...	7	...	...	...
10–15	**161**	79	82	**139**	78	61	**20**	1	19	**2**	...	**2**
15–20	**151**	94	57	**89**	80	9	**60**	14	46	**2**	...	**2**
20–30	**310**	204	106	**108**	106	2	**173**	93	80	**29**	5	**24**
30–40	**213**	138	75	**27**	27	...	**136**	101	35	**50**	10	**40**
40–50	**145**	92	53	**10**	10	...	**84**	64	20	**51**	18	**33**
50–60	**65**	40	25	**2**	2	...	**35**	31	4	**28**	7	**21**
60 and over ...	**38**	15	23	...	...	...	**12**	12	...	**26**	3	**23**
Tribal.												
All ages ...	**1,067**	**566**	**501**	**557**	**329**	**228**	**399**	**200**	**199**	**111**	**37**	**74**
0–1	**27**	13	14	**27**	13	14	...	...	...	...	...	...
1–2	**29**	12	17	**29**	12	17	...	...	...	...	...	...
2–3	**31**	15	16	**31**	15	16	...	...	...	...	...	...
3–4	**31**	18	13	**31**	18	13	...	...	...	...	...	...
4–5	**27**	15	12	**27**	15	12	...	...	...	...	...	...
Total 0–5 ...	**145**	73	72	**145**	73	72	...	...	...	...	...	...
5–10	**152**	82	70	**152**	82	70	...	...	...	...	...	...
10–15	**146**	79	67	**142**	79	63	**4**	...	4	...	...	...
15–20	**100**	49	51	**62**	44	18	**36**	5	31	**2**	...	**2**
20–30	**207**	99	108	**52**	47	5	**139**	46	93	**16**	6	**10**
30–40	**160**	95	65	**4**	4	...	**130**	80	50	**26**	11	**15**
40–50	**92**	54	38	...	...	...	**66**	48	18	**26**	6	**20**
50–60	**39**	20	19	...	...	...	**17**	14	3	**22**	6	**16**
60 and over ...	**26**	15	11	...	...	...	**7**	7	...	**19**	8	**11**

TABLE VII.

Age, Sex & Civil Condition.

Shimoga District.

AGE	POPULATION			UNMARRIED			MARRIED			WIDOWED		
	Persons	Males	Females	Persons	Males	Females	Persons	Males	Females	Persons	Males	Females
1	2	3	4	5	6	7	8	9	10	11	12	13
All Religions.												
All ages ...	**519,987**	**274,981**	**245,006**	**257,466**	**156,408**	**101,058**	**192,490**	**99,546**	**92,944**	**70,031**	**19,027**	**51,004**
0–1	**14,134**	6,980	7,164	**14,134**	6,980	7,164	...	...	...	...	...	...
1–2	**13,949**	6,835	7,114	**13,949**	6,835	7,114	...	...	...	...	...	...
2–3	**13,720**	6,645	7,075	**13,720**	6,645	7,075	...	...	...	...	...	...
3–4	**13,432**	6,575	6,857	**13,432**	6,575	6,857	...	...	...	...	...	...
4–5	**13,605**	6,794	6,811	**13,605**	6,794	6,811	...	...	...	...	...	...
Total 0–5 ...	**68,840**	33,829	35,011	**68,840**	33,829	35,011	...	...	...	...	...	...
5–10	**67,470**	33,735	33,735	**65,869**	33,697	32,172	**1,549**	35	1,514	**52**	3	**49**
10–15	**65,755**	33,919	31,836	**59,164**	33,737	25,427	**6,361**	174	6,187	**230**	8	**222**
15–20	**51,984**	27,225	24,759	**28,131**	23,629	4,502	**22,347**	3,460	18,887	**1,506**	136	1,370
20–30	**100,963**	53,214	47,749	**26,516**	24,513	2,003	**65,155**	26,962	38,193	**9,292**	1,739	7,553
30–40	**75,649**	43,897	31,752	**5,786**	4,875	911	**53,321**	34,782	18,539	**16,542**	4,240	12,302
40–50	**46,350**	26,637	19,713	**1,937**	1,386	551	**27,006**	20,313	6,693	**17,407**	4,938	12,469
50–60	**26,073**	13,851	12,222	**807**	511	296	**11,458**	9,171	2,287	**13,808**	4,169	9,639
60 and over ...	**16,903**	8,674	8,229	**416**	231	185	**5,293**	4,649	644	**11,194**	3,794	7,400
Hindu.												
All ages ...	**464,350**	**244,909**	**219,441**	**228,614**	**138,884**	**89,730**	**171,095**	**88,263**	**82,832**	**64,641**	**17,762**	**46,879**
0–1	**12,644**	6,243	6,401	**12,644**	6,243	6,401	...	...	...	...	...	...
1–2	**12,280**	6,016	6,264	**12,280**	6,016	6,264	...	...	...	...	...	...
2–3	**12,029**	5,810	6,219	**12,029**	5,810	6,219	...	...	...	...	...	...
3–4	**11,793**	5,756	6,037	**11,793**	5,756	6,037	...	...	...	...	...	...
4–5	**11,990**	5,987	6,003	**11,990**	5,987	6,003	...	...	...	...	...	...
Total 0–5 ...	**60,736**	29,812	30,924	**60,736**	29,812	30,924	...	...	...	...	...	...
5–10	**59,748**	29,783	29,965	**58,244**	29,752	28,492	**1,454**	28	1,426	**50**	3	47
10–15	**58,518**	30,088	28,430	**52,477**	29,928	22,549	**5,823**	152	5,671	**218**	8	210
15–20	**46,439**	24,232	22,207	**24,996**	21,002	3,994	**20,038**	3,107	16,931	**1,405**	123	1,282
20–30	**90,383**	47,479	42,904	**23,757**	21,870	1,887	**57,926**	23,982	33,944	**8,700**	1,627	7,073
30–40	**68,018**	39,359	28,659	**5,390**	4,504	886	**47,260**	30,882	16,378	**15,368**	3,973	11,395
40–50	**41,808**	24,001	17,807	**1,854**	1,317	537	**23,939**	18,053	5,886	**16,015**	4,631	11,384
50–60	**23,510**	12,428	11,082	**767**	483	284	**10,060**	8,034	2,026	**12,683**	3,911	8,772
60 and over ...	**15,190**	7,727	7,463	**393**	216	177	**4,595**	4,025	570	**10,202**	3,486	6,716
Musalman.												
All ages ...	**40,960**	**22,174**	**18,786**	**21,256**	**12,939**	**8,317**	**15,812**	**8,333**	**7,479**	**3,892**	**902**	**2,990**
0–1	**1,064**	528	536	**1,064**	528	536	...	...	...	...	...	...
1–2	**1,198**	588	610	**1,198**	588	610	...	...	...	...	...	...
2–3	**1,238**	622	616	**1,238**	622	616	...	...	...	...	...	...
3–4	**1,194**	606	588	**1,194**	606	588	...	...	...	...	...	...
4–5	**1,192**	595	597	**1,192**	595	597	...	...	..	...	...	...
Total 0–5 ...	**5,886**	2,939	2,947	**5,886**	2,939	2,947	...	...	...	...	...	...
5–10	**5,692**	2,910	2,782	**5,638**	2,904	2,734	**53**	6	47	**1**	...	**1**
10–15	**5,346**	2,820	2,526	**4,954**	2,806	2,148	**384**	14	370	**8**	...	**8**
15–20	**4,104**	2,212	1,892	**2,338**	1,963	375	**1,700**	239	1,461	**66**	10	**56**
20–30	**7,788**	4,238	3,550	**2,073**	1,993	80	**5,300**	2,163	3,137	**415**	82	**333**
30–40	**5,599**	3,323	2,276	**277**	264	13	**4,486**	2,869	1,617	**836**	190	**646**
40–50	**3,345**	1,950	1,395	**54**	45	9	**2,292**	1,691	601	**999**	214	**785**
50–60	**1,892**	1,056	836	**23**	17	6	**1,054**	866	188	**815**	173	**642**
60 and over ...	**1,308**	726	582	**13**	8	5	**543**	485	58	**752**	233	**519**
Christian.												
All ages ...	**4,084**	**2,355**	**1,729**	**2,038**	**1,268**	**770**	**1,716**	**1,011**	**705**	**330**	**76**	**254**
0–1	**123**	60	63	**123**	60	63	...	...	...	...	...	...
1–2	**131**	65	66	**131**	65	66	...	...	...	...	...	...
2–3	**108**	50	58	**108**	50	58	...	...	...	...	...	...
3–4	**100**	48	52	**100**	48	52	...	...	...	...	...	...
4–5	**93**	48	45	**93**	48	45	...	...	...	...	...	...
Total 0–5 ...	**555**	271	284	**555**	271	284	...	...	...	...	...	...
5–10	**468**	244	224	**465**	244	221	**3**	...	**3**	...	...	...
10–15	**448**	239	209	**419**	237	182	**28**	**2**	26	**1**	...	**1**
15–20	**421**	239	182	**260**	213	47	**153**	25	128	**8**	**1**	**7**
20–30	**890**	529	361	**274**	254	20	**577**	266	311	**39**	9	**30**
30–40	**655**	432	223	**48**	39	9	**537**	378	159	**70**	15	**55**
40–50	**373**	230	143	**9**	6	3	**270**	211	59	**94**	13	**81**
50–60	**183**	110	73	**5**	2	3	**106**	88	18	**72**	20	**52**
60 and over ...	**91**	61	30	**3**	2	**1**	**42**	41	**1**	**46**	18	**28**

TABLE VII.
Age, Sex, & Civil Condition.

Shimoga District—*concld.*

AGE	POPULATION			UNMARRIED			MARRIED			WIDOWED		
	Persons	Males	Females	Persons	Males	Females	Persons	Males	Females	Persons	Males	Females
1	2	3	4	5	6	7	8	9	10	11	12	13
Jain.												
All ages ...	**2,731**	**1,526**	**1,205**	**1,289**	**877**	**412**	**965**	**512**	**453**	**477**	**137**	**340**
0–1	**65**	26	39	**65**	26	39	...	...	...	...	...	...
1–2	**53**	31	22	**53**	31	22	...	...	...	...	...	...
2–3	**59**	34	25	**59**	34	25	...	...	...	...	...	...
3–4	**61**	31	30	**61**	31	30	...	...	...	...	...	...
4–5	**49**	23	26	**49**	23	26	...	...	...	...	...	...
Total 0–5 ...	**287**	145	142	**287**	145	142	...	...	...	...	...	...
5–10	**315**	155	160	**294**	155	139	**20**	...	20	**1**	...	1
10–15	**344**	186	158	**294**	184	110	**48**	2	46	**2**	...	2
15–20	**316**	179	137	**164**	148	16	**137**	31	106	**15**	...	15
20–30	**559**	320	239	**171**	169	2	**320**	140	180	**68**	11	57
30–40	**416**	252	164	**51**	50	1	**245**	172	73	**120**	30	90
40–50	**269**	158	111	**16**	15	1	**120**	99	21	**133**	44	89
50–60	**151**	89	62	**9**	8	1	**56**	49	7	**86**	32	54
60 and over ...	**74**	42	32	**3**	3	...	**19**	19	...	**52**	20	32
Tribal.												
All ages ...	**7,857**	**4,014**	**3,843**	**4,266**	**2,438**	**1,828**	**2,900**	**1,426**	**1,474**	**691**	**150**	**541**
0–1	**238**	123	115	**238**	123	115	...	...	...	...	...	...
1–2	**286**	134	152	**286**	134	152	...	...	...	...	...	...
2–3	**285**	129	156	**285**	129	156	...	...	...	...	...	...
3–4	**284**	134	150	**284**	134	150	...	...	...	...	...	...
4–5	**281**	141	140	**281**	141	140	...	...	...	...	...	...
Total 0–5 ...	**1,374**	661	713	**1,374**	661	713	...	...	...	...	...	...
5–10	**1,246**	642	604	**1,227**	641	586	**19**	1	18	...	...	...
10–15	**1,099**	586	513	**1,020**	582	438	**78**	4	74	**1**	...	1
15–20	**703**	363	340	**373**	303	70	**318**	58	260	**12**	2	10
20–30	**1,342**	647	695	**241**	227	14	**1,031**	410	621	**70**	10	60
30–40	**961**	531	430	**20**	18	2	**793**	481	312	**148**	32	116
40–50	**555**	298	257	**4**	3	1	**385**	259	126	**166**	36	130
50–60	**337**	168	169	**3**	1	2	**182**	134	48	**152**	33	119
60 and over ...	**240**	118	122	**4**	2	2	**94**	79	15	**142**	37	105

TABLE VII

Age, Sex & Civil Condition.

Civil and Military Station, Bangalore.

AGE	POPULATION			UNMARRIED			MARRIED			WIDOWED		
	Persons	Males	Females	Persons	Males	Females	Persons	Males	Females	Persons	Males	Females
1	2	3	4	5	6	7	8	9	10	11	12	13
All Religions.												
All ages ...	134,113	69,409	64,704	69,065	40,003	29,062	53,202	26,855	26,347	11,846	2,551	9,295
0–1	3,548	1,765	1,783	3,548	1,765	1,783	...	...	...	...	...	...
1–2	3,908	1,945	1,963	3,908	1,945	1,963	...	...	...	...	...	...
2–3	4,048	2,013	2,035	4,048	2,013	2,035	...	...	...	...	...	...
3–4	3,870	1,919	1,951	3,870	1,919	1,951	...	...	...	...	...	...
4–5	3,641	1,831	1,810	3,641	1,831	1,810	...	...	...	...	...	...
Total 0–5 ...	19,015	9,473	9,542	19,015	9,473	9,542	...	...	...	...	...	...
5–10	16,938	8,658	8,280	16,756	8,648	8,108	177	10	167	5	...	5
10–15	15,595	7,875	7,720	14,480	7,830	6,650	1,098	44	1,054	17	1	16
15–20	13,742	6,839	6,903	8,112	5,877	2,235	5,468	942	4,526	162	20	142
20–30	25,695	13,271	12,424	8,200	6,663	1,537	16,502	6,450	10,052	993	158	835
30–40	17,801	9,748	8,053	1,472	1,019	453	14,335	8,353	5,982	1,994	376	1,618
40–50	11,805	6,342	5,463	476	246	230	8,517	5,612	2,905	2,812	484	2,328
50–60	7,194	3,804	3,390	268	127	141	4,284	3,123	1,161	2,642	554	2,088
60 and over ...	6,328	3,399	2,929	286	120	166	2,821	2,321	500	3,221	958	2,263
Hindu.												
All ages ...	74,004	38,537	35,467	36,112	21,332	14,780	31,118	15,778	15,340	6,774	1,427	5,347
0–1	2,140	1,047	1,093	2,140	1,047	1,093	...	...	...	...	...	...
1–2	2,282	1,108	1,174	2,282	1,108	1,174	...	...	...	...	...	...
2–3	2,408	1,193	1,215	2,408	1,193	1,215	...	...	...	...	...	...
3–4	2,250	1,116	1,134	2,250	1,116	1,134	...	...	...	...	...	...
4–5	2,049	1,025	1,024	2,049	1,025	1,024	...	...	...	...	...	...
Total 0–5 ...	11,129	5,489	5,640	11,129	5,489	5,640	...	...	...	...	...	...
5–10	9,307	4,745	4,562	9,165	4,740	4,425	139	5	134	3	...	3
10–15	8,317	4,219	4,098	7,555	4,193	3,362	751	26	725	11	...	11
15–20	7,414	3,734	3,680	3,847	3,088	759	3,464	633	2,831	103	13	90
20–30	14,222	7,354	6,868	3,644	3,216	428	9,964	4,040	5,924	614	98	516
30–40	10,139	5,676	4,463	505	416	89	8,443	5,041	3,402	1,191	219	972
40–50	6,567	3,613	2,954	149	112	37	4,790	3,227	1,563	1,628	274	1,354
50–60	3,825	2,041	1,784	64	45	19	2,238	1,675	563	1,523	321	1,202
60 and over ...	3,084	1,666	1,418	54	33	21	1,329	1,131	198	1,701	502	1,199
Musalman.												
All ages ...	28,625	15,398	13,227	14,966	8,962	6,004	11,400	5,900	5,500	2,259	536	1,723
0–1	641	324	317	641	324	317	...	...	...	...	...	...
1–2	809	402	407	809	402	407	...	...	...	...	...	...
2–3	815	395	420	815	395	420	...	...	...	...	...	...
3–4	820	390	430	820	390	430	...	...	...	...	...	...
4–5	824	403	421	824	403	421	...	...	...	...	...	...
Total 0–5 ...	3,909	1,914	1,995	3,909	1,914	1,995	...	...	...	...	...	...
5–10	3,827	1,936	1,891	3,800	1,933	1,867	25	3	22	2	...	2
10–15	3,527	1,795	1,732	3,293	1,785	1,508	230	9	221	4	1	3
15–20	2,946	1,552	1,394	1,785	1,384	401	1,131	165	966	30	3	27
20–30	5,485	2,919	2,566	1,753	1,579	174	3,539	1,307	2,232	193	33	160
30–40	3,782	2,180	1,602	304	272	32	3,102	1,825	1,277	376	83	293
40–50	2,488	1,489	999	71	57	14	1,858	1,320	538	559	112	447
50–60	1,407	850	557	23	19	4	891	723	168	493	108	385
60 and over ...	1,254	763	491	28	19	9	624	548	76	602	196	406
Christian.												
All ages ...	30,022	14,652	15,370	17,253	9,263	7,990	10,063	4,831	5,232	2,706	558	2,148
0–1	728	374	354	728	374	354	...	...	...	...	...	...
1–2	775	414	361	775	414	361	...	...	...	...	...	...
2–3	780	403	377	780	403	377	...	...	...	...	...	...
3–4	759	392	367	759	392	367	...	...	...	...	...	...
4–5	736	384	352	736	384	352	...	...	...	...	...	...
Total 0–5 ...	3,778	1,967	1,811	3,778	1,967	1,811	...	...	...	...	...	...
5–10	3,641	1,889	1,752	3,629	1,887	1,742	12	2	10	...	...	...
10–15	3,587	1,768	1,819	3,480	1,760	1,720	106	8	98	1	...	1
15–20	3,202	1,452	1,750	2,383	1,335	1,048	791	113	678	28	4	24
20–30	5,669	2,816	2,853	2,705	1,793	912	2,783	998	1,785	181	25	156
30–40	3,686	1,772	1,914	648	320	328	2,631	1,386	1,245	407	66	341
40–50	2,613	1,159	1,454	248	72	176	1,773	999	774	592	88	504
50–60	1,895	878	1,017	178	61	117	1,118	699	419	599	118	481
60 and over ...	1,951	951	1,000	204	68	136	849	626	223	898	257	641

Civil and Military Station, Bangalore—*concld.*

AGE	POPULATION			UNMARRIED			MARRIED			WIDOWED		
	Persons	Males	Females	Persons	Males	Females	Persons	Males	Females	Persons	Males	Females
1	2	3	4	5	6	7	8	9	10	11	12	13
Jain.												
All ages ...	**814**	**484**	**330**	**359**	**250**	**109**	**384**	**213**	**171**	**71**	**21**	**50**
0–1	**19**	10	9	**19**	10	9	...	...	...	...	...	...
1–2	**24**	11	13	**24**	11	13	...	...	...	...	...	...
2–3	**21**	11	10	**21**	11	10	...	...	...	...	...	...
3–4	**16**	9	7	**16**	9	7	...	...	...	...	...	...
4–5	**18**	10	8	**18**	10	8	...	...	...	...	...	...
Total 0–5 ...	**98**	51	47	**98**	51	47	...	...	...	...	...	...
5–10	**79**	46	33	**79**	46	33	...	...	...	...	...	...
10–15	**85**	51	34	**73**	50	23	11	1	10	1	...	1
15–20	**115**	73	42	**53**	50	3	61	23	38	1	...	1
20–30	**195**	116	79	**47**	45	2	144	69	75	4	2	2
30–40	**108**	73	35	**3**	3	...	92	64	28	13	6	7
40–50	**81**	49	32	**5**	4	1	54	39	15	22	6	16
50–60	**33**	17	16	**1**	1	...	14	11	3	18	5	13
60 and over ...	**20**	8	12	...	...	...	8	6	2	12	2	10

MYSORE CENSUS 1931.

TABLE VIII.—Civil Condition by Age for Selected Castes, Tribes and Races.

NOTE 1.—The Castes, Tribes and Races appearing in this table are those for which on account of their proportion in the population, details were given in the Census Tables of 1921.

NOTE 2.—Komati which appeared as a separate Caste in 1921 is now merged in Vaisya.

NOTE 3.—Changes in the names of Castes under Religion Hindu approved by Government since the last Census, are indicated below :—

1931		1921
Adikarnataka	..	Holeya Madiga
Banajara	..	Lambani
Gangakula	..	Besta
Visvakarma	..	Panchala
Yadava	...	Golla

TABLE VIII.

Civil Condition by Age.

TABLE

Civil Condition by Age for

Serial No.	Caste, Tribe or Race	Locality	Sex	Population dealt with	Unmarried: Total	0—6	7—13	14—16	17—23	24—43	44 and over
	1	2	3	4	5	6	7	8	9	10	11
	Hindu.										
1	Adikarnataka.	MYSORE STATE, INCLUDING C. AND M. STN., BANGALORE	Male	509,898	283,948	93,385	93,532	34,411	40,177	21,095	1,348
			Female	490,428	206,067	96,210	85,576	13,471	5,520	4,171	1,119
2		Civil and Military Station, Bangalore...	Male	18,267	7,434	2,679	2,282	649	1,225	517	82
			Female	13,344	5,718	2,657	2,113	401	346	166	35
1	Agasa ...	MYSORE STATE, INCLUDING C. AND M. STN., BANGALORE	Male	55,879	30,707	9,962	9,966	3,952	4,562	2,145	130
			Female	53,611	21,487	10,302	9,337	1,296	385	138	29
2		Civil and Military Station, Bangalore...	Male	629	356	143	118	89	46	9	1
			Female	561	257	129	110	10	4	3	1
1	Banajiga ...	MYSORE STATE, INCLUDING C. AND M. STN., BANGALORE	Male	77,779	41,641	12,938	13,065	4,910	7,069	3,344	315
			Female	74,471	28,292	13,427	12,147	1,586	506	437	189
2		Civil and Military Station, Bangalore...	Male	3,913	2,172	687	633	202	484	156	10
			Female	3,591	1,484	715	626	83	46	9	5
1	Beda ...	MYSORE STATE, INCLUDING C. AND M. STN., BANGALORE	Male	153,590	87,337	28,143	27,041	10,733	12,632	8,059	729
			Female	147,873	62,121	27,778	26,608	4,061	1,381	1,626	667
2		Civil and Military Station, Bangalore...	Male	70	38	14	6	8	6	4	...
			Female	55	18	7	10	1	...	...	...
1	Brahmin ...	MYSORE STATE, INCLUDING C. AND M. STN., BANGALORE	Male	126,542	66,751	23,018	21,298	8,164	10,656	3,030	585
			Female	118,621	42,975	23,974	18,246	493	135	89	38
2		Civil and Military Station, Bangalore...	Male	1,945	1,015	328	298	114	202	76	2
			Female	1,477	566	299	241	22	2	1	1
1	Darzi ...	MYSORE STATE, INCLUDING C. AND M. STN., BANGALORE	Male	10,488	5,899	2,249	1,992	725	742	170	21
			Female	10,039	4,338	2,362	1,761	144	47	19	5
2		Civil and Military Station, Bangalore...	Male	1,237	728	250	257	86	101	25	9
			Female	1,071	508	280	195	23	3	5	2
1	Devanga ...	MYSORE STATE, INCLUDING C. AND M. STN., BANGALORE	Male	30,002	16,495	5,706	5,298	2,076	2,455	891	69
			Female	29,300	11,926	5,837	5,127	739	150	55	18
2		Civil and Military Station, Bangalore...	Male	35	22	5	8	1	2	6	...
			Female	28	8	3	4	...	...	...	1
1	Gangakula.	MYSORE STATE, INCLUDING C. AND M. STN., BANGALORE	Male	88,356	48,151	15,676	16,220	6,356	6,692	2,989	218
			Female	85,947	34,083	16,207	14,401	1,883	785	606	201
2		Civil and Military Station, Bangalore...	Male	86	41	15	9	4	9	4	...
			Female	77	28	13	13	2	...	...	...
1	Ganiga ...	MYSORE STATE, INCLUDING C. AND M. STN., BANGALORE	Male	22,620	12,213	3,941	4,006	1,562	1,855	798	51
			Female	22,340	8,516	4,222	3,715	399	106	56	18
2		Civil and Military Station, Bangalore...	Male	208	119	43	36	14	18	6	2
			Female	399	108	49	47	9	2	1	...
1	Idiga ...	MYSORE STATE, INCLUDING C. AND M. STN., BANGALORE	Male	50,076	28,455	7,618	8,635	3,913	4,833	3,263	193
			Female	44,593	17,766	7,773	8,070	1,363	380	138	37
2		Civil and Military Station, Bangalore...	Male	182	94	28	32	8	20	6	...
			Female	122	43	19	22	...	1	1	...
1	Jogi ...	MYSORE STATE, INCLUDING C. AND M. STN., BANGALORE	Male	7,627	4,106	1,476	1,310	496	479	312	33
			Female	7,382	3,026	1,499	1,283	162	52	23	7
2		Civil and Military Station, Bangalore...	Male	2	...	...	...	...	...	...	...
			Female	...	...	...	...	...	...	...	...
1	Kshatriya...	MYSORE STATE, INCLUDING C. AND M. STN., BANGALORE	Male	21,304	11,760	3,559	3,596	1,416	2,125	972	92
			Female	19,704	7,747	3,766	3,242	489	152	65	33
2		Civil and Military Station, Bangalore...	Male	688	371	98	94	26	92	55	6
			Female	482	182	87	71	9	7	5	3

Selected Castes, Tribes and Races. — **Civil Condition by Age.**

Married							Widowed							
Total	0—6	7—13	14—16	17—23	24—43	44 and over	Total	0—6	7—13	14—16	17—23	24—43	44 and over	Serial No.
12	13	14	15	16	17	18	19	20	21	22	23	24	25	
202,048 *207,423*	**7** *24*	**139** *6,061*	**637** *15,220*	**11,929** *53,517*	**128,412** *112,293*	**60,924** *20,308*	**23,902** *76,938*	... *1*	**2** *59*	**15** *318*	**275** *2,686*	**7,766** *30,419*	**15,844** *43,455*	1
5,359 *5,592*	2 ...	3 *84*	14 *316*	316 *1,575*	3,440 *3,003*	1,584 *614*	474 *2,034*	... ...	... *1*	... *5*	7 *77*	128 *709*	389 *1,242*	2
22,198 *22,631*	**2** *8*	**14** *628*	**78** *1,966*	**1,552** *5,929*	**13,729** *11,902*	**6,823** *2,198*	**2,974** *9,493*	... ...	... *10*	**1** *42*	**27** *335*	**949** *3,705*	**1,997** *5,401*	1
254 *224*	... ...	2 *2*	... *23*	22 *63*	152 *93*	78 *43*	19 *80*	... ...	... ...	... *1*	... *3*	4 *28*	15 *48*	2
31,565 *32,279*	**1** *2*	**14** *938*	**68** *2,630*	**1,936** *8,637*	**19,359** *16,625*	**10,187** *3,447*	**4,573** *13,900*	... ...	... *14*	... *56*	**78** *436*	**1,286** *4,982*	**3,209** *8,412*	1
1,584 *1,596*	... ...	2 *31*	1 *125*	121 *486*	1,001 *793*	459 *161*	157 *511*	... ...	... *1*	... *1*	3 *12*	50 *187*	104 *310*	2
56,822 *59,808*	**1** *1*	**34** *1,548*	**156** *4,455*	**3,207** *15,755*	**35,903** *31,882*	**17,521** *6,167*	**9,431** *25,944*	... *1*	**1** *42*	**5** *166*	**84** *1,198*	**2,751** *10,238*	**6,590** *14,299*	1
84 *32*	... ...	1 *1*	... *3*	4 *10*	18 *15*	11 *3*	8 *5*	... ...	... ...	... ...	... ...	1 *1*	2 *4*	2
52,721 *52,054*	**1** *6*	**33** *3,156*	**159** *6,980*	**5,702** *14,815*	**30,553** *21,295*	**16,273** *5,802*	**7,070** *23,592*	... *1*	... *37*	**5** *178*	**55** *1,140*	**1,426** *7,811*	**5,584** *14,425*	1
863 *719*	... ...	... *20*	4 *89*	107 *216*	531 *330*	221 *64*	67 *192*	... ...	... ...	... *2*	... *8*	22 *57*	45 *125*	2
4,198 *4,310*	**1** ...	**7** *168*	**19** *552*	**508** *1,283*	**2,469** *1,902*	**1,194** *405*	**391** *1,391*	... ...	... *1*	... *12*	**9** *49*	**90** *491*	**292** *838*	1
475 *446*	... ...	2 *13*	1 *48*	48 *131*	295 *211*	129 *43*	34 *117*	... ...	... ...	... *2*	1 *5*	8 *31*	25 *79*	2
11,678 *12,270*	... *1*	**5** *342*	**64** *1,250*	**1,055** *3,261*	**7,021** *6,055*	**3,533** *1,361*	**1,829** *5,104*	... ...	... *3*	... *14*	**23** *170*	**545** *1,986*	**1,261** *2,931*	1
12 *17*	... ...	... ...	... *1*	1 *5*	6 *10*	5 *1*	1 *3*	... ...	... ...	... ...	... ...	... *2*	1 *1*	2
35,859 *36,614*	**3** *1*	**17** *1,494*	**121** *3,136*	**2,474** *9,505*	**21,899** *18,920*	**11,345** *3,558*	**4,346** *15,250*	... ...	**1** *12*	**3** *60*	**55** *481*	**1,396** *5,741*	**2,891** *8,956*	1
41 *37*	... ...	... ...	... *3*	2 *12*	22 *19*	17 *3*	4 *12*	... ...	... ...	... ...	... *1*	1 *6*	3 *5*	2
9,329 *9,648*	... ...	**6** *367*	**14** *858*	**734** *2,613*	**5,647** *4,751*	**2,928** *1,059*	**1,078** *4,176*	... ...	**1** *6*	... *30*	**12** *141*	**261** *1,442*	**804** *2,557*	1
81 *126*	... ...	... *5*	... *13*	9 *41*	54 *60*	18 *7*	8 *65*	... ...	... *1*	... ...	... *3*	1 *20*	7 *41*	2
18,828 *17,577*	... ...	**17** *561*	**63** *1,648*	**1,128** *5,005*	**12,746** *9,204*	**4,874** *1,159*	**2,793** *9,250*	... ...	... *12*	**3** *59*	**31** *398*	**1,215** *4,156*	**1,544** *4,625*	1
83 *56*	... ...	... *1*	... *8*	9 *19*	58 *22*	16 *6*	5 *23*	... ...	... ...	... *1*	... *1*	2 *10*	3 *11*	2
3,051 *3,293*	... ...	**2** *90*	**21** *272*	**175** *857*	**1,867** *1,747*	**986** *327*	**370** *1,063*	... ...	... *3*	... *4*	**4** *37*	**128** *344*	**238** *675*	1
2 ...	... ...	... ...	... ...	... ...	2 ...	... ...	... ...	... ...	... ...	... ...	... ...	... ...	... ...	2
8,508 *8,293*	**1** *1*	**3** *232*	**15** *728*	**612** *2,296*	**5,079** *4,154*	**2,798** *882*	**1,036** *3,664*	... ...	... *2*	... *14*	**18** *142*	**309** *1,308*	**709** *2,198*	1
299 *239*	1 ...	... *5*	3 *25*	29 *68*	179 *109*	87 *32*	18 *61*	... ...	... ...	... ...	2 *2*	4 *21*	12 *38*	2

TABLE VIII.

Civil Condition by Age.

TABLE

Civil Condition by Age for

Serial No.	Caste, Tribe or Race	Locality	Sex	Population dealt with	Unmarried: Total	0—6	7—13	14—16	17—23	24—43	44 and over
	1	2	3	4	5	6	7	8	9	10	11
	Hindu *—contd.*										
1	Kumbara...	MYSORE STATE, INCLUDING C. AND M. STN., BANGALORE	Male	24,824	13,554	4,323	4,517	1,732	2,010	898	74
			Female	23,833	9,430	4,551	4,066	592	137	50	34
2		Civil and Military Station, Bangalore...	Male	74	33	13	11	...	8	1	...
			Female	95	36	21	11	4	...	...	...
1	Kunchatiga.	MYSORE STATE, INCLUDING C. AND M. STN., BANGALORE	Male	59,207	33,359	10,474	10,578	4,102	5,032	2,947	296
			Female	57,357	23,079	11,002	10,210	1,472	267	87	41
2		Civil and Military Station, Bangalore...	Male	154	88	25	37	9	14	3	...
			Female	117	48	20	25	2	...	1	...
1	Lingayat ...	MYSORE STATE, INCLUDING C. AND M. STN., BANGALORE	Male	390,652	220,181	67,399	67,914	29,566	35,532	18,126	1,644
			Female	380,150	148,746	69,353	65,896	10,144	2,160	801	392
2		Civil and Military Station, Bangalore...	Male	576	810	97	105	40	52	15	1
			Female	514	206	101	85	14	4	2	...
1	Mahratta...	MYSORE STATE, INCLUDING C. AND M. STN., BANGALORE	Male	31,696	17,422	5,557	5,540	2,018	2,871	1,330	106
			Female	28,832	11,358	5,576	4,967	545	150	83	37
2		Civil and Military Station, Bangalore...	Male	777	406	122	123	33	96	31	1
			Female	659	259	120	121	12	6	...	...
1	Meda ...	MYSORE STATE, INCLUDING C. AND M. STN., BANGALORE	Male	3,819	2,053	663	666	256	291	156	21
			Female	3,713	1,556	719	680	108	28	17	4
2		Civil and Military Station, Bangalore...	Male	133	71	29	23	10	8	1	...
			Female	127	53	29	23	1	...	...	...
1	Mudali ...	MYSORE STATE, INCLUDING C. AND M. STN., BANGALORE	Male	16,773	9,161	2,891	2,676	924	1,838	783	47
			Female	14,959	5,973	2,876	2,441	447	147	42	20
2		Civil and Military Station, Bangalore...	Male	4,690	2,665	765	762	235	646	239	18
			Female	4,127	1,727	787	680	176	63	14	7
1	Nagartha...	MYSORE STATE, INCLUDING C. AND M. STN., BANGALORE	Male	4,258	2,232	744	666	272	381	143	26
			Female	4,129	1,447	688	625	104	19	8	3
2		Civil and Military Station, Bangalore...	Male	164	98	31	27	13	19	4	4
			Female	184	73	40	30	1	1	...	1
1	Nayinda ...	MYSORE STATE, INCLUDING C. AND M. STN., BANGALORE	Male	23,797	12,829	4,303	4,201	1,556	1,964	761	44
			Female	22,419	8,706	4,377	3,712	455	107	42	13
2		Civil and Military Station, Bangalore...	Male	455	240	86	66	29	48	10	1
			Female	455	193	109	71	9	2	2	...
1	Neygi ...	MYSORE STATE, INCLUDING C. AND M. STN., BANGALORE	Male	27,918	15,299	5,263	4,902	1,845	2,287	896	106
			Female	26,539	10,458	5,189	4,435	632	124	59	19
2		Civil and Military Station, Bangalore...	Male	72	26	5	6	5	6	4	...
			Female	59	18	12	5	1	...	...	...
1	Satani ...	MYSORE STATE, INCLUDING C. AND M. STN., BANGALORE	Male	11,658	6,229	1,904	1,957	906	981	436	45
			Female	11,444	4,234	2,129	1,862	178	39	20	6
2		Civil and Military Station, Bangalore...	Male	19	13	3	5	1	2	2	...
			Female	15	4	2	2	...	...	...	...
1	Tigala ...	MYSORE STATE, INCLUDING C. AND M. STN., BANGALORE	Male	46,792	26,680	9,407	9,010	3,114	3,688	1,393	68
			Female	43,908	19,212	9,377	8,425	1,036	264	87	23
2		Civil and Military Station, Bangalore...	Male	2,234	1,191	419	341	88	257	79	7
			Female	1,967	814	419	323	40	24	8	...
1	Uppara ...	MYSORE STATE, INCLUDING C. AND M. STN., BANGALORE	Male	59,207	33,298	10,982	10,954	4,444	4,290	2,466	162
			Female	57,154	23,367	11,054	9,992	1,550	483	233	55
2		Civil and Military Station, Bangalore...	Male	...	...	...	...	...	...	...	...
			Female	1	...	...	...	...	...	...	...

VIII. **TABLE VIII.**

Selected Castes, Tribes and Races.—*contd.* **Civil Condition by Age,**

Married							Widowed							
Total	0—6	7—13	14—16	17—23	24—43	44 and over	Total	0—6	7—13	14—16	17—23	24—43	44 and over	Serial No.
12	13	14	15	16	17	18	19	20	21	22	23	24	25	
10,106 10,180	... 2	7 413	32 907	720 2,656	6,303 5,217	3,044 985	1,164 4,223	... ...	... 7	... 22	8 139	357 1,650	799 2,405	1
39 36	... ...	... 3	... 2	7 9	24 19	8 3	2 23	... ...	... ...	... ...	... 1	2 14	... 8	2
22,357 23,485	1 9	11 628	77 1,905	1,250 6,374	13,587 11,960	7,431 2,609	3,491 10,793	... ...	... 12	3 45	29 335	891 4,064	2,568 6,337	1
58 51	... ...	... ...	... 6	4 13	27 27	27 5	8 18	... ...	... ...	... ...	... 1	3 3	5 14	2
146,077 150,040	4 18	61 4,620	351 12,806	8,960 42,453	90,114 74,698	46,587 15,445	24,394 81,364	... 1	3 86	13 326	225 2,902	6,963 31,992	17,190 46,057	1
235 224	... ...	... 7	... 28	18 64	133 107	84 18	31 84	... ...	... ...	... ...	... 1	6 25	25 58	2
12,531 12,278	... 1	9 375	60 1,138	780 3,396	7,870 6,114	3,812 1,254	1,743 5,196	... ...	... 3	1 26	25 180	585 1,913	1,182 3,074	1
340 299	... ...	... 6	1 23	45 91	194 145	100 34	31 101	... ...	... ...	... 1	... 1	11 35	20 64	2
1,538 1,592	... ...	... 58	14 149	119 443	971 795	434 147	228 565	... ...	... ...	... 3	2 19	76 200	150 343	1
8 59	... ...	... 3	1 3	5 17	32 32	20 4	4 15	... ...	... ...	... ...	... ...	... 4	4 11	2
6,928 6,687	... ...	4 127	12 469	393 1,904	4,359 3,518	2,160 669	684 2,299	... ...	... 3	... 6	5 70	194 810	485 1,410	1
1,849 1,770	... ...	... 15	4 114	118 498	1,108 907	619 236	176 630	... ...	... 1	... 3	... 13	46 208	130 405	2
1,712 1,706	... 1	2 38	4 132	105 502	1,001 847	600 186	314 976	... ...	... ...	... ...	4 39	76 332	234 605	1
59 83	... ...	... 1	... 6	5 25	28 41	26 10	7 28	... ...	... ...	... ...	... 1	1 9	6 18	2
9,784 10,146	... 4	13 317	32 891	722 2,706	6,017 5,196	3,000 1,032	1,184 3,567	... 1	... 8	1 18	18 92	346 1,297	819 2,151	1
209 196	... ...	1 3	1 18	16 64	130 88	61 23	6 66	... ...	... ...	... 1	1 1	1 24	4 40	2
11,001 11,510	... 2	4 374	31 1,055	945 3,175	6,590 5,601	3,431 1,303	1,618 4,571	... ...	1 4	1 15	21 149	453 1,710	1,142 2,693	1
45 29	... ...	... ...	... 4	5 9	34 14	6 2	1 12	... ...	... ...	... ...	... 1	... 5	1 6	2
4,604 4,934	... 2	1 206	15 496	312 1,283	2,754 2,442	1,522 505	825 2,276	... ...	... 3	... 10	6 82	204 838	615 1,343	1
6 5	... ...	... ...	... ...	... 2	5 3	1 ...	... 6	... ...	... ...	... ...	... ...	... 1	... 5	2
18,096 18,301	... 4	8 359	58 1,459	1,123 5,023	11,261 9,554	5,646 1,902	2,016 6,395	... ...	... 4	1 21	22 184	494 2,292	1,499 3,894	1
958 873	... ...	1 13	3 76	70 273	622 418	262 93	85 280	... ...	... ...	... ...	2 4	21 114	62 162	2
22,870 23,530	1 4	12 680	74 1,764	1,474 6,248	14,600 12,528	6,709 2,306	3,039 10,257	... ...	... 5	2 54	50 350	1,041 4,095	1,946 5,753	1
... 1	... ...	... ...	... ...	... ...	... 1	... ...	... ...	... ...	... ...	... ...	... ...	... ...	... ...	2

TABLE VIII.

Civil Condition by Age.

TABLE

Civil Condition by Age for

Serial No.	Caste, Tribe or Race	Locality	Sex	Population dealt with	Unmarried						
					Total	0—6	7—13	14—16	17—23	24—43	44 and over
	1	2	3	4	5	6	7	8	9	10	11
	Hindu —*concld.*										
1	Vakkaliga...	MYSORE STATE, INCLUDING C. AND M. STN., BANGALORE	Male	663,718	366,424	115,551	119,422	48,743	56,674	24,550	1,484
			Female	648,546	255,156	119,937	111,397	17,168	4,814	1,378	462
2		Civil and Military Station, Bangalore...	Male	2,092	1,136	340	332	122	261	72	9
			Female	1,941	798	405	317	49	17	7	3
1	Vaisya ...	MYSORE STATE, INCLUDING C. AND M. STN., BANGALORE	Male	23,344	12,340	4,136	3,741	1,563	1,948	795	157
			Female	20,891	7,307	4,437	2,744	55	28	26	17
2		Civil and Military Station, Bangalore...	Male	878	446	129	115	70	84	40	8
			Female	740	246	128	105	7	1	3	2
1	Viswakarma	MYSORE STATE, INCLUDING C. AND M. STN., BANGALORE	Male	74,370	40,765	12,424	12,898	5,258	6,670	3,233	282
			Female	69,299	26,767	12,756	11,879	1,531	388	171	42
2		Civil and Military Station, Bangalore...	Male	677	354	100	118	44	73	19	...
			Female	615	234	109	106	15	3	1	...
1	Vodda ...	MYSORE STATE, INCLUDING C. AND M. STN., BANGALORE	Male	84,527	46,505	15,849	15,545	5,863	6,220	2,870	158
			Female	80,349	33,580	16,367	14,410	1,995	539	205	64
2		Civil and Military Station, Bangalore...	Male	356	186	65	63	19	33	6	...
			Female	349	148	85	56	5	2	...	...
1	Yadava ...	MYSORE STATE, INCLUDING C. AND M. STN., BANGALORE	Male	88,561	49,733	16,586	15,552	6,158	6,278	4,859	300
			Female	85,640	34,407	16,236	14,688	2,494	684	223	82
2		Civil and Military Station, Bangalore...	Male	459	245	72	88	24	41	19	1
			Female	428	181	94	63	15	4	4	1
	Hindu and Tribal.										
1	Banajara ... (Hindu)	MYSORE STATE, INCLUDING C. AND M. STN., BANGALORE	Male	26,170	15,586	5,769	5,495	1,928	1,737	629	28
			Female	24,539	12,015	5,799	5,118	844	177	48	29
2		Civil and Military Station, Bangalore...	Male	4	1	...	...	...	1	...	...
			Female	8	3	3	...	...	...	...	...
1	Banajara ... (Tribal)	MYSORE STATE, INCLUDING C. AND M. STN., BANGALORE	Male	6,967	4,176	1,563	1,419	495	505	185	9
			Female	6,692	3,200	1,604	1,329	208	42	11	6
2		Civil and Military Station, Bangalore...	Male	...	...	...	...	...	...	...	...
			Female	...	...	...	...	...	...	...	...
	Banajara ... (Total)	MYSORE STATE, INCLUDING C. AND M. STN., BANGALORE	Male	33,137	19,762	7,332	6,914	2,423	2,242	814	37
			Female	31,231	15,215	7,403	6,447	1,052	219	59	35
		Civil and Military Station, Bangalore...	Male	4	1	...	...	...	1	...	...
			Female	8	3	3	...	...	...	...	...
1	Koracha ... (Hindu)	MYSORE STATE, INCLUDING C. AND M. STN., BANGALORE	Male	5,319	2,803	954	928	363	366	181	11
			Female	4,919	1,963	1,005	814	106	19	14	5
2		Civil and Military Station, Bangalore...	Male	93	52	18	16	3	12	3	...
			Female	74	24	14	10	...	...	...	...
1	Koracha (Tribal)	MYSORE STATE, INCLUDING C. AND M. STN., BANGALORE	Male	965	518	186	189	62	51	28	2
			Female	882	358	199	145	11	2	1	...
2		Civil and Military Station, Bangalore...	Male	...	...	...	...	...	...	...	...
			Female	...	...	...	...	...	...	...	...
	Koracha ... (Total)	MYSORE STATE, INCLUDING C. AND M. STN., BANGALORE	Male	6,284	3,321	1,140	1,117	425	417	209	13
			Female	5,801	2,321	1,204	959	117	21	15	5
		Civil and Military Station, Bangalore...	Male	93	52	18	16	3	12	3	...
			Female	74	24	14	10	...	...	...	...
1	Korama ... (Hindu)	MYSORE STATE, INCLUDING C. AND M. STN., BANGALORE	Male	6,893	3,700	1,294	1,250	462	486	198	10
			Female	6,714	2,655	1,287	1,143	155	46	15	9
2		Civil and Military Station, Bangalore...	Male	36	22	11	6	2	3	...	...
			Female	26	9	3	5	1	...	...	...
1	Korama ... (Tribal)	MYSORE STATE, INCLUDING C. AND M. STN., BANGALORE	Male	1,801	977	325	354	123	114	60	1
			Female	1,716	743	353	306	59	19	6	...
2		Civil and Military Station, Bangalore...	Male	...	...	...	...	...	...	...	...
			Female	...	...	...	...	...	...	...	...
	Korama ... (Total)	MYSORE STATE, INCLUDING C. AND M. STN., BANGALORE	Male	8,694	4,677	1,619	1,604	585	600	258	11
			Female	8,430	3,398	1,640	1,449	214	65	21	9
		Civil and Military Station, Bangalore...	Male	36	22	11	6	2	3	...	...
			Female	26	9	3	5	1	...	...	...

VIII. **TABLE VIII.**

Selected Castes, Tribes and Races. —*contd.* **Civil Condition by Age.**

Married							Widowed							
Total	0—6	7—13	14—16	17—23	24—43	44 and over	Total	0—6	7—13	14—16	17—23	24—43	44 and over	Serial No.
12	13	14	15	16	17	18	19	20	21	22	23	24	25	
266,351 272,374	6 38	171 9,999	853 21,031	16,411 69,315	161,829 141,819	87,081 30,172	30,943 121,016	... 3	8 98	12 397	244 3,171	8,284 42,329	22,395 75,018	1
883 836	... ...	1 13	3 53	75 267	536 416	268 87	73 307	... ...	... 1	... 1	3 7	16 84	54 214	2
9,581 9,541	... 3	3 719	45 1,279	1,045 2,507	5,458 4,009	3,030 1,024	1,423 4,043	... ...	... 9	... 34	18 182	303 1,484	1,102 2,334	1
378 342	... ...	... 12	2 42	47 94	208 155	121 39	54 152	... ...	... 1	... ...	1 3	15 53	38 95	2
29,540 29,387	... 6	16 1,100	98 2,817	1,990 7,808	18,034 14,921	9,402 2,735	4,065 13,145	... ...	2 15	1 66	60 534	1,275 5,226	2,727 7,304	1
292 291	... ...	... 9	... 38	19 95	183 132	90 17	31 90	... ...	... ...	... ...	... 4	9 29	22 57	2
34,167 35,561	... 4	17 815	108 2,597	2,169 9,137	21,044 19,403	10,829 3,605	3,855 11,208	... ...	2 10	1 56	70 333	1,228 3,959	2,554 6,850	1
154 152	... ...	... 2	... 16	18 39	89 81	47 14	16 49	... ...	... ...	... ...	1 2	3 12	12 35	2
33,916 35,259	2 6	18 817	109 2,376	1,751 8,852	20,726 18,960	11,310 4,248	4,912 15,974	... ...	5 18	8 80	43 619	1,295 5,958	3,561 9,299	1
188 180	... ...	... 3	... 13	7 55	117 81	64 28	26 67	... ...	... ...	... ...	1 ...	7 31	18 36	2
9,543 9,825	2 2	4 98	35 517	446 2,469	6,299 5,794	2,757 945	1,041 2,699	... ...	... 1	2 6	28 46	351 904	660 1,742	1
3 4	... ...	... ...	... ...	1 1	1 3	1 ...	... 1	... ...	... ...	... ...	... 1	... ...	... ...	2
2,564 2,681	... 1	1 28	5 140	146 745	1,671 1,491	741 276	227 811	... ...	1 ...	... 1	4 16	73 294	149 500	1
... ...	... ...	... ...	... ...	... ...	... ...	... ...	... ...	... ...	... ...	... ...	... ...	... ...	... ...	2
12,107 12,506	2 3	5 126	40 657	592 3,214	7,970 7,285	3,498 1,221	1,268 3,510	... ...	1 1	2 7	32 62	424 1,198	809 2,242	
3 4	... ...	... ...	... ...	1 1	1 3	1 ...	... 1	... ...	... ...	... ...	... 1	... ...	... ...	
2,215 2,247	... ...	2 49	12 159	135 536	1,320 1,273	746 230	301 709	... ...	... ...	... 4	5 23	82 228	214 454	1
40 40	... ...	... ...	... 4	2 8	22 25	16 3	1 10	... ...	... ...	... ...	... ...	... 1	1 9	2
411 423	... ...	1 31	6 39	41 104	234 215	129 34	36 101	... ...	... ...	... ...	1 2	13 33	22 66	1
... ...	... ...	... ...	... ...	... ...	... ...	... ...	... ...	... ...	... ...	... ...	... ...	... ...	... ...	2
2,626 2,670	... ...	3 80	18 198	176 640	1,554 1,488	875 264	337 810	... ...	... ...	... 4	6 25	95 261	236 520	
40 40	... ...	... ...	... 4	2 8	22 25	16 3	1 10	... ...	... ...	... ...	... ...	... 1	1 9	
2,827 3,062	... ...	6 96	15 237	212 772	1,712 1,625	882 332	366 997	... ...	... ...	... 4	8 33	111 337	247 623	1
12 13	... ...	... ...	... 1	... 5	7 5	5 2	2 4	... ...	... ...	... ...	... 1	1 1	1 2	2
722 756	... ...	... 14	2 50	37 176	442 433	241 83	102 217	... ...	... 1	... 1	1 10	34 74	67 131	1
... ...	... ...	... ...	... ...	... ...	... ...	... ...	... ...	... ...	... ...	... ...	... ...	... ...	... ...	2
3,549 3,818	... ...	6 110	17 287	249 948	2,154 2,058	1,123 415	468 1,214	... ...	... 1	... 5	9 43	145 411	314 754	
12 13	... ...	... ...	... 1	... 5	7 5	5 2	2 4	... ...	... ...	... ...	... 1	1 1	1 2	

TABLE VIII.

Civil Condition by Age.

TABLE

Civil Condition by Age for

Serial No.	Caste, Tribe or Race	Locality	Sex	Population dealt with	Unmarried: Total	0—6	7—13	14—16	17—23	24—43	44 and over
	1	2	3	4	5	6	7	8	9	10	11
	Hindu and Tribal —*concld.*										
1	Kuruba ... (Hindu)	MYSORE STATE, INCLUDING C. AND M. STN., BANGALORE	Male	**218,058**	**119,072**	**38,803**	**39,341**	**15,953**	16,695	7,749	**531**
			Female	***213,269***	***82,595***	***40,477***	***35,442***	***4,836***	***1,114***	***549***	***178***
2		Civil and Military Station, Bangalore...	Male	588	321	114	108	27	56	16	...
			Female	*533*	*215*	*110*	*87*	*12*	*4*	*2*	...
1	Kuruba ... (Tribal)	MYSORE STATE, INCLUDING C. AND M. STN., BANGALORE	Male	**2,398**	1,197	**445**	**401**	**135**	**161**	**54**	**1**
			Female	***2,205***	***904***	***471***	***357***	***48***	***17***	***10***	***1***
2		Civil and Military Station, Bangalore...	Male	...	...	...	...	...	...	...	...
			Female	...	...	...	...	...	...	...	...
	Kuruba ... (Total)	MYSORE STATE, INCLUDING C. AND M. STN., BANGALORE	Male	**220,456**	**120,269**	**39,248**	**39,742**	**16,088**	**16,856**	**7,803**	**532**
			Female	***215,474***	***83,499***	***40,948***	***35,799***	***4,883***	***1,131***	***559***	***179***
		Civil and Military Station, Bangalore...	Male	588	321	114	108	27	56	16	...
			Female	*533*	*215*	*110*	*87*	*12*	*4*	*2*	...
	Musalman										
1	Labbai	MYSORE STATE, INCLUDING C. AND M. STN., BANGALORE	Male	**7,906**	**4,306**	**955**	**1,182**	**533**	1,028	**588**	**20**
			Female	***4,391***	***2,019***	***971***	***839***	***145***	***39***	***16***	***9***
2		Civil and Military Station, Bangalore...	Male	809	458	111	126	70	102	46	3
			Female	*531*	*239*	*115*	*92*	*20*	*8*	*3*	*1*
1	Mughal ...	MYSORE STATE, INCLUDING C. AND M. STN., BANGALORE	Male	**5,890**	**3,482**	**1,120**	**1,143**	**399**	**600**	**206**	**14**
			Female	***5,130***	***2,437***	***1,158***	***1,013***	***192***	***57***	***13***	***4***
2		Civil and Military Station, Bangalore...	Male	341	208	46	65	23	48	24	2
			Female	*280*	*130*	*64*	*53*	*13*	*7*	*2*	...
1	Pathan ...	MYSORE STATE, INCLUDING C. AND M. STN., BANGALORE	Male	**29,654**	**17,644**	**5,808**	**5,627**	**1,985**	**2,930**	**1,234**	**60**
			Female	***25,953***	***12,068***	***5,845***	***5,078***	***840***	***216***	***68***	***21***
2		Civil and Military Station, Bangalore...	Male	1,798	1,045	291	311	100	214	122	7
			Female	*1,445*	*690*	*326*	*279*	*57*	*25*	*8*	*1*
1	Pinjari ...	MYSORE STATE, INCLUDING C. AND M. STN., BANGALORE	Male	**5,458**	**3,104**	**1,094**	**975**	**367**	**433**	**227**	**8**
			Female	***5,173***	***2,260***	***1,110***	***958***	***135***	***40***	***14***	***3***
2		Civil and Military Station, Bangalore...	Male	7	5	1	...	...	1	2	1
			Female	*4*	*2*	*2*	...	...	...	...	...
1	Saiyad ...	MYSORE STATE, INCLUDING C. AND M. STN., BANGALORE	Male	**39,146**	**22,864**	**7,528**	**7,393**	**2,551**	**3,774**	**1,520**	**98**
			Female	***34,584***	***15,950***	***7,723***	***6,655***	***1,121***	***308***	***80***	***63***
2		Civil and Military Station, Bangalore ...	Male	2,107	1,223	382	373	121	216	122	9
			Female	*1,778*	*821*	*349*	*352*	*72*	*35*	*11*	*2*
1	Sheik ...	MYSORE STATE, INCLUDING C. AND M. STN., BANGALORE	Male	**118,538**	**69,377**	**22,585**	**22,235**	**8,269**	11,394	**4,632**	**262**
			Female	***105,871***	***47,840***	***22,659***	***20,185***	***3,495***	***1,107***	***320***	***74***
2		Civil and Military Station, Bangalore ...	Male	9,637	5,642	1,659	1,699	562	1,107	577	38
			Female	*8,830*	*3,952*	*1,393*	*1,652*	*464*	*319*	*107*	*17*
	Christian										
1	Anglo-Indian	MYSORE STATE, INCLUDING C. AND M. STN., BANGALORE	Male	**3,781**	**2,515**	**628**	**791**	**366**	**441**	**220**	**69**
			Female	***4,528***	***2,700***	***583***	***751***	***358***	***539***	***297***	***172***
2		Civil and Military Station, Bangalore...	Male	2,401	1,659	337	587	293	251	131	60
			Female	*3,119*	*1,865*	*318*	*518*	*267*	*375*	*236*	*151*
1	European and Allied Races.	MYSORE STATE, INCLUDING C. AND M. STN., BANGALORE	Male	**3,144**	**1,893**	**206**	**209**	**81**	**561**	**754**	**82**
			Female	***2,267***	***1,076***	***241***	***224***	***80***	***144***	***202***	***185***
2		Civil and Military Station, Bangalore...	Male	2,486	1,643	158	177	74	516	669	49
			Female	*1,722*	*825*	*189*	*182*	*67*	*118*	*137*	*132*
1	Indian Christian.	MYSORE STATE, INCLUDING C. AND M. STN., BANGALORE	Male	**38,239**	**22,640**	**7,182**	**6,563**	**2,340**	**4,390**	**1,996**	**169**
			Female	***35,579***	***17,497***	***7,013***	***6,278***	***1,927***	***1,387***	***718***	***174***
2		Civil and Military Station, Bangalore...	Male	9,815	5,961	2,027	1,923	549	1,033	369	60
			Female	*10,529*	*5,300*	*1,819*	*1,780*	*683*	*571*	*350*	*97*

VIII.

Selected Castes, Tribes and Races.—*contd.*

TABLE VIII

Civil Condition by Age.

Married							Widowed							
Total	0—6	7—13	14—16	17—23	24—43	44 and over	Total	0—6	7—13	14—16	17—23	24—43	44 and over	Serial No.
12	13	14	15	16	17	18	19	20	21	22	23	24	25	
87,483 90,494	2 14	54 3,163	265 7,423	5,782 23,808	54,142 46,850	27,188 9,236	11,553 40,180	... ...	1 47	7 128	207 1,096	3,250 15,068	8,088 23,841	1
243 239	... ...	... 6	... 16	15 69	149 127	79 21	24 79	... ...	... ...	... ...	... 2	3 29	21 48	2
1,111 1,080	... ...	... 22	2 81	75 289	724 590	310 98	90 221	... ...	... ...	... 2	4 13	33 78	53 128	1
... ...	... ...	... ...	... ...	... ...	... ...	... ...	... ...	... ...	... ...	... ...	... ...	... ...	... ...	2
88,544 91,574	2 14	54 3,185	267 7,504	5,857 24,097	54,866 47,440	27,498 9,334	11,643 40,401	... ...	1 47	7 130	211 1,109	3,283 15,146	8,141 23,969	1
243 239	... ...	... 6	... 16	15 69	149 127	79 21	24 79	... ...	... ...	... ...	... 2	3 29	21 48	2
3,398 1,860	... ...	... 34	3 175	186 532	2,144 966	1,065 153	202 512	... ...	... ...	... 2	2 19	55 163	145 328	1
388 231	... ...	... 3	... 20	17 69	208 118	108 21	18 61	... ...	... ...	... ...	... ...	5 21	13 40	2
2,223 2,094	... ...	2 26	5 156	125 571	1,323 1,125	768 216	185 599	... ...	... ...	... 3	2 16	43 185	140 395	1
124 102	... ...	1 4	1 12	2 27	69 53	51 6	9 39	... ...	... ...	... ...	... ...	2 10	7 29	2
11,128 10,737	... ...	7 136	23 849	557 2,977	6,727 5,674	3,814 1,101	882 3,148	... ...	... 4	... 13	10 87	244 976	628 2,068	1
685 582	... ...	1 5	2 33	23 163	411 316	248 65	68 173	... ...	... ...	... ...	... 3	21 49	47 121	2
2,138 2,238	... ...	3 57	11 178	145 554	1,281 1,202	698 247	216 675	... ...	... 1	... 2	2 24	68 249	146 399	1
2 2	... ...	... ...	... ...	... 1	1 1	1 ...	... ...	... ...	... ...	... ...	... ...	... ...	... ...	2
15,078 14,331	... 2	5 165	27 1,135	791 3,960	9,138 7,555	5,117 1,514	1,204 4,303	... ...	1 1	1 8	15 111	385 1,417	802 2,766	1
815 725	... ...	... 7	3 45	44 189	462 426	306 58	69 232	... ...	... ...	... ...	1 12	16 85	52 135	2
45,223 44,306	... 5	23 519	87 3,450	2,381 12,112	28,053 23,790	14,679 4,430	3,938 13,725	... ...	... 9	1 52	61 359	1,151 4,292	2,725 9,013	1
3,641 3,704	... ...	4 22	7 273	179 1,053	2,164 2,003	1,287 353	354 1,174	... ...	... 3	... 3	4 36	93 350	257 752	2
1,107 1,281	... ...	... ...	2 7	28 140	475 694	602 440	159 547	... ...	... ...	... ...	1 9	20 120	138 418	1
634 808	... ...	... ...	... 2	12 71	210 386	412 349	108 446	... ...	... ...	... ...	1 7	11 97	96 342	2
1,143 931	... ...	... ...	... ...	16 53	484 495	643 383	108 260	... ...	... ...	... ...	... 1	10 47	98 212	1
708 670	... ...	... ...	... ...	12 42	281 341	415 287	85 227	... ...	... ...	... ...	... 1	7 41	78 185	2
14,421 13,480	... ...	7 60	31 644	698 3,790	9,382 7,582	4,303 1,404	1,178 4,602	... ...	... ...	... 9	14 139	338 1,613	826 2,841	1
3,489 3,754	... ...	4 17	11 175	189 981	2,229 2,032	1,056 549	365 1,475	... ...	... ...	... 2	6 39	99 417	260 1,017	2

TABLE VIII.

Civil Condition by Age.

TABLE

Civil Condition by Age for

Serial No.	Caste, Tribe or Race	Locality	Sex	Population dealt with	Unmarried						
					Total	0—6	7—13	14—16	17—23	24—43	44 and over
	1	2	3	4	5	6	7	8	9	10	11
	Jain										
1	Digambara	MYSORE STATE, INCLUDING C. AND M. STN., BANGALORE	Male	**6,596**	**3,722**	**1,082**	**1,141**	**462**	**602**	**372**	**63**
			Female	***6,183***	***2,261***	***1,070***	***1,010***	***140***	***26***	***13***	***2***
2		Civil and Military Station, Bangalore...	Male	47	26	6	6	5	9	...	...
			Female	*34*	*11*	*7*	*4*	...	...	...	...
1	Swetambara.	MYSORE STATE, INCLUDING C. AND M. STN., BANGALORE	Male	**2,030**	**1,115**	**221**	**233**	**178**	**318**	**148**	**17**
			Female	***849***	***310***	***169***	***129***	***7***	***2***	***3***	...
2		Civil and Military Station, Bangalore...	Male	272	142	39	36	24	31	11	1
			Female	*195*	*67*	*37*	*28*	*1*	*1*	...	...
1	Sada ...	MYSORE STATE, INCLUDING C. AND M. STN., BANGALORE	Male	**6,900**	**3,792**	**1,080**	**1,170**	**457**	**645**	**380**	**60**
			Female	***6,446***	***2,423***	***1,115***	***1,121***	***148***	***24***	***12***	***3***
2		Civil and Military Station, Bangalore...	Male	56	28	9	9	2	6	1	1
			Female	*39*	*13*	*5*	*7*	...	*1*	...	...
1	**Parsi**	MYSORE STATE, INCLUDING C. AND M. STN., BANGALORE	Male	**169**	**112**	**33**	**28**	**16**	**17**	**16**	**2**
			Female	***162***	***93***	***27***	***27***	***10***	***20***	***7***	***2***
2		Civil and Military Station, Bangalore...	Male	120	85	26	26	8	12	11	2
			Female	*124*	*73*	*23*	*23*	*9*	*10*	*6*	*2*
1	**Sikh**	MYSORE STATE, INCLUDING C. AND M. STN., BANGALORE	Male	**63**	**22**	**8**	**4**	**6**	**3**	**1**	...
			Female	***37***	***15***	***8***	***5***	***2***	...	...	...
2		Civil and Military Station, Bangalore...	Male	29	2	...	1	1	...	...	...
			Female	*3*	*1*	*1*	...	...	...	...	...
1	**Jew**	MYSORE STATE, INCLUDING C. AND M. STN., BANGALORE	Male	**13**	**6**	**2**	**2**	**1**	**1**	...	...
			Female	***26***	***18***	***5***	***6***	***4***	***3***	...	...
2		Civil and Military Station, Bangalore...	Male	6	3	2	1	...	...	...	...
			Female	*15*	*11*	*5*	*3*	*1*	*2*	...	...
1	**Buddhist**	MYSORE STATE, INCLUDING C. AND M. STN., BANGALORE	Male	**640**	**363**	**146**	**98**	**29**	**64**	**26**	...
			Female	***599***	***270***	***139***	***79***	***34***	***11***	***7***	...
2		Civil and Military Station, Bangalore...	Male	143	83	28	27	6	12	10	...
			Female	*117*	*65*	*30*	*19*	*9*	*5*	*2*	...
1	**Others**	MYSORE STATE, INCLUDING C. AND M. STN., BANGALORE	Male	**51**	**31**	**11**	**6**	**3**	**5**	**4**	**2**
			Female	***55***	***29***	***5***	***9***	***4***	***7***	***4***	...
2		Civil and Military Station, Bangalore...	Male	40	23	10	5	1	3	4	...
			Female	*51*	*29*	*5*	*9*	*4*	*7*	*4*	...

Selected Castes, Tribes and Races.—*concld.* **Civil Condition by Age.**

Married							Widowed							
Total	0—6	7—13	14—16	17—23	2 —43	44 and over	Total	0—6	7—13	14—16	17—23	24—43	44 and over	Serial No.
12	13	14	15	16	17	18	19	20	21	22	23	24	25	
2,454	...	3	7	219	1,462	763	420	...	...	...	2	128	290	1
2,492	*2*	*105*	*284*	*702*	*1,113*	*286*	*1,430*	...	*2*	*8*	*56*	*585*	*779*	
20	...	...	...	4	13	3	1	...	...	...	...	...	1	2
19	...	...	*1*	*4*	*11*	*3*	*4*	...	...	...	...	*2*	*2*	
836	...	3	2	133	524	174	79	...	...	...	1	31	47	1
423	...	*14*	*39*	*137*	*219*	*14*	*116*	...	...	*2*	*9*	*36*	*69*	
116	...	...	1	25	66	24	14	...	...	...	...	7	7	2
97	...	...	*12*	*34*	*48*	*3*	*31*	...	...	*2*	*3*	*8*	*18*	
2,635	...	2	6	156	1,539	932	473	...	...	5	7	118	343	1
2,681	...	*78*	*216*	*751*	*1,318*	*318*	*1,342*	...	*1*	*4*	*51*	*445*	*841*	
28	...	...	...	6	18	4	...	...	...	...	...	...	...	2
19	...	...	...	*5*	*12*	*2*	*7*	...	...	...	*1*	...	*6*	
49	1	...	...	...	24	24	8	...	...	...	...	1	7	1
55	...	*1*	...	*7*	*31*	*16*	*14*	...	...	...	...	*2*	*12*	
32	...	...	...	...	16	16	3	...	...	...	...	...	3	2
39	...	...	...	*4*	*25*	*10*	*12*	...	...	...	...	*2*	*10*	
38	...	...	2	11	17	8	3	...	...	...	...	...	3	1
18	...	...	*1*	*4*	*9*	*4*	*4*	...	...	...	...	*3*	*1*	
25	...	...	2	8	13	2	2	...	...	...	...	...	2	2
2	...	...	...	*1*	...	*1*	...	...	...	...	...	...	...	
7	...	...	...	...	2	5	...	...	...	...	...	...	...	1
8	...	...	*1*	*1*	*4*	*2*	...	...	...	...	...	...	...	
3	...	...	...	...	2	1	...	...	...	...	...	...	...	2
4	...	...	...	...	*3*	*1*	...	...	...	...	...	...	...	
266	...	1	1	16	180	68	11	...	...	...	...	4	7	1
255	...	*4*	*18*	*76*	*131*	*26*	*74*	...	...	*1*	*4*	*24*	*45*	
57	...	...	...	8	39	15	3	...	...	...	...	2	1	2
42	...	...	*1*	*12*	*24*	*5*	*10*	...	...	...	...	*4*	*6*	
19	...	...	...	1	10	8	1	...	...	...	...	...	1	1
20	...	...	...	*3*	*12*	*5*	*6*	...	...	...	...	*3*	*3*	
16	...	...	...	1	7	8	1	...	...	...	...	...	1	2
17	...	...	...	*3*	*9*	*5*	*5*	...	...	...	...	*2*	*3*	

MYSORE CENSUS, 1931.

TABLE IX.

Infirmities.

Part I.—Distribution by Age.

Part II.—Distribution by Districts.

NOTE 1.—In part I, details are given for (i) Mysore State including the Civil and Military Station, Bangalore, and (ii) Mysore State excluding the Civil and Military Station, Bangalore.

NOTE 2.—Of the persons returned in this Table, a few have been found to be afflicted with two or more infirmities. Such persons have been shown under each of the infirmities, but have been reckoned singly for purposes of columns 2 to 4. Information concerning these has been given separately.

TABLE IX.
Infirmities.
Part I—Distribution by Age.

TABLE IX.

Infirmities.

Part I.—Distribution by Age.

Mysore State including Civil and Military Station, Bangalore.

Age	Population Afflicted			Insane			Deaf-Mutes			Blind			Lepers		
	Persons	Males	Females	Persons	Males	Females	Persons	Males	Females	Persons	Males	Females	Persons	Males	Females
1	2	3	4	5	6	7	8	9	10	11	12	13	14	15	16
All Ages ...	**12,954**	**7,358**	**5.596**	**1,782**	**1,050**	**732**	**3,950**	**2.254**	**1,696**	**6,553**	**3,556**	**2,997**	**733**	**536**	**197**
0—1 ...	27	14	13	2	...	2	6	3	3	18	10	8	1	1	...
1—2 ...	41	25	16	4	4	...	6	4	2	29	16	13	2	1	1
2—3 ...	65	31	34	2	...	2	28	14	14	35	17	18	...	...	...
3—4 ...	112	64	48	3	3	...	63	35	28	48	28	20	...	...	...
4—5 ...	219	126	93	17	10	7	124	70	54	74	44	30	5	3	2
0—5 ...	**464**	**260**	**204**	**28**	**17**	**11**	**227**	**126**	**101**	**204**	**115**	**89**	**8**	**5**	**3**
5—10 ...	1,211	680	531	130	69	61	661	364	297	416	242	174	13	9	4
10—15 ...	1,313	737	576	171	94	77	666	365	301	469	272	197	12	10	2
15—20 ...	1,116	636	480	191	115	76	474	268	206	433	242	191	30	20	10
20—25 ...	1,106	643	463	192	123	69	437	250	187	443	248	195	41	26	15
25—30 ...	1,056	597	459	209	131	78	359	196	163	431	231	200	65	41	24
30—35 ...	1,003	579	424	210	135	75	302	176	126	414	215	199	80	55	25
35—40 ...	899	556	343	185	111	74	231	152	79	398	226	172	94	74	20
40—45 ...	806	485	321	148	82	66	183	114	69	385	217	168	92	73	19
45—50 ...	703	407	296	95	52	43	121	75	46	404	215	189	84	65	19
50—55 ...	603	340	263	69	39	30	93	55	38	382	200	182	60	46	14
55—60 ...	628	331	297	62	30	32	68	43	25	442	219	223	57	40	17
60—65 ...	603	308	295	41	21	20	58	35	23	456	219	237	49	34	15
65—70 ...	468	245	223	22	12	10	33	17	16	389	198	191	26	18	8
70 and over	975	554	421	29	19	10	37	18	19	887	497	390	22	20	2

Mysore State excluding Civil and Military Station, Bangalore.

Age	Population Afflicted			Insane			Deaf-Mutes			Blind			Lepers		
	Persons	Males	Females	Persons	Males	Females	Persons	Males	Females	Persons	Males	Females	Persons	Males	Females
1	2	3	4	5	6	7	8	9	10	11	12	13	14	15	16
All Ages ...	**12,747**	**7,244**	**5,503**	**1,752**	**1,030**	**722**	**3,895**	**2.218**	**1.677**	**6,441**	**3,502**	**2,939**	**723**	**532**	**191**
0—1 ...	27	14	13	2	...	2	6	3	3	18	10	8	1	1	...
1—2 ...	41	25	16	4	4	...	6	4	2	29	16	13	2	1	1
2—3 ...	63	30	33	2	...	2	26	13	13	35	17	18	...	...	...
3—4 ...	112	64	48	3	3	...	63	35	28	48	28	20	...	...	...
4—5 ...	216	125	91	17	10	7	122	69	53	74	44	30	4	3	1
0—5 ...	**459**	**258**	**201**	**28**	**17**	**11**	**223**	**124**	**99**	**204**	**115**	**89**	**7**	**5**	**2**
5—10 ...	1.197	671	526	126	67	59	652	358	294	415	241	174	13	9	4
10—15 ...	1.300	729	571	169	93	76	659	360	299	465	270	195	12	10	2
15—20 ...	1.103	628	475	188	113	75	469	265	204	428	239	189	30	20	10
20—25 ...	1.095	634	461	189	121	68	434	247	187	439	245	194	40	25	15
25—30 ...	1.046	590	456	208	130	78	357	195	162	426	227	199	63	40	23
30—35 ...	991	570	421	207	132	75	301	175	126	407	210	197	79	55	24
35—40 ...	884	546	338	182	109	73	226	149	77	391	221	170	94	74	20
40—45 ...	789	476	313	145	80	65	176	111	65	378	213	165	92	73	19
45—50 ...	689	399	290	93	51	42	117	73	44	398	211	187	82	64	18
50—55 ...	595	335	260	67	38	29	92	54	38	378	197	181	59	46	13
55—60 ...	613	323	290	61	29	32	66	41	25	432	215	217	55	39	16
60—65 ...	588	302	286	40	20	20	56	34	22	444	215	229	49	34	15
65—70 ...	453	239	214	20	11	9	32	16	16	377	194	183	26	18	8
70 and over	945	544	401	29	19	10	35	16	19	859	489	370	22	20	2

TABLE IX.

Infirmities—*concld.*

Part II.—Distribution by Districts.

TABLE IX.
Infirmities.
Part II—Distribution by Districts.

District or State	POPULATION AFFLICTED			INSANE			DEAF-MUTES			BLIND			LEPERS		
	Persons	Males	Females	Persons	Males	Females	Persons	Males	Females	Persons	Males	Females	Persons	Males	Females
1	2	3	4	5	6	7	8	9	10	11	12	13	14	15	16
MYSORE STATE, INCLUDING CIVIL AND MILITARY STATION, BANGALORE.	**12,954**	**7,358**	**5,596**	**1.782**	**1,050**	**732**	**3.950**	**2,254**	**1,696**	**6,553**	**3,556**	**2,997**	**733**	**536**	**197**
MYSORE STATE, EXCLUDING CIVIL AND MILITARY STATION, BANGALORE.	**12,747**	**7,244**	**5.508**	**1.752**	**1,030**	**722**	**3.895**	**2,218**	**1,677**	**6,441**	**3,502**	**2,939**	**723**	**532**	**191**
Bangalore City ...	**501**	**308**	**193**	213	128	85	76	46	30	125	72	53	91	63	28
Bangalore District ...	**1,854**	**1,091**	**763**	227	124	103	640	376	264	855	485	370	138	110	28
Kolar Gold Fields (City)	**119**	**70**	**49**	14	8	6	28	17	11	71	43	28	7	3	4
Kolar District ...	**1,946**	**1,106**	**841**	257	137	120	506	287	219	1,005	553	452	186	129	57
Tumkur District ...	**2,072**	**1,157**	**915**	203	126	77	616	349	267	1,201	644	557	62	46	16
Mysore City ...	**209**	**133**	**76**	35	20	15	64	34	30	110	79	31	...	...	...
Mysore District ...	**2,317**	**1,307**	**1,010**	232	127	105	733	422	311	1,246	669	577	113	94	19
Chitaldrug District ...	**1,516**	**871**	**645**	239	155	84	457	273	184	784	415	369	50	38	12
Hassan District ...	**889**	**477**	**412**	72	45	27	337	174	163	465	248	217	18	12	6
Kadur District ...	**505**	**275**	**230**	77	42	35	173	99	74	231	119	112	26	15	11
Shimoga District ...	**819**	**450**	**369**	183	118	65	265	141	124	348	175	173	32	22	10
Civil and Military Station, Bangalore.	**207**	**114**	**93**	**30**	**20**	**10**	**55**	**36**	**19**	**112**	**54**	**58**	**10**	**4**	**6**

Persons afflicted with two or more infirmities.

Infirmities	Persons	Males	Females
1	2	3	4
Insane and Deaf-mutes	34	22	12
Insane and Blind	8	4	4
Insane and Leper	2	...	2
Deaf-mute and Leper	2	1	1
Deaf-mute and Blind	15	8	7
Blind and Leper	3	3	...
Total ...	**64**	**38**	**26**

MYSORE CENSUS, 1931.

TABLE X—Occupation.

NOTE 1.—In this Table the Occupations have been arranged in 4 Classes, 12 Sub-classes, 55 Orders and 195 Groups. The Table deals with the whole population of the State.

NOTE 2.—The following Groups which are blank for the whole State are omitted from the Table.

Number.		*Name.*	
8	... ...	Cultivators of jhum, taungya and shifting areas.	
9	... ...	Cultivation of Cinchona.	
31	... ...	Exploitation of Lead, silver and zinc.	
35	... ...	Do	Coal.
36	... ...	Do	Petroleum.
38	... ...	Do	Mica.
39	... ...	Do	Precious and semi-precious stones.
41	... ...	Do	Other non-metallic minerals.
69	... ...	Manufacture and refining of mineral oils.	
79	... ...	Manufacturers of opium.	
80	... ...	Do	of ganja.
101	... ...	Persons concerned with aerodromes and aeroplanes.	
155	... ...	Navy.	

NOTE 3.—Separate figures in regard to persons undergoing rigorous and other kinds of imprisonment are available only for the Cities of Bangalore and Mysore. In all other cases the imprisonment has been treated as other than rigorous. Prisoners undergoing rigorous imprisonment are shown as working dependants and appear in the corresponding total at the head of the table. All other classes of prisoners appear under the group number as earners. In the total, however, they are included not under the head earners but under non-working dependants.

TABLE X.

Occupation

District or State	Total Population	Total of all Classes — Total Population — Total earners (Principal occupation)		Total working dependants		Total non-working dependants		Total earners with subsidiary occupation		Class A.—Production of Raw Materials — Total of Class A — Total earners (Principal occupation)		Total working dependants		Total following occupation as subsidiary to other	
		Males	Females	Males	Females	Males	Females	Males	Females	Males	Females	Males	Females	Males	Females
	1	2	3	4	5	6	7	8	9	10	11	12	13	14	15
MYSORE STATE, INCLUDING CIVIL AND MILITARY STATION, BANGALORE.	6,557,302	1,936,622	413,388	126,295	509,925	1,291,046	2,280,026	222,912	20,199	1,461,138	255,026	111,751	461,685	75,563	8,331
MYSORE STATE, EXCLUDING CIVIL AND MILITARY STATION, BANGALORE.	6,423,189	1,898,976	405,817	126,205	509,380	1,259,373	2,223,438	221,819	20,137	1,459,283	254,786	111,743	461,670	75,276	8,330
Bangalore City ...	172,357	48,871	9,276	989	2,962	42,820	68,439	672	69	2,322	346	24	90	212	3
Bangalore District ...	908,056	262,690	41,414	15,039	27,718	184,176	877,024	34,086	1,506	206,660	19,227	18,462	24,936	12,449	568
Kolar Gold Fields (City)...	85,103	27,807	2,955	282	42	17,012	37,055	1,063	139	14,521	789	228	57	380	9
Kolar District ...	763,934	230,331	37,781	19,344	51,707	189,587	285,184	36,367	1,762	185,864	22,325	17,649	43,654	12,613	756
Tumkur District ...	861,405	249,168	47,582	24,402	110,871	165,574	263,808	32,602	2,694	204,594	31,181	22,003	101,481	10,680	1,090
Mysore City ...	107,142	29,973	5,581	476	316	26,323	44,444	1,580	160	3,677	319	120	21	654	15
Mysore District ...	1,403,984	393,515	91,890	29,183	89,929	281,140	518,327	50,083	4,023	322,954	54,081	26,145	82,879	16,878	1,446
Chitaldrug District ...	656,569	187,588	49,112	9,777	64,409	189,421	206,262	17,610	2,265	143,780	34,609	8,701	59,159	6,000	1,162
Hassan District ...	596,937	179,105	39,608	16,276	93,718	105,365	162,965	24,906	5,246	148,308	29,642	14,213	86,985	7,341	2,545
Kadur District ...	347,715	126,148	41,069	2,628	80,355	55,618	91,904	7,963	960	102,510	33,795	2,288	28,316	2,809	268
Shimoga District ...	519,987	164,265	39,549	7,859	87,381	102,537	168,126	14,317	1,313	124,078	28,522	6,910	34,162	5,260	479
Civil and Military Station, Bangalore.	134,113	37,646	7,571	90	545	31,673	56,588	1,093	62	1,855	240	8	15	287	1

TABLE X.

Occupation—*contd.*

District or State	Total of Sub-class I—Exploitation of Animals and Vegetation						Order 1.—Pasture and Agriculture: Total of Order 1						Order 1 (a).—Ordinary Cultivation: Total of Order 1 (a)					
	Total earners (Principal occupation)		Total working dependants		Total following occupation as subsidiary to other		Total earners (Principal occupation)		Total working dependants		Total following occupation as subsidiary to other		Total earners (Principal occupation)		Total working dependants		Total following occupation as subsidiary to other	
	Males	Females	Males	Females	Males	Females	Males	Females	Males	Females	Males	Females	Males	Females	Males	Females	Males	Females
	16	17	18	19	20	21	22	23	24	25	26	27	28	29	30	31	32	33
MYSORE STATE, INCLUDING CIVIL AND MILITARY STATION, BANGALORE.	**1,449,860**	**254,599**	**111,742**	**461,683**	**75,014**	**8,325**	**1,448,872**	**254,486**	**111,693**	**461,649**	**74,055**	**8,299**	**1,384,483**	**232,412**	**53,093**	**441,808**	**42,528**	**5,847**
MYSORE STATE, EXCLUDING CIVIL AND MILITARY STATION, BANGALORE.	**1,448,007**	**254.359**	**111,734**	**461,668**	**74,727**	**8,324**	**1,447,037**	**254,246**	**111,685**	**461,634**	**73,768**	**8,298**	**1,383,243**	**232,292**	**53,093**	**441,803**	**42,249**	**5,846**
Bangalore City ...	2,322	346	21	90	212	2	2,315	346	21	90	210	3	1,498	199	14	80	198	3
Bangalore District ...	206,640	19,226	13,462	24,936	12,447	563	206,561	19,218	13,462	24,935	12,377	568	200,202	17,718	8,690	22,044	4,981	366
Kolar Gold Fields (City)...	4,277	427	228	37	201	9	4,276	427	228	37	201	9	4,101	390	226	29	114	9
Kolar District ...	185,670	22,322	17.647	43,654	12,548	756	185,612	22,322	17,643	43,654	12,187	753	180,172	20.910	6.494	88,518	7,129	515
Tumkur District ...	204,567	81,179	22,002	101,481	10,669	1,090	204,585	81,170	22,001	101,479	10,561	1,089	197,910	80,252	11,269	98,562	6,000	550
Mysore City ...	3,674	819	120	21	645	15	3,665	819	120	19	637	15	2,549	240	53	8	572	9
Mysore District ...	322,901	54,075	26,141	82,879	16,856	1.445	322,572	54,025	26,126	82,871	16,383	1,440	314,574	51 5 4	11,157	78.224	7,784	1,025
Chitaldrug District ...	1,43,505	34,539	8.701	59,157	5,772	1.156	143,480	34,585	8,701	59,157	5,751	1,156	137,981	33,841	6,328	58,542	4.358	967
Hassan District ...	148,258	29,647	14,213	86,935	7,336	2,545	148,052	29,628	14,187	86,914	7,209	2,538	189,224	21,236	8,077	84,088	4,973	1,802
Kadur District ...	102,344	33,767	2,288	28,316	2,803	263	102,256	33,756	2,288	28,316	2,795	253	84,898	24,661	1,274	27,725	1,755	160
Shimoga District ...	128,851	28,522	6,905	34,162	5,243	479	128,683	28,505	6,905	34,162	5,157	479	120,184	28,271	4,546	38,988	4,440	440
Civil and Military Station, Bangalore.	**1.853**	**240**	**8**	**15**	**287**	**1**	**1,835**	**240**	**8**	**15**	**287**	**1**	**1.240**	**120**	**...**	**5**	**279**	**1**

TABLE X.

Occupation—*contd.*

District or State	Order I (a).—Ordinary Cultivation—*contd.* Group I.—Non-cultivating proprietors taking rent in money or kind: Total earners (Principal occupation) Males	Total earners (Principal occupation) Females	Total working dependants Males	Total working dependants Females	Total following occupation as subsidiary to other Males	Total following occupation as subsidiary to other Females	2. Estate Agents and managers of owners: Total earners (Principal occupation) Males	Total earners (Principal occupation) Females	Total working dependants Males	Total working dependants Females	Total following occupation as subsidiary to other Males	Total following occupation as subsidiary to other Females	3. Estate Agents and managers of Government: Total earners (Principal occupation) Males	Total earners (Principal occupation) Females	Total working dependants Males	Total working dependants Females	Total following occupation as subsidiary to other Males	Total following occupation as subsidiary to other Females
	34	35	36	37	38	39	40	41	42	43	44	45	46	47	48	49	50	51
MYSORE STATE, INCLUDING CIVIL AND MILITARY STATION, BANGALORE.	**27,240**	**16,034**	**337**	**4,503**	**5,977**	**275**	**103**	**19**	**6**	...	**59**	...	**1**	...	...	...	**1**	...
MYSORE STATE, EXCLUDING CIVIL AND MILITARY STATION, BANGALORE.	**27,021**	**16,006**	**337**	**4,503**	**5,892**	**275**	**103**	**19**	**6**	...	**59**	...	**1**	...	...	...	**1**	...
Bangalore City ...	481	87	3	1	115	1	1	...	...	...	...	...	...	...	...	...	...	...
Bangalore District ...	3,613	2,138	33	26	1,146	31	...	...	...	...	...	...	...	...	...	...	...	...
Kolar Gold Fields (City)...	18	42	...	1	16	2	...	...	...	...	...	...	...	...	...	...	...	...
Kolar District ...	4,238	2,258	61	161	1,061	49	...	...	...	...	1	...	1	...	...	...	...	...
*Tumkur District ...	5,001	2,922	60	43	854	39	47	...	6	...	21	...	...	...	...	...	...	...
Mysore City ...	530	174	10	3	287	2	...	...	...	...	...	...	...	...	...	...	...	...
Mysore District ...	5,082	3,745	39	46	857	68	1	...	...	...	...	...	...	...	...	...	1	...
Chitaldrug District ...	2,445	1,046	88	549	442	31	...	...	...	...	...	...	...	...	...	...	...	...
Hassan District ...	1,454	1,451	2	3,554	383	27	10	11	...	...	7	...	...	...	...	...	...	...
Kadur District ...	2,112	672	2	4	206	3	10	8	...	...	1	...	...	...	...	...	...	...
Shimoga District ...	2,097	1,271	39	115	525	22	34	...	...	...	29	...	...	...	...	...	...	...
Civil and Military Station, Bangalore.	**219**	**28**	...	...	**85**	...	...	...	...	...	...	...	...	...	...	...	...	...

TABLE X.

Occupation—*contd.*

Order I (a).—Ordinary Cultivation—*contd.*

District or State	4. Rent collectors, clerks, etc. — Total earners (Principal occupation)		Total working dependants		Total following occupation as subsidiary to other		5. Cultivating Owners — Total earners (Principal occupation)		Total working dependants		Total following occupation as subsidiary to other		6. Tenant cultivators — Total earners (Principal occupation)		Total working dependants		Total following occupation as subsidiary to other	
	Males	Females	Males	Females	Males	Females	Males	Females	Males	Females	Males	Females	Males	Females	Males	Females	Males	Females
	52	53	54	55	56	57	58	59	60	61	62	63	64	65	66	67	68	69
MYSORE STATE, INCLUDING CIVIL AND MILITARY STATION, BANGALORE.	**51**	**13**	...	**2**	**3**	**4**	**1,083,605**	**75,334**	**25,646**	**232,090**	**14,898**	**541**	**130,368**	**18,306**	**7,375**	**44,055**	**7,036**	**514**
MYSORE STATE, EXCLUDING CIVIL AND MILITARY STATION, BANGALORE.	**50**	**13**	...	**2**	**3**	**4**	**1,083,180**	**75,312**	**25,646**	**232,090**	**14,885**	**541**	**129,886**	**18,277**	**7,375**	**44,055**	**6,857**	**513**
Bangalore City ...	...	...	...	...	...	...	778	32	6	71	63	2	228	5	5	8	16	...
Bangalore District ...	2	...	...	...	1	...	168,193	7,460	1,027	310	1,864	47	16,759	967	242	99	730	24
Kolar Gold Fields (City)...	...	...	...	...	...	...	3,643	189	7	...	56	...	158	21	8	...	11	...
Kolar District ...	5	...	...	...	1	...	148,978	7,087	2,857	8,470	2,332	79	15,535	1,062	584	571	965	31
Tumkur District ...	1	...	...	...	...	...	162,356	10,868	7,263	73,427	2,338	89	14,684	1,505	2,842	15,617	688	40
Mysore City ...	...	...	...	...	...	...	1,104	37	30	5	170	4	505	5	9	...	74	...
Mysore District ...	...	...	...	...	...	...	269,327	18,934	1,287	665	3,044	84	17,750	1,872	1,730	88	1,854	42
Chitaldrug District ...	38	7	...	...	...	1	98,488	7,735	3,734	86,686	1,574	92	12,923	1,939	1,203	15,351	545	143
Hassan District ...	...	5	...	2	...	3	117,490	11,072	6,265	67,843	1,644	92	8,207	871	580	2,750	922	192
Kadur District ...	4	1	...	...	1	...	43,975	3,171	984	23,242	527	9	13,129	1,737	152	2,572	317	18
Shimoga District ...	...	...	...	...	...	...	68,858	8,727	2,186	21,871	1,273	48	80,008	8,798	625	7,004	1,235	23
Civil and Military Station, Bangalore.	1	...	...	...	...	...	**425**	**22**	...	...	**13**	...	**482**	**29**	...	...	**179**	**1**

TABLE X.

Occupation—*contd.*

District or State	Order 1 (a).—Ordinary cultivation—*concld.*						Order 1 (b).—Cultivation of special crops, fruit, etc., (Planters, managers, clerks and labourers)											
	7. Agricultural labourers						Total of Order 1 (b)						10. Cocoanut					
	Total earners (Principal occupation)		Total working dependants		Total following occupation as subsidiary to other		Total earners (Principal occupation)		Total working dependants		Total following occupation as subsidiary to other		Total earners (Principal occupation)		Total working dependants		Total following occupation as subsidiary to other	
	Males	Females	Males	Females	Males	Females	Males	Females	Males	Females	Males	Females	Males	Females	Males	Females	Males	Females
	70	71	72	73	74	75	76	77	78	79	80	81	82	83	84	85	86	87
MYSORE STATE, INCLUDING CIVIL AND MILITARY STATION, BANGALORE.	143,115	127,706	19,729	161,158	14,554	4,513	32,190	15,025	668	859	7,889	489	10	1	...	...	2	...
MYSORE STATE, EXCLUDING CIVIL AND MILITARY STATION, BANGALORE.	143,002	127,665	19,729	161,153	14,552	4,513	31,688	14,930	667	854	7,882	489	10	1	...	...	2	...
Bangalore City ...	60	75	...	...	4	...	721	121	8	9	7	...	...	...	...	...	...	...
Bangalore District ...	11,685	7,158	2,388	21,609	1,240	264	3,036	263	243	241	2,894	35	...	...	...	...	...	...
Kolar Gold Fields (City)...	282	188	216	28	81	7	71	9	1	...	45	...	...	...	...	...	...	...
Kolar District ...	11,420	10,508	3,042	29,816	2,769	356	918	167	114	199	1,181	25	...	...	...	...	...	...
Tumkur District ...	15,821	14,957	1,568	9,475	2,099	382	294	56	62	15	376	6	5	...	...	...	...	...
Mysore City ...	410	24	4	...	41	3	955	68	13	3	45	8	8	...	...	...	...	...
Mysore District ...	22,414	27,523	8,101	77,480	2,478	831	2,340	193	71	7	1,288	16	...	...	...	...	...	...
Chitaldrug District ...	24,092	23,114	1,298	5,956	1,792	700	249	58	21	3	198	4	1	1	...	...	2	...
Hassan District ...	12,068	10,826	1,280	9,939	2,017	1,488	7,048	5,048	78	122	1,109	320	1	...	...	...	...	...
Kadur District ...	25,668	18,672	186	1,907	708	180	15,812	8,848	41	247	419	50	...	...	...	...	...	...
Shimoga District ...	19,137	14,480	1,696	5,498	1,378	252	744	99	20	8	380	30	...	...	...	...	...	...
Civil and Military Station, Bangalore.	113	41	...	5	2	...	502	95	1	5	7	...	...	...	...	...	...	...

TABLE X.

Occupation—*contd.*

District or State	11. Coffee						12. Ganja						13. Pan-vine					
	Total earners (Principal occupation)		Total working dependants		Total following occupation as subsidiary to other		Total earners (Principal occupation)		Total working dependants		Total following occupation as subsidiary to other		Total earners (Principal occupation)		Total working dependants		Total following occupation as subsidiary to other	
	Males	Females	Males	Females	Males	Females	Males	Females	Males	Females	Males	Females	Males	Females	Males	Females	Males	Females
	88	89	90	91	92	93	94	95	96	97	98	99	100	101	102	103	104	105
MYSORE STATE, INCLUDING CIVIL AND MILITARY STATION, BANGALORE.	18,967	10,369	80	292	1,180	249	1	1	...	...	...	...	845	64	17	8	626	2
MYSORE STATE, EXCLUDING CIVIL AND MILITARY STATION, BANGALORE.	18,957	10,368	80	292	1,180	249	1	1	...	...	...	...	844	64	17	8	626	2
Bangalore City ...	4	...	...	...	...	...	...	...	...	...	...	...	...	...	...	...	...	...
Bangalore District ...	7	...	...	...	...	...	...	...	...	...	...	...	115	...	6	...	278	...
Kolar Gold Fields (City)...	...	...	...	...	...	...	...	...	...	...	...	...	...	...	...	...	...	...
Kolar District ...	...	...	...	...	...	...	...	...	...	...	...	...	32	2	...		101	1
Tumkur District ...	5	...	1	...	...	...	1	...	...	...	...	...	24	2	3	...	64	...
Mysore City ...	4	1	...	...	...	...	...	...	...	...	...	...	522	...	6	...	7	...
Mysore District ...	17	1	...	...	1	...	...	1	...	...	...	...	2	...	...	...	72	...
Chitaldrug District ...	...	1	...	...	...	...	...	...	...	...	...	...	83	8	2	1	53	...
Hassan District ...	5,509	3,795	50	59	911	217	...	...	...	...	...	...	15	8	...	...	32	1
Kadur District ...	13,411	6,570	29	233	268	32	...	...	...	...	...	...	40	42	...	7	10	...
Shimoga District ...	...	...	...	...	...	...	...	...	...	...	...	...	11	2	...	...	9	...
Civil and Military Station, Bangalore.	10	1	...	...	...	...	...	...	...	...	...	...	1	...	...	...	...	...

Order 1 (b).—Cultivation of special crops, fruit, etc., (Planters, managers, clerks and labourers)—*contd.*

TABLE X.

Occupation—*contd.*

District or State	Order 1 (b).—Cultivation of special crops, fruit, etc., (Planters, managers, clerks and labourers)—*concld.*																	
	14. Rubber						15. Tea						16. Market gardeners, flower and fruit growers					
	Total earners (Principal occupation)		Total working dependants		Total following occupation as subsidiary to other		Total earners (Principal occupation)		Total working dependants		Total following occupation as subsidiary to other		Total earners (Principal occupation)		Total working dependants		Total following occupation as subsidiary to other	
	Males	Females	Males	Females	Males	Females	Males	Females	Males	Females	Males	Females	Males	Females	Males	Females	Males	Females
	106	107	108	109	110	111	112	113	114	115	116	117	118	119	120	121	122	123
MYSORE STATE, INCLUDING CIVIL AND MILITARY STATION, BANGALORE.	**5**	...	...	...	...	...	**1,257**	**2,146**	**1**	**22**	...	**6**	**11,105**	**2,444**	**570**	**537**	**6,081**	**232**
MYSORE STATE, EXCLUDING CIVIL AND MILITARY STATION, BANGALORE.	**2**	...	...	...	...	...	**1,252**	**2,145**	**1**	**22**	...	**6**	**10,622**	**2,351**	**569**	**532**	**6,074**	**232**
Bangalore City ...	2	...	...	...	...	...	...	...	...	...	...	...	715	121	8	9	7	...
Bangalore District ...	...	...	...	...	...	...	...	...	...	...	...	...	2,914	263	237	241	2,616	85
Kolar Gold Fields (City)...	...	...	...	...	...	...	...	...	...	...	...	...	71	9	1	...	45	...
Kolar District ...	...	...	...	...	...	...	...	...	...	...	...	...	886	165	114	199	1,080	24
Tumkur District ...	...	...	...	...	...	...	...	...	...	...	...	...	259	54	58	15	312	6
Mysore City ...	...	...	...	...	...	...	...	...	...	...	...	...	426	67	7	3	38	3
Mysore District ...	...	...	...	...	...	...	...	...	...	...	...	...	2,821	191	71	7	1,160	16
Chitaldrug District ...	...	...	...	...	...	...	...	...	...	...	...	...	165	48	19	2	138	4
Hassan District ...	...	...	...	...	...	...	651	357	...	22	...	...	872	888	23	41	166	102
Kadur District ...	...	...	...	...	...	...	601	1,788	1	...	...	6	1,260	448	11	7	141	12
Shimoga District ...	...	...	...	...	...	...	...	...	...	...	...	...	733	97	20	8	371	30
Civil and Military Station, Bangalore.	**3**	...	...	...	...	...	**5**	**1**	...	...	...	...	**483**	**93**	**1**	**5**	**7**	...

TABLE X.

Occupation—*contd.*

District or State	Order 1 (c).—Forestry																	
	Total of Order 1 (c)						17. Forest Officers, Rangers, Guards, etc.						18. Wood-cutters and Charcoal-burners					
	Total earners (Principal occupation)		Total working dependants		Total following occupation as subsidiary to other		Total earners (Principal occupation)		Total working dependants		Total following occupation as subsidiary to other		Total earners (Principal occupation)		Total working dependants		Total following occupation as subsidiary to other	
	Males	Females	Males	Females	Males	Females	Males	Females	Males	Females	Males	Females	Males	Females	Males	Females	Males	Females
	124	125	126	127	128	129	130	131	132	133	134	135	136	137	138	139	140	141
MYSORE STATE, INCLUDING CIVIL AND MILITARY STATION, BANGALORE.	2,749	1,094	268	1,126	1,019	484	1,470	23	5	5	187	2	574	149	10	34	204	6
MYSORE STATE, EXCLUDING CIVIL AND MILITARY STATION, BANGALORE.	2,677	1,087	268	1,126	1,018	484	1,467	23	5	5	187	2	506	149	10	34	203	6
Bangalore City ...	30	...	...	...	...	...	5	...	...	...	...	...	21	...	...	...	...	...
Bangalore District ...	184	51	...	1	86	5	80	...	...	...	13	...	39	...	...	...	33	...
Kolar Gold Fields (City)...	1	4	...	...	7	...	1	...	...	...	...	...	...	3	...	...	7	...
Kolar District ...	258	370	175	689	134	47	85	...	...	1	18	...	11	1	...	...	2	...
Tumkur District ...	356	271	12	38	289	256	55	...	...	...	12	...	15	8	...	7	15	2
Mysore City ...	42	...	...	...	1	...	32	...	...	...	1	...	5	...	...	...	...	...
Mysore District ...	579	56	3	40	129	2	534	20	3	4	93	2	85	3	...	...	13	...
Chitaldrug District ...	283	283	26	47	221	163	67	...	...	...	2	...	108	105	9	27	61	4
Hassan District ...	90	10	16	150	12	2	86	...	1	...	9	...	2	...	...	...	3	...
Kadur District ...	356	42	31	161	77	9	147	3	...	...	9	...	196	29	...	...	51	...
Shimoga District ...	498	...	5	...	62	...	375	...	1	...	30	...	71	...	1	...	18	...
Civil and Military Station, Bangalore.	72	7	...	...	1	...	3	...	...	...	...	...	68	...	...	...	1	...

TABLE X.

Occupation—*contd.*

District or State	Order 1(c)—Forestry—*concld.*												Order 1 (d).—Stock raising					
	19. Collectors of Forest produce						20. Collectors of lac						Total of Order 1 (d)					
	Total earners (Principal occupation)		Total working dependants		Total following occupation as subsidiary to other		Total earners (Principal occupation)		Total working dependants		Total following occupation as subsidiary to other		Total earners (Principal occupation)		Total working dependants		Total following occupation as subsidiary to other	
	Males	Females	Males	Females	Males	Females	Males	Females	Males	Females	Males	Females	Males	Females	Males	Females	Males	Females
	142	143	144	145	146	147	148	149	150	151	152	153	154	155	156	157	158	159
MYSORE STATE, INCLUDING CIVIL AND MILITARY STATION, BANGALORE.	**698**	**920**	**253**	**1,087**	**627**	**476**	**7**	**2**	...	...	**1**	...	**28,145**	**5,079**	**57,391**	**17,530**	**12,258**	**1,006**
MYSORE STATE, EXCLUDING CIVIL AND MILITARY STATION, BANGALORE.	**697**	**913**	**253**	**1,087**	**627**	**476**	**7**	**2**	...	...	**1**	...	**28,124**	**5,061**	**57,384**	**17,525**	**12,258**	**1,006**
Bangalore City ...	1	...	...	...	...	...	...	...	...	...	...	...	66	26	2	1	5	...
Bangalore District ...	64	51	...	1	40	5	1	...	...	...	...	...	2,663	859	9,503	2,627	1,348	68
Kolar Gold Fields (City)...	...	1	...	...	...	...	...	...	...	...	...	...	103	24	1	8	35	...
Kolar District ...	162	367	175	688	114	47	...	2	...	...	...	...	3,941	770	10,826	4,174	2,134	128
Tumkur District ...	280	263	12	81	261	254	6	...	...	...	1	...	5,910	575	10,658	2,814	2,157	121
Mysore City ...	5	...	...	...	...	...	...	...	...	...	...	...	119	11	54	8	19	3
Mysore District ...	10	33	...	36	23	...	...	...	...	...	...	...	4,654	1,769	14,712	4,420	3,642	207
Chitaldrug District ...	108	178	17	20	158	159	...	...	...	...	...	...	4,967	353	2,331	565	984	22
Hassan District ...	2	10	15	150	...	2	...	...	...	...	...	...	1,690	334	6,021	2,554	1,115	414
Kadur District ...	13	10	31	161	17	9	...	...	...	...	...	...	1,709	205	942	183	544	34
Shimoga District ...	52	...	8	...	14	...	...	...	...	...	...	...	2,302	135	2,334	171	275	9
Civil and Military Station, Bangalore.	1	7	...	...	...	...	...	...	...	...	...	...	21	18	7	5	...	...

TABLE X.

Occupation—*contd.*

District or State	Order 1 (d).—Stock-raising—*concld.*																	
	21. Cattle and buffalo breeders and keepers						22. Breeders of transport animals						23. Herdsmen, shepherds and breeders of other animals					
	Total earners (Principal occupation)		Total working dependants		Total following occupation as subsidiary to other		Total earners (Principal occupation)		Total working dependants		Total following occupation as subsidiary to other		Total earners (Principal occupation)		Total working dependants		Total following occupation as subsidiary to other	
	Males	Females	Males	Females	Males	Females	Males	Females	Males	Females	Males	Females	Males	Females	Males	Females	Males	Females
	160	161	162	163	164	165	166	167	168	169	170	171	172	173	174	175	176	177
MYSORE STATE, INCLUDING CIVIL AND MILITARY STATION, BANGALORE.	53	28	...	...	17	3	29	...	...	2	1	...	28,063	5,051	57,391	17,528	12,240	1,003
MYSORE STATE, EXCLUDING CIVIL AND MILITARY STATION, BANGALORE.	53	28	...	...	17	3	29	...	...	2	1	..	28,042	5,033	57,384	17,523	12,240	1,003
Bangalore City ...	14	13	...	...	...	...	...	...	...	...	...	...	52	18	2	1	5	...
Bangalore District ...	...	14	...	...	...	3	...	...	...	...	...	...	2,663	845	9,508	2,627	1,348	65
Kolar Gold Fields (City)	2	...	...	...	...	...	...	...	...	...	...	...	101	24	1	8	35	...
Kolar District ...	...	...	...	...	...	...	1	...	...	2	1	...	3,940	770	10,826	4,172	2,133	128
Tumkur District ...	...	...	...	...	...	...	...	...	...	...	...	...	5,910	575	10,658	2,814	2,157	121
Mysore City ...	...	...	...	...	...	...	5	...	...	...	...	...	114	11	54	8	19	3
Mysore District ...	...	...	...	...	...	...	14	...	...	...	...	...	4,640	1,769	14,712	4,420	3,642	207
Chitaldrug District ...	2	...	...	...	1	...	...	...	...	...	...	...	4,965	358	2,331	565	983	22
Hassan District ...	8	...	...	...	4	...	...	...	...	...	...	...	1,687	334	6,021	2,554	1,111	414
Kadur District ...	27	1	...	...	11	...	4	...	...	...	...	...	1,678	204	942	183	533	34
Shimoga District ...	5	...	...	...	1	...	5	...	...	...	...	...	2,292	135	2,334	171	274	9
Civil and Military Station, Bangalore.	...	...	...	...	...	...	...	...	...	...	...	...	21	18	7	5	...	...

TABLE X.

Occupation—*contd.*

District or State	Order I (e) :—Raising of small animals and insects.																	
	Total of order I (e)						24. Birds, bees, etc.						25. Silk worms					
	Total earners (Principal occupation)		Total working dependants		Total following occupation as subsidiary to other		Total earners (Principal occupation)		Total working dependants		Total following occupation as subsidiary to other		Total earners (Principal occupation)		Total working dependants		Total following occupation as subsidiary to other	
	Males	Females	Males	Females	Males	Females	Males	Females	Males	Females	Males	Females	Males	Females	Males	Females	Males	Females
	178	179	180	181	182	183	184	185	186	187	188	189	190	191	192	193	194	195
MYSORE STATE, INCLUDING CIVIL AND MILITARY STATION, BANGALORE.	1,305	876	273	326	10,361	473	1	4	...	...	1	...	1,288	872	273	326	10,360	473
MYSORE STATE, EXCLUDING CIVIL AND MILITARY STATION, BANGALORE.	1,305	876	273	326	10,361	473	1	4	...	...	1	...	1,288	872	273	326	10,360	473
Bangalore City ...	...	...	...	...	...	...	...	...	...	...	...	...	...	...	...	...	...	...
Bangalore District ...	476	322	26	22	3,068	89	...	...	...	...	1	...	476	322	26	22	3,067	89
Kolar Gold Fields (City)	...	...	...	...	...	...	...	...	...	...	...	...	...	...	...	...	...	...
Kolar District ...	323	105	34	74	1,909	38	...	3	...	...	...	...	323	102	34	74	1,909	38
Tumkur District ...	65	16	30	50	1,739	156	...	1	...	...	...	...	65	15	30	50	1,739	156
Mysore City ...	...	...	...	...	...	...	...	...	...	...	...	...	...	...	...	...	...	...
Mysore District ...	425	433	183	180	3,645	190	...	...	...	...	...	...	424	433	183	180	3,645	190
Chitaldrug District ...	...	...	...	...	...	...	...	...	...	...	...	...	...	...	...	...	...	...
Hassan District ...	...	...	...	...	...	...	...	...	...	...	...	...	...	...	...	...	...	...
Kadur District ...	11	...	...	...	...	...	1	...	...	...	...	...	...	...	...	...	...	...
Shimoga District ...	5	...	...	...	...	...	...	...	...	...	...	...	...	...	...	...	...	...
Civil and Military Station, Bangalore.	...	...	...	...	...	...	...	...	...	...	...	...	...	...	...	...	...	...

TABLE X.

Occupation—*contd.*

District or State	Order I (e):—Raising of small animals and insects—*concld.*						Order 2:—Fishing and Hunting											
	26. Lac cultivation						Total of Order 2.						27. Fishing and pearling					
	Total earners (Principal occupation)		Total working dependants		Total following occupation as subsidiary to other		Total earners (Principal occupation)		Total working dependants		Total following occupation as subsidiary to other		Total earners (Principal occupation)		Total working dependants		Total following occupation as subsidiary to other	
	Males	Females	Males	Females	Males	Females	Males	Females	Males	Females	Males	Females	Males	Females	Males	Females	Males	Females
	196	197	198	199	200	201	202	203	204	205	206	207	208	209	210	211	212	213
MYSORE STATE, INCLUDING CIVIL AND MILITARY STATION, BANGALORE.	**16**	...	...	...	...	...	**988**	**113**	**49**	**34**	**959**	**26**	**896**	**100**	**48**	**33**	**887**	**16**
MYSORE STATE, EXCLUDING CIVIL AND MILITARY STATION, BANGALORE.	**16**	...	...	...	...	...	**970**	**113**	**49**	**34**	**959**	**26**	**881**	**100**	**48**	**33**	**887**	**16**
Bangalore City ...	...	...	...	...	...	...	7	...	...	...	2	...	7	...	...	...	2	...
Bangalore District ...	...	...	...	...	...	...	79	13	...	1	70	...	70	5	...	1	58	...
Kolar Gold Fields (City)	...	...	...	...	...	...	1	...	...	...	...	...	1	...	...	...	...	...
Kolar District ...	...	...	...	...	...	...	58	...	4	...	56	3	56	...	4	...	55	3
Tumkur District ...	...	...	...	...	...	...	32	9	1	2	108	1	23	9	...	2	104	1
Mysore City ...	...	...	...	...	...	...	9	...	...	2	8	...	8	...	...	2	7	...
Mysore District ...	1	...	...	...	...	...	329	50	18	8	473	5	307	45	18	7	423	5
Chitaldrug District ...	...	...	...	...	...	...	25	4	...	...	21	...	21	4	...	...	20	...
Hassan District ...	...	...	...	...	...	...	201	9	26	21	127	7	176	9	26	21	126	5
Kadur District ...	10	...	...	...	...	...	58	11	...	...	8	10	42	11	...	...	8	2
Shimoga District ...	5	...	...	...	...	...	171	17	...	...	86	...	170	17	...	...	84	...
Civil and Military Station, Bangalore.	...	...	...	...	...	...	18	...	...	...	...	...	15	...	...	...	...	...

TABLE X.

Occupation—*contd.*

District or State	Order 2 :—Fishing and Hunting—*concld.* 28. Hunting: Total earners (Principal occupation) Males	Females	Total working dependants Males	Females	Total following occupation as subsidiary to other Males	Females	Total of Sub-class II:—Exploitation of minerals: Total earners (Principal occupation) Males	Females	Total working dependants Males	Females	Total following occupation as subsidiary to other Males	Females	Order 3 :—Metallic minerals. Total of Order 3: Total earners (Principal occupation) Males	Females	Total working dependants Males	Females	Total following occupation as subsidiary to other Males	Females
	214	215	216	217	218	219	220	221	222	223	224	225	226	227	228	229	230	231
MYSORE STATE, INCLUDING CIVIL AND MILITARY STATION, BANGALORE.	**92**	**13**	**1**	**1**	**72**	**10**	**11,278**	**427**	**9**	**2**	**549**	**6**	**10,336**	**349**	**8**	...	**291**	...
MYSORE STATE, EXCLUDING CIVIL AND MILITARY STATION, BANGALORE.	**89**	**13**	**1**	**1**	**72**	**10**	**11,276**	**427**	**9**	**2**	**549**	**6**	**10,334**	**349**	**8**	...	**291**	...
Bangalore City ...	...	...	...	...	...	...	...	...	...	...	...	...	...	...	...	...	...	...
Bangalore District ...	9	8	...	...	12	...	20	1	...	...	2	...	2	1	...	...	...	...
Kolar Gold Fields (City)	...	...	...	...	...	...	10,244	312	...	...	179	...	10,244	312	...	...	179	...
Kolar District ...	2	...	...	...	1	...	214	3	2	...	70	...	210	3	2	...	66	...
Tumkur District ...	9	...	1	...	4	...	27	2	1	...	11	...	1	...	...	...	...	...
Mysore City ...	1	...	...	...	1	...	3	...	...	...	9	...	3	...	...	...	9	...
Mysore District ...	22	5	...	1	50	...	53	6	1	...	22	...	51	...	1	...	14	...
Chitaldrug District ...	4	...	...	...	1	...	275	70	...	2	228	6	3	...	...	...	...	...
Hassan District ...	25	...	...	...	1	2	55	5	...	...	5	...	54	5	...	...	3	...
Kadur District ...	16	...	...	...	...	8	166	28	...	...	6	...	151	28	...	...	3	...
Shimoga District ...	1	...	...	...	2	...	219	...	5	...	17	...	215	...	5	...	17	...
Civil and Military Station, Bangalore.	3	...	...	...	...	...	2	...	...	...	...	...	2	...	...	...	...	...

TABLE X.

Occupation—*contd.*

District or State	Order 3:—Metallic minerals—*contd.*																	
	29. Gold						30. Iron						32. Manganese					
	Total earners (Principal occupation)		Total working dependants		Total following occupation as subsidiary to other		Total earners (Principal occupation)		Total working dependants		Total following occupation as subsidiary to other		Total earners (Principal occupation)		Total working dependants		Total following occupation as subsidiary to other	
	Males	Females	Males	Females	Males	Females	Males	Females	Males	Females	Males	Females	Males	Females	Males	Females	Males	Females
	232	233	234	235	236	237	238	239	240	241	242	243	244	245	246	247	248	249
MYSORE STATE, INCLUDING CIVIL AND MILITARY STATION, BANGALORE.	10,460	315	2	...	257	...	354	27	5	...	20	...	60	3	...	...	...	...
MYSORE STATE, EXCLUDING CIVIL AND MILITARY STATION, BANGALORE.	10,458	315	2	...	257	...	354	27	5	...	20	...	60	3	...	...	...	...
Bangalore City ...	...	...	...	...	...	...	...	...	...	...	...	...	...	...	...	...	...	...
Bangalore District ...	1	...	...	...	...	...	...	1	...	...	...	...	...	...	...	...	...	...
Kolar Gold Fields (City)...	10,242	312	...	...	179	...	...	...	...	...	...	...	...	...	...	...	...	...
Kolar District ...	210	3	2	...	66	...	...	...	...	...	...	...	...	...	...	...	...	...
Tumkur District ...	...	...	...	...	...	...	...	...	...	...	...	...	1	...	...	...	...	...
Mysore City ...	3	...	...	...	9	...	...	...	...	...	...	...	...	...	...	...	...	...
Mysore District ...	...	...	...	...	...	...	1	...	...	...	...	...	7	...	...	...	...	...
Chitaldrug District ...	...	...	...	...	...	...	...	...	...	...		...	3	...	...	...	...	...
Hassan District ...	2	...	...	...	3	...	...	...	...	...	...	...	45	3	...	...	...	...
Kadur District ...	...	...	...	...	...	...	146	26	...	...	3	...	...	...	...	...	...	...
Shimoga District ...	...	...	...	...	...	...	207	...	5	...	17	...	4	...	...	...	...	...
Civil and Military Station, Bangalore.	2	...	...	...	...	...	...	...	...	...	...	...	...	...	...	...	...	...

TABLE X.

Occupation—*contd.*

District or State	Order 3:—Metallic minerals—*concld.*												Order 4:—Non-metallic minerals					
	33. Tin and Wolfram						34. Other metallic minerals						Total of Order 4					
	Total earners (Principal occupation)		Total working dependants		Total following occupation as subsidiary to other		Total earners (Principal occupation)		Total working dependants		Total following occupation as subsidiary to other		Total earners (Principal occupation)		Total working dependants		Total following occupation as subsidiary to other	
	Males	Females	Males	Females	Males	Females	Males	Females	Males	Females	Males	Females	Males	Females	Males	Females	Males	Females
	250	251	252	253	254	255	256	257	258	259	260	261	262	263	264	265	266	267
MYSORE STATE, INCLUDING CIVIL AND MILITARY STATION, BANGALORE.	17	4	...	...	...	...	45	...	1	...	14	...	342	78	1	2	258	6
MYSORE STATE, EXCLUDING CIVIL AND MILITARY STATION, BANGALORE.	17	4	...	...	...	...	45	...	1	...	14	...	342	78	1	2	258	6
Bangalore City ...	...	...	...	...	...	...	...	...	...	...	...	...	...	...	...	...	...	...
Bangalore District ...	...	...	...	...	...	...	1	...	...	...	...	...	18	...	...	...	2	...
Kolar Gold Fields (City) ...	2	...	...	...	...	...	...	...	...	...	...	...	...	...	...	...	...	...
Kolar District ...	...	...	...	...	...	...	...	...	...	...	...	...	4	...	...	...	4	...
Tumkur District ...	...	...	...	...	...	...	...	...	...	...	...	...	26	2	1	...	11	...
Mysore City ...	...	...	...	...	...	...	...	...	...	...	...	...	...	...	...	...	...	...
Mysore District ...	...	...	...	...	...	...	43	...	1	...	14	...	2	6	...	...	8	...
Chitaldrug District ...	...	...	...	...	...	...	...	...	...	...	...	...	272	70	...	2	228	6
Hassan District ...	6	2	...	...	...	...	1	...	...	...	...	...	1	...	...	...	2	...
Kadur District ...	5	2	...	...	...	...	...	...	...	...	...	...	15	...	...	...	3	...
Shimoga District ...	4	...	...	...	...	...	...	...	...	...	...	...	4	...	...	...	...	...
Civil and Military Station, Bangalore,	...	...	...	...	...	...	...	...	...	...	...	...	...	...	...	...	...	...

TABLE X.

Occupation—*contd.*

District or State	Order 4.—Non-metallic minerals—concld.												Class B.—Preparation and supply of material substances					
	37. Building materials (including stone, materials for cement-manufacture and clays.)						40. Salt, saltpetre and other saline substances.						Total of Class B.					
	Total earners (Principal occupation)		Total working dependants		Total following occupation as subsidiary to other		Total earners (Principal occupation)		Total working dependants		Total following occupation as Subsidiary to other		Total earners (Principal occupation)		Total working dependants		Total following occupation as subsidiary to other	
	Males	Females	Males	Females	Males	Females	Males	Females	Males	Females	Males	Females	Males	Females	Males	Females	Males	Females
	268	269	270	271	272	273	274	275	276	277	278	279	280	281	282	283	284	285
MYSORE STATE, INCLUDING CIVIL AND MILITARY STATION, BANGALORE.	49	...	...	...	7	...	293	78	1	2	251	6	270,977	80,717	7,780	34,952	99,593	6,815
MYSORE STATE, EXCLUDING CIVIL AND MILITARY STATION, BANGALORE.	49	...	...	...	7	...	293	78	1	2	251	6	253,695	77,934	7,729	34,781	99,087	6,768
Bangalore City ...	...	...	...	...	...	...	...	...	...	...	...	...	29,282	5,641	384	1,287	309	51
Bangalore District ...	18	...	...	...	2	...	...	...	...	...	...	...	31,056	12,576	727	1,846	14,248	616
Kolar Gold Fields (City)...	...	...	...	...	...	...	...	...	...	...	...	...	6,225	1,068	2	4	450	16
Kolar District ...	2	...	...	...	...	...	2	...	...	...	4	...	24,846	6,926	986	6,517	15,572	598
Tumkur District ...	1	...	...	...	...	...	13	2	1	...	11	...	25,785	7,414	1,390	6,216	14,810	899
Mysore City ...	...	...	...	...	...	...	...	...	...	...	...	...	13,364	3,004	15	266	604	106
Mysore District ...	...	...	...	...	...	...	2	6	...	...	8	...	40,483	19,959	1,369	4,463	23,509	1,718
Chitaldrug District ...	...	...	...	...	...	...	272	70	...	2	228	6	29,248	8,687	575	4,873	8,345	708
Hassan District ...	1	...	...	...	2	...	...	...	...	...	...	...	17,500	4,628	1,240	5,858	11,238	1,212
Kadur District ...	15	...	...	...	3	...	...	...	...	...	...	...	13,156	2,698	285	1,915	3,598	249
Shimoga District ...	...	...	...	...	...	...	4	...	...	...	...	...	22,750	5,338	666	2,536	6,409	600
Civil and Military Station, Bangalore.	...	...	...	...	...	...	...	...	...	...	...	...	17,282	2,783	51	171	506	47

TABLE X.

Occupation—*contd.*

District or State	Total of Sub-class III.— Industry						Order 5.—Textiles											
							Total of Order 5						42. Cotton ginning, cleaning and pressing					
	Total earners (Principal occupation)		Total working dependants		Total following occupation as subsidiary to other		Total earners (Principal occupation)		Total working dependants		Total following occupation as subsidiary to other		Total earners (Principal occupation)		Total working dependants		Total following occupation as subsidiary to other	
	Males	Females	Males	Females	Males	Females	Males	Females	Males	Females	Males	Females	Males	Females	Males	Females	Males	Females
	286	287	288	289	290	291	292	293	294	295	296	297	298	299	300	301	302	303
MYSORE STATE, INCLUDING CIVIL AND MILITARY STATION, BANGALORE.	**160,360**	**40,786**	**5,493**	**28,947**	**55,535**	**3,281**	**34,442**	**12,553**	**1,436**	**13,240**	**10,032**	**1,008**	**361**	**168**	**3**	...	**35**	**42**
MYSORE STATE, EXCLUDING CIVIL AND MILITARY STATION, BANGALORE.	**151,145**	**39,417**	**5,453**	**28,802**	**55,130**	**3,250**	**34,266**	**12,526**	**1,456**	**13,232**	**10,030**	**1,008**	**361**	**168**	**3**	...	**35**	**42**
Bangalore City ...	17,827	3,955	247	1,218	142	31	9,059	2,896	103	1,120	53	15	3	1	...	...	...	...
Bangalore District ...	19,468	5,191	462	1,419	7,746	228	4,251	1,509	59	858	1,519	94	...	...	...	...	...	...
Kolar Gold Fields (City)...	4,118	548	....	4	205	2	13	...	...	...	16	...	...	...	...	...	...	...
Kolar District ...	13,252	2,837	613	4,233	9,319	246	2,787	753	156	2,066	1,773	101	4	...	...	...	...	...
Tumkur District ...	16,014	3,917	1,025	5,789	9,103	516	4,502	1,553	358	2,315	1,909	216	6	...	...	...	1	...
Mysore City ...	6,122	924	71	75	117	43	699	166	10	12	8	25	2	...	...	...	...	...
Mysore District ...	25,231	9,828	869	3,127	12,095	840	4,621	2,600	156	1,138	2,269	181	11	...	...	...	...	...
Chitaldrug District ...	20,107	5,568	497	3,872	5,335	460	6,005	2,163	122	2,018	1,120	173	266	167	...	...	17	42
Hassan District ...	10,394	2,328	964	5,098	6,068	507	1,424	531	332	2,188	1,018	189	69	...	3	...	17	...
Kadur District ...	6,622	1,528	253	1,892	1,826	146	458	101	90	1,046	169	11	...	...	...	...	...	...
Shimoga District ...	11,990	2,793	452	2,080	3,174	231	497	254	70	476	176	3	...	...	...	...	...	...
Civil and Military Station, Bangalore.	**9,215**	**1,369**	**40**	**145**	**405**	**31**	**176**	**27**	...	**8**	**2**	...	...	...	...	...	...	...

TABLE X.

Occupation—*contd.*

District or State	Order 5.—Textiles—Contd.																	
	43. Cotton spinning, sizing and weaving						44. Jute pressing, spinning and weaving						46. Rope, twine, string and other fibres					
	Total earners (Principal occupation)		Total working dependants		Total following occupation as subsidiary to other		Total earners (Principal occupation)		Total working dependants		Total following occupation as subsidiary to other		Total earners (Principal occupation)		Total working dependants		Total following occupation as subsidiary to other	
	Males	Females	Males	Females	Males	Females	Males	Females	Males	Females	Males	Females	Males	Females	Males	Females	Males	Females
	304	305	306	307	308	309	310	311	312	313	314	315	316	317	318	319	320	321
MYSORE STATE, INCLUDING CIVIL AND MILITARY STATION, BANGALORE.	**23,568**	**6,804**	**1,049**	**8,156**	**3,876**	**439**	**28**	**3**	**1**	**5**	**12**	**3**	**632**	**579**	**38**	**200**	**552**	**145**
MYSORE STATE, EXCLUDING CIVIL AND MILITARY STATION, BANGALORE.	**23,480**	6,790	**1,049**	**8,155**	**3,874**	**439**	**28**	**3**	**1**	**5**	**12**	**3**	**632**	**579**	**38**	**200**	552	**145**
Bangalore City ...	6,098	1,547	58	143	11	1	...	...	...	...	...	...	34	...	...	...	...	...
Bangalore District ...	3,654	912	49	443	474	58	...	...	...	...	1	...	78	208	3	37	105	17
Kolar Gold Fields (City)...	4	...	...	...	5	...	...	...	...	...	...	...	1	...	...	...	...	...
Kolar District ...	2,145	496	106	751	710	9	4	1	...	...	...	...	106	59	9	14	166	58
Tumkur District ...	2,327	488	187	1,194	608	64	18	2	1	5	11	1	97	57	12	16	72	12
Mysore City ...	665	164	9	12	5	25	...	...	...	...	...	...	...	...	...	...	3	...
Mysore District ...	3,806	2,022	121	761	1,023	98	...	...	...	...	...	...	35	112	6	88	108	48
Chitaldrug District ...	2,377	685	82	1,541	406	30	6	...	...	...	...	...	142	95	1	28	65	18
Hassan District ...	1,174	404	290	2,020	454	153	...	...	...	...	...	2	44	23	1	17	11	...
Kadur District ...	350	29	87	821	76	5	...	...	...	...	...	...	15	4	...	...	5	...
Shimoga District ...	290	48	60	469	102	1	...	...	...	...	...	...	80	21	6	...	17	2
Civil and Military Station, Bangalore.	88	14	...	1	2	...	...	...	...	...	...	...	...	...	...	...	...	...

TABLE X.

Occupation—*contd.*

District or State	Order 5.—Textiles - Contd.																	
	46. Wool carding, spinning and weaving						47. Silk spinning and weaving						48. Hair (horse-hair) etc.					
	Total earners (Principal occupation)		Total working dependants		Total following occupation as subsidiary to other		Total earners (Principal occupation)		Total working dependants		Total following occupation as subsidiary to other		Total earners (Principal occupation)		Total working dependants		Total following occupation as subsidiary to other	
	Males	Females	Males	Females	Males	Females	Males	Females	Males	Females	Males	Females	Males	Females	Males	Females	Males	Females
	322	323	324	325	326	327	328	329	330	331	332	333	334	335	336	337	338	339
MYSORE STATE, INCLUDING CIVIL AND MILITARY STATION, BANGALORE.	**5,831**	**2,841**	**249**	**3,194**	**4,590**	**341**	**3,435**	**1,899**	**106**	**1,560**	**924**	**28**	**1**	...	...	...	...	...
MYSORE STATE, EXCLUDING CIVIL AND MILITARY STATION, BANGALORE.	**5,806**	**2,841**	**249**	**3,194**	**4,590**	**341**	**3,413**	**1,897**	**106**	**1,560**	**924**	**28**	**1**	...	...	...	...	...
Bangalore City ...	701	4	...	...	...	...	1,834	1,222	37	914	36	14	...	...	...	...	...	...
Bangalore District ...	248	119	2	339	399	2	239	174	5	26	534	13	...	...	...	...	...	...
Kolar Gold Fields (City)...	8	...	...	...	11	...	...	...	...	...	...	...	...	...	...	...	...	...
Kolar District ...	292	178	36	1,296	782	33	175	14	4	8	95	1	...	...	...	...	...	...
Tumkur District ...	1,939	800	136	847	1,189	139	87	208	22	253	22	...	1	...	...	...	...	...
Mysore City ...	9	1	...	...	...	...	4	1	...	...	...	...	...	...	...	...	...	...
Mysore District ...	498	444	25	288	937	44	257	4	4	1	201	...	...	...	...	...	...	...
Chitaldrug District ...	1,841	1,071	31	'189	598	83	748	144	8	255	32	...	...	...	...	...	...	...
Hassan District ...	87	101	12	17	533	34	43	3	26	99	2	...	...	...	...	...	...	...
Kadur District ...	92	67	3	225	88	6	1	...	...	...	...	...	...	...	...	...	...	...
Shimoga District ...	91	56	4	3	53	...	25	132	...	4	2	...	...	...	...	...	...	...
Civil and Military Station, Bangalore.	25	...	...	...	...	...	22	2	...	...	...	...	...	...	...	...	...	...

TABLE X

Occupation—*contd.*

District or State	Order 5.—Textiles—*concld.*												Order 6.—Hides, skins and hard materials from the animal kingdom					
	49. *Dyeing, bleaching, printing, preparation and sponging of textiles*						50. Lace, crepe, embroideries, fringes, etc., and insufficiently described textile industries						Total of Order 6					
	Total earners (Principal occupation)		Total working dependants		Total *following* occupation as subsidiary to other		Total earners (Principal occupation)		Total working dependants		Total following occupation as subsidiary to other		Total earners (Principal occupation)		Total working dependants		Total following occupation as subsidiary to other	
	Males	Females	Males	Females	Males	Females	Males	Females	Males	Females	Males	Females	Males	Females	Males	Females	Males	Females
	340	341	342	343	344	345	346	347	348	349	350	351	352	353	354	355	356	357
MYSORE STATE, INCLUDING CIVIL AND MILITARY STATION, BANGALORE.	**240**	**106**	**2**	**51**	**18**	**6**	**346**	**153**	**8**	**74**	**25**	**4**	**3,111**	**347**	**48**	**8**	**1,193**	**29**
MYSORE STATE, EXCLUDING CIVIL AND MILITARY STATION, BANGALORE.	**231**	**105**	**2**	**51**	**18**	**6**	**314**	**143**	**8**	**67**	**25**	**4**	**3,075**	**347**	**48**	**8**	**1,192**	**29**
Bangalore City ...	143	4	...	1	1	...	256	118	8	62	5	...	97	...	...	...	...	...
Bangalore District ...	23	96	...	13	6	4	9	...	...	...	...	...	1,004	246	9	4	1	...
Kolar Gold Fields (City)...	...	...	...	...	...	...	...	...	...	...	...	...	...	...	...	...	...	...
Kolar District ...	6	3	1	2	7	2	5	2	...	5	13	3	30	1	1	...	45	...
Tumkur District ...	18	2	...	...	3	...	9	1	...	...	3	...	352	9	8	...	352	...
Mysore City ...	19	...	1	...	...	...	...	...	...	...	...	...	52	...	1	...	7	...
Mysore District ...	2	...	...	...	...	...	12	18	...	...	...	1	104	3	1	...	4	...
Chitaldrug District ...	9	...	...	...	1	...	16	1	...	...	1	...	1,016	38	17	...	671	17
Hassan District ...	...	...	...	35	...	...	7	...	...	...	1	...	53	7	2	4	25	10
Kadur District ...	...	...	...	...	...	...	...	1	...	...	...	...	11	...	...	...	1	...
Shimoga District ...	11	...	...	...	...	...	...	2	...	...	2	...	356	43	9	...	86	2
Civil and Military Station, Bangalore.	9	1	...	...	...	...	32	10	...	7	...	...	36	...	...	...	1	...

TABLE X

Occupation—*contd*

District or State	Order 6.— Hides, skins and hard materials from the animal kingdom—*concld*																	
	51. Working in leather						52. Furriers and persons occupied with feathers, and bristles; brush makers						53. Bone, ivory, horn, shell, etc., workers (except buttons).					
	Total earners (Principal occupation)		Total working dependants		Total following occupation as Subsidiary to other		Total earners (Principal occupation)		Total working dependants		Total following occupation as Subsidiary to other		Total earners (Principal occupation)		Total working dependants		Total following occupation as Subsidiary to other	
	Males	Females	Males	Females	Males	Females	Males	Females	Males	Females	Males	Females	Males	Females	Males	Females	Males	Females
	358	359	360	361	362	363	364	365	366	367	368	369	370	371	372	373	374	375
MYSORE STATE, INCLUDING CIVIL AND MILITARY STATION, BANGALORE.	3,092	344	47	8	1,188	29	6	...	...	...	...	...	13	3	1	...	5	...
MYSORE STATE, EXCLUDING CIVIL AND MILITARY STATION, BANGALORE.	3,060	344	47	8	1,187	29	2	...	...	...	...	...	13	3	1	...	5	...
Bangalore City ...	93	...	...	...	...	...	1	...	...	...	...	...	3	...	...	...	...	...
Bangalore District ...	1,004	246	9	4	1	...	...	...	...	...	...	...	...	...	...	...	...	...
Kolar Gold Fields (City)...	...	...	...	...	...	...	...	...	...	...	...	...	...	...	...	...	...	...
Kolar District ...	30	1	1	...	45	...	...	...	...	...	...	...	...	...	...	...	...	...
Tumkur District ...	352	9	8	...	351	...	...	...	...	...	...	...	...	...	...	...	1	...
Mysore City ...	42	...	...	...	7	...	...	...	...	...	...	...	10	...	1	...	...	...
Mysore District ...	104	...	1	...	...	...	...	...	...	...	...	...	...	3	...	...	4	...
Chitaldrug District ...	1,016	38	17	...	671	17	...	...	...	...	...	...	...	...	...	...	...	...
Hassan District ...	52	7	2	4	25	10	1	...	...	...	...	...	...	...	...	...	...	...
Kadur District ...	11	...	...	...	1	...	...	...	...	...	...	...	...	...	...	...	...	...
Shimoga District ...	356	43	9	...	86	2	...	...	...	...	...	...	...	...	...	...	...	...
Civil and Military Station, Bangalore.	32	...	...	...	1	...	4	...	...	...	...	...	...	...	...	...	...	...

TABLE X

Occupation—*contd*

District or State	Order 7.—Wood																	
	Total of Order 7						54. Sawyers						55. Carpenters, turners and joiners, etc.					
	Total earners (Principal occupation)		Total working dependants		Total following occupation as subsidiary to other		Total earners (Principal Occupation)		Total working dependants		Total following occupation as Subsidiary to other		Total earners (Principal occupation)		Total working dependants		Total following occupation as subsidiary to other	
	Males	Females	Males	Females	Males	Females	Males	Females	Males	Females	Males	Females	Males	Females	Males	Females	Males	Females
	376	377	378	379	380	381	382	383	384	385	386	387	388	389	390	391	392	393
MYSORE STATE, INCLUDING CIVIL AND MILITARY STATION, BANGALORE.	**17,123**	**4,705**	**392**	**1,478**	**6,007**	**425**	**1,481**	**3**	**8**	...	**271**	...	**11,225**	**57**	**170**	**64**	**3,697**	**20**
MYSORE STATE, EXCLUDING CIVIL AND MILITARY STATION, BANGALORE.	**16,115**	**4,615**	**390**	**1,478**	**5,877**	**425**	**1,440**	**3**	**8**	...	**271**	...	**10,424**	**55**	**168**	**64**	**3,568**	**20**
Bangalore City ...	1,189	89	12	17	13	6	11	...	...	...	...	...	1,042	6	7	1	8	...
Bangalore District ...	1,196	666	18	45	636	13	35	...	...	...	17	...	607	1	7	...	380	1
Kolar Gold Fields (City)...	427	3	...	...	12	...	7	...	...	...	...	...	414	1	...	...	12	...
Kolar District ...	910	199	29	862	618	14	28	1	...	...	29	...	487	...	8	9	339	...
Tumkur District ...	993	353	44	154	684	42	106	1	1	...	32	...	502	2	19	1	472	2
Mysore City ...	836	116	8	6	12	3	90	...	...	...	...	...	572	8	2	1	10	3
Mysore District ...	3,670	1,776	119	248	1,918	184	64	1	...	...	17	...	2,730	9	52	6	1,140	3
Chitaldrug District ...	1,459	415	46	109	408	38	114	...	...	...	20	...	800	4	15	...	275	1
Hassan District ...	1,784	182	53	204	776	35	395	...	6	...	93	...	1,089	8	13	...	438	4
Kadur District ...	1,259	320	10	43	255	23	249	...	...	...	23	...	689	4	2	...	152	1
Shimoga District ...	2,892	496	51	295	545	67	341	...	1	...	40	...	1,492	12	43	46	347	5
Civil and Military Station, Bangalore.	**1,008**	**90**	**2**	...	**130**	...	**41**	...	...	...	...	...	**801**	**2**	**2**	...	**129**	...

TABLE X.

Occupation—*contd.*

District or State	Order 7—Wood—*concld.*						Order 8—Metals											
	56. Basket makers and other industries of woody materials, including leaves and thatchers and builders working with bamboo, reeds or similar materials						Total of Order 8						57. Smelting, forging and rolling of iron and other metals					
	Total earners (Principal occupation)		Total working dependants		Total following occupation as subsidiary to other		Total earners (Principal occupation)		Total working dependants		Total following occupation as subsidiary to other		Total earners (Principal occupation)		Total working dependants		Total following occupation as subsidiary to other	
	Males	Females	Males	Females	Males	Females	Males	Females	Males	Females	Males	Females	Males	Females	Males	Females	Males	Females
	394	395	396	397	398	399	400	401	402	403	404	405	406	407	408	409	410	411
MYSORE STATE, INCLUDING CIVIL AND MILITARY STATION, BANGALORE.	**4,417**	**4,645**	**214**	**1,414**	**2,039**	**405**	**8,556**	**125**	**152**	**65**	**2,626**	**7**	**255**	**4**	**3**	**14**	**24**	**1**
MYSORE STATE, EXCLUDING CIVIL AND MILITARY STATION, BANGALORE.	**4,251**	**4,557**	**214**	**1,414**	**2,038**	**405**	**7,980**	**124**	**152**	**65**	**2,545**	**7**	**246**	**3**	**3**	**14**	**24**	**1**
Bangalore City ...	136	83	5	16	5	6	352	1	2	...	4	...	15	...	1	...	...	...
Bangalore District ...	554	665	11	45	239	12	963	4	24	4	412	...	1	...	...	...	...	...
Kolar Gold Fields (City)...	6	2	...	...	...	...	465	3	...	...	14	...	...	...	...	...	...	...
Kolar District ...	395	198	21	353	250	14	710	13	36	21	390	3	...	...	...	...	...	...
Tumkur District ...	385	350	24	153	180	40	1,008	26	17	13	497	1	6	...	...	...	1	...
Mysore City ...	174	108	6	5	2	...	244	9	...	...	9	...	...	...	...	...	...	...
Mysore District ...	876	1,766	67	237	761	181	1,380	20	21	1	500	...	14	...	...	...	1	...
Chitaldrug District ...	545	411	31	109	113	37	986	20	27	5	167	...	21	...	...	...	3	...
Hassan District ...	300	174	34	204	250	31	534	7	11	2	244	2	22	...	2	...	...	...
Kadur District ...	321	316	8	43	80	22	441	9	...	...	103	1	31	...	...	...	1	1
Shimoga District ...	559	464	7	249	158	62	897	12	14	19	205	...	136	3	...	14	18	...
Civil and Military Station, Bangalore.	**166**	**88**	...	...	**1**	...	**576**	**1**	...	...	**81**	...	**9**	**1**	...	...	...	...

TABLE X.

Occupation—*contd.*

District or State	Order 8—Metals—*contd.*																	
	58. Makers of arms, guns, etc.						59. Blacksmiths, other workers in iron, makers of implements						60. Workers in brass, copper and bell metal					
	Total earners (Principal occupation)		Total working dependants		Total following occupation as subsidiary to other		Total earners (Principal occupation)		Total working dependants		Total following occupation as subsidiary to other		Total earners (Principal occupation)		Total working dependants		Total following occupation as subsidiary to other	
	Males	Females	Males	Females	Males	Females	Males	Females	Males	Females	Males	Females	Males	Females	Males	Females	Males	Females
	412	413	414	415	416	417	418	419	420	421	422	423	424	425	426	427	428	429
MYSORE STATE, INCLUDING CIVIL AND MILITARY STATION, BANGALORE.	**24**	...	...	...	**10**	...	**6,244**	**81**	**131**	**42**	**2,351**	**5**	**923**	**21**	**13**	...	**118**	...
MYSORE STATE, EXCLUDING CIVIL AND MILITARY STATION, BANGALORE.	**24**	...	...	...	**10**	...	**5,913**	**81**	**131**	**42**	**2,270**	**5**	**835**	**21**	**13**	...	**118**	...
Bangalore City ...	9	...	...	...	...	...	149	1	...	...	2	...	111	...	1	...	2	...
Bangalore District ...	1	...	...	...	...	...	780	4	24	4	371	...	50	...	...	...	11	...
Kolar Gold Fields (City)...	...	...	...	...	...	...	401	...	...	...	14	...	41	...	...	...	...	...
Kolar District ...	...	...	...	...	2	...	607	5	26	21	362	2	47	6	7	...	10	...
Tumkur District ...	...	...	...	...	1	...	789	26	16	13	421	1	63	...	...	...	36	...
Mysore City ...	...	...	...	...	...	...	106	...	...	...	2	...	58	8	...	...	3	...
Mysore District ...	...	...	...	...	...	...	1,011	12	16	1	451	...	224	4	4	...	32	...
Chitaldrug District ...	...	...	...	...	...	...	753	13	27	1	161	...	17	1	...	...	...	...
Hassan District ...	...	...	...	...	3	...	391	6	9	2	222	2	67	1	...	...	7	...
Kadur District ...	9	...	...	...	3	...	325	9	...	...	97	...	66	...	...	...	2	...
Shimoga District ...	5	...	...	...	1	...	601	5	13	...	167	...	91	1	1	...	15	...
Civil and Military Station, Bangalore.	..	...	...	...	...	...	**331**	...	...	...	**81**	...	**88**	...	...	...	...	...

TABLE X.

Occupation—*contd.*

District or State	Order 8.—Metals.—*concld.*												Order 9.—Ceramics					
	61. Workers in other metals (except precious metals).						62. Workers in mints, die-sinkers, etc.						Total of Order 9					
	Total earners (Principal occupation)		Total working dependants		Total following occupation as subsidiary to other		Total earners (Principal occupation)		Total working dependants		Total following occupation as subsidiary to other		Total earners (Principal occupation)		Total working dependants		Total following occupation as subsidiary to other	
	Males	Females	Males	Females	Males	Females	Males	Females	Males	Females	Males	Females	Males	Females	Males	Females	Males	Females
	430	431	432	433	434	435	436	437	438	439	440	441	442	443	444	445	446	447
MYSORE STATE, INCLUDING CIVIL AND MILITARY STATION, BANGALORE.	1,022	19	5	9	94	1	88	...	...	...	29	...	7,395	4,355	436	2,742	4,027	351
MYSORE STATE, EXCLUDING CIVIL AND MILITARY STATION, BANGALORE.	874	19	5	9	94	1	88	...	...	...	29	...	7,255	4,321	436	2,740	4,027	346
Bangalore City ...	68	...	...	...	...	...	...	...	...	...	...	...	44	4	1	...	...	...
Bangalore District ...	69	...	...	...	3	...	62	...	...	...	27	...	1,131	642	63	83	426	14
Kolar Gold Fields (City)...	23	3	...	...	...	...	...	...	...	...	...	...	11	1	...	...	15	2
Kolar District ...	56	2	3	...	16	1	...	...	...	...	...	...	680	343	31	186	564	17
Tumkur District ...	150	...	1	...	38	...	...	...	...	...	...	...	701	316	63	617	525	27
Mysore City ...	80	1	...	...	4	...	...	...	...	...	...	...	124	44	...	4	5	...
Mysore District ...	108	4	1	...	14	...	28	...	...	...	2	...	2,097	1,902	110	682	1,397	146
Chitaldrug District ...	192	6	...	4	3	...	3	...	...	...	...	...	851	408	27	210	221	9
Hassan District ...	54	...	...	...	12	...	...	...	...	...	...	...	720	347	73	464	414	63
Kadur District ...	10	...	...	...	...	...	...	...	...	...	...	...	335	95	45	305	262	25
Shimoga District ...	64	3	...	5	4	...	...	...	...	...	...	...	561	219	23	239	198	43
Civil and Military Station, Bangalore.	148	...	...	...	...	...	...	...	...	...	...	...	140	34	...	2	...	5

TABLE X.

Occupation—*contd.*

District or State	Order 9 :—Ceramics—*concld.*																	
	63. Potters and makers of earthen-ware						64. Brick and tile makers						65. Other workers in ceramics					
	Total earners (Principal occupation)		Total working dependants		Total following occupation as subsidiary to other		Total earners (Principal occupation)		Total working dependants		Total following occupation as subsidiary to other		Total earners (Principal occupation)		Total working dependants		Total following occupation as subsidiary to other	
	Males	Females	Males	Females	Males	Females	Males	Females	Males	Females	Males	Females	Males	Females	Males	Females	Males	Females
	448	449	450	451	452	453	454	455	456	457	458	459	460	461	462	463	464	465
MYSORE STATE, INCLUDING CIVIL AND MILITARY STATION, BANGALORE.	**7,120**	**4,254**	**436**	**2,742**	**3,986**	**348**	**269**	**101**	...	...	**38**	**3**	**6**	...	...	...	**3**	...
MYSORE STATE, EXCLUDING CIVIL AND MILITARY STATION, BANGALORE	**7,077**	**4,220**	**436**	**2,740**	**3,986**	**343**	**172**	**101**	...	...	**38**	**3**	**6**	...	...	...	**3**	...
Bangalore City ...	37	4	1	...	...	...	7	...	...	...	...	...	...	...	...	...	...	...
Bangalore District ...	1,095	547	63	83	398	14	96	95	...	...	28	...	...	...	...	...	...	...
Kolar Gold Fields (City)...	8	1	...	...	15	2	3	...	...	...	...	...	...	...	...	...	...	...
Kolar District	680	343	31	186	563	17	...	...	...	...	1	...	...	...	...	...	...	...
Tumkur District ...	699	316	63	617	525	27	2	...	...	...	...	...	...	...	...	...	...	...
Mysore City	101	44	...	4	4	...	23	...	...	...	1	...	...	...	...	...	...	...
Mysore District ...	2,096	1,901	110	632	1,397	146	...	1	...	...	...	...	1	...	...	...	...	...
Chitaldrug District ...	899	407	27	210	217	9	7	1	...	...	1	...	5	...	...	...	3	...
Hassan District ...	696	343	73	464	407	60	24	4	...	...	7	3	...	...	...	...	...	...
Kadur District ...	329	95	45	305	262	25	6	...	...	...	...	...	...	...	...	...	...	...
Shimoga District ...	557	219	23	239	198	43	4	...	...	...	...	...	...	...	...	...	...	...
Civil and Military Station, Bangalore	**43**	**34**	...	**2**	...	**5**	**97**	...	...	...	...	...	...	...	...	...	...	...

TABLE X.

Occupation—*contd.*

District or State	Order 10:—Chemical products properly so-called and analogous																	
	Total of Order 10						66. Manufacture of matches, fire works and other explosives						67. Manufacture of aerated and mineral waters and ice					
	Total earners (Principal occupation)		Total working dependants		Total following occupation as subsidiary to other		Total earners (Principal occupation)		Total working dependants		Total following occupation as subsidiary to other		Total earners (Principal occupation)		Total working dependants		Total following occupation as subsidiary to other	
	Males	Females	Males	Females	Males	Females	Males	Females	Males	Females	Males	Females	Males	Females	Males	Females	Males	Females
	466	467	468	469	470	471	472	473	474	475	476	477	478	479	480	481	482	483
MYSORE STATE, INCLUDING CIVIL AND MILITARY STATION, BANGALORE.	**2,031**	**680**	**138**	**619**	**2,000**	76	**91**	**6**	**5**	...	**86**	...	**145**	**2**	**1**	...	**15**	...
MYSORE STATE, EXCLUDING CIVIL AND MILITARY STATION, BANGALORE.	**2,002**	**678**	**138**	**619**	**2,000**	76	**87**	**6**	**5**	...	**86**	...	**130**	**2**	**1**	...	**15**	...
Bangalore City ...	111	22	...	...	3	...	2	...	...	...	...	...	16	...	...	...	1	...
Bangalore District ...	353	121	14	15	343	8	1	...	...	...	...	...	1	...	...	...	...	...
Kolar Gold Fields (City) ...	15	...	...	...	...	...	...	...	...	...	...	...	6	...	...	...	...	...
Kolar District ...	330	72	23	199	404	7	1	...	...	...	1	...	7	...	...	...	1	...
Tumkur District ...	243	68	35	78	482	17	28	...	5	...	79	...	1	...	...	...	1	...
Mysore City ...	80	5	1	...	6	...	2	1	...	...	...	...	26	...	...	...	...	...
Mysore District ...	404	286	32	224	562	27	3	...	...	...	1	...	13	2	...	...	1	...
Chitaldrug District ...	60	12	1	...	11	...	4	...	...	...	1	...	3	...	1	...	...	...
Hassan District ...	171	69	30	103	150	16	4	...	...	...	3	...	8	...	...	...	...	...
Kadur District ...	107	16	2	...	23	...	...	...	...	...	...	...	24	...	...	...	3	...
Shimoga District ...	128	7	...	...	16	1	42	5	...	...	1	...	25	...	...	...	8	...
Civil and Military Station, Bangalore.	29	2	...	...	...	...	4	...	...	...	...	...	15	...	...	...	...	...

TABLE X.

Occupation—*contd.*

District or State	Order 10.—Chemical products properly so-called and analogous—*concld.* 68. Manufacture and refining of vegetable oils: Total earners (Principal occupation) Males	Females	Total working dependants Males	Females	Total following occupation as subsidiary to other Males	Females	70. Others: Total earners (Principal occupation) Males	Females	Total working dependants Males	Females	Total following occupation as subsidiary to other Males	Females	Order 11.—Food Industries. Total of Order 11: Total earners (Principal occupation) Males	Females	Total working dependants Males	Females	Total following occupation as subsidiary to other Males	Females
	484	485	486	487	488	489	490	491	492	493	494	495	496	497	498	499	500	501
MYSORE STATE, INCLUDING CIVIL AND MILITARY STATION, BANGALORE.	**1,748**	**660**	**132**	**619**	**1,899**	**76**	**47**	**12**	...	...	...	...	**7,276**	**2,369**	**198**	**401**	**1,624**	**226**
MYSORE STATE, EXCLUDING CIVIL AND MILITARY STATION, BANGALORE.	**1,738**	**658**	**132**	**619**	**1,899**	**76**	**47**	**12**	...	...	...	...	**5,987**	**2,215**	**197**	**396**	**1,623**	**201**
Bangalore City ...	82	12	...	...	2	...	11	10	...	...	...	...	408	99	...	3	9	...
Bangalore District ...	351	121	14	15	343	8	...	...	...	...	...	...	595	247	14	44	167	8
Kolar Gold Fields (City)...	9	...	...	...	...	...	...	...	...	...	...	...	98	19	...	1	1	...
Kolar District... ...	321	72	23	199	402	7	1	...	...	...	...	...	486	81	9	15	138	8
Tumkur District ...	214	68	30	78	402	17	...	...	...	...	...	...	731	215	41	68	204	36
Mysore City	33	8	1	...	6	...	19	1	...	...	...	...	362	77	2	5	1	1
Mysore District ...	387	284	32	224	560	27	1	...	...	...	...	...	1,139	711	61	119	423	71
Chitaldrug District ...	49	12	...	...	10	...	4	...	...	...	...	...	408	109	8	2	77	6
Hassan District ...	158	69	30	103	147	16	1	...	...	...	...	...	755	235	57	120	369	33
Kadur District ...	79	15	2	...	20	...	4	1	...	...	...	...	559	122	1	...	117	18
Shimoga District ...	55	2	...	...	7	1	6	...	...	...	...	...	446	300	4	19	122	20
Civil and Military Station, Bangalore.	**10**	**2**	...	...	...	...	...	...	...	...	...	...	**1,289**	**154**	**1**	**5**	**1**	**25**

TABLE X.

Occupation—*contd.*

District or State	Order 11—Food Industries—*contd.*																	
	71. Rice-pounders and huskers and flour-grinders						72. Grain Parchers, etc.						73. Butchers					
	Total earners (Principal occupation)		Total working dependants		Total following occupation as subsidiary to other		Total earners (Principal occupation)		Total working dependants		Total following occupation as subsidiary to other		Total earners (Principal occupation)		Total working dependants		Total following occupation as subsidiary to other	
	Males	Females	Males	Females	Males	Females	Males	Females	Males	Females	Males	Females	Males	Females	Males	Females	Males	Females
	502	503	504	505	506	507	508	509	510	511	512	513	514	515	516	517	518	519
MYSORE STATE, INCLUDING CIVIL AND MILITARY STATION, BANGALORE.	465	1,164	10	68	122	64	279	99	2	5	38	17	1,386	25	4	...	29	...
MYSORE STATE, EXCLUDING CIVIL AND MILITARY STATION, BANGALORE.	459	1,162	10	68	122	64	279	99	2	5	38	17	658	21	4	...	29	...
Bangalore City ...	72	32	...	...	...	...	28	27	...	2	...	...	142	7	...	...	...	...
Bangalore District ...	8	105	1	3	...	4	16	3	...	...	5	...	30	1	...	...	4	...
Kolar Gold Fields (City)...	5	4	...	...	...	...	...	1	...	...	...	...	82	...	...	...	...	...
Kolar District ...	29	67	5	13	42	8	13	...	...	...	5	...	53	...	1	...	...	...
Tumkur District ...	14	47	1	2	10	6	29	6	2	...	13	4	65	...	2	...	11	...
Mysore City ...	52	67	1	5	...	1	31	...	...	...	...	...	66	7	...	...	...	...
Mysore District ...	70	420	1	26	47	22	18	2	...	2	5	1	40	4	1	...	1	...
Chitaldrug District ...	25	44	...	1	5	4	46	19	...	...	2	...	63	2	...	...	2	...
Hassan District ...	84	71	...	3	11	3	28	4	...	1	3	2	36	...	...	...	4	...
Kadur District ...	49	90	...	...	6	1	30	26	...	...	1	10	33	...	...	...	2	...
Shimoga District ...	51	215	1	15	1	15	40	11	...	...	4	...	48	...	...	...	5	...
Civil and Military Station, Bangalore.	6	2	...	...	...	...	...	...	...	...	...	...	728	4	...	...	...	...

TABLE X.

Occupation—*contd.*

District or State	Order 11—Food Industries—*contd.*																	
	74. Makers of sugar, molasses and gur						75. Sweetmeat and condiment makers						76. Toddy drawers.					
	Total earners (Principal occupation)		Total working dependants		Total following occupation as subsidiary to other		Total earners (Principal occupation)		Total working dependants		Total following occupation as subsidiary to other		Total earners (Principal occupation)		Total working dependants		Total following occupation as subsidiary to other	
	Males	Females	Males	Females	Males	Females	Males	Females	Males	Females	Males	Females	Males	Females	Males	Females	Males	Females
	520	521	522	523	524	525	526	527	528	529	530	531	532	533	534	535	536	537
MYSORE STATE, INCLUDING CIVIL AND MILITARY STATION, BANGALORE.	**85**	**3**	...	**1**	**226**	...	**165**	**20**	...	**4**	**51**	...	**2,613**	**19**	**33**	...	**821**	**4**
MYSORE STATE, EXCLUDING CIVIL AND MILITARY STATION, BANGALORE.	**85**	**3**	...	**1**	**226**	...	**165**	**8**	...	...	**51**	...	**2,603**	**19**	**33**	...	**821**	**4**
Bangalore City ...	...	...	...	...	...	...	28	8	...	...	...	...	2	...	...	...	2	...
Bangalore District ...	...	...	...	...	2	...	...	...	...	...	...	...	218	3	...	...	81	...
Kolar Gold Fields (City)...	...	...	...	...	...	...	...	...	...	...	...	...	5	...	...	...	1	...
Kolar District ...	12	2	...	...	2	...	1	...	...	...	...	...	360	4	3	...	78	...
Tumkur District ...	2	1	...	...	15	...	...	...	...	...	...	...	444	5	6	...	106	1
Mysore City ...	...	...	...	...	...	...	...	...	...	...	...	...	7	...	...	...	...	...
Mysore District ...	53	...	...	1	174	...	...	...	...	...	...	...	349	1	2	...	122	1
Chitaldrug District ...	8	...	...	...	...	...	4	...	...	...	...	...	237	4	4	...	54	...
Hassan District ...	10	...	...	...	30	...	4	...	...	...	...	...	481	...	17	...	242	...
Kadur District ...	...	...	...	...	...	...	1	...	...	...	...	...	429	1	...	...	103	2
Shimoga District ...	...	...	...	...	3	...	127	...	...	...	51	...	71	1	1	...	82	...
Civil and Military Station, Bangalore.	...	...	...	...	...	...	...	**12**	...	4	...	...	10	...	...	...	...	...

TABLE X.

Occupation—*contd.*

District or State	Order 11—Food Industries—*concld.*																	
	77. Brewers and distillers						78. Manufacturers of Tobacco						81. Others					
	Total earners (Principal occupation)		Total working dependants		Total following occupation as subsidiary to other		Total earners (Principal occupation)		Total working dependants		Total following occupation as subsidiary to other		Total earners (Principal occupation)		Total working dependants		Total following occupation as subsidiary to other	
	Males	Females	Males	Females	Males	Females	Males	Females	Males	Females	Males	Females	Males	Females	Males	Females	Males	Females
	538	539	540	541	542	543	544	545	546	547	548	549	550	551	552	553	554	555
MYSORE STATE, INCLUDING CIVIL AND MILITARY STATION, BANGALORE.	**27**	**2**	...	...	...	...	**1,800**	**971**	**149**	**321**	**332**	**139**	**456**	**66**	...	**2**	**5**	**2**
MYSORE STATE, EXCLUDING CIVIL AND MILITARY STATION, BANGALORE.	**19**	**2**	...	...	...	...	**1,577**	**850**	**148**	**320**	**331**	**114**	**142**	**51**	...	**2**	**5**	**2**
Bangalore City ...	6	...	...	...	...	...	72	7	...	1	5	...	58	18	...	...	2	...
Bangalore District ...	8	...	...	...	...	...	295	132	13	41	73	4	20	3	...	...	2	...
Kolar Gold Fields (City) ...	...	...	...	...	...	...	...	..	...	...	...	...	6	14	...	1	...	...
Kolar District ...	1	...	...	...	...	...	8	5	...	1	5	...	9	3	...	1	1	...
Tumkur District ...	...	...	...	...	...	...	177	156	30	66	49	25	...	...	...	...	...	...
Mysore City ...	...	...	...	...	...	...	171	3	1	...	1	...	35	...	...	...	...	...
Mysore District ...	...	...	...	...	...	...	602	271	57	90	74	45	7	13	...	...	...	2
Chitaldrug District ...	1	...	...	...	...	...	24	40	4	1	14	2	...	...	...	...	...	...
Hassan District ...	...	...	...	...	...	...	110	160	40	116	79	28	2	...	...	...	...	...
Kadur District ...	...	...	...	...	...	...	12	5	1	...	5	5	5	...	...	...	...	...
Shimoga District ...	3	2	...	...	...	...	106	71	2	4	26	5	...	...	...	...	...	...
Civil and Military Station, Bangalore.	**8**	...	...	...	...	...	**223**	**121**	**1**	**1**	**1**	**25**	**314**	**15**	...	...	...	...

TABLE X.

Occupation—*contd.*

District or State	Order 12.—Industries of dress and the toilet.																	
	Total of Order 12						82. Boot, shoe, sandal and clog makers						83. Tailors, milliners, dressmakers and darners.					
	Total earners (Principal occupation)		Total working dependants		Total following occupation as subsidiary to other		Total earners (Principal occupation)		Total working dependants		Total following occupation as subsidiary to other		Total earners (Principal occupation)		Total working dependants		Total following occupation as subsidiary to other	
	Males	Females	Males	Females	Males	Females	Males	Females	Males	Females	Males	Females	Males	Females	Males	Females	Males	Females
	556	557	558	559	560	561	562	563	564	565	566	567	568	569	570	571	572	573
MYSORE STATE, INCLUDING CIVIL AND MILITARY STATION, BANGALORE.	**30,199**	**6,308**	**1,502**	**8,918**	**14,219**	**645**	**3,727**	**121**	**46**	**5**	**1,727**	**24**	**8,792**	**1,432**	**271**	**488**	**1,231**	**110**
MYSORE STATE, EXCLUDING CIVIL AND MILITARY STATION, BANGALORE.	**27,655**	**5,978**	**1,478**	**8,818**	**14,187**	**644**	**3,256**	**107**	**46**	**4**	**1,708**	**24**	**7,512**	**1,380**	**249**	**488**	**1,226**	**109**
Bangalore City ...	1,989	300	51	62	26	5	282	...	6	...	...	...	857	34	30	5	9	3
Bangalore District ...	3,884	680	142	335	2,212	75	328	7	4	...	69	...	969	203	26	78	216	7
Kolar Gold Fields (City)...	556	64	...	3	58	...	52	...	...	...	2	...	211	18	...	...	3	...
Kolar District ...	3,047	669	172	899	2,623	68	101	...	3	...	116	...	817	164	25	69	173	12
Tumkur District ...	3,287	693	297	2,219	2,285	96	379	4	3	1	338	2	741	146	25	49	209	24
Mysore City ...	1,187	161	20	40	25	11	196	12	1	...	...	...	579	60	14	24	9	8
Mysore District ...	5,130	1,546	202	630	2,874	177	531	22	6	...	220	1	1,014	279	31	67	199	19
Chitaldrug District ...	3,789	828	101	1,204	1,136	54	936	25	10	1	554	12	698	130	8	22	86	7
Hassan District ...	1,681	399	233	2,002	1,577	45	101	1	3	...	59	...	561	101	35	111	150	3
Kadur District ...	1,097	217	65	445	365	31	136	12	...	...	66	...	383	79	8	3	56	12
Shimoga District ...	2,008	421	195	979	1,006	82	264	24	10	2	284	9	682	166	47	60	116	14
Civil and Military Station, Bangalore.	**2,544**	**330**	**24**	**100**	**32**	**1**	**471**	**14**	...	**1**	**19**	...	**1,280**	**52**	**22**	...	**5**	**1**

TABLE X.

Occupation—*contd.*

District or State	Order 12.—Industries of dress and the toilet.—*contd.*																	
	84. Embroiderers, hat-makers and makers of other articles of wear.						85. Washing and cleaning.						86. Barbers, hair-dressers and wig-makers.					
	Total earners (Principal occupation)		Total working dependants		Total following occupation as subsidiary to other		Total earners (Principal occupation)		Total working dependants		Total following occupation as subsidiary to other		Total earners (Principal occupation)		Total working dependants		Total following occupation as subsidiary to other	
	Males	Females	Males	Females	Males	Females	Males	Females	Males	Females	Males	Females	Males	Females	Males	Females	Males	Females
	574	575	576	577	578	579	580	581	582	583	584	585	586	587	588	589	590	591
MYSORE STATE, INCLUDING CIVIL AND MILITARY STATION, BANGALORE.	**98**	**80**	**4**	**96**	**5**	**6**	**10,648**	**4,396**	**925**	**8,280**	**7,212**	**471**	**6,729**	**16**	**246**	**1**	**3,989**	...
MYSORE STATE, EXCLUDING CIVIL AND MILITARY STATION, BANGALORE.	**72**	**46**	**4**	**18**	**5**	**6**	**10,183**	**4,176**	**923**	**8,259**	**7,209**	**471**	**6,429**	**16**	**246**	**1**	**3,985**	...
Bangalore City ...	14	9	3	3	...	1	442	155	7	50	3	...	396	1	2	...	14	...
Bangalore District ...	2	3	...	1	...	...	1,580	435	83	243	1,267	66	962	...	28	...	641	...
Kolar Gold Fields (City)...	...	...	...	...	...	...	175	46	...	3	25	...	118	...	...	...	28	...
Kolar District ...	6	4	...	4	...	...	1,325	486	80	826	1,286	53	783	1	63	...	1,025	...
Tumkur District ...	33	3	1	3	4	2	1,355	492	242	2,160	1,215	63	727	6	23	1	515	...
Mysore City ...	16	2	...	...	1	2	211	86	2	16	...	1	185	1	3	...	15	...
Mysore District ...	...	12	...	2	...	1	2,374	1,207	120	537	1,718	153	1,198	...	45	...	731	...
Chitaldrug District ...	...	5	...	5	...	...	1,392	645	67	1,176	317	34	755	7	16	...	178	...
Hassan District ...	1	2	...	...	...	...	602	280	151	1,891	922	40	415	...	44	...	446	...
Kadur District ...	...	2	...	...	...	...	269	121	57	442	134	17	305	...	...	...	109	...
Shimoga District ...	...	4	...	...	...	...	458	223	114	915	322	44	585	...	22	...	283	...
Civil and Military Station, Bangalore.	**26**	**34**	...	**78**	...	...	**465**	**220**	**2**	**21**	**3**	...	**300**	...	...	...	**4**	...

TABLE X.

Occupation—*contd.*

District or State	Order 12.—Industries of dress and the toilet—*concld.* 87. Other industries connected with the toilet. Total earners (Principal occupation) Males	Females	Total working dependants Males	Females	Total following occupation as subsidiary to other Males	Females	Order 13.—Furniture Industries. Total of Order 13. Total earners (Principal occupation) Males	Females	Total working dependants Males	Females	Total following occupation as subsidiary to other Males	Females	88. Cabinet-makers, carriage painters, etc. Total earners (Principal occupation) Males	Females	Total working dependants Males	Females	Total following occupation as subsidiary to other Males	Females
	592	593	594	595	596	597	598	599	600	601	602	603	604	605	606	607	608	609
MYSORE STATE, INCLUDING CIVIL AND MILITARY STATION, BANGALORE.	**205**	**263**	**10**	**48**	**55**	**34**	**164**	**6**	**1**	**5**	**23**	...	**59**	...	...	...	**8**	...
MYSORE STATE, EXCLUDING CIVIL AND MILITARY STATION, BANGALORE.	**203**	**253**	**10**	**48**	**54**	**34**	**162**	**6**	**1**	**5**	**23**	...	**59**	...	...	...	**8**	...
Bangalore City ...	48	101	3	4	...	1	81	3	1	...	...	...	9	...	...	...	...	...
Bangalore District ...	43	32	1	13	19	2	7	...	...	...	3	...	2	...	...	...	...	...
Kolar Gold Fields (City)...	...	...	...	...	...	...	3	...	...	...	...	...	2	...	...	...	...	...
Kolar District ...	15	14	1	...	23	3	17	3	...	5	12	...	2	...	...	...	...	...
Tumkur District ...	52	42	3	5	4	5	3	...	...	...	...	...	...	...	...	...	...	...
Mysore City ...	...	...	...	...	...	...	25	...	...	...	1	...	24	...	...	...	1	...
Mysore District ...	13	26	...	24	6	3	10	...	...	...	1	...	8	...	...	...	1	...
Chitaldrug District ...	8	16	...	...	1	1	4	...	...	...	...	...	1	...	...	...	...	...
Hassan District ...	1	15	...	...	...	2	6	...	...	...	5	...	5	...	...	...	5	...
Kadur District ...	4	3	...	...	...	2	6	...	...	...	1	...	6	...	...	...	1	...
Shimoga District ...	19	4	2	2	1	15	...	...	...	...	...	...	...	...	...	...	...	...
Civil and Military Station, Bangalore.	2	10	...	...	1	...	2	...	...	...	...	...	...	...	...	...	...	...

TABLE X.

Occupation.—*contd.*

District or State	Order 13.—Furniture Industries—*concld.* 89. Upholsterers. tent-makers, etc. Total earners (Principal occupation) Males	Females	Total working dependants Males	Females	Total following occupation as subsidiary to other Males	Females	Order 14.—Building Industries 90. Lime burners, cement workers; Excavators and well-sinkers; Stone cutters and dressers; Brick layers and masons; Builders (other than buildings made of bamboo or similar materials), painters, decorators of houses, tilers, plumbers, etc. Total earners (Principal occupation) Males	Females	Total working dependants Males	Females	Total following occupation as subsidiary to other Males	Females	Order 15.—Construction of means of transport. Total of Order 15 Total earners (Principal occupation) Males	Females	Total working dependants Males	Females	Total following occupation as subsidiary to other Males	Females
	610	611	612	613	614	615	616	617	618	619	620	621	622	623	624	625	626	627
MYSORE STATE, INCLUDING CIVIL AND MILITARY STATION, BANGALORE.	**105**	**6**	**1**	**5**	**15**	...	**27,102**	**6,806**	**515**	**1,218**	**8,504**	**453**	**937**	**8**	**12**	...	**287**	**7**
MYSORE STATE, EXCLUDING CIVIL AND MILITARY STATION, BANGALORE.	**103**	**6**	**1**	**5**	**15**	...	**25,530**	**6,620**	**515**	**1,218**	**8,377**	**453**	**703**	**7**	**12**	...	**287**	**7**
Bangalore City ...	72	3	1	...	...	...	2,257	255	38	5	12	...	65	...	1	...	1	...
Bangalore District ...	5	...	...	...	3	...	3,496	930	54	27	1,329	11	59	...	1	...	17	...
Kolar Gold Fields (City)...	1	...	...	...	...	...	1,612	100	...	...	83	...	17	...	...	...	...	...
Kolar District ...	15	3	...	5	12	...	2,467	576	98	405	2,245	25	23	...	...	...	2	...
Tumkur District ...	3	...	...	...	...	...	2,177	568	80	244	1,417	76	16	...	1	...	24	1
Mysore City ...	1	...	...	...	...	...	1,111	70	5	2	32	1	83	2	...	...	...	...
Mysore District ...	2	...	...	...	...	...	2,591	686	58	108	858	38	145	4	3	...	95	6
Chitaldrug District ...	3	...	...	...	...	...	3,868	1,445	115	318	1,270	152	53	...	...	...	23	...
Hassan District ...	1	...	...	...	...	...	1,710	467	28	5	558	102	35	...	3	...	38	...
Kadur District ...	...	...	...	...	...	...	1,242	564	5	52	128	36	149	1	1	...	79	...
Shimoga District ...	...	...	...	...	...	...	2,999	957	34	52	445	12	58	...	2	...	8	...
Civil and Military Station, Bangalore.	**2**	...	...	...	...	...	**1,572**	**186**	...	...	**127**	...	**234**	**1**	...	...	...	...

TABLE X.

Occupation.—*contd.*

District or State	Order 15. Construction of means of transport—*concld.*																	
	91. Persons engaged in making, assembling or repairing motor vehicles or cycles.						92. Carriage, cart, palki, etc. makers and wheel-wrights.						93. Ship, boat, aeroplane builders.					
	Total earners (Principal occupation)		Total working dependants		Total following occupation as subsidiary to other		Total earners (Principal occupation)		Total working dependants		Total following occupation as subsidiary to other		Total earners (Principal occupation)		Total working dependants		Total following occupation as subsidiary to other	
	Males	Females	Males	Females	Males	Females	Males	Females	Males	Females	Males	Females	Males	Females	Males	Females	Males	Females
	628	629	630	631	632	633	634	635	636	637	638	639	640	641	642	643	644	645
MYSORE STATE, INCLUDING CIVIL AND MILITARY STATION, BANGALORE.	484	...	3	...	18	...	451	8	9	...	267	7	2	...	...	...	2	...
MYSORE STATE, EXCLUDING CIVIL AND MILITARY STATION, BANGALORE.	266	...	3	...	18	...	435	7	9	...	267	7	2	...	...	...	2	...
Bangalore City ...	48	...	1	...	1	...	16	...	...	...	...	...	1	...	...	...	...	...
Bangalore District ...	54	...	...	...	2	...	5	...	1	...	15	...	...	...	...	...	...	...
Kolar Gold Fields (City)...	14	...	...	...	...	...	3	...	...	...	...	...	...	...	...	...	...	...
Kolar District ...	18	...	...	...	...	...	5	...	...	...	2	...	...	...	...	...	...	...
Tumkur District ...	5	...	...	...	...	...	11	...	1	...	24	1	...	...	...	...	...	...
Mysore City ...	77	...	...	...	...	...	6	2	...	...	...	...	...	...	...	...	...	...
Mysore District ...	16	...	...	...	8	...	128	4	3	...	85	6	1	...	...	...	2	...
Chitaldrug District ...	10	...	...	...	1	...	43	...	...	...	22	...	...	...	...	...	...	...
Hassan District ...	12	...	...	...	...	...	23	...	3	...	38	...	...	...	...	...	...	...
Kadur District ...	1	...	...	...	3	...	148	1	1	...	76	...	...	...	...	...	...	...
Shimoga District ...	11	...	2	...	3	...	47	...	...	...	5	...	...	...	...	...	...	...
Civil and Military Station, Bangalore.	218	...	...	...	...	...	16	1	...	...	...	...	...	...	...	...	...	...

TABLE X.

Occupation—*contd.*

District or State	Order 16:—Production and transmission of physical force. 94. Heat, light, electricity, motive power, etc., Gas works and electric light and power. Total earners (Principal occupation) Males	Females	Total working dependants Males	Females	Total following occupation as subsidiary to other Males	Females	Order 17:—Miscellaneous and undefined Industries. Total of Order 17. Total earners (Principal occupation) Males	Females	Total working dependants Males	Females	Total following occupation as subsidiary to other Males	Females	95. Printers, engravers, book-binders, etc. Total earners (Principal occupation) Males	Females	Total working dependants Males	Females	Total following occupation as subsidiary to other Males	Females
	646	647	648	649	650	651	652	653	654	655	656	657	658	659	660	661	662	663
MYSORE STATE, INCLUDING CIVIL AND MILITARY STATION, BANGALORE.	869	2	6	...	7	...	21,155	2,522	637	253	4,986	54	1,336	17	13	30	49	...
MYSORE STATE, EXCLUDING CIVIL AND MILITARY STATION, BANGALORE.	785	1	6	...	6	...	19,630	1,979	624	223	4,956	54	1,016	13	12	...	26	...
Bangalore City ...	66	...	1	...	...	...	2,109	286	37	11	21	5	596	3	7	...	3	...
Bangalore District ...	196	1	1	...	2	...	2,333	145	63	4	679	5	13	...	1	...	3	...
Kolar Gold Fields (City)...	210	...	...	...	...	...	691	358	...	...	6	...	66	...	...	...	...	...
Kolar District ...	31	...	2	...	1	...	1,784	127	56	75	509	3	24	2	...	...	2	...
Tumkur District ...	6	...	...	...	...	...	1,995	116	81	81	724	4	20	...	...	...	2	...
Mysore City ...	121	...	1	...	...	...	1,198	274	23	6	11	2	218	...	2	...	5	...
Mysore District ...	138	...	1	...	3	...	3,802	292	105	32	1,191	10	6	...	...	...	2	...
Chitaldrug District ...	2	...	...	...	...	...	1,606	130	33	11	231	11	9	...	...	...	...	...
Hassan District ...	...	...	...	...	...	...	1,521	84	142	1	894	12	8	...	...	...	1	...
Kadur District ...	...	...	...	...	...	...	958	33	34	1	323	1	15	...	2	...	5	...
Shimoga District ...	15	...	...	...	...	...	1,683	84	50	1	367	1	41	8	...	...	3	...
Civil and Military Station, Bangalore.	84	1	...	...	1	...	1,525	543	13	30	30	...	320	4	1	30	23	...

TABLE X.

Occupation—*contd.*

District or State	Order 17:—Miscellaneous and undefined Industries—*contd.*																	
	96. Makers of musical instruments.						97. Makers of clocks and surgical or scientific instruments, etc.						98. Makers of jewellery and ornaments.					
	Total earners (Principal occupation)		Total working dependants		Total following occupation as subsidiary to other		Total earners (Principal occupation)		Total working dependants		Total following occupation as subsidiary to other		Total earners (Principal occupation)		Total working dependants		Total following occupation as subsidiary to other	
	Males	Females	Males	Females	Males	Females	Males	Females	Males	Females	Males	Females	Males	Females	Males	Females	Males	Females
	664	665	666	667	668	669	670	671	672	673	674	675	676	677	678	679	680	681
MYSORE STATE, INCLUDING CIVIL AND MILITARY STATION, BANGALORE.	**78**	...	...	...	**13**	...	**120**	...	...	...	**17**	...	**16,285**	**277**	**604**	**157**	**4,791**	**29**
MYSORE STATE, EXCLUDING CIVIL AND MILITARY STATION, BANGALORE.	**61**	...	...	...	**13**	...	**89**	...	...	...	**16**	...	**15,790**	**276**	**592**	**157**	**4,789**	**29**
Bangalore City ...	23	...	...	...	1	...	25	...	...	...	...	...	1,072	21	30	2	7	...
Bangalore District ...	2	...	...	...	3	...	3	...	...	...	1	...	2,054	18	57	...	666	5
Kolar Gold Fields (City)	2	...	...	...	...	...	11	...	...	...	4	...	70	...	...	...	2	...
Kolar District ...	1	...	...	...	...	...	5	...	...	...	3	...	1,550	34	55	50	490	...
Tumkur District ...	4	...	...	...	3	...	3	...	...	...	2	...	1,887	42	79	79	681	2
Mysore City ...	11	...	...	...	1	...	25	...	...	...	1	...	558	8	17	5	3	2
Mysore District ...	7	...	...	...	4	...	3	...	...	...	1	...	3,482	52	98	9	1,166	10
Chitaldrug District ...	1	...	...	...	...	...	2	...	...	...	...	...	1,460	49	33	11	217	2
Hassan District ...	3	...	...	...	1	...	4	...	...	...	3	...	1,436	22	142	...	887	6
Kadur District ...	1	...	...	...	...	...	4	...	...	...	...	...	843	11	31	1	312	1
Shimoga District ...	6	...	...	...	...	...	4	...	...	...	1	...	1,428	19	50	...	358	1
Civil and Military Station, Bangalore.	17	...	...	...	...	...	31	...	...	...	1	...	495	1	12	...	2	...

TABLE X.

Occupation—*contd.*

District or State	Order 17.—Miscellaneous and undefined Industries—*concld.*												Total of Sub-class IV.—Transport.					
	99. Other miscellaneous and undefined industries (toy-making, taxidermy, etc.)						100. Scavenging.											
	Total earners (Principal occupation)		Total working dependants		Total following occupation as subsidary to other		Total earners (Principal occupation)		Total working dependants		Total following occupation as subsidary to other		Total earners (Principal occupation)		Total working Dependants		Total following occupation as subsidary to other	
	Males	Females	Males	Females	Males	Females	Males	Females	Males	Females	Males	Females	Males	Females	Males	Females	Males	Females
	682	683	684	685	686	687	688	689	690	691	692	693	694	695	696	697	698	699
MYSORE STATE, INCLUDING CIVIL AND MILITARY STATION, BANGALORE.	**246**	**101**	**5**	**11**	**8**	**6**	**3,090**	**2,127**	**15**	**55**	**108**	**19**	**22,383**	**1,834**	**564**	**427**	**14,287**	**150**
MYSORE STATE, EXCLUDING CIVIL AND MILITARY STATION, BANGALORE.	**228**	**101**	**5**	**11**	**8**	**6**	**2,446**	**1,589**	**15**	**55**	**104**	**19**	**20,409**	**1,758**	**564**	**427**	**14,259**	**149**
Bangalore City ...	49	35	...	9	...	5	344	227	...	...	10	...	2,691	61	4	9	25	...
Bangalore District ...	94	...	...	...	2	...	167	127	5	4	4	...	1,909	105	80	12	2,471	6
Kolar Gold Fields (City)...	...	...	...	...	...	...	542	358	...	...	...	...	620	15	...	...	125	...
Kolar District ...	...	...	...	...	1	...	204	91	1	25	13	3	1,955	328	74	361	1,623	30
Tumkur District ...	12	36	1	1	2	1	119	38	1	1	34	1	1,124	8	94	1	1,453	1
Mysore City ...	15	1	2	1	1	...	371	265	2	...	...	...	2,077	6	15	...	233	...
Mysore District ...	38	...	2	...	1	...	266	240	5	23	17	...	3,010	696	173	38	4,485	27
Chitaldrug District ...	5	4	...	...	...	...	129	77	...	...	14	9	1,212	216	8	5	643	14
Hassan District ...	2	...	...	...	...	...	68	62	...	1	2	6	1,631	101	43	...	1,678	68
Kadur District ...	1	16	...	...	1	...	94	56	1	..	5	...	1,531	44	14	...	507	2
Shimoga District ...	12	9	...	...	...	...	142	48	...	1	5	...	2,649	238	59	1	1,016	1
Civil and Military Station, Bangalore.	**18**	...	...	...	...	...	**644**	**538**	...	...	4	...	**1,974**	**76**	...	...	**28**	**1**

TABLE X.

Occupation- *contd.*

District or State	Order 19.—Transport by water—*concld.*																	
	Total of Order 19						102. Ship-owners, boat-owners and their employees, officers, mariners, etc., Ships brokers, boatmen and tow men.						103. Persons (other than labourers) employed in harbours, docks, rivers and canals, including pilots.					
	Total earners (Principal occupation)		Total working dependants		Total following occupation as subsidiary to other		Total earners (Principal occupation)		Total working dependants		Total following occupation as subsidiary to other		Total earners (Principal occupation)		Total working dependants		Total following occupation as subsidiary to other	
	Males	Females	Males	Females	Males	Females	Males	Females	Males	Females	Males	Females	Males	Females	Males	Females	Males	Females
	700	701	702	703	704	705	706	707	708	709	710	711	712	713	714	715	716	717
MYSORE STATE, INCLUDING CIVIL AND MILITARY STATION, BANGALORE.	748	403	28	17	269	17	151	2	3	...	81	...	10	...	...	...	9	...
MYSORE STATE, EXCLUDING CIVIL AND MILITARY STATION, BANGALORE.	748	403	28	17	269	17	151	2	3	...	81	...	10	...	...	...	9	...
Bangalore City ...	...	...	...	...	...	...	...	...	...	...	...	...	...	...	...	...	...	...
Bangalore District ...	3	...	...	...	...	...	3	...	...	...	...	...	...	...	...	...	...	...
Kolar Gold Fields (City)...	...	...	...	...	...	...	...	...	...	...	...	...	...	...	...	...	...	...
Kolar District ...	1	...	...	...	2	...	1	...	...	...	...	...	...	...	...	...	1	...
Tumkur District ...	17	...	...	...	...	...	...	...	...	...	...	...	...	...	...	...	...	...
Mysore City ...	1	...	...	...	...	...	1	...	...	...	...	...	...	...	...	...	...	...
Mysore District ...	662	396	28	17	253	17	94	2	3	...	69	...	10	...	...	...	7	...
Chitaldrug District ...	5	...	...	...	...	...	5	...	...	...	...	...	...	...	...	...	...	...
Hassan District ...	10	7	...	...	3	...	8	...	...	...	3	...	...	...	...	...	...	...
Kadur District ...	3	...	...	...	2	...	2	...	...	...	1	...	...	...	...	...	...	...
Shimoga District ...	46	...	...	...	9	...	37	...	...	...	8	...	...	...	...	...	1	...
Civil and Military Station, Bangalore.	...	...	...	...	...	...	...	...	...	...	...	...	...	...	...	...	...	...

TABLE X.

Occupation—*contd.*

District or State	Order 19.—Transport by water—*concld.*						Order 20.—Transport by road											
	104. Labourers employed on harbours, docks, rivers and canals.						Total of Order 20						105. Persons (other than labourers) employed on the construction and maintenance of roads and bridges.					
	Total earners (Principal occupation)		Total working dependants		Total following occupation as subsidiary to other		Total earners (Principal occupation)		Total working dependants		Total following occupation as subsidiary to other		Total earners (Principal occupation)		Total working dependants		Total following occupation as subsidiary to other	
	Males	Females	Males	Females	Males	Females	Males	Females	Males	Females	Males	Females	Males	Females	Males	Females	Males	Females
	718	719	720	721	722	723	724	725	726	727	728	729	730	731	732	733	734	735
MYSORE STATE, INCLUDING CIVIL AND MILITARY STATION, BANGALORE.	**587**	**401**	**25**	**17**	**179**	**17**	**13,382**	**1,195**	**517**	**400**	**13,468**	**133**	**294**	**78**	**3**	**1**	**120**	**4**
MYSORE STATE, EXCLUDING CIVIL AND MILITARY STATION, BANGALORE.	**587**	**401**	**25**	**17**	**179**	**17**	**12,163**	**1,128**	**517**	**400**	**13,441**	**132**	**285**	**78**	**3**	**1**	**120**	**4**
Bangalore City ...	...	...	...	...	...	...	1,216	50	2	9	21	...	10	...	...	...	...	...
Bangalore District ...	...	...	...	...	...	...	1,263	105	76	12	2,353	6	8	1	...	1	15	1
Kolar Gold Fields (City)...	...	...	...	...	...	...	388	3	...	...	125	...	...	...	...	...	...	...
Kolar District ...	...	...	...	...	1	...	1,149	316	70	351	1,549	30	5	...	...	...	6	...
Tumkur District ...	17	...	...	...	...	...	810	7	90	1	1,365	1	64	...	2	...	31	...
Mysore City ...	...	...	...	...	...	...	956	4	15	...	228	...	4	...	...	...	1	...
Mysore District ...	558	394	25	17	177	17	1,777	289	143	21	4,130	10	13	...	...	...	3	...
Chitaldrug District ...	...	...	...	...	...	...	729	215	7	5	601	14	50	28	1	...	29	...
Hassan District ...	2	7	...	...	...	...	1,085	93	43	...	1,617	68	47	40	...	...	32	3
Kadur District ...	1	...	...	...	1	...	1,026	31	14	...	487	2	47	...	...	...	2	...
Shimoga District ...	9	...	...	...	...	...	1,769	65	57	1	965	1	37	9	...	...	1	...
Civil and Military Station, Bangalore.	...	...	...	...	...	...	**1,219**	**67**	...	...	**27**	**1**	**9**	...	...	...	...	...

TABLE X

Occupation—*contd*

Order 20.—Transport by road—*contd*.

District or State	106. Labourers employed on roads and bridges.						107. Owners, managers, and employees (excluding personal servants) connected with mechanically driven vehicles (including trams).						108. Owners, managers and employees (excluding personal servants) connected with other vehicles.					
	Total earners (Principal occupation)		Total working dependants		Total following occupation as subsidiary to other		Total earners (Principal occupation)		Total working dependants		Total following occupation as subsidiary to other		Total earners (Principal occupation)		Total working dependants		Total following occupation as subsidiary to other	
	Males	Females	Males	Females	Males	Females	Males	Females	Males	Females	Males	Females	Males	Females	Males	Females	Males	Females
	736	737	738	739	740	741	742	743	744	745	746	747	748	749	750	751	752	753
MYSORE STATE, INCLUDING CIVIL AND MILITARY STATION, BANGALORE.	**1,815**	**1,075**	**65**	**390**	**818**	**117**	**1,056**	**4**	**7**	...	**137**	...	**10,120**	**37**	**436**	**9**	**12,349**	**12**
MYSORE STATE, EXCLUDING CIVIL AND MILITARY STATION, BANGALORE.	**1,727**	**1,013**	**65**	**390**	**818**	**116**	**973**	**3**	**7**	...	**137**	...	**9,081**	**34**	**436**	**9**	**12,322**	**12**
Bangalore City ...	31	39	...	9	...	...	158	2	...	...	...	...	1,017	9	2	...	21	...
Bangalore District ...	172	103	7	10	171	3	44	...	...	...	4	...	1,089	1	69	1	2,163	2
Kolar Gold Fields (City)...	60	3	...	...	...	...	13	...	...	...	...	...	310	...	...	...	125	...
Kolar District ...	414	315	42	345	267	28	84	...	3	...	1	...	646	1	25	6	1,275	2
Tumkur District ...	62	6	...	...	5	...	66	...	...	...	3	...	586	1	82	1	1,290	1
Mysore City ...	129	...	...	...	2	...	120	...	3	...	83	...	708	4	12	...	142	...
Mysore District ...	108	228	3	21	87	4	94	...	...	...	...	...	1,526	11	140	...	4,040	6
Chitaldrug District ...	186	183	2	5	205	14	68	...	1	...	2	...	420	4	3	...	360	...
Hassan District ...	33	53	2	...	52	65	60	...	...	...	9	...	945	...	41	...	1,524	...
Kadur District ...	111	29	...	...	14	2	110	1	...	...	33	...	737	1	14	...	438	...
Shimoga District ...	421	54	9	...	15	...	156	...	...	...	2	...	1,152	2	48	1	944	1
Civil and Military Station, Bangalore.	**88**	**62**	...	...	...	1	**83**	1	...	...	...	...	**1,039**	**3**	...	...	**27**	...

TABLE X.

Occupation—*contd.*

District or State	Order 20—Transport by road—*concld.*																	
	109. Palki, etc., bearers and owners.						110. Pack elephant, camel, mule, ass and bullock, owners and drivers.						111. Porters and messengers.					
	Total earners (Principal occupation)		Total working dependants		Total following occupation as subsidiary to other		Total earners (Principal occupation)		Total working dependants		Total following occupation as subsidiary to other		Total earners (Principal occupation)		Total working dependants		Total following occupation as subsidiary to other	
	Males	Females	Males	Females	Males	Females	Males	Females	Males	Females	Males	Females	Males	Females	Males	Females	Males	Females
	754	755	756	757	758	759	760	761	762	763	764	765	766	767	768	769	770	771
MYSORE STATE, INCLUDING CIVIL AND MILITARY STATION, BANGALORE.	3	1	...	...	3	...	78	...	6	...	41	...	16	...	...	...	...	...
MYSORE STATE, EXCLUDING CIVIL AND MILITARY STATION, BANGALORE.	3	...	...	...	3	...	78	...	6	...	41	...	16	...	...	...	...	...
Bangalore City ...	...	...	...	...	...	...	...	...	...	...	...	...	...	...	...	...	...	...
Bangalore District ...	...	...	...	...	...	...	...	...	...	...	...	...	...	...	...	...	...	...
Kolar Gold Fields (City)...	...	...	...	...	...	...	...	...	...	...	...	...	...	...	...	...	...	...
Kolar District ...	...	...	...	...	...	...	...	...	...	...	...	...	...	...	...	...	...	...
Tumkur District ...	...	...	...	...	...	...	18	...	6	...	36	...	14	...	...	...	...	...
Mysore City ...	...	...	...	...	...	...	...	...	...	...	...	...	...	...	...	...	...	...
Mysore District ...	...	...	...	...	...	...	36	...	...	...	...	...	...	...	...	...	...	...
Chitaldrug District ...	...	...	...	...	...	...	5	...	...	...	5	...	...	...	...	...	...	...
Hassan District ...	...	...	...	...	...	...	...	...	...	...	...	...	...	...	...	...	...	...
Kadur District ...	...	...	...	...	...	...	19	...	...	...	...	...	2	...	...	...	...	...
Shimoga District ...	3	...	...	...	3	...	...	...	...	...	...	...	...	...	...	...	...	...
Civil and Military Station, Bangalore.	...	1	...	...	...	...	...	...	...	...	...	...	...	...	...	...	...	...

TABLE X.

Occupation—*contd.*

District or State	Order 21. Transport by rail																	
	Total of Order 21						112. Railway employees of all kinds other than coolies.						113. Labourers employed on railway construction and maintenance and coolies and porters employed on railway premises.					
	Total earners (Principal occupation)		Total working dependants		Total following occupation as subsidiary to other		Total earners (Principal occupation)		Total working dependants		Total following occupation as subsidiary to other		Total earners (Principal occupation)		Total working dependants		Total following occupation as subsidiary to other	
	Males	Females	Males	Females	Males	Females	Males	Females	Males	Females	Males	Females	Males	Females	Males	Females	Males	Females
	772	773	774	775	776	777	778	779	780	781	782	783	784	785	786	787	788	789
MYSORE STATE, INCLUDING CIVIL AND MILITARY STATION, BANGALORE.	**6,651**	**221**	**18**	**10**	**390**	...	**4,907**	**44**	**16**	**4**	**262**	...	**1,744**	**177**	**2**	**6**	**128**	...
MYSORE STATE, EXCLUDING CIVIL AND MILITARY STATION, BANGALORE.	**6,198**	**221**	**18**	**10**	**389**	...	**4,662**	**44**	**16**	**4**	**262**	...	**1,536**	**177**	**2**	**6**	**127**	...
Bangalore City ...	1,276	10	2	...	4	...	1,082	7	2	...	2	...	194	3	...	...	2	...
Bangalore District ...	530	...	4	...	97	...	317	...	4	...	56	...	213	...	...	...	41	...
Kolar Gold Fields (City)...	171	10	...	...	...	...	112	9	...	...	...	...	59	1	...	...	...	...
Kolar District	658	11	4	10	48	...	609	10	3	4	43	...	49	1	1	6	5	...
Tumkur District ...	188	1	3	...	59	...	94	...	3	...	27	...	94	1	...	...	32	...
Mysore City	1,001	1	...	...	5	...	736	1	...	...	2	...	265	...	...	...	3	...
Mysore District ...	445	1	2	...	78	...	434	1	2	...	78	...	11	...	...	...	...	...
Chitaldrug District ...	362	1	1	...	18	...	318	1	1	...	17	...	44	...	...	...	1	...
Hassan District ...	440	1	...	...	43	...	379	1	...	...	30	...	61	...	...	...	13	...
Kadur District ...	419	13	...	...	9	...	405	11	...	...	6	...	14	2	...	...	3	...
Shimoga District ...	708	172	2	...	28	...	176	3	1	...	1	...	532	169	1	...	27	...
Civil and Military Station, Bangalore.	**453**	...	...	...	1	...	**245**	...	...	...	...	...	**208**	...	...	...	1	...

TABLE X.

Occupation—*contd.*

District or State	Order 22. Post Office, Telegraph and Telephone services. 114. Post Office, Telegraph, and Telephone services. Total earners (Principal occupation) Males	Females	Total working dependants Males	Females	Total following occupation as subsidiary to other Males	Females	Total of Sub-class V—Trade. Total earners (Principal occupation) Males	Females	Total working dependants Males	Females	Total following occupation as subsidiary to other Males	Females	Order 23. Banks, establishments of credit, exchange and insurance. 115. Bank managers, money lenders, exchange and insurance agents, money changers and brokers and their employees. Total earners (Principal occupation) Males	Females	Total working dependants Males	Females	Total following occupation as subsidiary to other Males	Females
	790	791	792	793	794	795	796	797	798	799	800	801	802	803	804	805	806	807
MYSORE STATE, INCLUDING CIVIL AND MILITARY STATION, BANGALORE.	**1,602**	**15**	**1**	..	**160**	...	**88,234**	**38,097**	**1,723**	**5,678**	**29,771**	**3,384**	**3,439**	**724**	**43**	**39**	**5,993**	**252**
MYSORE STATE, EXCLUDING CIVIL AND MILITARY STATION, BANGALORE.	**1,300**	**6**	**1**	...	**160**	...	**82,141**	**36,759**	**1,712**	**5,552**	**29,698**	**3,369**	**3,102**	**704**	**43**	**39**	**5,991**	**252**
Bangalore City ...	199	1	...	...	..	...	8,764	1,625	83	60	142	20	519	31	2	...	40	...
Bangalore District ...	113	...	...	...	21	...	9,679	7,280	185	415	4,081	382	258	111	3	...	873	36
Kolar Gold Fields (City)...	66	2	...	...	...	...	1,487	500	2	...	120	14	159	6	...	...	17	..
Kolar District... ...	147	1	...	...	24	...	9,639	3,761	299	1,923	4,630	317	255	51	7	22	825	19
Tumkur District ..	109	...	1	...	29	...	8,647	3,489	271	426	4,254	382	381	113	1	2	925	31
Mysore City	119	1	...	...	...	...	5,165	2,074	69	191	254	63	195	36	2	2	53	3
Mysore District ..	126	...	...	...	24	...	12,242	9,495	327	1,298	6,929	851	373	159	6	7	1,290	68
Chitaldrug District ...	116	...	...	...	24	...	7,929	2,908	70	496	2,367	234	363	51	1	...	668	25
Hassan District ...	96	...	...	...	15	...	5,475	2,199	233	265	3,492	637	185	70	16	6	611	17
Kadur District ...	83	...	...	...	9	...	5,003	1,126	18	23	1,260	101	98	31	...	...	228	12
Shimoga District ...	126	1	...	...	14	..	8,111	2,307	155	455	2,219	368	321	45	5	...	461	11
Civil and Military Station, Bangalore.	**302**	**9**	...	...	...	...	**6,093**	**1,338**	**11**	**26**	**73**	**15**	**337**	**20**	...	...	**2**	...

TABLE X.

Occupation.—*contd.*

District or State	Order 24. Brokerage commission and export. 116. Brokers, commission agents, commercial travellers, warehouse owners and employees. Total earners (Principal occupation) Males	Total earners (Principal occupation) Females	Total working dependants Males	Total working dependants Females	Total following occupation as subsidiary to other Males	Total following occupation as subsidiary to other Females	Order 25. Trade in textiles. 117. Trade in piece-goods, wool, cotton, silk, hair and other textiles. Total earners (Principal occupation) Males	Total earners (Principal occupation) Females	Total working dependants Males	Total working dependants Females	Total following occupation as subsidiary to other Males	Total following occupation as subsidiary to other Females	Order 26. Trade in skins, leather and furs. 118. Trade in skins, leather, furs, feathers, horn, etc., and the articles made from these. Total earners (Principal occupation) Males	Total earners (Principal occupation) Females	Total working dependants Males	Total working dependants Females	Total following occupation as subsidiary to other Males	Total following occupation as subsidiary to other Females
	808	809	810	811	812	813	814	815	816	817	818	819	820	821	822	823	824	25
MYSORE STATE, INCLUDING CIVIL AND MILITARY STATION, BANGALORE.	**1,141**	**6**	**3**	...	**188**	**1**	**7,302**	**593**	**93**	**195**	**1,803**	**83**	**1,213**	**9**	**9**	**1**	**426**	**4**
MYSORE STATE, EXCLUDING CIVIL AND MILITARY STATION, BANGALORE.	**1,038**	**4**	**3**	...	**182**	**1**	**6,789**	**581**	**93**	**195**	**1,794**	**83**	**1,025**	**9**	**9**	**1**	**426**	**4**
Bangalore City ...	149	...	1	...	6	...	849	3	6	...	4	...	15	...	...	...	1	...
Bangalore District ...	39	...	...	...	30	...	980	22	...	9	200	1	229	1	1	...	71	...
Kolar Gold Fields (City) ...	14	...	...	...	...	...	75	1	...	...	1	...	17	...	...	...	...	...
Kolar District ...	50	1	1	...	20	...	847	53	8	23	254	6	201	...	5	1	103	...
Tumkur District ...	56	2	1	...	38	...	726	66	10	2	180	4	145	5	...	...	64	3
Mysore City ...	328	...	...	...	14	...	390	6	4	4	5	1	32	...	...	...	...	...
Mysore District ...	60	1	...	...	36	...	897	355	59	156	773	67	105	...	...	...	81	...
Chitaldrug District ...	230	...	...	...	14		732	18	4	...	144	2	124	1	3	...	56	1
Hassan District ...	26	...	...	...	10	1	325	10	1	...	67	...	46	...	...	...	40	...
Kadur District ...	40	...	...	...	1	...	275	12	...	...	58	1	20	2	...	...	2	...
Shimoga District ..	46	...	...	...	12	...	693	35	1	1	108	1	91	...	...	...	8	...
Civil and Military Station, Bangalore.	**103**	**2**	...	...	**6**	...	**513**	**12**	...	...	**9**	...	**188**	...	...	...	...	...

TABLE X.

Occupation—*con td.*

District or State	Order 27. Trade in wood																	
	Total of Order 27						119. Trade in wood (not fire-wood).						120. Trade in barks.					
	Total earners (Principal occupation)		Total working dependants		Total following occupation as subsidiary to other		Total earners (Principal occupation)		Total working dependants		Total following occupation as subsidiary to other		Total earners (Principal occupation)		Total working dependants		Total following occupation as subsidiary to other	
	Males	Females	Males	Females	Males	Females	Males	Females	Males	Females	Males	Females	Males	Females	Males	Females	Males	Females
	826	827	828	829	830	831	832	833	834	835	836	837	838	839	840	841	842	843
MYSORE STATE, INCLUDING CIVIL AND MILITARY STATION, BANGALORE.	**878**	**304**	**6**	**19**	**153**	**21**	**253**	**160**	...	**9**	**29**	**4**	**422**	**53**	**3**	**3**	**81**	**10**
MYSORE STATE, EXCLUDING CIVIL AND MILITARY STATION, BANGALORE.	**828**	**299**	**6**	**19**	**152**	**21**	**222**	**157**	...	**9**	**29**	**4**	**420**	**51**	**3**	**3**	**80**	**10**
Bangalore City ...	59	...	...	...	...	...	37	...	...	...	...	...	...	...	...	...	...	...
Bangalore District ...	39	19	1	1	15	...	3	...	...	...	...	...	14	9	...	1	7	...
Kolar Gold Fields (City) ...	11	...	...	...	1	...	7	...	...	...	1	...	4	...	...	...	...	...
Kolar District ...	66	35	...	4	12	1	18	...	...	...	4	...	42	15	...	2	3	...
Tumkur District ...	205	2	1	...	43	...	1	...	...	...	...	...	184	...	1	...	37	...
Mysore City ...	39	...	...	...	...	...	34	...	...	...	...	...	...	...	...	...	...	...
Mysore District ...	36	11	2	5	19	6	8	...	...	...	5	...	2	...	...	...	...	...
Chitaldrug District ...	280	192	2	9	41	14	45	157	...	9	1	4	171	27	2	...	32	10
Hassan District ...	20	...	...	...	13	...	13	...	...	...	13	...	...	...	...	...	...	...
Kadur District ...	21	9	...	...	4	...	13	...	...	...	1	...	...	...	...	...	1	...
Shimoga District ...	52	1	...	...	4	...	48	...	...	...	4	...	3	...	...	...	...	...
Civil and Military Station, Bangalore.	**50**	**5**	...	...	**1**	...	**31**	**3**	...	...	...	...	**2**	...	...	...	**1**	...

TABLE X.

Occupation—*contd.*

District or State	Order 27. Trade in wood.—*concld.*												Order 28. Trade in metals					
	121. Trade in bamboos and canes.						122. Trade in thatches and other forest produce.						123. Trade in metals, machinery, knives, tools, etc.					
	Total earners (Principal occupation)		Total working dependants		Total following occupation as subsidiary to other		Total earners (Principal occupation)		Total working dependants		Total following occupation as subsidiary to other		Total earners (Principal occupation)		Total working dependants		Total following occupation as subsidiary to other	
	Males	Females	Males	Females	Males	Females	Males	Females	Males	Females	Males	Females	Males	Females	Males	Females	Males	Females
	844	845	846	847	848	849	850	851	852	853	854	855	856	857	858	859	860	861
MYSORE STATE, INCLUDING CIVIL AND MILITARY STATION, BANGALORE	**100**	**66**	**3**	**3**	**33**	**3**	**103**	**25**	...	**4**	**10**	**4**	**545**	**20**	**33**	**1**	**102**	**1**
MYSORE STATE, EXCLUDING CIVIL AND MILITARY STATION, BANGALORE.	**83**	**66**	**3**	**3**	**33**	**3**	**103**	**25**	...	**4**	**10**	**4**	**513**	**17**	**33**	**1**	**101**	**1**
Bangalore City ...	13	...	...	...	...	...	9	...	...	...	...	...	82	1	...	...	...	...
Bangalore District ...	3	7	1	...	...	...	19	3	...	...	8	...	42	...	...	...	3	...
Kolar Gold Fields (City)	...	...	...	...	...	...	...	...	...	...	...	...	8	...	...	...	...	...
Kolar District ...	8	15	...	...	4	...	3	5	...	2	1	1	52	2	...	...	5	1
Tumkur District ...	16	1	...	...	5	...	4	1	...	...	1	...	46	3	...	1	10	...
Mysore City ...	5	...	...	...	...	...	...	...	...	...	...	...	48	2	...	...	1	...
Mysore District ...	26	32	2	3	14	3	...	9	...	2	...	3	73	6	...	...	18	...
Chitaldrug District ...	2	1	...	...	8	...	62	7	...	...	...	...	14	1	...	...	1	...
Hassan District ...	1	...	...	...	...	...	6	...	...	...	...	...	69	...	33	...	32	...
Kadur District ...	8	9	...	...	2	...	...	...	...	...	...	...	13	2	...	...	2	...
Shimoga District ...	1	1	...	...	...	...	...	...	...	...	...	...	71	...	...	...	29	...
Civil and Military Station, Bangalore.	**17**	...	...	...	...	...	...	...	...	...	...	...	**32**	**3**	...	...		...

TABLE X.

Occupation—*contd.*

District or State	Order 29.—Trade in pottery, bricks and tiles.						Order 30.—Trade in chemical products.						Order 31.—Hotels, cafes, restaurants, etc.					
	124. Trade in pottery, bricks and tiles.						125. Drugs, dyes, paints, petroleum, explosives, etc.						Total of Order 31					
	Total earners (Principal occupation)		Total working dependants		Total following occupation as subsidiary to other		Total earners (Principal occupation)		Total working dependants		Total following occupation as subsidiary to other		Total earners (Principal occupation)		Total working dependants		Total following occupation as subsidiary to other	
	Males	Females	Males	Females	Males	Females	Males	Females	Males	Females	Males	Females	Males	Females	Males	Females	Males	Females
	862	863	864	865	866	867	868	869	870	871	872	873	874	875	876	877	878	879
MYSORE STATE, INCLUDING CIVIL AND MILITARY STATION, BANGALORE.	**100**	**36**	**6**	**33**	**62**	**2**	**227**	**30**	**3**	**7**	**52**	**1**	**6,730**	**1,378**	**95**	**109**	**739**	**63**
MYSORE STATE, EXCLUDING CIVIL AND MILITARY STATION, BANGALORE.	**98**	**36**	**6**	**33**	**62**	**2**	**192**	**30**	**3**	**7**	**52**	**1**	**6,216**	**1,179**	**95**	**108**	**739**	**60**
Bangalore City ...	5	1	...	...	...	...	40	4	...	2	...	...	1,057	146	5	3	7	...
Bangalore District ...	1	...	...	...	5	...	9	1	...	...	1	...	522	147	17	3	81	5
Kolar Gold Fields (City)...	...	...	...	...	...	...	2	...	...	...	...	...	164	40	...	...	5	...
Kolar District ...	...	...	...	...	...	...	23	...	...	...	5	...	354	75	3	16	79	4
Tumkur District ...	37	20	6	1	20	...	26	6	...	...	12	...	551	150	20	21	136	9
Mysore City ...	...	...	...	...	...	...	27	2	...	...	...	...	600	127	9	1	11	1
Mysore District ...	7	...	...	...	...	...	2	1	...	1	12	1	768	354	5	36	170	22
Chitaldrug District ...	1	...	...	...	...	...	22	1	...	...	2	...	558	36	11	1	42	3
Hassan District ...	35	3	...	32	11	...	23	14	3	4	16	...	396	44	8	16	70	12
Kadur District ...	2	...	...	...	...	2	7	...	...	...	...	...	541	24	7	...	54	1
Shimoga District ...	10	12	...	...	26	...	11	1	...	...	4	...	705	30	10	11	84	3
Civil and Military Station, Bangalore.	2	...	...	...	...	...	35	...	...	...	...	...	514	199	...	1	...	3

TABLE X.

Occupation—*contd.*

District or State	Order 31.—Hotels, cafes, restaurants—*concld.*																	
	126. Vendors of wine, liquors, aerated waters and ice.						127. Owners and Managers of hotels, cook shops, sarais, etc. (and employees).						128. Hawkers of drink and food stuffs.					
	Total earners (Principal occupation)		Total working dependants		Total following occupation as subsidiary to other		Total earners (Principal occupation)		Total working dependants		Total following occupation as subsidiary to other		Total earners (Principal occupation)		Total working dependants		Total following occupation as subsidiary to other	
	Males	Females	Males	Females	Males	Females	Males	Females	Males	Females	Males	Females	Males	Females	Males	Females	Males	Females
	880	881	882	883	884	885	886	887	888	889	890	891	892	893	894	895	896	897
MYSORE STATE, INCLUDING CIVIL AND MILITARY STATION, BANGALORE.	**2,239**	**203**	**34**	**24**	**538**	**19**	**4,179**	**548**	**61**	**49**	**163**	**25**	**312**	**627**	...	**36**	**38**	**19**
MYSORE STATE, EXCLUDING CIVIL AND MILITARY STATION, BANGALORE.	**2,130**	**192**	**34**	**24**	**538**	**19**	**3,836**	**532**	**61**	**49**	**163**	**25**	**250**	**455**	...	**35**	**38**	**16**
Bangalore City ...	101	2	...	...	3	...	902	97	5	3	3	...	51	47	...	...	1	...
Bangalore District ...	287	22	17	1	65	2	212	28	...	...	15	1	23	97	...	2	1	2
Kolar Gold Fields (City) ...	53	...	...	...	5	...	108	28	...	...	...	...	3	12	...	...	...	...
Kolar District ...	143	26	2	16	61	2	205	31	1	...	13	...	6	18	...	...	5	2
Tumkur District ...	347	42	3	3	118	2	195	12	17	...	15	...	9	96	...	18	3	7
Mysore City ...	34	3	...	...	1	...	560	86	9	1	10	1	6	88	...	...	...	...
Mysore District ...	315	52	3	4	131	3	397	171	2	17	21	16	56	131	...	15	18	3
Chitaldrug District ...	258	17	2	...	35	1	266	15	9	1	6	...	34	4	...	...	1	2
Hassan District ...	133	10	3	...	37	6	258	23	5	16	32	6	5	11	...	...	1	...
Kadur District ...	201	8	4	...	37	...	332	16	3	...	17	1	8	...	...	...	...	...
Shimoga District ...	255	10	...	...	45	3	401	25	10	11	31	...	49	1	...	...	8	...
Civil and Military Station, Bangalore.	**109**	**11**	...	...	...	...	**343**	**16**	...	...	...	...	**62**	**172**	...	**1**	...	**3**

TABLE X.

Occupation—*contd.*

District or State	Order 32.—Other trade in food stuffs																	
	Total of Order 32						129. Grain and pulse dealers.						130. Dealers in sweetmeats sugar and spices.					
	Total earners (Principal occupation)		Total working dependants		Total following occupation as subsidiary to other		Total earners (Principal occupation)		Total working dependants		Total following occupation as subsidiary to other		Total earners (Principal occupation)		Total working dependants		Total following occupation as subsidiary to other	
	Males	Females	Males	Females	Males	Females	Males	Females	Males	Females	Males	Females	Males	Females	Males	Females	Males	Females
	898	899	900	901	902	903	904	905	906	907	908	909	910	911	912	913	914	915
MYSORE STATE, INCLUDING CIVIL AND MILITARY STATION, BANGALORE.	**23,210**	**19,387**	**505**	**2,376**	**7,369**	**1,676**	**6,326**	**1,272**	**71**	**39**	**1,224**	**79**	**2,249**	**617**	**50**	**34**	**780**	**50**
MYSORE STATE, EXCLUDING CIVIL AND MILITARY STATION, BANGALORE.	**21,218**	**18,656**	**500**	**2,352**	**7,341**	**1,666**	**5,809**	**1,249**	**69**	**39**	**1,221**	**78**	**1,993**	**557**	**49**	**34**	**778**	**49**
Bangalore City ...	2,298	866	11	39	59	20	952	148	1	2	...	...	105	8	1	...	1	...
Bangalore District ...	2,384	4,518	39	273	1,041	191	166	17	1	...	43	2	76	25	3	1	9	...
Kolar Gold Fields (City)...	374	346	2	...	37	13	25	2	...	...	3	...	15	7	...	...	1	...
Kolar District ...	3,444	2,202	136	795	1,407	186	288	41	6	21	103	8	59	11	...	6	19	...
Tumkur District ...	1,988	1,318	63	135	1,010	162	812	220	7	3	228	18	295	177	12	20	275	18
Mysore City ...	1,207	1,165	21	117	48	20	198	7	...	1	4	...	71	5	...	...	2	...
Mysore District ...	2,785	4,706	100	765	1,700	406	463	150	7	9	208	10	159	39	2	2	30	...
Chitaldrug District ...	2,051	7,116	18	45	457	91	714	376	10	2	140	15	342	96	4	1	96	11
Hassan District ...	982	922	47	109	790	334	221	57	12	...	189	14	194	50	1	...	140	13
Kadur District ...	1,290	552	9	14	276	53	785	83	8	...	124	8	270	46	1	...	91	...
Shimoga District ...	2,415	945	54	60	516	190	1,185	153	17	1	179	3	407	93	25	4	114	7
Civil and Military Station, Bangalore.	**1,992**	**731**	**5**	**24**	**28**	**10**	**517**	**23**	**2**	...	**3**	**1**	**256**	**60**	**1**	...	**2**	**1**

TABLE X.

Occupation—*contd.*

District or State	Order 32.—Other trade in food stuffs																	
	131. Dealers in dairy products, eggs and poultry.						132. Dealers in animals for food.						133. Dealers in fodder for animals.					
	Total earners (Principal occupation)		Total working dependants		Total following occupation as subsidiary to other		Total earners (Principal occupation)		Total working dependants		Total following occupation as subsidiary to other		Total earners (Principal occupation)		Total working dependants		Total following occupation as subsidiary to other	
	Males	Females	Males	Females	Males	Females	Males	Females	Males	Females	Males	Females	Males	Females	Males	Females	Males	Females
	916	917	918	919	920	921	922	923	924	925	926	927	928	929	930	931	932	933
MYSORE STATE, INCLUDING CIVIL AND MILITARY STATION, BANGALORE.	**2,186**	**8,607**	**58**	**912**	**686**	**822**	**434**	**162**	**5**	**11**	**190**	**29**	**234**	**1,204**	**32**	**180**	**55**	**207**
MYSORE STATE, EXCLUDING CIVIL AND MILITARY STATION, BANGALORE.	**1,802**	**8,419**	**58**	**898**	**678**	**821**	**413**	**162**	**5**	**11**	**190**	**29**	**218**	**979**	**32**	**180**	**54**	**201**
Bangalore City ...	485	272	6	12	28	10	2	2	...	...	...	...	16	86	...	...	...	3
Bangalore District ...	466	2,270	10	120	246	97	51	79	...	4	5	7	71	296	2	44	27	22
Kolar Gold Fields (City)...	50	102	2	...	5	4	11	...	...	...	...	...	5	57	...	...	...	8
Kolar District ...	80	917	7	198	92	54	34	...	...	...	12	1	49	247	30	96	13	20
Tumkur District ...	100	421	10	56	49	53	69	23	2	...	30	2	7	3	...	1	2	4
Mysore City ...	179	458	5	33	20	6	1	...	...	...	...	...	12	70	...	2	...	...
Mysore District ...	112	2,382	10	378	102	230	63	16	3	3	31	1	17	104	...	15	4	24
Chitaldrug District ...	65	307	2	15	27	44	35	26	...	3	64	...	12	35	...	9	1	8
Hassan District ...	20	588	...	58	25	194	26	3	...	...	30	18	15	34	...	4	3	42
Kadur District ...	49	336	...	12	23	35	28	1	...	...	...	...	...	8	...	...	1	...
Shimoga District ...	246	366	6	16	61	94	108	12	...	1	18	..	14	39	...	9	3	70
Civil and Military Station, Bangalore.	**384**	**188**	...	**14**	**8**	**1**	**21**	...	...	...	...	...	**16**	**225**	...	...	**1**	**6**

TABLE X.

Occupation—*contd.*

District or State	Order 32. Other trade in food stuffs—*contd.* 134. Dealers in other food stuffs. Total earners (Principal occupation) Males	Females	Total working dependants Males	Females	Total following occupation as subsidiary to other Males	Females	135. Dealers in tobacco. Total earners (Principal occupation) Males	Females	Total working dependants Males	Females	Total following occupation as subsidiary to other Males	Females	136. Dealers in opium. Total earners (Principal occupation) Males	Females	Total working dependants Males	Females	Total following occupation as subsidiary to other Males	Females
	934	935	936	937	938	939	940	941	942	943	944	945	946	947	948	949	950	951
MYSORE STATE, INCLUDING CIVIL AND MILITARY STATION, BANGALORE.	**9,517**	**7,097**	**201**	**1,100**	**3,818**	**460**	**2,217**	**421**	**88**	**100**	**604**	**29**	**9**	**4**	...	...	**2**	...
MYSORE STATE, EXCLUDING CIVIL AND MILITARY STATION, BANGALORE.	**8,979**	**6,877**	**199**	**1,090**	**3,806**	**459**	**1,959**	**410**	**88**	**100**	**602**	**29**	**8**	...	...	...	**2**	...
Bangalore City ...	715	347	2	22	29	7	69	8	1	3	1	...	...	...	..	...	...	...
Bangalore District ...	1,381	1,788	21	94	684	62	167	43	2	10	27	1	1	...	...	...	...	...
Kolar Gold Fields (City)...	251	173	...	...	28	1	17	5	...	...	...	...	...	...	...	...	...	...
Kolar District ...	2,700	950	67	466	1,131	101	229	36	26	8	36	2	1	...	...	...	...	...
Tumkur District ...	335	433	29	52	344	67	378	40	3	3	80	...	1	...	...	...	...	...
Mysore City	622	579	4	72	15	14	121	46	12	9	7	...	2	...	...	...	...	...
Mysore District ...	1,747	1,952	62	340	1,139	140	221	63	16	18	185	1	...	..	...	...	...	...
Chitaldrug District ...	553	210	2	6	73	11	323	65	...	9	52	2	2	...	...	...	2	...
Hassan District ...	327	107	10	9	219	34	176	83	24	38	183	19	...	...	...	..	...	...
Kadur District ...	49	59	...	...	21	8	112	19	...	2	15	2	...	...	...	...	..	...
Shimoga District ...	299	279	2	29	123	14	146	2	4	...	16	2	1	...	...	...	...	...
Civil and Military Station, Bangalore.	**538**	**220**	**2**	**10**	**12**	**1**	**258**	**11**	...	...	**2**	...	**1**	**4**	...	...	...	...

TABLE X.

Occupation—*contd.*

District or State	Order 32. Other trade in food stuffs—*concld.* 137. Dealers in ganja: Total earners (Principal occupation) Males	Females	Total working dependants Males	Females	Total following occupation as subsidiary to other Males	Females	Order 33. Trade in clothing and toilet articles 138. Trade in ready-made clothing and other articles of dress and the toilet (hats, umbrellas, ready-made shoes, purfume, etc.): Total earners (Principal occupation) Males	Females	Total working dependants Males	Females	Total following occupation as subsidiary to other Males	Females	Order 34. Trade in furniture Total of Order 34: Total earners (Principal occupation) Males	Females	Total working dependants Males	Females	Total following occupation as subsidiary to other Males	Females
	952	953	954	955	956	957	958	959	960	961	962	963	964	965	966	967	968	969
MYSORE STATE, INCLUDING CIVIL AND MILITARY STATION, BANGALORE.	**38**	**3**	...	...	**10**	...	**788**	**348**	**32**	**57**	**99**	**3**	**716**	**18**	...	...	**79**	**2**
MYSORE STATE, EXCLUDING CIVIL AND MILITARY STATION, BANGALORE.	**37**	**3**	...	...	**10**	...	**714**	**327**	**32**	**57**	**99**	**3**	**546**	**17**	...	...	**77**	**2**
Bangalore City ...	4	...	...	...	...	...	155	131	13	7	...	...	83	2	...	...	...	...
Bangalore District ...	5	...	...	...	...	...	20	20	1	2	6	...	68	...	...	...	4	1
Kolar Gold Fields (City)...	...	...	...	...	...	...	1	...	...	...	...	...	13	...	...	...	3	...
Kolar District... ...	4	...	...	...	1	...	105	75	9	43	17	3	24	1	...	...	16	...
Tumkur District ...	1	1	...	...	2	...	24	5	1	2	3	...	40	...	...	...	17	...
Mysore City	1	...	...	...	...	...	67	31	2	2	2	...	92	12	...	...	...	1
Mysore District ...	3	...	...	...	1	...	11	28	...	1	8	...	50	...	...	...	15	...
Chitaldrug District ...	5	1	...	...	2	...	16	16	...	...	8	...	43	...	...	...	1	...
Hassan District ...	3	...	...	...	1	...	70	4	...	...	18	...	95	2	...	...	20	...
Kadur District ...	2	...	...	...	1	...	95	1	...	...	10	...	17	...	...	...	1	...
Shimoga District ...	9	1	...	...	2	...	150	16	6	...	27	...	21	...	...	...	...	...
Civil and Military Station, Bangalore.	1	...	...	...	...	...	**74**	**21**	...	...	...	...	**170**	**1**	...	...	**2**	...

TABLE X.

Occupation—*contd.*

District or State	Order 34.—Trade in furniture—*concld.* 129. Trade in furniture, carpets, curtains and bedding. Total earners (Principal occupation) Males	Females	Total working dependants Males	Females	Total following occupation as subsidiary to other Males	Females	140. Hardware, cooking utensils, porcelain, crockery, glass ware, bottles, articles for gardening, etc. Total earners (Principal occupation) Males	Females	Total working dependants Males	Females	Total following occupation as subsidiary to other Males	Females	Order 35.—Trade in building materials. 141. Trade in building materials (other than bricks, tiles, and woody materials). Total earners (Principal occupation) Males	Females	Total working dependants Males	Females	Total following occupation as subsidiary to other Males	Females
	970	971	972	973	974	975	976	977	978	979	980	981	982	983	984	985	986	987
MYSORE STATE, INCLUDING CIVIL AND MILITARY STATION, BANGALORE.	**161**	...	...	...	**13**	**1**	**555**	**18**	...	...	**66**	**1**	**485**	**427**	**12**	**107**	**259**	**36**
MYSORE STATE, EXCLUDING CIVIL AND MILITARY STATION, BANGALORE.	**100**	...	...	...	**11**	**1**	**446**	**17**	...	...	**66**	**1**	**481**	**360**	**12**	**107**	**259**	**35**
Bangalore City ...	39	...	...	...	...	...	44	2	...	...	...	...	24	13	...	...	...	...
Bangalore District ...	9	...	...	...	...	1	59	...	...	...	4	...	140	78	6	3	47	5
Kolar Gold Fields (City)...	...	...	...	...	...	...	13	...	...	...	3	...	...	3	...	...	...	...
Kolar District ...	6	...	...	...	2	...	18	1	...	...	14	...	69	85	2	80	79	5
Tumkur District ...	12	...	...	...	4	...	28	...	...	...	13	...	37	23	...	2	14	2
Mysore City ...	6	...	...	...	...	...	86	12	...	...	...	1	13	25	...	...	1	...
Mysore District ...	1	...	...	...	1	...	49	...	...	...	14	...	146	91	3	21	89	23
Chitaldrug District ...	...	...	...	...	...	...	43	...	...	...	1	...	3	19	...	...	1	...
Hassan District ...	5	...	...	...	3	...	90	2	...	...	17	...	18	13	...	1	16	...
Kadur District ...	8	...	...	...	1	...	9	...	...	...	...	...	11	7	...	...	...	...
Shimoga District ...	14	...	...	...	...	...	7	...	...	...	...	...	20	3	1	...	12	...
Civil and Military Station, Bangalore.	**61**	...	...	...	**2**	...	**109**	**1**	...	...	...	...	**4**	**67**	...	...	...	**1**

TABLE X.

Occupation—*contd.*

District or State	Order 36. Trade in means of transport																	
	Total of Order 36						142. Dealers and hirers in mechanical transport, motors, cycles, etc.,						143. Dealers and hirers, in other carriages, carts, boats, etc.					
	Total earners (Principal occupation)		Total working dependants		Total following occupation as subsidiary to other		Total earners (Principal occupation)		Total working dependants		Total following occupation as subsidiary to other		Total earners (principal occupation)		Total working dependants		Total following occupation as subsidiary to other	
	Males	Females	Males	Females	Males	Females	Males	Females	Males	Females	Males	Females	Males	Females	Males	Females	Males	Females
	988	989	990	991	992	993	994	995	996	997	998	999	1000	1001	1002	1003	1004	1005
MYSORE STATE, INCLUDING CIVIL AND MILITARY STATION, BANGALORE.	**1,493**	**48**	**15**	**108**	**963**	**7**	**200**	...	...	...	**7**	...	**324**	**1**	**8**	**5**	**191**	**1**
MYSORE STATE, EXCLUDING CIVIL AND MILITARY STATION, BANGALORE.	**1,404**	**48**	**13**	**108**	**963**	**7**	**121**	...	...	...	**7**	...	**317**	**1**	**7**	**5**	**191**	**1**
Bangalore City ...	177	...	1	...	5	...	63	...	...	...	...	...	102	...	1	...	5	...
Bangalore District ...	173	3	...	...	143	1	12	...	...	...	2	...	6	...	...	...	7	1
Kolar Gold Fields (City)...	4	...	..	...	3	...	1	...	...	...	...	...	...	...	...	...	...	...
Kolar District ...	422	13	4	10	285	...	1	...	...	...	...	...	12	...	2	...	22	...
Tumkur District ...	50	5	4	...	76	...	10	...	...	...	4	...	6	...	4	...	19	...
Mysore City ...	38	...	...	...	2	...	18	...	...	...	...	...	...	...	...	...	...	...
Mysore District ...	161	1	4	...	216	...	6	...	...	...	...	...	35	...	...	...	61	...
Chitaldrug District ...	183	28	...	90	51	3	4	...	...	...	...	...	105	...	...	...	...	...
Hassan District ...	43	...	...	...	152	...	3	...	...	...	...	...	7	...	...	...	76	...
Kadur District ...	35	1	...	2	1	3	1	...	...	...	...	...	33	1	...	...	...	...
Shimoga District ...	118	2	...	6	29	...	2	...	...	...	1	...	11	...	...	5	1	...
Civil and Military Station, Bangalore.	**89**	...	**2**	...	...	...	**79**	...	...	...	...	...	**7**	...	**1**	...	...	...

TABLE X.

Occupation—*contd.*

District or State	Order 36. Trade in means of transport						Order 37. Trade in fuel						Order 38. Trade in articles of luxury and those pertaining to letters and the arts and sciences.					
	144. Dealers and hirers of elephants, camels, horses, cattle, asses, mules, etc.						145. Dealers in firewood charcoal, cowdung, etc.						Total of Order 38.					
	Total earners (Principal occupation)		Total working dependants		Total following occupation as subsidiary to other		Total earners (Principal occupation)		Total working dependants		Total following occupation as subsidiary to other		Total earners (Principal occupation)		Total working dependants		Total following occupation as subsidiary to other	
	Males	Females	Males	Females	Males	Females	Males	Females	Males	Females	Males	Females	Males	Females	Males	Females	Males	Females
	1006	1007	1008	1009	1010	1011	1012	1013	1014	1015	1016	1017	1018	1019	1020	1021	1022	1023
MYSORE STATE, INCLUDING CIVIL AND MILITARY STATION, BANGALORE.	**969**	**47**	**7**	**103**	**765**	**6**	**2,210**	**3,802**	**133**	**1,011**	**1,445**	**543**	**3,591**	**1,220**	**87**	**667**	**946**	**88**
MYSORE STATE, EXCLUDING CIVIL AND MILITARY STATION, BANGALORE.	**966**	**47**	**6**	**103**	**765**	**6**	**2,057**	**3,751**	**133**	**1,011**	**1,443**	**542**	**3,305**	**1,192**	**87**	**667**	**943**	**88**
Bangalore City ...	12	...	...	...	...	...	173	39	1	2	2	...	552	42	5	4	3	...
Bangalore District ...	155	3	...	...	134	...	356	828	36	53	288	78	326	150	2	13	101	7
Kolar Gold Fields (City) ...	3	...	...	...	3	...	27	19	...	...	3	...	25	8	...	...	38	...
Kolar District ...	409	13	2	10	263	...	241	416	21	46	248	30	506	205	28	564	299	15
Tumkur District ...	34	5	...	...	53	...	123	322	29	118	162	57	294	106	6	10	133	2
Mysore City ...	20	...	...	...	2	...	72	140	1	8	12	36	260	189	14	28	50	...
Mysore District ...	120	1	4	...	155	...	122	655	3	55	105	104	322	151	6	29	114	6
Chitaldrug District ...	74	23	...	90	51	3	179	360	8	321	56	31	343	125	1	6	55	4
Hassan District ...	33	...	...	...	76	..	82	294	2	69	42	61	210	93	22	3	88	52
Kadur District ...	1	...	...	2	1	3	304	87	1	...	214	7	155	42	...	1	35	1
Shimoga District ...	105	2	...	1	27	...	378	591	31	349	311	143	312	81	3	9	34	1
Civil and Military Station, Bangalore.	**3**	...	**1**	...	...	...	**153**	**51**	...	...	**2**	**1**	**286**	**28**	...	...	**3**	...

TABLE X.

Occupation—*contd.*

District or State	Order 38. Trade in articles of luxury, and those pertaining to letters and the arts and sciences—*concld.*																	
	146. Dealers in precious stones, jewellery (real and imitation), clocks, optical instruments, etc.						147. Dealers in common bangles, bead necklaces, fans, small articles, toys, hunting and fishing tackle, flowers, etc.						148. Publishers, book-sellers, stationers, dealers in music, pictures, musical instruments and curiosities.					
	Total earners (Principal occupation)		Total working dependants		Total following occupation as subsidiary to other		Total earners (Principal occupation)		Total working dependants		Total following occupation as subsidiary to other		Total earners (Principal occupation)		Total working dependants		Total following occupation as subsidiary to other	
	Males	Females	Males	Females	Males	Females	Males	Females	Males	Females	Males	Females	Males	Females	Males	Females	Males	Females
	1024	1025	1026	1027	1028	1029	1030	1031	1032	1033	1034	1035	1036	1037	1038	1039	1040	1041
MYSORE STATE, INCLUDING CIVIL AND MILITARY STATION, BANGALORE.	**721**	**62**	**16**	**2**	**95**	...	**2,670**	**1,147**	**68**	**665**	**843**	**88**	**200**	**11**	**3**	...	**8**	...
MYSORE STATE, EXCLUDING CIVIL AND MILITARY STATION, BANGALORE.	**582**	**60**	**16**	**2**	**94**	...	**2 557**	**1,122**	**68**	**665**	**841**	**88**	**166**	**10**	**3**	...	**8**	...
Bangalore City ...	153	1	1	...	...	...	321	39	4	4	...	...	78	2	...	...	3	...
Bangalore District ...	28	8	...	...	1	...	297	142	2	13	100	7	1	...	...	...	...	...
Kolar Gold Fields (City) ...	4	...	...	...	34	...	20	8	...	...	4	...	1	...	...	...	...	...
Kolar District ...	57	8	1	2	9	...	447	194	27	562	281	15	2	3	...	...	2	...
Tumkur District ...	21	4	2	...	4	...	264	101	4	10	129	2	9	1	...	...	...	...
Mysore City ...	35	8	...	...	...	...	202	180	14	28	50	...	23	1	...	...	...	...
Mysore District ...	28	4	...	...	6	...	290	147	3	29	107	6	4	...	3	...	1	...
Chitaldrug District ...	60	6	...	...	1	...	264	116	1	6	53	4	19	3	...	...	1	...
Hassan District ...	71	3	12	...	27	...	133	90	10	3	61	52	6	...	...	...	...	...
Kadur District ...	52	6	...	...	9	...	101	36	...	1	26	1	2	...	...	...	...	...
Shimoga District ...	73	12	...	...	3	...	218	69	3	9	30	1	21	...	...	...	1	...
Civil and Military Station, Bangalore.	139	2	...	...	1	...	113	25	...	...	2	...	34	1	...	...	...	...

TABLE X.

Occupation—*contd.*

District or State	Order 39. Trade of other sorts																	
	Total of Order 39						149. Dealers in rags, stable refuse, etc.						150. General store-keepers and shop-keepers otherwise unspecified					
	Total earners (Principal occupation)		Total working dependants		Total following occupation as subsidiary to other		Total earners (Principal occupation)		Total working dependants		Total following occupation as subsidiary to other		Total earners (Principal occupation)		Total working dependants		Total following occupation as subsidiary to other	
	Males	Females	Males	Females	Males	Females	Males	Females	Males	Females	Males	Females	Males	Females	Males	Females	Males	Females
	1042	1043	1044	1045	1046	1047	1048	1049	1050	1051	1052	1053	1054	1055	1056	1057	1058	1059
MYSORE STATE, INCLUDING CIVIL AND MILITARY STATION, BANGALORE.	**34,166**	**9,747**	**648**	**848**	**9,093**	**601**	**15**	**53**	**4**	**13**	**2**	**2**	**19,980**	**5,820**	**285**	**243**	**4,293**	**328**
MYSORE STATE, EXCLUDING CIVIL AND MILITARY STATION, BANGALORE.	**32,615**	**9,549**	**644**	**847**	**9,074**	**601**	**14**	**53**	**4**	**13**	**2**	**2**	**18,571**	**5,624**	**281**	**242**	**4,274**	**328**
Bangalore City ...	2,527	346	38	3	15	...	1	...	...	...	...	...	2,350	315	36	3	15	...
Bangalore District ...	4,098	1,382	79	58	1,122	62	...	15	...	7	...	...	2,122	743	16	27	490	31
Kolar Gold Fields (City) ...	593	77	...	...	12	1	1	...	...	...	...	...	338	14	...	...	12	...
Kolar District ...	2,980	547	75	319	983	47	...	...	...	...	...	...	1,057	259	9	40	197	22
Tumkur District ...	3,918	1,343	129	132	1,411	112	...	2	...	...	...	...	2,381	851	65	67	767	72
Mysore City ...	1,762	339	16	29	55	1	...	...	...	...	...	...	638	135	9	2	26	1
Mysore District ...	6,324	2,946	139	222	2,283	148	...	5	...	3	...	1	2,062	1,295	52	41	760	52
Chitaldrug District ...	2,787	944	22	24	770	60	1	...	...	...	...	...	2,243	840	20	18	612	55
Hassan District ...	2,850	730	101	35	1,496	130	4	31	4	3	2	1	1,364	407	29	22	682	65
Kadur District ...	2,079	356	1	6	374	21	7	...	...	...	...	...	1,397	248	1	4	198	11
Shimoga District ...	2,697	539	44	19	553	19	...	...	...	...	...	...	2,619	517	44	18	520	19
Civil and Military Station, Bangalore.	**1,551**	**198**	**4**	**1**	**19**	...	**1**	...	...	...	...	...	**1,409**	**196**	**4**	**1**	**19**	...

TABLE X.

Occupation—*contd.*

District or State	Order 39. Trade of other sorts—*concld.*												Total of Class C.					
	151. Itinerant traders, pedlars and hawkers (of other than food, etc.).						152. Other trades (including farmers of pounds, tools and markets).						Public Administration and Liberal Arts.					
	Total earners (Principal occupation)		Total working dependants		Total following occupation as subsidiary to other		Total earners (Principal occupation)		Total working dependants		Total following occupation as subsidiary to other		Total earners (Principal occupation)		Total working dependants		Total following occupation as subsidiary to other	
	Males	Females	Males	Females	Males	Females	Males	Females	Males	Females	Males	Females	Males	Females	Males	Females	Males	Females
	1060	1061	1062	1063	1064	1065	1066	1067	1068	1069	1070	1071	1072	1073	1074	1075	1076	1077
MYSORE STATE, INCLUDING CIVIL AND MILITARY STATION, BANGALORE.	**253**	**288**	**3**	**57**	**224**	**63**	**13,918**	**3,586**	**356**	**535**	**4,574**	**208**	**79,891**	**5,157**	**727**	**375**	**33,054**	**769**
MYSORE STATE, EXCLUDING CIVIL AND MILITARY STATION, BANGALORE.	**243**	**288**	**3**	**57**	**224**	**63**	**13,787**	**3,584**	**356**	**535**	**4,574**	**208**	**72,158**	**4,393**	**724**	**374**	**33,019**	**765**
Bangalore City ...	22	...	...	...	...	...	154	31	2	...	...	...	7,822	595	18	19	59	...
Bangalore District ...	19	26	...	1	5	8	1,957	598	63	23	627	23	8,188	448	56	21	4,858	60
Kolar Gold Fields (City)...	3	...	...	...	...	...	251	63	...	...	...	1	1,062	158	...	...	149	4
Kolar District ...	40	3	3	4	17	1	1,888	285	63	275	769	24	7,374	516	143	218	6,241	94
Tumkur District ...	10	91	...	35	2	...	1,527	399	64	30	642	40	7,360	371	101	27	5,230	89
Mysore City ...	...	...	...	...	...	...	1,124	204	7	27	29	...	8,079	596	40	20	144	...
Mysore District ...	23	38	...	13	30	1	4,289	1,608	87	165	1,493	94	9,979	571	120	27	6,057	222
Chitaldrug District ...	15	19	...	3	4	1	528	85	2	3	154	4	5,867	311	64	17	2,419	79
Hassan District ...	80	104	...	...	155	62	1,402	188	68	10	657	12	5,548	328	124	17	4,663	189
Kadur District ...	3	...	...	...	...	...	672	108	...	2	181	10	3,725	192	11	...	1,160	13
Shimoga District ...	28	7	...	1	11	...	50	15	...	...	22	...	7,154	307	52	8	2,089	15
Civil and Military Station, Bangalore.	10	...	...	...	...	...	**131**	**2**	...	...	...	...	**7,733**	**764**	**3**	**1**	**35**	**4**

TABLE X.

Occupation—*contd.*

District or State	Total of Sub-class VI. Public Force						Order 40. Army											
							Total of Order 40						153. Army (Imperial)					
	Total earners (Principal occupation)		Total working dependants		Total following occupation as subsidiary to other		Total earners (Principal occupation)		Total working dependants		Total following occupation as subsidiary to other		Total earners (Principal occupation)		Total working dependants		Total following occupation as subsidiary to other	
	Males	Females	Males	Females	Males	Females	Males	Females	Males	Females	Males	Females	Males	Females	Males	Females	Males	Females
	1078	1079	1080	1081	1082	1083	1084	1085	1086	1087	1088	1089	1090	1091	1092	1093	1094	1095
MYSORE STATE, INCLUDING CIVIL AND MILITARY STATION, BANGALORE.	**16,694**	**309**	**73**	**49**	**4,050**	**149**	**6,925**	**20**	**5**	**1**	**12**	...	**4,324**	**18**	...	**1**	...	...
MYSORE STATE, EXCLUDING CIVIL AND MILITARY STATION, BANGALORE.	**11,832**	**302**	**73**	**49**	**4,050**	**149**	**2,607**	**13**	**5**	**1**	**12**	...	**13**	**11**	...	**1**	...	...
Bangalore City ...	1,095	...	...	...	...	...	48	...	...	...	...	...	6	...	...	...	...	...
Bangalore District ...	1,782	19	1	1	385	6	946	...	...	...	...	...	...	...	...	...	...	...
Kolar Gold Fields (City)...	318	...	...	...	12	...	13	...	...	...	...	...	...	...	...	...	...	...
Kolar District... ...	1,044	16	7	36	626	17	116	...	...	...	3	...	...	...	...	...	...	...
Tumkur District ...	1,238	37	8	4	960	31	94	...	...	...	2	...	1	...	...	...	...	...
Mysore City	1,527	3	2	...	3	...	958	2	2	...	3	...	...	...	...	...	...	...
Mysore District ...	1,044	63	7	4	592	50	83	11	...	1	1	...	...	11	...	1	...	...
Chitaldrug District ...	1,131	60	5	...	541	26	55	...	...	...	3	..	...	...	...	...	...	...
Hassan District ...	878	8	37	4	527	3	94	...	3	...	...	...	6	...	...	...	...	...
Kadur District ...	495	21	...	...	126	6	28	...	...	...	...	...	...	...	...	...	...	...
Shimoga District ...	1,280	75	6	...	336	10	172	...	...	...	...	...	...	...	...	...	...	...
Civil and Military Station, Bangalore.	**4,862**	**7**	...	...	...	...	**4,318**	**7**	...	...	...	...	**4,311**	**7**	...	...	...	...

TABLE X.

Occupation—*contd.*

District or State	Order 40. Army—*concld.*						Order 42. Air Force						Order 43. Police					
	154. Army (Indian States)						156. Air Force						Total of Order 43					
	Total earners (Principal occupation)		Total working dependants		Total following occupation as subsidiary to other		Total earners (Principal occupation)		Total working dependants		Total following occupation as subsidiary to other		Total earners (Principal occupation)		Total working dependants		Total following occupation as subsidiary to other	
	Males	Females	Males	Females	Males	Females	Males	Females	Males	Females	Males	Females	Males	Females	Males	Females	Males	Females
	1096	1097	1098	1099	1100	1101	1102	1103	1104	1105	1106	1107	1108	1109	1110	1111	1112	1113
MYSORE STATE, INCLUDING CIVIL AND MILITARY STATION, BANGALORE.	**2,601**	**2**	**5**	...	**12**	...	**1**	...	...	...	...	...	**9,768**	**289**	**68**	**48**	**4,088**	**149**
MYSORE STATE, EXCLUDING CIVIL AND MILITARY STATION, BANGALORE.	**2,594**	**2**	**5**	...	**12**	...	...	...	...	...	...	...	**9,225**	**289**	**68**	**48**	**4,088**	**149**
Bangalore City ...	42	...	...	...	...	...	...	...	...	...	...	...	1,047	...	...	...	...	...
Bangalore District ...	946	...	...	...	...	...	...	...	...	...	...	...	836	19	1	1	385	6
Kolar Gold Fields (City)...	13	...	...	...	...	...	...	...	...	...	...	...	305	...	...	...	12	...
Kolar District ...	116	...	...	...	3	...	...	...	...	...	...	...	928	16	7	36	625	17
Tumkur District ...	93	...	...	...	2	...	...	...	...	...	...	...	1,144	37	8	4	958	31
Mysore City ...	958	2	2	...	3	...	...	...	...	...	...	...	569	1	...	...	...	...
Mysore District ...	83	...	...	...	1	...	...	...	...	...	...	...	961	52	7	3	531	50
Chitaldrug District ...	55	...	...	...	3	...	...	...	...	...	...	...	1,076	60	5	...	588	26
Hassan District ...	88	...	3	...	...	...	...	...	...	...	...	...	784	8	34	4	527	3
Kadur District ...	28	...	...	...	...	...	...	...	...	...	...	...	467	21	...	...	126	6
Shimoga District ...	172	...	...	...	...	...	...	...	...	...	...	...	1,108	75	6	...	336	10
Civil and Military Station, Bangalore.	7	...	...	...	...	...	1	...	...	...	...	...	**543**	...	...	...	...	...

TABLE X.

Occupation—*contd.*

District or State	Order 48. Police												Total of Sub-class VII. Public Administration					
	157. Police						158. Village watchmen											
	Total earners (Principal occupation)		Total working dependants		Total following occupation as subsidiary to other		Total earners (Principal occupation)		Total working dependants		Total following occupation as subsidiary to other		Total earners (Principal occupation)		Total working dependants		Total following occupation as subsidiary to other	
	Males	Females	Males	Females	Males	Females	Males	Females	Males	Females	Males	Females	Males	Females	Males	Females	Males	Females
	1114	1115	1116	1117	1118	1119	1120	1121	1122	1123	1124	1125	1126	1127	1128	1129	1130	1131
MYSORE STATE, INCLUDING CIVIL AND MILITARY STATION, BANGALORE.	**6,825**	...	...	...	**120**	...	**2,943**	**289**	**68**	**48**	**3,918**	**149**	**31,772**	**883**	**145**	**101**	**18,624**	**453**
MYSORE STATE, EXCLUDING CIVIL AND MILITARY STATION, BANGALORE.	**6,285**	...	...	...	**120**	...	**2,940**	**289**	**68**	**48**	**3,918**	**149**	**30,605**	**877**	**145**	**101**	**18,624**	**453**
Bangalore City ...	1,023	...	...	...	...	...	24	...	...	...	...	...	4,068	8	...	...	2	...
Bangalore District ...	642	...	...	...	21	...	194	19	1	1	364	6	3,208	85	11	3	3,084	32
Kolar Gold Fields (City)...	302	...	...	...	...	...	3	...	...	...	12	...	403	11	...	...	112	2
Kolar District... ...	672	...	...	...	21	...	256	16	7	36	604	17	3,468	108	53	67	4,334	56
Tumkur District ...	589	...	...	...	11	...	555	87	8	4	947	31	2,774	50	18	7	2,443	35
Mysore City	567	...	...	...	...	...	2	1	...	...	...	...	3,953	180	...	...	26	...
Mysore District ...	739	...	...	...	13	...	222	52	7	3	518	50	4,192	228	18	12	3,326	152
Chitaldrug District ..	508	...	...	...	8	...	568	60	5	...	530	26	2,355	65	29	6	1,136	31
Hassan District ...	435	...	...	...	26	...	349	8	34	4	501	3	2,180	88	11	6	2,823	140
Kadur District ...	287	...	...	...	1	...	180	21	...	...	125	6	1,499	15	...	...	622	3
Shimoga District ...	521	...	...	...	19	...	587	75	6	...	317	10	2,505	39	5	...	866	2
Civil and Military Station, Bangalore.	**540**	...	...	...	...	...	**3**	...	...	...	...	...	**1,167**	**6**	...	...	...	...

TABLE X.

Occupation—*contd.*

District or State	Order 44.—Public Administration—*contd.*																	
	Total of Order 44						159. Service of the State						160. Service of Indian and Foreign States					
	Total earners (Principal occupation)		Total working dependants		Total following occupation as subsidiary to other		Total earners (Principal occupation)		Total working dependants		Total following occupation as subsidiary to other		Total earners (Principal occupation)		Total working dependants		Total following occupation as subsidiary to other	
	Males	Females	Males	Females	Males	Females	Males	Females	Males	Females	Males	Females	Males	Females	Males	Females	Males	Females
	1132	1133	1134	1135	1136	1137	1138	1139	1140	1141	1142	1143	1144	1145	1146	1147	1148	1149
MYSORE STATE, INCLUDING CIVIL AND MILITARY STATION, BANGALORE.	**31,772**	**883**	**145**	**101**	**18,624**	**453**	**262**	**13**	...	...	**17**	**1**	**19,958**	**325**	...	...	**506**	**2**
MYSORE STATE, EXCLUDING CIVIL AND MILITARY STATION, BANGALORE.	**30,605**	**877**	**145**	**101**	**18,624**	**453**	**92**	**9**	...	...	**17**	**1**	**19,218**	**325**	...	...	**506**	**2**
Bangalore City ...	4,068	8	...	...	2	...	21	...	...	...	...	...	3,647	6	...	...	...	...
Bangalore District ...	3,208	85	11	3	3,034	32	38	6	...	...	...	1	1,449	12	...	...	43	...
Kolar Gold Fields (City)...	408	11	...	...	112	2	...	...	...	...	...	...	277	3	...	...	2	...
Kolar District ...	3,468	108	53	67	4,334	56	21	...	...	...	...	...	1,238	16	...	...	42	...
Tumkur District ...	2,774	50	18	7	2,443	35	...	1	...	...	4	...	1,356	5	...	...	130	...
Mysore City ...	3,958	180	...	...	26	...	...	...	...	...	...	...	3,570	179	...	...	18	...
Mysore District ...	4,192	228	18	12	3,326	152	...	...	...	...	...	...	2,580	51	...	...	150	2
Chitaldrug District ...	2,355	65	29	6	1,136	31	1	...	...	...	1	...	1,160	11	...	...	23	...
Hassan District ...	2,180	88	11	6	2,823	140	5	1	...	...	...	...	1,167	33	...	...	14	...
Kadur District ...	1,499	15	...	...	522	3	6	...	...	...	7	...	1,071	1	...	...	1	...
Shimoga District ...	2,505	39	5	...	866	2	...	1	...	...	5	...	1,703	8	...	...	83	...
Civil and Military Station, Bangalore.	1,167	6	...	...	...	...	170	4	...	...	...	...	740	...	...	...	...	...

TABLE X.

Occupation—*contd.*

District or State	Order 44.—Public Administration—*concld.* 161. Municipal and other local (not village) service: Total earners (Principal occupation) Males	Females	Total working dependants Males	Females	Total following occupation as subsidiary to other Males	Females	162. Village officials and servants other than watchmen: Total earners (Principal occupation) Males	Females	Total working dependants Males	Females	Total following occupation as subsidiary to other Males	Females	Tota[illegible]-class VIII. Professi[illegible] Liberal Arts. Po[illegible]: Total earners (Principal occupation) Males	Females	Total working dependants Males	Females	Total following occupation as subsidiary to other Males	Females
	1150	1151	1152	1153	1154	1155	1156	1157	1158	1159	1160	1161	1162	1163	1164	1165	1166	1167
MYSORE STATE, INCLUDING CIVIL AND MILITARY STATION, BANGALORE.	**2,065**	**31**	...	...	**72**	**3**	**9,487**	**514**	**145**	**101**	**18,029**	**447**	**31,425**	**3,965**	**509**	**225**	**10,380**	**167**
MYSORE STATE, EXCLUDING CIVIL AND MILITARY STATION, BANGALORE.	**1,822**	**31**	...	...	**72**	**3**	**9,473**	**512**	**145**	**101**	**18,029**	**447**	**29,721**	**3,214**	**506**	**224**	**10,345**	**163**
Bangalore City ...	318	2	...	...	...	...	82	...	...	...	2	...	2,659	587	13	19	57	...
Bangalore District ...	154	9	...	...	22	...	1,567	58	11	3	2,969	31	3,198	344	44	17	1,439	22
Kolar Gold Fields (City)...	77	2	...	...	...	...	49	6	...	...	110	2	341	147	...	...	25	2
Kolar District ...	144	7	...	...	12	3	2,065	85	53	67	4,280	53	2,862	392	83	115	1,279	21
Tumkur District ...	168	...	...	...	12	...	1,250	44	18	7	2,297	35	3,348	284	75	16	1,827	23
Mysore City ...	334	...	...	...	5	...	49	1	...	...	3	...	2,599	418	38	20	115	...
Mysore District ...	159	2	...	...	4	...	1,453	175	18	12	3,172	150	4,743	280	95	11	2,199	20
Chitaldrug District ...	133	...	...	...	1	...	1,061	54	29	6	1,111	31	2,881	186	90	11	742	22
Hassan District ...	96	...	...	...	11	...	912	54	11	6	2,798	140	2,490	232	76	7	1,813	46
Kadur District ...	89	8	...	...	1	...	333	6	...	...	518	3	1,731	156	11	...	512	4
Shimoga District ...	150	1	...	...	4	...	652	29	5	...	774	2	3,369	193	41	8	837	3
Civil and Military Station, Bangalore.	**243**	...	...	...	...	...	**14**	**2**	...	...	...	...	**1,704**	**751**	**3**	**1**	**35**	**4**

TABLE X.

Occupation—*contd.*

District or State	Order 45.—Religion																	
	Total of Order 45						163. Priests, ministers, etc.						164. Monks, nuns, religious mendicants.					
	Total earners (Principal occupation)		Total working dependants		Total following occupation as subsidiary to other		Total earners (Principal occupation)		Total working dependants		Total following occupation as subsidiary to other		Total earners (Principal occupation)		Total working dependants		Total following occupation as subsidiary to other	
	Males	Females	Males	Females	Males	Females	Males	Females	Males	Females	Males	Females	Males	Females	Males	Females	Males	Females
	1168	1169	1170	1171	1172	1173	1174	1175	1176	1177	1178	1179	1180	1181	1182	1183	1184	1185
MYSORE STATE, INCLUDING CIVIL AND MILITARY STATION, BANGALORE.	**8,246**	**417**	**333**	**61**	**6,100**	**81**	**3,026**	**75**	**112**	**8**	**1,913**	**10**	**271**	**52**	**14**	**1**	**136**	**1**
MYSORE STATE, EXCLUDING CIVIL AND MILITARY STATION, BANGALORE.	**7,920**	**358**	**333**	**61**	**6,088**	**79**	**2,842**	**68**	**112**	**8**	**1,905**	**10**	**254**	**45**	**14**	**1**	**136**	**1**
Bangalore City ...	419	32	4	3	17	...	301	4	1	...	15	...	11	8	...	...	...	...
Bangalore District ...	974	38	35	3	892	8	256	4	7	...	196	...	2	7	...	...	2	...
Kolar Gold Fields (City) ...	53	9	...	...	17	1	39	5	...	...	10	...	...	1	...	...	...	1
Kolar District ...	873	52	49	35	744	9	373	17	13	6	324	3	22	9	2	1	16	...
Tumkur District ...	880	26	58	5	1,128	6	318	9	18	2	331	3	65	3	3	...	18	...
Mysore City ...	407	9	24	3	36	...	287	1	21	...	27	...	1	...	1	...	...	...
Mysore District ...	1,617	67	74	2	1,284	12	378	6	18	...	320	3	14	...	1	...	16	...
Chitaldrug District ...	575	25	18	...	401	2	229	9	2	...	142	...	96	8	5	...	29	...
Hassan District ...	695	46	28	7	793	41	118	3	16	...	178	1	34	8	...	...	39	...
Kadur District ...	546	31	10	...	328	3	222	1	6	...	168	...	5	1	...	...	2	...
Shimoga District ...	881	23	33	3	448	2	321	9	11	...	209	...	4	...	2	...	14	...
Civil and Military Station, Bangalore.	**326**	**59**	...	...	12	**2**	**184**	7	...	...	**8**	...	17	7	...	...	...	...

TABLE X.

Occupation—*contd.*

District or State	Order 45—Religion—concld.												Order 46. Law					
	165. Other religious workers						166. Servants in religious edifices, burial and burning grounds, pilgrim conductors, circumcisers, etc.						Total of Order 46.					
	Total earners (Principal occupation)		Total working dependants		Total following occupation as subsidiary to other		Total earners (Principal occupation)		Total working dependants		Total following occupation as subsidiary to other		Total earners (Principal occupation)		Total working dependants		Total following occupation as subsidiary to other	
	Males	Females	Males	Females	Males	Females	Males	Females	Males	Females	Males	Females	Males	Females	Males	Females	Males	Females
	1186	1187	1188	1189	1190	1191	1192	1193	1194	1195	1196	1197	1198	1199	1200	1201	1202	1203
MYSORE STATE, INCLUDING CIVIL AND MILITARY STATION, BANGALORE.	**283**	**57**	**5**	**2**	**164**	**2**	**4,666**	**233**	**202**	**50**	**3,887**	**68**	**1,140**	**6**	**1**	...	**95**	**1**
MYSORE STATE, EXCLUDING CIVIL AND MILITARY STATION, BANGALORE.	**264**	**26**	**5**	**2**	**163**	...	**4,560**	**219**	**202**	**50**	**3,884**	**68**	**1,095**	**6**	**1**	...	**95**	**1**
Bangalore City ...	19	8	...	2	...	...	88	12	3	1	2	...	229	...	...	...	1	...
Bangalore District ...	10	...	...	...	...	...	706	27	28	3	694	3	61	...	...	...	7	...
Kolar Gold Fields (City) ...	...	...	...	...	...	...	14	3	...	...	7	...	18	...	...	...	1	...
Kolar District ...	10	7	...	...	2	...	468	19	34	28	402	6	93	...	...	...	6	...
Tumkur District ...	44	1	5	...	42	...	453	13	32	3	787	3	103	2	...	...	15	...
Mysore City ...	...	...	...	...	...	...	119	8	2	3	9	...	165	...	...	...	5	...
Mysore District ...	15	7	...	...	2	...	1,210	54	55	2	946	9	111	...	1	...	14	...
Chitaldrug District ...	11	...	...	...	29	...	239	8	11	...	201	2	67	...	...	...	12	...
Hassan District ...	18	...	...	...	3	...	525	35	13	7	578	40	93	3	...	...	23	1
Kadur District ...	41	2	...	...	49	...	278	27	4	...	119	3	61	1	...	...	...	...
Shimoga District ...	96	1	...	...	36	...	460	13	20	3	189	2	94	...	...	...	11	...
Civil and Military Station, Bangalore.	**19**	**31**	...	...	**1**	**2**	**106**	**14**	...	...	**3**	...	**45**	...	...	...	...	...

TABLE X.

Occupation.—*contd.*

District or State	Order 46. Law—*contd.*												Order 47. Medicine					
	167. Lawyers of all kinds, including Qazis, Law Agents and Mukhtiars.						168. Lawyers, clerks, petition-writers, etc.						Total of Order 47.					
	Total earners (Principal occupation)		Total working dependants		Total following occupation as subsidiary to other		Total earners (Principal occupation)		Total working dependants		Total following occupation as subsidiary to other		Total earners (Principal occupation)		Total working dependants		Total following occupation as subsidiary to other	
	Males	Females	Males	Females	Males	Females	Males	Females	Males	Females	Males	Females	Males	Females	Males	Females	Males	Females
	1204	1205	1206	1207	1208	1209	1210	1211	1212	1213	1214	1215	1216	1217	1218	1219	1220	1221
MYSORE STATE, INCLUDING CIVIL AND MILITARY STATION, BANGALORE.	797	...	...	...	58	...	343	6	1	...	37	1	3,525	1,338	20	66	840	51
MYSORE STATE, EXCLUDING CIVIL AND MILITARY STATION, BANGALORE.	761	...	...	...	58	...	334	6	1	...	37	1	3,209	1,073	20	65	834	50
Bangalore City ...	142	...	...	...	...	...	87	...	...	...	1	...	498	222	1	13	3	...
Bangalore District ...	36	...	...	...	5	...	25	...	...	...	2	...	289	106	2	12	168	12
Kolar Gold Fields (City) ...	9	...	...	...	...	...	9	...	...	...	1	...	59	61	...	...	...	...
Kolar District ...	89	...	...	...	4	...	4	...	...	...	2	...	297	105	4	23	222	6
Tumkur District ...	69	...	...	...	6	...	34	2	...	...	9	...	294	88	1	3	95	8
Mysore City ...	124	...	...	...	3	...	41	...	...	...	2	...	450	142	5	1	21	...
Mysore District ...	72	...	...	...	5	...	39	...	1	...	9	...	499	88	6	7	218	7
Chitaldrug District ...	53	...	...	...	9	...	14	...	...	...	3	...	201	70	...	4	28	13
Hassan District ...	67	...	...	...	17	...	26	3	...	...	6	1	202	74	1	...	43	4
Kadur District ...	41	...	...	...	...	...	20	1	...	...	...	...	157	44	...	...	14	...
Shimoga District ...	59	...	...	...	9	...	35	...	...	...	2	...	268	78	...	2	27	...
Civil and Military Station, Bangalore.	36	...	...	...	...	...	9	...	...	...	...	...	316	265	...	1	6	1

TABLE X.

Occupation—*contd.*

District or State	Order 47. Medicine—*contd.*																	
	169. Registered medical practitioners including occulists.						170. Other persons practising the healing arts without being registered.						171. Dentists.					
	Total earners (Principal occupation)		Total working dependants		Total following occupation as subsidiary to other		Total earners (Principal occupation)		Total working dependants		Total following occupation as subsidiary to other		Total earners (Principal occupation)		Total working dependants		Total following occupation as subsidiary to other	
	Males	Females	Males	Females	Males	Females	Males	Females	Males	Females	Males	Females	Males	Females	Males	Females	Males	Females
	1222	1223	1224	1225	1226	1227	1228	1229	1230	1231	1232	1233	1234	1235	1236	1237	1238	1239
MYSORE STATE, INCLUDING CIVIL AND MILITARY STATION, BANGALORE.	**520**	**54**	**2**	...	**22**	**3**	**1,689**	**66**	**11**	**15**	**778**	**14**	**34**	**1**	...	...	**7**	...
MYSORE STATE, EXCLUDING CIVIL AND MILITARY STATION, BANGALORE.	**443**	**34**	**2**	...	**19**	**2**	**1,585**	**64**	**11**	**15**	**775**	**14**	**21**	...	...	...	**7**	...
Bangalore City ...	65	9	...	...	...	...	219	11	...	...	3	...	6	...	...	...	...	...
Bangalore District ...	27	2	...	...	2	...	189	11	2	...	159	5	9	...	...	...	2	...
Kolar Gold Fields (City) ...	15	2	...	...	...	...	14	1	...	...	...	...	2	...	...	...	...	...
Kolar District ...	24	6	...	...	...	...	175	12	4	13	212	2	2	...	...	...	5	...
Tumkur District ...	44	...	...	...	8	1	145	8	...	...	88	1	...	...	...	...	...	...
Mysore City ...	51	5	1	...	1	...	156	1	1	1	20	...	...	...	...	...	...	...
Mysore District ...	58	3	1	...	4	...	309	10	4	1	209	4	...	...	...	...	...	...
Chitaldrug District ...	29	2	...	...	3	...	119	4	...	...	25	1	1	...	...	...	...	...
Hassan District ...	58	2	...	...	...	1	57	2	...	...	36	1	1	...	...	...	...	...
Kadur District ...	42	1	...	...	1	...	80	...	...	...	5	...	...	...	...	...	...	...
Shimoga District ...	30	2	...	...	...	...	122	4	...	...	24	...	...	...	...	...	...	...
Civil and Military Station, Bangalore.	**77**	**20**	...	...	**3**	**1**	**104**	**2**	...	...	**3**	...	**13**	**1**	...	...	...	...

TABLE X.

Occupation—*contd.*

District or State	Order 47. Medicine—*concld.*												Order 48. Instruction					
	172. Midwives, vaccinators, compounders, nurses, masseurs, etc.						173. Veterinary surgeons						Total of Order 48					
	Total earners (Principal occupation)		Total working dependants		Total following occupation as subsidiary to other		Total earners (Principal occupation)		Total working dependants		Total following occupation as subsidiary to other		Total earners (Principal occupation)		Total working dependants		Total following occupation as subsidiary to other	
	Males	Females	Males	Females	Males	Females	Males	Females	Males	Females	Males	Females	Males	Females	Males	Females	Males	Females
	1240	1241	1242	1243	1244	1245	1246	1247	1248	1249	1250	1251	1252	1253	1254	1255	1256	1257
MYSORE STATE, INCLUDING CIVIL AND MILITARY STATION, BANGALORE.	**1,027**	**1,204**	**5**	**51**	**23**	**33**	**255**	**13**	**2**	...	**10**	**1**	**13,665**	**1,811**	**47**	**49**	**1,211**	**8**
MYSORE STATE, EXCLUDING CIVIL AND MILITARY STATION, BANGALORE.	**917**	**962**	**5**	**50**	**23**	**33**	**243**	**13**	**2**	...	**10**	**1**	**13,101**	**1,428**	**47**	**49**	**1,206**	**8**
Bangalore City ...	188	202	1	18	...	...	15	...	...	...	...	...	976	292	3	2	4	...
Bangalore District ...	44	93	...	12	3	7	20	...	...	...	2	...	1,498	152	3	1	155	2
Kolar Gold Fields (City) ...	25	58	...	...	...	...	3	...	...	...	...	...	120	75	...	...	3	...
Kolar District ...	70	86	...	10	2	4	26	1	...	...	3	...	1,210	164	12	23	96	1
Tumkur District ...	100	71	1	3	2	6	5	4	...	...	2	...	1,670	134	5	6	259	3
Mysore City ...	158	136	1	...	...	...	85	...	2	...	...	...	1.226	248	4	14	13	...
Mysore District ...	80	74	1	6	...	2	52	1	...	...	...	1	1,996	97	3	1	270	...
Chitaldrug District ...	45	64	...	4	...	12	7	...	...	...	...	...	1,211	67	1	...	76	1
Hassan District ...	78	70	1	...	5	2	8	...	...	...	3	...	1,139	79	16	...	205	...
Kadur District ...	29	43	...	...	8	...	6	...	...	...	...	...	703	48	...	...	37	1
Shimoga District ...	100	65	...	2	3	...	16	7	...	...	...	...	1,352	72	...	2	88	...
Civil and Military Station, Bangalore.	**110**	**242**	...	**1**	...	...	**12**	...	...	...	...	...	**564**	**383**	...	...	**5**	...

TABLE X.

Occupation—*contd.*

District or State	Order 48. Instruction—*concld.*												Order 49. Letters, arts and sciences (other than 44).					
	174. Professors and teachers of all kinds.						175. Clerks and servants connected with education.						Total of Order 49					
	Total earners (Principal occupation)		Total working dependants		Total following occupation as subsidiary to other		Total earners (Principal occupation)		Total working dependants		Total following occupation as subsidiary to other		Total earners (Principal occupation)		Total working dependants		Total following occupation as subsidiary to other	
	Males	Females	Males	Females	Males	Females	Males	Females	Males	Females	Males	Females	Males	Females	Males	Females	Males	Females
	1258	1259	1260	1261	1262	1263	1264	1265	1266	1267	1268	1269	1270	1271	1272	1273	1274	1275
MYSORE STATE, INCLUDING CIVIL AND MILITARY STATION, BANGALORE.	**12,415**	**1,548**	**40**	**37**	**1,101**	**7**	**1,250**	**263**	**7**	**12**	**110**	**1**	**4,849**	**393**	**108**	**49**	**2,134**	**26**
MYSORE STATE, EXCLUDING CIVIL AND MILITARY STATION, BANGALORE.	**11,924**	**1,182**	**40**	**37**	**1,096**	**7**	**1,177**	**246**	**7**	**12**	**110**	**1**	**4,396**	**349**	**105**	**49**	**2,122**	**25**
Bangalore City ...	848	229	3	2	3	...	128	63	...	...	1	...	542	41	5	1	32	...
Bangalore District ...	1,425	128	3	...	146	2	73	24	...	1	9	...	376	48	4	1	217	5
Kolar Gold Fields (City) ...	118	74	...	...	3	...	2	1	...	...	...	...	91	2	...	...	4	1
Kolar District ...	1,150	147	10	17	88	...	60	17	2	6	8	1	389	71	18	34	211	5
Tumkur District ...	1,521	106	2	2	227	3	149	28	3	4	32	...	401	39	11	2	330	6
Mysore City ...	1,069	223	4	13	13	...	187	25	...	1	...	...	351	14	5	2	40	...
Mysore District ...	1,988	80	2	1	261	...	58	17	1	...	9	...	520	28	11	1	418	1
Chitaldrug District ...	1,117	49	1	...	71	1	94	18	...	...	5	...	327	24	11	7	225	6
Hassan District ...	927	60	15	...	163	...	212	29	1	...	42	...	361	30	31	...	249	...
Kadur District ...	663	48	...	...	37	1	40	...	...	...	...	...	264	32	1	...	133	...
Shimoga District ...	1,178	38	...	2	84	...	174	24	...	...	4	...	774	20	8	1	263	1
Civil and Military Station, Bangalore.	**491**	**366**	...	...	**5**	...	**73**	**17**	...	...	...	...	**453**	**44**	**3**	...	**12**	**1**

TABLE X

Occupation—*contd.*

District or State	Order 49. Letters, arts and sciences (other than 44)—*contd.*																	
	176. Public scribes, stenographers, etc.						177. Architects, surveyors, engineers and their employees (not being State servants).						178. Authors, editors, journalists and photographers.					
	Total earners (Principal occupation)		Total working dependants		Total following occupation as subsidiary to other		Total earners (Principal occupation)		Total working dependants		Total following occupation as subsidiary to other		Total earners (Principal occupation)		Total working dependants		Total following occupation as subsidiary to other	
	Males	Females	Males	Females	Males	Females	Males	Females	Males	Females	Males	Females	Males	Females	Males	Females	Males	Females
	1276	1277	1278	1279	1280	1281	1282	1283	1284	1285	1286	1287	1288	1289	1290	1291	1292	1293
MYSORE STATE, INCLUDING CIVIL AND MILITARY STATION, BANGALORE.	89	23	1	...	8	2	113	...	...	...	6	...	299	4	2	...	20	...
MYSORE STATE, EXCLUDING CIVIL AND MILITARY STATION, BANGALORE.	77	3	1	...	8	2	82	...	...	...	6	...	199	3	2	...	18	...
Bangalore City ...	24	1	1	...	2	...	33	...	...	...	...	...	57	1	1	...	...	...
Bangalore District ...	2	...	...	...	...	...	...	...	...	...	...	...	6	...	...	...	2	...
Kolar Gold Fields (City) ...	21	...	...	...	...	1	17	...	...	...	...	...	13	...	...	...	1	...
Kolar District	...	...	...	...	...	...	4	...	...	...	4	...	4	...	...	...	2	...
Tumkur District ...	1	...	...	...	1	1	2	...	...	...	2	...	17	...	...	...	3	...
Mysore City	9	...	...	...	2	...	...	...	...	...	...	...	67	2	...	...	4	...
Mysore District ...	10	...	...	...	...	...	...	...	...	...	...	...	8	...	1	...	2	...
Chitaldrug District ...	...	...	...	...	...	...	3	...	...	...	...	...	10	...	...	...	2	...
Hassan District ...	...	...	...	...	...	...	3	...	...	...	...	...	6	...	...	...	...	...
Kadur District ...	...	2	...	...	...	...	1	...	...	...	...	...	1	...	...	...	...	...
Shimoga District ...	10	...	...	...	3	...	19	...	...	...	...	...	10	...	...	...	2	...
Civil and Military Station, Bangalore.	12	20	...	...	...	...	31	...	...	...	...	...	100	1	...	...	2	...

TABLE X.

Occupation—*contd.*

District or State	Order 49. Letters, arts and sciences (other than 44)—*contd.*																	
	179. Artists, sculptors and image-makers.						180. Scientists (astronomers, botanists, etc.)						181. Horoscope casters, astrologers, fortune-tellers, wizards, witches and mediums.					
	Total earners (Principal occupation)		Total working dependants		Total following occupation as subsidiary to other		Total earners (Principal occupation)		Total working dependants		Total following occupation as subsidiary to other		Total earners (Principal occupation)		Total working dependants		Total following occupation as subsidiary to other	
	Males	Females	Males	Females	Males	Females	Males	Females	Males	Females	Males	Females	Males	Females	Males	Females	Males	Females
	1294	1295	1296	1297	1298	1299	1300	1301	1302	1303	1304	1305	1306	1307	1308	1309	1310	1311
MYSORE STATE, INCLUDING CIVIL AND MILITARY STATION, BANGALORE.	**290**	**10**	**4**	**3**	**48**	**4**	**48**	**23**	**5**	...	**2**	...	**388**	**43**	**2**	**8**	**249**	**6**
MYSORE STATE, EXCLUDING CIVIL AND MILITARY STATION, BANGALORE.	**205**	**9**	**4**	**3**	**47**	**4**	**34**	**23**	**5**	...	**2**	...	**361**	**43**	**2**	**8**	**249**	**6**
Bangalore City ...	39	3	...	...	...	...	15	...	...	...	...	...	29	...	...	...	3	...
Bangalore District ...	28	...	...	...	1	...	...	...	...	...	...	...	23	15	...	...	13	4
Kolar Gold Fields (City)...	...	...	...	...	...	...	15	...	...	...	...	...	5	2	...	...	...	...
Kolar District... ...	18	...	1	...	6	...	...	...	...	...	...	...	7	10	...	7	8	2
Tumkur District ...	10	1	...	1	9	2	...	...	...	...	...	...	26	4	...	...	55	...
Mysore City	24	...	1	...	...	...	...	...	...	...	...	...	20	1	...	1	8	...
Mysore District ...	14	1	1	...	13	...	1	...	...	...	1	...	57	8	1	...	35	...
Chitaldrug District ...	6	3	...	2	1	1	...	...	...	...	...	...	15	...	...	...	5	...
Hassan District ...	14	...	...	...	5	...	3	23	5	...	1	...	72	1	...	...	54	...
Kadur District ...	9	...	...	...	1	...	...	...	...	...	...	...	28	1	...	...	18	...
Shimoga District ...	13	1	1	...	11	1	...	...	...	...	...	...	77	1	1	...	50	...
Civil and Military Station, Bangalore.	**85**	**1**	...	...	**1**	...	**14**	...	...	...	...	...	**27**	...	...	...	...	...

TABLE X.

Occupation—*contd.*

District or State	Order 49—Letters, arts and sciences (other than 44)—*concld.*																	
	182. Musicians (composers and performers other than military), actors, dancers, etc.						183. Managers and employees of places of public entertainments, race courses, societies, clubs.						184. Conjurors, acrobates, recitors, exhibitors of curiosities and wild animals, etc.					
	Total earners (Principal occupation)		Total working dependants		Total following occupation as subsidiary to other		Total earners (Principal occupation)		Total working dependants		Total following occupation as subsidiary to other		Total earners (Principal occupation)		Total working dependants		Total following occupation as subsidiary to other	
	Males	Females	Males	Females	Males	Females	Males	Females	Males	Females	Males	Females	Males	Females	Males	Females	Males	Females
	1312	1313	1314	1315	1316	1317	1318	1319	1320	1321	1322	1323	1324	1325	1326	1327	1328	1329
MYSORE STATE, INCLUDING CIVIL AND MILITARY STATION, BANGALORE.	**2,157**	**126**	**57**	**2**	**1,568**	**8**	**831**	**75**	**17**	**27**	**126**	**4**	**634**	**89**	**20**	**9**	**107**	**2**
MYSORE STATE, EXCLUDING CIVIL AND MILITARY STATION, BANGALORE:	**2,063**	**107**	**57**	**2**	**1,560**	**7**	**741**	**72**	**14**	**27**	**125**	**4**	**634**	**89**	**20**	**9**	**107**	**2**
Bangalore City ...	192	31	2	1	27	...	140	3	1	...	...	...	13	2	...	...	...	...
Bangalore District ...	174	12	1	...	179	...	81	16	3	1	13	1	62	5	...	....	9	...
Kolar Gold Fields (City)...	12	...	...	...	3	...	8	...	...	...	...	...	...	...	...	...	...	...
Kolar District ...	150	21	9	1	148	1	139	31	5	25	39	2	67	9	3	1	4	...
Tumkur District ...	144	8	7	...	219	...	46	8	1	...	16	1	153	18	3	1	25	2
Mysore City ...	197	1	3	...	23	...	30	10	1	1	1	...	4	...	...	...	2	...
Mysore District ...	318	12	5	...	318	1	68	3	2	...	47	...	44	4	1	1	2	...
Chitaldrug District ...	191	6	9	...	191	5	87	...	...	...	1	...	65	15	2	5	25	...
Hassan District ...	162	...	15	...	159	...	21	...	...	...	5	...	80	6	11	...	26	...
Kadur District ...	162	9	1	...	104	...	8	...	...	...	...	...	55	20	...	...	10	...
Shimoga District ...	361	7	5	...	189	...	163	1	1	...	3	...	91	10	...	1	5	...
Civil and Military Station, Bangalore.	**94**	**19**	...	...	**8**	**1**	**90**	**3**	**3**	...	**1**	...	...	...	...	...	...	...

TABLE X.

Occupation—*contd.*

District or State	Class D—Miscellaneous: Total of Class D						Total of Sub class IX Persons living on their income.						Order 50. Persons living principally on their income. 185. Proprietors (other than agricultural land), fund and scholarships holders and pensioners					
	Total earners (Principal occupation)		Total working dependants		Total following occupation as subsidiary to other		Total earners (Principal occupation)		Total working dependants		Total following occupation as subsidiary to other		Total earners (Principal occupation)		Total working dependants		Total following occupation as subsidiary to other	
	Males	Females	Males	Females	Males	Females	Males	Females	Males	Females	Males	Females	Males	Females	Males	Females	Males	Females
	1330	1331	1332	1333	1334	1335	1336	1337	1338	1339	1340	1341	1342	1343	1344	1345	1346	1347
MYSORE STATE, INCLUDING CIVIL AND MILITARY STATION, BANGALORE.	**124,616**	**72,488**	**6,037**	**12,913**	**14,702**	**4,284**	**5,909**	**1,187**	**16**	**55**	**820**	**39**	**5,909**	**1,187**	**16**	**55**	**820**	**39**
MYSORE STATE, EXCLUDING CIVIL AND MILITARY STATION, BANGALORE.	**113,840**	**68,704**	**6,009**	**12,555**	**14,437**	**4,274**	**4,197**	**778**	**14**	**55**	**689**	**34**	**4,197**	**778**	**14**	**55**	**689**	**34**
Bangalore City ...	8,945	2,694	618	1,566	92	15	1,173	298	5	19	45	11	1,173	298	5	19	45	11
Bangalore District ...	16,786	9,163	794	910	2,481	267	339	25	3	2	111	...	339	25	3	2	111	...
Kolar Gold Fields (City)...	5,999	995	2	1	84	110	227	14	...	...	26	...	227	14	...	...	26	...
Kolar District ...	12,227	8,014	566	1,318	2,561	819	381	41	3	7	126	2	381	41	3	7	126	2
Tumkur District ...	11,429	8,616	908	3,147	1,892	616	278	46	1	7	88	4	278	46	1	7	88	4
Mysore City ...	4,853	1,662	161	38	178	39	876	158	1	7	88	10	876	158	1	7	88	10
Mysore District ...	20,099	17,279	1,549	2,560	3,639	688	218	80	1	11	64	3	213	80	1	11	64	3
Chitaldrug District ...	8,698	5,506	437	860	846	316	176	26	...	2	44	1	176	26	...	2	44	1
Hassan District ...	7,749	5,010	699	1,408	1,664	1,300	136	24	...	...	42	2	136	24	...	...	42	2
Kadur District ...	6,752	4,384	44	122	401	435	174	22	...	...	37	...	174	22	...	...	37	...
Shimoga District ...	10,308	5,382	231	625	809	219	224	54	...	...	18	1	224	54	...	...	18	1
Civil and Militay Station, Bangalore.	**10,776**	**3,784**	**28**	**358**	**265**	**10**	**1,712**	**409**	**2**	...	**131**	**5**	**1,712**	**409**	**2**	...	**131**	**5**

TABLE X.

Occupation—*contd.*

District or State	Total of Sub-class X—Domestic service						Order 51.—Domestic service											
							Total Order 51						186. Private motor-drivers and cleaners					
	Total earners (Principal occupation)		Total working dependants		Total following occupation as subsidiary to other		Total earners (Principal occupation)		Total working dependants		Total following occupation as subsidiary to other		Total earners (Principal occupation)		Total working dependants		Total following occupation as subsidiary to other	
	Males	Females	Males	Females	Males	Females	Males	Females	Males	Females	Males	Females	Males	Females	Males	Females	Males	Females
	1348	1349	1350	1351	1352	1353	1354	1355	1356	1357	1358	1359	1360	1361	1362	1363	1364	1365
MYSORE STATE, INCLUDING CIVIL AND MILITARY STATION, BANGALORE.	**32,088**	**6,898**	**1,909**	**6,029**	**1,351**	**1,194**	**32,088**	**6,898**	**1,909**	**6,029**	**1,351**	**1,194**	**3,399**	**77**	**14**	...	**90**	...
MYSORE STATE, EXCLUDING CIVIL AND MILITARY STATION, BANGALORE.	**27,183**	**4,972**	**1,887**	**5,675**	**1,317**	**1,192**	**27,183**	**4,972**	**1,887**	**5,675**	**1,317**	**1,182**	**2,541**	**75**	**12**	...	**72**	...
Bangalore City ...	1,650	523	24	1,498	12	1	1,650	523	24	1,498	12	1	447	...	...	...	...	...
Bangalore District ...	4,196	333	328	103	144	11	4,196	333	328	103	144	11	191	...	1	...	18	...
Kolar Gold Fields (City)...	2,018	538	2	...	54	108	2,018	538	2	...	54	103	313	74	...	...	2	...
Kolar District ...	2,295	293	88	72	103	19	2,295	293	88	72	103	19	125	...	...	...	6	...
Tumkur District ...	2,674	422	267	2,165	111	59	2,674	422	267	2,165	111	59	126	...	5	...	16	...
Mysore City ...	1,752	381	22	14	21	14	1,752	381	22	14	21	14	482	...	2	...	...	...
Mysore District ...	4,565	579	680	771	321	43	4,565	579	680	771	321	43	164	...	2	...	12	...
Chitaldrug District ...	1,783	204	61	110	115	35	1,783	204	61	110	115	35	118	...	...	...	2	...
Hassan District ...	2,557	844	352	821	302	801	2,557	844	352	821	302	801	177	...	1	...	8	...
Kadur District ...	1,646	446	8	92	54	93	1,646	446	8	92	54	93	239	...	1	...	8	...
Shimoga District ...	2,047	409	55	29	80	8	2,047	409	55	29	80	8	159	1	...	...	...	...
Civil and Military Station, Bangalore.	**4,905**	**1,926**	**22**	**354**	**34**	**2**	**4,905**	**1,926**	**22**	**354**	**34**	**2**	**858**	**2**	**2**	...	**18**	...

TABLE X.

Occupation—*contd.*

District or State	Order 51. Domestic service — 187. Other domestic service: Total earners (Principal occupation)		Total working dependants		Total following occupation as subsidiary to other		Total of Sub-class XI Insufficiently described occupations: Total earners (Principal occupation)		Total working dependants		Total following occupation as subsidiary to other		Order 52.—General terms which do not indicate a definite Occupation — Total of Order 52: Total earners (Principal occupatoin)		Total working dependants		Total following occupation as subsidiary to other	
	Males	Females	Males	Females	Males	Females	Males	Females	Males	Females	Males	Females	Males	Females	Males	Females	Males	Females
	1866	1367	1368	1369	1370	1371	1372	1373	1374	1375	1376	1377	1378	1379	1380	1381	1382	1383
MYSORE STATE, INCLUDING CIVIL AND MILITARY STATION, BANGALORE.	**28,689**	**6,821**	**1,895**	**6,029**	**1,261**	**1,194**	**76,658**	**57,218**	**3,537**	**6,737**	**10,748**	**2,533**	**76,658**	**57,218**	**3,537**	**6,737**	**10,748**	**2,533**
MYSORE STATE, EXCLUDING CIVIL AND MILITARY STATION, BANGALORE.	**24,642**	**4,897**	**1,875**	**5,675**	**1,245**	**1,192**	**72,775**	**55,863**	**3,533**	**6,733**	**10,648**	**2,530**	**72,775**	**55,863**	**3,533**	**6,733**	**10,648**	**2,530**
Bangalore City ...	1,203	523	24	1,498	12	1	5,804	1,644	110	33	28	2	5,804	1,644	110	33	28	2
Bangalore District ...	4,005	383	327	108	126	11	10,612	7,754	460	794	2,001	211	10,612	7,754	460	794	2,001	211
Kolar Gold Fields (City)...	1,705	464	2	...	52	108	3,656	383	...	1	3	2	3,656	388	...	1	3	2
Kolar District ...	2,170	293	88	72	97	19	7,669	6,102	474	1,230	2,057	287	7,669	6,102	474	1,230	2,057	297
Tumkur District ...	2,548	422	262	2,165	95	59	7,197	7,127	640	949	1,361	454	7,197	7,127	640	949	1,361	454
Mysore City ...	1,270	381	20	14	21	14	2,026	989	47	14	64	14	2,026	989	47	14	64	14
Mysore District ...	4,401	579	678	771	309	43	14,106	16,161	868	1,778	2,850	571	14,106	16,161	868	1,778	2,850	571
Chitaldrug District ...	1,665	204	61	110	113	35	5,706	4,315	876	731	515	155	5,706	4,315	376	731	515	155
Hassan Dirtrict ...	2,380	844	351	821	294	801	4,338	3,739	346	587	1,140	470	4,338	3,739	346	587	1,140	470
Kadur District ...	1,407	446	7	92	46	93	4,563	3,701	36	30	289	300	4,563	3,701	36	30	289	300
Shimoga District ...	1,888	408	55	29	80	8	7,098	3,948	176	586	390	114	7,098	3,948	176	586	390	114
Civil and Military Station, Bangalore.	**4,047**	**1,924**	**20**	**354**	**16**	**2**	**3,883**	**1,355**	**4**	**4**	**100**	**3**	**3,883**	**1,355**	**4**	**4**	**100**	**3**

TABLE X.

Occupation—*contd.*

Order 52. General terms which do not indicate a definite occupation—*contd.*

District or State	188. Manufacturers, business men and contractors otherwise unspecified.						189. Cashiers, accountants, book-keepers, clerks and other employees in unspecified offices and ware houses and shops						190. Machanics otherwise unspecified					
	Total earners (Principal occupation)		Total working dependants		Total following occupation as subsidiary to other		Total earners (Principal occupation)		Total working dependants		Total following occupation as subsidiary to other		Total earners (Principal occupation)		Total working dependants		Total following occupation as subsidiary to other	
	Males	Females	Males	Females	Males	Females	Males	Females	Males	Females	Males	Females	Males	Females	Males	Females	Males	Females
	1384	1385	1386	1387	1388	1389	1390	1391	1392	1393	1394	1395	1396	1397	1398	1399	1400	1401
MYSORE STATE, INCLUDING CIVIL AND MILITARY STATION, BANGALORE.	**2,986**	**74**	**14**	**9**	**454**	**4**	**6,549**	**337**	**24**	**114**	**212**	**7**	**1,753**	**66**	**6**	...	**61**	**2**
MYSORE STATE, EXCLUDING CIVIL AND MILITARY STATION, BANGALORE.	**2,783**	**25**	**13**	**9**	**454**	**1**	**5,289**	**320**	**24**	**114**	**182**	**7**	**1,280**	**64**	**5**	...	**2**	**2**
Bangalore City ...	294	3	...	...	9	...	1,949	1	7	...	4	...	317	...	1	...	...	...
Bangalore District ...	123	2	...	...	74	...	72	3	...	...	16	...	11	...	...	...	...	...
Kolar Gold Fields (City) ...	1,072	3	...	...	1	...	318	9	...	...	...	...	720	...	...	...	...	...
Kolar District ...	154	...	2	1	43	...	177	1	5	...	37	...	46	5	...	...	...	...
Tumkur District ...	80	...	1	...	60	...	225	1	...	...	22	...	11	...	4	...	1	...
Mysore City ...	254	6	...	...	11	...	293	...	4	...	3	...	83	...	...	...	...	...
Mysore District ...	232	5	2	...	123	1	116	...	...	...	17	...	6	...	...	...	1	...
Chitaldrug District ...	65	...	...	...	17	...	1,281	288	5	111	18	...	19	7	...	...	...	...
Hassan District ...	153	...	5	...	72	...	231	11	3	...	22	7	23	...	...	...	...	...
Kadur District ...	215	2	3	...	23	...	413	6	...	...	26	...	6	...	...	...	...	...
Shimoga District ...	141	4	...	8	21	...	214	...	...	...	17	...	36	52	...	...	...	2
Civil and Military Station, Bangalore.	203	49	1	...	...	3	1,260	17	...	...	30	...	473	2	1	...	59	...

TABLE X.

Occupation—*contd.*

District or State	Order 52. General terms which do not indicate a definite occupation—*concld.* 191 Labourers and workmen otherwise unspecified.						Total of Sub-class XII—Un productive.						Order 53. Inmates of jails, asylums and almshouses. *192. Inmates of jails, asylums and alms houses.					
	Total earners (Principal occupation)		Total working dependants		Total following occupation as subsidiary to other		Total earners (Principal occupation)		Total working dependants		Total following occupation as subsidiary to other		Total earners (Principal occupation)		Total working dependants		Total following occupation as subsidiary to other	
	Males	Females	Males	Females	Males	Females	Males	Females	Males	Females	Males	Females	Males	Females	Males	Females	Males	Females
	1402	1403	1404	1405	1406	1407	1408	1409	1410	1411	1412	1413	1414	1415	1416	1417	1418	1419
MYSORE STATE, INCLUDING CIVIL AND MILITARY STATION, BANGALORE.	**65,370**	**56,741**	**3,493**	**6,614**	**10,021**	**2,520**	**9,961**	**7,185**	**575**	**92**	**1,783**	**518**	**507**	**17**	**570**	**16**	...	...
MYSORE STATE, EXCLUDING CIVIL AND MILITARY STATION, BANGALORE.	**63,423**	**55,454**	**3,491**	**6,610**	**10,010**	**2,520**	**9,685**	**7,091**	**575**	**92**	**1,783**	**518**	**506**	**17**	**570**	**16**	...	...
Bangalore City ...	3,244	1,640	102	33	15	2	318	234	479	16	7	1	287	13	479	13	...	...
Bangalore District ...	10,406	7,749	460	794	1,911	211	1,639	1,051	8	11	225	45	18	1	...	...	...	...
Kolar Gold Fields (City)...	1,546	371	...	1	2	2	98	60	...	...	1	...	...	...	...	...	...	...
Kolar District... ...	7,292	6,096	467	1,229	1,977	237	1,882	1,578	1	9	275	61	11	2	...	...	...	...
Tumkur District ...	6,881	7,126	639	949	1,278	454	1,280	1,021	...	26	322	99	30	...	...	...	...	...
Mysore City	1,396	983	39	14	50	14	199	139	91	3	5	1	61	1	91	3	...	...
Mysore District ...	13,750	16,156	866	1,778	2,709	570	1,215	459	...	...	404	21	23	...	...	...	...	...
Chitaldrug District ...	4,341	4,020	371	617	480	155	1,028	960	...	17	172	125	11	...	...	...	...	...
Hassan District ...	3,931	3,728	338	587	1,046	463	718	403	1	...	180	27	11	...	...	...	...	...
Kadur District ...	3,929	3,693	33	30	190	300	369	215	...	...	71	42	31	...	...	...	...	...
Shimoga District ...	6,707	3,892	176	578	352	112	939	971	...	10	121	96	23	...	...	...	...	...
Civil and Military Station, Bangalore.	1,947	1,287	2	4	11	...	276	94	...	...	...	...	1	...	...	...	...	...

*Order 53.—All earners in group 192 have been excluded from the total earners and included among non-working Dependents at the head of the table.

TABLE X.

Occupation—*concld.*

District or State	Order 54. Beggars, vagrants, prostitutes																		Order 55. Other unclassfied non-productive industries					
	Total of Order 54						193. Beggars and vagrants						194. Procurers and prostitutes						195. Other unclassfied non-productive industries					
	Total earners (Principal occupation)		Total working dependants		Total following occupation as subsidiary to other		Total earners (Principal occupation)		Total working dependants		Total following occupation as subsidiary to other		Total earners (Principal occupation)		Total working dependants		Total following occupation as subsidiary to other		Total earners (Principal occupation)		Total working dependants		Total following occupation as subsidiary to other	
	Males	Females	Males	Females	Males	Females	Males	Females	Males	Females	Males	Females	Males	Females	Males	Females	Males	Females	Males	Females	Males	Females	Males	Females
	1420	1421	1422	1423	1424	1425	1426	1427	1428	1429	1430	1431	1432	1433	1434	1435	1436	1437	1438	1439	1440	1441	1442	1443
MYSORE STATE, INCLUDING CIVIL AND MILITARY STATION, BANGALORE.	**9,828**	**7,148**	**1**	**70**	**1,762**	**518**	**9,804**	**5,560**	...	...	**1,730**	**278**	**24**	**1,588**	**1**	**70**	**32**	**240**	**133**	**37**	**4**	**6**	**21**	...
MYSORE STATE, EXCLUDING CIVIL AND MILITARY STATION, BANGALORE.	**9,552**	**7,054**	**1**	**70**	**1,762**	**518**	**9,528**	**5,466**	...	...	**1,730**	**278**	**24**	**1,588**	**1**	**70**	**32**	**240**	**133**	**37**	**4**	**6**	**21**	...
Bangalore City ...	315	234	...	3	1	1	315	163	...	...	1	1	...	71	...	3	...	...	3	...	...	...	6	...
Bangalore District ...	1,619	1,051	...	11	224	45	1,619	1,023	...	...	224	44	...	28	...	11	...	1	20	...	3	...	1	...
Kolar Gold Fields (City)...	98	60	...	...	1	...	98	60	...	...	1	...	...	...	...	...	...	...	...	...	...	...	...	...
Kolar District... ...	1,791	1,551	...	6	273	61	1,791	1,518	...	...	272	58	...	33	...	6	1	3	91	27	1	3	2	...
Tumkur District ...	1,273	1,021	...	26	320	99	1,273	806	...	...	320	50	...	215	...	26	...	49	7	...	...	...	2	...
Mysore City	196	199	...	...	5	1	196	92	...	...	5	1	...	57	...	...	...	...	3	...	...	...	...	...
Mysore District ...	1,213	459	...	...	404	21	1,213	439	...	...	404	21	...	20	...	...	...	...	2	...	...	...	...	...
Chitaldrug District ...	1,027	960	...	17	172	125	1,017	566	...	...	171	44	10	394	...	17	1	81	1	...	...	...	...	...
Hassan District ...	718	400	1	...	180	27	704	323	...	...	150	17	14	77	1	...	30	10	...	3	...	...	...	...
Kadur District ...	366	211	...	...	62	42	366	145	...	...	62	21	...	66	...	...	...	21	3	4	...	...	9	...
Shimoga District ...	936	968	...	7	120	96	936	341	...	...	120	21	...	627	...	7	...	75	3	3	...	3	1	...
Civil and Military Station, Bangalore.	**276**	**94**	...	...	...	...	**276**	**94**	...	...	...	...	...	...	...	...	...	...	...	...	...	...	...	...

MYSORE CENSUS, 1931.

TABLE XI. A—Occupation by Caste, Tribe or Race.

(a) European and Allied Races

(b) Anglo-Indians

TABLE XI A.

Occupation by Caste, Tribe or Race—*contd.*

District or State	Total Population	Total of all Sub-classes: Population dealt with: Total earners (Principal occupations) Males	Total earners (Principal occupations) Females	Total working dependants Males	Total working dependants Females	Non-working dependants Both sexes	Total earners with Subsidiary occupation Males	Total earners with Subsidiary occupation Females	Recorded Principal Occupation of earners (by Sub-classes and Orders): Total of Sub-class I Exploitation of Animals and Vegetation Males	Total of Sub-class I Females	Total of Order 1 Pasture and Agriculture Males	Total of Order 1 Females	Order 1 (a) Cultivation Males	Order 1 (a) Females	Order 1 (b) Cultivation of Special crops Males	Order 1 (b) Females	Order 1 (c) Forestry Males	Order 1 (c) Females	Order 1 (d) Stock raising Males	Order 1 (d) Females	Order 1 (e) Rearing of small animals and insects Males	Order 1 (e) Females
1	2	3	4	5	6	7	8	9	10	11	12	13	14	15	16	17	18	19	20	21	22	23
(a) EUROPEAN & ALLIED RACES.																						
Mysore State, including C. & M. Station, Bangalore.	**5,411**	**2,438**	**406**	...	...	**2,517**	**12**	**2**	**86**	**3**	**85**	**3**	**4**	**2**	**80**	**1**	**1**	...	...	...	...	...
Mysore State, excluding C. & M. Station. Bangalore.	**1,253**	**573**	**120**	...	...	**560**	**4**	**2**	**71**	**3**	**70**	**3**	**4**	**2**	**66**	**1**	...	...	...	...	...	...
Bangalore City	300	86	56	...	...	158	...	...	8	...	3	...	...	...	3	...	...	...	...	...	...	...
Bangalore District	95	15	9	...	...	71	...	...	5	2	5	2	4	2	1	...	...	...	...	...	...	...
Kolar Gold Fields (City) ...	574	337	1	...	...	236	...	...	...	...	...	...	...	...	...	...	...	...	...	...	...	...
Kolar District	24	8	9	...	...	7	1	...	...	...	...	...	...	...	...	...	...	...	...	...	...	...
Tumkur District	9	4	1	...	...	4	...	...	...	...	...	...	...	...	...	...	...	...	...	...	—	...
Mysore City	101	32	24	...	...	45	2	2	...	...	...	...	...	...	...	...	...	...	...	...	...	...
Mysore District	27	21	1	...	...	5	1	...	7	...	6	...	...	...	6	...	...	...	...	...	...	...
Chitaldrug District	2	1	1	...	...	...	...	...	...	...	...	...	...	...	...	...	...	...	...	...	...	...
Hassan District	40	24	8	...	...	8	...	...	17	...	17	...	...	...	17	...	...	...	...	...	...	...
Kadur District	67	42	5	...	...	20	...	...	39	1	39	1	...	...	39	1	...	...	...	...	...	...
Shimoga District	14	3	5	...	...	6	...	...	...	...	...	...	...	...	...	...	...	...	...	...	...	...
Civil & Miltary Station, Bangalore. ...	4,158	1,915	286	...	...	1,957	8	...	15	...	15	...	...	...	14	...	1	...	...	...	...	...
(b) ANGLO-INDIANS.																						
Mysore State, including C. & M. Station, Bangalore.	**8,309**	**1,547**	**600**	**4**	**108**	**6,050**	**27**	**5**	**12**	**3**	**12**	**3**	**2**	**1**	**8**	**2**	**2**	...	...	...	...	...
Mysore State, excluding C. & M. Station, Bangalore.	**2,789**	**676**	**159**	**3**	...	**1,951**	**3**	**2**	**8**	**1**	**8**	**1**	**2**	**1**	**4**	...	**2**	...	...	...	...	...
Bangalore City	416	77	62	...	...	277	...	...	1	...	1	...	...	...	1	...	...	...	...	...	...	...
Bangalore District	221	13	8	1	...	199	1	...	...	...	...	...	...	...	...	...	...	...	...	...	...	...
Kolar Gold Fields (City) ...	1,541	418	39	...	...	1,084	2	1	...	...	...	...	...	...	...	...	...	...	...	...	...	...
Kolar District	53	12	5	...	...	36	...	...	1	1	1	1	1	1	...	...	...	...	...	...	...	...
Tumkur District	31	8	4	...	...	19	...	...	...	...	...	...	...	...	...	...	...	...	...	...	...	...
Mysore City	327	76	28	1	...	222	...	...	1	...	1	...	...	1	...	...	...	...	...	...	...	...
Mysore District	85	34	6	1	...	44	...	...	...	...	...	...	...	...	...	...	...	...	...	...	...	...
Chitaldrug District	20	10	2	...	...	8	...	1	...	...	...	...	...	...	...	...	...	...	...	...	...	...
Hassan District	57	14	3	...	...	40	...	...	...	...	...	...	...	...	...	...	...	...	...	...	...	...
Kadur District	15	7	1	...	...	7	...	...	3	...	3	...	...	...	3	...	...	...	...	...	...	...
Shimoga District	23	7	1	...	...	15	...	...	2	...	2	...	...	...	...	...	2	...	...	...	...	...
Civil & Military Station, Bangalore.	5,520	871	441	1	108	4,099	24	3	4	2	4	2	...	...	4	2	...	...	...	...	...	...

TABLE XI. A.

Occupation by Caste, Tribe or Race—*contd.*

District or State	Recorded Principal Occupation of earners (by Sub-classes and Orders)																					
	Order 2 Fishing and Hunting		Total of Sub-class II Exploitation of Minerals		Order 3 Metallic Minerals		Order 4 Non-Metallic Minerals		Total of Sub-class III Industry		Order 5 Textiles		Order 6 Hides, Skins, etc.		Order 7 Wood		Order 8 Metals		Order 9 Ceramics		Order 10 Chemical Products	
	Males	Females	Males	Females	Males	Females	Males	Females	Males	Females	Males	Females	Males	Females	Males	Females	Males	Females	Males	Females	Males	Females
	24	25	26	27	28	29	30	31	32	33	34	35	36	37	38	39	40	41	42	43	44	45
(a) EUROPEAN & ALLIED RACES.																						
Mysore State, including C. & M. Station, Bangalore.	1	...	165	...	163	...	2	...	74	6	17	...	...	...	2	...	2	...	...	...	2	...
Mysore State, excluding C. & M. Station, Bangalore.	1	...	164	...	162	...	2	...	28	...	14	...	...	...	1	...	2	...	...	...	1	...
Bangalore City	...	...	...	...	...	...	...	...	13	...	13	...	...	...	...	...	...	...	...	...	...	...
Bangalore District	...	...	...	...	...	...	...	...	...	...	...	...	...	...	...	...	...	...	...	...	...	...
Kolar Gold Fields (City)	...	...	162	...	160	...	2	...	9	...	...	...	...	...	1	...	2	...	...	...	1	...
Kolar District	...	...	...	...	...	...	...	...	1	...	...	...	...	...	...	...	...	...	...	...	...	...
Tumkur District	...	...	...	...	...	...	...	...	...	...	...	...	...	...	...	...	...	...	...	...	...	...
Mysore City	...	...	...	...	...	...	...	...	4	...	1	...	...	...	...	...	...	...	...	...	...	...
Mysore District	1	...	...	...	...	...	...	...	1	...	...	...	...	...	...	...	...	...	...	...	...	...
Chitaldrug District ...	...	...	1	...	1	...	...	...	...	...	...	...	...	...	...	...	...	...	...	...	...	...
Hassan District	...	...	...	...	...	...	...	...	...	...	...	...	...	...	...	...	...	...	...	...	...	...
Kadur District	...	...	...	...	...	...	...	...	...	...	...	...	...	...	...	...	...	...	...	...	...	...
Shimoga District	...	...	1	...	1	...	...	...	...	...	...	...	...	...	...	...	...	...	...	...	...	...
Civil & Military Station, Bangalore.	...	...	1	...	1	...	...	...	46	6	3	...	...	...	1	...	...	...	...	...	1	...
(b) ANGLO-INDIANS.																						
Mysore State, including C. & M. Station, Bangalore.	...	...	171	...	168	...	3	...	170	45	6	...	2	...	20	3	23	...	1	...	2	...
Mysore State, excluding C. & M. Station, Bangalore.	...	...	170	...	167	...	3	...	88	8	4	...	1	...	15	3	17	...	1	...	1	...
Bangalore City	...	...	...	...	...	...	...	...	5	...	4	...	...	...	...	...	...	...	...	...	...	...
Bangalore District	...	...	...	...	...	...	...	...	...	...	...	...	...	...	...	...	...	...	...	...	...	...
Kolar Gold Fields (City)	...	...	168	...	165	...	3	...	59	6	...	...	...	...	13	3	15	...	...	...	...	...
Kolar District	...	...	1	...	1	...	...	...	2	...	...	...	...	...	1	...	...	...	...	...	...	...
Tumkur District	...	...	...	...	...	...	...	...	2	...	...	...	...	...	...	...	...	...	1	...	1	...
Mysore City	...	...	...	...	...	...	...	...	4	2	...	...	1	...	...	...	...	...	...	...	...	...
Mysore District	...	...	...	...	...	...	...	...	13	...	...	...	...	...	...	...	1	...	...	...	...	...
Chitaldrug District ...	...	...	...	...	...	...	...	...	...	...	...	...	...	...	...	...	...	...	...	...	...	...
Hassan District	...	...	1	...	1	...	...	...	2	...	...	...	...	...	1	...	1	...	...	...	...	...
Kadur District	...	...	...	...	...	...	...	...	1	...	...	...	...	...	...	...	...	...	...	...	...	...
Shimoga District	...	...	...	...	...	...	...	...	...	...	...	...	...	...	...	...	...	...	...	...	...	...
Civil & Military Station, Bangalore.	...	...	1	...	1	...	...	...	82	37	2	...	1	...	5	...	6	...	...	...	1	...

TABLE XI. A.

Occupation by Caste, Tribe or Race—*contd.*

District or State	Recorded Principal Occupation of earners (by Sub-classes and Orders)																			
	Order 11 Food Industries		Order 12 Industries of dress and toilet		Order 13 Furniture Industries		Order 14 Building Industries		Order 15 Construction of means of transport		Order 16 Production and transmission of physical force		Order 17 Miscellaneous Industries		Total of Sub-class IV Transport		Order 18 Transport by air		Order 19 Transport by water	
	Males	Females	Males	Females	Males	Females	Males	Females	Males	Females	Males	Females	Males	Females	Males	Females	Males	Females	Males	Females
	46	47	48	49	50	51	52	53	54	55	56	57	58	59	60	61	62	63	64	65
(a) EUROPEAN & ALLIED RACES.																				
Mysore State, including C. & M. Station, Bangalore.	21	...	3	6	...	...	4	...	8	...	9	...	6	...	72	4	...	...	...	...
Mysore State, excluding C. & M. Station, Bangalore.	1	...	...	...	...	...	2	...	...	...	4	...	3	...	29	...	...	...	...	...
Bangalore City	...	...	...	...	...	...	...	...	...	...	...	...	...	...	13	...	...	...	...	...
Bangalore District ...	...	...	...	...	...	...	...	...	...	...	...	...	...	...	1	...	...	...	...	...
Kolar Gold Fields (City) ...	...	...	...	...	...	...	2	...	...	...	3	...	...	...	6	...	...	...	...	...
Kolar District	...	...	...	...	...	...	...	...	...	...	1	...	...	...	1	...	...	...	...	...
Tumkur District	...	...	...	...	...	...	...	...	...	...	...	...	...	...	...	...	...	...	...	...
Mysore City	...	...	...	...	...	...	...	...	...	...	...	...	3	...	1	...	...	...	...	...
Mysore District	1	...	...	...	...	...	...	...	...	...	...	...	...	...	2	...	...	...	...	...
Chitaldrug District ...	...	...	...	...	...	...	...	...	...	...	...	...	...	...	...	...	...	...	...	...
Hassan District	...	...	...	...	...	...	...	...	...	...	...	...	...	...	5	...	...	...	...	...
Kadur District	...	...	...	...	...	...	...	...	...	...	...	...	...	...	...	...	...	...	...	...
Shimoga District	...	...	...	...	...	...	...	...	...	...	...	...	...	...	...	...	...	...	...	...
Civil & Military Station, Bangalore.	20	...	3	6	...	...	2	...	8	...	5	...	3	...	43	4	...	...	...	...
(b) ANGLO-INDIANS.																				
Mysore State, including C. & M. Station, Bangalore.	11	...	4	42	...	...	20	...	25	...	47	...	9	...	262	9	...	...	2	...
Mysore State, excluding C. & M. Station, Bangalore.	1	...	2	5	...	...	13	...	...	...	33	...	...	...	162	1	...	...	2	...
Bangalore City	1	...	...	...	...	...	...	...	...	...	...	...	...	...	48	...	...	...	...	...
Bangalore District ...	...	...	...	...	...	...	...	...	...	...	...	...	...	...	5	...	...	...	...	...
Kolar Gold Fields (City) ...	...	...	1	3	...	...	10	...	...	...	20	...	...	...	29	1	...	...	...	...
Kolar District	...	...	...	...	...	...	...	...	...	...	1	...	...	...	8	...	...	...	...	...
Tumkur District	...	...	...	...	...	...	...	...	...	...	...	...	...	...	4	...	...	...	...	...
Mysore City	...	...	...	2	...	...	2	...	...	...	1	...	...	...	32	...	...	...	...	...
Mysore District	...	...	1	...	...	...	...	...	...	...	11	...	...	...	10	...	...	...	2	...
Chitaldrug District ...	...	...	...	...	...	...	...	...	...	...	...	...	...	...	8	...	...	...	...	...
Hassan District	...	...	...	...	...	...	...	...	...	...	...	...	...	...	11	...	...	...	...	...
Kadur District	...	...	...	...	...	...	1	...	...	...	...	...	...	...	3	...	...	...	...	...
Shimoga District	...	...	...	...	...	...	...	...	...	...	...	...	...	...	4	...	...	...	...	...
Civil & Military Station, Bangalore.	10	...	2	37	...	...	7	...	25	...	14	...	9	...	100	8	...	...	...	...

TABLE XI. A.

Occupation by Caste, Tribe or Race—contd

District or State	Recorded Principal Occupation of earners (by Sub-classes and Orders)																			
	Order 20 Transport by road		Order 21 Transport by rail		Order 22 Post office, Telegraph and Telephone services		Total of Sub-class V Trade		Order 23 Banks		Order 24 Brokerage commission and export		Order 25 Trade in textiles		Order 26 Trade in skins, leather and furs		Order 27 Trade in wood		Order 28 Trade in metals	
	Males	Females	Males	Females	Males	Females	Males	Females	Males	Females	Males	Females	Males	Females	Males	Females	Males	Females	Males	Females
	66	67	68	69	70	71	72	73	74	75	76	77	78	79	80	81	82	83	84	85
(a) EUROPEAN & ALLIED RACES.																				
Mysore State, including C. & M. Station, Bangalore.	8	1	39	...	25	3	81	23	14	9	14	...	...	...	...	...	7	...	...	...
Mysore State, excluding C. & M. Station, Bangalore.	3	...	24	...	2	...	29	3	6	2	6	...	...	...	...	...	7	...	...	...
Bangalore City	1	...	12	...	...	...	8	...	2	...	...	...	...	...	...	...	...	...	...	...
Bangalore District	1	...	...	...	...	...	2	1	2	1	...	...	...	...	...	...	...	...	...	...
Kolar Gold Fields (City) ...	1	...	4	...	1	...	13	...	...	...	6	...	...	...	...	...	7	...	...	...
Kolar District	...	...	1	...	...	...	1	...	...	...	...	...	...	...	...	...	...	...	...	...
Tumkur District	...	...	...	...	...	...	...	...	...	...	...	...	...	...	...	...	...	...	...	...
Mysore City	...	...	...	...	1	...	5	2	2	1	...	...	...	...	...	...	...	...	...	...
Mysore District	...	...	2	...	...	...	...	...	...	...	...	...	...	...	...	...	...	...	...	...
Chitaldrug District	...	...	...	...	...	...	...	...	...	...	...	...	...	...	...	...	...	...	...	...
Hassan District	...	...	5	...	...	...	...	...	...	...	...	...	...	...	...	...	...	...	...	...
Kadur District	...	...	...	...	...	...	...	...	...	...	...	...	...	...	...	...	...	...	...	...
Shimoga District	...	...	...	...	...	...	...	...	...	...	...	...	...	...	...	...	...	...	...	...
Civil & Military Station, Bangalore.	5	1	15	...	23	3	52	20	8	7	8	...	...	...	...	...	...	...	...	...
(b) ANGLO-INDIANS.																				
Mysore State, including C. & M. Station, Bangalore.	2	2	178	...	80	7	88	29	8	10	21	2	1	...	...	...	...	...	...	...
Mysore State, exculding C. & M. Station, Bangalore.	2	...	125	...	33	1	11	5	1	4	4	...	...	...	...	...	...	...	...	...
Bangalore City	...	...	47	...	1	...	1	...	...	...	1	...	...	...	...	...	...	...	...	...
Bangalore District	...	...	5	...	...	...	2	5	1	4	...	...	...	...	...	...	...	...	...	...
Kolar Gold Fields (City) ...	...	...	1	...	28	1	5	...	...	...	3	...	...	...	...	...	...	...	...	...
Kolar District	...	...	8	...	...	...	...	...	...	...	...	...	...	...	...	...	...	...	...	...
Tumkur District	1	...	3	...	...	...	1	...	...	...	...	...	...	...	...	...	...	...	...	...
Mysore City	1	...	30	...	1	...	2	...	...	...	...	...	...	...	...	...	...	...	...	...
Mysore District	...	...	8	...	...	...	...	...	...	...	...	...	...	...	...	...	...	...	...	...
Chitaldrug District	...	...	6	...	2	...	...	...	...	...	...	...	...	...	...	...	...	...	...	...
Hassan District	...	...	11	...	...	...	...	...	...	...	...	...	...	...	...	...	...	...	...	...
Kadur District	...	...	3	...	...	...	...	...	...	...	...	...	...	...	...	...	...	...	...	...
Shimoga District	...	...	3	...	1	...	...	...	...	...	...	...	...	...	...	...	...	...	...	...
Civil & Military Station, Bangalore.	...	2	53	...	47	6	77	24	7	6	17	2	1	...	...	...	...	...	...	...

TABLE XI. A.

Occupation by Caste, Tribe or Race—*contd.*

District or State	Recorded Principal Occupation of earners (by Sub-classes and Orders)																			
	Order 29 Trade in pottery, bricks and tiles		Order 30 Trade in chemical products		Order 31 Hotels, restaurants, etc.		Order 32 Other trade in food stuffs		Order 33 Trade in clothing and toilet articles		Order 34 Trade in furniture		Order 35 Trade in building materials		Order 36 Trade in means of transport		Order 37 Trade in fuel		Order 38 Trade in articles of luxury	
	Males	Females	Males	Females	Males	Females	Males	Females	Males	Females	Males	Females	Males	Females	Males	Females	Males	Females	Males	Females
	86	87	88	89	90	91	92	93	94	95	96	97	98	99	100	101	102	103	104	105
(a) EUROPEAN & ALLIED RACES.																				
Mysore State, including C. & M. Station, Bangalore.	...	...	10	...	7	11	3	3	...	...	...	...	...	...	4	...	...	...	3	...
Mysore State, excluding C. & M. Station, Bangalore.	...	...	5	...	2	1	...	...	...	...	...	...	...	...	...	...	...	...	...	...
Bangalore City	...	...	4	...	...	...	...	...	...	...	...	...	...	...	...	...	...	...	...	...
Bangalore District ...	...	...	...	...	...	...	...	...	...	...	...	...	...	...	...	...	...	...	...	...
Kolar Gold Fields (City) ...	...	...	...	...	...	...	...	...	...	...	...	...	...	...	...	...	...	...	...	...
Kolar District	...	...	...	...	...	...	...	...	...	...	...	...	...	...	...	...	...	...	...	...
Tumkur District	...	...	...	...	...	...	...	...	...	...	...	...	...	...	...	...	...	...	...	...
Mysore City	...	...	1	...	2	1	...	...	...	...	...	...	...	...	...	...	...	...	...	...
Mysore District	...	...	...	...	...	...	...	...	...	...	...	...	...	...	...	...	...	...	...	...
Chitaldrug District ...	...	...	...	...	...	...	...	...	...	...	...	...	...	...	...	...	...	...	...	...
Hassan District	...	...	...	...	...	...	...	...	...	...	...	...	...	...	...	...	...	...	...	...
Kadur District	...	...	...	...	...	...	...	...	...	...	...	...	...	...	...	...	...	...	...	...
Shimoga District	...	...	...	...	...	...	...	...	...	...	...	...	...	...	...	...	...	...	...	...
Civil & Military Station, Bangalore.	...	...	5	...	5	10	3	3	...	...	...	...	...	...	4	...	...	...	3	...
(b) ANGLO-INDIANS.																				
Mysore State, including C. & M. Station, Bangalore.	1	...	10	...	10	6	6	4	2	...	1	...	...	...	11	...	2	...	8	1
Mysore State, excluding C. & M. Station, Bangalore.	...	...	...	...	3	1	1	1	...	...	...	...	...	...	...	...	...	...	...	...
Bangalore City	...	...	...	...	...	...	...	...	...	...	...	...	...	...	...	...	...	...	...	...
Bangalore District ...	...	...	...	...	...	...	...	1	...	...	...	...	...	...	...	...	...	...	...	...
Kolar Gold Fields (City) ...	...	...	...	...	1	...	...	...	...	...	...	...	...	...	...	...	...	...	...	...
Kolar District	...	...	...	...	...	...	...	...	...	...	...	...	...	...	...	...	...	...	...	...
Tumkur District	...	...	...	...	...	...	...	...	...	...	...	...	...	...	...	...	...	...	...	...
Mysore City	...	...	...	...	2	...	...	...	...	...	...	...	...	...	...	...	...	...	...	...
Mysore District	...	...	...	...	...	...	...	...	...	...	...	...	...	...	...	...	...	...	...	...
Chitaldrug District ...	...	...	...	...	...	...	...	...	...	...	...	...	...	...	...	...	...	...	...	...
Hassan District	...	...	...	...	...	...	...	...	...	...	...	...	...	...	...	...	...	...	...	...
Kadur District	...	...	...	...	...	...	...	...	...	...	...	...	...	...	...	...	...	...	...	...
Shimoga District	...	...	...	...	...	...	...	...	...	...	...	...	...	...	...	...	...	...	...	...
Civil & Military Station, Bangalore.	1	...	10	...	7	6	5	3	2	...	1	...	...	...	11	...	2	...	8	1

TABLE XI. A

Occupation by Caste, Tribe or Race.
(a) European and Allied Races
(b) Anglo-Indians

TABLE XI. A.

Occupation by Caste, Tribe" or Race—*contd.*

Recorded Principal Occupation of earners (by Sub-classes and Orders)

District or State	Order 39 Trade of other sorts		Total of Sub-class VI Public Force		Order 40 Army		Order 41 Navy		Order 42 Air Force		Order 43 Police		Sub-class VII Order 44 Public Administration		Total of Sub-class VIII Professions and Liberal Arts		Order 45 Religion		Order 46 Law	
	Males	Females	Males	Females	Males	Females	Males	Females	Males	Females	Males	Females	Males	Females	Males	Females	Males	Females	Males	Females
	106	107	108	109	110	111	112	113	114	115	116	117	118	119	120	121	122	123	124	125
(a) EUROPEAN & ALLIED RACES.																				
Mysore State, including C. & M. Station, Bangalore.	19	...	1,309	...	1,296	...	...	...	1	...	12	...	58	2	231	250	64	52	...	...
Mysore State, excluding C. & M. Station, Bangalore.	3	...	14	...	11	...	...	...	...	...	3	...	16	1	114	103	35	35	...	...
Bangalore City	2	...	7	...	4	...	...	...	...	...	3	...	6	...	22	56	8	20	...	...
Bangalore District	...	...	1	...	1	...	...	...	...	...	...	...	3	...	3	6	2	3	...	...
Kolar Gold Fields (City) ...	...	...	5	...	5	...	...	...	...	...	...	...	1	...	58	1	3	...	...	...
Kolar District	1	...	...	...	...	...	...	...	...	...	...	...	...	...	4	7	3	2	...	...
Tumkur District	...	...	...	...	...	...	...	...	...	...	...	...	...	...	4	1	4	1	...	...
Mysore City	...	...	1	...	1	...	...	...	...	...	...	...	5	1	12	14	6	...	...	...
Mysore District	...	...	...	...	...	...	...	...	...	...	...	...	1	...	6	1	6	1	...	...
Chitaldrug District ...	...	...	...	...	...	...	...	...	...	...	...	...	...	...	...	1	...	1	...	...
Hassan District	...	...	...	...	...	...	...	...	...	...	...	...	...	...	2	8	1	4	...	...
Kadur District	...	...	...	...	...	...	...	...	...	...	...	...	...	...	2	4	1	2	...	...
Shimoga District	...	...	...	...	...	...	...	...	...	...	...	...	...	...	1	4	1	1	...	...
Civil & Military Station, Bangalore.	16	...	1,295	...	1,285	...	...	...	1	...	9	...	42	1	117	147	29	17	...	...
(b) ANGLO-INDIANS.																				
Mysore State, including C. & M. Station, Bangalore.	7	6	36	...	25	...	...	...	...	...	11	...	66	3	163	341	15	22	2	...
Mysore State, excluding C. & M. Station, Bangalore.	2	...	9	...	3	...	...	...	...	...	6	...	23	1	36	127	4	4	1	...
Bangalore City	...	...	1	...	...	...	...	...	...	...	1	...	4	...	2	58	...	1	...	...
Bangalore District	...	...	2	...	2	...	...	...	...	...	...	...	1	...	1	1	...	...	...	...
Kolar Gold Fields (City) ...	1	...	2	...	1	...	...	...	...	...	1	...	11	...	20	29	...	...	1	...
Kolar District	...	...	...	...	...	...	...	...	...	...	...	...	...	...	...	4	...	2	...	...
Tumkur District	1	...	...	...	...	...	...	...	...	...	...	...	...	...	...	4	...	...	...	...
Mysore City	...	...	2	...	...	...	...	...	...	...	2	...	7	1	8	19	...	...	...	...
Mysore District	...	...	...	...	...	...	...	...	...	...	...	...	...	...	4	6	4	1	...	...
Chitaldrug District ...	...	...	2	...	...	...	...	...	...	...	2	...	...	...	...	2	...	...	...	...
Hassan District	...	...	...	...	...	...	...	...	...	...	...	...	...	...	...	2	...	...	...	...
Kadur District	...	...	...	...	...	...	...	...	...	...	...	...	...	...	...	1	...	...	...	...
Shimoga District	...	...	...	...	...	...	...	...	...	...	...	...	...	...	1	1	...	...	...	...
Civil & Military Station, Bangalore.	5	6	27	...	22	...	...	...	...	...	5	...	43	2	127	214	11	18	1	...

TABLE XI. A.

Occupation by Caste, Tribe or Race—*concld.*

District or State	Recorded Principal Occupation of earners (by Sub-classes and Orders)																			
	Order 47 Medicine		Order 48 Instruction		Order 49 Letters, Arts and Sciences		Sub-class IX Order 50 Persons living on their income		Sub-class X Order 51 Domestic service		Sub-class XI Order 52 Insufficiently described Occupations		Total of Sub-class XII Unproductive		Order 53 Inmates of jails, asylums and alm houses		Order 54 Beggars		Order 55 Other unclassified non-productive industries	
	Males	Females	Males	Females	Males	Females	Males	Females	Males	Females	Males	Females	Males	Females	Males	Females	Males	Females	Males	Females
	126	127	128	129	130	131	132	133	134	135	136	137	138	139	140	141	142	143	144	145
(a) EUROPEAN & ALLIED RACES.																				
Mysore State, including C. & M. Station, Bangalore.	30	90	51	97	86	11	320	106	11	1	80	11	1	...	1	...	...	...	...	...
Mysore State, excluding C. & M. Station, Bangalore.	9	30	12	36	58	2	23	4	11	...	73	6	1	...	1	...	...	...	...	...
Bangalore City	4	19	1	15	9	2	12	...	...	...	1	...	1	...	1	...	...	...	...	...
Bangalore District	...	2	1	1	...	...	...	...	...	...	...	...	...	...	...	...	...	...	...	...
Kolar Gold Fields (City) ...	3	...	5	1	47	...	5	...	11	...	67	...	...	...	...	...	...	...	...	...
Kolar District	1	2	...	3	...	...	1	2	...	...	...	...	...	...	...	...	...	...	...	...
Tumkur District	...	...	...	...	...	...	...	...	...	...	..	...	...	...	...	...	...	...	...	...
Mysore City	1	1	5	18	...	...	3	1	...	...	1	6	...	...	...	...	...			
Mysore District	...	...	...	...	...	...	...	...	...	...	4	...	...	...	...	...	...	...	...	...
Chitaldrug District ...	...	...	...	...	...	...	...	...	...	...	...	...	...	...	...	...	...	...	...	...
Hassan District	...	3	...	1	1	...	...	...	...	...	...	...	...	...	...	...	...	...	...	...
Kadur District	...	...	...	2	1	...	1	...	...	...	...	...	...	...	...	...	...	...	...	...
Shimoga District	...	3	...	...	...	...	1	1	...	...	...	...	...	...	...	...	...	...	...	...
Civil & Military Station, Bangalore.	21	60	39	61	28	9	297	102	...	1	7	5	...	...	...	...	...	...	...	...
(b) ANGLO-INDIANS.																				
Mysore State, including C. & M. Station, Bangalore.	37	157	22	141	87	21	332	136	57	18	190	15	...	1	...	1	...	...	...	...
Mysore State, excluding C. & M. Station, Bangalore.	9	75	2	47	20	1	21	6	30	4	118	5	...	1	...	1	...	...	...	...
Bangalore City	...	46	...	10	2	1	10	2	3	1	2	...	...	1	...	1	...	...	...	...
Bangalore District	...	...	1	1	...	...	...	...	1	2	1	...	...	...	...	...	...	...	...	...
Kolar Gold Fields (City) ...	7	10	...	19	12	...	7	3	13	...	104	...	...	...	...	...	...	...	...	...
Kolar District	...	1	...	1	...	...	...	...	...	...	...	...	...	...	...	...	...	...	...	...
Tumkur District	...	...	...	4	...	...	...	...	...	...	1	...	...	...	...	...	...	...	...	...
Mysore City	2	12	...	7	6	...	4	1	10	...	6	5	...	...	...	...	...	...	...	...
Mysore District	...	3	...	2	...	...	...	...	3	...	4	...	...	...	...	...	...	...	...	...
Chitaldrug District ...	...	2	...	...	...	...	...	...	...	...	...	...	...	...	...	...	...	...	...	...
Hassan District	...	...	...	2	...	...	...	...	...	1	...	...	...	...	...	...	...	...	...	...
Kadur District	...	1	...	...	...	...	...	...	...	...	...	...	...	...	...	...	...	...	...	...
Shimoga District	...	...	1	1	...	...	...	...	...	...	...	...	...	...	...	...	...	...	...	...
Civil & Military Station, Bangalore.	28	82	20	94	67	20	311	130	27	14	72	10	...	...	...	...	...	...	...	...

MYSORE CENSUS 1931.

TABLE XIII.—Literacy by Religion and Age.

NOTE 1.—In the case of Mysore State including the Civil and Military Station, Bangalore, and Mysore State excluding the Civil and Military Station, Bangalore, details are given for the total population and each religion. For cities and districts, figures are given for the total population and the following religions :—Hindu, Musalman, Christian, Jain and Tribal.

NOTE 2.—Literacy among Christians by Race is indicated below :—

Race	Persons	Males	Females
Total ...	31,286	18,935	12,351
Anglo-Indian	6,257	2,774	3,483
European	4,769	2,839	1,930
Indian Christian ...	20,260	13,322	6,938

NOTE 3.—Information regarding literacy in Vernaculars was not collected in the Civil and Military Station, Bangalore. Details for languages other than English are therefore given for the State excluding the Civil and Military Station and for the Districts and Cities other than the Civil and Military Station.

NOTE 4.—Languages appearing as Hindustani and Hindi in this Table appear as Western Hindi and Eastern Hindi respectively in the India Tables.

TABLE XIII.—Literacy by Religion and Age.

Number	District	AGE	POPULATION											
			Total			Literate			Illiterate			English		
			Persons	Males	Females	Persons	Males	Females	Persons	Males	Females	Persons	Males	Females
	1	2	3	4	5	6	7	8	9	10	11	12	13	14
	MYSORE STATE INCLUDING CIVIL AND MILITARY STATION, BANGALORE.	**All Religions.**												
1		All ages ...	**6,557,302**	**3,353,963**	**3,203,339**	**594,526**	**505,219**	**89,307**	**5,962,776**	**2,848,744**	**3,114,032**	**92,046**	**78,494**	**13,562**
2		0–5 ...	**929,960**	455,854	474,106	...	...	...	**929,960**	455,854	474,106	...	...	...
3		5–10 ...	**882,466**	440,978	441,488	**25,834**	18,254	7,580	**856,632**	422,724	433,908	**1,466**	875	591
4		10–15 ...	**814,673**	420,275	394,398	**82,395**	64,234	18,161	**732,278**	356,041	376,237	**10,083**	7,843	2,240
5		15–20 ...	**602,622**	305,621	297,001	**78,955**	62,184	16,141	**523,667**	242,807	280,860	**16,621**	14,057	2,564
6		20 and over ...	**3,327,581**	1,731,235	1,596,346	**407,342**	359,917	47,425	**2,920,239**	1,371,318	1,548,921	**63,876**	55,719	8,157
		Hindu (Brahmanic).												
1		All ages ...	**6,015,759**	**3,066,255**	**2,949,504**	**487,755**	**427,424**	**60,331**	**5,528,004**	**2,638,831**	**2,889,173**	**65,094**	**60,285**	**4,809**
2		0–5 ...	**847,529**	415,099	432,430	...	...	...	**847,529**	415,099	432,430	...	...	...
3		5–10 ...	**806,987**	402,395	404,592	**21,264**	15,667	5,597	**785,723**	386,728	398,995	**655**	472	183
4		10–15 ...	**746,551**	384,510	362,041	**68,738**	55,684	13,054	**677,813**	328,826	348,987	**7,298**	6,213	1,085
5		15–20 ...	**550,111**	278,179	271,932	**64,959**	53,608	11,351	**485,152**	224,571	260,581	**12,686**	11,557	1,129
6		20 and over ...	**3,064,581**	1,586,072	1,478,509	**332,794**	302,465	30,329	**2,731,787**	1,283,607	1,448,180	**44,455**	42,043	2,412
		Arya.												
1		All ages ...	**45**	**36**	**9**	**31**	**27**	**4**	**14**	**9**	**5**	**25**	**21**	**4**
2		0–5 ...	**3**	2	1	...	...	...	**3**	2	1	...	...	...
3		5–10 ...	**8**	6	2	**1**	1	...	**7**	5	2	...	...	...
4		10–15 ...	**8**	7	1	**8**	7	1	...	...	...	**5**	4	1
5		15–20 ...	**9**	8	1	**9**	8	1	...	...	...	**9**	8	1
6		20 and over ...	**17**	13	4	**13**	11	2	**4**	2	2	**11**	9	2
		Brahmo.												
1		All ages ...	**76**	**41**	**35**	**41**	**25**	**16**	**35**	**16**	**19**	**30**	**22**	**8**
2		0–5 ...	**16**	8	8	...	...	...	**16**	8	8	...	...	...
3		5–10 ...	**8**	5	3	**3**	2	1	**5**	3	2	...	...	...
4		10–15 ...	**11**	8	3	**6**	4	2	**5**	4	1	**3**	2	1
5		15–20 ...	**8**	4	4	**7**	4	3	**1**	...	1	**6**	4	2
6		20 and over ...	**33**	16	17	**25**	15	10	**8**	1	7	**21**	16	5
		Hindu (Total.)												
1		All ages ...	**6,015,880**	**3,066,332**	**2,949,548**	**487,827**	**427,476**	**60,351**	**5,528,053**	**2,638,856**	**2,889,177**	**65,149**	**60,328**	**4,821**
2		0–5 ...	**847,548**	415,109	432,439	...	...	...	**847,548**	415,109	432,439	...	...	...
3		5–10 ...	**(807,003**	402,406	404,597	**21,268**	15,670	5,598	**785,735**	386,736	398,999	**655**	472	183
4		10–15 ...	**746,570**	384,525	362,045	**68,752**	55,695	13,057	**677,818**	328,830	348,988	**7,306**	6,219	1,087
5		15–20 ...	**550,128**	278,191	271,937	**64,975**	53,620	11,355	**485,153**	224,571	260,582	**12,701**	11,569	1,132
6		20 and over ...	**3,064,631**	1,586,101	1,478,530	**332,832**	3,02,491	30,341	**2,731,799**	1,288,610	1,448,189	**44,487**	42,068	2,419
		Musalman												
1		All ages ...	**398,628**	**213,381**	**185,247**	**67,332**	**51,876**	**15,456**	**331,296**	**161,505**	**169,791**	**6,711**	**6,174**	**537**
2		0–5 ...	**61,921**	30,436	31,485	...	...	...	**61,921**	30,436	31,485	...	...	...
3		5–10 ...	**57,145**	29,284	27,861	**2,778**	1,633	1,145	**54,367**	27,651	26,716	**81**	48	33
4		10–15 ...	**50,954**	26,955	23,999	**8,820**	5,761	3,059	**42,134**	21,194	20,940	**656**	538	118
5		15–20 ...	**38,074**	20,184	17,890	**8,743**	6,134	2,609	**29,331**	14,050	15,281	**1,125**	1,003	122
6		20 and over ...	**190,534**	106,522	84,012	**46,991**	38,348	8,643	**143,543**	68,174	75,369	**4,849**	4,585	264
		Christian.												
1		All ages ...	**87,538**	**45,164**	**42.374**	**31,286**	**18,935**	**12,351**	**56,252**	**26,229**	**30,023**	**19,138**	**11,116**	**8,022**
2		0–5 ...	**12,449**	6,339	6,110	...	...	...	**12,449**	6,339	6,110	...	...	...
3		5–10 ...	**10,904**	5,520	5,384	**1,485**	731	754	**9,419**	4,789	4,630	**714**	347	367
4		10–15 ...	**10,345**	5,180	5,165	**3,750**	1,956	1,794	**6,595**	3,224	3,371	**2,015**	1,009	1,006
5		15–20 ...	**9,134**	4,490	4,644	**4,143**	2,175	1,968	**4,991**	2,315	2,676	**2,603**	1,322	1,281
6		20 and over ...	**44,706**	23,635	21,071	**21,908**	14,073	7,835	**22,798**	9,562	13,236	**13,806**	8.438	5,368
		Jain.												
1		All ages ...	**29,613**	**15,920**	**13,693**	**7,120**	**6,212**	**908**	**22,493**	**9,708**	**12,785**	**603**	**583**	**20**
2		0–5 ...	**3,729**	1,869	1,860	...	...	...	**3,729**	1,869	1,860	...	...	...
3		5–10 ...	**3,685**	1,857	1,828	**239**	174	65	**3,446**	1,683	1,763	**4**	2	2
4		10–15 ...	**3,555**	1,899	1,656	**938**	726	212	**2,617**	1,173	1,444	**54**	50	4
5		15–20 ...	**3,015**	1,669	1,346	**959**	797	162	**2,056**	872	1,184	**127**	125	2
6		20 and over ...	**15,629**	8,626	7,003	**4,984**	4,515	469	**10,645**	4,111	6,534	**418**	406	12
		Tribal.*												
1		All ages ...	**23,828**	**12,230**	**11,598**	**236**	**225**	**11**	**23,592**	**12,005**	**11,587**	**9**	**9**	...
2		0–5 ...	**4,008**	1,942	2,066	...	...	...	**4,008**	1,942	2,066	...	...	...
3		5–10 ...	**3,512**	1,798	1,714	**16**	16	...	**3,496**	1,782	1,714	...	...	...
4		10–15 ...	**3,048**	1,618	1,430	**46**	45	1	**3,002**	1.573	1,429	...	...	...
5		15–20 ...	**2,073**	999	1,074	**32**	32	...	**2,041**	967	1,074	**3**	3	...
6		20 and over ...	**11,187**	5,873	5,314	**142**	132	10	**11,045**	5,741	5,304	**6**	6	...
		Buddhist.												
1		All ages ...	**1,239**	**640**	**599**	**383**	**304**	**79**	**856**	**336**	**520**	**173**	**143**	**30**
2		0–5 ...	**226**	117	109	...	...	...	**226**	117	109	...	...	...
3		5–10 ...	**153**	82	71	**32**	22	10	**121**	60	61	**2**	2	...
4		10–15 ...	**132**	64	68	**46**	32	14	**86**	32	54	**17**	12	5
5		15–20 ...	**128**	53	75	**52**	30	22	**76**	23	53	**25**	18	7
6		20 and over ...	**600**	324	276	**253**	220	33	**347**	104	243	**129**	111	18

* See Note 2 to Table V.

Number	District	AGE	POPULATION											
			Total			Literate			Illiterate			English		
			Persons	Males	Females	Persons	Males	Females	Persons	Males	Females	Persons	Males	Females
	1	2	3	4	5	6	7	8	9	10	11	12	13	14
	MYSORE STATE, INCLUDING CIVIL AND MILITARY STATION, BANGALORE.	**Sikh.**												
1		All ages ...	100	63	37	46	43	3	54	20	34	10	9	1
2		0-5 ...	14	6	8	...	...	...	14	6	8	...	...	...
3		5-10 ...	7	4	3	1	1	...	6	3	3	...	...	...
4		10-15 ...	9	5	4	2	2	...	7	3	4	...	...	...
5		15-20 ...	16	12	4	9	7	2	7	5	2	1	1	...
6		20 and over ...	54	36	18	34	33	1	20	3	17	9	8	1
		Parsi.												
1		All ages ...	331	169	162	233	118	115	98	51	47	206	110	96
2		0-5 ...	45	25	20	...	...	...	45	25	20	...	...	...
3		5-10 ...	41	21	20	14	7	7	27	14	13	10	4	6
4		10-15 ...	42	22	20	32	14	18	10	8	2	30	13	17
5		15-20 ...	36	17	19	31	15	16	5	2	3	28	14	14
6		20 and over ...	167	84	83	156	82	74	11	2	9	138	79	59
		Jew.												
1		All ages ...	39	13	26	26	10	16	13	3	10	25	10	15
2		0-5 ...	5	1	4	...	...	...	5	1	4	...	...	...
3		5-10 ...	7	2	5	...	...	...	7	2	5	...	...	...
4		10-15 ...	7	2	5	6	2	4	1	...	1	5	2	3
5		15-20 ...	5	1	4	5	1	4	...	...	...	5	1	4
6		20 and over ...	15	7	8	15	7	8	...	...	...	15	7	8
		Others.												
1		All ages ...	106	51	55	37	20	17	69	31	38	22	12	10
2		0-5 ...	15	10	5	...	...	...	15	10	5	...	...	...
3		5-10 ...	9	4	5	1	...	1	8	4	4	...	...	...
4		10-15 ...	11	5	6	3	1	2	8	4	4	...	...	...
5		15-20 ...	13	5	8	6	3	3	7	2	5	3	1	2
6		20 and over ...	58	27	31	27	16	11	31	11	20	19	11	8
	MYSORE STATE, EXCLUDING CIVIL AND MILITARY STATION, BANGALORE.	**All Religions.**												
1		All ages ...	6,423,189	3,284,554	3,138,635	557,262	479,219	78,043	5,865,927	2,805,335	3,060,592	72,937	65,125	7,812
2		0-5 ...	910,945	446,381	464,564	...	...	...	910,945	446,381	464,564	...	...	...
3		5-10 ...	865,528	432,320	433,208	24,532	17,568	6,969	840,996	414,757	426,239	952	609	343
4		10-15 ...	799,078	412,400	386,678	78,351	61,915	16,436	720,727	350,485	370,242	8,042	6,597	1,445
5		15-20 ...	588,880	298,782	290,098	73,910	59,709	14,201	514,970	239,073	275,897	13,875	12,250	1,625
6		20 and over ...	3,258,758	1,694,671	1,564,087	380,469	340,032	40,437	2,878,289	1,354,639	1,523,650	50,068	45,669	4,399
		Hindu (Brahmanic).												
1		All ages ...	5,941,783	3,027,732	2,914,051	472,642	415,170	57,472	5,469,141	2,612,562	2,856,579	58,971	54,718	4,253
2		0-5 ...	836,405	409,613	426,792	...	...	...	836,405	409,613	426,792	...	...	...
3		5-10 ...	797,683	397,651	400,032	20,815	15,392	5,423	776,868	382,259	394,609	574	411	163
4		10-15 ...	738,238	380,293	357,945	67,183	54,684	12,499	671,055	325,609	345,446	6,711	5,749	962
5		15-20 ...	542,700	274,447	268,253	62,800	52,042	10,758	479,900	222,405	257,495	11,682	10,698	984
6		20 and over ...	3,026,757	1,565,728	1,461,029	321,844	293,052	28,792	2,704,913	1,272,676	1,432,237	40,004	37,860	2,144
		Arya.												
1		All ages ...	34	30	4	25	23	2	9	7	2	19	17	2
2		0-5 ...	1	1	...	...	...	...	1	1	...	...	...	...
3		5-10 ...	6	5	1	1	1	...	5	4	1	...	...	...
4		10-15 ...	7	7	...	7	7	...	...	...	...	4	4	...
5		15-20 ...	8	7	1	8	7	1	...	...	...	8	7	1
6		20 and over ...	12	10	2	9	8	1	3	2	1	7	6	1
		Brahmo.												
1		All ages ...	59	33	26	34	21	13	25	12	13	23	17	6
2		0-5 ...	13	6	7	...	...	...	13	6	7	...	...	...
3		5-10 ...	7	5	2	3	2	1	4	3	1	...	...	...
4		10-15 ...	8	6	2	5	3	2	3	3	...	2	1	1
5		15-20 ...	6	3	3	6	3	3	...	...	...	5	3	2
6		20 and over ...	25	13	12	20	13	7	5	...	5	16	13	3
		Hindu (Total).												
1		All ages ...	5,941,876	3,027,795	2,914,081	472,701	415,214	57,487	5,469,175	2,612,581	2,856,594	59,013	54,752	4,261
2		0-5 ...	836,419	409,620	426,799	...	...	...	836,419	409,620	426,799	...	...	...
3		5-10 ...	797,696	397,661	400,035	20,819	15,395	5,424	776,877	382,266	394,611	574	411	163
4		10-15 ...	738,253	380,306	357,947	67,195	54,694	12,501	671,058	325,612	345,446	6,717	5,754	963
5		15-20 ...	542,714	274,457	268,257	62,814	52,052	10,762	479,900	222,405	257,495	11,695	10,708	987
6		20 and over ...	3,026,794	1,565,751	1,461,043	321,873	293,073	28,800	2,704,921	1,272,678	1,432,243	40,027	37,879	2,148
		Musalman.												
1		All ages ...	370,003	197,983	172,020	59,597	46,304	13,293	310,406	151,679	158,727	4,863	4,508	355
2		0-5 ...	58,012	28,522	29,490	...	...	...	58,012	28,522	29,490	...	...	...
3		5-10 ...	53,318	27,348	25,970	2,522	1,513	1,009	50,796	25,835	24,961	49	31	18
4		10-15 ...	47,427	25,160	22,267	7,979	5,274	2,705	39,448	19,886	19,562	476	400	76
5		15-20 ...	35,128	18,632	16,496	7,792	5,546	2,246	27,336	13,086	14 250	866	778	88
6		20 and over ...	176,118	98,321	77,797	41,304	33,971	7,333	134,814	64,850	70,464	3,472	3,299	173

LITERATE IN																					
Kannada			Telugu			Tamil			Hindi*			Hindustani*			Marathi			Others			
Persons	Males	Females	Persons	Males	Females	Persons	Males	Females	Persons	Males	Females	Persons	Males	Females	Persons	Males	Females	Persons	Males	Females	Number
15	16	17	18	19	20	21	22	23	24	25	26	27	28	29	30	31	32	33	34	35	
...	...	...	...	...	...	...	...	...	...	...	...	...	...	...	...	...	...	...	...	...	1
...	...	...	...	...	...	...	...	...	...	...	...	...	...	...	...	...	...	...	...	...	2
...	...	...	...	...	...	...	...	...	...	...	...	...	...	...	...	...	...	...	...	...	3
...	...	...	...	...	...	...	...	...	...	...	...	...	...	...	...	...	...	...	...	...	4
...	...	...	...	...	...	...	...	...	...	...	...	...	...	...	...	...	...	...	...	...	5
...	...	...	...	...	...	...	...	...	...	...	...	...	...	...	...	...	...	...	...	...	6
...	...	...	...	...	...	...	...	...	...	...	...	...	...	...	...	...	...	...	...	...	1
...	...	...	...	...	...	...	...	...	...	...	...	...	...	...	...	...	...	...	...	...	2
...	...	...	...	...	...	...	...	...	...	...	...	...	...	...	...	...	...	...	...	...	3
...	...	...	...	...	...	...	...	...	...	...	...	...	...	...	...	...	...	...	...	...	4
...	...	...	...	...	...	...	...	...	...	...	...	...	...	...	...	...	...	...	...	...	5
...	...	...	...	...	...	...	...	...	...	...	...	...	...	...	...	...	...	...	...	...	6
...	...	...	...	...	...	...	...	...	...	...	...	...	...	...	...	...	...	...	...	...	1
...	...	...	...	...	...	...	...	...	...	...	...	...	...	...	...	...	...	...	...	...	2
...	...	...	...	...	...	...	...	...	...	...	...	...	...	...	...	...	...	...	...	...	3
...	...	...	...	...	...	...	...	...	...	...	...	...	...	...	...	...	...	...	...	...	4
...	...	...	...	...	...	...	...	...	...	...	...	...	...	...	...	...	...	...	...	...	5
...	...	...	...	...	...	...	...	...	...	...	...	...	...	...	...	...	...	...	...	...	6
...	...	...	...	...	...	...	...	...	...	...	...	...	...	...	...	...	...	...	...	...	1
...	...	...	...	...	...	...	...	...	...	...	...	...	...	...	...	...	...	...	...	...	2
...	...	...	...	...	...	...	...	...	...	...	...	...	...	...	...	...	...	...	...	...	3
...	...	...	...	...	...	...	...	...	...	...	...	...	...	...	...	...	...	...	...	...	4
...	...	...	...	...	...	...	...	...	...	...	...	...	...	...	...	...	...	...	...	...	5
...	...	...	...	...	...	...	...	...	...	...	...	...	...	...	...	...	...	...	...	...	6
472,073	414,507	57,566	17,837	15,741	2,096	26,474	21,262	5,212	2,599	2,148	451	48,538	35,419	13,119	2,570	2,049	521	10,295	8,830	1,465	1
...	...	...	...	...	...	...	...	...	...	...	...	...	...	...	...	...	...	...	...	...	2
21,057	15,505	5,552	248	188	60	826	514	312	63	40	23	2,254	1,303	951	41	23	18	112	66	46	3
68,588	55,732	12,856	915	694	221	2,284	1,531	753	238	158	75	6,779	4,205	2,574	127	76	51	637	436	201	4
62,432	51,626	10,806	1,563	1,175	388	3,079	2,260	819	362	305	57	6,717	4,077	2,640	256	162	94	1,269	1,013	256	5
319,996	291,644	28,352	15,111	13,684	1,427	20,285	16,957	3,328	1,941	1,645	296	32,788	25,834	6,954	2,146	1,788	358	8,277	7,315	962	6
442,793	389,610	53,183	16,726	14,767	1,959	17,440	14,198	3,242	1,273	1,057	216	618	564	54	2,400	1,912	488	5,715	5,284	431	1
...	...	...	...	...	...	...	...	...	...	...	...	...	...	...	...	...	...	...	...	...	2
20,069	14,869	5,200	230	176	54	541	354	187	30	19	11	4	4	...	38	21	17	44	26	18	3
65,006	53,074	12,932	856	648	208	1,455	1,029	426	117	77	40	19	17	2	117	70	47	260	208	52	4
58,633	48,583	10,050	1,432	1,064	368	2,028	1,516	512	175	149	26	65	47	18	237	150	87	661	573	88	5
299,085	273,084	26,001	14,208	12,879	1,329	13,416	11,299	2,117	951	812	189	530	496	34	2,008	1,671	337	4,750	4,477	273	6
17	16	1	5	5	...	5	5	...	3	3	...	...	...	...	2	2	...	2	1	1	1
...	...	...	...	...	...	...	...	...	...	...	...	...	...	...	...	...	...	...	...	...	2
1	1	...	...	...	...	...	...	...	...	...	...	...	...	...	...	...	...	...	...	...	3
7	7	...	1	1	...	...	...	...	...	...	...	...	...	...	...	...	...	...	...	...	4
7	6	1	2	2	...	4	4	...	1	1	...	...	...	...	1	1	...	...	...	...	5
2	2	...	2	2	...	1	1	...	2	2	...	...	...	...	1	1	...	2	1	1	6
32	20	12	1	1	...	5	3	2	...	...	...	1	1	...	...	...	...	3	3	...	1
...	...	...	...	...	...	...	...	...	...	...	...	...	...	...	...	...	...	...	...	...	2
3	2	1	...	...	...	...	...	...	...	...	...	...	...	...	...	...	...	...	...	...	3
4	2	2	...	...	...	1	1	...	...	...	...	...	...	...	...	...	...	...	...	...	4
6	3	3	...	...	...	2	1	1	...	...	...	...	...	...	...	...	...	2	2	...	5
19	13	6	1	1	...	2	1	1	...	...	...	1	1	...	...	...	...	1	1	...	6
442,842	389,646	53,196	16,732	14,773	1,959	17,450	14,206	3,244	1,276	1,060	216	619	565	54	2,402	1,914	488	5,720	5,288	432	1
...	...	...	...	...	...	...	...	...	...	...	...	...	...	...	...	...	...	...	...	...	2
20,073	14,872	5,201	230	176	54	541	354	187	30	19	11	4	4	...	38	21	17	44	26	18	3
65,017	53,083	11,934	857	649	208	1,456	1,030	426	117	77	40	19	17	2	117	70	47	260	208	52	4
58,646	48,592	10,054	1,434	1,066	368	2,034	1,521	518	176	150	26	65	47	18	238	151	87	663	575	88	5
299,106	273,099	26,007	14,211	12,882	1,329	13,419	11,301	2,118	953	814	139	531	497	34	2,009	1,672	337	4,753	4,479	274	6
15,824	15,070	754	633	615	18	2,682	2,567	115	830	646	184	47,781	34,749	13,032	36	32	4	2,916	2,122	794	1
...	...	...	...	...	...	...	...	...	...	...	...	...	...	...	...	...	...	...	...	...	2
307	243	64	4	4	...	26	21	5	21	12	9	2,246	1,295	951	...	...	...	49	24	25	3
1,560	1,345	215	24	19	5	124	110	14	80	52	28	6,757	4,186	2,571	1	1	...	246	120	126	4
1,908	1,799	109	86	85	1	290	267	23	100	74	26	6,631	4,013	2,618	1	1	...	375	241	134	5
12,049	11,683	366	519	507	12	2,242	2,169	73	629	508	121	32,147	25,255	6,892	34	30	4	2,246	1,737	509	6

* See note 4 on title page.

Number	State	AGE	POPULATION: Total: Persons	Total: Males	Total: Females	Literate: Persons	Literate: Males	Literate: Females	Illiterate: Persons	Illiterate: Males	Illiterate: Females	English: Persons	English: Males	English: Females
	1	2	3	4	5	6	7	8	9	10	11	12	13	14
	MYSORE STATE, EXCLUDING CIVIL AND MILITARY STATION, BANGALORE.	**Christian.**												
1		All ages ...	**57,516**	**30,512**	**27,004**	**17,551**	**11,271**	**6,280**	**39,965**	**19,241**	**20,724**	**8,340**	**5,199**	**3,141**
2		0-5 ...	**8,671**	4,372	4,299	...	...	...	**8,671**	4,372	4,299	...	...	...
3		5-10 ...	**7,263**	3,631	3,632	**912**	448	464	**6,351**	3,183	3,168	**323**	163	160
4		10-15 ...	**6,758**	3,412	3,346	**2,187**	1,177	1,010	**4,571**	2,235	2,336	**787**	390	397
5		15-20 ...	**5,932**	3,038	2,894	**2,312**	1,295	1,017	**3,620**	1,743	1,877	**1,169**	627	542
6		20 and over ...	**28,892**	16,059	12,833	**12,140**	8,351	3,789	**16,752**	7,708	9,044	**6,061**	4,019	2,042
		Jain.												
1		All ages ...	**28,799**	**15,436**	**13,363**	**6,807**	**5,915**	**892**	**21,992**	**9,521**	**12,471**	**548**	**529**	**19**
2		0-5 ...	**3,631**	1,818	1,813	...	...	...	**3,631**	1,818	1,813	...	...	...
3		5-10 ...	**3,606**	1,811	1,795	**235**	171	64	**3,371**	1,640	1,731	**4**	2	2
4		10-15 ...	**3,470**	1,848	1,622	**912**	703	209	**2,558**	1,145	1,413	**52**	49	3
5		15-20 ...	**2,900**	1,596	1,304	**906**	749	157	**1,994**	847	1,147	**118**	116	2
6		20 and over ...	**15,192**	8,363	6,829	**4,754**	4,292	462	**10,438**	4,071	6,367	**374**	362	12
		Tribal.												
1		All ages ...	**23,828**	**12,230**	**11,598**	**236**	**225**	**11**	**23,592**	**12,005**	**11,587**	**9**	**9**	...
2		0-5 ...	**4,008**	1,942	2,066	...	...	...	**4,008**	1,942	2,066	...	...	...
3		5-10 ...	**3,512**	1,798	1,714	**16**	16	...	**3,496**	1,782	1,714	...	...	...
4		10-15 ...	**3,048**	1,618	1,430	**46**	45	1	**3,002**	1,573	1,429	...	...	...
5		15-20 ...	**2,073**	999	1,074	**32**	32	...	**2,041**	967	1,074	**3**	3	...
6		20 and over ...	**11,187**	5,873	5,314	**142**	132	10	**11,045**	5,741	5,304	**6**	6	...
		Buddhist.												
1		All ages ...	**979**	**497**	**482**	**276**	**225**	**51**	**703**	**272**	**431**	**99**	**84**	**15**
2		0-5 ...	**180**	95	85	...	...	...	**180**	95	85	...	...	...
3		5-10 ...	**117**	62	55	**25**	17	8	**92**	45	47	...	...	...
4		10-15 ...	**100**	45	55	**24**	18	6	**76**	27	49	**5**	3	2
5		15-20 ...	**105**	45	60	**35**	23	12	**70**	22	48	**13**	11	2
6		20 and over ...	**477**	250	227	**192**	167	25	**285**	83	202	**81**	70	11
		Sikh.												
1		All ages ...	**68**	**34**	**34**	**20**	**19**	**1**	**48**	**15**	**33**	**1**	**1**	...
2		0-5 ...	**13**	6	7	...	...	...	**13**	6	7	...	...	...
3		5-10 ...	**7**	4	3	**1**	1	...	**6**	3	3	...	...	...
4		10-15 ...	**8**	4	4	**2**	2	...	**6**	2	4	...	...	...
5		15-20 ...	**9**	6	3	**5**	4	1	**4**	2	2	...	...	...
6		20 and over ...	**31**	14	17	**12**	12	...	**19**	2	17	**1**	1	...
		Parsi.												
1		All ages ...	**87**	**49**	**38**	**60**	**39**	**21**	**27**	**10**	**17**	**51**	**37**	**14**
2		0-5 ...	**9**	5	4	...	...	...	**9**	5	4	...	...	...
3		5-10 ...	**5**	3	2	**2**	2	...	**3**	1	2	**2**	2	...
4		10-15 ...	**8**	4	4	**3**	1	2	**5**	3	2	**2**	...	2
5		15-20 ...	**15**	7	8	**11**	7	4	**4**	...	4	**8**	6	2
6		20 and over ...	**50**	30	20	**44**	29	15	**6**	1	5	**39**	29	10
		Jew.												
1		All ages ...	**18**	**7**	**11**	**13**	**6**	**7**	**5**	**1**	**4**	**13**	**6**	**7**
2		0-5 ...	**1**	...	1	...	...	...	**1**	...	1	...	...	...
3		5-10 ...	**3**	1	2	...	...	...	**3**	1	2	...	...	...
4		10-15 ...	**4**	1	3	**3**	1	2	**1**	...	1	**3**	1	2
5		15-20 ...	**3**	1	2	**3**	1	2	...	...	...	**3**	1	2
6		20 and over ...	**7**	4	3	**7**	4	3	...	...	...	**7**	4	3
		Others.												
1		All ages ...	**15**	**11**	**4**	**1**	**1**	...	**14**	**10**	**4**	...	...	...
2		0-5 ...	**1**	1	...	...	...	...	**1**	1	...	...	...	...
3		5-10 ...	**1**	1	...	...	...	...	**1**	1	...	...	...	...
4		10-15 ...	**2**	2	...	...	...	...	**2**	2	...	...	...	...
5		15-20 ...	**1**	1	...	...	...	...	**1**	1	...	...	...	...
6		20 and over ...	**10**	6	4	**1**	1	...	**9**	5	4	...	...	...
	BANGALORE CITY.	**All Religions.**												
1		All ages ...	**172,357**	**91,680**	**80,677**	**52,509**	**39,314**	**13,195**	**119,848**	**52,366**	**67,482**	**19,900**	**16,914**	**2,986**
2		0-5 ...	**24,270**	11,982	12,288	...	...	...	**24,270**	11,982	12,288	...	...	...
3		5-10 ...	**20,870**	10,564	10,306	**3,006**	1,746	1,260	**17,864**	8,818	9,046	**381**	245	136
4		10-15 ...	**19,553**	10,185	9,368	**6,837**	4,391	2,446	**12,716**	5,794	6,922	**2,265**	1,675	590
5		15-20 ...	**18,870**	10,165	8,705	**8,224**	5,831	2,393	**10,646**	4,334	6,312	**3,958**	3,283	675
6		20 and over ...	**88,794**	48,784	40,010	**34,442**	27,346	7,096	**54,352**	21,438	32,914	**13,296**	11,711	1,585
		Hindu.												
1		All ages ...	**144,529**	**76,645**	**67,884**	**43,213**	**32,810**	**10,403**	**101,316**	**43,835**	**57,481**	**16,737**	**14,771**	**1,966**
2		0-5 ...	**20,319**	9,971	10,348	...	...	...	**20,319**	9,971	10,348	...	...	...
3		5-10 ...	**17,409**	8,813	8,596	**2,572**	1,503	1,069	**14,837**	7,310	7,527	**281**	184	97
4		10-15 ...	**16,367**	8,547	7,820	**5,730**	3,750	1,980	**10,637**	4,797	5,840	**1,928**	1,482	446
5		15-20 ...	**15,858**	8,589	7,269	**6,999**	5,087	1,912	**8,859**	3,502	5,357	**3,467**	3,007	460
6		20 and over ...	**74,576**	40,725	33,851	**27,912**	22,470	5,442	**46,664**	18,255	28,409	**11,061**	10,098	963

LITERATE IN

Kannada			Telugu			Tamil			Hindi			Hindustani			Marathi			Others			
Persons	Males	Females	Persons	Males	Females	Persons	Males	Females	Persons	Males	Females	Persons	Males	Females	Persons	Males	Females	Persons	Males	Females	Number
15	16	17	18	19	20	21	22	23	24	25	26	27	28	29	30	31	32	33	34	35	
7,690	4,895	2,795	440	326	114	6,036	4,237	1,799	18	15	3	87	58	29	76	59	17	609	426	183	1
...	...	...	...	...	...	...	...	...	...	...	...	...	...	...	...	...	...	...	...	...	2
439	215	224	14	8	6	237	125	112	...	...	...	2	2	...	3	2	1	8	7	1	3
1,164	654	510	31	24	7	682	374	308	...	...	...	1	1	...	2	...	2	34	17	17	4
1,145	643	502	41	24	17	718	448	270	2	2	...	5	3	2	9	6	3	54	31	23	5
4,942	3,383	1,559	354	270	84	4,399	3,290	1,109	16	13	3	79	52	27	62	51	11	513	371	142	6
5,458	4,652	806	28	23	5	34	31	3	461	413	48	26	25	1	29	27	2	1,009	975	34	1
...	...	...	...	...	...	...	...	...	...	...	...	...	...	...	...	...	...	...	...	...	2
231	158	63	...	...	...	1	1	...	11	8	3	...	...	...	...	...	...	10	8	2	3
799	608	196	3	2	1	...	...	...	34	27	7	...	...	...	3	3	...	96	91	5	4
697	557	140	2	...	2	3	2	1	82	77	5	12	11	1	3	1	2	170	163	7	5
3,741	3,334	407	23	21	2	30	28	2	334	301	33	14	14	...	23	23	...	733	713	20	6
229	219	10	3	3	...	6	5	1	1	1	...	...	...	...	4	3	1	...	...	...	1
...	...	...	...	...	...	...	...	...	...	...	...	...	...	...	...	...	...	...	...	...	2
16	16	...	...	...	...	...	...	...	...	...	...	...	...	...	...	...	...	...	...	...	3
46	45	1	...	...	...	...	...	...	...	...	...	...	...	...	1	1	...	...	...	...	4
31	31	...	...	...	...	1	1	...	...	...	...	...	...	...	1	1	...	...	...	...	5
136	127	9	3	3	...	5	4	1	1	1	...	...	...	...	2	1	1	...	...	...	6
11	8	3	...	...	...	262	213	49	2	2	...	5	5	...	...	...	...	...	...	...	1
...	...	...	...	...	...	...	...	...	...	...	...	...	...	...	...	...	...	...	...	...	2
1	1	...	...	...	...	21	13	8	...	...	...	...	...	...	...	...	...	...	...	...	3
1	1	...	...	...	...	22	17	5	...	...	...	...	...	...	...	...	...	...	...	...	4
1	1	...	...	...	...	32	20	12	...	...	...	...	...	...	...	...	...	...	...	...	5
8	5	3	...	...	...	187	163	24	2	2	...	5	5	...	...	...	...	...	...	...	6
13	12	1	1	1	...	...	...	...	9	9	...	1	1	...	...	...	...	1	1	...	1
...	...	...	...	...	...	...	...	...	...	...	...	...	...	...	...	...	...	...	...	...	2
...	...	...	...	...	...	...	...	...	1	1	...	...	...	...	...	...	...	...	...	...	3
1	1	...	...	...	...	...	...	...	2	2	...	...	...	...	...	...	...	...	...	...	4
4	3	1	...	...	...	...	...	...	2	2	...	...	...	...	...	...	...	...	...	...	5
8	8	...	1	1	...	...	...	...	4	4	...	1	1	...	...	...	...	1	1	...	6
3	3	...	...	...	...	4	3	1	2	2	...	13	12	1	11	8	3	36	17	19	1
...	...	...	...	...	...	...	...	...	...	...	...	...	...	...	...	...	...	...	...	...	2
...	...	...	...	...	...	...	...	...	...	...	...	2	2	...	...	...	...	1	1	...	3
...	...	...	...	...	...	...	...	...	...	...	...	...	...	...	...	...	...	1	...	1	4
...	...	...	...	...	...	1	1	...	...	...	...	2	2	...	2	1	1	7	3	4	5
3	3	...	...	...	...	3	2	1	2	2	...	9	8	1	9	7	2	27	13	14	6
3	2	1	...	...	...	...	...	...	...	...	...	5	3	2	12	6	6	3	...	3	1
...	...	...	...	...	...	...	...	...	...	...	...	...	...	...	...	...	...	...	...	...	2
...	...	...	...	...	...	...	...	...	...	...	...	...	...	...	...	...	...	...	...	...	3
...	...	...	...	...	...	...	...	...	...	...	...	2	1	1	3	1	2	...	...	...	4
...	...	...	...	...	...	...	...	...	...	...	...	2	1	1	2	1	1	...	...	...	5
3	2	1	...	...	...	...	...	...	...	...	...	1	1	...	7	4	3	3	...	3	6
...	...	...	...	...	...	...	...	...	...	...	...	1	1	...	...	...	...	1	1	...	1
...	...	...	...	...	...	...	...	...	...	...	...	...	...	...	...	...	...	...	...	...	2
...	...	...	...	...	...	...	...	...	...	...	...	...	...	...	...	...	...	...	...	...	3
...	...	...	...	...	...	...	...	...	...	...	...	...	...	...	...	...	...	...	...	...	4
...	...	...	...	...	...	...	...	...	...	...	...	...	...	...	...	...	...	...	...	...	5
...	...	...	...	...	...	...	...	...	...	...	...	1	1	...	...	...	...	1	1	...	6
37,517	28,007	9,510	3,935	3,153	782	7,168	5,445	1,723	334	272	62	5,338	4,050	1,288	1,028	784	244	2,034	1,668	366	1
...	...	...	...	...	...	...	...	...	...	...	...	...	...	...	...	...	...	...	...	...	2
2,472	1,419	1,053	60	37	23	215	135	80	6	4	2	236	137	99	23	7	16	28	15	13	3
5,402	3,479	1,923	212	134	78	568	361	207	19	6	13	613	382	231	62	31	31	127	91	36	4
6,322	4,528	1,794	492	385	157	895	621	274	50	41	9	664	444	220	109	67	42	335	269	66	5
23,321	18,581	4,740	3,171	2,647	524	5,490	4,328	1,162	259	221	38	3,825	3,087	738	834	679	155	1,544	1,298	251	6
35,312	26,549	8,763	3,716	2,983	733	5,786	4,472	1,314	269	227	42	73	61	12	994	761	233	1,194	1,014	180	1
...	...	...	...	...	...	...	...	...	...	...	...	...	...	...	...	...	...	...	...	...	2
2,350	1,360	990	54	33	21	175	110	65	5	4	1	...	...	...	22	7	15	11	6	5	3
5,108	3,328	1,780	200	126	74	440	288	152	14	5	9	3	3	...	57	29	28	68	45	23	4
5,966	4,333	1,633	475	329	146	738	522	216	38	31	7	9	5	4	103	65	38	226	187	39	5
21,888	17,528	4,360	2,987	2,495	492	4,433	3,552	881	212	187	25	61	53	8	812	660	152	889	776	113	6

Number	District	AGE	POPULATION											
			Total			Literate			Illiterate			English		
			Persons	Males	Females	Persons	Males	Females	Persons	Males	Females	Persons	Males	Females
	1	2	3	4	5	6	7	8	9	10	11	12	13	14
	BANGALORE CITY.	**Musalman.**												
1		All ages ...	**19,831**	**10,975**	**8,856**	**5,600**	**4,307**	**1,293**	**14,231**	**6,668**	**7,563**	**1,093**	**959**	**134**
2		0–5 ...	**2,802**	1,418	1,384	...	...	...	**2,802**	1,418	1,384	...	...	...
3		5–10 ...	**2,510**	1,268	1,242	**239**	138	101	**2,271**	1,130	1,141	**27**	18	**9**
4		10–15 ...	**2,275**	1,191	1,084	**632**	395	237	**1,643**	796	847	**122**	82	**40**
5		15–20 ...	**2,121**	1,153	968	**693**	483	210	**1,428**	670	758	**168**	135	**33**
6		20 and over ...	**10,123**	5,945	4,178	**4,036**	3,291	745	**6,087**	2,654	3,433	**776**	**724**	**52**
		Christian.												
1		All ages ...	**6,754**	**3,291**	**3,463**	**3,038**	**1,655**	**1,383**	**3,716**	**1,636**	**2,080**	**1,913**	**1,043**	**870**
2		0–5 ...	**1,008**	522	486	...	...	...	**1,008**	522	486	...	...	...
3		5–10 ...	**815**	402	413	**165**	84	81	**650**	318	332	**71**	42	**29**
4		10–15 ...	**767**	354	413	**384**	175	209	**383**	179	204	**195**	95	**100**
5		15–20 ...	**720**	308	412	**423**	176	247	**297**	132	165	**290**	110	**180**
6		20 and over ...	**3,444**	1,705	1,739	**2,066**	1,220	846	**1,378**	485	893	**1,357**	796	**561**
		Jain.												
1		All ages ...	**1,153**	**724**	**429**	**612**	**510**	**102**	**541**	**214**	**327**	**127**	**118**	**9**
2		0–5 ...	**135**	69	66	...	...	...	**135**	69	66	...	...	...
3		5–10 ...	**124**	75	49	**26**	17	9	**98**	58	40	**2**	1	**1**
4		10–15 ...	**132**	88	44	**87**	69	18	**45**	19	26	**15**	14	**1**
5		15–20 ...	**156**	107	49	**99**	77	22	**57**	30	27	**27**	26	**1**
6		20 and over ...	**606**	385	221	**400**	347	53	**206**	88	168	**83**	77	**6**
	BANGALORE DISTRICT.	**All Religions.**												
1		All ages ...	**908,056**	**461,905**	**446,151**	**61,675**	**53,862**	**7,813**	**846,381**	**408,043**	**438,338**	**4,558**	**4,216**	**342**
2		0–5 ...	**138,291**	67,865	70,426	...	...	...	**138,291**	67,865	70,426	...	...	...
3		5–10 ...	**126,495**	63,267	63,228	**2,603**	1,960	643	**123,892**	61,807	62,585	**40**	33	**7**
4		10–15 ...	**111,923**	57,640	54,283	**8,671**	6,930	1,741	**103,252**	50,710	52,542	**520**	474	**46**
5		15–20 ...	**79,621**	39,593	40,028	**8,134**	6,739	1,395	**71,487**	32,854	38,633	**917**	855	**62**
6		20 and over ...	**451,726**	233,540	218,186	**42,267**	38,233	4,034	**409,459**	195,307	214,152	**3,081**	2,854	**227**
		Hindu.												
1		All ages ...	**833,552**	**422,950**	**410,602**	**52,145**	**46,839**	**5,306**	**781,407**	**376,111**	**405,296**	**3,760**	**3,612**	**148**
2		0–5 ...	**125,584**	61,645	63,939	...	...	...	**125,584**	61,645	63,939	...	...	...
3		5–10 ...	**115,228**	57,534	57,694	**2,175**	1,713	462	**113,053**	55,821	57,232	**35**	28	7
4		10–15 ...	**102,194**	52,516	49,678	**7,323**	6,077	1,246	**94,871**	46,439	48,432	**461**	426	35
5		15–20 ...	**72,790**	36,052	36,738	**6,787**	5,790	997	**66,003**	30,262	35,741	**778**	748	30
6		20 and over ...	**417,756**	215,203	202,553	**35,860**	33,259	2,601	**381,896**	181,944	199,952	**2,486**	2.410	76
		Musalman.												
1		All ages ...	**60,276**	**31,744**	**28,532**	**7,833**	**5,815**	**2,018**	**52,443**	**25,929**	**26,514**	**426**	402	**24**
2		0–5 ...	**10,361**	5,075	5,286	...	...	...	**10,361**	5,075	5,286	...	...	...
3		5–10 ...	**9,293**	4,741	4,552	**376**	219	157	**8,917**	4,522	4,395	**3**	3	...
4		10–15 ...	**7,992**	4,226	3,766	**1,142**	709	433	**6,850**	3,517	3,333	**40**	38	**2**
5		15–20 ...	**5,574**	2,916	2,658	**1,139**	821	318	**4,435**	2,095	2,340	**93**	88	**5**
6		20 and over ...	**27,056**	14,786	12,270	**5,176**	4,066	1,110	**21,880**	10,720	11,160	**290**	273	17
		Christian.												
1		All ages ...	**8,036**	**4,067**	**3,969**	**1,096**	**682**	**414**	**6,940**	**3,385**	**3,555**	**349**	**179**	**170**
2		0–5 ...	**1,342**	638	704	...	...	...	**1,342**	638	704	...	...	...
3		5–10 ...	**1,138**	582	556	**32**	15	17	**1,106**	567	539	**2**	**2**	...
4		10–15 ...	**1,009**	525	484	**109**	65	44	**900**	460	440	**18**	**9**	**9**
5		15–20 ...	**717**	354	363	**126**	64	62	**591**	290	301	**42**	15	**27**
6		20 and over ...	**3,830**	1,968	1,862	**829**	538	291	**3,001**	1,430	1,571	**287**	153	134
		Jain.												
1		All ages ...	**3,532**	**1,777**	**1,755**	**584**	**510**	**74**	**2,948**	**1,267**	**1,681**	**22**	**22**	...
2		0–5 ...	**526**	263	263	...	...	...	**526**	263	263	...	...	...
3		5–10 ...	**473**	221	252	**19**	12	7	**454**	209	245	...	...	...
4		10–15 ...	**425**	211	214	**93**	75	18	**332**	136	196	**1**	1	...
5		15–20 ...	**327**	170	157	**81**	63	18	**246**	107	139	**4**	4	...
6		20 and over ...	**1,781**	912	869	**391**	360	31	**1,390**	552	838	**17**	**17**	...
		Tribal.												
1		All ages ...	**2,645**	**1,357**	**1,288**	**13**	**12**	**1**	**2,632**	**1,345**	**1,287**	...	...	...
2		0–5 ...	**476**	243	233	...	...	...	**476**	243	233	...	...	...
3		5–10 ...	**362**	188	174	**1**	1	...	**361**	187	174	...	...	...
4		10–15 ...	**301**	161	140	**4**	4	...	**297**	157	140	...	...	...
5		15–20 ...	**212**	100	112	**1**	1	...	**211**	99	112	...	...	...
6		20 and over ...	**1,294**	665	629	**7**	6	**1**	**1,287**	659	628	...	...	...
	K. G. F. CITY.	**All Religions.**												
1		All ages ...	**85,103**	**45,051**	**40,052**	**15,100**	**12,223**	**2,877**	**70,003**	**32,828**	**37,175**	**4,034**	**2,984**	**1,050**
2		0–5 ...	**12,693**	6,286	6,407	...	...	...	**12,693**	6,286	6,407	...	...	...
3		5–10 ...	**10,443**	5,205	5,238	**734**	447	287	**9,709**	4,758	4,951	**185**	89	96
4		10–15 ...	**9,176**	4,659	4,517	**1,660**	1,136	524	**7,516**	3,523	3,993	**382**	242	140
5		15–20 ...	**7,980**	4,091	3,889	**1,818**	1,422	396	**6,162**	2,669	3,493	**573**	439	134
6		20 and over ...	**44,811**	24,810	20,001	**10,888**	9,218	1,670	**33,923**	15,592	18,331	**2,894**	2,214	680

LITERATE IN																					
Kannada			Telugu			Tamil			Hindi			Hindustani			Marathi			Others			
Persons	Males	Females	Persons	Males	Females	Persons	Males	Females	Persons	Males	Females	Persons	Males	Females	Persons	Males	Females	Persons	Males	Females	Number
15	16	17	18	19	20	21	22	23	24	25	26	27	28	29	30	31	32	33	34	35	
681	636	45	104	102	2	270	253	17	24	16	8	5,231	3,963	1,268	4	2	2	367	259	108	1
...	...	...	...	...	...	...	...	...	...	...	...	...	...	...	...	...	...	...	...	...	2
14	5	9	1	1	...	2	1	1	...	...	...	233	134	99	...	...	...	8	2	6	3
37	32	5	3	3	...	8	8	...	2	1	1	612	379	233	...	...	...	22	13	9	4
86	78	8	4	4	...	24	22	2	3	2	1	649	436	213	...	...	...	39	24	15	5
544	521	23	96	94	2	236	222	14	19	13	6	3,737	3,014	723	4	2	2	298	220	78	6
1,227	601	626	112	67	45	1,097	708	389	6	5	1	24	17	7	16	9	7	163	107	56	1
...	...	...	...	...	...	...	...	...	...	...	...	...	...	...	...	...	...	...	...	...	2
88	43	45	5	3	2	37	23	14	...	...	...	2	2	...	1	...	1	4	4	...	3
200	76	124	9	5	4	118	64	54	...	...	...	1	1	...	2	...	2	9	6	8	4
219	81	138	12	2	10	132	76	56	1	1	...	2	2	...	2	...	2	20	13	7	5
720	401	319	86	57	29	810	545	265	5	4	1	19	12	7	11	9	2	130	84	46	6
296	221	75	3	1	2	...	...	...	34	23	11	2	2	...	4	4	...	292	277	15	1
...	...	...	...	...	...	...	...	...	...	...	...	...	...	...	...	...	...	...	...	...	2
23	14	9	...	...	...	...	...	...	1	...	1	...	...	...	...	...	...	5	3	2	3
55	41	14	...	...	...	...	...	...	3	...	3	...	...	...	1	1	...	28	27	1	4
50	35	15	1	...	1	...	...	...	8	7	1	...	...	...	...	...	...	46	42	4	5
168	131	37	2	1	1	...	...	...	22	16	6	2	2	...	3	3	...	213	205	8	6
53,296	47,846	5,450	1,058	926	132	1,327	1,060	267	157	123	34	6,963	4,998	1,965	118	92	26	406	321	85	1
...	...	...	...	...	...	...	...	...	...	...	...	...	...	...	...	...	...	...	...	...	2
2,228	1,754	474	5	4	1	30	13	17	5	4	1	348	195	153	1	1	...	4	2	2	3
7,621	6,262	1,359	34	22	12	81	45	36	22	14	8	1,052	632	420	1	1	...	27	10	17	4
6,905	5,880	1,025	66	43	23	109	73	36	19	15	4	1,005	698	307	13	6	7	39	28	11	5
36,542	33,950	2,592	953	857	96	1,107	929	178	111	90	21	4,558	3,473	1,085	103	84	19	336	281	55	6
50,873	45,763	5,110	960	839	121	788	675	113	90	71	19	44	39	5	110	87	23	200	193	7	1
...	...	...	...	...	...	...	...	...	...	...	...	...	...	...	...	...	...	...	...	...	2
2,152	1,693	459	5	4	1	13	11	2	5	4	1	...	...	...	1	1	...	1	1	...	3
7,242	6,013	1,229	32	21	11	38	27	11	11	9	2	...	...	...	1	1	...	7	7	...	4
6,561	5,591	970	62	39	23	52	38	14	8	4	4	4	2	2	10	4	6	11	9	2	5
34,918	32,466	2,452	861	775	86	685	599	86	66	54	12	40	37	3	98	81	17	181	176	5	6
1,397	1,280	117	25	25	...	231	225	6	63	48	15	6,911	4,954	1,957	...	...	...	156	100	56	1
...	...	...	...	...	...	...	...	...	...	...	...	...	...	...	...	...	...	...	...	...	2
40	37	3	...	...	...	...	...	...	...	...	...	348	195	153	...	...	...	3	1	2	3
204	123	81	1	1	...	7	5	2	11	5	6	1,052	632	420	...	...	...	19	3	16	4
188	180	8	...	...	...	35	32	3	10	10	...	1,000	696	304	...	...	...	19	12	7	5
965	940	25	24	24	...	189	188	1	42	33	9	4,511	3,431	1,080	...	...	...	115	84	31	6
432	284	148	68	57	11	307	159	148	2	2	...	6	3	3	8	5	3	48	26	22	1
...	...	...	...	...	...	...	...	...	...	...	...	...	...	...	...	...	...	...	...	...	2
16	11	5	...	...	...	17	2	15	...	...	...	...	...	...	...	...	...	...	...	...	3
78	47	31	1	...	1	36	13	23	...	...	...	...	...	...	...	...	...	1	...	1	4
74	45	29	4	4	...	22	3	19	1	1	...	1	...	1	3	2	1	9	7	2	5
264	181	83	63	53	10	232	141	91	1	1	...	5	3	2	5	3	2	38	19	19	6
578	504	74	5	5	...	1	1	...	2	2	...	...	...	...	...	...	...	1	1	...	1
...	...	...	...	...	...	...	...	...	...	...	...	...	...	...	...	...	...	...	...	...	2
19	12	7	...	...	...	...	...	...	...	...	...	...	...	...	...	...	...	...	...	...	3
93	75	18	...	...	...	...	...	...	...	...	...	...	...	...	...	...	...	...	...	...	4
81	63	18	...	...	...	...	...	...	...	...	...	...	...	...	...	...	...	...	...	...	5
385	354	31	5	5	...	1	1	...	2	2	...	...	...	...	...	...	...	1	1	...	6
13	12	1	...	...	...	...	...	...	...	...	...	...	...	...	...	...	...	...	...	...	1
...	...	...	...	...	...	...	...	...	...	...	...	...	...	...	...	...	...	...	...	...	2
1	1	...	...	...	...	...	...	...	...	...	...	...	...	...	...	...	...	...	...	...	3
4	4	...	...	...	...	...	...	...	...	...	...	...	...	...	...	...	...	...	...	...	4
1	1	...	...	...	...	...	...	...	...	...	...	...	...	...	...	...	...	...	...	...	5
7	6	1	...	...	...	...	...	...	...	...	...	...	...	...	...	...	...	...	...	...	6
1,673	1,383	290	749	659	90	9,529	8,030	1,499	146	127	19	1,028	784	244	38	33	5	1,007	903	104	1
...	...	...	...	...	...	...	...	...	...	...	...	...	...	...	...	...	...	...	...	...	2
102	62	40	18	14	4	424	273	151	4	4	...	39	20	19	...	...	...	19	11	8	3
207	147	60	45	27	18	1,141	818	323	10	6	4	113	67	46	...	...	...	52	37	15	4
179	143	36	59	47	12	1,250	1,029	221	17	16	1	97	58	39	1	...	1	61	45	16	5
1,185	1,031	154	627	571	56	6,714	5,910	804	115	101	14	779	639	140	37	33	4	875	810	65	6

Number	District	AGE	POPULATION											
			Total			Literate			Illiterate			English		
			Persons	Males	Females	Persons	Males	Females	Persons	Males	Females	Persons	Males	Females
	1	2	3	4	5	6	7	8	9	10	11	12	13	14
	KOLAR GOLD FIELDS CITY.	**Hindu.**												
1		All ages ...	**62,313**	**32,695**	**29,618**	**8,035**	**7,008**	**1,027**	**54,278**	**25,687**	**28,591**	**1,098**	**1,014**	**84**
2		0–5 ...	**8,972**	4,395	4,577	...	...	...	**8,972**	4,395	4,577	...	...	...
3		5–10 ...	**7,560**	3,759	3,801	**363**	250	113	**7,197**	3,509	3,688	**11**	8	3
4		10–15 ...	**6,679**	3,386	3,293	**951**	713	238	**5,728**	2 673	3,055	**143**	116	27
5		15–20 ...	**5,770**	2,950	2,820	**1,022**	861	161	**4,748**	2,089	2,659	**235**	220	15
6		20 and over ...	**33,332**	18,205	15,127	**5,699**	5,184	515	**27,633**	13,021	14,612	**709**	670	39
		Musalman.												
1		All ages ...	6,771	**4,045**	**2,726**	**1,761**	**1,498**	**263**	**5,010**	**2,547**	**2,463**	**186**	**174**	**12**
2		0–5 ...	**969**	480	489	...	...	...	**969**	480	489	...	...	...
3		5–10 ...	**842**	436	406	**55**	33	22	**787**	403	384	**2**	...	2
4		10–15 ...	**730**	392	338	**170**	121	49	**560**	271	289	**22**	20	2
5		15–20 ...	**607**	346	261	**157**	122	35	**450**	224	226	**18**	17	1
6		20 and over ...	**3,623**	2,391	1,232	**1,379**	1,222	157	**2,244**	1,169	1,075	**144**	137	7
		Christian.												
1		All ages ...	**14,651**	**7,579**	**7,072**	**4,883**	**3,349**	**1,534**	**9,768**	**4,230**	**5,538**	**2,658**	**1,712**	**946**
2		0–5 ...	**2,498**	1,278	1,220	...	...	...	**2,498**	1,278	1,220	...	...	...
3		5–10 ...	**1,883**	926	957	**292**	148	144	**1,591**	778	813	**172**	81	91
4		10–15 ...	**1,626**	813	813	**502**	271	231	**1,124**	542	582	**212**	101	111
5		15–20 ...	**1,452**	720	732	**580**	393	187	**872**	327	545	**306**	190	116
6		20 and over ...	**7,192**	3,842	3,350	**3,509**	2,537	972	**3,683**	1,305	2,378	**1,968**	1,340	628
		Jain.												
1		All ages ...	**447**	**262**	**185**	**176**	**166**	**10**	**271**	**96**	**175**	**15**	**15**	...
2		0–5 ...	**83**	41	42	...	...	...	**83**	41	42	...	...	...
3		5–10 ...	**52**	27	25	**4**	4	...	**48**	23	25	...	...	...
4		10–15 ...	**48**	26	22	**17**	15	2	**31**	11	20	**4**	4	...
5		15–20 ...	**53**	34	19	**28**	27	1	**25**	7	18	**4**	4	...
6		20 and over ...	**211**	134	77	**127**	120	7	**84**	14	70	**7**	7	...
		Tribal.												
1		All ages ...	**1**	**1**	...	...	...	...	**1**	**1**	...	...	...	...
2		0–5 ...	...	...	...	...	...	...	...	...	...	...	...	...
3		5–10 ...	...	...	...	...	...	...	...	...	...	...	...	...
4		10–15 ...	...	...	...	...	...	...	...	...	...	...	...	...
5		15–20 ...	...	...	...	...	...	...	...	...	...	...	...	...
6		20 and over ...	**1**	1	...	...	...	...	**1**	1	...	...	...	...
	KOLAR DISTRICT.	**All Religions.**												
1		All ages ...	**7,63,934**	**389,262**	**374,672**	**54,769**	**47,561**	**7,208**	**709,165**	**341,701**	**367,464**	**5,886**	**5,332**	**554**
2		0–5 ...	**103,793**	50,591	53,202	...	...	...	**103,793**	50,591	53,202	...	...	...
3		5–10 ...	**99,568**	49,869	49,699	**2,333**	1,690	643	**97,235**	48,179	49,056	**59**	41	18
4		10–15 ...	**88,360**	45,408	42,952	**7,268**	5,791	1,477	**81,092**	39,617	41,475	**638**	504	134
5		15–20 ...	**64,861**	32,182	32,679	**6,740**	5,426	1,314	**58,121**	26,756	31,365	**1,058**	916	142
6		20 and over ...	**407,352**	211,212	196,140	**38,428**	34,654	3,774	**368,924**	176,558	192,366	**4,131**	3,871	260
		Hindu.												
1		All ages ...	696,319	**353,912**	**342,407**	**44,849**	**40,087**	**4,762**	**651,470**	**313,825**	**337,645**	**4,728**	**4,530**	**198**
2		0–5 ...	**92,942**	45,270	47,672	...	...	...	**92,942**	45,270	47,672	...	...	...
3		5–10 ...	**89,517**	44,704	44,813	**1,822**	1,393	429	**87,695**	43,311	44,384	**34**	27	7
4		10–15 ...	**79,707**	40,879	38,828	**5,826**	4,846	980	**73,881**	36,033	37,848	**451**	403	48
5		15–20 ...	**58,750**	29,068	29,682	**5,412**	4,543	869	**53,338**	24,525	28,813	**846**	798	48
6		20 and over ...	**375,403**	193,991	181 412	**31,789**	29,305	2,484	**343,614**	164,686	178,928	**3,397**	3,302	95
		Musalman.												
1		All ages ...	**58,760**	**30,790**	**27,970**	**7,945**	**6,110**	**1,835**	**50,815**	**24,680**	**26,135**	**487**	**452**	**35**
2		0–5 ...	**9,664**	4,722	4,942	...	...	...	**9,664**	4,722	4,942	...	...	...
3		5–10 ...	**8,839**	4,564	4,275	**397**	235	162	**8,442**	4,329	4,113	6	2	4
4		10–15 ...	**7,533**	3,956	3,577	**1,083**	731	352	**6,450**	3,225	3,225	47	39	8
5		15–20 ...	**5,249**	2,681	2,568	**1,038**	715	323	**4,211**	1,966	2,245	60	52	8
6		20 and over ...	**27,475**	14,867	12,608	**5,427**	4,429	998	**22,048**	10,438	11,610	**374**	359	15
		Christian.												
1		All ages ...	**2,679**	**1,319**	**1,360**	**1,094**	**561**	**533**	**1,585**	**758**	**827**	**621**	**302**	**319**
2		0–5 ...	**427**	223	204	...	...	...	**427**	223	204	...	...	...
3		5–10 ...	**408**	199	209	**89**	40	49	**319**	159	160	19	12	7
4		10–15 ...	**378**	180	198	**237**	112	125	**141**	68	73	**139**	62	77
5		15–20 ...	**308**	134	174	**182**	78	104	**126**	56	70	**142**	57	85
6		20 and over ...	**1,158**	583	575	**586**	331	255	**572**	252	320	**321**	171	150
		Jain.												
1		All ages ...	**6,052**	**3,173**	**2,879**	**879**	**801**	**78**	**5,173**	**2,372**	**2,801**	**50**	**48**	**2**
2		0–5 ...	**741**	367	374	...	...	...	**741**	367	374	...	...	...
3		5–10 ...	**783**	388	395	**25**	22	3	**758**	366	392	...	...	...
4		10–15 ...	**724**	382	342	**122**	102	20	**602**	280	322	1	...	1
5		15–20 ...	**546**	295	251	**108**	90	18	**438**	205	233	10	9	1
6		20 and over ...	**3,258**	1,741	1,517	**624**	587	37	**2,634**	1,154	1,480	**39**	39	...

LITERATE IN																					
Kannada			Telugu			Tamil			Hindi			Hindustani			Marathi			Others			
Persons	Males	Females	Persons	Males	Females	Persons	Males	Females	Persons	Males	Females	Persons	Males	Females	Persons	Males	Females	Persons	Males	Females	Number
15	16	17	18	19	20	21	22	23	24	25	26	27	28	29	30	31	32	33	34	35	
1,509	1,254	255	651	573	78	5,549	4,881	668	21	17	4	33	23	10	32	29	3	499	435	64	1
...	...	...	...	...	...	...	...	...	...	...	...	...	...	...	...	...	...	...	...	...	2
97	59	38	16	13	3	255	176	79	...	...	...	...	...	...	...	...	...	11	5	6	3
194	136	58	34	17	17	720	562	158	1	...	1	1	...	1	...	...	...	18	9	9	4
167	134	33	50	39	11	789	680	109	1	1	...	5	...	5	1	...	1	28	17	11	5
1,051	925	126	551	504	47	3,785	3,463	322	19	16	3	27	23	4	31	29	2	442	404	38	6
89	82	7	32	32	...	479	469	10	50	39	11	979	749	229	2	...	2	321	308	13	1
...	...	...	...	...	...	...	...	...	...	...	...	...	...	...	...	...	...	...	...	...	2
4	2	2	...	...	...	8	7	1	...	...	...	39	20	19	...	...	...	7	5	2	3
9	9	...	5	5	...	27	26	1	4	2	2	112	67	45	...	...	...	20	16	4	4
6	6	...	3	3	...	51	51	...	5	4	1	91	57	34	...	...	...	13	12	1	5
70	65	5	24	24	...	393	385	8	41	33	8	736	605	131	2	...	2	281	275	6	6
72	44	28	65	53	12	3,247	2,470	777	1	1	...	11	6	5	4	4	...	87	65	22	1
...	...	...	...	...	...	...	...	...	...	...	...	...	...	...	...	...	...	...	...	...	2
1	1	...	2	1	1	141	78	63	...	...	...	...	...	...	...	...	...	1	1	...	3
4	2	2	6	5	1	374	214	160	...	...	...	...	...	...	...	...	...	2	1	1	4
6	3	3	6	5	1	377	277	100	...	...	...	...	...	...	...	...	...	4	1	3	5
61	38	23	51	42	9	2,355	1,901	454	1	1	...	11	6	5	4	4	...	80	62	18	6
1	1	...	1	1	...	10	9	1	73	69	4	1	1	...	...	...	...	100	95	5	1
...	...	...	...	...	...	...	...	...	...	...	...	...	...	...	...	...	...	...	...	...	2
...	...	...	...	...	...	...	...	...	5	4	...	...	...	...	...	...	...	...	...	...	3
...	...	...	...	...	...	...	...	...	4	4	1	...	...	...	...	...	...	12	11	1	4
...	...	...	...	...	...	2	2	...	11	11	...	1	1	...	...	...	...	16	15	1	5
1	1	...	1	1	...	8	7	1	53	50	3	...	...	...	...	...	...	72	69	3	6
...	...	...	...	...	...	...	...	...	...	...	...	...	...	...	...	...	...	...	...	...	1
...	...	...	...	...	...	...	...	...	...	...	...	...	...	...	...	...	...	...	...	...	2
...	...	...	...	...	...	...	...	...	...	...	...	...	...	...	...	...	...	...	...	...	3
...	...	...	...	...	...	...	...	...	...	...	...	...	...	...	...	...	...	...	...	...	4
...	...	...	...	...	...	...	...	...	...	...	...	...	...	...	...	...	...	...	...	...	5
...	...	...	...	...	...	...	...	...	...	...	...	...	...	...	...	...	...	...	...	...	6
42,244	37,506	4,738	6,779	6,383	396	1,299	1,061	238	203	156	47	6,193	4,461	1,732	70	61	9	746	615	131	1
...	...	...	...	...	...	...	...	...	...	...	...	...	...	...	...	...	...	...	...	...	2
1,873	1,408	470	84	72	12	37	17	20	10	7	3	338	197	141	1	1	...	8	2	6	3
5,938	4,907	1,031	294	251	43	66	43	23	19	12	7	918	586	332	3	2	1	43	22	21	4
5,356	4,514	842	467	405	62	112	75	37	22	14	8	771	462	309	3	2	1	69	49	20	5
29,077	26,682	2,395	5,934	5,655	279	1,084	926	158	152	123	29	4,166	3,216	950	63	56	7	626	542	84	6
39,075	34,768	4,307	6,478	6,106	372	940	765	175	47	44	3	27	23	4	67	59	8	487	463	24	1
...	...	...	...	...	...	...	...	...	...	...	...	...	...	...	...	...	...	...	...	...	2
1,726	1,321	405	78	68	10	25	7	18	1	1	...	...	...	...	1	1	...	1	1	...	3
5,539	4,606	933	274	235	39	53	35	18	6	6	...	2	2	...	3	2	1	12	10	2	4
4,988	4,198	790	446	385	61	76	51	25	5	5	...	2	1	1	3	2	1	32	27	5	5
26,822	24,643	2,179	5,680	5,418	262	786	672	114	35	32	3	23	20	3	60	54	6	442	425	17	6
1,769	1,699	70	214	210	4	209	206	3	154	110	44	6,155	4,431	1,724	1	1	...	167	66	101	1
...	...	...	...	...	...	...	...	...	...	...	...	...	...	...	...	...	...	...	...	...	2
53	32	21	2	2	...	3	3	...	9	6	3	338	197	141	...	...	...	6	...	6	3
181	153	28	8	5	3	5	4	1	13	6	7	916	584	332	...	...	...	23	5	18	4
211	206	5	15	15	...	15	15	...	17	9	8	769	461	308	...	...	...	21	7	14	5
1,324	1,308	16	189	188	1	186	184	2	115	89	26	4,132	3,189	943	1	1	...	117	54	63	6
606	321	285	82	62	20	148	88	60	1	1	...	11	7	4	1	...	1	15	9	6	1
...	...	...	...	...	...	...	...	...	...	...	...	...	...	...	...	...	...	...	...	...	2
69	28	41	4	2	2	9	7	2	...	...	...	...	...	...	...	...	...	...	...	...	3
105	54	51	10	9	1	8	4	4	...	...	...	...	...	...	...	...	...	1	...	1	4
67	37	30	6	5	1	21	9	12	...	...	...	...	...	...	...	...	...	1	...	1	5
365	202	163	62	46	16	110	68	42	1	1	...	11	7	4	1	...	1	13	9	4	6
792	716	76	5	5	...	2	2	...	1	1	...	...	...	...	1	1	...	77	77	...	1
...	...	...	...	...	...	...	...	...	...	...	...	...	...	...	...	...	...	...	...	...	2
25	22	3	...	...	...	...	...	...	...	...	...	...	...	...	...	...	...	1	1	...	3
113	94	19	2	2	...	...	...	...	...	...	...	...	...	...	...	...	...	7	7	...	4
90	73	17	...	...	...	...	...	...	...	...	...	...	...	...	...	...	...	15	15	...	5
564	527	37	3	3	...	2	2	...	1	1	...	...	...	...	1	1	...	54	54	...	6

Number	District	AGE	POPULATION: Total: Persons	Total: Males	Total: Females	Literate: Persons	Literate: Males	Literate: Females	Illiterate: Persons	Illiterate: Males	Illiterate: Females	English: Persons	English: Males	English: Females
	1	2	3	4	5	6	7	8	9	10	11	12	13	14
	KOLAR DISTRICT.	**Tribal.**												
1		All ages ...	**122**	67	**55**	**2**	**2**	...	**120**	**65**	**55**	...	...	...
2		0–5 ...	**18**	8	10	...	...	...	**18**	8	10	...	...	...
3		5–10 ...	**21**	14	7	...	...	...	**21**	14	7	...	...	...
4		10–15 ...	**18**	11	7	...	...	...	**18**	11	7	...	...	...
5		15–20 ...	**8**	4	4	...	...	...	**8**	4	4	...	...	...
6		20 and over ...	**57**	30	27	**2**	2	...	**55**	28	27	...	...	...
	TUMKUR DISTRICT.	**All Religions.**												
1		All ages ...	**861,405**	**439,144**	**422,261**	**72,308**	**63,769**	**8,539**	**789,097**	**375,375**	**413,722**	**5,603**	**5,276**	**327**
2		0–5 ...	**127,378**	62,753	64,625	...	...	...	**127,378**	62,753	64,625	...	...	...
3		5–10 ...	**119,478**	59,568	59,910	**2,962**	2,260	702	**116,516**	57,308	59,208	**36**	30	6
4		10–15 ...	**107,861**	55,421	52,440	**10,368**	8,511	1,857	**97,493**	46,910	50,583	**719**	648	71
5		15–20 ...	**76,238**	38,272	37,966	**9,327**	7,697	1,630	**66,911**	30,575	36,336	**1,306**	1,237	69
6		20 and over ...	**430,450**	223,130	207,320	**49,651**	45,301	4,350	**380,799**	177,829	202,970	**3,542**	3 361	181
		Hindu.												
1		All ages ...	**806,673**	**410,649**	**396,024**	**63,158**	**56,667**	**6,491**	**743,515**	**353,982**	**389,533**	**4,845**	**4,615**	**230**
2		0–5 ...	**118,585**	58,382	60,203	...	...	...	**118,585**	58,382	60,203	...	...	...
3		5–10 ...	**111,199**	55,373	55,826	**2,581**	2,006	575	**108,618**	53,367	55,251	**31**	27	4
4		10–15 ...	**100,554**	51,591	48,963	**8,964**	7,569	1,395	**91,590**	44,022	47,568	**629**	570	59
5		15–20 ...	**71,232**	35,707	35,525	**8,113**	6,828	1,285	**63,119**	28,879	34,240	**1,131**	1,081	50
6		20 and over ...	**405,103**	209,596	195,507	**43,500**	40,264	3,236	**361,603**	169,332	192,271	**3,054**	2,937	117
		Musalman.												
1		All ages ...	**44,390**	**23,116**	**21,274**	**6,895**	**5,341**	**1,554**	**37,495**	**17,775**	**19,720**	**392**	**383**	**9**
2		0–5 ...	**7,344**	3,642	3,702	...	...	...	**7,344**	3,642	3,702	...	...	...
3		5–10 ...	**6,872**	3,504	3,368	**273**	183	90	**6,599**	3,321	3,278	**2**	2	...
4		10–15 ...	**6,034**	3,167	2,867	**1,033**	675	358	**5,001**	2,492	2,509	**40**	40	...
5		15–20 ...	**4,069**	2,100	1,969	**950**	669	281	**3,119**	1,431	1,688	**106**	103	3
6		20 and over ...	**20,071**	10,703	9,368	**4,639**	3,814	825	**15,432**	6,889	8,543	**244**	238	6
		Christian.												
1		All ages ...	**1,620**	**892**	**728**	**801**	**495**	**306**	**819**	**397**	**422**	**269**	**186**	**83**
2		0–5 ...	**273**	140	133	...	...	...	**273**	140	133	...	...	...
3		5–10 ...	**240**	126	114	**49**	24	25	**191**	102	89	**3**	1	2
4		10–15 ...	**205**	124	81	**150**	101	49	**55**	23	32	**37**	26	11
5		15–20 ...	**150**	87	63	**109**	73	36	**41**	14	27	**49**	33	16
6		20 and over ...	**752**	415	337	**493**	297	196	**259**	118	141	**180**	126	54
		Jain.												
1		All ages ...	**7,340**	**3,814**	**3,526**	**1,434**	**1,248**	**186**	**5,906**	**2,566**	**3,340**	**94**	**92**	**2**
2		0–5 ...	**917**	460	457	...	...	...	**917**	460	457	...	...	...
3		5–10 ...	**958**	473	485	**59**	47	12	**899**	426	473	...	...	...
4		10–15 ...	**898**	461	437	**216**	161	55	**682**	300	382	**13**	12	1
5		15–20 ...	**684**	332	352	**153**	125	28	**531**	207	324	**20**	20	...
6		20 and over ...	**3,883**	2,088	1,795	**1,006**	915	91	**2,877**	1,173	1,704	**61**	60	1
		Tribal.												
1		All ages ...	**1,381**	**672**	**709**	**19**	**17**	**2**	**1,362**	**655**	**707**	...	...	...
2		0–5 ...	**259**	129	130	...	...	...	**259**	129	130	...	...	...
3		5–10 ...	**209**	92	117	...	...	...	**209**	92	117	...	...	...
4		10–15 ...	**170**	78	92	**5**	5	...	**165**	73	92	...	...	...
5		15–20 ...	**103**	46	57	**2**	2	...	**101**	44	57	...	...	...
6		20 and over ...	**640**	327	313	**12**	10	2	**628**	317	311	...	...	...
	MYSORE CITY.	**All Religions.**												
1		All ages ...	**107,142**	**56,772**	**50,370**	**32,595**	**23,858**	**8,737**	**74,547**	**32,914**	**41,633**	**12,093**	**10,688**	**1,405**
2		0–5 ...	**13,759**	6,821	6,938	...	...	...	**13,759**	6,821	6,938	...	...	...
3		5–10 ...	**13,695**	7,091	6,604	**1,969**	1,177	792	**11,726**	5,914	5,812	**152**	89	63
4		10–15 ...	**13,024**	6,947	6,077	**4,936**	3,281	1,655	**8,088**	3,666	4,422	**1,486**	1,204	282
5		15–20 ...	**11,036**	5,975	5,061	**5,068**	3,611	1,457	**5,968**	2,364	3,604	**2,410**	2,098	312
6		20 and over ...	**55,628**	29,938	25,690	**20,622**	15,789	4,833	**35,006**	14,149	20,857	**8,045**	7,297	748
		Hindu.												
1		All ages ...	**84,789**	**44,734**	**40,055**	**26,094**	**19,585**	**6,509**	**58,695**	**25,149**	**33,546**	**9,989**	**9,085**	**904**
2		0–5 ...	**10,860**	5,348	5,512	...	...	...	**10,860**	5,348	5,512	...	...	...
3		5–10 ...	**10,817**	5,603	5,214	**1,628**	995	633	**9,189**	4,608	4,581	**105**	70	35
4		10–15 ...	**10,317**	5,539	4,778	**3,980**	2,701	1,279	**6,337**	2,838	3,499	**1,260**	1,062	198
5		15–20 ...	**8,701**	4,780	3,921	**4,047**	2,980	1,067	**4,654**	1,800	2,854	**2,028**	1,814	214
6		20 and over ...	**44,094**	23,464	20,630	**16,439**	12,909	3,530	**27,655**	10,555	17,100	**6,596**	6,139	457
		Musalman.												
1		All ages ...	**17,772**	**9,661**	**8,111**	**4,422**	**3,042**	**1,380**	**13,350**	**6,619**	**6,731**	**939**	**865**	**74**
2		0–5 ...	**2,310**	1,167	1,143	...	...	...	**2,310**	1,167	1,143	...	...	...
3		5–10 ...	**2,307**	1,199	1,108	**226**	130	96	**2,081**	1,069	1,012	**3**	...	3
4		10–15 ...	**2,130**	1,114	1,016	**636**	415	221	**1,494**	699	795	**90**	78	12
5		15–20 ...	**1,784**	915	869	**660**	430	230	**1,124**	485	639	**169**	148	21
6		20 and over ...	**9,241**	5,266	3,975	**2,900**	2,067	833	**6,341**	3,199	3,142	**677**	639	38

LITERATE IN																					
Kannada			Telugu			Tamil			Hindi			Hindustani			Marathi			Others			
Persons	Males	Females	Persons	Males	Females	Persons	Males	Females	Persons	Males	Females	Persons	Males	Females	Persons	Males	Females	Persons	Males	Females	Number
15	16	17	18	19	20	21	22	23	24	25	26	27	28	29	30	31	32	33	34	35	
2	2	...	...	...	...	...	...	...	...	...	...	...	...	...	...	...	...	...	...	...	1
...	...	...	...	...	...	...	...	...	...	...	...	...	...	...	...	...	...	...	...	...	2
...	...	...	...	...	...	...	...	...	...	...	...	...	...	...	...	...	...	...	...	...	3
...	...	...	...	...	...	...	...	...	...	...	...	...	...	...	...	...	...	...	...	...	4
...	...	...	...	...	...	...	...	...	...	...	...	...	...	...	...	...	...	...	...	...	5
2	2	...	...	...	...	...	...	...	...	...	...	...	...	...	...	...	...	...	...	...	6
65,994	59,075	6,919	2,071	1,882	189	431	325	106	217	165	52	5,436	4,015	1,421	105	91	14	581	442	139	1
...	...	...	...	...	...	...	...	...	...	...	...	...	...	...	...	...	...	...	...	...	2
2,700	2,091	609	35	28	7	7	5	2	3	2	1	241	154	87	2	2	...	3	2	1	3
9,363	7,866	1,497	189	163	26	18	10	8	19	12	7	854	521	333	6	6	...	33	14	19	4
8,541	7,211	1,330	159	128	31	41	20	21	22	19	3	763	505	258	7	6	1	91	62	29	5
45,390	41,907	3,483	1,688	1,563	125	365	290	75	173	132	41	3,578	2,835	743	90	77	13	454	364	90	6
61,538	55,214	6,324	1,959	1,784	175	286	203	83	80	64	16	75	73	2	103	89	14	226	218	8	1
...	...	...	...	...	...	...	...	...	...	...	...	...	...	...	...	...	...	...	...	...	2
2,555	1,985	570	33	27	6	6	4	2	2	2	...	1	1	...	2	2	...	1	1	...	3
8,776	7,408	1,373	182	159	23	14	7	7	8	7	1	1	1	...	6	6	...	6	3	3	4
7,975	6,723	1,252	143	113	30	27	9	18	11	10	1	5	5	...	7	6	1	30	27	3	5
42,232	39,103	3,129	1,601	1,485	116	239	183	56	59	45	14	68	66	2	88	75	13	189	187	2	6
2,342	2,203	139	92	85	7	91	87	4	131	95	36	5,360	3,942	1,418	1	1	...	305	177	128	1
...	...	...	...	...	...	...	...	...	...	...	...	...	...	...	...	...	...	...	...	...	2
40	35	5	1	1	...	1	1	...	1	...	1	240	153	87	...	...	...	2	1	1	3
226	202	24	5	3	2	3	3	...	10	4	6	853	520	333	...	...	...	25	10	15	4
312	291	21	15	15	...	11	10	1	10	8	2	758	500	258	...	...	...	58	32	26	5
1,764	1,675	89	71	66	5	76	73	3	110	83	27	3,509	2,769	740	1	1	...	220	134	86	6
717	446	271	10	5	5	51	32	19	...	...	...	1	...	1	...	...	...	6	5	1	1
...	...	...	...	...	...	...	...	...	...	...	...	...	...	...	...	...	...	...	...	...	2
46	24	22	1	...	1	...	...	...	...	...	...	...	...	...	...	...	...	...	...	...	3
145	98	47	1	1	...	1	...	1	...	...	...	...	...	...	...	...	...	...	...	...	4
102	73	29	1	...	1	3	1	2	...	...	...	...	...	...	...	...	...	...	...	...	5
424	251	173	7	4	3	47	31	16	...	...	...	1	...	1	...	...	...	6	5	1	6
1,380	1,197	183	8	6	2	3	3	...	6	6	...	...	...	...	1	1	...	44	42	2	1
...	...	...	...	...	...	...	...	...	...	...	...	...	...	...	...	...	...	...	...	...	2
59	47	12	...	...	...	...	...	...	...	...	...	...	...	...	...	...	...	...	...	...	3
211	158	63	1	...	1	...	...	...	1	1	...	...	...	...	...	...	...	2	1	1	4
150	122	28	...	...	...	...	...	...	1	1	...	...	...	...	...	...	...	3	3	...	5
960	870	90	7	6	1	3	3	...	4	4	...	...	...	...	1	1	...	39	38	1	6
17	15	2	2	2	...	...	...	...	...	...	...	...	...	...	...	...	...	...	...	...	1
...	...	...	...	...	...	...	...	...	...	...	...	...	...	...	...	...	...	...	...	...	2
...	...	...	...	...	...	...	...	...	...	...	...	...	...	...	...	...	...	...	...	...	3
5	5	...	...	...	...	...	...	...	...	...	...	...	...	...	...	...	...	...	...	...	4
2	2	...	...	...	...	...	...	...	...	...	...	...	...	...	...	...	...	...	...	...	5
10	8	2	2	2	...	...	...	...	...	...	...	...	...	...	...	...	...	...	...	...	6
26,539	20,054	6,485	839	674	165	2,038	1,431	607	635	521	114	5,638	3,788	1,850	304	236	68	1,672	1,431	241	1
...	...	...	...	...	...	...	...	...	...	...	...	...	...	...	...	...	...	...	...	...	2
1,637	987	650	18	16	2	44	28	16	15	6	9	223	128	95	8	7	1	20	12	8	3
4,162	2,856	1,306	38	20	18	166	80	86	63	41	22	603	385	218	14	10	4	141	118	23	4
4,245	3,134	1,111	82	58	24	223	129	94	115	102	13	1,144	417	727	37	26	11	219	186	33	5
16,495	13,077	3,418	701	580	121	1,605	1,194	411	442	372	70	3,668	2,858	810	245	193	52	1,292	1,115	177	6
24,572	18,576	5,996	797	640	157	1,510	1,108	402	530	425	105	100	94	6	262	201	61	1,165	1,085	80	1
...	...	...	...	...	...	...	...	...	...	...	...	...	...	...	...	...	...	...	...	...	2
1,561	948	613	17	15	2	30	23	7	13	4	9	2	2	...	6	5	1	6	1	5	3
3,891	2,671	1,220	35	17	18	69	29	40	53	32	21	2	1	1	12	9	3	80	74	6	4
3,918	2,906	1,012	77	54	23	144	93	51	99	89	10	8	7	1	33	22	11	163	150	13	5
15,202	12,051	3,151	668	554	114	1,267	963	304	365	300	65	88	84	4	211	165	46	916	860	56	6
823	775	48	7	7	...	46	44	2	41	34	7	5,520	3,678	1,842	1	1	...	431	303	128	1
...	...	...	...	...	...	...	...	...	...	...	...	...	...	...	...	...	...	...	...	...	2
6	6	...	...	...	...	...	...	...	...	...	...	220	125	95	...	...	...	14	11	3	3
75	65	10	...	...	...	...	...	...	6	5	1	601	384	217	...	...	...	55	42	13	4
91	83	8	...	...	...	3	3	...	7	5	2	1,135	409	726	1	1	...	49	32	17	5
651	621	30	7	7	...	43	41	2	28	24	4	3,564	2,760	804	...	...	...	313	218	95	6

Number	District	AGE	POPULATION — Total — Persons	Total — Males	Total — Females	Literate — Persons	Literate — Males	Literate — Females	Illiterate — Persons	Illiterate — Males	Illiterate — Females	English — Persons	English — Males	English — Females
	1	2	3	4	5	6	7	8	9	10	11	12	13	14
	MYSORE CITY.	**Christian.**												
1		All ages ...	3,947	1,956	1,991	1,713	933	780	2,234	1,023	1,211	1,028	621	407
2		0–5 ...	512	267	245	...	...	...	512	267	245	...	...	...
3		5–10 —	497	243	254	97	39	58	400	204	196	42	18	24
4		10–15 ...	501	239	262	285	141	144	216	98	118	128	59	69
5		15–20 ...	468	218	250	296	147	149	172	71	101	178	104	74
6		20 and over ...	1,969	989	980	1,035	606	429	934	383	551	680	440	240
		Jain.												
1		All ages ...	549	372	177	316	265	51	233	107	126	97	94	3
2		0–5 ...	65	33	32	...	...	...	65	33	32	...	...	...
3		5–10 ...	66	42	24	15	10	5	51	32	19	1	...	1
4		10–15 ...	64	48	16	28	20	8	36	28	8	4	4	...
5		15–20 ...	72	56	16	57	49	8	15	7	8	28	28	...
6		20 and over ...	282	193	89	216	186	30	66	7	59	64	62	2
		Tribal.												
1		All ages ...	7	6	1	1	1	...	6	5	1	...	...	...
2		0–5 ...	...	...	...	...	...	...	...	...	...	...	...	...
3		5–10 ...	...	...	...	...	...	...	...	...	...	...	...	...
4		10–15 ...	...	...	...	...	...	...	...	...	...	...	...	...
5		15–20 ...	...	...	...	...	...	...	...	...	...	...	...	...
6		20 and over ...	7	6	1	1	1	...	6	5	1	...	...	...
	MYSORE DISTRICT.	**All Religions.**												
1		All ages ...	1,403,984	703,838	700,146	70,962	62,745	8,217	1,333,022	641,093	691,929	5,350	5,070	280
2		0–5 ...	196,556	97,738	100,818	...	...	...	196,556	97,738	100,818	...	...	...
3		5–10 ...	193,075	96,699	96,376	3,023	2,375	648	190,052	94,324	95,728	24	16	8
4		10–15 ...	179,097	92,838	86,259	9,888	8,173	1,715	169,209	84,665	84,544	501	461	40
5		15–20 ...	125,816	63,025	62,791	8,725	7,191	1,534	117,091	55,834	61,257	863	801	62
6		20 and over ...	707,440	353,538	353,902	49,326	45,006	4,320	658,114	308,532	349,582	3,962	3,792	170
		Hindu.												
1		All ages ...	1,348,180	674,201	673,979	62,617	56,294	6,323	1,285,563	617,907	667,656	4,774	4,575	199
2		0–5 ...	190,458	93,656	96,802	...	...	...	190,458	93,656	96,802	...	...	...
3		5–10 ...	185,177	92,625	92,552	2,699	2,181	518	182,478	90,444	92,034	20	14	6
4		10–15 ...	171,909	89,036	82,873	8,953	7,577	1,376	162,956	81,459	81,497	466	435	31
5		15 20 ...	120,571	60,269	60,302	7,719	6,496	1,223	112,852	53,773	59,079	791	742	49
6		20 and over ...	680,065	338,615	341,450	43,246	40,040	3,206	636,819	298,575	338,244	3,497	3,384	113
		Musalman.												
1		All ages ...	43,485	23,231	20,254	6,852	5,276	1,576	36,633	17,955	18,678	258	242	16
2		0–5 ...	6,293	3,175	3,118	...	...	...	6,293	3,175	3,118	...	...	...
3		5–10 ...	6,271	3,228	3,043	259	152	107	6,012	3,076	2,936	...	...	...
4		10–15	5,721	3,041	2,680	767	486	281	4,954	2,555	2,399	20	16	4
5		15–20 ...	4,069	2,192	1,877	808	556	252	3,261	1,636	1,625	29	24	5
6		20 and over ...	21,131	11,595	9,536	5.018	4,082	936	16,113	7,513	8,600	209	202	7
		Christian.												
1		All ages ...	3,375	1,828	1,547	778	577	201	2,597	1,251	1,346	271	208	63
2		0–5 ...	498	258	240	...	...	...	498	258	240	...	...	...
3		5–10 ...	462	239	223	33	17	16	429	222	207	3	1	2
4		10–15 ...	414	212	202	90	57	33	324	155	169	14	9	5
5		15–20 ...	341	184	157	114	80	34	227	104	123	40	32	8
6		20 and over ...	1,660	935	725	541	423	118	1,119	512	607	214	166	48
		Jain.												
1		All ages ...	2,514	1,250	1,264	678	563	115	1,836	687	1,149	44	42	2
2		0–5 ...	347	178	169	...	...	...	347	178	169	...	...	...
3		5–10 ...	317	162	155	26	19	7	291	143	148	1	1	...
4		10–15 ...	292	150	142	77	52	25	215	98	117	1	1	...
5		15–20 ...	239	122	117	79	55	24	160	67	93	3	3	...
6		20 and over ...	1,319	638	681	496	437	59	823	201	622	39	37	2
		Tribal.												
1		All ages ...	6,390	3,312	3,078	27	26	1	6,363	3,286	3,077	2	2	...
2		0–5 ...	952	468	484	...	...	...	952	468	484	...	...	...
3		5–10 ...	845	444	401	6	6	...	839	438	401	...	...	...
4		10–15 ...	758	398	360	1	1	...	757	397	360	...	...	...
5		15–20 ...	591	255	336	1	1	...	590	254	336	...	...	...
6		20 and over ...	3,244	1,747	1,497	19	18	1	3,225	1,729	1,496	2	2	...
	CHITALDRUG DISTRICT.	**All Religions.**												
1		All ages ...	656,569	336,786	319,783	56,170	51,171	4,999	600,399	285,615	314,784	3,556	3,394	162
2		0–5 ...	98,572	47,795	50,777	...	...	...	98,572	47,795	50,777	...	...	...
3		5–10 ...	89,502	44,499	45,003	2,093	1,628	465	87,409	42,871	44,538	11	10	1
4		10–15 ...	81,562	42,109	39,453	8,330	7,098	1,232	73,232	35,011	38,221	370	337	33
5		15–20 ...	61,093	30,779	30,314	7,465	6,482	983	53,628	24,297	29,331	739	714	25
6		20 and over ...	325,840	171,604	154,236	38,282	35,963	2,319	287,558	135,641	151,917	2,436	2,333	103

LITERATE IN

Kannada			Telugu			Tamil			Hindi			Hindustani			Marathi			Others			
Persons	Males	Females	Persons	Males	Females	Persons	Males	Females	Persons	Males	Females	Persons	Males	Females	Persons	Males	Females	Persons	Males	Females	Number
15	16	17	18	19	20	21	22	23	24	25	26	27	28	29	30	31	32	33	34	35	
901	511	390	34	26	8	468	269	199	1	...	1	12	11	1	34	31	3	21	...	21	1
...	...	...	...	...	...	...	...	...	...	...	...	...	...	...	...	...	...	...	...	...	2
54	22	32	1	1	...	13	4	9	...	...	...	...	...	...	2	2	...	...	...	...	3
168	100	68	3	3	...	97	51	46	...	...	...	...	...	...	...	...	...	3	...	3	4
193	109	84	5	4	1	75	32	43	...	...	...	...	...	...	4	4	...	1	...	1	5
486	280	206	25	18	7	283	182	101	1	...	1	12	11	1	28	25	3	17	...	17	6
231	183	48	1	1	...	7	7	...	53	52	1	2	2	...	1	1	...	44	43	1	1
...	...	...	...	...	...	...	...	...	...	...	...	...	...	...	...	...	...	...	...	...	2
15	10	5	...	...	...	1	1	...	1	1	...	...	...	...	...	...	...	...	...	...	3
26	18	8	...	...	...	...	...	...	2	2	...	...	...	...	...	...	...	2	2	...	4
42	35	7	...	...	...	...	...	...	8	7	1	1	1	...	...	...	...	4	4	...	5
148	120	28	1	1	...	6	6	...	42	42	...	1	1	...	1	1	...	38	37	1	6
1	1	...	...	...	...	...	...	...	...	...	...	...	...	...	...	...	...	...	...	...	1
...	...	...	...	...	...	...	...	...	...	...	...	...	...	...	...	...	...	...	...	...	2
...	...	...	...	...	...	...	...	...	...	...	...	...	...	...	...	...	...	...	...	...	3
...	...	...	...	...	...	...	...	...	...	...	...	...	...	...	...	...	...	...	...	...	4
...	...	...	...	...	...	...	...	...	...	...	...	...	...	...	...	...	...	...	...	...	5
1	1	...	...	...	...	...	...	...	...	...	...	...	...	...	...	...	...	...	...	...	6
64,344	57,827	6,517	527	443	84	1,882	1,591	291	194	171	23	5,531	4,071	1,460	113	92	21	1,084	893	191	1
...	...	...	...	...	...	...	...	...	...	...	...	...	...	...	...	...	...	...	...	...	2
2,786	2,244	542	3	1	2	23	16	7	5	3	2	218	120	98	...	...	...	11	5	6	3
9,226	7,796	1,430	15	10	5	87	60	27	13	10	3	646	387	259	1	...	1	60	28	32	4
7,941	6,679	1,262	43	24	19	172	118	54	14	9	5	659	430	229	3	1	2	140	99	41	5
44,391	41,108	3,283	466	408	58	1,600	1,397	203	162	149	13	4,008	3,134	874	109	91	18	873	761	112	6
61,570	55,408	6,162	493	415	78	1,121	916	205	104	96	8	70	67	3	104	84	20	593	576	17	1
...	...	...	...	...	...	...	...	...	...	...	...	...	...	...	...	...	...	...	...	...	2
2,685	2,172	513	3	1	2	12	10	2	1	1	...	...	...	...	...	...	...	3	2	1	3
8,915	7,549	1,366	15	10	5	39	26	13	7	6	1	...	...	...	1	...	1	22	22	...	4
7,591	6,405	1,186	41	24	17	89	52	37	5	3	2	7	5	2	3	1	2	61	55	6	5
42,379	39,282	3,097	434	380	54	981	828	153	91	86	5	63	62	1	100	83	17	507	497	10	6
1,616	1,426	90	15	14	1	569	528	41	83	68	15	5,456	4,001	1,455	5	5	...	441	283	158	1
...	...	...	...	...	...	...	...	...	...	...	...	...	...	...	...	...	...	...	...	...	2
38	30	8	...	...	...	7	4	3	4	2	2	218	120	98	...	...	...	7	3	4	3
151	140	11	...	...	...	41	31	10	6	4	2	646	387	259	...	...	...	37	6	31	4
176	155	21	...	...	...	60	52	8	8	5	3	652	425	227	...	...	...	73	41	32	5
1,151	1,101	50	15	14	1	461	441	20	65	57	8	3,940	3,069	871	5	5	...	324	233	91	6
555	405	150	15	10	5	183	140	43	3	3	...	4	2	2	3	2	1	38	23	15	1
...	...	...	...	...	...	...	...	...	...	...	...	...	...	...	...	...	...	...	...	...	2
31	17	14	...	...	...	4	2	2	...	...	...	...	...	...	...	...	...	1	...	1	3
82	54	28	...	...	...	7	3	4	...	...	...	...	...	...	...	...	...	1	...	1	4
90	60	30	2	...	2	23	14	9	...	...	...	...	...	...	...	...	...	6	3	3	5
352	274	78	13	10	3	149	121	28	3	3	...	4	2	2	3	2	1	30	20	10	6
671	557	114	2	2	...	4	3	1	2	2	...	1	1	...	1	1	...	12	11	1	1
...	...	...	...	...	...	...	...	...	...	...	...	...	...	...	...	...	...	...	...	...	2
26	19	7	...	...	...	...	...	...	...	...	...	...	...	...	...	...	...	...	...	...	3
77	52	25	...	...	...	...	...	...	...	...	...	...	...	...	...	...	...	...	...	...	4
79	55	24	...	...	...	...	...	...	...	...	...	...	...	...	...	...	...	...	...	...	5
489	431	58	2	2	...	4	3	1	2	2	...	1	1	...	1	1	...	12	11	1	6
23	23	...	1	1	...	5	4	1	1	1	...	...	...	...	...	...	...	...	...	...	1
...	...	...	...	...	...	...	...	...	...	...	...	...	...	...	...	...	...	...	...	...	2
6	6	...	...	...	...	...	...	...	...	...	...	...	...	...	...	...	...	...	...	...	3
1	1	...	...	...	...	...	...	...	...	...	...	...	...	...	...	...	...	...	...	...	4
1	1	...	...	...	...	...	...	...	...	...	...	...	...	...	...	...	...	...	...	...	5
15	15	...	1	1	...	5	4	1	1	1	...	...	...	...	...	...	...	...	...	...	6
52,659	48,408	4,251	779	696	83	435	336	99	176	152	24	2,430	1,832	598	214	175	39	410	365	45	1
...	...	...	...	...	...	...	...	...	...	...	...	...	...	...	...	...	...	...	...	...	2
1,995	1,573	422	5	2	3	5	2	3	3	3	...	91	50	41	1	1	...	2	2	...	3
7,940	6,844	1,096	19	14	5	21	8	13	8	5	3	390	266	124	18	8	5	30	22	8	4
7,070	6,227	843	58	36	22	27	14	13	27	23	4	356	249	107	14	6	8	44	37	7	5
35,654	33,764	1,890	697	644	53	382	312	70	138	121	17	1,593	1,267	326	186	160	26	334	304	30	6

Number	District	AGE	POPULATION											
			Total			Literate			Illiterate			English		
			Persons	Males	Females	Persons	Males	Females	Persons	Males	Females	Persons	Males	Females
	1	2	3	4	5	6	7	8	9	10	11	12	13	14
	CHITALDRUG DISTRICT.	**Hindu.**												
1		All ages ...	614,755	314,839	299,916	50,884	46,667	4,217	563,871	268,172	295,699	3,186	3,052	134
2		0-5 ...	91,200	44,371	46,829	...	...	...	91,200	44,371	46,829	...	...	...
3		5-10 ...	83,448	41,399	42,049	1,944	1,527	417	81,504	39,872	41,632	8	7	1
4		10-15 ...	76,356	39,288	37,068	7,649	6,572	1,077	68,707	32,716	35,991	340	308	32
5		15-20 ...	57,144	28,740	28,404	6,803	5,959	844	50,341	22,781	27,560	674	650	24
6		20 and over ...	306,607	161,041	145,566	34,488	32,609	1,879	272,119	128,432	143,687	2,164	2,087	77
		Musalman.												
1		All ages ...	36,841	19 271	17,570	4,510	3,848	662	32,331	15,423	16,908	260	257	3
2		0-5 ...	6,524	3,026	3,498	...	...	...	6,524	3,026	3,498	...	...	...
3		5-10 ...	5,343	2,734	2,609	127	82	45	5,216	2,652	2,564	...	...	...
4		10-15 ...	4,597	2,473	2,124	578	441	137	4,019	2,032	1,987	22	22	...
5		15-20 ...	3,488	1,793	1,695	566	446	120	2,922	1,347	1,575	56	56	...
6		20 and over ...	16,889	9,245	7,644	3,239	2,879	360	13,650	6,366	7,284	182	179	3
		Christian.												
1		All ages ...	515	275	240	211	148	63	304	127	177	77	54	23
2		0-5 ...	98	44	54	...	...	...	98	44	54	...	...	...
3		5-10 ...	62	31	31	7	6	1	55	25	30	2	2	...
4		10-15 ...	52	29	23	29	23	6	23	6	17	5	4	1
5		15-20 ...	52	25	27	18	10	8	34	15	19	4	3	1
6		20 and over ...	251	146	105	157	109	48	94	37	57	66	45	21
		Jain.												
1		All ages ...	1,180	696	484	518	464	54	662	232	430	25	24	1
2		0-5 ...	146	74	72	...	...	...	146	74	72	...	...	...
3		5-10 ...	140	79	61	11	9	2	129	70	59	...	...	...
4		10-15 ...	144	85	59	66	54	12	78	31	47	3	3	...
5		15-20 ...	136	83	53	70	59	11	66	24	42	4	4	...
6		20 and over ...	614	375	239	371	342	29	243	33	210	18	17	1
		Tribal.												
1		All ages ...	3,269	1,699	1,570	39	38	1	3,230	1,661	1,569	1	1	...
2		0-5 ...	602	279	323	...	...	...	602	279	323	...	...	...
3		5-10 ...	508	255	253	3	3	...	505	252	253	...	...	...
4		10-15 ...	413	234	179	8	8	...	405	226	179	...	...	...
5		15-20 ...	273	138	135	8	8	...	265	130	135	1	1	...
6		20 and over ...	1,473	793	680	20	19	1	1,453	774	679	...	...	...
	HASSAN DISTRICT.	**All Religions.**												
1		All ages ...	596,937	300,746	296,191	51,875	45,863	6,012	545,062	254,883	290,179	4,237	3,986	251
2		0-5 ...	80,528	39,292	41,236	...	...	...	80,528	39,292	41,236	...	...	...
3		5-10 ...	80,219	39,531	40,688	2,140	1,612	528	78,079	37,919	40,160	18	14	4
4		10-15 ...	78,177	40,141	38,036	7,764	6,360	1,404	70,413	33,781	36,632	469	430	39
5		15-20 ...	56,405	29,030	27,375	6,692	5,551	1,141	49,713	23,479	26,234	707	655	52
6		20 and over ...	301,608	152,752	148,856	35,279	32,340	2,939	266,329	120,412	145,917	3,043	2,887	156
		Hindu.												
1		All ages ...	567,139	284,490	282 649	45,729	41,149	4,580	521,410	243,341	278,069	3,619	3,470	149
2		0-5 ...	75,962	37,046	38,916	...	...	...	75,962	37,046	38,916	...	...	...
3		5-10 ...	76,267	37,506	38,761	1,923	1,490	433	74,344	36,016	38,328	15	14	1
4		10-15 ...	74,512	38,164	36,348	6,923	5,816	1,107	67,589	32,348	35,241	433	395	38
5		15-20 ...	53,495	27,416	26,079	5,898	5,015	883	47,597	22,401	25,196	606	568	38
6		20 and over ...	286,903	144,358	142,545	30,985	28,828	2,157	255,918	115,530	140,388	2,565	2,493	72
		Musalman.												
1		All ages ...	21,487	11,835	9,652	4,172	3,273	899	17,315	8,562	8,753	260	238	22
2		0-5 ...	3,414	1,693	1,721	...	...	...	3,414	1,693	1,721	...	...	...
3		5-10 ...	2,868	1,488	1,380	145	87	58	2,723	1,401	1,322	...	...	...
4		10-15 ...	2,616	1,438	1,178	576	383	193	2,040	1,055	985	23	22	1
5		15-20 ...	2,066	1,160	906	531	366	165	1,535	794	741	53	47	6
6		20 and over ...	10,523	6,056	4,467	2,920	2,437	483	7,603	3,619	3,984	184	169	15
		Christian.												
1		All ages ...	5,280	2,840	2,440	1,168	766	402	4,112	2,074	2,038	304	224	80
2		0-5 ...	720	351	369	...	...	...	720	351	369	...	...	...
3		5-10 ...	680	336	344	41	15	26	639	321	318	3	...	3
4		10-15 ...	668	336	332	152	76	76	516	260	256	5	5	...
5		15-20 ...	541	286	255	148	67	81	393	219	174	34	26	8
6		20 and over ...	2,671	1,531	1,140	827	608	219	1,844	923	921	262	193	69
		Jain.												
1		All ages ...	1,941	1,044	897	789	658	131	1,152	386	766	54	54	...
2		0-5 ...	250	121	129	...	...	...	250	121	129	...	...	...
3		5-10 ...	235	120	115	29	18	11	206	102	104	...	...	...
4		10-15 ...	238	132	106	111	83	28	127	49	78	8	8	...
5		15-20 ...	220	124	96	112	100	12	108	24	84	14	14	...
6		20 and over ...	998	547	451	537	457	80	461	90	371	32	32	...

LITERATE IN																					
Kannada			Telugu			Tamil			Hindi			Hindustani			Marathi			Others			
Persons	Males	Females	Persons	Males	Females	Persons	Males	Females	Persons	Males	Females	Persons	Males	Females	Persons	Males	Females	Persons	Males	Females	Number
15	16	17	18	19	20	21	22	23	24	25	26	27	28	29	30	31	32	33	34	35	
49,626	45,524	4,102	702	626	76	292	219	73	30	24	6	28	26	2	190	155	35	166	159	7	1
...	...	...	...	...	...	...	...	...	...	...	...	...	...	...	...	...	...	...	...	...	2
1,938	1,525	413	5	2	3	3	...	3	...	...	...	...	...	...	1	1	...	...	...	...	3
7,616	6,552	1,064	17	12	5	11	3	8	2	...	2	1	1	...	12	7	5	5	3	2	4
6,747	5,924	823	50	30	20	19	9	10	1	...	1	1	1	...	11	5	6	10	9	1	5
33,325	31,523	1,802	630	582	48	259	207	52	27	24	3	26	24	2	166	142	24	151	147	4	6
2,540	2,475	65	61	58	3	66	63	3	77	61	16	2,388	1,794	594	7	7	...	89	62	27	1
...	...	...	...	...	...	...	...	...	...	...	...	...	...	...	...	...	...	...	...	...	2
43	37	6	...	...	...	...	...	...	...	...	...	91	50	41	...	...	...	...	...	...	3
245	229	16	2	2	...	...	...	...	4	3	1	385	263	122	...	...	...	8	2	6	4
265	257	8	5	4	1	4	3	1	14	11	3	354	245	109	...	...	...	13	8	5	5
1,987	1,952	35	54	52	2	62	60	2	59	47	12	1,556	1,236	322	7	7	...	68	52	16	6
122	85	37	14	11	3	76	53	23	...	...	...	5	3	2	2	1	1	12	8	4	1
...	...	...	...	...	...	...	...	...	...	...	...	...	...	...	...	...	...	...	...	...	2
4	3	1	...	...	...	2	2	...	...	...	...	...	...	...	...	...	...	...	...	...	3
22	18	4	...	...	...	10	5	5	...	...	...	...	...	...	...	...	...	...	...	...	4
10	6	4	2	2	...	4	2	2	...	...	...	...	...	...	...	...	...	...	...	...	5
86	58	28	12	9	3	60	44	16	...	...	...	5	3	2	2	1	1	12	8	4	6
332	286	46	2	1	1	1	1	...	69	67	2	5	5	...	11	9	2	135	130	5	1
...	...	...	...	...	...	...	...	...	...	...	...	...	...	...	...	...	...	...	...	...	2
7	5	2	...	...	...	...	...	...	3	3	...	...	...	...	...	...	...	1	1	...	3
49	37	12	...	...	...	...	...	...	2	2	...	...	...	...	1	1	...	17	17	...	4
40	32	8	1	...	1	...	...	...	12	12	...	1	1	...	3	1	2	21	20	1	5
236	212	24	1	1	...	1	1	...	52	50	2	4	4	...	7	7	...	96	92	4	6
39	38	1	...	...	...	...	...	...	...	...	...	...	...	...	...	...	...	...	...	...	1
...	...	...	...	...	...	...	...	...	...	...	...	...	...	...	...	...	...	...	...	...	2
3	3	...	...	...	...	...	...	...	...	...	...	...	...	...	...	...	...	...	...	...	3
8	8	...	...	...	...	...	...	...	...	...	...	...	...	...	...	...	...	...	...	...	4
8	8	...	...	...	...	...	...	...	...	...	...	...	...	...	...	...	...	...	...	...	5
20	19	1	...	...	...	...	...	...	...	...	...	...	...	...	...	...	...	...	...	...	6
46,903	41,917	4,986	285	238	47	754	640	114	189	156	33	3,020	2,161	859	77	64	13	621	590	31	1
...	...	...	...	...	...	...	...	...	...	...	...	...	...	...	...	...	...	...	...	...	2
1,992	1,526	466	2	...	2	8	4	4	2	1	1	135	79	56	1	...	1	7	6	1	3
7,250	6,039	1,211	10	7	3	23	17	6	22	19	3	475	288	187	3	3	...	38	33	5	4
5,192	4,235	957	21	18	3	76	55	21	32	31	1	409	251	158	9	5	4	74	68	6	5
32,469	30,117	2,352	252	213	39	647	564	83	133	105	28	2,001	1,543	458	64	56	8	502	483	19	6
44,177	39,680	4,497	254	210	44	365	306	59	41	32	9	23	23	...	65	52	13	286	275	11	1
...	...	...	...	...	...	...	...	...	...	...	...	...	...	...	...	...	...	...	...	...	2
1,921	1,489	432	2	...	2	3	1	2	1	1	...	...	...	...	1	...	1	3	2	1	3
6,901	5,801	1,100	10	7	3	11	6	5	8	5	3	1	1	...	2	2	...	14	10	4	4
4,849	3,973	876	18	15	3	27	20	7	2	1	1	3	3	...	9	5	4	15	14	1	5
30,506	28,417	2,089	224	188	36	324	279	45	30	25	5	19	19	...	53	45	8	254	249	5	6
1,182	1,142	40	17	17	...	227	219	8	60	51	9	2,989	2,133	856	5	5	...	135	124	11	1
...	...	...	...	...	...	...	...	...	...	...	...	...	...	...	...	...	...	...	...	...	2
10	8	2	...	...	...	...	...	...	...	...	...	135	79	56	...	...	...	1	1	...	3
104	96	8	...	...	...	8	8	...	3	3	...	474	287	187	...	...	...	9	8	1	4
130	127	3	3	3	...	29	26	3	5	5	...	404	247	157	...	...	...	21	19	2	5
938	911	27	14	14	...	190	185	5	52	43	9	1,976	1,520	456	5	5	...	104	96	8	6
894	560	334	14	11	3	159	112	47	1	1	...	6	4	2	1	1	...	76	69	7	1
...	...	...	...	...	...	...	...	...	...	...	...	...	...	...	...	...	...	...	...	...	2
32	11	21	...	...	...	5	3	2	...	...	...	...	...	...	...	...	...	1	1	...	3
144	69	75	...	...	...	4	3	1	...	...	...	...	...	...	...	...	...	...	...	...	4
122	55	67	...	...	...	19	8	11	...	...	...	1	1	...	...	...	...	5	3	2	5
596	425	171	14	11	3	131	98	33	1	1	...	5	3	2	1	1	...	70	65	5	6
634	519	115	...	...	...	2	2	...	87	72	15	2	1	1	6	6	...	124	122	2	1
...	...	...	...	...	...	...	...	...	...	...	...	...	...	...	...	...	...	...	...	...	2
27	16	11	...	...	...	...	...	...	1	...	1	...	...	...	...	...	...	2	2	...	3
101	73	28	...	...	...	...	...	...	11	11	...	...	...	...	1	1	...	15	15	...	4
87	76	11	...	...	...	...	...	...	25	25	...	1	...	1	...	...	...	33	32	1	5
419	354	65	...	...	...	2	2	...	50	36	14	1	1	...	5	5	...	74	73	1	6

Number	District	AGE		POPULATION											
				Total			Literate			Illiterate			English		
				Persons	Males	Females	Persons	Males	Females	Persons	Males	Females	Persons	Males	Females
	1	2		3	4	5	6	7	8	9	10	11	12	13	14
		Tribal.													
1	HASSAN DISTRICT.	All ages	...	1,089	536	553	17	17	...	1,072	519	553	...	...	...
2		0–5	...	182	81	101	...	...	...	182	81	101	...	...	...
3		5–10	...	169	81	88	2	2	...	167	79	88	...	...	...
4		10–15	...	143	71	72	2	2	...	141	69	72	...	...	...
5		15–20	...	83	44	39	3	3	...	80	41	39	...	...	...
6		20 and over	...	512	259	253	10	10	...	502	249	253	...	...	...
		All Religions.													
1	KADUR DISTRICT	All ages	...	347,715	184,389	163,326	37,227	32,402	4,825	310,488	151,987	158,501	3,597	3,359	238
2		0–5	...	44,265	21,429	22,836	...	...	...	44,265	21,429	22,836	...	...	...
3		5–10	...	44,713	22,292	22,421	1,768	1,284	484	42,945	21,008	21,937	28	26	2
4		10–15	...	44,590	23,133	21,457	5,503	4,423	1,080	39,087	18,710	20,377	326	295	31
5		15–20	...	34,976	18,445	16,531	4,820	3,952	868	30,156	14,493	15,663	568	524	44
6		20 and over	...	179,171	99,090	80,081	25,136	22,743	2,393	154,035	76,347	77,688	2,675	2,514	161
		Hindu.													
1		All ages	...	319,277	167,771	151,506	30,831	27,340	3,491	288,446	140,431	148,015	2,694	2,581	113
2		0–5	...	40,801	19,724	21,077	...	...	...	40,801	19,724	21,077	...	...	...
3		5–10	...	41,326	20,562	20,764	1,480	1,127	353	39,846	19,435	20,411	21	20	1
4		10–15	...	41,140	21,272	19,868	4,696	3,890	806	36,444	17,382	19,062	269	248	21
5		15–20	...	31,964	16,654	15,310	4,019	3,361	658	27,945	13,293	14,652	458	436	22
6		20 and over	...	164,046	89,559	74,487	20,636	18,962	1,674	143,410	70,597	72,813	1,946	1,877	69
		Musalman.													
1		All ages	...	19,430	11,141	8,289	4,394	3,455	939	15,036	7,686	7,350	296	285	11
2		0–5	...	2,445	1,185	1,260	...	...	...	2,445	1,185	1,260	...	...	...
3		5–10	...	2,481	1,276	1,205	230	126	104	2,251	1,150	1,101	4	4	...
4		10–15	...	2,453	1,342	1,111	640	423	217	1,813	919	894	31	27	4
5		15–20	...	1,997	1,164	833	580	439	141	1,417	725	692	56	55	1
6		20 and over	...	10,054	6,174	3,880	2,944	2,467	477	7,110	3,707	3,403	205	199	6
		Christian.													
1		All ages	...	6,575	4,110	2,465	1,585	1,256	329	4,990	2,854	2,136	595	481	114
2		0–5	...	740	380	360	...	...	...	740	380	360	...	...	...
3		5–10	...	610	303	307	49	26	23	561	277	284	3	2	1
4		10–15	...	690	361	329	117	78	39	573	283	290	25	19	6
5		15–20	...	762	483	279	160	103	57	602	380	222	51	30	21
6		20 and over	...	3,773	2,583	1,190	1,259	1,049	210	2,514	1,534	980	516	430	86
		Jain.													
1		All ages	...	1,360	798	562	411	348	63	949	450	499	9	9	...
2		0–5	...	134	67	67	...	...	...	134	67	67	...	...	...
3		5–10	...	143	69	74	9	5	4	134	64	70	...	...	...
4		10–15	...	161	79	82	49	32	17	112	47	65	1	1	...
5		15–20	...	151	94	57	60	49	11	91	45	46	3	3	...
6		20 and over	...	771	489	282	293	262	31	478	227	251	5	5	...
		Tribal.													
1		All ages	...	1,067	566	501	...	...	...	1,067	566	501	...	...	...
2		0–5	...	145	73	72	...	...	...	145	73	72	...	...	...
3		5–10	...	152	82	70	...	...	...	152	82	70	...	...	...
4		10–15	...	146	79	67	...	...	...	146	79	67	...	...	...
5		15–20	...	100	49	51	...	...	...	100	49	51	...	...	...
6		20 and over	...	524	283	241	...	...	...	524	283	241	...	...	...
		All Religions.													
1	SHIMOGA DISTRICT.	All ages	...	519,987	274,981	245,006	52,072	46,451	5,621	467,915	228,530	239,385	4,123	3,906	217
2		0–5	...	68,840	33,829	35,011	...	...	...	68,840	33,829	35,011	...	...	...
3		5–10	...	67,470	33,735	33,735	1,901	1,384	517	65,569	32,351	33,218	18	16	2
4		10–15	...	65,755	33,919	31,836	7,126	5,821	1,305	58,629	28,098	30,531	366	327	39
5		15–20	...	51,984	27,225	24,759	6,897	5,807	1,090	45,087	21,418	23,669	776	728	48
6		20 and over	...	265,938	146,273	119,665	36,148	33,439	2,709	229,790	112,834	116,956	2,963	2,835	128
		Hindu.													
1		All ages	...	464,350	244,909	219,441	45,146	40,768	4,378	419,204	204,141	215,063	3,583	3,447	136
2		0–5	...	60,736	29,812	30,924	...	...	...	60,736	29,812	30,924	...	...	...
3		5–10	...	59,748	29,783	29,965	1,632	1,210	422	58,116	28,573	29,543	13	12	1
4		10–15	...	58,518	30,088	28,430	6,200	5,183	1,017	52,318	24,905	27,413	337	309	28
5		15–20	...	46,439	24,232	22,207	5,995	5,132	863	40,444	19,100	21,344	681	644	37
6		20 and over	...	238,909	130,994	107,915	31,319	29,243	2,076	207,590	101,751	105,839	2,552	2,482	70
		Musalman.													
1		All ages	...	40,960	22,174	18,786	5,213	4,339	874	35,747	17,835	17,912	266	251	15
2		0–5	...	5,886	2,939	2,947	...	...	...	5,886	2,939	2,947	...	...	...
3		5–10	...	5,692	2,910	2,782	195	128	67	5,497	2,782	2,715	2	2	...
4		10–15	...	5,346	2,820	2,526	722	495	227	4,624	2,325	2,299	19	16	3
5		15–20	...	4,104	2,212	1,892	670	499	171	3,434	1,713	1,721	58	53	5
6		20 and over	...	19,932	11,293	8,639	3,626	3,217	409	16,306	8,076	8,230	187	180	7

LITERATE IN																					
Kannada			Telugu			Tamil			Hindi			Hindustani			Marathi			Others			
Persons	Males	Females	Persons	Males	Females	Persons	Males	Females	Persons	Males	Females	Persons	Males	Females	Persons	Males	Females	Persons	Males	Females	Number
15	16	17	18	19	20	21	22	23	24	25	26	27	28	29	30	31	32	33	34	35	
16	16	...	...	...	...	1	1	...	...	...	...	...	...	...	...	...	...	...	...	...	1
...	...	...	...	...	...	...	...	...	...	...	...	...	...	...	...	...	...	...	...	...	2
2	2	...	...	...	...	...	...	...	...	...	...	...	...	...	...	...	...	...	...	...	3
2	2	...	...	...	...	...	...	...	...	...	...	...	...	...	...	...	...	...	...	...	4
2	2	...	...	...	...	1	1	...	...	...	...	...	...	...	...	...	...	...	...	...	5
10	10	...	...	...	...	...	...	...	...	...	...	...	...	...	...	...	...	...	...	...	6
32,991	29,223	3,768	237	197	40	742	627	115	149	122	27	3,235	2,338	897	136	111	25	740	695	45	1
...	...	...	...	...	...	...	...	...	...	...	...	...	...	...	...	...	...	...	...	...	2
1,548	1,166	382	3	3	...	8	4	4	7	4	3	210	112	98	...	...	...	5	5	...	3
4,944	4,082	862	7	5	2	37	30	7	14	10	4	548	338	210	3	2	1	43	35	8	4
4,332	3,621	711	19	9	10	74	54	20	19	14	5	419	284	135	13	6	7	98	89	9	5
22,167	20,354	1,813	208	180	28	623	539	84	109	94	15	2,058	1,604	454	120	103	17	594	566	28	6
30,263	26,861	3,402	228	188	40	351	276	75	31	28	3	24	20	4	128	105	23	322	314	8	1
...	...	...	...	...	...	...	...	...	...	...	...	...	...	...	...	...	...	...	...	...	2
1,473	1,120	353	2	2	...	4	2	2	1	1	...	...	...	...	...	...	...	3	3	...	3
4,673	3,872	801	7	5	2	19	14	5	5	5	...	1	1	...	3	2	1	14	13	1	4
3,974	3,331	643	19	9	10	21	11	10	2	2	...	3	...	3	13	6	7	37	35	2	5
20,143	18,538	1,605	200	172	28	307	249	58	23	20	3	20	19	1	112	97	15	268	263	5	6
1,290	1,241	49	3	3	...	267	258	9	60	50	10	3,208	2,316	892	4	4	...	224	212	12	1
...	...	...	...	...	...	...	...	...	...	...	...	...	...	...	...	...	...	...	...	...	2
19	14	5	...	...	...	2	2	...	5	3	2	210	112	98	...	...	...	...	...	...	3
135	124	11	...	...	...	9	9	...	4	3	1	547	337	210	...	...	...	10	9	1	4
182	172	10	...	...	...	38	35	3	6	4	2	416	284	132	...	...	...	37	34	3	5
954	931	23	3	3	...	218	212	6	45	40	5	2,035	1,583	452	4	4	...	177	169	8	6
1,179	911	268	5	5	...	122	92	30	1	1	...	3	2	1	2	1	1	83	61	22	1
...	...	...	...	...	...	...	...	...	...	...	...	...	...	...	...	...	...	...	...	...	2
45	24	21	1	1	...	2	...	2	...	...	...	...	...	...	...	...	...	1	1	...	3
100	64	36	...	...	...	9	7	2	...	...	...	...	...	...	...	...	...	12	7	5	4
135	85	50	...	...	...	14	8	6	...	...	...	...	...	...	...	...	...	4	1	3	5
899	738	161	4	4	...	97	77	20	1	1	...	3	2	1	2	1	1	66	52	14	6
258	209	49	1	1	...	2	1	1	57	43	14	...	...	...	...	...	...	107	107	...	1
...	...	...	...	...	...	...	...	...	...	...	...	...	...	...	...	...	...	...	...	...	2
8	5	3	...	...	...	...	...	...	1	...	1	...	...	...	...	...	...	1	1	...	3
36	22	14	...	...	...	...	...	...	5	2	3	...	...	...	...	...	...	6	6	...	4
44	36	8	...	...	...	1	...	1	11	8	3	...	...	...	...	...	...	19	19	...	5
170	146	24	1	1	...	1	1	...	40	33	7	...	...	...	...	...	...	81	81	...	6
...	...	...	...	...	...	...	...	...	...	...	...	...	...	...	...	...	...	...	...	...	1
...	...	...	...	...	...	...	...	...	...	...	...	...	...	...	...	...	...	...	...	...	2
...	...	...	...	...	...	...	...	...	...	...	...	...	...	...	...	...	...	...	...	...	3
...	...	...	...	...	...	...	...	...	...	...	...	...	...	...	...	...	...	...	...	...	4
...	...	...	...	...	...	...	...	...	...	...	...	...	...	...	...	...	...	...	...	...	5
...	...	...	...	...	...	...	...	...	...	...	...	...	...	...	...	...	...	...	...	...	6
47,913	43,261	4,652	578	490	88	869	716	153	199	183	16	3,726	2,921	805	367	310	57	994	907	87	1
...	...	...	...	...	...	...	...	...	...	...	...	...	...	...	...	...	...	...	...	...	2
1,724	1,280	444	15	11	4	25	17	8	3	2	1	175	111	64	4	4	...	5	4	1	3
6,535	5,454	1,081	52	41	11	76	59	17	24	23	1	567	353	214	21	13	8	43	26	17	4
6,349	5,454	895	97	72	25	100	72	28	25	21	4	430	279	151	47	37	10	99	81	18	5
33,305	31,073	2,232	414	366	48	668	568	100	147	137	10	2,554	2,178	376	295	256	39	847	796	51	6
44,327	40,049	4,278	494	409	85	462	385	77	33	32	1	122	116	6	347	292	55	582	556	26	1
...	...	...	...	...	...	...	...	...	...	...	...	...	...	...	...	...	...	...	...	...	2
1,615	1,200	415	15	11	4	15	10	5	1	1	...	1	1	...	4	4	...	4	4	...	3
6,162	5,152	1,010	51	40	11	42	33	9	2	2	...	7	7	...	20	12	8	14	12	2	4
5,910	5,074	836	53	29	24	52	36	16	4	4	...	18	18	...	45	35	10	50	45	5	5
30,640	28,623	2,017	375	329	46	353	306	47	26	25	1	96	90	6	278	241	37	514	495	19	6
2,195	2,111	84	63	62	1	227	215	12	87	74	13	3,585	2,788	797	6	6	...	280	228	52	1
...	...	...	...	...	...	...	...	...	...	...	...	...	...	...	...	...	...	...	...	...	2
40	37	3	...	...	...	3	3	...	2	1	1	174	110	64	...	...	...	1	...	1	3
193	172	21	...	...	...	16	16	...	17	16	1	559	346	213	...	...	...	18	6	12	4
261	244	17	41	41	...	20	18	2	15	11	4	403	253	150	1	1	...	32	20	12	5
1,701	1,658	43	22	21	1	188	178	10	53	46	7	2,449	2,079	370	5	5	...	229	202	27	6

Number	District	AGE	POPULATION											
			Total			Literate			Illiterate			English		
			Persons	Males	Females	Persons	Males	Females	Persons	Males	Females	Persons	Males	Females
	1	2	3	4	5	6	7	8	9	10	11	12	13	14
	SHIMOGA DISTRICT.	**Christian.**												
1		All ages ...	**4,084**	**2,355**	**1,729**	**1,184**	**849**	**335**	**2,900**	**1,506**	**1,394**	**255**	**189**	**66**
2		0-5 ...	**555**	271	284	...	...	...	**555**	271	284	...	...	...
3		5-10 ...	**468**	244	224	**58**	34	24	**410**	210	200	**3**	2	1
4		10-15 ...	**448**	239	209	**132**	78	54	**316**	161	155	**9**	1	8
5		15-20 ...	**421**	239	182	**156**	104	52	**265**	135	130	**33**	27	6
6		20 and over ...	**2,192**	1,362	830	**838**	633	205	**1,354**	729	625	**210**	159	51
		Jain.												
1		All ages ...	**2,731**	**1,526**	**1,205**	**410**	**382**	**28**	**2,321**	**1,144**	**1,177**	**11**	**11**	...
2		0-5 ...	**287**	145	142	...	...	...	**287**	145	142	...	...	...
3		5-10 ...	**315**	155	160	**12**	8	4	**303**	147	156	...	...	...
4		10-15 ...	**344**	186	158	**46**	40	6	**298**	146	152	**1**	1	...
5		15-20 ...	**316**	179	137	**59**	55	4	**257**	124	133	**1**	1	...
6		20 and over ...	**1,469**	861	608	**293**	279	14	**1,176**	582	594	**9**	9	...
		Tribal.												
1		All ages ...	**7,857**	**4,014**	**3,843**	**118**	**112**	**6**	**7 739**	**3,902**	**3,837**	**6**	**6**	...
2		0-5 ...	**1,374**	661	713	...	...	...	**1,374**	661	713	...	...	...
3		5-10 ...	**1,246**	642	604	**4**	4	...	**1,242**	638	604	...	...	...
4		10-15 ...	**1,099**	586	513	**26**	25	1	**1,073**	561	512	...	...	...
5		15-20 ...	**703**	363	340	**17**	17	...	**686**	346	340	**2**	2	...
6		20 and over ...	**3,436**	1,762	1,673	**71**	66	5	**3,364**	1,696	1,668	**4**	4	...
	CIVIL AND MILITARY STATION, BANGALORE.	**All Religions.**												
1		All ages ...	**134,113**	**69,409**	**64,704**	**37,264**	**26,000**	**11,264**	**96,849**	**43,409**	**53,440**	**19,109**	**13,369**	**5,740**
2		0-5 ...	**19,015**	9,473	9,542	...	...	...	**19,015**	9,473	9,542	...	...	...
3		5-10 ...	**16,938**	8,658	8,280	**1,302**	691	611	**15,636**	7,967	7,669	**514**	266	248
4		10-15 ...	**15,595**	7,875	7,720	**4,044**	2,319	1,725	**11,551**	5,556	5,995	**2,041**	1,246	795
5		15-20 ...	**13,742**	6,839	6,903	**5,045**	3,105	1,940	**8,697**	3,734	4,963	**2,746**	1,807	939
6		20 and over ...	**68,823**	36,564	32,259	**26,873**	19,885	6,988	**41,950**	16,679	25,271	**13,808**	10,050	3,758
		Hindu.												
1		All ages ...	**74,004**	**38,537**	**35,467**	**15,126**	**12,262**	**2,864**	**58,878**	**26,275**	**32,603**	**6,136**	**5,576**	**560**
2		0-5 ...	**11,129**	5,489	5,640	...	...	...	**11,129**	5,489	5,640	...	...	...
3		5-10 ...	**9,307**	4,745	4,562	**449**	275	174	**8,858**	4,470	4,388	**81**	61	20
4		10-15 ...	**8,317**	4,219	4,098	**1,557**	1,001	556	**6,760**	3,218	3,542	**589**	465	124
5		15-20 ...	**7,414**	3,734	3,680	**2,161**	1,568	593	**5,253**	2,166	3,087	**1,006**	861	145
6		20 and over ...	**37,837**	20,350	17,487	**10,959**	9,418	1,541	**26,878**	10,932	15,946	**4,460**	4,189	271
		Musalman.												
1		All ages ...	**28,625**	**15,398**	**13,227**	**7,735**	**5,572**	**2,163**	**20,890**	**9,826**	**11,064**	**1,848**	**1,666**	**182**
2		0-5 ...	**3,909**	1,914	1,995	...	...	...	**3,909**	1,914	1,995	...	...	...
3		5-10 ...	**3,827**	1,936	1,891	**256**	120	136	**3,571**	1,816	1,755	**32**	17	15
4		10-15 ...	**3,527**	1,795	1,732	**841**	487	354	**2,686**	1,308	1,378	**180**	138	42
5		15-20 ...	**2,946**	1,552	1,394	**951**	588	363	**1,995**	964	1,031	**259**	225	34
6		20 and over ...	**14,416**	8,201	6,215	**5,687**	4,377	1,310	**8,729**	3,824	4,905	**1,377**	1,286	91
		Christian.												
1		All ages ...	**30,022**	**14,652**	**15,370**	**13,735**	**7,664**	**6,071**	**16,287**	**6,988**	**9,299**	**10,798**	**5,917**	**4,881**
2		0-5 ...	**3,778**	1,967	1,811	...	...	...	**3,778**	1,967	1,811	...	...	...
3		5-10 ...	**3,641**	1,889	1,752	**573**	283	290	**3,068**	1,606	1,462	**391**	184	207
4		10-15 ...	**3,587**	1,768	1,819	**1,563**	779	784	**2,024**	989	1,035	**1,228**	619	609
5		15-20 ...	**3,202**	1,452	1,750	**1,831**	880	951	**1,371**	572	799	**1,434**	695	739
6		20 and over ...	**15,814**	7,576	8,238	**9,768**	5,722	4,046	**6,046**	1,854	4,192	**7,745**	4,419	3,326
		Jain.												
1		All ages ...	**814**	**484**	**330**	**313**	**297**	**16**	**501**	**187**	**314**	**55**	**54**	**1**
2		0-5 ...	**98**	51	47	...	...	...	**98**	51	47	...	...	...
3		5-10 ...	**79**	46	33	**4**	3	1	**75**	43	32	...	...	...
4		10-15 ...	**85**	51	34	**26**	23	3	**59**	28	31	**2**	1	1
5		15-20 ...	**115**	73	42	**53**	48	5	**62**	25	37	**9**	9	...
6		20 and over ...	**437**	263	174	**230**	223	7	**207**	40	167	**44**	44	...

LITERATE IN *																					
Kannada			Telugu			Tamil			Hindi			Hindustani			Marathi			Others			
Persons	Males	Females	Persons	Males	Females	Persons	Males	Females	Persons	Males	Females	Persons	Males	Females	Persons	Males	Females	Persons	Males	Females	Number
15 -	16	17	18	19	20	21	22	23	24	25	26	27	28	29	30	31	32	33	34	35	
985	727	258	21	19	2	178	114	64	2	1	1	4	3	1	5	5	...	60	53	7	1
...	...	...	...	...	...	...	...	...	...	...	...	...	...	...	...	...	...	...	...	...	2
53	31	22	...	...	...	7	4	3	...	...	...	...	...	...	...	...	...	...	...	...	3
116	72	44	1	1	...	18	10	8	...	...	...	...	...	...	...	...	...	5	3	2	4
127	89	38	3	2	1	28	18	10	...	...	...	1	...	1	...	...	...	4	3	1	5
689	535	154	17	16	1	125	82	43	2	1	1	3	3	...	5	5	...	51	47	4	6
285	259	26	...	...	...	2	2	...	77	76	1	13	13	...	4	4	...	73	70	3	1
...	...	...	...	...	...	...	...	...	...	...	...	...	...	...	...	...	...	...	...	...	2
12	8	4	...	...	...	...	...	...	...	...	...	...	...	...	...	...	...	...	...	...	3
38	33	5	...	...	...	...	...	...	5	5	...	...	...	...	...	...	...	7	5	2	4
34	30	4	...	...	...	...	...	...	6	6	...	8	8	...	...	...	...	13	13	...	5
201	188	13	...	...	...	2	2	...	66	65	1	5	5	...	4	4	...	53	52	1	6
118	112	6	...	...	...	...	...	...	...	...	...	...	...	...	4	3	1	...	...	...	1
...	...	...	...	...	...	...	...	...	...	...	...	...	...	...	...	...	...	...	...	...	2
4	4	...	...	...	...	...	...	...	...	...	...	...	...	...	...	...	...	...	...	...	3
26	25	1	...	...	...	...	...	...	...	...	...	...	...	...	1	1	...	...	...	...	4
17	17	...	...	...	...	...	...	...	...	...	...	...	...	...	1	1	...	...	...	...	5
71	66	5	...	...	...	...	...	...	...	...	...	...	...	...	2	1	1	...	...	...	6
...	...	...	...	...	...	...	...	...	...	...	...	...	...	...	...	...	...	...	...	...	1
...	...	...	...	...	...	...	...	...	...	...	...	...	...	...	...	...	...	...	...	...	2
...	...	...	...	...	...	...	...	...	...	...	...	...	...	...	...	...	...	...	...	...	3
...	...	...	...	...	...	...	...	...	...	...	...	...	...	...	...	...	...	...	...	...	4
...	...	...	...	...	...	...	...	...	...	...	...	...	...	...	...	...	...	...	...	...	5
...	...	...	...	...	...	...	...	...	...	...	...	...	...	...	...	...	...	...	...	...	6
...	...	...	...	...	...	...	...	...	...	...	...	...	...	...	...	...	...	...	...	...	1
...	...	...	...	...	...	...	...	...	...	...	...	...	...	...	...	...	...	...	...	...	2
...	...	...	...	...	...	...	...	...	...	...	...	...	...	...	...	...	...	...	...	...	3
...	...	...	...	...	...	...	...	...	...	...	...	...	...	...	...	...	...	...	...	...	4
...	...	...	...	...	...	...	...	...	...	...	...	...	...	...	...	...	...	...	...	...	5
...	...	...	...	...	...	...	...	...	...	...	...	...	...	...	...	...	...	...	...	...	6
...	...	...	...	...	...	...	...	...	...	...	...	...	...	...	...	...	...	...	...	...	1
...	...	...	...	...	...	...	...	...	...	...	...	...	...	...	...	...	...	...	...	...	2
...	...	...	...	...	...	...	...	...	...	...	...	...	...	...	...	...	...	...	...	...	3
...	...	...	...	...	...	...	...	...	...	...	...	...	...	...	...	...	...	...	...	...	4
...	...	...	...	...	...	...	...	...	...	...	...	...	...	...	...	...	...	...	...	...	5
...	...	...	...	...	...	...	...	...	...	...	...	...	...	...	...	...	...	...	...	...	6
...	...	...	...	...	...	...	...	...	...	...	...	...	...	...	...	...	...	...	...	...	1
...	...	...	...	...	...	...	...	...	...	...	...	...	...	...	...	...	...	...	...	...	2
...	...	...	...	...	...	...	...	...	...	...	...	...	...	...	...	...	...	...	...	...	3
...	...	...	...	...	...	...	...	...	...	...	...	...	...	...	...	...	...	...	...	...	4
...	...	...	...	...	...	...	...	...	...	...	...	...	...	...	...	...	...	...	...	...	5
...	...	...	...	...	...	...	...	...	...	...	...	...	...	...	...	...	...	...	...	...	6
...	...	...	...	...	...	...	...	...	...	...	...	...	...	...	...	...	...	...	...	...	1
...	...	...	...	...	...	...	...	...	...	...	...	...	...	...	...	...	...	...	...	...	2
...	...	...	...	...	...	...	...	...	...	...	...	...	...	...	...	...	...	...	...	...	3
...	...	...	...	...	...	...	...	...	...	...	...	...	...	...	...	...	...	...	...	...	4
...	...	...	...	...	...	...	...	...	...	...	...	...	...	...	...	...	...	...	...	...	5
...	...	...	...	...	...	...	...	...	...	...	...	...	...	...	...	...	...	...	...	...	6

* See note 3 on the title page.

MYSORE CENSUS, 1931.

TABLE XIV—Literacy by Selected Castes, Tribes, or Races.

NOTE.—Regarding the selection of castes for presentation in this Table see Notes 1, 2 and 3 to Table VIII.

TABLE XIV.

Literacy by Selected Castes, Tribes, or Races.

TABLE XIV.

Literacy by Selected Castes, Tribes, or Races.

Caste, Tribe or Race	Locality	Population (Seven years and over)									Literate in English (Seven years and over)		
		Total			Literate			Illiterate					
		Persons	Males	Females	Persons	Males	Females	Persons	Males	Females	Persons	Males	Females
1	2	3	4	5	6	7	8	9	10	11	12	13	14
Hindu. Adikarnataka	Mysore State, including C. and M. Stn., Bangalore.	810,699	416,506	394,193	14,667	13,472	1,195	796,032	403,034	392,998	2,088	1,994	94
	C. & M. Stn., Bangalore ...	21,273	10,586	10,687	2,629	2,230	399	18,644	8,356	10,288	788	722	66
Agasa	Mysore State, including C. and M. Stn., Bangalore.	89,226	45,925	43,301	2,948	2,814	134	86,278	43,111	43,167	89	88	1
	C. & M. Stn., Bangalore ...	918	486	432	106	99	7	812	387	425	11	10	1
Banajiga	Mysore State, including C. and M. Stn., Bangalore.	125,882	64,840	61,042	20,237	17,472	2,765	105,645	47,368	58,277	2,868	2,628	240
	C. & M. Stn., Bangalore ...	6,102	3,226	2,876	1,943	1,549	394	4,159	1,677	2,482	728	658	70
Beda	Mysore State, including C. and M. Stn., Bangalore.	245,539	125,446	120,093	7,827	7,319	508	237,712	118,127	119,585	274	259	15
	C. & M. Stn., Bangalore ...	104	56	48	24	17	7	80	39	41	6	5	1
Brahmin	Mysore State, including C. and M. Stn., Bangalore.	198,163	103,523	94,640	113,633	81,044	32,589	84,530	22,479	62,051	38,319	35,053	3,266
	C. & M. Stn., Bangalore ...	2,795	1,617	1,178	1,821	1,320	501	974	297	677	1,178	1,051	127
Darzi	Mysore State, including C. and M. Stn., Bangalore.	15,915	8,238	7,677	3,973	3,559	414	11,942	4,679	7,263	336	324	12
	C. & M. Stn., Bangalore ...	1,778	987	791	302	270	32	1,476	717	759	67	66	1
Devanga	Mysore State, including C. and M. Stn., Bangalore.	47,758	24,296	23,462	8,948	8,304	644	38,810	15,992	22,818	391	364	27
	C. & M. Stn., Bangalore ...	55	30	25	15	14	1	40	16	24	4	4	...
Gangakula	Mysore State, including C. and M. Stn., Bangalore.	142,416	72,677	69,739	4,629	4,334	295	137,787	68,343	69,444	235	226	9
	C. & M. Stn., Bangalore ...	135	71	64	28	17	11	107	54	53	9	6	3
Ganiga	Mysore State, including C. and M. Stn., Bangalore.	36,797	18,679	18,118	3,542	3,326	216	33,255	15,353	17,902	160	154	6
	C. & M. Stn., Bangalore ...	415	165	250	25	16	9	390	149	241	6	5	1
Idiga	Mysore State, including C. and M. Stn., Bangalore.	79,273	42,458	36,815	3,477	3,332	145	75,796	39,126	36,670	85	84	1
	C. & M. Stn., Bangalore ...	257	154	103	48	39	4	214	115	99	9	9	...
Jogi	Mysore State, including C. and M. Stn., Bangalore.	11,934	6,051	5,883	256	246	10	11,678	5,805	5,873	8	7	1
	C. & M. Stn., Bangalore ...	2	2	...	...	...	...	2	2	...	...	...	...
Kshatriya	Mysore State, including C. and M. Stn., Bangalore.	33,681	17,744	15,937	9,355	7,993	1,362	24,326	9,751	14,575	1,813	1,637	176
	C. & M Stn., Bangalore ...	984	589	395	347	296	51	637	293	344	163	151	12
Kumbara	Mysore State, including C. and M. Stn., Bangalore.	39,781	20,501	19,280	2,092	1,998	94	37,689	18,503	19,186	46	42	4
	C. & M. Stn., Bangalore ...	135	61	74	20	18	2	115	43	72	8	7	1
Kunchatiga	Mysore State, including C. and M., Stn., Bangalore.	95,078	48,732	46,346	8,950	8,504	446	86,128	40,228	45,900	481	466	15
	C. & M. Stn., Bangalore ...	226	129	97	67	55	12	159	74	85	32	30	2
Lingayat	Mysore State, including C. and M. Stn., Bangalore.	634,027	323,249	310,778	104,076	97,356	6,720	529,951	225,893	304,058	4,694	4,526	168
	C. & M. Stn., Bangalore ...	892	479	413	285	229	56	607	250	357	104	98	6

TABLE XIV.

Literacy by Selected Castes, Tribes, or Races—*contd.*

TABLE XIV.

Literacy by Selected Castes, Tribes, or Races.

Caste, Tribe or Race	Locality	Population (seven years and over): Total: Persons	Total: Males	Total: Females	Literate: Persons	Literate: Males	Literate: Females	Illiterate: Persons	Illiterate: Males	Illiterate: Females	Literate in English (Seven years and over): Persons	Males	Females
1	2	3	4	5	6	7	8	9	10	11	12	13	14
Hindu— *contd.*													
Mahratta	Mysore State, including C. and M. Stn., Bangalore.	**49,394**	**26,139**	**23,256**	**7,253**	**6,545**	**708**	**42,141**	**19,594**	**22,547.**	**1,100**	**1,031**	**69**
	C. & M. Stn., Bangalore ...	1,194	655	539	397	342	55	797	318	484	163	148	15
Meda	Mysore State, including C. and M. Stn., Bangalore.	**6,150**	**3,156**	**2,994**	**232**	**215**	**17**	**5,918**	**2,941**	**2,977**	**14**	**14**	...
	C. & M. Stn., Bangalore ...	202	104	98	2	2	...	200	102	98	...	...	...
Mudali	Mysore State, including C. and M. Stn., Bangalore.	**25,965**	**13,882**	**12,083**	**9,852**	**7,583**	**2,269**	**16,113**	**6,299**	**9,814**	**3,534**	**3,206**	**328**
	C. & M. Stn., Bangalore ...	7,265	3,925	3,340	3,699	2,833	866	3,566	1,092	2,474	1,674	1,531	143
Nagartha	Mysore State, including C. and M. Stn., Bangalore.	**6,954**	**3,514**	**3,440**	**2,108**	**1,885**	**223**	**4,846**	**1,629**	**3,217**	**225**	**220**	**5**
	C. & M. Stn., Bangalore ...	277	133	144	27	24	3	250	109	141	9	8	1
Nayinda	Mysore State including C. and M. Stn., Bangalore.	**37,531**	**19,494**	**18,037**	**3,252**	**3,063**	**189**	**34,279**	**16,431**	**17,848**	**138**	**132**	**6**
	C. & M. Stn., Bangalore ...	715	369	346	152	132	20	563	237	326	31	29	2
Neygi	Mysore State, including C. and M. Stn., Bangalore.	**44,003**	**22,655**	**21,348**	**7,221**	**6,792**	**429**	**36,782**	**15,863**	**20,919**	**379**	**353**	**26**
	C. & M. Stn., Bangalore ...	114	67	47	45	38	7	69	29	40	18	18	...
Satani	Mysore State, including C. and M. Stn., Bangalore.	**19,067**	**9,754**	**9,313**	**3,968**	**3,708**	**260**	**15,099**	**6,046**	**9,053**	**203**	**196**	**7**
	C. & M. Stn., Bangalore ...	29	16	13	11	9	2	18	7	11	3	3	...
Tigala	Mysore State, including C. and M. Stn., Bangalore.	**71,912**	**37,385**	**34,527**	**2,517**	**2,382**	**135**	**69,395**	**35,003**	**34,392**	**172**	**168**	**4**
	C. & M. Stn., Bangalore ...	3,363	1,815	1,548	298	263	35	3,065	1,552	1,513	66	63	3
Uppara	Mysore State, including C. and M. Stn., Bangalore.	**94,320**	**48,224**	**46,096**	**2,588**	**2,505**	**83**	**91,732**	**45,719**	**46,013**	**74**	**72**	**2**
	C. & M. Stn., Bangalore ...	1	...	1	...	...	...	1	...	1	...	...	...
Vakkaliga	Mysore State, including C. and M. Stn., Bangalore.	**1,076,729**	**548,161**	**528,568**	**69,528**	**66,727**	**2,801**	**1,007,201**	**481,434**	**525,767**	**3,047**	**2,909**	**138**
	C. & M. Stn., Bangalore ...	3,288	1,752	1,536	648	560	88	2,640	1,192	1,448	213	192	21
Vaisya	Mysore State, including C. and M. Stn., Bangalore.	**35,659**	**19,208**	**16,451**	**17,355**	**15,198**	**2,157**	**18,304**	**4,010**	**14,294**	**2,542**	**2,469**	**73**
	C. & M. Stn., Bangalore ...	1,361	749	612	780	668	112	581	81	500	335	318	17
Viswakarma	Mysore State, including C. and M. Stn., Bangalore.	**118,483**	**61,946**	**56,537**	**20,756**	**19,503**	**1,253**	**97,727**	**42,443**	**55,284**	**552**	**532**	**20**
	C. & M. Stn., Bangalore ...	1,083	577	506	286	259	27	797	318	479	56	49	7
Vodda	Mysore State, including C. and M. Stn., Bangalore.	**132,656**	**68,678**	**63,978**	**1,391**	**1,336**	**55**	**131,265**	**67,342**	**63,923**	**50**	**46**	**4**
	C. & M. Stn., Bangalore ...	555	291	264	19	18	1	536	273	263	1	1	...
Yadava	Mysore State, including C. and M. Stn., Bangalore.	**141,371**	**71,973**	**69,398**	**4,668**	**4,384**	**284**	**136,703**	**67,589**	**69,114**	**336**	**319**	**17**
	C. & M. Stn., Bangalore ...	721	387	334	182	151	31	539	236	303	65	56	9

TABLE XIV.

Literacy by Selected Castes, Tribes, or Races.

TABLE XIV.

Literacy by Selected Castes, Tribes, or Races.

Caste Tribe or Race	Locality	Population (Seven years and over)									Literate in English (Seven years and over)		
		Total			Literate			Illiterate					
		Persons	Males	Females	Persons	Males	Females	Persons	Males	Females	Persons	Males	Females
1	2	3	4	5	6	7	8	9	10	11	12	13	14
Hindu and Tribal													
Banajara (Hindu)	Mysore State, including C. and M. Stn., Bangalore.	39,137	20,399	18,738	381	353	28	38,756	20,046	18,710	9	9	...
	C. & M. Stn., Bangalore ...	9	4	5	...	...	...	9	4	5	...	...	...
Banajara (Tribal)	Mysore State, including C. and M. Stn., Bangalore.	10,491	5,404	5,087	105	99	6	10,386	5,305	5,081	4	4	...
	C. & M. Stn., Bangalore ...	...	...	...	...	...	...	...	...	...	...	...	...
Banajara (Total)	Mysore State, including C. and M, Stn. Bangalore.	49,628	25,803	23,825	486	452	34	49,142	25,351	23,791	13	13	...
	C. & M. Stn., Bangalore ...	9	4	5	...	...	...	9	4	5	...	...	...
Koracha (Hindu)	Mysore State, including C. and M. Stn., Bangalore.	8,279	4,365	3,914	257	247	10	8,022	4,118	3,904	12	12	...
	C. & M. Stn., Bangalore ...	135	75	60	22	22	...	113	53	60	5	5	...
Koracha (Tribal)	Mysore State, including C. and M. Stn., Bangalore.	1,462	779	683	15	15	...	1,447	764	683	...	...	...
	C. & M. Stn., Bangalore ...	...	...	...	...	...	...	...	...	...	...	...	...
Koracha (Total)	Mysore State, including C. and M. Stn., Bangalore.	9,741	5,144	4,597	272	262	10	9,469	4,882	4,587	12	12	...
	C. & M. Stn., Bangalore ...	135	75	60	22	22	...	113	53	60	5	5	...
Korama (Hindu)	Mysore State, including C. and M, Stn., Bangalore.	11,026	5,599	5,427	229	221	8	10,797	5,378	5,419	3	3	...
	C. & M. Stn., Bangalore ...	48	25	23	9	9	...	39	16	23	1	1	...
Korama (Tribal)	Mysore State, including C. and M. Stn., Bangalore.	2,839	1,476	1,363	71	68	3	2,768	1,408	1,360	...	...	...
	C. & M. Stn., Bangalore ...	...	...	...	...	...	...	...	...	...	...	...	...
Korama (Total)	Mysore State, including C. and M. Stn., Bangalore.	13,865	7,075	6,790	300	289	11	13,565	6,786	6,779	3	3	...
	C. & M. Stn., Bangalore ...	48	25	23	9	9	...	39	16	23	1	1	...
Kuruba (Hindu)	Mysore State, including C. and M. Stn., Bangalore.	352,031	179,253	172,778	12,775	12,325	450	339,256	166,928	172,328	613	606	7
	C. & M. Stn., Bangalore ...	897	474	423	141	129	12	756	345	411	42	42	...
Kuruba (Tribal)	Mysore State, including C. and M. Stn., Bangalore.	3,687	1,953	1,734	23	23	...	3,664	1,930	1,734	3	3	...
	C. & M. Stn., Bangalore ...	...	...	...	...	...	...	...	...	...	...	...	...
Kuruba (Total)	Mysore State, including C. and M. Stn., Bangalore.	355,718	181,206	174,512	12,798	12,348	450	342,920	168,858	174,062	616	609	7
	C. & M. Stn., Bangalore ...	697	474	423	141	129	12	756	345	411	42	42	...
Musalman.													
Labbai	Mysore State, including C. and M. Stn., Bangalore,	10,371	6,951	3,420	3,599	3,162	437	6,772	3,789	2,983	194	192	2
	C. & M. Stn., Bangalore ...	1,114	698	416	593	472	121	521	226	295	93	91	2
Mughal	Mysore State, including C. and M. Stn., Bangalore.	8,742	4,770	3,972	2,138	1,562	576	6,604	3,208	3,396	286	236	50
	C. & M. Stn., Bangalore ...	511	295	216	230	154	76	281	141	140	97	74	23

TABLE XIV.

Literacy by Selected Castes, Tribes or Races—*concld.*

Caste, Tribe or Race	Locality	POPULATION (Seven years and over)									Literate in English (Seven years and over)		
		Total			Literate			Illiterate					
		Persons	Males	Females	Persons	Males	Females	Persons	Males	Females	Persons	Males	Females
1	2	3	4	5	6	7	8	9	10	11	12	13	14
Musalman—*concld.* Pathan	Mysore State, including C. and M. Stn., Bangalore.	**43,954**	**23,846**	**20,108**	**8,511**	**6,563**	**1,948**	**35,443**	**17,283**	**18,160**	**754**	**710**	**44**
	C. & M. Stn., Bangalore ...	2,632	1,507	1,125	873	614	259	1,759	893	866	174	169	5
Pinjari	Mysore State, including C. and M. Stn., Bangalore.	**8,427**	**4,364**	**4,063**	**597**	**562**	**35**	**7,830**	**3,802**	**4,028**	**14**	**13**	**1**
	C. & M. Stn., Bangalore ...	8	6	2	6	5	1	2	1	1	4	3	1
Saiyad	Mysore State, including C. and M. Stn., Bangalore.	**58,477**	**31,618**	**26,859**	**13,379**	**9,927**	**3,452**	**45,098**	**21,691**	**23,407**	**1,472**	**1,355**	**117**
	C. & M. Stn., Bangalore ...	3,154	1,725	1,429	1,357	735	622	1,797	990	807	289	254	35
Sheik	Mysore State, including C. and M. Stn., Bangalore.	**179,160**	**95,953**	**83,207**	**37,452**	**28,958**	**8,494**	**141,708**	**66,995**	**74,713**	**3,644**	**3,363**	**281**
	C. & M. Stn., Bangalore ...	15,415	7,978	7,437	4,215	3,207	1,008	11,200	4,771	6,429	1,009	923	86
Christian. Anglo-Indian	Mysore State, including C. and M. Stn., Bangalore.	**7,098**	**3,153**	**3,945**	**6,221**	**2,764**	**3,457**	**877**	**389**	**488**	**6,073**	**2,694**	**3,379**
	C. & M. Stn., Bangalore ...	4,865	2,064	2,801	4,272	1,801	2,471	593	263	330	4,181	1,768	2,413
European and Allied Races	Mysore State, including C. and M. Stn., Bangalore.	**4,964**	**2,938**	**2,026**	**4,756**	**2,832**	**1,924**	**208**	**107**	**102**	**4,668**	**2,782**	**1,886**
	C. & M. Stn., Bangalore ...	3,811	2,278	1,533	3,665	2,201	1,464	146	77	69	3,613	2,174	1,439
Indian Christian	Mysore State, including C. and M. Stn., Bangalore.	**59,623**	**31,057**	**28,566**	**20,010**	**13,198**	**6,812**	**39,613**	**17,359**	**21,754**	**8,341**	**5,608**	**2,733**
	C. & M. Stn., Bangalore ...	16,498	7,788	8,710	5,733	3,622	2,111	10,765	4,166	6,599	3,004	1,975	1,029
Jain. Digambara	Mysore State, including C. and M. Stn., Bangalore.	**10,625**	**5,514**	**5,111**	**3,748**	**3,081**	**667**	**6,877**	**2,433**	**4,444**	**365**	**355**	**10**
	C. & M. Stn., Bangalore ...	68	41	27	19	19	...	49	22	27	...	...	...
Swetambara	Mysore State, including C. and M. Stn., Bangalore.	**2,489**	**1,809**	**680**	**1,498**	**1,417**	**81**	**991**	**392**	**599**	**103**	**101**	**2**
	C. & M. Stn., Bangalore ...	391	233	158	197	185	12	194	48	146	46	46	...
Sada	Mysore State, including C. and M. Stn., Bangalore.	**11,151**	**5,820**	**5,331**	**1,621**	**1,489**	**132**	**9,530**	**4,331**	**5,199**	**109**	**104**	**5**
	C. & M. Stn., Bangalore ...	81	47	34	34	32	2	47	15	32	5	4	1
Parsi.	Mysore State, including C. and M. Stn., Bangalore.	**270**	**135**	**135**	**224**	**110**	**114**	**46**	**25**	**21**	**205**	**109**	**96**
	C. & M. Stn., Bangalore ...	195	94	101	163	70	93	32	24	8	152	70	82
Sikh.	Mysore State, including C. and M. Stn., Bangalore.	**84**	**55**	**29**	**46**	**43**	**3**	**38**	**12**	**26**	**10**	**9**	**1**
	C. and M. Stn., Bangalore ...	31	29	2	26	24	2	5	5	...	9	8	1
Jew.	Mysore State, including C. and M. Stn, Bangalore.	**32**	**11**	**21**	**24**	**9**	**15**	**8**	**2**	**6**	**23**	**9**	**14**
	C. and M. Stn., Bangalore ...	14	4	10	11	3	8	3	1	2	11	3	8
Buddhist.	Mysore State, including C. and M. Stn., Bangalore.	**954**	**494**	**460**	**379**	**300**	**79**	**575**	**194**	**381**	**173**	**143**	**30**
	C. and M. Stn., Bangalore ...	202	115	87	106	78	28	96	37	59	74	59	15
Others.	Mysore State including C. and M. Stn., Bangalore.	**90**	**40**	**50**	**35**	**19**	**16**	**55**	**21**	**34**	**20**	**10**	**10**
	C. and M. Stn., Bangalore ...	76	30	46	34	18	16	42	12	30	20	10	10

MYSORE CENSUS, 1931.

TABLE XV(i)—Language.

TABLE XV (i).

Language.

District or State	Population			A.—Vernaculars of India											
				Total			Tibeto—Chinese Family								
							Tibetan Group			Non-pronominalised Himalayan Group			Burma Group		
							Tibetan			Newari			Burmese		
	Persons	Males	Females	Persons	Males	Females	Persons	Males	Females	Persons	Males	Females	Persons	Males	Females
	1	2	3	4	5	6	7	8	9	10	11	12	13	14	15
MYSORE STATE, INCLUDING CIVIL AND MILITARY STATION, BANGALORE ...	**6,557,302**	**3,353,963**	**3,203,339**	**6,541,837**	**3,345,943**	**3,195,894**	1	...	1	35	32	3	3	2	1
MYSORE STATE, EXCLUDING CIVIL AND MILITARY STATION, BANGALORE ...	**6,423,189**	**3,284,554**	**3,138,635**	**6,417,873**	**3,281,615**	**3,136,258**	1	...	1	2	2	...	2	2	...
Bangalore City	172,357	91,680	80,677	171,469	91,275	80,194	1	...	1	...	...	...	1	1	...
Bangalore District	908,056	461,905	446,151	907,742	461,768	445,974	...	...	...	2	2	...	...	...	...
Kolar Gold Fields (City)	85,103	45,051	40,052	82,967	43,878	39,089	...	...	...	...	...	...	...	...	...
Kolar District	763,934	389,262	374,672	763,824	389,209	374,615	...	...	...	...	...	...	1	1	...
Tumkur District	861,405	439,144	422,261	861,342	439,112	422,230	...	...	...	...	...	...	...	...	...
Mysore City	107,142	56,772	50,370	106,606	56,543	50,063	...	...	...	...	...	...	...	...	...
Mysore District	1,408,984	708,838	700,146	1,408,768	708,705	700,063	...	...	...	...	...	...	...	...	...
Chitaldrug District	656,569	336,786	319,783	656,523	336,754	319,769	...	...	...	...	...	...	...	...	...
Hassan District	596,937	300,746	296,191	596,645	300,538	296,107	...	...	...	...	...	...	...	...	...
Kadur District	347,715	184,889	163,826	347,275	184,087	163,238	...	...	...	...	...	...	...	...	...
Shimoga District	519,987	274,981	245,006	519,712	274,796	244,916	...	...	...	...	...	...	...	...	...
Civil and Military Station, Bangalore	*134,113*	*69,409*	*64,704*	*123,964*	*64,328*	*59,636*	...	...	...	*33*	*30*	*3*	*1*	...	*1*

TABLE XV (i).

Language—*contd.*

District or State	A—Vernaculars of India														
	Dravidian Family														
	Dravida Group														
	Tamil												Malayalam		
	Total			Tamil			Korama			Koracha					
	Persons	Males	Females	Persons	Males	Females	Persons	Males	Females	Persons	Males	Females	Persons	Males	Females
	16	17	18	19	20	21	22	23	24	25	26	27	28	29	30
MYSORE STATE, INCLUDING CIVIL AND MILITARY STATION, BANGALORE ...	**313,685**	**161,918**	**151,767**	**307,462**	**158,707**	**148,755**	**2,519**	**1,250**	**1,269**	**3,704**	**1,961**	**1,743**	**8,513**	**6,842**	**1,671**
MYSORE STATE, EXCLUDING CIVIL AND MILITARY STATION, BANGALORE ...	**254,989**	**132,155**	**122,834**	**248,769**	**128,946**	**119,823**	**2,519**	**1,250**	**1,269**	**3,701**	**1,959**	**1,742**	**7,619**	**6,218**	**1,401**
Bangalore City	38,966	20,501	18,465	38,922	20,477	18,445	9	9	...	35	15	20	567	430	137
Bangalore District	60,150	30,844	29,306	59,016	30,289	28,727	791	386	405	343	169	174	145	95	50
Kolar Gold Fields (City)	50,365	26,273	24,092	50,356	26,268	24,088	...	...	...	9	5	4	1,761	1,396	365
Kolar District	36,234	18,189	18,045	35,609	17,894	17,715	261	128	133	364	167	197	65	48	17
Tumkur District	5,402	2,801	2,601	4,735	2,455	2,280	325	165	160	342	181	161	34	33	1
Mysore City	13,676	7,099	6,577	13,676	7,099	6,577	...	...	...	...	...	...	175	150	25
Mysore District	19,490	10,098	9,392	19,006	9,875	9,131	435	197	238	49	26	23	464	405	59
Chitaldrug District	4,710	2,575	2,135	3,035	1,614	1,421	408	264	144	1,267	697	570	48	34	14
Hassan District	12,257	6,324	5,933	11,948	6,160	5,788	118	64	54	191	100	91	1,393	1,187	206
Kadur District	6,946	3,848	3,098	6,812	3,785	3,027	22	10	12	112	53	59	1,830	1,531	299
Shimoga District	6,793	3,603	3,190	5,654	3,080	2,624	150	27	123	989	546	443	1,137	909	228
Civil and Military Station, Bangalore	***58,696***	***29,763***	***28,933***	***58,693***	***29,761***	***28,932***	...	...	...	***3***	***2***	***1***	***894***	***624***	***270***

TABLE XV(i).

Language—*contd.*

District or State	A.—Vernaculars of India—*contd.*														
	Dravidian Family—*concld.*												Indo-European Family		
	Dravida Group—*concld.*									Andhra Language			Eastern Group		
	Kannada			Coorgi			Tulu			Telugu			Pashto		
	Persons	Males	Females	Persons	Males	Females	Persons	Males	Females	Persons	Males	Females	Persons	Males	Females
	31	32	33	34	35	36	37	38	39	40	41	42	43	44	45
MYSORE STATE, INCLUDING CIVIL AND MILITARY STATION, BANGALORE ..	**4,578,801**	**2,322,597**	**2,256,204**	**440**	**293**	**147**	**45,168**	**28,441**	**16,727**	**1,030,926**	**527,576**	**503,350**	**71**	**61**	**10**
MYSORE STATE, EXCLUDING CIVIL AND MILITARY STATION, BANGALORE ...	**4,570,838**	**2,318,483**	**2,252,355**	**389**	**247**	**142**	**45,162**	**28,439**	**16,723**	**1,009,153**	**516,367**	**492,786**	**64**	**54**	**10**
Bangalore City	56,071	30,145	25,926	33	14	19	124	83	41	39,659	20,631	19,028	18	18	...
Bangalore District	590,379	299,092	291,287	4	4	...	17	11	6	177,751	90,310	87,441	27	22	5
Kolar Gold Fields (City)	6,353	3,230	3,123	...	...	...	6	1	5	16,934	8,732	8,202	...	...	...
Kolar District	192,074	97,111	94,963	...	...	...	32	19	13	466,349	237,780	228,569	...	...	...
Tumkur District	686,464	349,034	337,430	9	4	5	31	19	12	111,204	57,139	54,065	...	...	...
Mysore City	56,691	29,852	26,839	87	48	39	245	188	57	9,988	5,244	4,744	4	3	1
Mysore District	1,313,391	656,393	656,998	65	51	14	107	81	26	22,748	11,695	11,053	5	2	3
Chitaldrug District	476,705	244,308	232,397	2	...	2	73	43	30	119,741	61,160	58,581	...	...	...
Hassan District	528,469	263,423	265,046	102	66	36	9,648	6,108	3,540	14,721	7,577	7,144	...	...	...
Kadur District	261,402	134,805	127,097	65	43	22	29,233	18,223	11,010	10,763	5,762	5,001	...	...	...
Shimoga District	402,839	211,590	191,249	22	17	5	5,646	3,663	1,983	19,295	10,337	8,958	10	9	1
Civil and Military Station, Bangalore	*7,963*	*4,114*	*3,849*	*51*	*46*	*5*	*6*	*2*	*4*	*21,773*	*11,209*	*10,564*	*7*	*7*	...

TABLE XV (i).

Language—*contd.*

District or State	A—Vernaculars of India—*contd.*																	
	Indo-European Family—*contd.*																	
	Eastern Group—*concld.*			Dard Group			North-Western Group									Southern Group		
	Balochi			Kashmiri			Lahnda			Sindhi			Kachchi (Sindhi)			Marathi		
	Persons	Males	Females	Persons	Males	Females	Persons	Males	Females	Persons	Males	Females	Persons	Males	Females	Persons	Males	Females
	46	47	48	49	50	51	52	53	54	55	56	57	58	59	60	61	62	63
MYSORE STATE, INCLUDING CIVIL AND MILITARY STATION, BANGALORE ...	**6**	**3**	**3**	**29**	**18**	**11**	**11**	**9**	**2**	**248**	**167**	**81**	**258**	**107**	**151**	**91,322**	**47,025**	**44,297**
MYSORE STATE, EXCLUDING CIVIL AND MILITARY STATION, BANGALORE ...	**6**	**3**	**3**	...	...	...	**7**	**6**	**1**	**230**	**156**	**74**	**145**	**46**	**99**	**87,112**	**44,798**	**42,314**
Bangalore City	2	...	2	...	...	...	7	6	1	78	63	15	19	16	3	12,911	6,678	6,233
Bangalore District	...	...	...	...	...	...	...	...	...	6	4	2	...	...	...	12,196	6,240	5,956
Kolar Gold Fields (City)	...	...	...	...	...	...	...	...	...	...	...	...	...	...	...	732	387	345
Kolar District	...	...	...	...	...	...	...	...	...	...	...	...	...	...	...	8,085	4,045	4,040
Tumkur District	...	...	...	...	...	...	...	...	...	...	...	...	20	20	...	8,309	4,193	4,116
Mysore City	...	...	...	...	...	...	...	...	...	124	75	49	...	...	...	6,081	3,256	2,825
Mysore District	4	3	1	...	...	...	...	...	...	...	...	...	...	...	...	7,568	3,817	3,751
Chitaldrug District	...	...	...	...	...	...	...	...	...	...	...	...	98	6	92	7,223	3,696	3,527
Hassan District	...	...	...	...	...	...	...	...	...	...	...	...	...	...	...	3,973	1,990	1,983
Kadur District	...	...	...	...	...	...	...	...	...	...	...	...	8	4	4	4,529	2,397	2,132
Shimoga District	...	...	...	...	...	...	...	...	...	22	14	8	...	...	...	15,505	8,099	7,406
Civil and Military Station, Bangalore	...	...	...	***29***	***18***	***11***	***4***	***3***	***1***	***18***	***11***	***7***	***113***	***61***	***52***	***4,210***	***2,227***	***1,983***

TABLE XV (i).

Language—*contd.*

District or State	A.—Vernaculars of India—*contd.*																	
	Indo-European Family—*contd.*																	
	Southern Group—*concld.*			Eastern Group									Mediate Group			Central Group		
	Konkani			Oriya			Bihari			Bengali			*Hindi			*Hindustani		
	Persons	Males	Females	Persons	Males	Females	Persons	Males	Females	Persons	Males	Females	Persons	Males	Females	Persons	Males	Females
	64	65	66	67	68	69	70	71	72	73	74	75	76	77	78	79	80	81
MYSORE STATE, INCLUDING CIVIL AND MILITARY STATION, BANGALORE ...	**16,295**	**9,912**	**6,383**	**1,388**	**709**	**679**	**1**	**1**	...	**207**	**115**	**92**	**6,915**	**3,909**	**3,006**	**382,876**	**202,493**	**180,383**
MYSORE STATE, EXCLUDING CIVIL AND MILITARY STATION, BANGALORE ...	**16,023**	**9,781**	**6,242**	**1,374**	**702**	**672**	**1**	**1**	...	**151**	**86**	**65**	**6,139**	**3,392**	**2,747**	**354,789**	**187,560**	**167,229**
Bangalore City	679	358	321	...	...	...	...	...	...	22	15	7	713	455	258	19,821	10,798	9,023
Bangalore District	84	66	18	44	29	15	...	...	...	111	53	58	558	291	267	60,796	31,890	28,906
Kolar Gold Fields (City)	37	15	22	...	...	...	...	...	...	1	1	...	98	57	41	6,201	3,493	2,708
Kolar District	39	24	15	131	62	69	...	...	...	...	...	...	466	246	220	58,775	30,763	28,012
Tumkur District	32	18	14	255	132	123	...	...	...	...	...	...	683	365	318	43,487	22,645	20,842
Mysore City	128	74	54	88	44	44	...	...	...	6	6	...	659	387	272	18,376	9,915	8,461
Mysore District	201	174	27	...	...	...	...	...	...	...	...	...	790	399	391	38,158	20,184	17,974
Chitaldrug District	399	186	213	395	207	188	1	1	...	1	1	...	576	304	272	32,976	17,261	15,715
Hassan District	1,043	687	356	193	98	95	...	...	...	...	...	...	485	256	229	19,548	10,335	9,213
Kadur District	6,559	4,094	2,465	220	109	111	...	...	...	3	3	...	403	235	168	17,439	9,364	8,075
Shimoga District	6,822	4,085	2,737	48	21	27	...	...	...	7	7	...	708	397	311	39,212	20,912	18,300
Civil and Military Station, Bangalore	*272*	*131*	*141*	*14*	*7*	*7*	...	...	...	*56*	*29*	*27*	*776*	*517*	*259*	*28,087*	*14,933*	*13,154*

* See note 4 on title page of table XIII.

TABLE XV(i).

Language—*contd.*

District or State	A.—Vernaculars of India—*contd.*																	
	Indo-European Family—*contd.*																	
	Central Group—*contd.*																	
	Rajasthani												Gujarathi					
	Total			Rajasthani			Marwari			Banjari			Total			Gujarathi		
	Persons	Males	Females	Persons	Males	Females	Persons	Males	Females	Persons	Males	Females	Persons	Males	Females	Persons	Males	Females
	82	83	84	85	86	87	88	89	90	91	92	93	94	95	96	97	98	99
MYSORE STATE, INCLUDING CIVIL AND MILITARY STATION, BANGALORE ...	**59,711**	**30,845**	**28,866**	**79**	**41**	**38**	**2,217**	**1,610**	**607**	**57,415**	**29,194**	**28,221**	**4,600**	**2,604**	**1,996**	**3,430**	**2,007**	**1,423**
MYSORE STATE, EXCLUDING CIVIL AND MILITARY STATION, BANGALORE ...	**59,421**	**30,675**	**28,746**	**76**	**40**	**36**	**1,932**	**1,443**	**489**	**57,413**	**29,192**	**28,221**	**4,130**	**2,347**	**1,783**	**2,986**	**1,765**	**1,221**
Bangalore City	323	239	84	40	18	22	273	219	54	10	2	8	1,415	793	622	654	413	241
Bangalore District	5,035	2,589	2,446	20	11	9	131	67	64	4,884	2,511	2,373	423	217	206	412	211	201
Kolar Gold Fields (City)	414	240	174	...	...	...	414	240	174	...	...	...	36	24	12	36	24	12
Kolar District	1,479	858	621	...	...	...	126	105	21	1,353	753	600	94	63	31	33	22	11
Tumkur District	5,215	2,613	2,602	2	1	1	62	54	8	5,151	2,558	2,593	176	89	87	163	82	81
Mysore City	103	81	22	13	9	4	62	57	5	28	15	13	174	120	54	160	112	48
Mysore District	437	226	211	1	1	...	...	...	...	436	225	211	339	176	163	330	173	157
Chitaldrug District	12,877	6,597	6,280	...	...	...	271	222	49	12,606	6,375	6,231	689	370	319	431	246	185
Hassan District	4,676	2,389	2,287	...	...	...	203	155	48	4,473	2,234	2,239	137	98	39	123	87	36
Kadur District	7,720	4,019	3,701	...	...	...	230	196	34	7,490	3,823	3,667	144	89	55	142	87	55
Shimoga District	21,142	10,824	10,318	...	...	...	160	128	32	20,982	10,696	10,286	503	308	195	502	308	194
Civil and Military Station, Bangalore	***290***	***170***	***120***	***3***	***1***	***2***	***285***	***167***	***118***	***2***	***2***	...	***470***	***257***	***213***	***444***	***242***	***202***

TABLE XV (i).

Language—*contd.*

District or State	A.—Vernaculars of India—*concld.*																	
	Indo-European Family—*concld.*																	
	Central Group—*concld.*															Pahari Group		
	Gujarathi									Panchali (Bhili)			Panjabi			Pahari (unspecified)		
	Memani			Nagari			Sourashtra											
	Persons	Males	Females	Persons	Males	Females	Persons	Males	Females	Persons	Males	Females	Persons	Males	Females	Persons	Males	Females
	100	101	102	103	104	105	106	107	108	109	110	111	112	113	114	115	116	117
MYSORE STATE, INCLUDING CIVIL AND MILITARY STATION, BANGALORE ...	3	2	1	403	201	202	764	394	370	11	6	5	275	238	37	10	3	7
MYSORE STATE, EXCLUDING CIVIL AND MILITARY STATION, BANGALORE ...	3	2	1	403	201	202	738	379	359	11	6	5	81	72	9	3	...	3
Bangalore City	...	...	...	92	42	50	669	338	331	...	...	...	35	30	5	3	...	3
Bangalore District	...	...	...	11	6	5	...	...	...	11	6	5	3	3	...	...	...	...
Kolar Gold Fields (City)	...	...	...	...	...	...	...	...	...	...	...	...	29	29	...	...	...	...
Kolar District	...	...	...	15	11	4	46	30	16	...	...	...	...	...	...	...	...	...
Tumkur District	...	...	...	13	7	6	...	...	...	...	...	...	...	...	...	...	...	...
Mysore City	...	...	...	...	...	...	14	8	6	...	...	...	1	1	...	...	...	...
Mysore District	...	...	...	...	...	...	9	3	6	...	...	...	1	1	...	...	...	...
Chitaldrug District	...	...	...	258	124	134	...	...	...	...	...	...	9	5	4	...	...	...
Hassan District	...	...	...	14	11	3	...	...	...	...	...	...	...	...	...	...	...	...
Kadur District	2	2	...	...	...	...	...	...	...	...	...	...	2	2	...	...	...	...
Shimoga District	1	...	1	...	...	...	...	...	...	...	...	...	1	1	...	...	...	...
Civil and Military Station, Bangalore	...	...	...	...	...	...	26	15	11	...	...	...	194	166	28	7	3	4

TABLE XV(i).

Language—*contd.*

District or State	A.—Vernaculars of India.—*concld.* Unclassed Languages: Gipsy Language (Ladar)			B.—Vernaculars of other Asiatic Countries and Africa. Total			Indo-European Family: Southern Group: Singhalese			Indo-European Family: Persian Group: Persian			Indo-European Family: Armenian Group: Armenian			Tibeto—Chinese Family: Chinese Group: Chinese			Semitic Family: Arabic		
	Persons	Males	Females	Persons	Males	Females	Persons	Males	Females	Persons	Males	Females	Persons	Males	Females	Persons	Males	Females	Persons	Males	Females
	118	119	120	121	122	123	124	125	126	127	128	129	130	131	132	133	134	135	136	137	138
MYSORE STATE, INCLUDING CIVIL AND MILITARY STATION, BANGALORE ...	**31**	**17**	**14**	**1,095**	**783**	**312**	**39**	**27**	**12**	**275**	**149**	**126**	**5**	**3**	**2**	**16**	**15**	**1**	**746**	**584**	**162**
MYSORE STATE, EXCLUDING CIVIL AND MILITARY STATION, BANGALORE ...	*31*	*17*	*14*	*900*	*679*	*221*	*17*	*12*	*5*	*134*	*77*	*57*	...	...	...	*9*	*9*	...	*737*	*580*	*157*
Bangalore City	1	1	...	32	19	13	5	1	4	17	9	8	...	...	...	9	9	...	...	...	...
Bangalore District	...	...	...	24	18	6	8	8	...	4	3	1	...	...	...	...	...	...	12	7	5
Kolar Gold Fields (City)	...	...	...	4	2	2	2	1	1	1	1	...	...	...	...	...	...	...	1	...	1
Kolar District	...	...	...	13	7	6	...	...	...	13	7	6	...	...	...	...	...	...	...	...	...
Tumkur District	21	7	14	22	13	9	...	...	...	...	...	...	...	...	...	...	...	...	22	13	9
Mysore City	...	...	...	30	10	20	1	1	...	15	6	9	...	...	...	...	...	...	13	3	10
Mysore District	...	...	...	89	50	39	...	...	...	54	30	24	...	...	...	...	...	...	35	20	15
Chitaldrug District	...	...	...	7	7	...	1	1	...	4	4	...	...	...	...	...	...	...	2	2	...
Hassan District	...	...	...	168	139	29	...	...	...	10	9	1	...	...	...	...	...	...	158	130	28
Kadur District	9	9	...	308	264	44	...	...	...	15	7	8	...	...	...	...	...	...	292	256	36
Shimoga District	...	...	...	203	150	53	...	...	...	1	1	...	...	...	...	...	...	...	202	149	53
Civil and Military Station, Bangalore	...	...	...	*195*	*104*	*91*	*22*	*15*	*7*	*141*	*72*	*69*	*5*	*3*	*2*	*7*	*6*	*1*	*9*	*4*	*5*

TABLE XV (i).

Language—*contd.*

District or State	B.—Vernaculars of other Asiatic Countries and Africa—*concld.*						C.—European Languages.														
	Semitic Family—*concld.*			Mongolian Family			Total			Indo-European Family											
				Japanese Group						Romance Group											
	Hebrew			Japanese						Italian			French			Spanish			Portuguese		
	Persons	Males	Females	Persons	Males	Females	Persons	Males	Females	Persons	Males	Females	Persons	Males	Females	Persons	Males	Females	Persons	Males	Females
	139	140	141	142	143	144	145	146	147	148	149	150	151	152	153	154	155	156	157	158	159
MYSORE STATE, INCLUDING CIVIL AND MILITARY STATION, BANGALORE ...	9	2	7	5	3	2	14,370	7,237	7,133	49	41	8	127	38	89	11	3	8	306	144	162
MYSORE STATE, EXCLUDING CIVIL AND MILITARY STATION, BANGALORE ...	...	...	...	3	1	2	4,416	2,260	2,156	42	40	2	56	13	43	8	3	5	93	55	38
Bangalore City	...	...	...	1	...	1	856	386	470	1	1	...	27	6	21	8	3	5	44	22	22
Bangalore District	...	...	...	...	...	...	290	119	171	...	...	...	14	4	10	...	...	...	...	...	...
Kolar Gold Fields (City)	...	...	...	...	...	...	2,182	1,171	961	39	37	2	7	1	6	...	...	...	6	4	2
Kolar District	...	...	...	...	...	...	97	46	51	...	...	...	1	1	...	...	...	...	1	...	1
Tumkur District	...	...	...	...	...	...	41	19	22	...	...	...	...	...	...	...	...	...	1	1	...
Mysore City	...	...	...	1	...	1	506	219	287	2	2	...	2	1	1	...	...	...	9	5	4
Mysore District	...	...	...	...	...	...	127	83	44	...	...	...	...	...	...	...	...	...	1	1	...
Chitaldrug District	...	...	...	...	...	...	39	25	14	...	...	...	...	...	...	...	...	...	3	3	...
Hassan District	...	...	...	...	...	...	124	69	55	...	...	...	4	...	4	...	...	...	10	5	5
Kadur District	...	...	...	1	1	...	132	88	44	...	...	...	1	...	1	...	...	...	18	14	4
Shimoga District	...	...	...	...	...	...	72	35	37	...	...	...	...	...	...	...	...	...	...	...	...
Civil and Military Station, Bangalore	9	2	7	2	2	...	9,954	4,977	4,977	7	1	6	71	25	46	3	...	3	213	89	124

TABLE XV (i).
Language.

TABLE XV (i).

Language—*concld.*

District or State	C.—European Languages.—*concld.*																				
	Indo-European Family—*concld.*																		Mongolian Family		
	Celtic Group						Balto-Slavonic Group			Teutonic Group									Ural-altic Group		
	Welsh			Irish			Russian			English			Danish			German			Hungarian		
	Persons	Males	Females	Persons	Males	Females	Persons	Males	Females	Persons	Males	Females	Persons	Males	Females	Persons	Males	Females	Persons	Males	Females
	160	161	162	163	164	165	166	167	168	169	170	171	172	173	174	175	176	177	178	179	180
MYSORE STATE, INCLUDING CIVIL AND MILITARY STATION, BANGALORE ...	8	7	1	5	3	2	1	...	1	13,825	6,987	6,838	7	3	4	30	11	19	1	...	1
MYSORE STATE, EXCLUDING CIVIL AND MILITARY STATION, BANGALORE ...	6	5	1	...	...	...	...	...	...	4,192	2,138	2,054	3	1	2	16	5	11	...	...	...
Bangalore City	...	...	...	...	...	...	...	...	...	770	351	419	1	1	...	5	2	3	...	...	...
Bangalore District	...	...	...	...	...	...	...	...	...	274	115	159	...	...	...	2	...	2	...	...	...
Kolar Gold Fields (City)	6	5	1	...	...	...	...	...	...	2,074	1,124	950	...	...	...	...	...	...	...	...	...
Kolar District	...	...	...	...	...	...	...	...	...	94	45	49	1	...	1	...	...	...	...	...	...
Tumkur District	...	...	...	...	...	...	...	...	...	40	18	22	...	...	...	...	...	...	...	...	...
Mysore City	...	...	...	...	...	...	...	...	...	487	210	277	1	...	1	5	1	4	...	...	...
Mysore District	...	...	...	...	...	...	...	...	...	126	82	44	...	...	...	...	...	...	...	...	...
Chitaldrug District	...	...	...	...	...	...	...	...	...	36	22	14	...	...	...	...	...	...	...	...	...
Hassan District	...	...	...	...	...	...	...	...	...	110	64	46	...	...	...	...	...	...	...	...	...
Kadur District	...	...	...	...	...	...	...	...	...	109	72	37	...	...	...	4	2	2	...	...	...
Shimoga District	...	...	...	...	...	...	...	...	...	72	35	37	...	...	...	...	...	...	...	...	...
Civil and Military Station, Bangalore	2	2	...	5	3	2	1	...	1	9,633	4,849	4,784	4	2	2	14	6	8	1	...	1

MYSORE CENSUS, 1931.

TABLE XV—PART II—Bilingualism.

NOTE 1.—This table is confined to only eight important mother-tongues in the State, *viz.*, Kannada, Telugu, Tamil, Marathi, Hindustani (which appears as Western Hindi in the India Tables,) Tulu, Konkani and Banajari (Rajasthani).

(*a*) The following languages returned as subsidiary have been omitted for the purpose of this table. The numbers speaking them are small and they are not in the nature of subsidiary languages in the State:—

Arabic
Balochi
Bengali
Burmese
Coorgi
Deccani
English
German
Greek
Gujarathi
Hindi (Eastern)
Ladar
Malayali
Oriya
Pashto
Portuguese
Panjabi
Sindhi
Spanish

(*b*) The following statement shows the number of persons who speak Gujarathi and Malayali respectively as mother-tongues, and also the number of persons who speak Kannada as subsidiary to these mother-tongues;—

	Gujarathi as mother-tongue		Kannada subsidiary to gujarathi		Malayali as mother-tongue		Kannada subsidiary to Malayali	
	Males	Females	Males	Females	Males	Females	Males	Females
Mysore State, including Civil and Military Station, Bangalore.	2,604	1,996	817	668	6,842	1,671	2,484	481
Civil and Military Station, Bangalore.	257	213	9	4	624	270	5	3

NOTE 2.—The figures in italics in columns 6-19 show the actual number of persons speaking only one subsidiary language and those in columns 20-27 more than one; other figures in columns 6-19 show the duplicated number.

TABLE XV.—PART II.

Bilingualism.

Area of Bilingualism	Mother-tongue.—Kannada																									
	Number of Persons speaking																									
	Mother-tongue		Total of Subsidiary Languages		Subsidiary Language														Two Subsidiary Languages		Three Subsidiary Languages		Four Subsidiary Languages		Five Subsidiary Languages	
					Telugu		Hindustani		Tamil		Marathi		Banajari		Tulu		Konkani									
	Males	Females	Males	Females	Males	Females	Males	Females	Males	Females	Males	Females	Males	Females	Males	Females	Males	Females	Males	Females	Males	Females	Males	Females	Males	Females
1	2	3	4	5	6	7	8	9	10	11	12	13	14	15	16	17	18	19	20	21	22	23	24	25	26	27
MYSORE STATE, INCLUDING CIVIL AND MILITARY STATION, BANGALORE.	**2,322,597**	**2,562,204**	**165,509** *159,274*	**129,393** *128,342*	**141,026** *136,405*	**121,911** *121,006*	**12,896** *9,485*	**1,313** *1,093*	**6,345** *3,328*	**3,204** *2,417*	**2,290** *1,935*	**1,530** *1,436*	**141** *141*	**87** *87*	**2,549** *2,475*	**1,194** *1,182*	**262** *227*	**154** *144*	... *4,356*	... *910*	... *887*	... *61*	... *35*	... *5*	... ...	... *1*
MYSORE STATE, EXCLUDING CIVIL AND MILITARY STATION, BANGALORE.	**2,318,483**	**2,252,355**	**163,588** *157,646*	**128,078** *127,106*	**140,023** *135,599*	**121,110** *120,276*	**12,763** *9,452*	**1,293** *1,082*	**5,571** *2,786*	**2,724** *2,015*	**2,279** *1,928*	**1,522** *1,428*	**141** *141*	**87** *87*	**2,549** *2,475*	**1,194** *1,182*	**262** *227*	**148** *138*	... *4,168*	... *831*	... *836*	... *61*	... *34*	... *5*	... ...	... *1*
Bangalore City ...	30,145	25,926	7,518 *5,947*	3,986 *3,681*	5,088 *3,888*	3,179 *2,914*	782 *164*	145 *95*	1,356 *388*	516 *265*	235 *156*	133 *120*	... ...	... ...	32 *27*	8 *8*	25 *22*	5 *5*	... *1,042*	... *245*	... *251*	... *27*	... *9*	... *2*	... ...	... ...
Bangalore District ...	299,092	291,287	38,953 *37,595*	30,247 *30,068*	35,582 *34,442*	29,387 *29,218*	2,240 *1,439*	112 *80*	1,018 *426*	642 *498*	103 *85*	102 *94*	3 *3*	2 *2*	7 *6*	2 *2*	... ...	... ...	... *1,032*	... *169*	... *160*	... *5*	... *2*	... ...	... ...	... ...
Kolar Gold Fields (City)	3,230	3,123	2,404 *2,312*	2,057 *2,018*	2,190 *2,051*	1,958 *1,920*	20 *5*	2 *1*	250 *174*	91 *56*	4 *1*	6 *3*	... ...	... ...	... ...	... ...	... ...	... ...	... *70*	... *37*	... *11*	... *1*	... ...	... ...	... ...	... ...
Kolar District ...	97,111	94,963	64,104 *63,144*	57,475 *57,257*	62,873 *62,052*	57,053 *56,847*	681 *87*	65 *25*	485 *136*	305 *144*	60 *30*	50 *32*	... ...	... ...	5 *5*	2 *1*	... ...	... ...	... *711*	... *198*	... *120*	... *10*	... *3*	... ...	... ...	... ...
Tumkur District ...	349,034	337,430	16,910 *16,606*	11,717 *11,679*	14,879 *14,660*	11,312 *11,281*	1,558 *1,323*	105 *89*	275 *178*	133 *118*	134 *115*	123 *114*	47 *47*	43 *43*	16 *16*	... ...	1 *1*	1 ...	... *229*	... *29*	... *36*	... *3*	... *1*	... ...	... ...	... *1*
Mysore City ...	29,852	26,839	1,936 *1,577*	642 *613*	469 *247*	301 *277*	949 *738*	63 *56*	418 *213*	197 *175*	86 *70*	70 *68*	... ...	... ...	18 *16*	11 *10*	1 *1*	... ...	... *229*	... *25*	... *59*	... *2*	... *4*	... ...	... ...	... ...
Mysore District ...	656,393	656,998	4,394 *3,985*	1,520 *1,490*	1,268 *1,027*	828 *806*	1,991 *1,745*	128 *113*	841 *624*	377 *353*	254 *230*	174 *173*	1 *1*	... ...	23 *23*	18 *18*	16 *4*	... ...	... *258*	... *24*	... *68*	... *3*	... *5*	... ...	... ...	... ...
Chitaldrug District ...	244,308	232,397	17,592 *17,310*	16,467 *16,419*	15,855 *15,671*	15,937 *15,905*	1,203 *983*	255 *231*	125 *77*	52 *33*	368 *297*	200 *186*	21 *21*	5 *5*	12 *10*	8 *8*	8 *8*	10 *10*	... *209*	... *37*	... *29*	... *1*	... *5*	... *3*	... ...	... ...
Hassan District ...	263,423	265,046	2,577 *2,391*	858 *820*	559 *459*	342 *321*	1,006 *896*	81 *65*	440 *346*	228 *210*	208 *191*	83 *72*	1 *1*	... ...	355 *338*	116 *113*	8 *7*	8 *8*	... *122*	... *24*	... *29*	... *7*	... *2*	... ...	... ...	... ...
Kadur District ...	134,305	127,097	3,162 *2,953*	1,078 *1,061*	450 *336*	274 *262*	762 *621*	72 *69*	172 *105*	80 *70*	83 *73*	59 *57*	34 *34*	22 *22*	1,651 *1,613*	569 *564*	10 *6*	2 ...	... *121*	... *17*	... *44*	... ...	... ...	... ...	... ...	... ...
Shimoga District ...	211,590	191,249	4,038 *3,826*	2,031 *2,001*	870 *766*	539 *525*	1,571 *1,451*	270 *258*	196 *119*	103 *93*	744 *680*	522 *509*	34 *34*	15 *15*	430 *421*	460 *458*	193 *178*	122 *115*	... *145*	... *26*	... *29*	... *2*	... *3*	... ...	... ...	... ...
Civil and Military Station, Bangalore.	**4,114**	**3,849**	**1,921** *1,628*	**1,315** *1,236*	**1,008** *806*	**801** *730*	**133** *33*	**20** *11*	**774** *542*	**480** *402*	**11** *7*	**8** *8*	... ...	... ...	... ...	... ...	... ...	**6** *6*	... *188*	... *79*	... *51*	... ...	... *1*	... ...	... ...	... ...

TABLE XV.—PART II.

Bilingualism—*contd.*

Area of Bilingualism	Mother-tongue.—Telugu																									
	Number of Persons speaking																									
	Mother-tongue		Total of subsidiary Languages		Subsidiary Language														Two Subsidiary Languages		Three Subsidiary Languages		Four Subsidiary Languages		Five Subsidiary Languages	
					Kannada		Hindustani		Tamil		Marathi		Banajari		Tulu		Konkani									
	Males	Females	Males	Females	Males	Females	Males	Females	Males	Females	Males	Females	Males	Females	Males	Females	Males	Females	Males	Females	Males	Females	Males	Females	Males	Females
1	2	3	4	5	6	7	8	9	10	11	12	13	14	15	16	17	18	19	20	21	22	23	24	25	26	27
MYSORE STATE, INCLUDING CIVIL AND MILITARY STATION, BANGALORE.	527,576	508,350	240,221 *234,046*	193,228 *191,554*	223,740 *218,754*	185,452 *183,922*	4,370 *1,309*	677 *337*	11,877 *8,474*	6,987 *5,668*	196 *81*	78 *26*	3 *3*	1 *1*	33 *11*	33 *2*	2 *2*	... ...	... *4,666*	... *1,525*	... *720*	... *70*	... *17*	... *3*	... ...	... ...
MYSORE STATE, EXCLUDING CIVIL AND MILITARY STATION, BANGALORE.	516,367	492,786	234,844 *229,310*	189,635 *188,156*	222,467 *217,767*	184,479 *183,089*	3,636 *941*	559 *279*	8,516 *5,670*	4,490 *3,344*	187 *77*	73 *22*	3 *3*	1 *1*	33 *11*	33 *2*	2 *2*	... ...	... *4,160*	... *1,362*	... *663*	... *54*	... *16*	... *3*	... ...	... ...
Bangalore City ...	20,631	19,028	14,090 *12,671*	11,214 *10,741*	11,469 *10,373*	9,877 *9,441*	547 *24*	60 *4*	2,025 *1,092*	1,274 *853*	44 *26*	3 ...	1 *1*	... ...	4 *1*	... ...	... ...	... ..	... *890*	... *415*	... *257*	... *26*	... *5*	... *2*	... ...	... ...
Bangalore District ...	90,310	87,441	57,547 *56,425*	45,570 *45,358*	54,065 *53,087*	45,068 *44,867*	649 *89*	127 *87*	2,806 *2,262*	368 *199*	23 *5*	12 *2*	... ...	... ...	 *1*	... ...	... ...	... ...	... *857*	... *194*	... *128*	... *9*	... *3*	... ...	... ...	... ...
Kolar Gold Fields (City)...	8,732	8,202	2,194 *2,008*	1,905 *1,858*	848 *691*	598 *560*	49 *15*	9 *1*	1,293 *1,127*	1,298 *1,246*	4 *4*	5 *4*	... ...	... ...	... ...	... ...	... ...	... ...	... *156*	... *47*	... *15*	... ...	... ...	... ...	... ...	... ...
Kolar District ...	237,780	228,569	47,419 *46,325*	29,822 *29,660*	44,761 *43,796*	28,817 *28,670*	1,322 *638*	110 *85*	1,801 *880*	847 *743*	34 *19*	18 *12*	... ...	... ...	1 ...	... ...	... ...	... ...	... *891*	... *138*	... *100*	... *12*	... *1*	... ...	... ...	... ...
Tumkur District ...	57,139	54,065	28,223 *27,946*	23,650 *23,564*	27,841 *27,592*	23,484 *23,400*	227 *55*	45 *14*	131 *37*	105 *63*	24 *13*	15 *2*	... ...	1 *1*	... ...	... ...	... ...	... ...	... *223*	... *83*	... *24*	... ...	... *2*	... *1*	... ...	... ...
Mysore City ...	5,244	4,744	4,577 *4,113*	4,085 *3,886*	4,040 *3,652*	3,830 *3,641*	247 *21*	69 *16*	285 *35*	184 *33*	5 ...	2 ...	... ...	... ...	... ...	... ...	... ...	... ...	... *348*	... *193*	... *55*	... *3*	... *2*	... ...	... ...	... ...
Mysore District ...	11,695	11,053	9,313 *9,095*	8,641 *8,558*	8,942 *8,756*	8.464 *8,383*	111 *35*	8 *4*	259 *115*	169 *90*	1 ...	... ...	... ...	... ...	... ...	... ...	... ...	... ...	... *160*	... *79*	... *29*	... *2*	... ...	... ...	... ...	... ...
Chitaldrug District ...	61,160	58.581	50,568 *50,355*	46,728 *46,694*	50,295 *50,104*	46,667 *46,640*	187 *24*	18 ...	69 *24*	38 *26*	13 *1*	... ...	2 *2*	... ...	2 *2*	... ...	... ...	... ...	... *183*	... *27*	... *15*	... *1*	... ...	... ...	... ...	... ...
Hassan District ...	7,577	7,144	6,827 *6,711*	6,265 *6,241*	6,636 *6,525*	6,216 *6,192*	102 *20*	8 ...	75 *44*	41 *25*	4 *4*	... ...	... ...	... ...	8 *5*	... ...	2 *2*	... ...	... *107*	... *24*	.. *3*	... ...	... *1*	... ...	... ...	... ...
Kadur District ...	5,762	5,001	4,913 *4,715*	4,206 *4,121*	4,692 *4,513*	4,101 *4,017*	94 *7*	2 *1*	107 *12*	72 *19*	7 ...	... ...	... ...	... ...	18 *2*	31 ...	... ...	... ...	... *166*	... *83*	... *13*	... *1*	... *2*	... ...	... ...	... ...
Shimoga District ...	10,337	8,958	9,173 *8,946*	7,554 *7,475*	8,878 *8,676*	7,357 *7,278*	101 20	73 67	165 *42*	104 *47*	28 *5*	18 *2*	... ...	... ...	1 ...	2 *2*	... ...	... ...	... *179*	... *79*	... *24*	... ...	... ...	... ...	... ...	... ...
Civil and Military Station, Bangalore.	11,209	10,564	5,377 *4,738*	3,593 *3,398*	1,273 *987*	973 *833*	734 *368*	118 *58*	3,361 *2,804*	2,497 *2,324*	9 *4*	5 *4*	... ...	... ...	.. ...	... ...	... ...	... ...	... *506*	... *163*	... *66*	... *16*	... *1*	... ...	... ...	... ...

TABLE XV.—PART II.

Bilingualism—*contd.*

Area of Bilingualism	Mother-tongue.—Hindustani																									
	Number of Persons speaking																									
	Mother-tongue		Total of subsidiary Languages		Subsidiary Language														Two Subsidiary Languages		Three Subsidiary Languages		Four Subsidiary Languages		Five Subsidiary Languages	
					Kannada		Telugu		Tamil		Marathi		Konkani		Banajari		Tulu									
	Males	Females	Males	Females	Males	Females	Males	Females	Males	Females	Males	Females	Males	Females	Males	Females	Males	Females	Males	Females	Males	Females	Males	Females	Males	Females
1	2	3	4	5	6	7	8	9	10	11	12	13	14	15	16	17	18	19	20	21	22	23	24	25	26	27
MYSORE STATE, INCLUDING CIVIL AND MILITARY STATION, BANGALORE.	**202,493**	**180,383**	**139,793** *131,325*	**91,248** *89,048*	**109,911** *102,993*	**74,875** *72,862*	**20,904** *14,517*	**13,912** *12,187*	**8,443** *5,943*	**2,286** *1,832*	**168** *70*	**50** *31*	**21** *5*	**1** ...	**2** ...	... ...	**344** *62*	**124** *30*	... *7,017*	... *2,013*	... *703*	... *92*	... *15*	... *1*	... ...	... ...
MYSORE STATE, EXCLUDING CIVIL AND MILITARY STATION, BANGALORE.	**187,560**	**167,229**	**133,900** *126,306*	**90,004** *87,918*	**109,398** *102,739*	**74,750** *72,770*	**19,987** *14,236*	**13,725** *12,081*	**3,990** *2,242*	**1,357** *1,005*	**158** *61*	**47** *29*	**21** *5*	**1** ...	**2** ...	... ...	**344** *62*	**124** *30*	... *6,343*	... *1,921*	... *603*	... *81*	... *15*	... *1*	... ...	... ...
Bangalore City ...	**10,798**	**9,023**	6,723 *5,482*	2,406 *2,148*	5,051 *4,140*	1,852 *1,649*	769 *115*	907 *137*	864 *276*	243 *143*	16 *5*	4 *3*	2 ...	... ...	... ...	... ...	1 *1*	... ...	... *651*	... *174*	... *292*	... *42*	... *2*	... ...	... ...	... ...
Bangalore District ...	**31,890**	**28,906**	19,483 *18,099*	12,489 *12,009*	17,011 *15,780*	10,984 *10,515*	2,148 *896*	1,407 *948*	311 *180*	95 *70*	12 ...	3 *3*	... ...	... ...	... ...	... ...	1 *1*	... ...	... *1,222*	... *466*	... *78*	... *7*	... *2*	... ...	... ...	... ...
Kolar Gold Fields (City)...	**3,493**	**2,708**	2,028 *1,785*	944 *900*	195 *89*	37 *26*	461 *275*	283 *244*	1,870 *1,197*	624 *587*	2 *1*	... ...	... ...	... ...	... ...	... ...	... ...	... ...	... *212*	... *42*	... *14*	... *1*	... ...	... ...	... ...	... ...
Kolar District ...	**30,763**	**28,012**	21,426 *18,586*	12,431 *11,853*	6,024 *3,422*	1,802 *1,266*	14,886 *12,185*	10,535 *9,973*	509 *236*	93 *52*	7 *1*	1 ...	... ...	... ...	... ...	... ...	... ...	... ...	... *2,645*	... *547*	... *96*	... *14*	... *1*	... *1*	... ...	... ...
Tumkur District ...	**22,645**	**20,842**	16,653 *16,363*	12,922 *12,208*	15,818 *15,541*	11,545 *11,434*	782 *531*	756 *646*	49 *19*	20 *16*	2 ...	... ...	... ...	... ...	2 ...	... ...	... ...	1 *1*	... *254*	... *108*	... *18*	... *3*	... ...	... ...	... ...	... ...
Mysore City ...	**9,915**	**8,461**	6,116 *5,997*	2,683 *2,660*	5,948 *5,844*	2,636 *2,619*	33 *4*	15 *4*	128 *40*	30 *19*	6 ...	2 ...	... ...	... ...	... ...	... ...	1 *1*	... ...	... *97*	... *13*	... *11*	... *5*	... ...	... ...	... ...	... ...
Mysore District ...	**20,184**	**17,974**	15,024 *14,775*	11,190 *11,108*	14,653 *14,456*	11,049 *10,970*	107 *37*	22 *11*	209 *46*	97 *29*	55 *36*	22 *19*	... ...	... ...	... ...	... ...	... ...	... ...	... *158*	... *76*	... *35*	... *3*	... *7*	... ...	... ...	... ...
Chitaldrug District ...	**17,261**	**15,715**	14,435 *13,912*	11,874 *11,637*	13,760 *13,263*	11,538 *11,306*	595 *129*	317 *97*	56 *12*	13 *1*	22 *5*	6 ...	1 *1*	... ...	... ...	... ...	1 ...	... ...	... *463*	... *229*	... *17*	... *4*	... *2*	... ...	... ...	... ...
Hassan District ...	**10,335**	**9,213**	7,972 *7,855*	6,085 *5,984*	7,737 *7,623*	5,994 *5,835*	59 *27*	34 *4*	113 *72*	41 *36*	3 ...	... ...	3 *3*	... ...	... ...	... ...	57 *16*	16 *8*	... *111*	... *101*	... *3*	... ...	... ...	... ...	... ...	... ...
Kadur District ...	**9,364**	**8,075**	7,489 *7,153*	5,418 *5,315*	6,971 *6,667*	5,257 *5,159*	58 *18*	22 *11*	189 *104*	52 *25*	13 *6*	1 ...	3 *1*	... ...	... ...	... ...	255 *43*	86 *18*	... *293*	... *101*	... *20*	... *1*	... *1*	... ...	... ...	... ...
Shimoga District ...	**20,912**	**18,300**	16,551 *16,296*	12,162 *12,096*	16,230 *15,974*	12,056 *11,991*	89 *19*	27 *6*	172 *60*	49 *27*	20 *7*	8 *4*	12 ...	1 ...	... ...	... ...	28 ...	21 *3*	... *217*	... *64*	... *19*	... *1*	... ...	... ...	... ...	... ...
Civil and Military Station, Bangalore.	**14,933**	**13,154**	**5,893** *5,019*	**1,244** *1,130*	**513** *254*	**125** *92*	**917** *281*	**187** *106*	**4,453** *3,701*	**929** *827*	**10** *9*	**3** *2*	... ...	... ...	... ...	... ...	... ...	... ...	... *674*	... *92*	... *100*	... *11*	... ...	... ...	... ...	... ...

TABLE XV.—PART II.

Bilingualism—*contd.*

Mother-tongue.—Tamil

Number of Persons speaking

Area of Bilingualism	Mother-tongue Males	Mother-tongue Females	Total of subsidiary Languages Males	Total of subsidiary Languages Females	Subsidiary Language: Kannada Males	Kannada Females	Telugu Males	Telugu Females	Hindustani Males	Hindustani Females	Marathi Males	Marathi Females	Banajari Males	Banajari Females	Tulu Males	Tulu Females	Konkani Males	Konkani Females	Two Subsidiary Languages Males	Two Subsidiary Languages Females	Three Subsidiary Languages Males	Three Subsidiary Languages Females	Four Subsidiary Languages Males	Four Subsidiary Languages Females	Five Subsidiary Languages Males	Five Subsidiary Languages Females
1	2	3	4	5	6	7	8	9	10	11	12	13	14	15	16	17	18	19	20	21	22	23	24	25	26	27
MYSORE STATE, INCLUDING CIVIL AND MILITARY STATION, BANGALORE.	161,918	151,767	89,559 77,722	72,587 65,648	59,235 48.669	50,424 43,635	23,908 14,906	20,205 13,903	6,310 3,100	1,846 1,201	121 28	81 54	9 9	2 2	71 30	22 6	5 ...	7 2	... 10,142	... 6,752	... 820	... 92	... 17	... 1	... 1	... ...
MYSORE STATE, EXCLUDING CIVIL AND MILITARY STATION, BANGALORE.	132,155	122,834	83,544 72,484	69,869 63,063	57,927 47.776	49,680 42,980	21.325 12,835	18,669 12,485	4,096 1,495	1,418 828	112 24	72 45	9 9	2 2	71 30	22 6	4 ...	6 1	... 9,588	... 6,627	... 710	... 88	... 16	... 1	... 1	... ...
Bangalore City ...	20,501	18,465	11,591 9,680	8,282 7,367	8,165 6,588	6,267 5,400	2,706 1,430	1,902 1,061	683 53	99 28	34 ...	14 6	... ...	... ...	2 1	... ...	1 ...	... ...	... 1,311	... 830	... 291	... 41	... 6	... 1	... ...	... ...
Bangalore District ...	30,844	29,306	23,943 20,196	20,420 17,779	16,638 13,041	14,503 11,872	6,785 3,382	5,805 3,221	507 214	109 52	13 2	2 ...	... ...	... ...	... ...	1 1	... ...	... ...	... 3,488	... 2,625	... 128	... 8	... 1	... ...	... ...	... ...
Kolar Gold Fields (City)...	26,273	24,092	2,227 2,013	1,468 1,406	307 178	168 119	1,602 1,429	1,259 1,205	312 215	39 23	5 2	2 ...	... ...	... ...	1 ...	... ...	... ...	... ...	... 164	... 56	... 25	... 3	... ...	... ...	... ...	... ...
Kolar District ...	18 189	18,045	14,972 12,445	13,913 11,882	6,221 3,831	5,392 3,377	8,539 6,136	8,475 6,458	200 46	41 23	12 ...	5 1	... ...	... ...	... ...	... ...	... ...	... ...	... 2,339	... 2,015	... 91	... 8	... 2	... ...	... ...	... ...
Tumkur District ...	2,801	2,601	2,564 2,281	2,371 2,259	2.170 1,900	2,082 1,972	288 99	265 158	96 3	17 12	9 8	6 6	1 1	1 1	... ...	... ...	... ...	... ...	... 258	... 108	... 11	... 2	... 1	... ...	... ...	... ...
Mysore City ...	7,099	6,577	5,846 5,462	4,677 4,519	5,387 5,053	4,443 4,299	184 25	116 18	264 34	80 22	11 5	38 31	... ...	... ...	... ...	... ...	... ...	... ...	... 306	... 140	... 39	... 9	... ...	... ...	... ...	... ...
Mysore District ...	10,098	9,392	8,539 7,848	7,821 7,469	6,970 6.304	6,738 6,390	350 131	284 183	1,216 743	797 548	3 3	2 ...	... ...	... ...	... ...	... ...	... ...	... ...	... 643	... 344	... 24	... 4	... ...	... ...	... ...	... ...
Chitaldrug District ...	2,575	2,135	2,486 2,156	2,023 1,828	2,123 1,821	1,796 1.604	257 29	202 26	98 ...	25 6	5 ...	... ...	... ...	... ...	3 3	... ...	... ...	... ...	... 279	... 189	... 21	... 3	... 3	... ...	... ...	... ...
Hassan District ...	6,324	5,933	5,259 5,041	4.674 4,619	4,947 4.734	4,571 4,506	114 63	43 23	188 45	51 37	2 ...	... ...	... ...	... ...	6 ...	4 ...	2 ...	5 1	... 180	... 49	... 19	... 3	... ...	... ...	... ...	... ...
Kadur District ...	3,848	3,098	3.000 2,604	2,002 1,853	2.422 2,056	1,753 1,607	239 51	147 44	283 99	85 53	3 ...	2 ...	... ...	... ...	53 25	15 4	... ...	... ...	... 352	... 141	... 19	... 4	... 2	... ...	... ...	... ...
Shimoga District ...	3,603	3,190	3,117 2,758	2,218 2,082	2,577 2,270	1,967 1,834	261 120	171 88	249 43	75 24	15 4	1 1	8 8	1 1	6 1	2 1	1 ...	1 ...	... 268	... 130	... 42	... 3	... 1	... ...	... 1	... ..
Civil and Military Station, Bangalore.	29,763	28,933	6,015 5,238	2,718 2,585	1,308 893	744 655	2,583 2,071	1.536 1,418	2,114 1,605	428 373	9 4	9 9	... ...	... ...	... ...	... ...	1 ...	1 1	... 554	... 125	... 110	... 4	... 1	... ...	... ...	... ...

TABLE XV.—PART II.

Bilingualism—*contd.*

Area of Bilingualism	Mother-tongue.—Marathi																									
	Number of Persons speaking																									
	Mother-tongue		Total of subsidiary Languages		Subsidiary Language														Two Subsidiary Languages		Three Subsidiary Languages		Four Subsidiary Languages		Five Subsidiary Languages	
					Kannada		Telugu		Hindustani		Tamil		Tulu		Konkani		Banajari									
	Males	Females	Males	Females	Males	Females	Males	Females	Males	Females	Males	Females	Males	Females	Males	Females	Males	Females	Males	Females	Males	Females	Males	Females	Males	Females
1	2	3	4	5	6	7	8	9	10	11	12	13	14	15	16	17	18	19	20	21	22	23	24	25	26	27
MYSORE STATE, INCLUDING CIVIL AND MILITARY STATION, BANGALORE.	**47,025**	**44,297**	**43,347** ***37,781***	**36,246** ***33,350***	**34,164** ***29,839***	**30,190** ***27,767***	**4,441** ***2,125***	**3,654** ***2,151***	**3,017** ***446***	**1,377** ***317***	**1,384** ***659***	**807** ***459***	**312** ***101***	**208** ***95***	**29** ***7***	**10** ***8***	... ...	... ...	... ***3,790***	... ***2,245***	... ***666***	... ***273***	... ***148***	... ***35***	... ...	... ...
MYSORE STATE, EXCLUDING CIVIL AND MILITARY STATION, BANGALORE.	**44,798**	**42,314**	**41,837** ***36,662***	**35,318** ***32,633***	**33,868** ***29,642***	**30,026** ***27,660***	**4,136** ***2,006***	**3,428** ***2,035***	**2,768** ***340***	**1,234** ***243***	**726** ***221***	**413** ***190***	**312** ***101***	**208** ***95***	**27** ***5***	**9** ***7***	... ...	... ...	... ***3,651***	... ***2,152***	... ***584***	... ***220***	... ***132***	... ***31***	... ...	... ...
Bangalore City ...	**6,678**	**6,233**	5,862 *4,802*	4,474 *3,971*	4,552 *3,802*	3,855 *3,458*	646 *105*	352 *44*	393 *41*	136 *19*	258 *61*	127 *38*	1 ...	2 ...	12 3	2 *1*	... ...	... ...	... *577*	... *334*	... *156*	... *68*	... *57*	... *15*	... ...	... ...
Bangalore District ...	**6,240**	**5,956**	5,895 *5,014*	4,395 *3,962*	4,800 *4,128*	3,741 *3,384*	537 *98*	460 *160*	478 *80*	138 *23*	85 *17*	56 *30*	... ...	... ...	... ...	... ...	... ...	... ...	... *529*	... *309*	... *134*	... *44*	... *28*	... *12*	... ...	... ...
Kolar Gold Fields (City) ...	**387**	**345**	436 *288*	258 *201*	113 *39*	48 *21*	118 *53*	88 *54*	38 *9*	16 ...	167 *88*	106 *76*	... ...	... ...	... ...	... ...	... ...	... ...	... *63*	... *43*	... *23*	... *7*	... *13*	... ...	... ...	... ...
Kolar District ...	**4,045**	**4,040**	3,938 *3,213*	3,420 *2,972*	1,764 *1,170*	1,441 *1,055*	1,993 *1,408*	1,898 *1,511*	138 *5*	62 *4*	43 *10*	19 *4*	... ...	... ...	... ...	... ...	... ...	... ...	... *519*	... *349*	... *97*	... *48*	... *4*	... *1*	... ...	... ...
Tumkur District ...	**4,193**	**4,116**	4,107 *3,839*	3,711 *3,465*	3,580 *3,364*	3,262 *3,039*	357 *233*	322 *194*	155 *20*	119 ...	12 ...	6 ...	3 *3*	2 *2*	... ...	... ...	... ...	... ...	... *177*	... *214*	... *35*	... *16*	... *7*	... ...	... ...	... ...
Mysore City ...	**3,256**	**2,825**	3,279 *2,795*	2,651 *2,384*	2,739 *2,301*	2,328 *2,079*	50 *3*	38 *11*	409 *17*	232 *14*	81 *31*	52 *26*	... ...	1 ...	... ...	... ...	... ...	... ...	... *412*	... *242*	... *21*	... *11*	... *10*	... *1*	... ...	... ...
Mysore District ...	**3,817**	**3,751**	3,351 *3,037*	3,031 *2,921*	2,965 *2,668*	2,793 *2,685*	31 *8*	15 *7*	331 *58*	214 *114*	24 *3*	9 *7*	... ...	... ...	... ...	... ...	... ...	... ...	... *287*	... *107*	... *12*	... ...	... *1*	... *1*	... ...	... ...
Chitaldrug District ...	**3,696**	**3,527**	3,617 *3,140*	3,323 *3,083*	3,069 *2,659*	3,056 *2,833*	265 *45*	180 *16*	267 *26*	79 *10*	16 ...	8 ...	... ...	... ...	... ...	... ...	... ...	... ...	... *351*	... *208*	... *51*	... *16*	... *8*	... ...	... ...	... ...
Hassan District ...	**1,990**	**1,983**	1,899 *1,742*	1,747 *1,674*	1,733 *1,584*	1,654 *1,588*	33 *1*	20 *8*	110 ...	63 *6*	8 *3*	1 ...	13 *7*	7 *4*	2 *2*	2 *2*	... ...	... ...	... *134*	... *59*	... *10*	... *7*	... *1*	... ...	... ...	... ...
Kadur District ...	**2,397**	**2,132**	2,222 *1,967*	1,865 *1,765*	1,840 *1,596*	1,635 *1,537*	38 *21*	28 *23*	165 *33*	83 *53*	7 *2*	12 *7*	170 *68*	104 *44*	2 ...	3 *2*	... ...	... ...	... *239*	... *98*	... *8*	... *1*	... ...	... ...	... ...	... ...
Shimoga District ...	**8,099**	**7,406**	7,231 *6,825*	6,443 *6,235*	6,713 *6,331*	6,213 *5,981*	68 *31*	27 *7*	289 *51*	92 ...	25 *6*	17 *2*	125 *23*	92 *45*	11 ...	2 *2*	... ...	... ...	... *363*	... *189*	... *17*	... *8*	... *3*	... *1*	... ...	... ...
Civil and Military Station, Bangalore.	**2,227**	**1,963**	**1,510** ***1,119***	**928** ***717***	**296** ***197***	**164** ***107***	**305** ***119***	**226** ***116***	**249** ***106***	**143** ***74***	**658** ***438***	**394** ***269***	... ...	... ...	**2** ***2***	**1** ***1***	... ...	... ...	... ***139***	... ***93***	... ***102***	... ***53***	... ***16***	... ***4***	... ...	... ...

TABLE XV.—PART II.

Bilingualism—*contd.*

Area of Bilingualism	Mother-tongue.—Banajari (Rajasthani) — Number of persons speaking																									
	Mother-tongue		Total of Subsidiary languages		Subsidiary Language														Two Subsidiary Languages		Three Subsidiary Languages		Four Subsidiary Languages		Five Subsidiary Languages	
					Kannada		Telugu		Hindustani		Tamil		Marathi		Tulu		Konkani									
	Males	Females	Males	Females	Males	Females	Males	Females	Males	Females	Males	Females	Males	Females	Males	Females	Males	Females	Males	Females	Males	Females	Males	Females	Males	Females
1	2	3	4	5	6	7	8	9	10	11	12	13	14	15	16	17	18	19	20	21	22	23	24	25	26	27
MYSORE STATE, INCLUDING CIVIL AND MILITARY STATION, BANGALORE.	29,194	28,221	26,429 *24,458*	22,778 *21,398*	22,889 *20,872*	19,977 *18,537*	1,729 *1,390*	1,458 *1,254*	1,729 *198*	1,236 *165*	1 ...	41 *19*	80 *79*	66 *66*	1 *1*	... ...	... ...	... ...	... *1,865*	... *1,334*	... *53*	... *23*	... ...	... ...	... ...	... ...
MYSORE STATE, EXCLUDING CIVIL AND MILITARY STATION, BANGALORE.	29,192	28,221	26,429 *24,458*	22,778 *21,398*	22,889 *20,872*	19,977 *18,537*	1,729 *1,390*	1,458 *1,254*	1,729 *198*	1,236 *165*	1 ...	41 *19*	80 *79*	66 *66*	1 *1*	... ...	... ...	... ...	... *1,865*	... *1,334*	... *53*	... *23*	... ...	... ...	... ...	... ...
Bangalore City ...	2	8	...	...	...	...	...	...	...	...	...	...	...	...	...	...	...	...	...	...	...	...	...	...	...	...
Bangalore District ...	2,511	2,373	2,376 *2,233*	2,073 *1,947*	2,133 *1,994*	1,850 *1,726*	68 *22*	54 *21*	185 *78*	165 *76*	... ...	4 ...	... ...	... ...	... ...	... ...	... ...	... ...	... *135*	... *122*	... *4*	... *2*	... ...	... ...	... ...	... ...
Kolar Gold Fields (City)...	...	...	...	...	...	...	...	...	...	...	...	...	...	...	...	...	...	...	...	...	...	...	...	...	...	...
Kolar District ...	753	600	670 *665*	509 *506*	15 *10*	15 *12*	655 *650*	494 *491*	... ...	... ...	... ...	... ...	... ...	... ...	... ...	... ...	... ...	... ...	... *5*	... *3*	... ...	... ...	... ...	... ...	... ...	... ...
Tumkur District ...	2,558	2,593	2,317 *2,175*	2,256 *2,157*	1,649 *1,526*	1,601 *1,522*	568 *502*	556 *522*	100 *23*	81 *34*	... ...	18 ...	... ...	... ...	... ...	... ...	... ...	... ...	... *106*	... *59*	... *18*	... *20*	... ...	... ...	... ...	... ...
Mysore City ...	15	13	...	...	...	...	...	...	...	...	...	...	...	...	...	...	...	...	...	...	...	...	...	...	...	...
Mysore District ...	225	211	196 *195*	168 *168*	195 *194*	167 *167*	... ...	... ...	... ...	... ...	1 ...	1 *1*	... ...	... ...	... ...	... ...	... ...	... ...	... *1*	... ...	... ...	... ...	... ...	... ...	... ...	... ...
Chitaldrug District ...	6,375	6,231	5,801 *5,268*	5,212 *4,938*	5,077 *4,473*	4,717 *4,361*	434 *209*	354 *220*	209 *2*	57 ...	... ...	18 *18*	80 *79*	66 *66*	1 *1*	... ...	... ...	... ...	... *475*	... *272*	... *29*	... *1*	... ...	... ...	... ...	... ...
Hassan District ...	2,234	2,239	1,887 *1,830*	1,950 *1,901*	1,823 *1,766*	1,901 *1,852*	8 *7*	... ...	56 ...	49 ...	... ...	... ...	... ...	... ...	... ...	... ...	... ...	... ...	... *57*	... *49*	... ...	... ...	... ...	... ...	... ...	... ...
Kadur District ...	3,823	3,667	3,411 *2,945*	3,569 *3,217*	2,925 *2,460*	3,197 *2,845*	1 ...	... ...	485 *20*	372 *20*	... ...	... ...	... ...	... ...	... ...	... ...	... ...	... ...	... *464*	... *352*	... *1*	... ...	... ...	... ...	... ...	... ...
Shimoga District ...	10,696	10,286	9,771 *9,147*	7,041 *6,564*	9,072 *8,449*	6,529 *6,052*	5 ...	... ...	694 *75*	512 *35*	... ...	... ...	... ...	... ...	... ...	... ...	... ...	... ...	... *622*	... *477*	... *1*	... ...	... ...	... ...	... ...	... ...
Civil and Military Station, Bangalore.	2	...	...	...	...	...	...	...	...	...	...	...	...	...	...	...	...	...	...	...	...	...	...	...	...	...

TABLE XV.—PART II.

Bilingualism—*contd.*

Area of Bilingualism	Mother-tongue.—Tulu																									
	Number of persons speaking																									
	Mother-tongue		Total of subsidiary languages		Subsidiary Language														Two Subsidiary Languages		Three Subsidiary Languages		Four Subsidiary Languages		Five Subsidiary Languages	
					Kannada		Telugu		Hindustani		Tamil		Marathi		Banajari		Konkani									
	Males	Females	Males	Females	Males	Females	Males	Females	Males	Females	Males	Females	Males	Females	Males	Females	Males	Females	Males	Females	Males	Females	Males	Females	Males	Females
1	2	3	4	5	6	7	8	9	10	11	12	13	14	15	16	17	18	19	20	21	22	23	24	25	26	27
MYSORE STATE, INCLUDING CIVIL AND MILITARY STATION, BANGALORE.	28,441 ...	16,727 ...	17,859 *17,729*	7,729 *7,707*	17,664 *17,541*	7,668 *7,646*	16 *3*	11 *6*	89 *21*	12 *6*	38 *8*	20 *11*	9 *6*	2 *2*	... ...	... ...	43 *27*	16 *14*	... *117*	... *22*	... *5*	... ...	... *1*	... ...	... ...	... ...
MYSORE STATE, EXCLUDING CIVIL AND MILITARY STATION, BANGALORE.	28,439 ...	16,723 ...	17,857 *17,727*	7,729 *7,707*	17,662 *17,539*	7,668 *7,646*	16 *3*	11 *6*	89 *21*	12 *6*	38 *8*	20 *11*	9 *6*	2 *2*	... ...	... ...	43 *27*	16 *14*	... *117*	... *22*	... *5*	... ...	... *1*	... ...	... ...	... ...
Bangalore City ...	83 ...	41 ...	83 *82*	41 *41*	77 *76*	38 *38*	1 *1*	1 *1*	... ...	... ...	3 *2*	2 *2*	2 *2*	... ...	... ...	... ...	... ...	... ...	... *1*	... ...	... ...	... ...	... ...	... ...	... ...	... ...
Bangalore District ...	11 ...	6 ...	14 *11*	3 *2*	10 *7*	2 *1*	... ...	... ...	2 ...	... ...	2 *1*	1 ...	... ...	... ...	... ...	... ...	... ...	... ...	... *3*	... *1*	... ...	... ...	... ...	... ...	... ...	... ...
Kolar Gold Fields (City) ...	1 ...	5 ...	2 *1*	10 *5*	1 ...	5 ...	... ...	... ...	... ...	... ...	1 ...	5 ...	... ...	... ...	... ...	... ...	... ...	... ...	... *1*	... *5*	... ...	... ...	... ...	... ...	... ...	... ...
Kolar District ...	19 ...	13 ...	18 *16*	11 *11*	16 *14*	10 *10*	1 ...	1 *1*	1 ...	... ...	... ...	... ...	... ...	... ...	... ...	... ...	... ...	... ...	... *2*	... ...	... ...	... ...	... ...	... ...	... ...	... ...
Tumkur District ...	19 ...	12 ...	16 *16*	8 *8*	16 *16*	8 *8*	... ...	... ...	... ...	... ...	... ...	... ...	... ...	... ...	... ...	... ...	... ...	... ...	... ...	... ...	... ...	... ...	... ...	... ...	... ...	... ...
Mysore City ...	188 ...	57 ...	184 *173*	... ...	172 *163*	... ...	3 ...	... ...	1 ...	... ...	8 *1*	... ...	... ...	... ...	... ...	... ...	... ...	... ...	... *7*	... ...	... *2*	... ...	... ...	... ...	... ...	... ...
Mysore District ...	81 ...	26 ...	78 *74*	24 *24*	71 *67*	24 *24*	1 ...	... ...	5 *2*	... ...	1 *1*	... ...	... ...	... ...	... ...	... ...	... ...	... ...	... *4*	... ...	... ...	... ...	... ...	... ...	... ...	... ...
Chitaldrug District ...	43 ...	30 ...	43 *37*	30 *25*	37 *31*	21 *16*	6 ...	9 *4*	... ...	... ...	... ...	... ...	... ...	... ...	... ...	... ...	... ...	... ...	... *6*	... *5*	... ...	... ...	... ...	... ...	... ...	... ...
Hassan District ...	6,108 ...	3,540 ...	4,234 *4,209*	1,838 *1,835*	4,203 *4,178*	1,826 *1,823*	2 *2*	... ...	22 *3*	3 *1*	6 *1*	7 *6*	... ...	1 *1*	... ...	... ...	1 ...	1 *1*	... *25*	... *3*	... ...	... ...	... ...	... ...	... ...	... ...
Kadur District ...	18,223 ...	11,010 ...	9,960 *9,904*	4,076 *4,069*	9,874 *9,813*	4,052 *4,045*	1 ...	... ...	40 *4*	5 *2*	15 *1*	4 *2*	... ...	... ...	... ...	... ...	39 *25*	15 *13*	... *58*	... *7*	... *2*	... ...	... *1*	... ...	... ...	... ...
Shimoga District ...	3,663 ...	1,983 ...	3,216 *3,204*	1,688 *1,687*	3,185 3,174	1,682 *1,681*	1 ...	... ...	18 *12*	4 *3*	2 *1*	1 *1*	7 *4*	1 *1*	... ...	... ...	3 *2*	... ...	... *10*	... *1*	... *1*	... ...	... ...	... ...	... ...	... ...
Civil and Military Station, Bangalore.	2 ...	4 ...	2 *2*	... ...	2 *2*	... ...	... ...	... ...	... ...	... ...	... ...	... ...	... ...	... ...	... ...	... ...	... ...	... ...	... ...	... ...	... ...	... ...	... ...	... ...	... ...	... ...

TABLE XV.—PART II.

Bilingualism—*concld.*

Area of Bilingualism	Mother-tongue.—Konkani — Number of Persons speaking — Mother-tongue		Total of Subsidiary Languages		Subsidiary Language — Kannada		Telugu		Hindustani		Tamil		Marathi		Banajari		Tulu		Two Subsidiary Languages		Three Subsidiary Languages		Four Subsidiary Languages		Five Subsidiary Languages	
	Males	Females	Males	Females	Males	Females	Males	Females	Males	Females	Males	Females	Males	Females	Males	Females	Males	Females	Males	Females	Males	Females	Males	Females	Males	Females
1	2	3	4	5	6	7	8	9	10	11	12	13	14	15	16	17	18	19	20	21	22	23	24	25	26	27
MYSORE STATE, INCLUDING CIVIL AND MILITARY STATION, BANGALORE.	9,912	6,383	9,515 *7,634*	5,484 *4,833*	6,678 *4,995*	4,178 *3,547*	28 *5*	11 *1*	499 *218*	52 *26*	114 *24*	45 *29*	104 *13*	63 *16*	... ...	... ...	2,092 *633*	1,135 *574*	... *1,620*	... *630*	... *117*	... *9*	... *9*	... *1*	... ...	... ...
MYSORE STATE, EXCLUDING CIVIL AND MILITARY STATION, BANGALORE.	9,781	6,212	9,442 *7,576*	5,426 *4,786*	6,651 *4,977*	4,153 *3,534*	24 *2*	11 *1*	478 *202*	38 *14*	93 *16*	32 *22*	104 *13*	57 *11*	... ...	... ...	2,092 *633*	1,135 *574*	... *1,609*	... *621*	... *115*	... *8*	... *9*	... *1*	... ...	... ...
Bangalore City ...	358	321	341 *281*	242 *210*	262 *211*	199 *172*	3 *1*	3 ...	22 *5*	12 *6*	11 *1*	7 *1*	39 *8*	19 ...	... ...	... ...	4 *1*	2 ...	... *49*	... *96*	... *4*	... *3*	... *1*	... ...	... ...	... ...
Bangalore District ...	66	18	78 *70*	6 *6*	59 *53*	6 *6*	3 *1*	... ...	4 ...	... ...	1 ...	... ...	1 ...	... ...	... ...	... ...	10 *10*	... ...	... *4*	... ...	... *2*	... ...	... ...	... ...	... ...	... ...
Kolar Gold Fields (City)...	15	22	15 *8*	13 *13*	8 *3*	9 *9*	... ...	... ...	2 ...	... ...	5 ...	4 *4*	... ...	... ...	... ...	... ...	... ...	... ...	... *3*	... ...	... *2*	... ...	... ...	... ...	... ...	... ...
Kolar District ...	24	15	33 *22*	15 *9*	21 *15*	7 *4*	2 ...	3 ...	4 ...	2 ...	4 *1*	2 *2*	1 ...	1 ...	... ...	... ...	1 ...	... ...	... *2*	... *1*	... *3*	... *1*	... *1*	... *1*	... ...	... ...
Tumkur District ...	18	14	15 *13*	12 *12*	11 *9*	10 *10*	... ...	... ...	*2* ...	... ...	2 *2*	2 *2*	... ...	... ...	... ...	... ...	... ...	... ...	... *2*	... ...	... ...	... ...	... ...	... ...	... ...	... ...
Mysore City ...	74	54	62 *49*	39 *37*	43 *34*	32 *30*	3 ...	... ...	4 *1*	1 *1*	7 *2*	5 *4*	3 *2*	... ...	... ...	... ...	2 ...	1 ...	... *8*	... *2*	... *1*	... ...	... *1*	... ...	... ...	... ...
Mysore District ...	174	27	166 *143*	20 *19*	134 *115*	18 *17*	3 ...	... ...	18 *8*	1 *1*	8 ...	1 ...	... ...	... ...	... ...	... ...	3 ...	... ...	... *17*	... *1*	... *3*	... ...	... ...	... ...	... ...	... ...
Chitaldrug District ...	186	213	159 *151*	85 *81*	143 *136*	80 *77*	1 ...	2 ...	12 *7*	2 ...	... ...	... ...	2 *1*	1 ...	... ...	... ...	1 ...	... ...	... *6*	... *4*	... *1*	... ...	... ...	... ...	... ...	... ...
Hassan District ...	687	356	677 *448*	313 *243*	349 *132*	176 *106*	... ...	... ...	21 *7*	... ...	... ...	... ...	3 ...	... ...	... ...	... ...	304 *87*	137 *67*	... *215*	... *70*	... *7*	... ...	... ...	... ...	... ...	... ...
Kadur District ...	4,094	2,465	4,034 *2,735*	2,316 *1,863*	2,026 *654*	1,374 *926*	9 ...	2 ...	303 *159*	11 *3*	39 *5*	4 *4*	6 ...	3 *3*	... ...	... ...	1,651 *508*	922 *477*	... *1,124*	... *447*	... *80*	... *3*	... *5*	... ...	... ...	... ...
Shimoga District ...	4,085	2,737	3,862 *3,656*	2,365 *2,293*	3,595 *3,415*	2,242 *2,177*	... ...	1 *1*	86 *15*	9 *1*	16 *5*	7 *5*	49 *2*	33 *8*	... ...	... ...	116 *27*	73 *30*	... *179*	... *70*	... *12*	... *1*	... *1*	... ...	... ...	... ...
Civil and Military Station, Bangalore.	131	141	73 *58*	58 *47*	27 *18*	25 *13*	4 *3*	... ...	21 *16*	14 *12*	21 *8*	13 *7*	... ...	6 *5*	... ...	... ...	... ...	... ...	... *11*	... *9*	... *2*	... *1*	... ...	... ...	... ...	... ...

MYSORE CENSUS, 1931.

TABLE XVI.—Religion.

NOTE— Distribution of Christian Population by Sect and Race is shown in Provincial Table III.

TABLE XVI.

Religion.

District or State	Population			Hindu												Jain			Sikh		
				Brahmanic			Arya			Brahmo			Total								
	Persons	Males	Females	Persons	Males	Females	Persons	Males	Females	Persons	Males	Females	Persons	Males	Females	Persons	Males	Females	Persons	Males	Females
1	2	3	4	5	6	7	8	9	10	11	12	13	14	15	16	17	18	19	20	21	22
MYSORE STATE, INCLUDING CIVIL AND MILITARY STATION, BANGALORE.	6,557,302	3,353,963	3,203,339	6,015,759	3,066,255	2,949,504	45	36	9	76	41	35	6,015,880	3,066,332	2,949,548	29,613	15,920	13,693	100	63	37
MYSORE STATE, EXCLUDING CIVIL AND MILITARY STATION, BANGALORE.	6,423,189	3,284,554	3,138,635	5,941.783	3,027,732	2,914.051	34	30	4	59	33	26	5,941,876	3,027.795	2,914,081	28,799	15.436	13,363	68	34	34
Bangalore City	172,357	91,680	80,677	144,436	76,582	67,854	34	30	4	59	33	26	144,529	76,645	67,884	1,153	724	429	...	...	...
Bangalore District	908,056	461,905	446,151	833,552	422.950	410.602	...	...	...	...	...	...	833,552	422,950	410,602	3,532	1,777	1,755	11	7	4
Kolar Gold Fields (City) ...	85,103	45,051	40,052	62.313	32,695	29.618	...	...	...	...	...	...	62,313	32,695	29,618	447	262	185	...	...	...
Kolar District	763,934	389,262	374,672	696,319	353,912	342,407	...	...	...	...	...	...	696,319	353,912	342,407	6,052	3,173	2,879	...	...	...
Tumkur District	861,405	439,144	422,261	806,673	410.649	396,024	...	...	...	...	...	...	806,673	410,649	396,024	7,340	3,814	3,526	...	...	...
Mysore City	107,142	56.772	50,370	84,789	44,734	40,055	...	...	...	...	...	...	84.789	44,734	40,055	549	372	177	17	11	6
Mysore District	1,403,984	703,838	700,146	1,348,180	674.201	673.979	...	...	...	...	...	...	1,348,180	674.201	673,979	2,514	1,250	1,264	40	16	24
Chitaldrug District	656,569	336,786	319,783	614.755	314,839	299.916	...	...	...	...	...	...	614,755	314,839	299,916	1,180	696	484	...	...	...
Hassan District	596,937	300,746	296,191	567,139	284,490	282.649	...	...	...	...	...	...	567,139	284,490	282,649	1,941	1,044	897	...	...	...
Kadur District	347,715	184,389	163,326	319,277	167,771	151,506	...	...	...	...	...	...	319,277	167,771	151,506	1,360	798	562	...	...	...
Shimoga District	519,987	274,981	245,006	464,350	244,909	219,441	...	...	...	...	...	...	464,350	244,909	219,441	2,731	1,526	1,205	...	...	...
Civil and Military Station, Bangalore.	134,113	69,409	64,704	73,976	38,523	35,453	11	6	5	17	8	9	74,004	38,537	35,467	814	484	330	32	29	3

TABLE XVI.

Religion—*concld.*

District or State	Buddhist			Christian			Parsi			Tribal†			Musalman			Jew			Others*		
	Persons	Males	Females	Persons	Males	Females	Persons	Males	Females	Persons	Males	Females	Persons	Males	Females	Persons	Males	Females	Persons	Males	Females
	23	24	25	26	27	28	29	30	31	32	33	34	35	36	37	38	39	40	41	42	43
MYSORE STATE, INCLUDING CIVIL AND MILITARY STATION, BANGALORE.	**1,239**	**640**	**599**	**87,538**	**45,164**	**42,374**	**331**	**169**	**162**	**23,828**	**12,230**	**11,958**	**398,628**	**213,381**	**185,247**	**39**	**13**	**26**	**106**	**51**	**55**
MYSORE STATE, EXCLUDING CIVIL AND MILITARY STATION, BANGALORE.	**979**	**497**	**482**	**57,516**	**30,512**	**27,004**	**87**	**49**	**38**	**23,828**	**12,230**	**11,598**	**370,003**	**197,983**	**172,020**	**18**	**7**	**11**	**15**	**11**	**4**
Bangalore City	**35**	18	17	**6,754**	3,291	3,463	**28**	11	17	...	...	...	**19,831**	10,975	8,856	**12**	5	7	**15**	11	4
Bangalore District	**2**	1	1	**8,036**	4,067	3,969	**2**	2	...	**2,645**	1,357	1,288	**60,276**	31,744	28,532	...	...	...	...	...	...
Kolar Gold Fields (City) ...	**920**	469	451	**14,651**	7,579	7,072	...	...	...	**1**	1	...	**6,771**	4,045	2,726	...	...	...	...	...	...
Kolar District	**2**	1	1	**2,679**	1,319	1,360	...	...	...	**122**	67	55	**58,760**	30,790	27,970	...	...	...	...	...	...
Tumkur District	...	...	...	**1,620**	892	728	**1**	1	...	**1,381**	672	709	**44,390**	23,116	21,274	...	...	...	...	...	...
Mysore City	**19**	7	12	**3,947**	1,956	1,991	**36**	23	13	**7**	6	1	**17,772**	9,661	8,111	**6**	2	4	...	...	...
Mysore District	...	...	...	**3,375**	1,828	1,547	...	...	...	**6,390**	3,312	3,078	**43,485**	23,231	20,254	...	...	...	...	...	...
Chitaldrug District	...	...	...	**515**	275	240	**9**	6	3	**3,269**	1,699	1,570	**36,841**	19,271	17,570	...	...	...	...	...	...
Hassan District	**1**	1	...	**5,280**	2,840	2,440	...	...	...	**1,089**	536	553	**21,487**	11,835	9,652	...	...	...	...	...	...
Kadur District	...	...	...	**6,575**	4,110	2,465	**6**	3	3	**1,067**	566	501	**19,430**	11,141	8,289	...	...	...	...	...	...
Shimoga District	...	...	...	**4,084**	2,355	1,729	**5**	3	2	**7,857**	4,014	3,843	**40,960**	22,174	18,786	...	...	...	...	...	...
Civil and Military Station, Bangalore.	**260**	**143**	**117**	**30,022**	**14,652**	**15,370**	**244**	**120**	**124**	...	...	...	**28,625**	**15,398**	**13,227**	**21**	**6**	**15**	**91**	**40**	**51**

**Vide* note 2 on the title page of Table VII.

† See note 2 on the title page of Table V.

MYSORE CENSUS, 1931.

TABLE XVII.—Caste, Tribe or Race.

NOTE.—Regarding the changes in the names of certain castes under Religion Hindu and the selection of castes *for presentation in this* Table, see *notes* 1, 2 *and* 3 *to* Table VIII. The total population of other Castes, Tribes or Races which are omitted under the different religions is indicated below :—

Religion	Males	Females
Hindu	20,710	16,636
Tribal	99	103
Musalman	6,789	4,145
Jain	394	215

Caste, Tribe or Race	Mysore State, including Civil and Military Station, Bangalore		Mysore State, excluding Civil and Military Station, Bangalore		Bangalore City		Bangalore District	
	Males	Females	Males	Females	Males	Females	Males	Females
1	2	3	4	5	6	7	8	9
ALL RELIGIONS ...	3,353,963	3,203,339	3,284,554	3,138,635	91,680	80,677	461,905	446,151
HINDU ...	3,066,332	2,949,548	3,027,795	2,914,081	76,645	67,884	422,950	410,602
TRIBAL ...	12,230	11,598	12,230	11,598	...	...	1,357	1,288
Hindu—								
1 Adikarnataka ...	509,898	490,428	496,631	477,084	6,548	5,946	80,622	78,421
2 Agasa ...	55,879	53,611	55,250	53,050	752	692	7,549	7,187
3 Banajiga ...	77,779	74,471	73,866	70,880	6,529	6,341	11,801	11,505
4 Beda ...	153,590	147,873	153,520	147,818	674	541	10,620	10,260
5 Brahmin ...	126,542	118,621	124,597	117,144	17,466	14,716	11,094	10,816
6 Darzi ...	10,488	10,039	9,251	8,968	611	584	796	729
7 Devanga ...	30,002	29,300	29,967	29,272	4,237	4,080	3,276	3,296
8 Gangakula ...	88,356	85,947	88,270	85,870	544	491	6,297	6,135
9 Ganiga ...	22,620	22,340	22,412	22,041	596	528	3,696	3,573
10 Idiga ...	50,076	44,593	49,894	44,471	142	141	2,719	2,744
11 Jogi ...	7,527	7,382	7,525	7,382	36	29	1,896	1,849
12 Kshatriya ...	21,304	19,704	20,616	19,222	3,658	3,425	2,822	2,678
13 Kumbara ...	24,824	23,833	24,750	23,738	97	73	3,277	3,314
14 Kunchatiga ...	59,207	57,357	59,053	57,240	654	659	6,543	6,535
15 Lingayat ...	390,652	380,150	390,076	379,636	3,078	2,541	23,211	22,362
16 Mahratta ...	31,696	28,832	30,919	28,173	2,570	1,973	5,018	4,817
17 Meda ...	3,819	3,713	3,686	3,586	74	66	415	430
18 Mudali ...	16,773	14,959	12,083	10,832	3,804	3 397	1,089	954
19 Nagartha ...	4,258	4,129	4,094	3,945	282	290	1,648	1,679
20 Nayinda ...	23,797	22,419	23,342	21,964	912	733	4,368	4,213
21 Neygi ...	27,918	26,539	27,846	26,480	3,515	3,398	3,757	3,506
22 Satani ...	11,658	11,444	11,639	11,429	161	136	2,018	2,074
23 Tigala ...	46,792	43,908	44,558	41,941	2,867	2,818	20,800	18,881
24 Uppara ...	59,207	57,154	59,207	57,153	230	217	972	922
25 Vakkaliga ...	663,718	648,546	661,626	646,605	7,118	5,876	141,972	138,981
26 Vaisya ...	23,344	20,891	22,466	20,151	2,270	1,883	2,039	1,945
27 Viswakarma ...	74,370	69,299	73,693	68,684	1,367	1,196	8,512	8,155
28 Vodda ...	84,527	80,349	84,171	80,000	738	655	15,689	14,991
29 Yadava ...	88,561	85,640	88,102	85,212	1,528	1,416	10,502	10,047
Hindu and Tribal—								
1 Banajara (Hindu) ...	26,170	24,539	26,166	24,531	10	7	1,860	1,718
Banajara (Tribal) ...	6,967	6,692	6,967	6,692	...	...	1,157	1,097
Banajara (Total) ...	33,137	31,231	33,133	31,223	10	7	3,017	2,815
2 Koracha (Hindu) ...	5,319	4,919	5,226	4,845	98	102	671	653
Koracha (Tribal) ...	965	882	965	882	...	...	11	11
Koracha (Total) ...	6,284	5,801	6,191	5,727	98	102	682	664
3 Korama (Hindu) ...	6,893	6,714	6,857	6,688	398	420	1,973	1,919
Korama (Tribal) ...	1,801	1,716	1,801	1,716	...	...	158	143
Korama (Total) ...	8,694	8,430	8,658	8,404	398	420	2,126	2,062
4 Kuruba (Hindu) ...	218,058	213,269	217,470	212,736	2,117	1,908	22,767	22,295
Kuruba (Tribal) ...	2,398	2,205	2,398	2,205	...	...	27	33
Kuruba (Total) ...	220,456	215,474	219,868	214,941	2,117	1,908	22,794	22,328
MUSALMAN ...	213,381	185,247	197,983	172,020	10,975	8,856	31,744	28,532
1 Labbai ...	7,906	4,391	7,097	3,860	307	99	571	304
2 Mughal ...	5,890	5,130	5,549	4,850	273	238	997	901
3 Pathan ...	29,654	25,953	27,856	24,508	1,442	1,186	6,618	5,731
4 Pinjari ...	5,458	5,173	5,451	5,169	85	35	238	209
5 Saiyad ...	39,146	34,584	37,039	32,806	2,276	1,861	7,415	6,617
6 Sheik ...	118,538	105,871	108,901	97,041	6,153	5,118	15,317	14,207
CHRISTIAN* ...	45,164	42,374	30,512	27,004	3,291	3,463	4,067	3,969
JAIN ...	15,920	13,693	15,436	13,363	724	429	1,777	1,755
1 Digambara ...	6,596	6,183	6,549	6,149	193	150	316	316
2 Swetambara ...	2,030	849	1,758	654	383	148	6	1
3 Sada ...	6,900	6,446	6,844	6,407	120	107	1,455	1,438
PARSI ...	169	162	49	38	11	17	2	...
SIKH ...	63	37	34	34	...	...	7	4
JEW ...	13	26	7	11	5	7	...	...
BUDDHIST ...	640	599	497	482	18	17	1	1
OTHERS ...	51	55	11	4	11	4	...	...

* For details by Race, see Provincial Table III.

Kolar Gold Fields (City)		Kolar District		Tumkur District		Mysore City		Mysore District		Chitaldrug District	
Males	Females	Males	Females	Males	Females	Males	Females	Males	Females	Males	Females
10	11	12	13	14	15	16	17	18	19	20	21
45,051	**40,052**	**389,262**	**374,672**	**439,144**	**422,261**	**56,772**	**50,370**	**703,838**	**700,146**	**336,786**	**319,783**
32,695	**29,618**	**358,912**	**342,407**	**410,649**	**396,024**	**44,734**	**40,055**	**674,201**	**673,979**	**314,839**	**299,916**
1	...	**67**	**55**	**672**	**709**	**6**	**1**	**3,312**	**3,078**	**1,699**	**1,570**
18,397	16,671	67,147	64,857	57,604	55,774	5,214	4,636	114,278	114,808	39,353	37,285
235	228	7,481	7,000	7,774	7,527	890	867	11,688	11,748	5,155	4,926
2,128	1,968	24,286	28,209	8,990	8,417	1,515	1,489	8,458	8,287	2,355	2,142
572	563	33,779	32,492	32,678	31,092	284	254	2,286	2,858	55,475	53,785
746	708	13,340	13,486	11,477	11,082	11,194	9,795	17,055	17,173	5,076	4,631
72	78	514	494	959	967	653	639	743	698	1,875	1,322
34	30	1,203	1,168	3,568	3,826	722	601	2,505	2,463	3,628	3,525
12	13	3,305	3,185	2,764	2,568	1,831	1,605	56,535	56,208	3,675	3,486
172	187	3,610	3,587	2,171	2,280	620	630	9,144	9,192	203	216
70	87	1,420	1,407	4,006	3,863	69	72	4,064	4,165	2,511	2,511
62	46	1,449	1,360	698	646	6	13	995	1,058	676	723
308	226	1,734	1,816	1,403	1,237	2,082	1,784	3,649	3,659	621	494
67	76	2,765	2,490	2,420	2,356	288	245	9,237	9,339	1,326	1,301
20	21	141	159	33,619	32,256	626	605	279	252	13,158	13,116
123	180	6,178	5,935	52,867	50,652	2,449	2,127	99,489	100,241	72,539	68,448
250	223	3,042	3,006	2,688	2,523	1,864	1,653	2,522	2,397	2,219	2,053
4	6	209	193	374	362	210	168	846	865	232	217
1,704	1,584	918	844	280	273	1,504	1,405	1,015	882	204	150
22	12	1,097	1,115	67	66	27	81	396	403	105	104
379	379	5,370	5,167	2,548	2,338	529	499	5,518	5,289	944	828
[illegible]	51	4,694	4,533	2,754	2,699	283	264	2,582	2,60,	3,915	3,641
81	41	919	921	2,357	2,271	132	152	2,417	2,884	579	552
787	595	6,270	5,976	12,924	12,274	86	62	623	685	53	82
86	80	1,552	1,495	7,621	7,422	238	172	26,045	25,628	7,573	7,277
2,458	2,840	94,278	91,618	73,096	72,296	6,283	5,635	191,024	191,328	9,960	8,751
109	96	6,511	5,958	4,183	3,675	822	748	894	803	2,703	2,488
227	225	5,848	5,564	7,286	6,995	1,551	1,454	21,590	21,592	6,088	5,407
965	924	17,896	17 260	10,083	9,587	90	76	5,465	5,210	16,489	15,784
667	658	11,358	11,051	28,851	27,809	584	592	1,182	1,259	25,885	25,193
1	...	594	601	2,812	2,774	..	..	100	82	6,139	5,901
	...	18	13	424	447			839	821	1,191	1,070
1	..	612	614	3,235	3,221			439	403	7,330	6,971
94	91	1,765	1,744	119	352	44	49	221	177	865	774
1	..	9	4	46	49			2	1	245	282
95	91	1,774	1,748	465	401	44	49	223	178	1,110	1,006
3	...	872	897	1,098	1,103	16	9	915	879	484	487
...	...	39	34	189	198	5	1	674	637	238	232
3	...	411	435	1.282	1.306	21	10	1.589	1,516	717	719
1,029	991	21,091	20,453	26.482	25,440	2,086	1,887	69,638	69,071	22,114	21.271
..	..			...	...	1	..	2,265	2,089	14	14
1,029	991	21,091	20,453	26,482	25,440	2,087	1,887	71,908	71.160	22.128	21,285
4,045	**2,726**	**30.790**	**27.970**	**23,116**	**21,274**	**9,661**	**8,111**	**23.231**	**20.254**	**19.271**	**17.570**
761	151	192	100	153	85	119	48	3,383	2.481	51	28
74	56	870	725	641	584	461	410	783	686	315	264
490	371	4.385	4.012	3,892	3,571	1,224	986	3.314	2,972	1.602	1.409
10	5	988	878	605	598	195	178	24	18	2,811	2,788
724	591	7,154	6,701	8,827	3,445	1,710	1,446	4,088	3,699	2,947	2,702
1,784	1,522	17,050	15,427	13.476	12.499	5,680	4,808	11,022	9,802	11,263	10,170
7,579	**7.072**	**1,319**	**1,360**	**892**	**728**	**1,956**	**1,991**	**1.828**	**1,547**	**275**	**240**
262	**185**	**3.173**	**2,879**	**3,814**	**3,526**	**372**	**177**	**1,250**	**1,264**	**696**	**484**
16	12	582	586	1,002	910	288	148	1,142	1,158	414	407
246	173	83	16	94	60	70	8	22	27	242	68
...	...	2,491	2.268	2,662	2,501	83	15	77	78		...
...	...	...	...	**1**	...	**23**	**13**	...	...	**6**	**3**
...	...	...	...	...	...	**11**	**6**	**16**	**24**	...	...
...	...	...	...	...	...	**2**	**4**	...	..	...	...
469	**451**	**1**	**1**	...	...	**7**	**12**	...	...	...	...
...	...	...	...	...	..	..	...	...	...	...	...

TABLE XVII.

Caste, Tribe or Race—*concld.*

Caste, Tribe or Race	Hassan District		Kadur District		Shimoga District		Civil and Military Station, Bangalore	
	Males	Females	Males	Females	Males	Females	Males	Females
	22	23	24	25	26	27	28	29
ALL RELIGIONS ...	**300,746**	**296,191**	**184,389**	**163,326**	**274,981**	**245,006**	**69,409**	**64,704**
HINDU	**284,490**	**282,649**	**167,771**	**151,506**	**244,909**	**219,441**	**38,537**	**35,467**
TRIBAL ...	**536**	**553**	**566**	**501**	**4,014**	**3,843**	...	...
Hindu.—								
1 Adikarnataka ...	48,506	47,256	34,901	29,713	24,066	21,767	13,267	13,344
2 Agasa	5,554	5,453	2,097	1,952	6,630	5,885	629	561
3 Banajiga	2,014	1,913	3,341	3,163	2,447	2,446	3,913	3,591
4 Beda	2,834	2,785	2,359	2,200	12,014	11,488	70	55
5 Brahmin	10,977	10,760	10,177	9,502	15,996	14,475	1,945	1,477
6 Darzi	717	719	665	639	2,146	2,099	1,237	1,071
7 Devanga	4,253	4,296	3,888	3,982	2,708	2,510	35	28
8 Gangakula ...	4,549	4,389	1,948	1,908	6,815	5,882	86	77
9 Ganiga	1,493	1,408	477	836	230	104	208	299
10 Idiga	4,339	3,794	5,147	3,468	25,407	22,219	182	122
11 Jogi	293	326	352	309	1,062	1,023	2	...
12 Kshatriya	944	937	1,361	1,226	2,084	1,740	688	482
13 Kumbara	2,094	2,016	1,662	1,366	1,517	1,162	74	95
14 Kunchatiga ...	1,009	995	820	179	2,684	2,463	154	117
15 Lingayat	42,808	42,792	32,711	32,527	54,623	51,881	576	514
16 Mahratta	1,359	1,179	1,616	1,267	7,776	7,082	677	659
17 Meda	392	405	400	372	530	502	133	127
18 Mudali	441	348	449	385	686	610	4,690	4,127
19 Nagartha	14	14	19	9	417	222	164	184
20 Nayinda	1,633	1,658	455	287	691	573	155	455
21 Neygi	3,789	3,498	1,414	*1,351	1,076	932	72	59
22 Satani	1,957	1,856	414	394	659	648	19	15
23 Tigala	354	359	240	224	104	85	2,234	1,967
24 Uppara	4,848	4,714	5,439	5,045	4,658	4,231	...	1
25 Vakkaliga	93,097	95,356	22,633	19,163	19,707	15,261	2,092	1,941
26 Vaisya	1,252	1,195	691	612	992	798	878	740
27 Viswakarma ...	8,410	7,754	4,617	3,698	8,197	6,644	677	615
28 Vodda	3,487	3,427	3,178	2,846	10,141	9,240	356	349
29 Yadava	3,465	3,592	1,867	1,747	2,218	1,848	459	428
Hindu and Tribal.—								
1 Banajara (Hindu) ...	2,199	2,182	3,906	3,645	8,545	7,621	4	8
Banajara (Tribal) ...	273	288	535	477	3,031	2,979	...	...
Banajara (Total) ...	2,472	2,470	4,441	4,122	11,576	10,600	4	8
2 Koracha (Hindu) ...	226	211	561	450	262	242	93	74
Koracha (Tribal) ...	37	31	...	...	614	554	...	...
Koracha (Total) ...	263	242	561	450	876	796	93	74
3 Korama (Hindu) ...	711	642	294	338	598	489	36	26
Korama (Tribal) ...	191	194	25	15	292	258	...	...
Korama (Total) ...	902	836	319	353	890	747	36	26
4 Kuruba (Hindu) ...	23,047	23,347	14,566	14,498	12,533	11,630	588	533
Kuruba (Tribal) ...	25	26	...	...	66	48	...	...
Kuruba (Total) ...	23,072	23,373	14,566	14,498	12,599	11,678	588	533
MUSALMAN	**11,835**	**9,652**	**11,141**	**8,289**	**22,174**	**18.786**	**15,398**	**13,227**
1 Labbai	453	218	825	229	282	122	809	531
2 Mughal	454	427	815	237	366	322	341	280
3 Pathan	1,159	1,039	842	70[illegible]	2,888	2,521	1,798	1,445
4 Pinjari ...	41	29	9	3	495	443	7	4
5 Saiyad	2,055	1,816	1,479	1,111	3,864	2,814	2,107	1,778
6 Sheik	6,526	5,531	6,563	5,698	14,067	12,259	9,637	8,830
CHRISTIAN	**2,840**	**2.440**	**4,110**	**2,465**	**2,355**	**1,729**	**14,652**	**15,370**
JAIN	**1,044**	**897**	**798**	**562**	**1,526**	**1,205**	**484**	**330**
1 Digambara ...	823	825	569	523	1,254	1,119	47	34
2 Swetambara ...	194	60	191	32	227	61	272	195
3 Sada	1	..	1	..	4	.	56	39
PARSI	...	...	**3**	**3**	**3**	**2**	**120**	**124**
SIKH	...	...	..	...			**29**	**3**
JEW	...	..	...	...	.	..	**6**	**15**
BUDDHIST ...	**1**	...	..	...	..	.	**143**	**117**
OTHERS	..	...	...	..	.	:	**40**	**51**

* For details by Race, see Provincial Table III.

MYSORE CENSUS, 1931.

TABLE XIX.—European and Allied Races and Anglo-Indians by Race and Age

NOTE 1.—The population under the European and Allied Races includes 5 Armenians returned in the Civil and Military Station, Bangalore.

NOTE 2.—Eight persons returned as Armenians in the Mysore District are included among Indian-Christians, since all of them are Indians by birth and their mother tongue is either Kannada or Tamil.

TABLE XIX—(a).

European and Allied Races by Age (Including Armenians).

District or State	Total			British Subjects																	
				All Ages			0—13		14—16		17—23		24—33		34—43		44—53		54 and over	
	Persons	Males	Females	Persons	Males	Females	Males	Females	Males	Females	Males	Females	Males	Females	Males	Females	Males	Females	Males	Females
1	2	3	4	5	6	7	8	9	10	11	12	13	14	15	16	17	18	19	20	21
1. **MYSORE STATE, INCLUDING CIVIL AND MILITARY STATION, BANGALORE**	**5,411**	**3,144**	**2,267**	**4,907**	**2,929**	**1,978**	**375**	**419**	**77**	**67**	**562**	**180**	**864**	**323**	**309**	**317**	**259**	**261**	**483**	**411**
2. **MYSORE STATE, EXCLUDING CIVIL AND MILITARY STATION, BANGALORE**	**1,253**	**708**	**545**	**878**	**534**	**344**	**42**	**55**	**3**	**4**	**35**	**24**	**107**	**72**	**121**	**74**	**113**	**64**	**113**	**51**
3. Bangalore City	300	129	171	260	122	138	22	32	2	3	6	7	26	29	27	31	11	22	25	14
4. Bangalore District	95	43	52	31	15	16	1	2	...	...	...	2	1	2	3	3	2	1	8	6
5. Kolar Gold Fields (City)	574	383	191	340	258	82	9	8	...	1	17	8	51	20	65	18	69	21	47	6
6. Kolar District	24	8	16	12	5	7	...	...	...	...	...	...	2	1	...	2	1	1	2	3
7. Tumkur District	9	4	5	9	4	5	...	1	...	...	...	...	1	...	1	2	1	...	1	2
8. Mysore City	101	43	58	89	38	51	5	8	...	...	1	1	5	8	8	8	9	12	9	11
9. Mysore District	35	20	7	26	19	7	...	...	...	...	4	...	2	1	1	3	8	1	4	2
10. Chitaldrug District	2	1	1	2	1	1	...	...	...	...	...	...	...	...	...	...	1	...	...	1
11. Hassan District	40	26	14	34	24	10	...	...	...	...	4	2	7	3	4	3	4	1	5	1
12. Kadur District	67	46	21	61	43	18	3	3	1	...	3	2	11	6	10	3	3	2	12	2
13. Shimoga District	14	5	9	14	5	9	2	1	...	...	...	2	...	2	2	1	1	3	...	...
14. Civil and Military Station, Bangalore ...	*4,158*	*2,436*	*1,722*	*4,029*	*2,395*	*1,634*	*333*	*384*	*74*	*63*	*527*	*156*	*757*	*251*	*188*	*243*	*146*	*197*	*370*	*360*

TABLE XIX—(a).

European and Allied Races by Age (Including Armenians)—*concld.*

District or State	Others																
	All Ages			0—13		14—16		17—23		24—33		34—43		44—53		54 and over	
	Persons	Males	Females	Males	Females	Males	Females	Males	Females	Males	Females	Males	Females	Males	Females	Males	Females
	22	23	24	25	26	27	28	29	30	31	32	33	34	35	36	37	38
1. **MYSORE STATE, INCLUDING CIVIL AND MILITARY STATION, BANGALORE** ...	**504**	**215**	**289**	**40**	**48**	**4**	**13**	**15**	**16**	**39**	**46**	**36**	**58**	**18**	**44**	**63**	**64**
2. **MYSORE STATE, EXCLUDING CIVIL AND MILITARY STATION, BANGALORE** ...	**375**	**174**	**201**	**38**	**39**	**4**	**9**	**14**	**13**	**32**	**30**	**31**	**49**	**13**	**32**	**42**	**29**
3. Bangalore City ...	40	7	33	...	...	...	...	...	2	1	8	3	13	...	6	3	4
4. Bangalore District ...	64	28	36	6	3	...	4	3	...	6	3	2	8	1	7	10	11
5. Kolar Gold Fields (City) ...	234	125	109	32	36	4	5	10	10	23	16	25	20	7	13	24	9
6. Kolar District ...	12	3	9	...	...	...	...	...	...	...	1	1	5	2	2	...	1
7. Tumkur District ...	...	...	...	...	...	...	...	...	...	...	...	...	...	...	...	...	...
8. Mysore City ...	12	5	7	...	...	...	...	1	...	...	2	...	1	1	1	3	3
9. Mysore District ...	1	1	...	...	...	...	...	...	...	1	...	...	...	...	...	...	...
10. Chitaldrug District ...	...	...	...	...	...	...	...	...	...	...	...	...	...	...	...	...	...
11. Hassan District ...	6	2	4	...	...	...	...	...	...	...	...	...	2	2	2	...	...
12. Kadur District ...	6	3	3	...	...	...	...	...	1	1	...	...	...	...	1	2	1
13. Shimoga District ...	...	...	...	...	...	...	...	...	...	...	...	...	...	...	...	...	...
14. *Civil and Military Station, Bangalore* ...	*129*	*41*	*88*	*2*	*9*	...	*4*	*1*	*3*	*7*	*16*	*5*	*9*	*5*	*12*	*21*	*35*

TABLE XIX—(b).

Anglo-Indians by Age.

District or State	All Ages			0—3		4—6		7—13		14—16		17—19		20—29		30—39		40—49		50—59		60—69		70 and over	
	Persons	Males	Females	Males	Females	Males	Females	Males	Females	Males	Females	Males	Females	Males	Females	Males	Females	Males	Females	Males	Females	Males	Females	Males	Females
	39	40	41	42	43	44	45	46	47	48	49	50	51	52	53	54	55	56	57	58	59	60	61	62	63
1. **MYSORE STATE, INCLUDING CIVIL AND MILITARY STATION, BANGALORE** ...	**8,309**	**3,781**	**4,528**	**341**	**320**	**287**	**263**	**792**	**751**	**367**	**365**	**257**	**366**	**472**	**732**	**348**	**476**	**261**	**485**	**297**	**403**	**236**	**239**	**123**	**128**
2. **MYSORE STATE, EXCLUDING CIVIL AND MILITARY STATION, BANGALORE** ...	**2,789**	**1,380**	**1,409**	**172**	**146**	**119**	**119**	**204**	**233**	**74**	**96**	**125**	**140**	**215**	**253**	**178**	**157**	**123**	**143**	**98**	**76**	**54**	**31**	**18**	**15**
3. Bangalore City ...	416	175	241	16	25	21	12	30	28	11	11	9	29	27	50	18	35	18	27	16	10	6	7	3	4
4. Bangalore District ...	221	127	94	21	8	10	4	31	10	9	4	3	8	6	17	23	10	5	15	10	10	5	5	1	3
5. Kolar Gold Fields (City) ...	1,541	778	763	101	92	75	78	106	135	37	47	70	60	147	187	91	88	60	74	50	36	35	13	6	8
6. Kolar District ...	53	26	27	2	1	1	2	1	4	2	3	4	...	4	6	6	3	4	3	2	4	...	1	...	...
7. Tumkur District ...	31	14	17	2	1	1	3	2	2	...	1	1	1	1	4	3	1	...	2	2	2	1	...	1	...
8. Mysore City ...	327	145	182	17	9	7	9	19	39	13	23	25	38	17	22	15	13	13	13	10	11	6	5	3	...
9. Mysore District ...	85	50	35	5	5	1	4	6	1	...	1	8	2	4	8	12	8	12	3	1	...	...	...	1	...
10. Chitaldrug District ...	20	14	6	1	1	...	1	1	...	...	...	1	...	3	1	3	...	3	1	2	2	...	...	...	...
11. Hassan District ...	57	28	29	3	2	3	5	5	8	2	2	2	1	2	5	4	4	5	2	2	...	...	...	...	...
12. Kadur District ...	15	10	5	1	1	...	...	1	1	...	...	1	...	1	2	2	...	3	...	1	1	...	...	...	...
13. Shimoga District ...	23	13	10	3	1	...	1	2	2	...	1	1	1	3	1	1	...	...	3	2	...	1	...	...	...
14. Civil and Military Station, Bangalore ...	*5,520*	*2,401*	*3,119*	*169*	*174*	*168*	*144*	*588*	*518*	*293*	*269*	*132*	*226*	*257*	*479*	*170*	*319*	*138*	*342*	*199*	*327*	*182*	*208*	*105*	*113*

MYSORE CENSUS 1931.

TABLE XX.—Summary figures for Cities and Districts.

NOTE 1.—Areas in square miles in column 2 of this Table differ slightly from those shown in 1921 Census Tables owing to accurate measurement and area computation of tracts not subjected to such processes before.

NOTE 2.—Number of persons per square mile for 1921 shown in column 10 of the Table is calculated upon the area shown in the Census Table for 1921.

NOTE 3.—The area figures since furnished by the Surveyor-General of India are given below:—

District	*Area in Sq. miles*
Bangalore (including the City, and C. and M. Station) ...	3,076
Kolar (including K. G. F. City)	3,127
Tumkur	4,054
Mysore (including the City)	5,463
Chitaldrug	4,179
Hassan	2,666
Kadur	2,775
Shimoga	4,083

NOTE 4.—Figures for the Jain religion are shown separately and the column "Others" includes the population of all other religions not shown in the table.

TABLE XX.

Summary figures for Districts.

District or State	Area in square miles	Population, 1931			Population, 1921	Percentage of Variation		Numbers of Persons per square mile in		Distribution by Religion											
										Hindu		Musalman		Christian		Jain		Tribal*		Others	
		Persons	Males	Females		1921 to 1931	1911 to 1921	1931	1921	Males	Females	Males	Females	Males	Females	Males	Females	Males	Females	Males	Females
1	2	3	4	5	6	7	8	9	10	11	12	13	14	15	16	17	18	19	20	21	22
MYSORE STATE, INCLUDING CIVIL AND MILITARY STATION, BANGALORE. ...	**29,325·48**	**6,557,302**	**3,353,963**	**3,203,339**	**5,978,892**	**+9·674**	**+2·974**	**224**	**203**	**3,066,332**	**2,949,548**	**213,381**	**185,247**	**45,164**	**42,374**	**15,920**	**13,693**	**12,230**	**11,598**	**936**	**879**
MYSORE STATE, EXCLUDING CIVIL AND MILITARY STATION, BANGALORE. ...	**29,311·98**	**6,423,189**	**3,284,554**	**3,138,635**	**5,859,952**	**+9·611**	**+2·709**	**219**	**199**	**3,027,795**	**2,914,081**	**197,983**	**172,020**	**30,512**	**27,004**	**15,436**	**13,363**	**12,230**	**11,598**	**598**	**569**
Bangalore City ...	11·82	172,357	91,680	80,677	118,556	+45·381	+33·738	14,582	12,147	76,615	67,884	10,975	8,856	8,291	3,463	724	429	...	...	45	45
Bangalore District ...	2,922·41	908,056	461,905	446,151	788,379	+15·180	+3·799	311	257	422,950	410,602	31,744	28,532	4,067	3,969	1,777	1,755	1,357	1,288	10	5
Kolar Gold Fields (City).	30·00	85,103	45,051	40,052	87,682	−2·941	+4·708	2,837	2,923	32,695	29,618	4,045	2,726	7,579	7,072	262	185	1	...	469	451
Kolar District ...	3,161·16	763,934	389,262	374,672	704,657	+8·412	+1·184	242	224	353,912	342,407	30,790	27,970	1,319	1,360	3,173	2,879	67	55	1	1
Tumkur District ...	4,082·14	861,405	439,144	422,261	778,122	+11·419	+5·137	211	190	410,649	396,024	28,116	21,274	892	728	3,814	3,526	672	709	1	...
Mysore City ...	10·00	107,142	56,772	50,370	83,951	+27·624	+17·733	10,714	8,837	44,734	40,065	9,661	8,111	1,956	1,991	372	177	6	1	43	35
Mysore District ...	5,491·79	1,403,984	703,838	700,146	1,319,368	+6·418	+3·824	256	240	674,201	673,979	23,231	20,254	1,828	1,547	1,250	1,264	3,312	3,078	16	24
Chitaldrug District ...	4,149·12	656,569	336,786	319,783	574,179	+14·349	+1·760	158	138	314,889	299,916	19,271	17,570	275	240	696	484	1,699	1,570	6	8
Hassan District ...	2,684·52	596,937	300,746	296,191	583,960	+2·222	+0·648	227	219	284,490	282,649	11,835	9,652	2,840	2,440	1,044	807	546	558	1	...
Kadur District ...	2,770·96	347,715	184,389	163,326	333,538	+4·250	−1·453	125	120	167,771	151,506	11,141	8,289	4,110	2,465	798	562	566	501	3	3
Shimoga District ...	4,048·06	519,987	274,981	245,006	492,560	+5·568	+4·674	128	122	244,909	219,441	22,174	18,786	2,355	1,729	1,526	1,205	4,014	3,848	3	2
Civil and Military Station, Bangalore ...	*13·50*	*134,113*	*69,409*	*64,704*	*118,940*	+12·756	+17·956	*9,934*	*8,784*	*38,537*	*35,467*	*15,398*	*13,227*	*14,652*	*15,370*	**484**	**330**	...	...	**338**	**310**

*See note 2 on the title page of Table V.

MYSORE CENSUS, 1931.

PROVINCIAL TABLE I.—Area and Population of Cities and Taluks.

NOTE 1.—This and the following Table compiled for use within the State present, by taluks as units, the more important statistics relating to population, density, literacy, etc. Territorial distribution of Christian population by Sect and Race which appeared as an Imperial Table at the last Census has now been treated as Provincial Table III. The other three Provincial Tables newly added, *viz.*, Rural and Cottage Industries, Classification of structures and Vaccination furnish by Districts and Cities, certain statistics specially collected in the State (excluding the Civil and Military Station, Bangalore).

NOTE 2.—During the last decade French-Rocks ceased to be a separate Sub-Taluk and was merged in Seringapatam Taluk, Koratagere Sub-Taluk was converted into a Taluk and Periyapatna was constituted into a separate Sub-Taluk. These and other changes involved transfers of villages from taluk to taluk and introduced alterations in the area of the taluks concerned. No adjustment has however been made in the figures of population for 1921 and of variation for 1911-21 in these cases.

NOTE 3.—Maddur was constituted into a separate taluk subsequent to this Census by the transfer of villages from the Mandya and Malvalli Taluks. The areas of these two taluks as reconstituted and the area of the newly constituted taluk of Maddur and their population on the basis of the present Census are indicated below :—

	Area in sq. miles.	*Population.*
Mandya	261·59	90,797
Maddur	246·83	90,259
Malvalli	325·90	106,671

PROVINCIAL TABLE I.

PROVINCIAL TABLE I.

Area and Population of Cities and Taluks.

Area and Population of Cities and Taluks.

City or Taluk	Area in square miles	Number of		Number of occupied houses	Population				Percentage of variation		Number of persons per square mile in 1931
		Towns	Villages		1931			1921 (both sexes)	1921 to 1931	1911 to 1921	
					Persons	Males	Females				
1	2	3	4	5	6	7	8	9	10	11	12
MYSORE STATE, INCLUDING CIVIL AND MILITARY STATION, BANGALORE.	**29,325·5**	**108**	**16,483**	**1,311,445**	**6,557,302**	**3,353,963**	**3,203,339**	**5,978,892**	**+9·7**	**+3·0**	**224**
MYSORE STATE, EXCLUDING CIVIL AND MILITARY STATION, BANGALORE.	**29,312·0**	**107**	**16,483**	**1,289,833**	**6,423,189**	**3,284,554**	**3,138,635**	**5,859,952**	**+9·6**	**+2·7**	**219**
Bangalore City ...	**11 8**	**1**	...	**34,657**	**172,357**	**91,680**	**80,677**	**118,556**	**+45·4**	**+33·7**	**14,582**
Bangalore District.	**2,922·4**	**13**	**2,478**	**176,955**	**908,056**	**461,905**	**446,151**	**788,379**	**+15·2**	**+3·8**	**311**
Bangalore Taluk ...	384·4	1	394	29,487	150,264	76,961	73,303	123,517	+21·7	+3·1	391
Hoskote do ...	272·1	1	317	15,113	81,934	41,828	40,106	75,272	+8·9	—0·6	301
Devanhalli do ...	229·8	2	241	11,989	66,584	33,831	32,753	60,909	+9·3	—2·8	290
Dodballapur do ...	310·2	1	271	15,911	82,948	42,308	40,640	74,619	+11·2	+1·1	267
Nelamangala do ...	255·7	2	285	15,466	78,460	39,917	38,543	70,284	+11·6	+2·3	306
Magadi do ...	353·1	1	311	20,457	102,910	52,433	50,477	86,402	+19·1	+3·6	288
Channapatna do ...	212·3	1	130	18,820	94,786	47,705	47,081	83,431	+13·6	+8·6	446
Closepet do ...	239·5	1	118	12,196	61,520	31,121	30,399	50,294	+22·3	+10·7	258
Kankanhalli do ...	470·1	1	228	23,830	121,673	61,838	59,835	104,303	+16·7	+9·8	258
Anekal do ...	190·3	2	183	13,686	66,977	33,963	33,014	59,848	+12·9	+2·2	352
Kolar Gold Fields (City)...	**30·0**	**1**	...	**19,448**	**85,103**	**45,051**	**40,052**	**87,682**	**—2·9**	**+4·7**	**2,837**
Kolar District.	**3,161·2**	**11**	**2,751**	**150,993**	**763,934**	**389,262**	**374,672**	**704,657**	**+8·4**	**+1·2**	**242**
Kolar Taluk ...	283·6	1	288	17,780	94,519	47,874	46,645	86,781	+8·9	+7·6	333
Mulbagal do ...	327·2	1	306	16,155	74,603	37,613	36,990	67,163	+11·1	—2·0	228
Srinivasapur do ...	324·9	1	289	13,487	70,568	35,901	34,667	62,674	+12·6	—2·3	217
Chintamani do ...	271·7	1	322	14,713	78,211	39,656	38,555	64,109	+22·0	+3·3	288
Sidlaghatta do ...	326·1	1	242	12,000	62,355	31,662	30,693	67,934	—8.2	—4·2	191
Bagepalli do ...	446·7	1	201	11,150	57,706	29,925	27,781	55,562	+3·9	+2·7	170
Gudibanda Sub-Taluk ...		1	94	3,799	18,226	9,422	8,804	17,899	+4·8	—2·0	
Goribidnur Taluk ...	343·3	1	215	20,836	101,594	52,358	49,236	93,675	+8·5	+3·5	296
Chikballapur do ...	250·0	1	212	12,468	62,208	31,622	30,586	58,689	+6·0	+3·4	249
Malur do ...	265·8	1	299	14,135	73,851	37,601	36,250	67,659	+9·2	—1·9	278
Bowringpet do ...	321·9	1	283	14,470	70,093	35,628	34,465	63,012	+11·2	+1·7	217
Tumkur District.	**4,082·1**	**10**	**2,381**	**171,184**	**861,405**	**439,144**	**422,261**	**773,122**	**+11·4**	**+5·1**	**211**
Tumkur Taluk ...	379·6	1	338	24,358	127,945	65,850	62,095	125,294	+2·1	+7·2	337
Madhugiri do ...	426·2	1	264	20,078	96,528	49,758	46,770	91,874	+5·1	+3·8	226
Koratagere do* ...	259·0	1	225	13,010	63,009	32,435	30,574	41,955	+50·2	+3·0	243
Sira do ...	600.0	1	217	20,017	100,458	51,228	49,230	93,324	+7·6	+4·5	167
Pavagada do ...	524·3	1	135	14,454	72,766	37,538	35,228	65,529	+11·0	+7·1	139
Chiknayakanhalli Taluk ...	519·9	1	196	14,383	68,734	35,132	33,602	60,498	+13·6	+5·2	132
Gubbi do ...	552·8	1	351	22,451	112,358	57,269	55,089	102,967	+9·1	+6·4	203
Tiptur do ...	438·7	1	230	14,831	74,403	37,610	36,793	63,051	+18·0	+2·5	270
Turuvekere (Sub-Taluk) ...		1	139	8,677	43,941	21,798	22,143	39,537	+11·1	+0·9	
Kunigal Taluk ...	382·4	1	286	18,925	101,263	50,526	50,737	89,093	+13·7	+6·3	265
Mysore City ...	**10·0**	**1**	...	**21,715**	**107,142**	**56,772**	**50,370**	**83,951**	**+27.6**	**+17·7**	**10,714**
Mysore District.	**5,491·8**	**26**	**2,709**	**291,050**	**1,403,984**	**703,838**	**700,146**	**1,319,368**	**+6·4**	**+3 8**	**256**
Mysore Taluk ...	311·9	...	136	15,609	76,669	38,946	37,723	67,961	+12·8	+4·8	245
Yedatore Taluk ...	237·0	3	144	19,655	93,572	46,483	47,089	88,797	+5·4	+5·1	395
Hunsur do ...	660·8	1	176	14,514	64,659	31,848	32,811	109,162	—40·8	—7·8	168
Periyapatna Sub-Taluk*...		1	147	10,554	46,068	23,091	22,977	...	...	...	
Hoggaddevanakote Tk. ...	619·9	2	173	13,757	58,481	28,890	29,591	58,554	- 0·1	—8·2	94
Gundlupet Taluk ...	544·3	1	132	17,385	82,118	41,107	41,011	79,524	+3·3	+1·8	151
Chamarajnagar Taluk ...	474·8	2	147	27,010	132,125	66,127	65,998	121,487	+8·8	+6·4	278
Nanjangud do ...	378·5	1	167	26,215	127,945	64,632	63,313	120,727	+6·0	+6·7	337
T.-Narsipur Taluk ...	226·4	4	121	20,513	103,424	52,442	50,982	95,162	+8·7	+3·0	457
Seringapatam Taluk ...	274·8	3	175	21,661	96,938	48,923	48,015	95,749	+1·2	+14·7	352
Mandya do ...	443·1	2	284	30,189	156,297	79,282	77,015	136,204	+14·8	+6·5	353
Nagamangala do ...	402·2	1	334	16,877	84,456	41,024	43,432	80,667	+4·7	+0·8	210
Krishnarajpete do ...	424·9	1	332	23,756	116,817	57,549	59,268	112,551	+3·8	+4·7	275
Malvalli do ...	391·2	2	213	26,130	131,430	66,963	64,467	120,689	+8·9	+11·5	336
Yelandur (Jahagir) ...	102·2	2	28	7,225	32,985	16,531	16,454	32,134	+2·7	—5·7	323

* See note 2 on the title page.

PROVINCIAL TABLE I.

Area and Population of Cities and Taluks—*concld.*

PROVINCIAL TABLE I.

Area and Population of Cities and Taluks.

City or Taluk	Area in square miles	Number of		Number of occupied houses	Population				Percentage of variation		Number of persons per square mile in 1931
		Towns	Villages		1931			1921 (both sexes)	1921 to 1931	1911 to 1921	
					Persons	Males	Females				
1	2	3	4	5	6	7	8	9	10	11	12
Chitaldrug District.	**4149·1**	**11**	**1,239**	**124,798**	**656,569**	**336,786**	**319,783**	**574,179**	**+14·4**	**+1·8**	**158**
Chitaldrug Taluk ...	530·6	1	162	20,698	108,268	55,923	52,345	98,259	+10·2	+5·4	204
Challakere do ...	796·2	2	154	17,754	94,605	48,922	45,683	85,556	+10·6	+6·6	119
Molakalmuru Taluk ...	294·1	1	79	7,877	39,580	20,402	19,178	36,483	+8·5	—7·0	135
Jagalur do ...	372·7	1	135	10,850	57,140	29,472	27,668	51,445	+11·1	—4·0	153
Davangere do ... }	556·8	2	155	18,351	93,981	48,238	45,743	76,501	+22·9	+0·2	247
Harihar (Sub-Taluk) ... }		1	76	7,776	43,378	22,394	20,984	38,418	+12·9	—8·9	
Holalkere Taluk ...	406·7	1	157	13,757	73,782	37,365	36,417	61,133	+20·7	—1·7	181
Hosadurga do ...	565·9	1	185	12,949	69,732	35,094	34,638	56,421	+23·6	+0·4	123
Hiriyur do ...	623·8	1	136	14,766	76,103	38,976	37,127	69,960	+8·8	+10·7	122
Hassan District.	**2634·5**	**12**	**2,252**	**122,435**	**596,937**	**300,746**	**296,191**	**583,960**	**+2·2**	**+0·7**	**227**
Hassan Taluk ... }	473·2	1	362	20,257	103,942	51,764	52,178	101,901	+2·0	+3·1	270
Alur (Sub-Taluk) ... }		1	157	5,161	24,235	12,285	11,950	27,240	—11·0	—1·7	
Arsikere Taluk ...	487·4	3	316	20,968	107,841	54,584	53,257	93,390	+15·5	+8·3	221
Belur do ...	339·2	1	348	14,927	67,923	34,961	32,962	71,152	—4·5	—3·4	200
Saklespur Taluk ...	439·4	1	266	11,196	50,750	27,697	23,053	51,042	—0·6	+0·9	115
Arkalgud do ...	258·5	2	245	16,224	74,289	37,308	36,986	79,498	—6·6	—2·7	287
Holenarsipur Taluk ...	232·4	1	198	13,093	66,489	33,046	33,443	64,032	+3·8	—0·5	286
Channarayapatna Taluk ...	404·4	2	360	20,609	101,468	49,106	52,362	95,710	+6·0	—1·5	251
Kadur District.	**2771·0**	**9**	**959**	**73,649**	**347,715**	**184,389**	**163,326**	**333,538**	**+4·3**	**—1·5**	**125**
Chikmagalur Taluk ...	638·1	1	212	17,818	80,092	42,593	37,499	80,329	—0·3	—2·1	126
Kadur do ...	536·0	2	245	18,146	91,211	45,753	45,458	82,011	+11·2	+1·2	170
Tarikere do ...	472·5	2	181	14,989	70,344	36,161	34,183	65,221	+7·9	—7·5	149
Koppa do ... }	649·7	1	100	7,007	33,410	19,059	14,351	35,845	—6·8	+2·6	79
Narasimharajpura (Sub-Tk.) }		1	64	3,409	17,759	10,083	7,676	17,112	+3·8	+2·4	
Mudigere Taluk ...	431·5	1	138	10,449	45,856	25,861	19,995	43,683	+5·0	+0·8	106
Sringeri (Jahgir) ...	43·2	1	24	1,831	9,043	4,879	4,164	9,337	—3·2	—5·7	209
Shimoga District.	**4048·1**	**12**	**1,714**	**102,949**	**519,987**	**274,981**	**245,006**	**492,560**	**+5·6**	**—4·7**	**128**
Shimoga Taluk ... }	693·5	2	232	18,349	86,342	45,745	40,597	74,369	+16·1	—0·7	151
Kumsi (Sub-Taluk) ... }		1	66	3,887	18,486	9,930	8,556	16,786	+10·1	—2·0	
Channagiri Taluk ...	466·4	1	186	16,518	86,375	43,698	42,677	76,552	+12·8	—8·0	185
Honnali do ...	331·3	2	145	13,077	70,449	36,065	34,384	64,125	+9·9	—6·2	212
Shikarpur do ...	429·7	2	136	12,136	55,110	28,886	26,224	55,523	—0·7	—12·0	128
Sorab do ...	447·1	1	255	12,406	58,949	31,118	27,831	58,901	+0·1	—11·6	132
Sagar do ...	668·9	1	252	10,061	54,412	29,786	24,626	51,550	+5·6	+1·0	81
Nagar do ...	530·9	1	199	6,292	34,948	19,181	15,767	38,180	—8·5	+1·4	66
Thirthahalli do ...	480·3	1	243	10,223	54,916	30,572	24,344	56,574	—2·9	+3·4	114
Civil and Military Station, Bangalore.	**13·5**	**1**	...	**21,612**	**134,113**	**69,409**	**64,704**	**118,940**	**+12·8**	**+18·0**	**9,934**

MYSORE CENSUS 1931.

PROVINCIAL TABLE II.—Population of Cities and Taluks by Religion and Literacy.

NOTE 1.—Under "Others" are included 63 Males and 37 Females belonging to the Sikh Religion, whose distribution by Population and Literacy, is as under:—

District or City	Population			Number of literate persons by age periods					
				0 to 15		15 to 20		20 and over	
	Persons	Males	Females	Males	Females	Males	Females	Males	Females
Bangalore District ...	**11**	7	4	...	...	...	...	3	...
Mysore City	**17**	11	6	3	...	1	...	3	...
Mysore District	**40**	16	24	...	...	3	1	6	...
Civil and Military Station, Bangalore.	**32**	29	3	...	...	3	1	21	1

NOTE 2.—The total population of Depressed Classes in the State is arrived at by adding together the figures under the head so described under Religion Hindu and those shown under the head Tribal.

PROVINCIAL TABLE II.

Population of Cities and Taluks by Religion and Literacy.

Taluk or City	Hindu												Musalman				Christian			
	Brahmins				Other Hindus				Depressed Classes											
	Number of Persons		Number Literate		Number of Persons		Number Literate		Number of Persons		Number Literate		Number of Persons		Number Literate		Number of Persons		Number Literate	
	Males	Females	Males	Females	Males	Females	Males	Females	Males	Females	Males	Females	Males	Females	Males	Females	Males	Females	Males	Females
1	2	3	4	5	6	7	8	9	10	11	12	13	14	15	16	17	18	19	20	21
MYSORE STATE, INCLUDING CIVIL AND MILITARY STATION, BANGALORE.	**126,542**	**118,621**	**88,526**	**32,919**	**2,306,983**	**2,223,878**	**323,106**	**26,112**	**632,807**	**607,049**	**15,845**	**1,320**	**213,381**	**185,247**	**51,876**	**15,456**	**45,164**	**42,374**	**18,935**	**12,351**
MYSORE STATE, EXCLUDING CIVIL AND MILITARY STATION, BANGALORE.	**124,597**	**117,144**	**87,193**	**32,413**	**2,284,147**	**2,203,689**	**314,487**	**24,158**	**619,051**	**593,248**	**13,534**	**916**	**197,983**	**172,020**	**46,304**	**13,293**	**30,512**	**27,004**	**11,271**	**6,280**
Bangalore City ...	**17,466**	**14,716**	**13,170**	**6,695**	**51,387**	**46,038**	**18,609**	**3,630**	**7,792**	**7,130**	**1,031**	**78**	**10,975**	**8,856**	**4,307**	**1,293**	**3,291**	**3,463**	**1,655**	**1,383**
Bangalore District.	**11,094**	**10,816**	**7,605**	**2,523**	**311,041**	**302,084**	**37,823**	**2,719**	**100,815**	**97,702**	**1,411**	**64**	**31,744**	**28,532**	**5,815**	**2,018**	**4,067**	**3,969**	**682**	**414**
Bangalore Taluk ...	1,199	1,090	771	261	45,962	43,559	5,519	485	21,659	21,465	458	16	5,427	4,502	1,367	443	2,556	2,536	369	243
Hoskote Do ...	1,114	1,045	731	212	26,924	25,989	2,817	181	9,638	9,862	93	11	4,026	3,614	312	191	126	126	20	2
Devanhalli Do ...	1,034	1,026	746	235	23,534	22,840	3,084	252	8,112	7,831	121	2	1,053	978	207	63	97	77	22	7
Dodballapur Do ...	1,218	1,159	856	285	29,896	28,688	5,283	379	8,832	8,641	99	6	1,899	1,738	552	219	111	108	48	69
Nelamangala Do ...	933	977	733	254	26,927	26,041	4,353	360	9,250	8,902	165	2	2,320	2,183	468	161	13	12	9	2
Magadi Do ...	1,579	1,644	1,048	326	35,502	34,517	4,630	326	9,847	9,227	94	2	4,108	4,018	462	174	141	120	31	13
Channapatna Do ...	1,158	1,106	815	288	34,750	34,659	3,060	161	7,609	7,484	106	5	4,114	3,742	875	207	68	87	23	30
Closepet Do ...	721	636	498	179	22,128	21,856	2,511	220	5,495	5,269	51	3	2,669	2,559	506	240	102	77	23	13
Kankanhalli Do ...	1,146	1,151	749	224	44,491	43,177	3,698	229	10,655	10,155	107	10	3,808	3,356	631	182	667	661	89	22
Anekal Do ...	942	982	658	259	20,927	20,508	2,873	176	9,715	9,346	117	7	2,025	1,837	435	118	186	165	48	13
Kolar Gold Fields (City) ...	**746**	**708**	**564**	**210**	**12,489**	**11,224**	**3,341**	**518**	**19,460**	**17,686**	**3,103**	**299**	**4,045**	**2,726**	**1,498**	**263**	**7,579**	**7,072**	**3,349**	**1,534**
Kolar District.	**13,340**	**13,486**	**9,393**	**2,787**	**252,798**	**244,062**	**29,678**	**1,914**	**87,774**	**84,859**	**1,016**	**61**	**30,790**	**27,970**	**6,110**	**1,835**	**1,319**	**1,360**	**561**	**533**
Kolar Taluk ...	2,350	2,360	1,638	503	29,043	28,357	4,238	332	10,625	10,441	170	7	5,300	4,866	1,199	461	485	572	268	369
Mulbagal Do ...	1,541	1,666	995	343	22,729	22,599	2,775	155	9,288	9,132	88	11	3,906	3,523	623	151	145	124	35	7
Srinivaspur Do ...	974	1,000	725	199	23,422	22,689	2,605	116	8,277	7,951	77	9	3,193	2,992	725	362	35	35	20	8
Chintamani Do ...	1,314	1,237	971	173	26,365	25,658	2,719	128	8,758	8,594	83	8	3,160	3,001	539	138	57	65	6	4
Sidlaghatta Do ...	925	949	679	173	22,439	21,877	2,468	167	6,491	6,161	74	1	1,762	1,668	374	137	34	29	15	8
Bagepalli Do ...	649	616	451	117	20,816	19,392	1,620	75	6,690	6,203	13	...	1,762	1,567	267	37	3	1	3	1
Gudibanda (Sub) Do ...	354	326	250	67	6,597	6,217	624	32	1,762	1,706	4	...	694	541	99	13	...	2	...	2
Goribidnur Do ...	1,736	1,705	1,205	350	34,091	31,931	1,051	200	10,625	10,101	69	4	2,807	2,566	541	86	65	68	17	14
Chikballapur Do ...	1,299	1,305	904	339	20,855	20,454	2,981	269	7,337	6,827	121	5	1,847	1,725	422	75	254	258	71	38
Malur Do ...	1,071	1,187	747	229	24,668	23,880	2,762	173	8,645	8,495	146	9	3,178	2,653	542	141	23	24	9	15
Bowringpet Do ...	1,127	1,135	828	294	21,773	21,018	2,895	262	9,273	9,248	171	7	3,181	2,868	779	231	218	182	117	67

PROVINCIAL TABLE II.

Population of Cities and Taluks by Religion and Literacy—*contd.*

Taluk or City	Jain				Tribal				Others			
	Number of Persons		Number Literate		Number of Persons		Number Literate		Number of Persons		Number Literate	
	Males	Females	Males	Females	Males	Females	Males	Females	Males	Females	Males	Females
	22	23	24	25	26	27	28	29	30	31	32	33
MYSORE STATE, INCLUDING CIVIL AND MILITARY STATION, BANGALORE.	**15,920**	**13,693**	**6,212**	**908**	**12,230**	**11,598**	**225**	**11**	**936**	**879**	**495**	**230**
MYSORE STATE, EXCLUDING CIVIL AND MILITARY STATION, BANGALORE.	**15,436**	**13,368**	**5,915**	**892**	**12,230**	**11,598**	**225**	**11**	**598**	**569**	**290**	**80**
Bangalore City ...	**724**	**429**	**510**	**102**	...	...	...	...	**45**	**45**	**32**	**14**
Bangalore District.	**1,777**	**1,755**	**510**	**74**	**1,357**	**1,288**	**12**	**1**	**10**	**5**	**4**	...
Bangalore Taluk ...	103	110	23	7	46	36	...	...	9	5	3	...
Hoskote Do ...	...	...	...	...	...	...	...	...	...	...	...	...
Devanhalli Do ...	1	1	1	1	...	...	...	...	...	...	...	...
Dodballapur Do ...	172	138	47	...	180	168	2	...	...	...	...	...
Nelamangala Do ...	424	423	145	21	...	...	...	...	...	...	...	...
Magadi Do ...	919	917	249	33	37	34	...	...	...	...	...	...
Channapatna Do ...	6	3	3	...	...	...	...	...	...	...	...	...
Closepet Do ...	5	2	3	2	...	...	...	...	1	...	1	...
Kankanhalli Do ...	3	2	3	2	1,070	1,033	7	1	...	...	...	...
Anekal Do ...	144	159	36	8	24	17	3	...	...	...	...	...
Kolar Gold Fields (City)...	**262**	**185**	**166**	**10**	**1**	...	...	...	**469**	**451**	**202**	**43**
Kolar District.	**3,173**	**2,879**	**801**	**78**	**67**	**55**	**2**	...	**1**	**1**	...	...
Kolar Taluk ...	52	23	36	5	19	21	...	...	...	...	...	...
Mulbagal Do ...	4	6	4	1	...	...	...	...	...	...	...	...
Srinivaspur Do ...	...	...	...	...	...	...	...	...	...	...	...	...
Chintamani Do ...	2	...	...	...	...	...	...	...	...	...	...	...
Sidlaghatta Do ...	...	...	...	...	8	9	2	...	...	...	...	...
Bagepalli Do ...	5	2	3	...	...	...	...	...	...	...	...	...
Gudibanda (Sub) Do ...	15	12	12	1	...	...	...	...	...	...	...	...
Goribidnur Do ...	3,012	2,801	681	65	22	14	...	...	...	...	...	...
Chikballapur Do ...	30	17	20	6	...	...	...	...	...	...	...	...
Malur Do ...	...	...	...	...	16	11	...	...	...	...	...	...
Bowringpet Do ...	53	13	45	...	2	...	...	...	1	1	...	...

Taluk or City	Number Literate						Literate in English	
	Aged 0 to 15		Aged 15 to 20		Aged 20 and over			
	Males	Females	Males	Females	Males	Females	Males	Females
	34	35	36	37	38	39	40	41
MYSORE STATE, INCLUDING CIVIL AND MILITARY STATION, BANGALORE.	**82,488**	**25,741**	**62,814**	**16,141**	**369,917**	**47,425**	**78,494**	**13,552**
MYSORE STATE, EXCLUDING CIVIL AND MILITARY STATION, BANGALORE.	**79,478**	**23,405**	**59,709**	**14,201**	**340,032**	**40,437**	**65,125**	**7,812**
Bangalore City ...	**6,137**	**3,706**	**5,831**	**2,393**	**27,346**	**7,096**	**16,914**	**2,986**
Bangalore District.	**8,890**	**2,384**	**6,739**	**1,395**	**38,283**	**4,034**	**4,216**	**342**
Bangalore Taluk ...	1,285	350	1,144	230	6,081	825	542	136
Hoskote Do ...	696	152	513	112	2,764	333	261	10
Devanhalli Do ...	712	181	522	104	2,947	275	543	27
Dodballapur Do ...	1,145	322	886	166	4,856	470	522	42
Nelamangala Do ...	1,054	286	754	143	4,065	391	386	3
Magadi Do ...	1,025	269	759	172	4,730	433	391	12
Channapatna Do ...	790	217	681	104	3,461	370	533	51
Closepet Do ...	705	253	434	95	2,454	309	397	19
Kankanhalli Do ...	864	200	566	142	3,849	323	209	22
Anekal Do ...	614	154	580	127	3,026	300	432	18
Kolar Gold Fields (City)...	**1,583**	**811**	**1,422**	**396**	**9,218**	**1,670**	**2,984**	**1,050**
Kolar District.	**7,481**	**2,120**	**5,426**	**1,314**	**34,654**	**3,774**	**5,332**	**554**
Kolar Taluk ...	1,392	582	976	302	5,181	793	1,262	347
Mulbagal Do ...	655	162	438	119	3,427	387	443	23
Srinivaspur Do ...	654	167	479	118	3,019	409	262	4
Chintamani Do ...	630	115	489	82	3,199	254	371	13
Sidlaghatta Do ...	577	148	415	97	2,620	246	339	14
Bagepalli Do ...	319	66	235	49	1,808	115	171	3
Gudibanda (Sub) Do ...	150	46	90	21	749	48	88	2
Goribidnur Do ...	897	188	762	147	4,905	384	512	15
Chikballapur Do ...	751	180	582	146	3,186	406	743	59
Malur Do ...	656	192	441	94	3,109	289	353	17
Bowringpet Do ...	800	279	519	139	3,456	443	788	57

PROVINCIAL TABLE II.

Population of Cities and Taluks by Religion and Literacy.—*contd.*

Taluk or City	Hindu												Musalman				Christian			
	Brahmins				Other Hindus				Depressed Class											
	Number of Persons		Number Literate		Number of Persons		Number Literate		Number of Persons		Number Literate		Number of Persons		Number Literate		Number of Persons		Number Literate	
	Males	Females	Males	Females	Males	Females	Males	Females	Males	Females	Males	Females	Males	Females	Males	Females	Males	Females	Males	Females
1	2	3	4	5	6	7	8	9	10	11	12	13	14	15	16	17	18	19	20	21
Tumkur District.	**11,477**	**11,032**	**7,970**	**3,001**	**327,211**	**315,397**	**47,513**	**3,424**	**71,961**	**69,595**	**1,184**	**66**	**23,116**	**21,274**	**5,341**	**1,554**	**892**	**728**	**495**	**306**
Tumkur Taluk ...	3,074	2,869	2,264	1,012	41,741	42,312	8,113	1,080	11,296	10,916	278	21	5,296	4,781	1,307	390	618	469	896	246
Madhugiri Do ...	1,433	1,278	981	297	35,544	33,246	4,466	214	9,065	8,758	79	3	1,812	1,643	474	112	16	16	7	4
Koratagere Do ...	795	786	548	169	23,856	22,549	3,149	230	5,871	5,502	95	5	1,307	1,123	267	84	4	4	3	2
Sira Do ...	780	755	588	191	37,686	36,465	5,776	284	9,514	9,007	153	4	2,822	2,628	819	274	31	40	5	5
Pavagada Do ...	751	749	530	170	27,124	25,109	2,587	166	8,504	8,308	47	1	975	901	185	42	11	8	3	3
Chiknayakanhalli Taluk...	774	733	483	151	27,516	26,474	5,197	335	5,329	5,031	117	5	1,460	1,313	329	66	8	8	4	3
Gubbi Do ...	1,158	1,218	767	303	44,708	43,006	6,617	369	8,246	7,940	96	3	2,836	2,695	412	74	72	50	29	24
Tiptur Do ...	1,230	1,183	836	266	29,597	29,233	5,970	357	4,369	4,741	101	8	1,647	1,523	449	178	88	95	29	10
Turuvekere (Sub) Do ...	508	472	365	149	17,906	18,246	1,689	109	2,405	2,493	41	9	745	715	127	33	10	8	6	3
Kunigal Do ...	974	1,039	658	293	38,533	38,757	5,958	280	6,762	6,899	177	7	4,166	3,952	942	306	39	30	13	6
Mysore City ...	**11,194**	**9,795**	**8,677**	**4,423**	**28,176**	**25,490**	**10,339**	**2,059**	**5,364**	**4,770**	**569**	**27**	**9,661**	**8,111**	**3,042**	**1,380**	**1,956**	**1,991**	**933**	**780**
Mysore District.	**17,055**	**17,173**	**11,237**	**3,876**	**536,172**	**535,650**	**42,811**	**2,314**	**120,974**	**121,156**	**2,246**	**133**	**23,231**	**20,254**	**5,276**	**1,576**	**1,828**	**1,547**	**577**	**201**
Mysore Taluk ...	576	529	371	73	30,473	29,621	1,792	69	7,013	6,851	118	9	762	622	127	11	107	90	67	18
Yedatore Do ...	1,313	1,292	826	305	36,295	36,795	3,256	144	6,656	6,910	66	2	1,862	1,709	386	124	122	122	34	10
Hunsur Do ...	628	659	401	156	23,460	24,433	2,421	178	5,518	5,688	113	3	1,733	1,563	517	252	162	141	44	16
Periyapatna (Sub) Do ...	413	395	264	122	17,110	17,207	747	24	4,341	4,262	12	...	1,184	1,066	156	55	3	4	1	1
Heggaddevanakote Taluk	601	650	415	109	18,267	18,947	1,635	105	7,046	7,288	79	3	992	847	228	18	63	63	14	5
Gundlupet Taluk ...	1,078	1,042	769	160	31,685	31,875	3,183	157	7,159	7,174	178	12	930	730	364	83	34	11	25	5
Chamrajnagar Do ...	1,916	1,945	1,195	323	48,102	48,016	4,016	211	12,544	12,792	216	14	2,142	1,851	496	139	436	433	70	38
Nanjangud Do ...	2,219	2,174	1,446	524	47,745	46,959	3,531	226	12,968	12,678	209	15	1,559	1,385	357	70	96	65	17	8
T.-Narsipur Do ...	1,258	1,348	850	329	37,263	36,220	2,791	221	11,425	11,296	208	15	2,443	2,082	546	244	49	32	18	7
Seringapatam Do ...	1,767	1,784	1,144	428	38,350	37,856	3,116	233	6,706	6,602	85	8	1,833	1,548	426	104	252	207	108	21
Mandya Taluk ...	1,522	1,445	1,061	350	64,853	63,296	4,525	186	10,753	10,398	388	11	1,839	1,606	522	161	236	174	71	20
Nagamangala Do ...	714	714	505	230	34,880	36,711	3,782	131	3,987	4,616	78	1	1,247	1,137	309	94	12	13	6	2
Krishnarajpete Do ...	1,530	1,713	980	428	47,179	48,639	4,578	206	7,254	7,509	88	4	1,496	1,329	395	126	64	48	13	2
Malvalli Do ...	1,139	1,055	732	255	49,933	48,370	2,605	174	12,964	12,540	330	36	2,634	2,284	344	77	181	113	118	47
Yelandur (Jahagir) ...	381	428	276	84	10,627	10,705	830	49	4,640	4,552	78	...	575	495	103	18	6	6	1	1
Chitaldrug District.	**5,075**	**4,681**	**3,664**	**1,574**	**246,434**	**235,054**	**41,844**	**2,590**	**63,330**	**60,181**	**1,159**	**53**	**19,271**	**17,570**	**3,848**	**662**	**275**	**240**	**148**	**63**
Chitaldrug Taluk ...	1,191	1,078	916	419	39,396	36,901	8,147	636	11,087	10,662	272	12	3,794	3,426	833	202	91	81	51	19
Challakere Do ...	578	554	401	182	36,480	34,039	4,500	228	9,441	8,850	145	4	1,677	1,585	557	84	14	18	9	8
Molakalmuru Do ...	236	252	173	74	15,175	14,384	2,045	122	3,529	3,270	93	1	1,436	1,295	292	16	13	12	9	2
Jagalur Do ...	214	221	165	53	21,081	19,853	3,537	108	6,165	5,738	126	...	1,642	1,495	243	81	2	2	...	...
Davangere Do ...	1,060	929	758	388	34,154	32,461	7,086	642	8,524	8,339	129	9	3,983	3,619	662	105	67	63	34	13
Harihar (Sub) Taluk ...	476	476	314	107	17,182	16,006	2,434	132	2,308	2,238	31	2	2,191	2,087	363	51	43	32	25	8
Holalkere Taluk ...	465	394	322	117	27,314	27,031	4,975	238	8,392	7,989	116	5	1,067	929	283	63	10	3	6	2
Hosdurga Do ...	465	450	333	116	27,667	27,622	3,950	176	5,539	5,309	57	2	1,317	1,138	287	43	10	15	4	4
Hiriyur Do ...	389	327	292	118	27,985	26,807	5,170	308	8,345	7,936	251	18	2,164	1,996	528	117	25	14	10	2

PROVINCIAL TABLE II.

Population of Cities and Taluks by Religion and Literacy—*contd.*

Taluk or City	Jain				Tribal				Others				Number Literate						Literate in English	
	Number of Persons		Number Literate		Number of Persons		Number Literate		Number of Persons		Number Literate		Aged 0 to 15		Aged 15 to 20		Aged 20 and over			
	Males	Females	Males	Females	Males	Females	Males	Females	Males	Females	Males	Females	Males	Females	Males	Females	Males	Females	Males	Females
	22	23	24	25	26	27	28	29	30	31	32	33	34	35	36	37	38	39	40	41
Tumkur District.	**3,814**	**3,526**	**1,248**	**186**	**672**	**709**	**17**	**2**	**1**	...	**1**	...	**10,771**	**2,559**	**7,697**	**1,630**	**45,301**	**4,350**	**5,276**	**827**
Tumkur Taluk...	830	748	325	74	...	...	...	...	...	...	...	...	2,429	913	1,668	501	8,586	1,409	2,346	217
Madhugiri Do ...	1,706	1,630	384	36	182	199	3	...	...	...	...	...	905	173	723	120	4,766	364	302	18
Koratagere Do ...	486	466	146	20	116	144	7	...	...	...	...	...	692	149	459	106	3,055	255	253	16
Sira Do ...	360	308	133	6	35	32	2	...	...	...	...	...	1,843	241	912	139	5,171	384	314	7
Pavagada Do ...	50	40	34	10	123	113	...	...	...	...	...	...	549	116	364	74	2,473	202	191	6
Chiknayakanhalli Do ...	37	41	26	1	8	2	...	...	...	...	...	...	1,081	172	762	107	4,313	282	316	8
Gubbi Do ...	190	171	113	21	9	9	...	...	...	...	...	...	1,034	186	864	170	6,166	439	328	16
Tiptur Do ...	24	8	15	1	55	60	...	...	...	...	...	...	1,224	230	1,017	152	5,159	433	716	29
Turuvekere (Sub) Do ...	113	90	60	13	111	119	5	2	...	...	...	...	418	94	231	76	1,644	148	9	...
Kunigal Do ...	18	29	12	4	33	31	...	...	1	...	1	...	1,096	286	697	176	3,968	434	501	10
Mysore City ...	**372**	**177**	**265**	**51**	**6**	**1**	**1**	...	**43**	**35**	**32**	**17**	**4,458**	**2,447**	**3,611**	**1,457**	**15,789**	**4,833**	**10,688**	**1,405**
Mysore District.	**1,250**	**1,264**	**563**	**115**	**3,312**	**3,078**	**26**	**1**	**16**	**24**	**9**	**1**	**10,548**	**2,363**	**7,191**	**1,534**	**45,006**	**4,320**	**5,070**	**280**
Mysore Taluk...	15	10	8	1	...	...	...	...	...	...	...	...	418	47	276	29	1,759	105	170	20
Yedatore Do ...	215	223	107	17	20	38	1	...	...	...	...	...	546	109	557	130	3,573	368	421	18
Hunsur Do ...	8	8	4	2	339	319	2	...	...	...	...	...	618	174	366	97	2,518	336	280	25
Periyapatna (Sub) Do ...	10	17	7	1	30	26	1	...	...	...	...	...	191	61	107	33	890	109	98	4
Heggaddevanakote Taluk	510	489	144	17	1,406	1,302	14	...	...	...	...	...	368	71	235	48	1,926	138	105	4
Gundlupet Do ...	26	21	7	2	195	158	...	...	...	...	...	...	742	154	530	80	3,254	185	207	5
Chamrajnagar Do ...	173	195	97	25	814	766	3	1	...	...	...	...	856	210	693	153	4,544	387	310	17
Nanjangud Do ...	45	32	31	7	...	...	...	...	...	...	...	...	971	272	650	161	3,970	417	715	41
T.-Narsipur Taluk ...	4	4	3	2	...	...	...	...	...	...	...	...	665	194	508	171	3,246	453	320	10
Seringapatam Taluk ...	5	1	2	...	10	17	...	...	...	...	...	...	777	245	563	155	3,541	394	609	42
Mandya Do ...	68	82	34	9	11	14	1	...	...	...	...	...	1,396	215	716	135	4,490	387	620	29
Nagamangala Do ...	156	170	107	30	978	71	3	...	...	...	...	...	922	141	544	90	3,324	258	240	5
Krishnarajpete Do ...	10	6	9	...	...	...	...	...	16	24	9	1	1,158	227	745	145	4,174	395	392	13
Malvalli Do ...	5	6	3	2	107	99	1	...	...	...	...	...	773	213	582	81	2,778	297	477	49
Yelandur (Jahgir) ...	...	...	...	...	302	268	...	...	...	...	...	...	152	30	119	26	1,019	96	106	3
Chitaldrug District.	**696**	**484**	**464**	**54**	**1,699**	**1,570**	**38**	**1**	**6**	**3**	**6**	**2**	**8,726**	**1,697**	**6,482**	**988**	**36,963**	**2,319**	**3,394**	**162**
Chitaldrug Taluk ...	98	29	73	6	266	203	...	...	...	...	...	...	1,976	460	1,355	232	6,961	602	1,011	64
Challakere Do ...	24	18	19	2	708	619	22	...	...	...	...	...	871	152	664	79	3,918	227	155	7
Molakalmuru Do ...	13	15	5	...	...	...	...	...	...	...	...	...	355	76	296	40	1,905	99	156	6
Jagalur Do ...	64	50	43	7	304	309	5	...	...	...	...	...	633	71	603	37	2,883	91	64	3
Davangere Do ...	209	121	139	14	236	208	2	1	5	3	5	2	1,430	393	1,079	246	6,806	540	1,055	60
Harihar (Sub) Do ...	26	8	19	2	167	137	9	...	1	...	1	...	461	84	433	76	2,302	142	206	11
Holalkere Do ...	112	117	80	16	5	4	...	...	...	...	...	...	971	132	704	83	4,107	226	202	1
Hosdurga Do ...	82	79	57	6	13	25	...	...	...	...	...	...	802	115	582	73	3,304	159	124	2
Hiriyur Do ...	68	47	29	1	...	...	...	...	...	...	...	...	1,227	214	766	117	4,277	233	331	8

PROVINCIAL TABLE II.

Population of Cities and Taluks by Religion and Literacy—*contd.*

Taluk or City	Hindus												Musalman				Christian			
	Brahmins				Other Hindus				Depressed Classes											
	Number of Persons		Number Literate		Number of Persons		Number Literate		Number of Persons		Number Literate		Number of Persons		Number Literate		Number of Persons		Number Literate	
	Males	Females	Males	Females	Males	Females	Males	Females	Males	Females	Males	Females	Males	Females	Males	Females	Males	Females	Males	Females
1	2	3	4	5	6	7	8	9	10	11	12	13	14	15	16	17	18	19	20	21
Hassan District.	**10,977**	**10,760**	**7,731**	**2,761**	**218,384**	**218,171**	**32,728**	**1,771**	**55,129**	**53,718**	**690**	**48**	**11,835**	**9,652**	**3,273**	**899**	**2,840**	**2,440**	**766**	**402**
Hassan Taluk ...	2,774	2,666	1,997	892	38,946	39,665	5,562	306	7,025	6,905	140	9	1,659	1.440	585	221	956	1,075	256	256
Alur (Sub) Do ...	273	284	200	90	8,455	8,216	1,254	71	2,888	2,887	12	1	565	478	135	25	91	73	13	4
Arsikere Do ...	1,686	1,472	1,144	286	40,940	40,659	6,755	309	8,639	8,420	129	16	2,605	2,067	585	99	273	254	111	64
Belur Do ...	1,059	1,000	751	239	21,191	20,330	4,050	178	10,344	9,700	71	11	1,745	1,486	535	228	433	277	135	16
Saklespur Do ...	566	513	481	213	15,477	12,799	3,339	347	8.857	8,057	118	4	1,797	1,044	580	90	935	616	209	44
Arkalgud Do ...	2,044	2,133	1,392	430	27,216	26,738	3,138	184	6,931	7,075	51	2	1,100	1,039	282	56	...	...	...	...
Hole-Narsipur Do ...	1,373	1,410	920	315	25,021	25,515	3,242	208	5,896	5,404	84	2	1,221	1,082	306	82	26	21	17	12
Channarayapatna Taluk...	1,202	1,282	846	296	41,196	44.249	5,088	173	5,054	5,270	85	3	1,143	1,016	315	103	126	124	25	6
Kadur District.	**10,177**	**9,502**	**6,640**	**2,086**	**114,754**	**105,012**	**20,145**	**1,364**	**42,840**	**36,992**	**555**	**41**	**11,141**	**8,289**	**3,455**	**939**	**4,110**	**2,465**	**1,256**	**329**
Chikmagalur Taluk ...	1,815	1,595	1,296	597	24,345	22,150	4,781	406	11,544	10,309	169	16	3,713	2,796	1,461	512	1,021	596	380	127
Kadur Do ...	1,034	950	662	238	36,098	36,413	5,677	279	6,875	6,589	123	6	1,632	1,426	297	68	92	77	40	22
Tarikere Do ...	874	880	651	295	25,888	24,999	5,486	230	6,540	5,792	106	4	2,076	1,871	423	111	185	140	87	36
Koppa Do ...	2,944	2,733	1.729	245	9,380	6,876	1,161	92	4,958	3,849	21	5	930	418	335	18	824	439	181	26
Narasimharajpura (Sub-Tk)	774	723	553	225	4,831	3,466	794	66	3,164	2,496	43	...	910	689	281	88	335	250	104	30
Mudigere Taluk ...	1,320	1,163	817	221	11,531	8,935	1,783	198	9,321	7,599	84	6	1,649	950	542	124	1,618	943	450	83
Sringeri (Jahgir) ...	1,416	1,468	922	265	2,731	2,174	513	93	138	358	9	4	281	199	116	18	35	20	14	5
Shimoga District.	**15,996**	**14,475**	**10,542**	**2,477**	**185,301**	**165,507**	**28,656**	**1,855**	**43,612**	**39,459**	**570**	**46**	**22,174**	**18,786**	**4,339**	**874**	**2,355**	**1,729**	**849**	**335**
Shimoga Taluk ...	3,522	3,076	2,618	1,000	25,291	22,494	4,986	485	9,565	8,794	170	21	6,221	5,331	1,477	391	997	833	429	198
Kumsi (Sub) Do ...	308	247	238	51	5,940	5,173	1,027	44	2,159	1,837	17	...	1,468	1,264	244	54	25	15	13	5
Channagiri Do ...	422	355	323	111	30,434	30,188	5,684	303	5,314	5,069	90	4	4,080	3,725	640	98	6	10	2	2
Honnali Do ...	328	286	226	40	26,784	25,822	4,674	167	6,309	5,810	76	9	2,212	2,046	346	57	26	24	18	7
Shikarpur Do ...	555	491	357	119	18,820	16,997	2,976	208	6,458	5,973	92	6	2,926	2,707	348	86	27	22	13	5
Sorab Do ...	1,171	1,077	707	98	22,248	19,768	3,117	143	5,896	5,423	78	2	1,554	1,386	248	86	98	44	25	11
Sagar Do ...	4,090	3,628	2,558	327	19,783	16,072	2,174	175	3,215	2,828	23	2	1,263	958	360	54	396	227	105	31
Nagar Do ...	1,820	1,742	1,082	162	14,549	11,774	1,706	60	1,689	1,448	10	...	684	487	130	3	273	171	72	15
Tirthahalli Do ...	3,780	3,560	2,436	569	21,502	17,219	3,412	270	2,977	2,277	14	2	1,766	882	546	45	507	383	172	61
Civil and Military Station, Bangalore.	**1,945**	**1,477**	**1 333**	**506**	**22,836**	**20,189**	**8,618**	**1,954**	**13,756**	**13,801**	**2,311**	**404**	**15,398**	**13,227**	**5,572**	**2,163**	**14,652**	**15,370**	**7,664**	**6,071**

PROVINCIAL TABLE II.

Population of Cities and Taluks by Religion and Literary—*concld.*

Taluk or City	Jain				Tribal				Others				Number Literate						Literate in English	
	Number of Persons		Number Literate		Number of Persons		Number Literate		Number of Persons		Number Literate		Aged 0 to 15		Aged 15 to 20		Aged 20 and over			
	Males	Females	Males	Females	Males	Females	Males	Females	Males	Females	Males	Females	Males	Females	Males	Females	Males	Females	Males	Females
	22	23	24	25	26	27	28	29	30	31	32	33	34	35	36	37	38	39	40	41
Hassan District.	**1,044**	**897**	**658**	**131**	**536**	**553**	**17**	...	**1**	...	...	...	**7,972**	**1,932**	**5,551**	**1,141**	**32,340**	**2,939**	**3,986**	**251**
Hassan Taluk ...	360	378	201	51	44	49	1	...	...	...	...	...	1,952	558	1,193	299	5,897	878	1,288	117
Alur Sub-Taluk ...	18	12	15	2	...	...	...	...	...	...	...	...	134	60	188	40	1,307	98	87	6
Arsikere Taluk ...	121	58	75	4	319	327	10	...	1	...	...	...	1,141	208	1,038	177	6,630	398	742	25
Belur Do ...	128	112	85	6	61	57	2	...	...	...	...	...	1,021	211	679	138	3,929	319	410	24
Saklespur Do ...	59	19	45	2	6	5	...	...	...	...	...	...	753	254	464	112	3,555	334	453	27
Arkalgud Do ...	10	1	7	...	...	...	...	...	...	...	...	...	866	205	595	148	3,361	319	240	4
Hole-Narsipur Do ...	9	11	6	2	...	...	...	...	...	...	...	...	952	224	569	116	3,054	281	488	40
Channarayapatna Taluk...	339	306	224	64	106	115	4	...	...	...	...	...	1,153	212	827	111	4,607	322	278	8
Kadur District.	**798**	**562**	**348**	**63**	**566**	**501**	...	...	**3**	**3**	**3**	**3**	**5,707**	**1,564**	**3,952**	**868**	**22,743**	**2,393**	**3,359**	**238**
Chikmagalur Taluk ...	152	50	111	18	...	...	...	...	3	3	3	3	1,417	532	1,039	261	5,695	886	1,329	135
Kadur Do ...	22	3	7	...	...	...	...	...	...	...	...	...	1,368	226	836	91	4,602	296	331	13
Tarikere Do ...	76	35	37	1	522	466	...	...	...	...	...	...	1,251	218	813	133	4,726	326	516	31
Koppa Do ...	69	37	19	...	4	...	...	...	...	...	...	...	528	128	424	72	2,494	186	282	11
Narasimharajpura (Sub-Tk.)	29	17	23	8	40	35	...	...	...	...	...	...	264	97	175	113	1,359	207	260	7
Mudigere Taluk ...	422	405	130	29	...	...	...	...	...	...	...	...	579	224	429	180	2,798	307	430	40
Sringeri (Jahgir) ...	28	15	21	7	...	...	...	...	...	...	...	...	300	139	236	68	1,069	185	211	1
Shimoga District.	**1,526**	**1,205**	**382**	**28**	**4,014**	**3,843**	**112**	**6**	**3**	**2**	**1**	...	**7,205**	**1,822**	**5,807**	**1,090**	**33,439**	**2,709**	**3,906**	**217**
Shimoga Taluk ...	126	52	74	7	20	15	...	...	3	2	1	...	1,773	693	1,253	394	6,729	1,015	2,302	165
Kumsi Sub-Taluk ...	30	20	18	2	...	...	...	...	...	...	...	...	238	30	209	34	1,105	92	88	4
Channagiri Taluk ...	10	...	3	...	3,402	3,330	73	4	...	...	...	...	1,240	216	898	99	4,677	207	205	1
Honnali Do ...	132	117	25	1	324	279	18	...	...	...	...	...	787	75	771	54	3,727	152	150	1
Shikarpur Do ...	80	25	52	1	20	6	1	...	...	...	...	...	558	141	408	86	2,873	198	189	7
Sorab Do ...	33	24	13	1	118	109	1	...	...	...	...	...	447	22	454	64	3,288	185	66	4
Sagar Do ...	1,039	903	153	4	...	...	...	...	...	...	...	...	721	176	643	95	4,009	322	342	9
Nagar Do ...	51	53	24	10	115	92	16	2	...	...	...	...	438	95	384	39	2,268	118	141	6
Tirthahalli Do ...	25	11	20	2	15	12	3	...	...	...	...	...	1,003	304	837	225	4,763	420	423	20
Civil and Military Station, Bangalore.	**484**	**330**	297	**16**	...	...	...	...	**338**	**310**	**205**	**150**	**3,010**	**2,336**	**3,105**	**1,940**	**19,885**	**6,988**	**13,369**	**5,740**

PROVINCIAL TABLE II.

Population of Cities and Taluks by Religion and Literary.

MYSORE CENSUS 1931.

PROVINCIAL TABLE III. Territorial Distribution of the Christian Population by Sect and Race.

PROVINCIAL TABLE III.

Territorial Distribution of the Christian Population by Sect and Race.

District or State	All Denominations									Anglican									Methodist								
	Total			Distribution by Race						Total			Distribution by Race						Total			Distribution by Race					
	Persons	Males	Females	European and Allied Races		Anglo-Indian		Indian		Persons	Males	Females	European and Allied Races		Anglo-Indian		Indian		Persons	Males	Females	European and Allied Races		Anglo-Indian		Indian	
				Males	Females	Males	Females	Males	Females				Males	Females	Males	Females	Males	Females				Males	Females	Males	Females	Males	Females
1	2	3	4	5	6	7	8	9	10	11	12	13	14	15	16	17	18	19	20	21	22	23	24	25	26	27	28
MYSORE STATE, INCLUDING CIVIL AND MILITARY STATION, BANGALORE.	**87,538**	**45,164**	**42,374**	**3,144**	**2,267**	**3,781**	**4,528**	**38,239**	**35,579**	**2,876**	**1,404**	**1,472**	**562**	**519**	**599**	**652**	**243**	**301**	**7,981**	**4,084**	**3,897**	**99**	**76**	**139**	**114**	**3,846**	**3,707**
MYSORE STATE, EXCLUDING CIVIL AND MILITARY STATION, BANGALORE.	**57,516**	**30,512**	**27,004**	**708**	**545**	**1,380**	**1,409**	**28,424**	**25,050**	**1,170**	**623**	**547**	**210**	**127**	**256**	**261**	**157**	**159**	**7,244**	**3,765**	**3,479**	**76**	**43**	**68**	**74**	**3,621**	**3,362**
Bangalore City ...	**6,754**	3,291	3,463	129	171	175	241	2,987	3,051	**155**	73	82	29	29	27	39	17	14	**271**	76	195	1	1	...	...	75	194
Bangalore District ...	**8,036**	4,067	3,969	43	52	127	94	3,807	3,823	**5**	2	3	2	2	...	1	...	...	**110**	35	75	...	...	...	...	35	75
Kolar Gold Fields (City)...	**14,651**	7,579	7,072	383	191	778	763	6,418	6,118	**886**	485	401	161	85	211	202	113	113	**1,428**	812	616	57	28	49	57	706	531
Kolar District ...	**2,679**	1,319	1,360	8	16	26	27	1,285	1,317	**1**	1	...	...	...	...	...	1	...	**634**	371	263	...	...	...	...	371	263
Tumkur District ...	**1,620**	892	728	4	5	14	17	874	706	**20**	8	12	...	...	2	6	6	6	**1,266**	707	559	1	2	...	...	706	557
Mysore City ...	**3,947**	1,956	1,991	43	58	145	182	1,768	1,751	**37**	20	17	7	8	12	7	1	2	**872**	442	430	17	12	17	16	403	402
Mysore District ...	**3,375**	1,828	1,547	20	7	50	35	1,758	1,505	**5**	3	2	...	...	...	...	3	2	**1,060**	547	513	...	...	2	1	545	512
Chitaldrug District ...	**515**	275	240	1	1	14	6	260	233	**1**	1	...	...	...	1	...	...	...	**120**	56	64	...	...	...	...	56	64
Hassan do ...	**5,280**	2,840	2,440	26	14	28	29	2,786	2,397	**35**	17	18	5	1	2	2	10	15	**880**	393	487	...	...	...	...	393	487
Kadur do ...	**6,575**	4,110	2,465	46	21	10	5	4,054	2,439	**15**	9	6	6	2	...	1	3	3	**204**	106	98	...	...	...	...	106	98
Shimoga do ...	**4,084**	2,355	1,729	5	9	13	10	2,337	1,710	**10**	4	6	...	...	1	2	3	4	**399**	220	179	...	...	...	...	220	179
Civil and Military Station, Bangalore.	**30,022**	**14,652**	**15,370**	**2,436**	**1,722**	**2,401**	**3,119**	**9,815**	**10,529**	**1,706**	**781**	**925**	**352**	**392**	**343**	**391**	**86**	**142**	**737**	**319**	**418**	**23**	**33**	**71**	**40**	**225**	**345**

PROVINCIAL TABLE III

Territorial Distribution of the Christian Population by Sect and Race—*contd.*

District or State	Roman Catholic									Romo-Syrian									Syrian (Others)								
	Total			Distribution by Race						Total			Distribution by Race						Total			Distribution by Race					
				European and Allied Races		Anglo-Indian		Indian					European and Allied Races		Anglo-Indian		Indian					European and Allied Races		Anglo-Indian		Indian	
	Persons	Males	Females	Males	Females	Males	Females	Males	Females	Persons	Males	Females	Males	Females	Males	Females	Males	Females	Persons	Males	Females	Males	Females	Males	Females	Males	Females
	29	30	31	32	33	34	35	36	37	38	39	40	41	42	43	44	45	46	47	48	49	50	51	52	53	54	55
MYSORE STATE, INCLUDING CIVIL AND MILITARY STATION, BANGALORE.	**52,347**	**27,309**	**25,038**	**364**	**375**	**1,376**	**1,724**	**25,569**	**22,939**	**122**	**50**	**72**	...	...	...	...	**50**	**72**	**58**	**34**	**24**	...	...	...	...	**34**	**24**
MYSORE STATE, EXCLUDING CIVIL AND MILITARY STATION, BANGALORE.	**37,956**	**20,563**	**17,393**	**174**	**108**	**669**	**654**	**19,720**	**16,631**	**114**	**48**	**66**	...	...	...	...	**48**	**66**	**46**	**27**	**19**	...	...	...	...	**27**	**19**
Bangalore City ...	**2,358**	1,244	1,114	17	25	50	54	1,177	1,085	**46**	19	27	...	...	...	...	19	27	...	...	...	...	...	...	...	...	...
Bangalore District ...	**6,231**	3,175	3,056	2	1	13	14	3,160	3,041	...	...	...	...	...	...	...	...	...	...	...	...	...	...	...	...	...	...
Kolar Gold Fields (City)	**10,705**	5,359	5,346	143	69	499	479	4,717	4,798	...	...	...	...	...	...	...	...	...	...	...	...	...	...	...	...	...	...
Kolar District ...	**257**	142	115	...	...	1	...	141	115	**68**	29	39	...	...	...	...	29	39	**18**	2	16	...	...	...	...	2	16
Tumkur District ...	**245**	119	126	...	...	...	1	119	125	...	...	...	...	...	...	...	...	...	**3**	3	...	...	...	...	...	3	...
Mysore City ...	**2,633**	1,325	1,308	6	6	83	86	1,236	1,216	...	...	...	...	...	...	...	...	...	**3**	2	1	...	...	...	...	2	1
Mysore District ...	**1,360**	795	565	3	3	2	1	790	561	...	...	...	...	...	...	...	...	...	**10**	10	...	...	...	...	...	10	...
Chitaldrug District ...	**283**	159	124	...	...	4	1	155	123	...	...	...	...	...	...	...	...	...	...	...	...	...	...	...	...	...	...
Hassan do ...	**4,283**	2,376	1,907	...	1	14	15	2,362	1,891	...	...	...	...	...	...	...	...	...	**7**	6	1	...	...	...	...	6	1
Kadur do ...	**6,152**	3,867	2,285	2	1	1	...	3,864	2,284	...	...	...	...	...	...	...	...	...	**1**	1	...	...	...	...	...	1	...
Shimoga do ...	**3,449**	2,002	1,447	1	2	2	3	1,999	1,442	...	...	...	...	...	...	...	...	...	**4**	3	1	...	...	...	...	3	1
Civil and Military Station, Bangalore.	**14,391**	**6,746**	**7,645**	**190**	**267**	**707**	**1,070**	**5,849**	**6,308**	**8**	**2**	**6**	...	...	...	...	**2**	**6**	**12**	**7**	**5**	...	...	...	...	**7**	**5**

PROVINCIAL TABLE III

Territorial Distribution of the Christian Population by Sect and Race—*concld.*

District or State	Sect not returned — Total — Persons	Sect not returned — Total — Males	Sect not returned — Total — Females	Sect not returned — European and Allied Races — Males	Sect not returned — European and Allied Races — Females	Sect not returned — Anglo-Indian — Males	Sect not returned — Anglo-Indian — Females	Sect not returned — Indian — Males	Sect not returned — Indian — Females	South India United Church — Total — Persons	South India United Church — Total — Males	South India United Church — Total — Females	South India United Church — European and Allied Races — Males	South India United Church — European and Allied Races — Females	South India United Church — Anglo-Indian — Males	South India United Church — Anglo-Indian — Females	South India United Church — Indian — Males	South India United Church — Indian — Females	Others — Total — Persons	Others — Total — Males	Others — Total — Females	Others — European and Allied Races — Males	Others — European and Allied Races — Females	Others — Anglo-Indian — Males	Others — Anglo-Indian — Females	Others — Indian — Males	Others — Indian — Females
	56	57	58	59	60	61	62	63	64	65	66	67	68	69	70	71	72	73	74	75	76	77	78	79	80	81	82
MYSORE STATE, INCLUDING CIVIL AND MILITARY STATION, BANGALORE.	**17,012**	**8,686**	**8,326**	**1,802**	**1,078**	**1,452**	**1,755**	**5,432**	**5,493**	**2,060**	**1,095**	**965**	**180**	**81**	**96**	**77**	**819**	**807**	**5,082**	**2,502**	**2,580**	**137**	**138**	**119**	**206**	**2,246**	**2,236**
MYSCRE STATE, EXCLUDING CIVIL AND MILITARY STATION, BANGALORE.	**4,801**	**2,394**	**2,407**	**144**	**164**	**294**	**325**	**1,956**	**1,918**	**1,634**	**825**	**809**	**11**	**4**	**5**	**7**	**809**	**798**	**4,551**	**2,267**	**2,284**	**93**	**99**	**88**	**88**	**2,086**	**2,097**
Bangalore City ...	**3,247**	1,522	1,725	63	97	92	143	1,367	1,485	**55**	22	33	...	...	...	1	22	22	**622**	335	287	19	19	6	4	310	264
Bangalore District ...	**92**	63	29	4	3	59	26	...	...	**847**	415	432	...	...	...	...	415	432	**751**	377	374	35	16	55	53	287	275
Kolar Gold Fields (City)...	...	...	...	...	...	...	...	...	...	**704**	374	330	11	4	5	5	358	321	**928**	549	379	11	5	14	19	524	355
Kolar District ...	**289**	151	138	4	5	22	19	125	114	**9**	5	4	...	...	...	...	5	4	**1,403**	618	785	4	11	3	8	611	766
Tumkur District ...	**81**	53	28	2	1	11	9	40	18	...	...	...	...	...	...	...	...	...	**5**	2	3	1	2	1	1	...	...
Mysore City ...	**139**	40	99	10	27	30	71	...	1	**5**	1	4	...	...	...	1	1	3	**258**	126	132	3	5	3	1	120	126
Mysore District ...	**382**	229	153	8	2	45	32	176	119	...	...	...	...	...	...	...	...	...	**558**	244	314	9	2	1	1	234	311
Chitaldrug District ...	**109**	57	52	...	1	8	5	49	46	...	...	...	...	...	...	...	...	...	**2**	2	...	1	...	1	...	...	...
Hassan do ...	**62**	42	20	15	5	12	12	15	3	...	...	...	...	...	...	...	...	...	**13**	6	7	6	7	...	...	...	...
Kadur do ...	**197**	122	75	84	17	8	4	80	54	...	...	...	...	...	...	...	...	...	**6**	5	1	4	1	1	...	...	...
Shimoga do ...	**203**	115	88	4	6	7	4	104	78	**14**	8	6	...	...	...	...	8	6	**5**	3	2	...	1	3	1	...	...
Civil and Military Station, Bangalore.	**12,211**	6,292	5,919	1,658	914	1,158	1,430	3,476	3,575	**426**	270	156	169	77	91	70	10	9	**531**	235	296	44	39	31	118	160	139

MYSORE CENSUS, 1931.

PROVINCIAL TABLE IV.—Rural and Cottage Industries.

NOTE.—See note 1 on the title page of Provincial Table I. This table presents statistics of 12 rural and cottage industries in which a comparatively large number of persons are engaged.

PROVINCIAL TABLE IV.

Rural and Cottage Industries.

District or State	Population	Total			Weaving in Cotton			Weaving in Silk			Weaving in Wool (Blankets)			Silk-worm rearing			Oil Mills		
		Number of families engaged in the Industry	Number of persons in the families	Number of persons actually engaged in the Industry	Number of families engaged in the Industry	Number of persons in the families	Number of persons actually engaged in the Industry	Number of families engaged in the Industry	Number of persons in the families	Number of persons actually engaged in the Industry	Number of families engaged in the Industry	Number of persons in the families	Number of persons actually engaged in the Industry	Number of families engaged in the Industry	Number of persons in the families	Number of persons actually engaged in the Industry	Number of families engaged in the Industry	Number of persons in the families	Number of persons actually engaged in the Industry
	1	2	3	4	5	6	7	8	9	10	11	12	13	14	15	16	17	18	19
Mysore State, Excluding Civil & Military Station, Bangalore.	**6,423,189**	**59,834**	**350,771**	**131,022**	**12,548**	**69,811**	**29.738**	**1,911**	**11,527**	**4,900**	**7,505**	**47,443**	**19,298**	**11,832**	**82,204**	**26,166**	**3,343**	**19,240**	**6,774**
Bangalore City ...	172,357	1,530	9,188	4,020	176	1,075	547	1,024	6,301	2,804	23	88	48	...	...	...	10	62	18
Bangalore District ...	908,056	10,088	61,979	21,813	1,971	10,899	4,554	555	3,284	1,282	476	3,196	1,105	3,802	26,876	3,754	566	3,589	1,168
Kolar Gold Fields (City)	85,103	48	255	82	4	20	4	...	...	...	5	24	5	...	...	...	2	20	5
Kolar District ...	763,934	6,462	41,883	13,930	1,392	7,561	3,324	31	163	88	791	4,481	2,061	1,691	16,258	3,657	508	2,784	945
Tumkur District ...	861,405	9,094	53,646	21,160	1,881	9,861	4,229	80	357	146	2,360	14,022	6,480	1,509	11,595	4,017	665	3,898	1,362
Mysore City ...	107,142	475	2,499	1,121	182	937	480	1	5	3	50	360	79	...	...	...	14	74	31
Mysore District ...	1,403,984	17,964	97,538	37,255	3,797	19,891	8,504	82	210	52	1,280	8,045	2,964	4,829	27,468	9,784	1,270	6,617	2.471
Chitaldrug District ...	656,569	6,649	39,467	14,906	1,740	10,526	4,364	155	1,018	429	1,917	12,062	4,789	1	5	4	33	177	60
Hassan District ...	596,937	3,875	21,793	8,608	873	5,754	2,528	...	...	...	833	3,020	1,214	...	...	...	212	1,475	572
Kadur District ...	347,715	1,790	9,610	3,539	302	1,805	744	12	59	32	290	1,607	397	...	...	...	53	282	119
Shimoga District ...	519,987	2,364	12,913	4,588	230	1,482	465	21	190	64	90	588	156	...	...	...	10	62	23

PROVINCIAL TABLE IV.

Rural and Cottage Industries

District or State	Pottery			Basket making			Goldsmithy			Blacksmithy			Carpentry			Mat-making			Leather Industry		
	Number of families engaged in the Industry	Number of persons in the families	Number of persons actually engaged in the Industry	Number of families engaged in the Industry	Number of persons in the families	Number of persons actually engaged in the Industry	Number of families engaged in the Industry	Number of persons in the families	Number of persons actually engaged in the Industry	Number of families engaged in the Industry	Number of persons in the families	Number of persons actually engaged in the Industry	Number of families engaged in the Industry	Number of persons in the families	Number of persons actually engaged in the Industry	Number of families engaged in the Industry	Number of persons in the families	Number of persons actually engaged in the Industry	Number of families engaged in the Industry	Number of persons in the families	Number of persons actually engaged in the Industry
	20	21	22	23	24	25	26	27	28	29	30	31	32	33	34	35	36	37	38	39	40
Mysore State, Excluding Civil & Military Station, Bangalore.	**7,210**	**37,758**	**17,610**	**2,940**	**14,742**	**6,952**	**3,454**	**13,376**	**5,406**	**3,787**	**20,754**	**6,320**	**2,930**	**15,743**	**4,295**	**1,077**	**5,472**	**1,882**	**1,297**	**7,701**	**1,681**
Bangalore City ...	4	14	6	57	271	135	110	618	207	17	120	66	67	422	140	...	...	...	42	217	49
Bangalore District ...	950	5,083	2,141	417	2,002	853	439	2,284	642	646	3,298	999	239	1,393	284	4	7	4	23	116	27
Kolar Gold Fields (City)	12	83	35	1	4	2	2	16	3	15	79	26	2	9	2	...	...	...	...	...	...
Kolar District ...	704	3,854	1,641	293	1,318	638	334	1,603	457	501	2,683	810	170	942	224	28	168	59	19	118	26
Tumkur District ...	816	4,323	1,917	321	1,723	751	400	1,960	608	588	3,280	1,036	301	1,730	378	87	391	125	86	506	111
Mysore City ...	60	319	157	79	358	219	19	85	40	17	98	30	41	203	64	4	14	6	8	46	12
Mysore District ...	2,570	12,646	6,662	670	3,446	1,470	848	4,693	1,247	758	4,208	1,205	986	5,104	1,391	709	3,511	1,171	265	1,499	384
Chitaldrug District ...	620	3,418	1,528	268	1,410	764	434	2,138	694	405	2,328	742	370	2,115	544	111	625	279	595	3,645	709
Hassan District ...	552	3,308	1,559	224	1,200	606	491	3,065	926	316	2,038	576	300	1,519	508	40	215	75	34	199	49
Kadur District ...	454	2,211	870	197	911	536	136	654	209	194	961	321	141	649	210	11	68	22	60	403	79
Shimoga District ...	468	2,549	1,094	413	2,099	978	241	1,260	373	330	1,661	509	313	1,657	550	83	473	141	165	952	235

MYSORE CENSUS, 1931.

PROVINCIAL TABLE V—Structures Classified by Nature of Roofing and use.

NOTE.—See Note 1 on the title page of Provincial Table I. This table presents statistics of structures in the State classified according to the nature of their roofing and the use to which they are put.

PROVINCIAL TABLE V.

Structures Classified by Nature of Roofing and use.

District or State	Nature of roofing									Total	Purposes served							
	Terrace	Terrace and tile	Mangalore tile	Country tile	Stone	Mud	Thatched	Zinc-sheet	Others		Dwelling houses	Cattle sheds	Public buildings	Government buildings	Shops	Temples	Vacant	Others
1	2	3	4	5	6	7	8	9	10	11	12	13	14	15	16	17	18	19
MYSORE STATE, EXCLUDING CIVIL AND MILITARY STATION, BANGALORE.	**17,826**	**2,039**	**25,276**	**561,769**	**52,657**	**354,927**	**469,432**	**17,377**	**23**	**1,501,326**	**1,232,619**	**75,087**	**15,806**	**14,052**	**20,238**	**53,756**	**80,848**	**8,918**
Bangalore City ...	4,878	587	5,300	286	187	7,210	2,442	306	...	21,196	17,481	32	165	160	2,603	188	447	120
Bangalore District ...	878	158	1,262	66,140	10,455	58,994	50,762	437	...	189,086	156,290	7,706	2,640	1,846	2,924	6,797	9,943	940
Kolar Gold Fields (City) ...	761	285	7,077	2,703	364	276	3,244	8,549	...	23,259	19,616	228	137	100	627	387	1,862	302
Kolar District ...	3,277	254	2,305	14,146	16,785	83,840	72,145	367	...	193,119	150,917	10,745	5,414	3,149	2,835	6,696	11,462	1,901
Tumkur District ...	2,046	126	633	32,694	11,098	139,634	43,019	107	1	229,358	176,018	18,326	3,449	1,838	2,647	9,206	14,877	2,997
Mysore City ...	2,641	335	2,931	14,576	224	23	1,132	19	...	21,881	17,529	58	241	443	2,267	181	1,002	160
Mysore District ...	2,190	199	563	223,379	5,453	13,756	75,638	415	...	321,593	276,479	10,752	1,792	2,267	2,564	9,890	17,307	542
Chitaldrug District ...	486	61	313	31,188	3,445	47,465	66,101	1,421	6	150,486	128,749	4,558	756	1,130	1,189	6,311	7,349	444
Hassan District ...	495	26	1,478	109,290	3,014	1,781	42,951	1,088	1	160,124	122,450	18,838	560	1,412	1,152	6,235	8,636	841
Kadur District ...	56	1	2,794	34,391	971	331	36,595	2,083	14	77,136	66,747	1,435	379	808	577	3,111	3,749	330
Shimoga District ...	118	7	620	32,976	761	1,617	75,403	2,585	1	114,088	100,342	2,409	273	899	853	4,756	4,214	341

MYSORE CENSUS, 1931.

PROVINCIAL TABLE VI.--Vaccination.

NOTE.—See note 1 on the title page of Provincial Table I. This table presents statistics of persons who have been vaccinated, who have not been vaccinated and have had small-pox, under certain age periods.

PROVINCIAL TABLE VI.

Vaccination.

District or State	Population			Age											
				0						1–4					
				Vaccinated		Not vaccinated		Persons who have had Small-pox		Vaccinated		Not vaccinated		Persons who have had Small-pox	
	Persons	Males	Females	Males	Females	Males	Females	Males	Females	Males	Females	Males	Females	Males	Females
1	2	3	4	5	6	7	8	9	10	11	12	13	14	15	16
MYSORE STATE, EXCLUDING CIVIL AND MILITARY STATION, BANGALORE.	6,423,189	3,284,554	3,138,635	7,330	7,515	34,644	36,121	1,919	1,759	172,866	177,082	140,141	153,653	39,545	41,505
Bangalore City ...	172,357	*91,680*	*80,677*	539	582	608	555	3	3	8,373	9,163	610	645	95	125
Bangalore District ...	908,056	*461,905*	*446,151*	1,403	1,341	4,840	5,049	222	215	31,959	32,990	17,319	19,073	4,976	5,442
Kolar Gold Fields (City)	85,103	*45,051*	*40,052*	395	413	235	228	1	1	4,906	4,947	117	186	3	2
Kolar District ...	763,934	*389,262*	*374,672*	795	852	3,535	3,839	123	163	21,179	21,423	15,162	17,264	3,924	4,139
Tumkur District ...	861,405	*439,144*	*422,261*	762	738	5,221	5,253	325	324	21,193	22,229	21,302	23,013	6,899	6,958
Mysore City ...	107,142	*56,772*	*50,370*	289	347	365	310	3	5	4,313	4,726	456	615	155	166
Mysore District ...	1,403,984	*703,838*	*700,146*	1,503	1,561	7,275	7,816	555	392	37,880	37,461	29,730	34,091	8,465	8,680
Chitaldrug District	656,569	*336,786*	*319.783*	434	441	4,016	4,064	307	295	12,621	13,380	17,624	18,906	7,742	8,456
Hassan District ...	596,937	*300,746*	*296,191*	545	529	3,458	3,722	179	173	12,392	12,593	15,526	16,524	8,307	8,652
Kadur District ...	347,715	*184,389*	*163,326*	284	299	1,963	2,143	86	78	6,874	7,188	8,677	9,231	1,328	1,389
Shimoga District ...	519,987	*274,981*	*245,006*	381	412	3,125	3,142	115	110	10,176	10,982	13,618	14,105	2,651	2,496

PROVINCIAL TABLE VI.

Vaccination.

District or State	Age											
	5—9						10 and over					
	Vaccinated		Not vaccinated		Persons who have had Small-pox		Vaccinated		Not vaccinated		Persons who have had Small-pox	
	Males	Females	Males	Females	Males	Females	Males	Females	Males	Females	Males	Females
	17	18	19	20	21	22	23	24	25	26	27	28
MYSORE STATE, EXCLUDING CIVIL AND MILITARY STATION, BANGALORE.	**266,690**	**262,850**	**78,920**	**85,899**	**86,643**	**92,825**	**1,296,234**	**1,123,767**	**268,132**	**280,132**	**891,490**	**875,527**
Bangalore City	10,084	10,541	447	168	167	168	67,284	55,813	1,021	1,279	1,999	1,635
Bangalore District	44,936	44,650	8,380	8,982	11,882	12,629	204,513	185,861	28,892	29,120	103,184	100,799
Kolar Gold Fields (City) ...	5,896	5,669	72	47	7	13	32,965	27,716	420	281	514	529
Kolar District	33,804	32,973	8,490	9,159	8,680	8,973	178,485	162,531	25,516	27,156	89,569	86,200
Tumkur District	33,147	31,613	12,255	12,724	14,753	15,988	124,083	102,966	37,968	39,350	161,253	161,105
Mysore City	6,587	6,641	125	173	314	277	40,749	34,625	639	891	2,277	1,694
Mysore District	62,055	60,035	16,317	17,878	19,352	20,638	285,275	266,715	61,034	65,061	174,397	179,818
Chitaldrug District	19,432	18,835	9,208	10,243	15,764	16,687	69,800	56,169	29,140	29,549	150,698	142,758
Hassan District	20,375	21,071	8,787	9,565	7,566	8,222	112,750	99,144	26,180	30,584	89,731	90,462
Kadur District	11,944	11,965	6,272	7,090	3,035	3,415	76,595	55,730	22,957	23,523	44,374	41,275
Shimoga District	18,981	18,837	8,637	9,870	5,623	5,815	103,715	76,597	34,415	33,388	73,544	69,252

WD 481—GPB—1,000—13-4-32